Travel North Carolina

FOURTH EDITION

Travel North Carolina

Going Native
in the Old North State

By Carolyn Sakowski,
Sue Clark, Angela Harwood,
Steve Kirk, Artie Sparrow,
and Anne Holcomb Waters

JOHN F.
BLAIR   WINSTON-SALEM, NORTH CAROLINA

JOHN F. BLAIR
PUBLISHER
1406 Plaza Drive
Winston-Salem, North Carolina 27103
www.blairpub.com

Manufactured in the United States of America

COVER IMAGES
FRONT COVER, LEFT SIDE TOP TO BOTTOM:

Latham Garden at Tryon Palace / *Photograph by Angela Harwood*
Biltmore Estate / *Courtesy of Biltmore Estate*
Bodie Island Lighthouse / *Photograph by Artie Sparrow*
Whitewater rafting / *Courtesy of Asheville Convention and Visitors Bureau*
Reynolda House Museum of American Art / *Courtesy of Reynolda House and*
Winston-Salem Convention and Visitors Bureau
Battleship North Carolina / *Courtesy of* Battleship North Carolina

RIGHT SIDE TOP TO BOTTOM:

Masonboro Island / *Courtesy of Wilmington/Cape Fear Coast Convention and Visitors Bureau*
Christmas tree farm / *Courtesy of Boone Convention and Visitors Bureau*

BACK COVER, LEFT TO RIGHT:

North Carolina mountains / *Photograph by Ben Clark*
The Executive Mansion / *Photograph by Elizabeth Kirk*
The beach at Ocracoke / *Photograph by Artie Sparrow*

Library of Congress Cataloging-in-Publication Data

Travel North Carolina : going native in the Old North State / by Carolyn Sakowski ... [et al.]. -- 4th ed.
   p.   cm.
Includes index.
ISBN 978-0-89587-379-8 (alk. paper)
1. North Carolina--Guidebooks. I. Sakowski, Carolyn, 1948-
F252.3.T73 2010
917.56'0444--dc22

2009043186

www.blairpub.com

BOOK DESIGN BY DEBRA LONG HAMPTON

*To Debbie Hampton, Margaret Couch,
Kim Byerly, and Heath Simpson,
without whom this book would not
have been possible*

Contents

Acknowledgments   xi
Introduction   xiii

The Coast   1

The Outer Banks   3
    Northern Banks and Beaches   5
    Roanoke Island   30
    Bodie Island   46
    Hatteras Island   50
    Ocracoke Island   64

The Coastal Plain   77
    Albemarle Region   81
    Elizabeth City   82
    Edenton   97
    Bath   110

    Neuse River Region   118
    New Bern   119
    Morehead City   138
    Beaufort   143
    Bogue Banks   153

    Cape Fear Coast   160
    Topsail Island   161
    Wilmington   169
    Wrightsville Beach   187
    Pleasure Island   194
    Southport and the Brunswick Islands   202

The Piedmont 213

The Triangle 215
    Raleigh 217
    Durham 237
    Chapel Hill and Carrboro 256
    Research Triangle Park 273
    Triangle Nearby 276

The Sandhills 283
    Fayetteville 284
    Pinehurst and Southern Pines 301

The Triad 315
    Winston-Salem 317
    Greensboro 340
    High Point 359
    Triad Nearby 367

Charlotte 377

The Mountains 415

The Blue Ridge Parkway 417

The High Country 427
    Alleghany County 431
    Ashe County 439
    Boone 447
    Blowing Rock 457
    Banner Elk, Beech Mountain, and Linville 465
    Spruce Pine and Burnsville 477

Asheville 487

The Southern Mountains 513
    Hendersonville 515
    Brevard 526
    Highlands 535
    Franklin 543

The Great Smoky Mountains 549

Great Smoky Mountains National Park 551
Bryson City 555
Cherokee 559
Maggie Valley 565
Waynesville 569

Appendix 575
Index 587

Acknowledgments

We would all like to thank our two interns—Sara Harris and Kate Sadler—for their help in checking facts for us.

Sue Clark would like to thank Dodie Stephens of the Asheville Convention and Visitors Bureau; Brad Campbell of Market Connections, representing the Brevard Chamber of Commerce and Visitor Center; Bob Kieltyka of the Highlands Visitor Center; Dave Tomsky of the Grand Bohemian Hotel; Kim and Sharon Shailer of the Balsam Mountain Inn; Mort White of the Hemlock Inn; Elizabeth and Robert Rankin of Snowbird Mountain Lodge; Patti and Gary Wiles of Cumberland Falls Bed and Breakfast; Clark Lovelace of the Greystone Inn; Jackie Whitman, my mom and traveling guru; and Chris, Chad, and Ben Clark, the world's best traveling companions—I'd go anywhere with you guys!

Angela Harwood would like to thank Anne Waters for being so thorough the first time around; Connie Nelson of the Cape Fear Coast Convention and Visitors Bureau for all her help; the employees at the Craven County Convention and Visitors Bureau, the Carteret County Tourism Bureau, the Harkers Island Visitor Center, the Southport–Oak Island Chamber of Commerce, and the South Brunswick Islands Chamber of Commerce; and most of all, my husband, Jeff, who accompanied me and made my research trips feel like vacations.

Steve Kirk would like to thank his predecessors on the Triangle and Sandhills sections—Deb Baldwin, Sheryl Monks, and John Tarleton—for their solid work. I also thank Kimberly Morrisette and Betsy Lash of the Durham Convention and Visitors Bureau; Caleb Miles and Lisa Long of the Pinehurst, Southern Pines, Aberdeen

Area Convention and Visitors Bureau; Dr. Boyd D. Cathey and Kim Cumber of the North Carolina State Archives; Patty Griffin of the Chapel Hill/Orange County Visitors Bureau; Brett Friedlander for his suggestions for the Fayetteville chapter; my daughter Elizabeth and Peter Jin for taking Raleigh photos; my wife, Mary, for her company and her navigational skills on research trips; and my daughter Rebecca.

Carolyn Sakowski would like to thank the following people for their assistance: Bob and Mary Choate; Mac Forehand of the Boone Convention and Visitors Bureau; and the staffs of North Carolina High Country Host, the Ashe County Chamber of Commerce, the Avery County Chamber of Commerce, the Beech Mountain Chamber of Commerce, the Blowing Rock Visitors Center, the Greensboro Area Convention and Visitors Bureau, the Yancey County Chamber of Commerce, and the Mitchell County Chamber of Commerce.

Artie Sparrow would like to thank Sunny Smith Nelson for doing such a great job on earlier editions of this book. Most of her original text remains, since I couldn't improve on it. I would also like to thank Alice Sink for her expertise on Manteo and her beautiful photographs; the Edenton–Chowan County Tourism Authority; the North Carolina Department of Cultural Resources; the Elizabeth City Area Convention and Visitors Bureau; Kathleen Wheeless and the staff of the Forsyth County Public Library for research assistance; my parents, Warren and Lydia Sparrow, for exposing me to the Outer Banks at an impressionable age and teaching me so many other things; and lastly, my wife, Julie James, for far more things than can be listed here.

Anne Holcomb Waters would like to thank Jenni Woomer for her insightful recommendations and assistance with the updates for Charlotte and vicinity. For their assistance with photos, I thank Laura Hill, the marketing and communications coordinator at the Charlotte Regional Visitors Authority; Casey Hough, media manager of the Winston-Salem Visitors Center; and Rod Hackney, public relations manager at North Carolina Zoological Park. As always, I am indebted to the great staff at John F. Blair, whom I am lucky to call friends. And lastly, I thank my family for their support and encouragement.

Introduction

Who better to publish a travel guide to North Carolina than the staff of a North Carolina publisher? As the staff of John F. Blair, Publisher, planned its future projects, we asked ourselves that very question. We looked around and realized that, collectively, we were in a better position to write about our state than some guy from New York City who popped in for one weekend and recorded his snap judgments.

When we decided to undertake this project, we also decided that we wanted the guide to reflect our individual personalities. That's why you may notice distinct styles for each section.

Here's a brief look at who we are:

Sue Clark is a native of Detroit. In March of her senior year at Oakland University in Rochester, Michigan, her father sent her pictures of dogwood trees in bloom. That was enough to entice her to move south. She's been here over 25 years and considers herself one of North Carolina's biggest fans. She has a B.A. in history with a minor in English from Oakland University. She recently graduated from Salem College with a Master of Arts degree in secondary education. She worked for John F. Blair for 14 years before becoming a teacher. She is married and has two sons. The Clark family loves to travel and especially enjoys camping in the mountains. Sue's hobbies include cooking and singing. Yankee by birth, Southern by choice, Sue plans to call North Carolina home for the rest of her life.

Angela Harwood revised the sections for the Neuse River region and the Cape Fear coast. A navy brat, she spent most of her school years moving from one coastal city to another from Maine to Florida and as far west as Louisiana, so she is no stranger to the sea. Her family eventually settled in Olive Branch, Mississippi, practically a suburb of Memphis. She pursued a degree in landscape architecture at Mississippi State University for three years before changing her major to English. She received her B.A. in English with a minor in history from the University of Mississippi at Oxford. Angela moved to North Carolina in 2004 to work for John F. Blair after meeting Carolyn Sakowski, Blair's president, at the Denver Publishing Institute. Now the

special-projects director and the design and production assistant, she enjoys traveling the state with her husband, Jeff, and their two dogs, Buff and Uma.

Steve Kirk updated the Triangle and Sandhills sections. A native of Upstate New
York, he received a B.A. from St. Lawrence University before moving south to pursue an M.F.A. at UNC-Greensboro. He has lived in North Carolina ever since. The
editor at John F. Blair for over 20 years, he is the author of *Scribblers: Stalking the
Authors of Appalachia* and *First in Flight: The Wright Brothers in North Carolina* and has
contributed to other volumes. He is married and has two daughters.

Carolyn Sakowski wrote the sections for Greensboro, High Point, and the High
Country. She was born in North Carolina and has lived in the state for over 50 years.
She grew up in Morganton, graduated from Queens University in Charlotte with a
B.A. in history, and got an M.A. in history from Appalachian State University in
Boone. She and her husband have an Avery County farm, which he inherited from
his grandfather. That's where they escape to mow the fields most weekends in sum-
mer and fall. She is also the author of *Touring the Western North Carolina Backroads*
and *Touring the East Tennessee Backroads*.

Artie Sparrow revised and updated the sections on the Outer Banks and the Albemarle region. He's a lifelong resident of North Carolina and has been making
trips to the Outer Banks for nearly 40 years. He holds a bachelor's degree in political
science from the University of North Carolina at Chapel Hill and furthers his education by reading voraciously on every subject imaginable. He works at John F. Blair as
an office assistant and relishes the varied experience that brings. He also enjoys long
bike rides and hikes, hanging out with his librarian wife and their two goofy dogs,
and listening to live music.

Anne Holcomb Waters is an Arkansas native who has lived and worked in North
Carolina since 1996. She is the former vice president of sales and marketing for
John F. Blair and a graduate of Randolph-Macon Woman's College. In 2005, she
moved to Salisbury with her husband, Andrew, and infant son, Eli. She owns the
Green Goat Gallery and Blue Ewe Yoga Studio across from the North Carolina
Transportation Museum in Spencer.

When discussing a format for the book, we decided we didn't want an inclusive
listing of every accommodation in each city. If you're looking for that kind of list,

we've provided contact information for local convention and visitor bureaus. What we've tried to do is avoid the chains, unless we've discovered something unique about a particular chain hotel or motel. We've looked for locally owned, one-of-a-kind places that visitors might be unaware of. We've done the same thing when choosing restaurants. We've tried to find the places that locals would put on their list if you asked them for the best places to eat. We couldn't include them all, but we've tried to offer a variety of cuisines and price ranges. We haven't charged any establishment a fee to be included in this book. We wanted to approach these places just like regular visitors would.

Because prices for food and lodging fluctuate, we've simply categorized each establishment as Deluxe, Expensive, Moderate, or Inexpensive, based on the scales below.

For accommodations, the breakdown is

Deluxe—Over $140 for a double room
Expensive—$100 to $140
Moderate—$70 to $100
Inexpensive—Under $70 (Few of these are left!)

Prices often vary according to the season. For example, you might find some good bargains on the coast if you decide to vacation there in the late fall or winter. In the mountains, the bargains come after the summer and fall foliage seasons but before ski season.

For restaurants, the breakdown is

Expensive—Over $20 for most entrées
Moderate—$12 to $20
Inexpensive—Under $12

Although we came to our sections with some previous knowledge of the areas we were writing about, we all learned even more about our state. Each of us is proud to live in North Carolina, and we're glad we can share our enthusiasm with you.

Carolyn Sakowski
President, John F. Blair, Publisher

The Coast

The beach near Buxton
PHOTOGRAPH BY JULIE JAMES

PREVIOUS PAGE:
Pamlico Sound between Ocracoke and Swan Quarter
PHOTOGRAPH BY ARTIE SPARROW

The Outer Banks

Northern Banks and Beaches

Roanoke Island

Bodie Island

Hatteras Island

Ocracoke Island

By Artie Sparrow

I don't remember my first visit to the Outer Banks. I was too young. However, my parents swear that my response to losing a kite on a Hatteras beach was to say, "That's okay. It's going off to Europe." To me, that symbolizes what the Outer Banks is all about: It's a place of endless possibilities where you can let your imagination run wild. No matter how young or old you are, when you're at the Outer Banks, you realize you're at either the end or the beginning of the world.

I have vivid memories of subsequent trips to the Outer Banks. It's a place to experience sensory overload in the most positive sense of that term: the sounds, sights, and smells are overwhelming. I once stayed in a hotel that apologized for not having a TV. I didn't mind because that seemed superfluous, given where I was. You'll have access to modern conveniences on the Outer Banks: WiFi, cell phone reception, cable TV, etc. But you'll probably find yourself caring a lot less about those things than you would in other places. Instead, you'll marvel at what are consistently rated some of the best beaches in America.

The Outer Banks is a place to find long, sandy beaches where you can sit in silence and hear nothing but nature; sand dunes larger than houses, where hang gliders with colorful wings take flight and hover over the waves; wildlife refuges where you can endlessly stroll the trails, soaking up some of the most tranquil and beautiful sights nature has to offer. It also has some of the friendliest people and most delicious restaurant food you'll ever find, along with a wealth of historical sites.

There is much to see and do on the Outer Banks, and you'll discover a new adventure with each visit. The Outer Banks can be whatever you want it to be—quiet, wind-swept dunes where you can find blissful solitude or a friendly, outgoing, and active vacation spot.

JUST THE FACTS

The two main roads on the Outer Banks are U.S. 158 and N.C. 12. U.S. 158 is also known as the Croatan Highway. N.C. 12 is also known as the Virginia Dare Trail, Beach Road, and Duck Road. The two parallel one another in the northern section of the Outer Banks. Note that local directions from these roads are customarily given by milepost, rather than by street number. Milepost 1 is in Kitty Hawk and Milepost 16 in Nags Head.

To reach the Banks from the north, follow either U.S. 17 or Va. 168 to U.S. 158. Take U.S. 158 East across the Wright Brothers Memorial Bridge over Currituck Sound. To reach the northern communities of Duck, Sanderling, and Corolla, turn left on N.C. 12. To go south toward Kitty Hawk, Kill Devil Hills, and Nags Head, turn right on either of the two main roads.

From the south, you can take either a land or a water route. Via land, follow U.S. 264 East to U.S. 64 East, which will lead you through Roanoke Island to Bodie Island. For a scenic trip, the ferry system is the way to go. The Swan Quarter ferry and the Cedar Island ferry both deliver travelers to Ocracoke, the southernmost island in the Outer Banks. Either ferry ride takes about two and a half hours. Reservations are required in the summer and are advisable year-round. From Ocracoke, travelers can take a free 40-minute ferry ride to

Hatteras Island to gain access to the rest of the Outer Banks. No reservations are required for the Hatteras ferry. For complete information on ferry schedules, fees, and crossing times, call 800-BY-FERRY or visit www.ncferry.org.

From central North Carolina, U.S. 64 leads directly across Roanoke Island to Nags Head. From there, travelers can turn left on either U.S. 158 or N.C. 12 to head up the coast toward Kill Devil Hills and points north or turn right on N.C. 12 to head south toward Hatteras Island.

The Dare County Regional Airport is located on Airport Road in Manteo. Its two runways are 3,290 feet and 4,300 feet in length. Fuel, services, restrooms, and an area for pilots to sleep are offered. For information, call 252-475-5570 or visit www.fly2mqi.com. Air charters are available to and from the airport from just about anywhere east of the Mississippi River. A few local shuttle services and car and limousine rentals are available at the airport as well. Additional paved runways are located at Kill Devil Hills, Hatteras Island, and Ocracoke Island, but no support services are available at those locations.

One of the best sources of information about the area is the Outer Banks Visitors Bureau, at One Visitors Center Circle off U.S. 64/264 in Manteo (27954). For information about the history, culture, and folklore of the area, call 877-629-4386 or visit www.outerbanks.org. Those interested in learning about Ocracoke Island should contact the Greater Hyde County Chamber of Commerce by calling 888-493-3826 or 252-926-9171 or by visiting www.hydecounty.org.

Northern Banks and Beaches

The Northern Banks boast some of the newest and oldest resort areas in North Carolina.

Nags Head was one of the first beach resorts on the East Coast. People began going there in the early 1800s, seeking ocean breezes to provide respite from sweltering Southern summers. The first complaints about excessive development destroying the quaint atmosphere of the Outer Banks were made around 1830. By contrast, almost all of the development north of Duck has taken place in the last 25 years, since there was no paved road to Corolla until 1984.

The northern Banks and beaches stretch from Corolla to Nags Head. Here, you'll discover the northernmost lighthouse on the Banks, the tallest sand dune on the East Coast, and the spot where man first took flight. Or you can just relax in your lounge chair and watch the day pass by. The northern Banks offer some of both the least-developed and most-developed seashore on the Outer Banks. Visitors thus have the opportunity to be alone or in the middle of everything.

Things to Do

Historic Places, Gardens, and Tours

Currituck Beach Lighthouse, located at 1101 Corolla Village Road in Corolla (27927), is the northernmost lighthouse on the Outer Banks and the last major brick lighthouse built on the Outer Banks. Its approximately 1 million bricks were left unpainted to distinguish it from its famous counterparts. Begun in 1873 and completed two years later, it served the 40-mile area of dark coastline between Cape Henry Lighthouse to the north in Virginia and Bodie Island Lighthouse to the south. The 162-foot Currituck Beach Lighthouse had a light visible at 18 nautical miles. Before the advent of electricity, it was powered by a mineral-oil lamp that consisted of five concentric wicks, the largest of which was four inches in diameter. The lighthouse keeper was required to physically move the huge lens every two and a half hours to keep the light flashing. Cranking by hand the weights that were suspended from a line beneath the lantern, he moved the light much in the way a grandfather clock's gears turn to make the hour chime. The beam flooded the night sky for three seconds before fading to black for 17 seconds. This not only warned passing ships of the treacherous coastline but also allowed them to decipher where they were on their journey.

The lighthouse is still a navigational tool for sailors today, emitting its beam from dusk until dawn, though the keeper doesn't have to crank the lens nowadays. Visitors are invited to climb the 214 steps to the top, weather permitting. An interpretive guide is on hand to share facts about the lighthouse.

Also on the grounds is the lighthouse keepers' home. Shipped by barge to the Banks already precut and labeled for easy assembly, the Victorian Stick-style dwelling was completed in 1876. Two keepers and their families moved in to share the duplex. Visitors are not allowed to tour the home, as it is undergoing restoration by Outer Banks Conservationists, Inc.

Currituck Beach Lighthouse
PHOTOGRAPH BY ARTIE SPARROW

Sunset over Currituck Sound
PHOTOGRAPH BY ARTIE SPARROW

Other structures on the property include cisterns for catching rainwater for household use, an outhouse, a chapel, and a schoolhouse. A museum shop is located in a second lighthouse keeper's home, built in 1870 at Long Point Lighthouse on Currituck Sound and shipped to its current location in 1920.

No keepers have lived here since the light was automated in 1939.

Currituck Beach Lighthouse and the museum shop are open daily from 9 A.M. to 5 P.M. from the week before Easter to the week after Thanksgiving. On Thursdays in summer, the lighthouse is open until 8 P.M. An admission fee is charged. Children must be at least four years old to climb the lighthouse. For more information, call 252-453-4939 or visit www.currituckbeachlight.com.

The **Whalehead Club**, at 1084 Lighthouse Drive in Corolla (27927), is located a short walk from the Currituck Beach Lighthouse. Completed in 1925 after three years and $383,000 in construction costs, it was for a time a private residence called Corolla Island, the first home on the Outer Banks to have a basement, an elevator, and a swimming pool.

The local legend surrounding that stunning home reads like a romance novel. Edward Collings Knight, Jr., a wealthy executive with the Pennsylvania Railroad and the American Sugar Refinery, married a beautiful, talented French huntress by the name of Marie Louise LeBel. Marie loved vacationing in what was one of the best duck- and waterfowl-hunting spots in the world (Currituck is Indian for "Land of the Wild Goose"), but when she tried to join a local hunt club, she was turned down due to her gender. So Marie convinced Edward to build her a home that would eclipse any hunt club on the Outer Banks.

Visitors to their dinner parties found numbered and signed Tiffany lighting fixtures, a custom-made dining-room table and chairs with a signature water lily design carved into the wood, and door handles and hinges molded to look like water lily buds. Five chimneys, a large library, cork floors, corduroy walls, copper shingles, and pink tiles on the walls of the kitchen were other features of the lavish Art Nouveau–style home.

The Whalehead Club began to fall into disrepair after the Knights' tenure. It was used for purposes ranging from a boys' school to a facility for testing solid rocket fuel for the nation's space program. The club was bought by Currituck County in 1992 and has been restored to its original grandeur as part of the 39-acre Currituck Heritage Park. The main house, the original boathouse, and the pedestrian footbridge are listed on the National Register of Historic Places.

The grounds are open from dawn until dusk. Tours of the club's first two floors and gallery are given from 9 A.M. to 5 P.M. daily from April through November and Monday through Saturday from December through March. A variety of other tours

Corolla Village, with Whalehead Club on the left and the Outer Banks Center for Wildlife Education on the right
PHOTOGRAPH BY ARTIE SPARROW

Dunes north of Corolla
PHOTOGRAPH BY ARTIE SPARROW

are offered, including the "Search and Find Tour," the docent-led standard tour, the "Behind the Scenes Tour," the "Nuts and Bolts Tour," the "Children's Treasure Hunt," and the "Legends, Lore, and Ghost Tour." The "Moonlight Ghost Tour" takes place at 7:30 P.M. the first Saturday of the month from November through April. Reservations are required for all except the regular tour. An admission fee is charged; children eight and younger are admitted free with an adult on the regular tour. For more information, call 252-453-9040 or visit www.whalehead.org.

Wright Brothers National Memorial, at Milepost 8 on U.S. 158 (North Croatan Highway) in Kill Devil Hills (27948), honors a moment that changed history. Orville and Wilbur Wright, bicycle shop owners from Dayton, Ohio, had dreams of flying while they worked on their spokes and gears. They began pursuing their dream in earnest in 1899, when Wilbur wrote to the Smithsonian Institution asking for information on flight. Then the brothers set about finding out for themselves how to fly. For three years, they tested various gliders around Kitty Hawk and Kill Devil Hills. They also built a wind tunnel back in Ohio to learn the aerodynamics that would enable them to get off the ground. As Wilbur once said, "It is possible to fly without motors, but not without knowledge and skill."

On December 14, 1903, the brothers were ready to test a powered machine. They flipped a coin to see who would fly first; Wilbur won. He eased himself into the plane and took off from the launching rail, but the plane climbed too steeply and stalled. For three days, they repaired the plane. On the morning of December 17, they once again took their 40-foot, 605-pound *Flyer* into the sand. Amid 27-mile-per-hour wind gusts, Orville took flight for the first time, staying aloft for 12 seconds and

120 feet. The brothers took turns flying after that. The fourth and final flight—by Wilbur—was the most successful, lasting 59 seconds and covering 852 feet. After that, a gust of wind overturned the plane and damaged it beyond repair.

The visitor center, administered by the National Park Service, is the first stop at Wright Brothers National Memorial. It contains full-scale reproductions of one of the brothers' gliders and the famous *Flyer* that made the first flight. Interpretive talks are given in the center. The gift shop on the premises offers books and memorabilia.

Guests can see how the brothers lived and worked by visiting the reconstructed camp buildings on the grounds. Near the camp buildings are markers commemorating the takeoff and landing points of the first four flights.

The centerpiece of the memorial, however, is the 60-foot granite monument atop the 90-foot Kill Devil Hill, from which the brothers launched hundreds of glider flights before they ever built their first powered machine. Visitors can walk to the top of the hill and gaze down upon the entire site. Bronze busts of the Wrights are on one side of the monument.

The memorial is open daily except Christmas. An admission fee is charged for visitors 17 and older. For more information, call 252-441-7430 or visit www.nps.gov/wrbr.

Colington Island, just south of Wright Brothers National Memorial, is the site of the first permanent settlement on the Outer Banks. Accessible by Colington Road off U.S. 158, the island features several seafood shops and campgrounds and offers visitors a nice photographic opportunity in a relatively undeveloped area of the Banks.

Museums and Science Centers

Outer Banks Center for Wildlife Education, at 1160 Village Lane in Corolla (27927), is a 22,000-square-foot facility located in Corolla Heritage Park. It features a waterfowl decoy gallery, an exhibit hall, and an auditorium with informational videos on the area's unique history, traditions, and natural resources. In the summer, it offers extensive programs on coastal wildlife and outdoor skills. The center is open Monday through Saturday from 9 A.M. to 5 P.M. Admission is free. For more information, call 252-453-0221 or visit www.ncwildlife.org/pg08_EducationWorkshops/Outer_Banks_Center.htm.

The **United States Army Corps of Engineers Field Research Facility**, at 1261 Duck Road in Duck (27949), is the home of the Waterways Experiment Station. Waves, winds, currents, and tides are monitored and recorded at this site from a pier that extends 1,840 feet into the ocean. Walking tours are given at 10 A.M. Monday through Friday from mid-June to August only; those who arrive after 10 A.M. will not be permitted within the facility due to security reasons. Admission is free. For more information, call 252-261-6840 or visit www.frf.usace.army.mil.

Corolla Wild Horse Museum, located in a restored schoolhouse at 1126 Schoolhouse Lane in Corolla (27927), shares the history and legacy of the Banker horses. The wild horses on the northern Banks, the descendants of Spanish mustangs, have been living here for over 500 years. They're currently confined to a large area north of Corolla. At the museum, you can see photographic exhibits that tell their story. This is also the place to learn the best way to see the horses. Numerous private companies offer excursions into the wild-horse area; the museum staff can tell you which are the most reputable and reliable. The museum is open Monday through Friday from 10 A.M. to 4 P.M.; call for winter hours. Call 252-453-8002 or visit www.corollawildhorses.com.

The pier at the United States Army Corps of Engineers Field Research Facility
PHOTOGRAPH BY ARTIE SPARROW

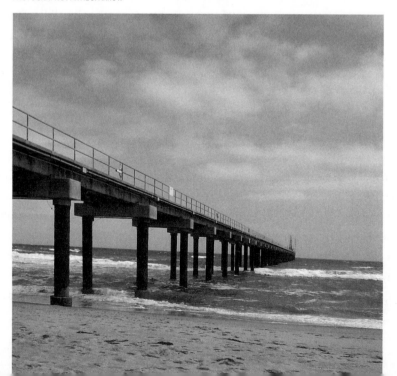

Special Shopping

Scarborough Faire, at 1177 Duck Road in Duck (27949), is an intimate shopping village nestled in the woods. If you're looking for the perfect gift, a great book, wickedly decadent fudge, or a wonderful meal, you'll find it here. The shopping center was established in the 1980s by Duck landowners who wanted to preserve the village atmosphere. Its 15 shops have something to delight anyone. For more information, visit www.scarboroughfaireinducknc.com.

Outer Barks, at 1171 Duck Road in Duck (27949), features the East Coast's largest selection of unique gifts for dog lovers. It's located in the Scarborough Lane Shoppes adjacent to Scarborough Faire. In addition to gifts, the shop hosts a weekly "Yappy Happy Hour" for dogs and their owners. For information, call 252-261-6279 or visit www.outerbarks.com.

North Carolina has seen a boom in wineries in the past decade, and the Banks claim two of their own on Knotts Island (27950), located northwest of Corolla in Currituck Sound.

Martin Vineyards, at 213 Martin Farm Lane, was started by the Martin family in 1977 as a peach and scuppernong grape farm. Today, it boasts a variety of wines from muscadine to Merlot. Wine tastings are offered year-round; the fee is waived with the purchase of a bottle. Visitors can pick their own fruit seasonally. From May through December, Martin Vineyards is open daily except Wednesday from noon to 5 P.M. From January through April, it is open weekdays except Wednesday from noon to 3 P.M. and weekends from noon to 5 P.M. For more information, call 252-429-3542 or visit www.martinvineyards.com.

Moonrise Bay Vineyard, at 134 Moonrise Bay Landing off N.C. 615 and Woodleigh Road, is named after the stunning moonrises owner Richard "Oakie" Morris and his wife, Kate, enjoy nightly over the quiet, starry sound. They created the winery as a hobby in 1997 and made it into a family business in 1999. Since then, it has grown to offer more than a dozen award-winning wines. Moonrise Bay is open for tours and tastings daily from noon to 5 P.M. and by appointment. Special-event dinners are also available by reservation. For more information, call 866-888-9463 or 252-429-9463 or visit www.moonrisebaywine.com.

The northern Banks are also home to an ever-growing arts community. More than 20 galleries are located between Duck and Nags Head alone. Gallery Row in

Nags Head features some of the best outlets in the state. Be sure to check out the Dare County Arts Council's website at www.darearts.org for a complete listing of the area's art events.

One of the best-known establishments is **Glenn Eure's Ghost Fleet Gallery**, near Milepost 10.5 at 210 East Driftwood Street in Nags Head (27959). Eure is a noted character in these parts, having created everything from the artwork on display to the building housing the gallery. Offerings here range from gallery showings to poetry readings and guest lectures. For more information, call 252-441-6584.

Seaside Art Gallery is located near Milepost 11 at 2716 South Virginia Dare Trail/N.C. 12 in Nags Head (27959). In addition to the work of local artists, visitors can view and purchase original pieces by the likes of Picasso, Whistler, Dali, and Renoir. Kids will enjoy the artwork by Warner Brothers Studios and Hanna Barbera Animation. For more information, call 252-441-5418 or visit www.seasideart.com.

You should also plan to visit **Lighthouse Gallery and Gifts**, at 301 East Driftwood Street in Nags Head (27959). This gallery offers original works of art, memorabilia, and books pertaining to lighthouses. For information, call 800-579-2827 or visit www.seabeacons.com.

Tanger Outlet Mall, at Milepost 16.5 on U.S. 158, is a good place to spend a rainy day or to hide out if you've had too much sun. Shoppers can find bargains from clothing retailers like Polo by Ralph Lauren and Gap and shoe manufacturers like Bass and Nine West. For information, visit www.tangeroutlet.com or call 252-441-5634.

Recreation

Swimming, fishing, kayaking, windsurfing, parasailing, surfing, water-skiing—the northern Banks is the place for great recreation. Watersports are the pastime of choice here. Thanks to the bounty of water, visitors find countless ways to keep wet. But please note that not all the beaches have lifeguards. And since the currents and tides have sunk over 1,500 ships and given the area the infamous nickname "Graveyard of the Atlantic," be sure to keep your wits about you while enjoying all the amusements the sea has to offer.

Kitty Hawk Sports is the watersports headquarters of the Outer Banks. Everything from swimwear to surfboards to kayaking gear is offered at its various stores in Corolla (252-453-4999 or 252-453-6900), Duck (252-261-8770), Kitty Hawk (252-261-0145), and Nags Head (252-441-6800 or 252-441-2756). Windsurfing and kayaking lessons are available, as is sailing, windsurfing, and kayaking rental equipment. For more information, visit www.kittyhawksports.com.

If fishing is your sport of choice, you'll be pleased to see the piers and marinas dotting the Banks. Indeed, the area is known as "the Billfish Capital of the World." Of course, piers are highly vulnerable to storm damage, so it's a good idea to call ahead and make sure the pier you plan on visiting is still there. Fees are charged at the piers to fish or just to watch others reel in their catch; weekly and seasonal passes are available.

Avalon Fishing Pier, at 2111 North Virginia Dare Trail in Kill Devil Hills (27948), is open spring, summer, and fall. Its website features a live webcam, daily fishing reports, and a chatroom. For information, call 252-441-7494 or visit www.avalonpier.com.

Nags Head Fishing Pier, at 3335 South Virginia Dare Trail in Nags Head (27959), is open year-round. It offers a tackle shop and a restaurant that will cook your catch for you. For information, call 252-441-5141 or visit www.nagsheadpier.com.

Roanoke Sound Pier, at 7665 South Virginia Dare Trail in Nags Head (27959) along the Manteo causeway, is known as a hot spot for crabbing and catching speckled trout, striped bass, and flounder. For information, call 252-441-5740 or visit www.fishingunlimited.net/SoundPier.html.

Jennette's Fishing Pier, at 7223 South Virginia Dare Trail in Nags Head (27959), is the granddaddy of Outer Banks fishing. Built in 1939, it withstood time and hurricanes to join the 21st century before Hurricane Isabel in September 2003 took out 540 feet of the pier. Renovations began in May 2009 and are scheduled to be completed by May 2011. The facility is owned and operated by the North Carolina Aquarium Society. It offers an ocean classroom and the largest trophy-fish collection in North Carolina. For information, call 252-441-6421 or visit www.jennettespier.net.

If you're feeling waterlogged, you'll be happy to note the many recreational opportunities to be had on land.

N.C. 12 ends just north of Corolla. After that, there are no paved roads in the 10-mile tract of undeveloped land that includes *Currituck National Wildlife Refuge*. Within the refuge are sandy beaches, grassy dunes, maritime forests, shrub thickets, and fresh and brackish marshes, along with a variety of birds, turtles, foxes, rabbits, wild boars, deer, and the famous wild horses of the northern Banks. The refuge can be reached on foot, in a kayak, or by driving up the beach in a four-wheel-drive vehicle. It is open year-round during daylight hours except for federal holidays. For information, visit www.fws.gov/currituck.

Currituck Banks National Estuarine Research Reserve is a 960-acre site north of Corolla off N.C. 12. A parking lot provides access to a 0.3-mile boardwalk that goes through a maritime forest and concludes at Currituck Sound. Visitors can also take the 1.5-mile primitive trail to explore more of the maritime forest. The warm Gulf Stream mixes with the cool Labrador Current off Currituck Banks. This creates a climate where Northern species reach the southern limit of their ranges and Southern species reach the northern limit of their ranges. The result is stunning biodiversity. For more information, visit www.nccoastalreserve.net.

Pine Island Audubon Sanctuary is a 6,000-acre wildlife sanctuary that stretches from Currituck Sound to the Atlantic Ocean. It can be accessed just north of Duck off N.C. 12 near The Sanderling. Visitors can take a self-guided hike along a 2.5-mile trail through sand dunes, sea oats, live oaks, and maritime marshes to discover what the northern Banks looked like a century ago, before development. Two observation platforms are stationed along the trail for resting and picture taking. For over a decade now, the Audubon Society has overseen the sanctuary and its more than 350 species of plants and 159 species of birds in an effort to conserve the state's natu-

Currituck Banks National Estuarine Research Reserve
PHOTOGRAPH BY ARTIE SPARROW

A flight of pelicans over the beach at Pine Island
PHOTOGRAPH BY ARTIE SPARROW

ral habitats. For information, visit www.nc.audubon.org/birds-science-education/pine-island or call 252-453-2838.

Duck Town Park, at 1240 Duck Road (27949) consists of 11 acres of sound-front property in the heart of Duck. Visitors enjoy trails, a gazebo, a public kayak/canoe launch, and an 1,800-foot boardwalk that provides gorgeous views of Currituck Sound, especially at sunset. For information, visit www.townofduck.com/ourtownpark.htm.

Nags Head Woods Ecological Preserve, at 701 West Ocean Acres Drive in Kill Devil Hills (27948), is a 1,092-acre maritime forest managed by the Nature Conservancy. It is located on the western shore of Nags Head off U.S. 158. The preserve, designated a national natural landmark by Congress in 1974, is home to over 50 bird species and an array of aquatic life, including the rare water violet. Visitors may be surprised to learn that the Outer Banks is the northern limit of the American alligator's habitat; the gators here are a bit smaller than their Florida counterparts. The preserve offers walking trails and a visitor center, where guests can pick up maps and learn about the research conducted on the grounds. It is open daily from dawn to dusk. Admission is free. For information, call 252-441-2525 or visit www.nature.org/wherewework/northamerica/states/northcarolina/preserves/art5618.html.

Jockey's Ridge State Park is located at 100 West Carolista Drive near Milepost 12 off U.S. 158 in Nags Head (27959). This 414-acre park features the tallest sand-dune system on the East Coast; its highest dune stands around 140 feet, depending on the prevailing winds. Used as a horse-racing track at the beginning of the 20th century, this land is now most famous for its kite-flying and hang-gliding opportunities. It was on dunes like these that the Wright brothers learned to fly; on a clear day, you can even see the granite monument at Wright Brothers National Memorial. The trails leading up the sand dunes offer a view of the entire width of Nags Head, all the way from Roanoke Sound to the Atlantic Ocean. This unbeatable panorama draws people to the "Sunset on the Ridge" program that park rangers present around 8 P.M. nearly every evening during summer. Visitors can bring a picnic dinner and enjoy the sunset as they learn how the dunes were formed and the story behind the ridge's name. The park offers a variety of educational programs, hiking trails, picnic facilities, restrooms, and a visitor center. The hours vary according to the season, so be sure to call before you visit. Admission is free. Call 252-441-7132 or visit www. jockeysridgestatepark.com.

Across the street from Jockey's Ridge State Park is the largest of more than a dozen *Kitty Hawk Kites* stores dotting the Outer Banks. The Nags Head location is home to the world's largest hang-gliding school. Here, instructors certified by the United States Hang Gliding Association teach an average of 10,000 students per year in beginning, intermediate, and advanced foot-launch and tandem hang gliding. Kitty Hawk Kites also offers guided outdoor activities including kayak ecotours and jet-boat tours. And the knowledgeable sales staff can help you find the perfect kite to use on the Outer Banks. For more information, call 877-359-8447 or visit www. kittyhawkkites.com.

Jockey's Ridge
PHOTOGRAPH BY ARTIE SPARROW

Getting off the sand and onto the greens is also possible on the Banks. Some very impressive golf courses are in the area.

The Currituck Club, at 620 Currituck Clubhouse Drive in Corolla (27927), features a Rees Jones–designed championship course. Call 252-453-9400 or visit www.currituckclubobx.org.

Duck Woods Country Club, at 50 South Dogwood Trail in Southern Shores (27949), is a venerable 18-hole course that has welcomed golfers since the late 1960s. Call 252-261-2744 or visit www.duckwoodscc.com.

Sea Scape Golf Links, at 300 Eckner Street in Kitty Hawk (27949), is located at the edge of a maritime forest. The course offers a nice view of the ocean from several holes. Call 252-261-2158 or visit www.seascapegolf.com.

Nags Head Golf Links, at 5615 South Seachase Drive in Nags Head (27959), has an 18-hole championship course designed by Bob Moore. Call 252-441-8073 or visit www.nagsheadgolflinks.com.

Seasonal Events

The Outer Banks prides itself on its good-time atmosphere, so the abundance of festivals and celebrations throughout the year should come as no surprise. As you may guess, many center around the area's greatest assets—the wind and water. From seafood feasts to sailing regattas, the Outer Banks knows how to throw a good party.

The nation's oldest hang-gliding competition occurs in Nags Head in mid-May. The *Annual Hang Gliding Spectacular and Air Games*, held at Jockey's Ridge State Park, offers an impressive and multicolored array of flyers. For more information, call 877-359-8447 or 252-441-4124 or visit www.hangglidingspectacular.com.

The *Outer Banks Pirate Festival* takes place in mid-September. It is hosted by Kitty Hawk Kites and Blackbeard's Crew, a living-history performance group that specializes in reenacting pirate raids. The festival features tales of the sea told by pirates, pirate training for children, and live cannon fire. For more information, see the events page of www.kittyhawk.com or visit www.blackbeardscrew.org.

The *Annual Nags Head Surf Fishing Club Invitational Tournament*, held in early October, has hosted many of the area's best competition fishermen for over 50 years. For information, visit www.nagsheadsurffishingclub.org.

Jockey's Ridge State Park, arguably the best kite-flying spot on earth, and Kitty Hawk Kites offer the ***Annual Outer Banks Stunt-Kite Competition*** in October. Sanctioned by the American Kiting Association, the event features workshops, demonstrations, and kite-flying ballets. For information, call 877-359-8447 or 252-441-4124 or visit the events page of www.kittyhawk.com. The good folks at Kitty Hawk Kites can tell you about the many other kite-flying competitions in the area, too.

Wings Over Water is a six-day wildlife festival that takes place in early November throughout the Outer Banks. Guided nature tours are offered at locations ranging from the area north of Corolla to Portsmouth Island, just south of Ocracoke. For information, visit www.wingsoverwater.org.

Places to Stay

The northern Banks and beaches offer a wide range of places to stay, from charming bed-and-breakfasts to steadfast, reliable chains. Families, honeymooners, and salty old fishermen alike will be able to find the places that fit them best. You'll discover that Corolla, Duck, Sanderling, Southern Shores, and Kitty Hawk have much to offer in the way of cottages and bed-and-breakfasts. Kill Devil Hills and Nags Head are where you'll find the majority of hotels and motels.

There are three seasons on the Banks. Peak season is Memorial Day through Labor Day. Off-season is Easter through Memorial Day in the spring and Labor Day through Thanksgiving in the fall. The winter season is Thanksgiving through Easter. Lodgings are crowded in summer and nearly uninhabited in winter. Rates for the same accommodations can vary by as much as $500 between peak season and winter. Minimum stays may be required at some places. Be sure to call well in advance to book your perfect spot. Two good resources to check before booking are the websites of the Outer Banks Visitors Bureau (www.outerbanks.org) and the Outer Banks Chamber of Commerce (www.outerbankschamber.com).

Resorts, Hotels, and Motels

The Sanderling. Deluxe. 1461 Duck Road in Duck, 27949 (877-650-4812 or 252-261-4111; www.thesanderling.com). Comprised of three inns, a spa, and a conference center, The Sanderling is one of the most lovely—and most expensive—places to stay on the Outer Banks. Featuring luxuriously appointed guest rooms and five three- and four-bedroom villas, the resort sits on 12 acres spanning the peninsula from Currituck Sound to the Atlantic Ocean. Many guests come here to enjoy the quiet, natural beauty of the area, though others say the full-service spa is the real draw. Guests are also pampered by the pool, the health club, the tennis courts, the sun deck, and the private beach. If you decide to stay here, you should definitely look into the adjoining Lifesaving Station Restaurant.

Hampton Inn & Suites Outer Banks. Deluxe/Expensive. 333 Audubon Drive in Corolla, 27927 (252-453-6565; www.hamptoninn-outerbanks.com). This beachfront hotel, conveniently located between Duck and Corolla, features 123 standard rooms and studio suites with complimentary high-speed Internet access for those who must check their e-mail while on vacation. Other amenities include an indoor pool, an outdoor pool, and a "lazy river" water ride that's great for cooling off. A guest laundromat is on the premises, as are exercise and game rooms. During the week, free On the Run™ breakfast bags are offered for those who can't wait to get out and explore. A daily complimentary continental breakfast is served in the dining room for those who prefer a more leisurely pace.

The Carolina Oceanfront. Expensive/Moderate. 401 North Virginia Dare Trail in Kill Devil Hills, 27948 (800-854-5286 or 252-480-2600; www.thecarolinaoceanfront. com). This clean, friendly hotel has three floors, 119 guest rooms, and an oceanfront pool. The rooms include refrigerators, microwaves, and coffee makers. A complimentary breakfast is offered each morning. This is among the more affordable options for families. According to hotel policy, an adult 21 or older must be booked for each room.

Days Inn & Suites Mariner. Expensive/Moderate. 1801 North Virginia Dare Trail in Kill Devil Hills, 27948 (800-329-7466 or 252-441-2021; www.outer-banks. com/days-mariner). Another of the many reliable chain lodgings along the northern Banks, this oceanfront hotel located a mile from Wright Brothers National Memorial offers standard, double, and king rooms and ocean-view suites featuring a kitchen, a living room, and two bedrooms. Kids will enjoy the outdoor pool, and those looking to get in some exercise can use the hotel's complimentary YMCA passes. Oregon Inlet Fishing Center parties receive a discount. Complimentary continental breakfast is served daily.

Salt Spray, Dreaming, and Abiding

Excerpted from *Duck: An Outer Banks Village*
by Judith D. Mercier

Clouds move in from the east. Tomorrow, they will linger over the sand, drench the dunes in a chilling rain. Maybe it was a stretch of gray October sky or the cold-hearted dimness of a February morning that first made me so curious about this place. It is always in nature's cheerlessness that I think about the earliest Bankers, the ones who settled what is now Duck and other towns in Dare County. I wonder how much courage this thin strip of sand can hold, how much it has already sapped over the years from the people who willingly risked it all on a chance as unsure as this wind-swept barrier island.

When those old-time Bankers passed on, they had no idea how valuable their sons' and daughters' inheritances would become. Even a thousand feet of waterfront property held no guarantee. There were never any sure bets here. Maybe the greatest virtue of this place has nothing to do with its ocean-view houses or sound-front lots, but with longings so intense they can't be shaken, blown off, or washed away. Maybe the Bankers' greatest bequest was their ability to be dreamers, to hold firm despite all the challenges and uncertainties, to abide.

It's the salt spray, I've been told, that can stunt the growth of plants along the Atlantic beachfront. On the Outer Banks, the habitat is too brutal for much of nature's greenery. But panic grass, sea elder, and evening primrose flourish on the frontal dunes in Duck. They know how to survive the harsh winds, the blowing sand, the shifts and changes that mark these shores. Dune plants thrive and spread because their roots grow down, then out. They dig deep. Maybe this is the legacy nature has left to the Bankers, old and new. It's a lesson that even the outsiders who have decided to stay, like David Stick, seem to have learned.

Bygone days may have proven that nothing comes easily to those who seek beginnings on the Outer Banks. Yet when I'm here, all the effort makes sense. The beauty, the mystery, the stories of aviators and dune builders, the adventures of dodging smoke bombs or digging for them under a sliver of white moon— all seem reason enough to hope that in this place, almost anything is possible.

View of the boardwalk at Duck Town Park
PHOTOGRAPH BY ARTIE SPARROW

No longer is it hard imagining what the Duck of the 1950s must have looked like—just a drowsy village with twenty-one property owners, one store, and probably fewer than a hundred residents. Approaching Duck Blind Villas, my car has sole possession of the road. Nothing moves in front of or behind me. It's nearly supper-time in the off-season, and Duck lulls. Only the faint pink glow of a sinking sun lingers over the Currituck. Streetlights will click on soon, but they haven't sensed night's coming yet.

It seems I could almost be driving into Duck's past. I envision the old village. The road is something other than smooth, black tar. I feel mounds of graded sand beneath the tires. The curves sharper and coming more quickly, I slow down, expecting rough spots ahead. Dozens of wild ducks streak a steel-gray sky. On the Currituck, a few hunters patch blinds with pine brush or pole their skiffs homeward through the shallow sound. On a front porch, neighborhood women spread a fishing net over their laps, their song a psalm for Sunday's service, their hands busy mending for the next day's catch. To the right and left, groves of oak grow without interruption. Their branches are bent and partially stripped of leaves. Like old sentries, they wave me in through the winter dusk.

Inns and Bed-and-Breakfasts

Advice 5¢. Deluxe. 11 Scarborough Lane in Duck, 27949 (800-238-4235 or 252-255-1050; www.advice5.com). This intimate and friendly inn is close to area shops and restaurants, making an evening stroll for ice cream a pleasure. Featuring four guest rooms and one suite, all with private baths and decks, the inn gives visitors a home-away-from-home feeling. A swimming pool, tennis courts, and a private walkway to the beach are available. Tea, coffee, and home-baked goods are provided for breakfast, and a lovely afternoon tea offers a respite from the sun. The inn hosts an annual 5K race around Thanksgiving, an event eagerly anticipated all over the Banks.

Cypress Moon Inn. Deluxe. 1206 Harbor Court in Kitty Hawk, 27949 (877-905-5060 or 252-261-5060; www.cypressmooninn.com). The proprietors of this inn have lived on the Outer Banks for more than a quarter-century, and they know how to make visitors feel at home. The inn's three guest rooms feature comfy queen-sized beds, private bathrooms, refrigerators, satellite television and radio, and, most importantly, gorgeous views of Kitty Hawk Sound. Guests can also enjoy the views from the inn's double-decker wraparound porches, from the hammocks stationed around the property, and from the kayaks furnished by the innkeepers. A full breakfast with vegetarian options is provided daily.

Bald View Bed-and-Breakfast. Deluxe/Expensive. 3805 Elijah Baum Road in Kitty Hawk, 27949 (252-255-2829; www.baldview.com). Bordering 11 acres of Kitty Hawk Sound and a maritime forest, this bed-and-breakfast offers a breather from the busy pace of the northern Banks. You'll feel like you're in a secluded retreat when you stay in one of the four guest rooms, each of which has a private bath and a television. The shared public rooms feature antiques, and the many family portraits hanging throughout the home have lots of stories behind them. The best feature, though, is the spectacular view of the sound. The ocean is only five minutes away, too. Breakfast is served every morning.

First Colony Inn. Deluxe/Expensive. 6720 South Virginia Dare Trail in Nags Head, 27959 (800-368-9390 or 252-441-2343; www.firstcolonyinn.com). One of the largest inns in Nags Head, First Colony opened its doors in 1932 and is now listed on the National Register. Its 27 guest rooms have earned the inn a Four Diamond rating from AAA. Each unique room is appointed with English antiques. Some feature a wet bar, a kitchenette, a whirlpool tub, a sitting room, or a private screened porch. Guests are invited to enjoy a few quiet moments reading in the library or taking in the salty air and the beautiful sunsets from the inn's gazebo on the dunes. A hot continental breakfast buffet is served daily in the breakfast room.

The Inn at Corolla Light. Deluxe/Expensive. 1066 Ocean Trail in Corolla, 27927 (800-215-0772 or 252-453-3340; www.corolla-inn.com). If you want to be away from the hustle and bustle of the Banks, this is the place. Located two miles from the end of N.C. 12, the inn offers 43 spacious rooms, each with its own bathroom and many with a whirlpool tub, a gas fireplace, and a kitchen and lounge area. The ocean, the sound, and Currituck Beach Lighthouse are all within walking distance, but guests are also free to use the inn's bicycles or the local trolley service to get there. A sports complex featuring an Olympic-sized swimming pool and clay tennis courts is only two blocks away, for those who want to work off their complimentary continental breakfast. The innkeepers' son, Bob, runs a wild horse tour that explores the uninhabited beaches and the wildlife north of Corolla.

Places to Eat

The restaurants along the northern Banks offer far more than the normal beach fare of fried seafood. You'll find an eclectic blend of Caribbean, Italian, French, Southwestern, and vegetarian cuisines. Everything from elegant wine dinners to burgers and fries is available. Since most restaurants recognize that guests are on vacation, casual, neat beach attire is the accepted form of dress. During the busy summer season, you can expect a wait for dinner almost anyplace. Reservations may be required at some restaurants and not accepted at others, so call ahead to be sure.

The Blue Point. Expensive. In the Waterfront Shops at 1240 Duck Road in Duck, 27949 (252-261-8090; www.goodfoodgoodwine.com). This restaurant, formerly known as The Blue Point Bar and Grill, quickly became a local favorite when it opened in 1989. You'll see why when you try its delicious Southern coastal cuisine, described by the classically trained chef as "cutting edge with a comfort factor." Many of the dishes rely on locally grown—and often organic—products. Reservations are accepted up to a month in advance; you should probably take advantage of this time window if you want to enjoy The Blue Point during summer. For a special treat, try to time your meal to coincide with a sunset over Currituck Sound, which can be spectacular. Lunch is served Tuesday through Sunday. Dinner is served Tuesday through Sunday from November to April and daily the rest of the year.

Elizabeth's Café and Winery. Expensive. In Scarborough Faire Shopping Village at 1177 Duck Road in Duck, 27949 (252-261-6145; www.elizabethscafe.com). Voted one of the top 100 restaurants of the 20th century by the International Restaurant and Hospitality Rating Bureau, Elizabeth's serves up haute cuisine without the attitude or the price. Guests can order international fare from a prix fixe menu that changes nightly or an à la carte menu. Wine dinners are also available, allowing guests to enjoy Elizabeth's special wines, given an Award of Excellence by *Wine Spectator* magazine. In fact, around 1,600 wines are on hand at any given time. Dinner is served Monday through Saturday during summer and Tuesday through Saturday the rest of the year.

Metropolis. Expensive. 520 Old Stoney Road in Corolla, 27927 (252-453-6167; www.metropolisobx.com). For a slow, leisurely, savory meal in Corolla, Metropolis is the place to go. Its extensive selection of light and heavy tapas varies depending on what's in season. Featuring a knowledgeable wait staff and an extensive martini menu, Metropolis is a wonderful place for a special meal. It is open daily during the busy season and offers very late hours.

Lifesaving Station Restaurant. Expensive/Moderate. On the grounds of The Sanderling at 1417 Duck Road in Duck, 27949 (252-261-4111; www.thesanderling. com/dining.aspx). This casual restaurant features traditional and coastal Southern cuisine prepared with the finest and freshest ingredients. The menu changes regularly to take advantage of what the season has to offer. Gourmet meals are paired with wines from the Lifesaving Station's wine room. Housed in what used to be the Caffey's Inlet Lifesaving Station and decorated with memorabilia from times gone by, the restaurant gives a sense of what the area was like before it became a tourist destination. An outdoor pavilion open on weekdays offers a casual dining experience. From the pavilion, guests can watch the sun set over the sound and take in the cool ocean breeze. Dinner reservations are recommended. Breakfast, lunch, and dinner are served daily; a three-course Sunday brunch is available as well.

Meridian 42. Expensive/Moderate. In Southern Shores Crossing Shopping Center at 1 Ocean Boulevard in Southern Shores, 27949 (www.meridian42.com; 252-261-0420). Once inside this airy, Mediterranean-inspired restaurant, you'll know you're about to experience a special meal. The dishes served here, some of the best along the Banks, take their inspiration from Barcelona, Spain, and Rome, Italy—cities located along the 42nd meridian, or latitude line. You'll definitely notice the emphasis on fresh local ingredients, including seafood caught from the Atlantic just that morning. All tapas, pastas, and baked goods are made on the premises to complement the large wine selection, for which Meridian 42 was named a *Wine Spectator* Award of Excellence recipient. Dinner is served Tuesday through Saturday. Reservations are accepted up to two weeks in advance.

Port O' Call Restaurant and Gaslight Saloon. Expensive/Moderate. Milepost 8.5, 504 South Virginia Dare Trail in Kill Devil Hills, 27948 (252-441-7484; www.outerbanksportocall.com). Feeding locals and tourists alike for over 20 years, this restaurant is an Outer Banks landmark. The plush Victorian atmosphere is unique, to say the least; velvet settees, Tiffany lamps, and copious artwork adorn the restaurant. The menu brags that it's the most extensive on the beach, featuring seafood seven ways, from baked to blackened to broiled to grilled to sautéed to steamed to fried. Angus beef, chicken, pasta dishes, soups, and salads round out the menu. You can await your table in the Gaslight Saloon or retreat there after dinner for a nightcap and live entertainment. The gift shop offers jewelry, nautical items, collector dolls, local and national artists' work, and Tiffany and Victorian lamps. Dinner is served nightly March through December. Seasonal live entertainment is offered.

Bad Bean Taqueria. Moderate. In Timbuck II Shopping Village at 785 Sunset Boulevard in Corolla, 27927 (252-453-4380; www.badbeanobx.com). Inspired by taquerias of the Pacific coast, the Bad Bean offers fresh local food. Its California-style burritos are genuinely giant, and its tacos filled with fresh local seafood are not to be missed. The Bad Bean also offers a wide selection of cold beers and special margaritas. It serves lunch and dinner daily from Memorial Day to Labor Day and Monday to Saturday the rest of the year.

Black Pelican Oceanfront Café. Moderate. Milepost 4, 3848 Virginia Dare Trail in Kitty Hawk, 27949 (877-890-6049 or 252-261-3171; www.blackpelican.com/main.cfm). The Black Pelican is housed in the 135-plus-year-old former lifesaving station and telegraph office where Orville and Wilbur Wright sent out to the world the news of their first flight. Diners can enjoy wood-oven pizzas and fresh local seafood. An on-site gift shop offers Wright brothers memorabilia. Lunch and dinner are served daily year-round.

Outer Banks Brewing Station. Moderate. Milepost 8.5, 600 South Croatan Highway in Kill Devil Hills, 27948 (252-449-2739; www.obbrewing.com). Besides brewing tasty seasonal beers with interesting names like "Hurley Burley Brown Ale" and "Huge Hefeweizen," this restaurant serves delicious homemade pasta dishes, grilled duck and steak, and fresh seafood. It also offers burgers and fries, if you're looking for more homey fare. It is the nation's first wind-powered brewpub. Live entertainment is offered most nights in the bar. Dinner is served daily except Tuesday.

The Rundown Café & Tsunami Surf Bar. Moderate. Milepost 1, 5218 Virginia Dare Trail in Kitty Hawk, 27949 (252-255-0026; www.thecoastalexplorer.com/RundownCafe). Housed in a structure that looks like a Caribbean beach house, The Rundown Café offers a menu heavy on fresh ingredients and local seafood. The entrées range from Jerk chicken to fish tacos to seasoned shrimp. Vegetarian dishes include deliciously spicy Thai noodles. Among the desserts are chocolate peanut butter pie and—what else?—Key lime pie. A children's menu is available, a feature you won't find at all Banks restaurants. Lunch and dinner are served daily from February through November.

Slice Pizzeria. Moderate. Milepost 8.5, 710 South Croatan Highway in Kill Devil Hills, 27948 (252-449-8888; www.slicepizzeriaobx.com). Slice opened in June 2008 and is already a favorite place for locals. Its pizza is baked in a stone oven. Slice offers traditional pizza along with Chicago-style deep-dish pizza and a variety of pasta dishes, subs, and calzones. Lunch and dinner are served daily.

Sugar Creek Soundfront Seafood Restaurant. Moderate. Milepost 16.5, 7340 South Virginia Dare Trail in Nags Head, 27959 (252-441-4963). Located on the sound on the Nags Head–Manteo Causeway, Sugar Creek features a great view of the water separating Roanoke Island from the northern Banks. It's been a local favorite for over two decades. Steaks and seafood are the specialties here. A lounge and a full bar serve up a variety of appetizers to guests waiting for an open table. Sugar Creek is open daily for lunch and dinner.

Awful Arthur's Oyster Bar. Moderate/Inexpensive. Milepost 6, 2106 North Virginia Dare Trail in Kill Devil Hills, 27948 (252-441-5955; www.awfularthursobx.com). Awful Arthur's is a casual hangout where you can get a dozen oysters at the steam bar or an entire meal in the adjoining restaurant. The local seafood, steaks, chicken, and pasta served here can be washed down with an assortment of beers.

Awful Arthur's T-shirts, a favorite of locals and frat guys, are sold in the neighboring gift shop. Lunch and dinner are offered daily year-round.

Sam and Omie's. Moderate/Inexpensive. Milepost 16.5, 7228 South Virginia Dare Trail in Nags Head, 27959 (252-441-7366; www.samandomies.net). Sam and Omie's has been an Outer Banks institution since 1937. Breakfast is the specialty here, as evidenced by the special "Omie-lettes" on the menu. This is also a nice place to select a quick but satisfying lunch from among the restaurant's "Samiches." You can't go wrong with one of the salads, the she-crab soup, the steamed local seafood, or the homemade desserts either. Sam and Omie's is open daily from March through November for breakfast, lunch, and dinner.

Roanoke Island

Surrounded by the waters of Roanoke Sound and Croatan Sound, Roanoke Island claims the honor of being the birthplace of English America. More than 400 years ago, intrepid explorers discovered this "goodliest land under the cope of heaven" and convinced Queen Elizabeth I to send settlers here to claim the land for England. Several attempts to settle the area were made—including one that saw the birth of the first English child on American soil—but none succeeded. Roanoke Island owes its heritage to the brave souls who gave up everything to seek out new opportunities and a new life in a strange land.

Manteo, named for one of the friendly Indians who helped the colonists, is the largest town on Roanoke Island. It prides itself on being a "walkable" community. Here, you will find the majority of shopping and dining opportunities on the island. Plan on spending a morning exploring the many shops on the waterfront, taking breakfast at one of the coffee shops, browsing the history section of the local bookstore, checking out the kayaking and windsurfing gear at the outdoor shops, and feeding the sea gulls that fly over Shallowbag Bay. You'll have chances to explore local history at Roanoke Island Festival Park and *The Lost Colony* outdoor drama as well.

Wanchese, to the south, is the other town on the island. It is much sleepier than

Marina in Manteo
PHOTOGRAPH BY ARTIE SPARROW

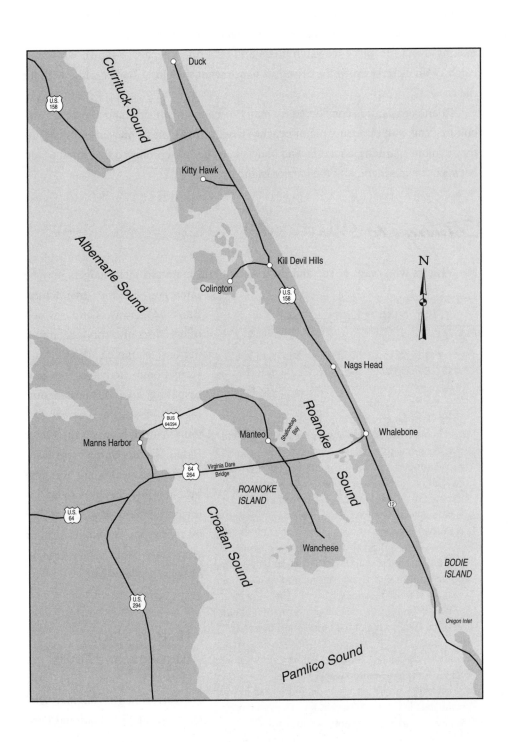

Manteo. Also named for a Native American who assisted the colonists, Wanchese is a fishing village. More than 20 million pounds of fish are caught here every year, making this a fun place to watch boats and fishermen depart or return with their catch. Wanchese is worth the drive just to see what the Outer Banks is like without the crowds.

Roanoke Island is considered by many to be the heart of Outer Banks art and culture. You won't find any major beaches here. Instead, plays, museums, living-history exhibits, gardens, concerts, and ballets keep people coming to this small island between the mainland and the barrier islands.

Things to Do

Visitors who want to see and do it all but still maintain their budgets may be interested in the free Outer Banks Getaway Card, which offers discounts on accommodations, shopping, dining, and recreational activities at participating area businesses during the off-season. The cards, a joint venture between the Outer Banks Visitors Bureau and Dare County businesses, are available by e-mailing the bureau at information@outerbanks.org or by filling out an online form at www.outerbanks.org/seasonal_savings/getaway_card.

JUST THE FACTS

From the north or the northern Banks, take U.S. 64/264 Bypass West over the Washington Baum Bridge. From the mainland, take U.S. 64/264 Bypass East over the Virginia Dare Memorial Bridge.

The Dare County Regional Airport is on Airport Road in Manteo. Its two runways are 3,290 feet and 4,300 feet in length. Fuel, services, restrooms, and an area for pilots to sleep are offered. For information, call 252-475-5570 or visit www.fly2mqi.com. Air charters are available to and from the airport from just about anywhere east of the Mississippi. A few local shuttle services and car and limousine rentals are available at the airport as well. Additional paved runways are located at Kill Devil Hills, Hatteras Island, and Ocracoke Island, though no support services are available at those locations.

Many different agencies offer information about the Outer Banks. One of the best is the Outer Banks Visitors Bureau (877-629-4386 or 252-473-2138; www.outerbanks.org), at One Visitors Center Circle off U.S. 64/264 in Manteo (27954). A useful page on the bureau's website lists the rates and availability of rental units in the area. The town of Manteo has its own website at www.townofmanteo.com.

Historic Places, Gardens, and Tours

Fort Raleigh National Historic Site, at 1401 National Park

Drive in Manteo (27954), is located off U.S. 64/264 at the northern end of the island. The site allows visitors to step back in time to see how the area looked over 400 years ago to the newly arrived English colonists, and to walk in the footsteps of those who attempted to tame this wild island, only to disappear without a trace. A visitor center administered by the National Park Service tells the story of the first colonists on Roanoke Island.

The English tried to settle the area many times, beginning in 1585 under the direction of Richard Grenville, a cousin of Sir Walter Raleigh, a leader in the move to explore the New World. Grenville led 600 men to found the first colony. He subsequently left a group of them under the direction of Ralph Lane to build fortifications while he returned to England. But relations with the natives soon turned sour. When Sir Francis Drake and his men visited the colony on their way home from Florida, the first colonists took advantage of the opportunity and returned to England.

Undeterred, Grenville came back a short time later with two years' worth of supplies and a smaller, more reliable group of settlers. Before returning to England, he gave the settlers strict instructions about establishing fortifications. It was this group of men who built what is now known as Fort Raleigh.

The appointed governor of the area, John White, came by boat in 1587 with a number of other colonists to further build the colony. He was undoubtedly shocked to find all the men missing and only one skeleton inhabiting the fort.

Despite the thousands of miles of ocean between him and Mother England and the many travel-weary wards in his care, the governor set about reestablishing the colony. White's colonists were families who had a vested interest in making the settlement permanent, in order to build themselves a better life. Included was White's own daughter, pregnant at the time with the now-famous Virginia Dare, the first English child born in the New World. Unfortunately, the colonists soon discovered they were unable to live off the land, which was much different from their native ground. The governor was thus forced to sail back to England for more provisions.

Mystery enters here. War was raging between England and Spain when White arrived home, and the Spanish Armada ensured that it wasn't until 1590 that he was able to return to the colony. Sailing back into the familiar bay, he was once again shocked to find Fort Raleigh uninhabited. At the entrance, he discovered the word *CROATOAN* carved on a post, but there was no cross with it—the colonists' agreed-upon signal of danger. Before he was able to search the nearby islands, Governor White was forced to return to England once more. To this day, no one knows what happened to the colonists of Roanoke Island. Theories abound as to their fate.

The earth embankments at Fort Raleigh, restored in 1950, are much as they

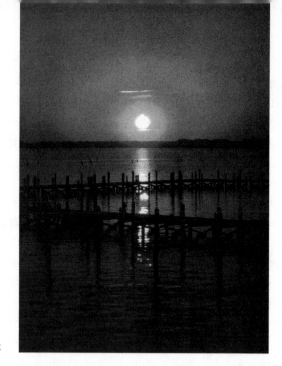

Sunset over Manteo
PHOTOGRAPH BY ALICE SINK

were when the colonists lived on Roanoke Island. The Lindsay Warren Visitor Center exhibits relics from the era of Governor White and Virginia Dare and offers maps of the area, books on the Lost Colony, and a 17-minute film on the history of Roanoke Island. The Waterside Theatre, located on the grounds, is the home of *The Lost Colony* outdoor drama during the summer. The site is open daily from sunrise to sunset from June to the end of August; the hours during the rest of the year are 9 A.M. to 5 P.M. The park is closed on Christmas. Admission is free, though a fee is charged to see *The Lost Colony*. For more information, call 252-473-5772 or visit www.nps.gov/fora.

The **Elizabethan Gardens**, at 1411 National Park Drive (27954), are located adjacent to the Waterside Theatre in the heart of Fort Raleigh National Historic Site. Created in 1951 by the Garden Club of North Carolina, the 10.5-acre gardens are a memorial to America's first English colonists. Designed by M. Umberto Innocenti and Richard Webel to bloom year-round, they feature plants native to the Outer Banks. Visitors enjoy an array of flowering shrubs, trees, plants, and herbs along the property's winding paths. Among the several gardens here are the formal Queen's Rose Garden (which features the "Lost Colony rose"), the Shakespearean Herb Garden, and the Great Lawn.

The centerpiece may well be the 15th-century Italian fountain, pool, and balustrade in the Sunken Garden, given by John Hay Whitney, a former ambassador to

Great Britain. Visitors can stop here to smell the flowers and listen to the gurgling fountain.

Situated next to Roanoke Sound is a 16th-century gazebo made of daub siding and thatched roofing. This area is said to be where the English flag was first raised in the New World.

The gardens are open daily year-round except for Thanksgiving, Christmas Eve, Christmas, and New Year's. Extended hours are offered during the summer. Admission is charged for adults and children ages six to 17. For more information, call 252-473-3234 or visit www.elizabethangardens.org.

Like Fort Raleigh National Historic Site, *Roanoke Island Festival Park* is dedicated to re-creating the history of the early colonists. It's located at 1 Festival Park (27954) on the 25-acre Ice Plant Island in Shallowbag Bay across from downtown Manteo.

Your first stop upon entering the visitor center will be the 8,500-square-foot *Roanoke Adventure Museum*, which features paintings, artifacts, relics, and interactive exhibits on the important figures and events in Roanoke Island's history. One of the best exhibits is the Civil War cannon found underwater off the island; it was so well packed with firing material that the gunpowder was still dry, meaning that the cannon was still ready for action. A Native American village, a Civil War encampment,

Roanoke Island Festival Park
COURTESY OF NORTH CAROLINA DEPARTMENT OF
CULTURAL RESOURCES

a pirate ship, a duck blind, and a 1950s general store are among the other exhibits. Children love the area where they can dress up in swashbuckling buccaneer and dainty m'lady costumes. Actors in period costumes trained in Elizabethan dialect are spread throughout the park to share stories of pioneering on Roanoke Island. Inquisitive children and adults can find out what it was like to survive in the hot, swampy, buggy conditions without any of the conveniences we depend upon today. The Native Americans' story is shared as well. A 50-minute film entitled *The Legend of Two-Path* tells what the people already settled on Roanoke Island thought of the "settlers" who appeared in 1585. Outside the museum are several trails leading to different exhibits, including a settlement site featuring historically costumed soldiers who share what the settlers did for shelter, food, and protection.

The most impressive feature of Roanoke Island Festival Park is perhaps the 69-foot ***Elizabeth II***. An authentic representation of the 16th-century *Elizabeth*, one of seven merchant ships used to sail to the colony, the *Elizabeth II* was built to commemorate the New World's quadricentennial. Interpretive guides on the three-mast, "50-tunne" Elizabethan ship share stories of what it was like to cross the Atlantic and try to settle the New World.

During the summer, the famed University of North Carolina School of the Arts uses the park to stage special dance, theater, and musical performances and films by some of the art world's up-and-coming stars. Past performances have included *A Midsummer Night's Dream*, *Cinderella*, and the musical *She Loves Me*. Three performances are generally given each day. In June and July, the morning offering includes

Elizabeth II
COURTESY OF NORTH CAROLINA DEPARTMENT OF CULTURAL RESOURCES

puppet shows and fairy and folk tales as part of the Children's Series. The afternoon performance is often a concert of chamber or jazz music in the park's art gallery. The evening performance—a dance recital, concert, or drama presented in the outdoor pavilion—is perhaps the highlight. Admission is free with admission to the park, though making a donation is a good way to ensure performances for the next year.

Roanoke Island Festival Park is open mid-February through December with the exception of Thanksgiving and Christmas. Hours vary seasonally. Admission is charged for adults and students; children age five and under are admitted free. For more information, call 252-475-1500 or visit www.roanokeisland.com.

Museums and Science Centers

The *North Carolina Aquarium at Roanoke Island*, at 374 Airport Road in Manteo (27954), is tucked away down a long, winding road off U.S. 64. It offers 68,000 square feet of freshwater and saltwater galleries. Creatures from North Carolina's rivers, marshes, sounds, and reefs are all highlighted.

The first stop inside the aquarium is the open-air natural-habitat atrium. Lined with real trees and topped with a huge skylight, the habitat gives a sense of the North Carolina wetlands. Wood ducks, river otters, and alligators all inhabit this area. Mists spray throughout the atrium periodically to keep the "wetlands" wet.

The centerpiece of the aquarium is undoubtedly the 285,000-gallon "Graveyard of the Atlantic" ocean tank, the largest in the state. Inside are the skeletal remains of a 53-foot re-created USS *Monitor* shipwreck, a one-third-scale replica of the famed Civil War ship now lying off Cape Hatteras. Created by a team of movie-set designers in Wilmington, the replica is covered with fiberglass orange, pink, and yellow corals, sponges, and sea fans. The fish inside the tank sometimes confuse the replica with the real thing and try to take a nip out of it. The sharks gliding stealthily by the 35-foot-long, five-and-a-half-inch-thick viewing window steal the show. Custom-made in Japan and set into place with a crane, the window wraps overhead, so viewers gets a sense of actually being in the water with the ship, the sharks, and other ocean creatures.

The aquarium's Discovery Gallery gives kids a chance to touch skates, rays, sea stars, crabs, urchins, and other invertebrates. Charts and graphics on the walls tell about the evolution and characteristics of each animal.

A theater, a gift shop, a shoreline boardwalk, and nature trails are also on the premises.

The aquarium is open daily year-round except for Thanksgiving, Christmas, and New Year's. A modest fee is charged for adults; children five and under and Aquarium Society members are admitted free. For information, call 866-332-3475 or 252-473-3494 or visit www.ncaquariums.com/roanoke-island.

The ***North Carolina Maritime Museum on Roanoke Island***, on the Manteo waterfront at 104 Fernando Street (27954), is a repository of information on the seafaring history and natural resources of the Outer Banks. During the summer, the museum offers educational programs on sailing and boat safety for children and adults. Visitors can also witness the art of boat restoration and construction at the George Washington Creef Boathouse, home to a working boat shop that relies on traditional boat-building and repair techniques. For information, call 252-475-1750 or visit www.ncmaritime.org/branches/roanoke_default.htm.

Nearby is the ***Roanoke Marshes Lighthouse***, the Banks' newest lighthouse, opened in 2004. It's a replica of a screw pile lighthouse built in 1877 to light the way for boats in Croatan Sound. The lighthouse served as both a guide for sailors and a residence for the keeper, thus explaining why it looks more like a cottage built over the water than a traditional lighthouse. Sailors in the sound now rely on the lighthouse's fourth-order Fresnel lens to light the night.

The museum and lighthouse operate on seasonal hours, so call ahead.

Roanoke Marshes Lighthouse in Manteo
PHOTOGRAPH BY ALICE SINK

Special Shopping

Downtown Manteo offers an array of browsing choices, from shops selling outdoor gear or local artwork to a unique independently owned bookstore. It's easy to spend a few leisurely hours wandering the shops and soaking up the culture. One of the best times to do this is during the town's "First Friday" events—held, as the name implies, on the first Friday of every month. Visitors can also listen to live music and enjoy a candlelight walking tour on these Fridays.

Island Produce, at 1 Patty Lane in Manteo (27954), offers a variety of local produce, homemade jams, relishes, pickles, honey, and roasted peanuts. This is the place to stock up on fresh, healthy food on your way to the Outer Banks. For information, call 252-473-4267 or visit www.ncbeaches.com/OuterBanks/Manteo/Shopping/FruitVegetableStands/IslandProduce.

Recreation

Downeast Rover, at 112 Musket Lane in Manteo (27954), is a reproduction of a 19th-century topsail schooner berthed on the waterfront adjacent to Roanoke Island Festival Park. The *Rover* offers daytime and sunset cruises that can accommodate up to 29 guests. Sailors aboard the 55-foot boat see Roanoke Island from a completely different perspective and get a close look at the local wildlife, including dolphins, ospreys, and herons. Below decks are accommodations for up to six adult passengers, for those who choose to charter the *Rover* for longer trips. Be sure to check availability, prices, and departure times for your preferred date. Call 866-724-5629 or 252-473-4866 or visit www.downeastrover.com.

Alligator River National Wildlife Refuge is located on Milltail Road off U.S. 64/264 in the Dare County mainland community of East Lake (27953). The refuge encompasses more than 150,000 acres of wetland separating the mainland from the Outer Banks. The Alligator River—actually a small sound—is part of the larger Albemarle Sound, one of the most important waterways in the state. Snaking from Alligator Lake in the Dismal Swamp to Albemarle Sound, the Alligator River is said to have received its name from the area's first settlers, who encountered quite a few of those stealthy, beady-eyed creatures. Little did the pioneers know that they were lucky—or unlucky, as the case may be—to have stumbled into the northernmost habitat of the American alligator. Wildlife specialists say the alligators in the Alligator River are smaller than their counterparts in Florida and Georgia, but that fact probably wouldn't have provided much comfort to the first men and women crossing these waters.

The refuge is also home to black bears, bobcats, bald eagles, white-tailed deer, and red wolves. The red wolf faced extinction as recently as 1996, but the numbers are growing today, thanks to a reintroduction project. All along the highway in the refuge, you'll see red wolf crossing signs, so take care to share the road with these shy creatures.

Admission to the refuge is free. Visitors can take advantage of the hiking and wildlife trails, the observation platforms, the fishing areas, and the wildlife drive for cars and bikes. Kayaking and canoeing are permitted; a guided canoe tour is available for a fee. The refuge is open daily year-round during daylight hours except for federal holidays. For information, visit www.alligatorriver.fws.gov. or call 252-473-1131.

Kitty Hawk Sports offers kayak ecotours led by trained guides. One of the best tours starts in Manteo and heads through Shallowbag Bay into the maritime forest. Kayakers learn useful information about local flora and fauna—like how to distinguish between bug-repellent plants and poison ivy. Call 252-441-6800 or visit www.kittyhawksports.com for more information.

Marinas line the Outer Banks. Those along Roanoke Island include *Manteo Waterfront Marina*, also known as Dough's Creek (252-473-3320), *Pirate's Cove Marina* (252-473-3906), *Salty Dawg Marina* (252-473-3405), and *Shallowbag Bay Marina* (252-473-4946) in Manteo and *Thicket Lump Marina* (252-473-4500) and *Broad Creek Fishing Center & Marina* (252-473-9991) in Wanchese.

Seasonal Events

The Lost Colony is headquartered at 1409 National Drive in Manteo (27954). First performed in 1937, this is the oldest outdoor drama in the United States. Over 4 million theatergoers have witnessed the passion and mystery surrounding the British colonists lost to the wilderness of Roanoke Island. Performed on the grounds of Fort Raleigh National Historic Site at the Waterside Theatre overlooking Roanoke

Sailboat on Shallowbag Bay
PHOTOGRAPH BY ALICE SINK

Sound, *The Lost Colony* tells the story of Governor John White; his daughter, Eleanor Dare; her daughter, Virginia Dare, the first English child born in America; and the native Algonquin Indians. The production includes dance, song, fighting, and fireworks. Guests witness how Sir Walter Raleigh convinced Queen Elizabeth I to support a settlement in the New World, only to be denied the chance to help build the colony; how the colonists became friends with the natives but later lost their allegiance; and how they came to the conclusion they could no longer survive at Fort Raleigh. Of course, you'll have to attend a performance to see what Pulitzer Prize–winning playwright Paul Green imagined to be the fate of the colonists.

If you're planning an evening at the Waterside Theatre, buy your tickets in advance and bring a supply of bug repellent. If you come prepared, you'll be justly rewarded with a tale of love, loss, and heroic courage.

The Lost Colony is performed Monday through Saturday at 8 P.M. from late May to late August. Children 11 and under accompanied by a paying adult are admitted free on Fridays and Mondays and for half price on Saturdays. Refunds are not given except in case of bad weather; performances are never canceled before 8:30 P.M. For more information, call 252-473-3414 or visit www.thelostcolony.org.

During summer, the Elizabethan Gardens and Roanoke Island Festival Park host a variety of plays in addition to *The Lost Colony*.

The several seasonal festivals on Roanoke Island are not to be missed.

The *Dare Day Festival* is held annually the first Saturday in June in downtown Manteo. It honors the memory of Virginia Dare and the other Lost Colonists. The festival features all-day entertainment, arts and crafts, food, dance, and live music. Call 252-475-5629 for more information.

The *Herbert Hoover Birthday Celebration*, held on August 10 and sponsored by Manteo Booksellers, honors our nation's 31st president. This is a quirky way to enjoy a day of book signings, live music, trivia, a "Herbie" shrine, and a "Herbert & Sherbet" birthday cake. Visit www.manteobooksellers.com or call 866-473-1222 or 252-473-1221 for more information.

Places to Stay

Roanoke Island is noted for its unique inns and bed-and-breakfasts. If you're looking for the tried-and-true chains, you may need to try up the road in Nags Head or Kitty Hawk. Rates vary seasonally.

Resorts, Hotels, and Motels

Elizabethan Inn. Expensive/Moderate/Inexpensive. 814 U.S. 64 in Manteo, 27954 (800-346-2466 or 252-473-2101; www.elizabethaninn.com). This 78-room, two-efficiency Tudor-style motel, located close to all of Roanoke Island's cultural offerings, boasts a wide range of amenities. Guests can enjoy an indoor heated pool, an outdoor pool, a whirlpool, a sauna, and a well-equipped gym. Complimentary bicycles are available for trips to the Manteo waterfront, Roanoke Island Festival Park, the North Carolina Aquarium, and Fort Raleigh National Historic Site. Breakfast is offered at the inn's Virginia Dare Restaurant. Pets are welcome in some of the rooms.

Duke of Dare Motor Lodge. Moderate/Inexpensive. 100 South Virginia Dare Road in Manteo, 27954 (252-473-2175). This no-frills 57-room motel offers the basics for a reasonable price. The Duke of Dare has been owned and operated by the same family for over 25 years. It features televisions, phones, and an outdoor pool.

Inns and Bed-and-Breakfasts

The Cameron House Inn. Deluxe. 300 Budleigh Street in Manteo, 27954 (800-279-8178 or 252-473-6596; www.cameronhouseinn.com). This restored 1919 Arts and Crafts–style bungalow features seven guest rooms with plush bedding, Oriental carpets, and individual bathrooms. The main inn's wraparound porch is the perfect place to read a book, take in the breeze off the water, and enjoy a quiet afternoon lazing in the restored 50-year-old porch swing. During winter, guests can enjoy rocking by the back porch's outdoor fireplace.

The White Doe Inn Bed-and-Breakfast. Deluxe. 319 Sir Walter Raleigh Street in Manteo, 27954 (800-473-6091 or 252-473-9851; www.whitedoeinn.com). Built in 1898 as the Theodore Meekins House and listed on the National Register of Historic Places in 1982, The White Doe is now a Three Diamond, three-story, eight-room Queen Anne–style inn. Each room is individually decorated with antiques and features amenities ranging from four-poster beds to private whirlpools to stained-glass windows to chandeliers. A complimentary four-course gourmet breakfast, afternoon tea, and bicycles are some of the extras. No stay would be complete without partaking of the inn's luxurious spa services, provided in the privacy of guests' own rooms.

Roanoke Island Inn. Deluxe/Expensive. 305 Fernando Street in Manteo, 27954 (877-473-5511 or 252-473-5511; www.roanokeislandinn.com). Built in the 1860s for the current innkeeper's great-great-grandmother, the Roanoke Island Inn grew steadily throughout the 20th century to accommodate the growing family and the guests who stayed here. This waterfront inn offers a bungalow and eight guest rooms, most of which have a view of the bay. Continental breakfast and access to the innkeeper's pantry ensure that guests are well fed. The inn is generally open from April to late October, though the owners charmingly advertise their season as ranging from "Easter 'til we're tired." If you're looking for a more secluded hideaway, ask the innkeepers about their Island Camp, a lovely house situated alone on an island south of the causeway. Guests must provide their own transportation by boat; a number of restaurants are located within boating distance.

Tranquil House Inn. Deluxe/Expensive. 405 Queen Elizabeth Street in Manteo, 27954 (800-458-7069 or 252-473-1404; www.tranquilinn.com). Guests staying here enjoy being in the middle of everything. The Tranquil House is located on the Shallowbag Bay waterfront in downtown Manteo. The majority of its 25 individually decorated rooms feature a view of the water. This turn-of-the-20th-century reproduction offers suites with sitting rooms, an upstairs porch with rocking chairs, evening wine and cheese, and complimentary continental breakfast. One of the best restaurants on the Outer Banks, 1587, sits conveniently next door.

Island House of Wanchese. Expensive/Moderate. 104 Old Wharf Road in Wanchese, 27981 (252-473-5619; www.islandhouse-bb.com). Located away from the hustle and bustle of Manteo in the quiet fishing village of Wanchese, this is the place to truly get away from it all. The three rooms and one suite have private baths, antique furnishings, Oriental rugs, televisions, VCRs, DVD players, and radios. Guests enjoy turn-down service at night and are welcomed in the morning with a home-cooked, Southern-style buffet breakfast. The guest pantry is open 24 hours a day. A screened porch, beach chairs, beach towels, beach showers, bicycles, and a freezer for your catch all make this seem like a home away from home. The inn is open year-round.

Scarborough House Inn. Moderate/Inexpensive. 323 Fernando Street in Manteo, 27954 (252-473-3849; www.scarboroughhouseinn.com). The keepers of this inn are as local as they come. The Scarboroughs boast lineages on both sides extending as far back as pre–Revolutionary War times. The photos of ancestors decorating the walls of the five rooms and the two-story guest house chronicle the story of Roanoke Island and the Outer Banks for close to a century. The rooms include antique beds covered with handmade spreads, gleaming pine floors, and modern amenities like refrigerators, microwaves, coffee makers, and televisions. Continental breakfast is included in the price of the stay.

Places to Eat

Though you won't find as many restaurants on Roanoke Island as on the northern Banks, you'll appreciate the good variety and tasty food. As you might expect, fresh seafood is available at just about every restaurant. Those who don't care for seafood will be able to find plenty to satisfy them as well.

1587. Expensive. 405 Queen Elizabeth Avenue in Manteo, 27954 (252-473-1587; www.1587.com). Named for the year the Lost Colonists arrived on Roanoke Island, this restaurant is one of the most sophisticated on the Banks. The cuisine at 1587 changes seasonally to reflect the local bounty. The chefs blend herbs grown in the restaurant's own garden with free-range chicken, certified Angus beef, and seafood from the Atlantic to create their unique dishes. Guests can enjoy the breeze off Shallowbag Bay and listen to the water lapping against the docks as they enjoy their evening meal. Dinner is served nightly year-round.

Stripers Bar and Grille. Expensive/Moderate. 1122 South Bay Club Drive in Manteo, 27954 (252-472-2222; www.stripersbarandgrille.com). Tucked away in Shallowbag Bay Marina, Stripers offers stunning views of the bay and some of the best seafood on the coast. Dinner is served daily. Lunch is offered on Saturday and brunch on Sunday.

Full Moon Café. Moderate. 208 Queen Elizabeth Avenue in Manteo, 27954 (252-473-6666; www.thefullmooncafe.com). Full Moon Café, located in a brick building under Manteo's clock tower, offers standard fare—delicious homemade salads, wraps, burgers, and seafood—in addition to an eclectic blend of world cuisines ranging from baked Brie to eggplant Napoleon. This is a terrific place to fill up without breaking the bank. Lunch and dinner are served daily.

Hurricane Mo's Restaurant and Raw Bar. Moderate. At Pirate's Cove Marina on the Manteo–Nags Head Causeway, 27954 (252-473-2266). Located at the point where Roanoke Island and Nags Head meet, this casual restaurant is a wonderful place to get a plate of oysters on the half shell and a cold beer and watch the boats come in. Fishermen and families alike are welcome here, and the service is gracious and helpful. Among the favorites are the generous seafood platters and the "Chicken Marsala Florentine" with spinach, sun-dried tomatoes, and mushrooms. Lunch and dinner are served daily during peak season.

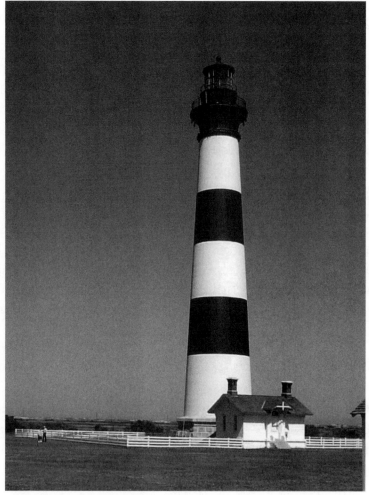

Bodie Island Lighthouse
PHOTOGRAPH BY ARTIE SPARROW

Bodie Island

Bodie Island provides a glimpse into what the Outer Banks looked like long before tourists arrived, when the only people inhabiting the area were the lighthouse keepers. It is a unique place, to say the least.

Bodie Island is really just the southern tip of the northern Banks and not an island at all. It was an island originally, but the inlets that surrounded it have filled in. The pronunciation of the name is also a little quirky. I've heard many lifelong North Carolinians pronounce it "Bo-dee," although the correct way of saying the name is "Body." As with every place on the Outer Banks, several explanations exist as to how the island was named. Some say the name honors the vast number of bodies that washed ashore from ships wrecked in the Graveyard of the Atlantic. Others a little less melodramatic claim it comes from the island's being a body of land. Still others say Bodie Island was named after a now-unknown person who helped build the lighthouse or was stationed there.

Established in 1953, Cape Hatteras National Seashore was the first national seashore in the country. It begins on Bodie Island and extends 75 miles through Hatteras and Ocracoke islands, covering over 30,000 acres. Some of the country's best fishing and surfing are found in the national seashore.

Things to Do

Historic Places, Gardens, and Tours

Encircled by its horizontal black and white bands, the ***Bodie Island Lighthouse*** has protected its small section of the coast since 1847. History has not always been kind to the lighthouse, though. Only 12 years after its creation, it was torn down and rebuilt because of improper construction. Two years later, in 1862, Confederate troops blew up the lighthouse so the Union wouldn't be able to use it. The lighthouse was rebuilt for the second (and so far last) time in 1871 at the staggering cost to Reconstruction North Carolina of $140,000. Shortly after it was reactivated, the lighthouse proved it was still on a bad-luck streak when a flock of wild geese flew into the lantern and damaged the lens.

Now long repaired, the 156-foot Bodie Island Lighthouse still flashes its 160,000-candlepower beacon 19 miles into the dark night over the Atlantic Ocean. The lighthouse is not open for climbing, but the keeper's quarters have been restored and now serve as a museum, gift shop, and visitor center for Cape Hatteras National Seashore. A nature trail winds through the marsh surrounding the lighthouse.

No admission fee is charged. The lighthouse grounds are open year-round with

JUST THE FACTS

Driving south from the northern Banks, take either U.S. 158 (Virginia Dare Trail) or N.C. 12 (the Beach Road). From Roanoke Island, take U.S. 64/264 East until you reach Whalebone Junction, then head south down N.C. 12.

Bodie Island has no airport. Charters into the area will need to land at the Dare Country Regional Airport on Roanoke Island.

Your best bet for gathering information is the Outer Banks Visitors Bureau (877-629-4386 or 252-473-2138; www.outerbanks.org), located at One Visitors Center Circle off U.S. 64/264 in Manteo (27954).

the exception of Christmas; hours are seasonal, so be sure to phone ahead. For more information, visit www.nps.gov/caha/bodie-island-light-station.htm or call 252-441-5711.

Recreation

Almost directly across N.C. 12 from the entrance to the Bodie Island Lighthouse is one of the best beaches on the Outer Banks, *Coquina Beach*. Named for the tiny white shells scattered all over, Coquina offers good swimming and surf fishing. Do take note that no lifeguard is on duty, so use common sense while visiting here.

Coquina Beach is rich in history. The *Laura A. Barnes*, built in 1918, was one of the last schooners constructed in the United States. It lies not far from where it grounded after a nor'easter blew it ashore in 1921. The crew survived thanks to the heroic actions of the men at the nearby lifesaving station. In 1973, the National Park Service moved the remains of the ship to their present location.

During World War II, this area came to be known as Torpedo Junction because the United States suffered such heavy losses to German submarines. America also made one of its greatest comebacks at this place, though, when it sank a German U-boat for the first time. The remains of that submarine now lie 15 miles offshore.

Oregon Inlet Fishing Center and Full-Service Marina, located just down N.C. 12 at the north end of the Herbert C. Bonner Bridge, is home to the largest and most modern fishing fleet on the East Coast. Serious fishermen from around the world come to this marina to charter boats for Gulf Stream fishing. Facilities include a general store, boat ramps and docks, and areas to clean your catch. If you're driving past in late afternoon, be sure to stop to see the boats come in with their daily catch of sea bass, mullet, bluefish, billfish, and even shark. The National Park Service administers a boat-launch facility adjacent to the marina that offers ample free parking. For more information, call 800-272-5199 or 252-441-6301 or visit www.fishingoregoninlet.com.

Outer Banks Fishing Pier, at 8901 Old Oregon Inlet Road in Nags Head (27959), is the closest pier to Oregon Inlet. The 600-foot structure, operated by Fishing Unlimited, includes a tackle shop, a grill, and an arcade. For more information, call 252-441-5740 or visit http://fishingunlimited.net/OuterBanksPier.html.

The National Park Service operates the only place to stay on Bodie Island, the *Oregon Inlet Campground*. Here, you'll find 120 sites serving tents, trailers, and motor homes with only the basics—cold showers, toilets, picnic tables, potable water, and grills. No utility connections are offered, but the reasonable price makes up for the no-frills accommodations. The campground is open from mid-April to mid-October. Availability is on a first-come, first-served basis, though reservations for groups of seven or more may be made by calling 252-441-7425, extension 230. The National Park Service recommends that campers using tents bring longer-than-normal tent stakes, due to the shifting sands and winds. Insect netting and bug spray are good ideas, too. For more information, call 252-473-2111 or visit www.nps.gov/caha/planyourvisit/campgrounds.htm.

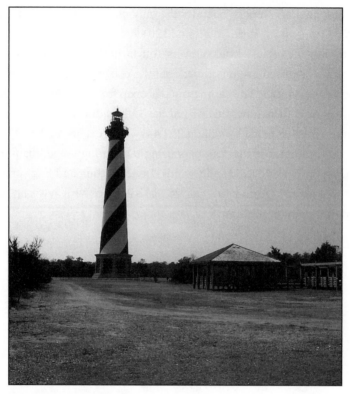

Cape Hatteras Lighthouse
PHOTOGRAPH BY ARTIE SPARROW

Hatteras Island

The largest island of the Outer Banks, Hatteras has a heritage rich in maritime history and lore. Even the trip between Bodie Island and Hatteras Island is a history lesson. Going from one island to the next, you'll cross Oregon Inlet, a body of water that came into existence in 1846 after a large storm blew a channel open. The *Oregon*, the first ship to sail through this passageway, gave the inlet its name. Oregon Inlet is now the main entrance to Pamlico Sound. The three-mile Herbert C. Bonner Bridge connects the two islands. The inlet requires constant dredging, as sand is perpetually deposited along the stone pillars of the bridge.

Once on Hatteras Island, you'll visit several small towns connected by N.C. 12: Rodanthe, Waves, Salvo, Avon, Buxton, Frisco, and Hatteras. Each has a story and flavor all its own.

The most recognized symbol of the island is the Cape Hatteras Lighthouse.

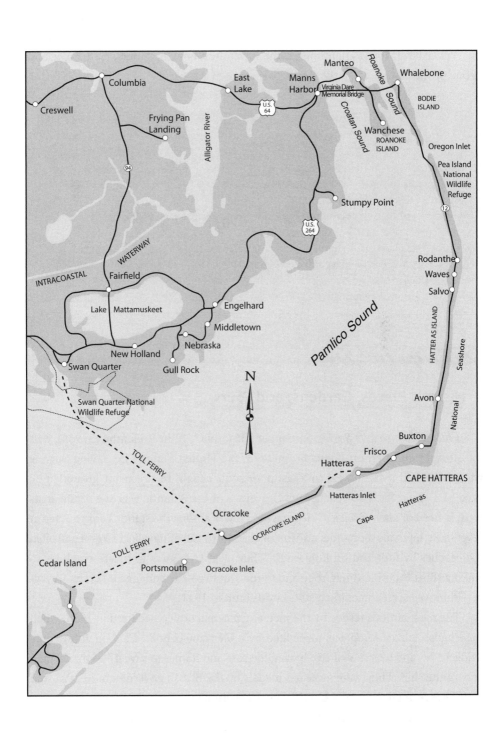

Threatened by the same winds and tides that created Oregon Inlet, the lighthouse underwent a monumental move in 1999 to preserve it from the forces of nature.

While hazardous to lighthouses, the waves are a boon to surfers. Hatteras Island is one of the best spots on the East Coast to catch a wave.

JUST THE FACTS

Driving south from the northern Banks, take either U.S. 158 (Virginia Dare Trail) or N.C. 12 (the Beach Road). From Roanoke Island, take U.S. 64/264 East to Whalebone Junction, then go south on N.C. 12.

Hatteras Island has no airport, so charters will need to land at the Dare Country Regional Airport on Roanoke Island.

The best place to turn for information is the Outer Banks Visitors Bureau (877-629-4386 or 252-473-2138; www.outerbanks.org), located at One Visitors Center Circle off U.S. 64/264 in Manteo (27954).

Things to Do

Historic Places, Gardens, and Tours

Chicamacomico Life Saving Station, at 23645 N.C. 12 in Rodanthe (27968), tells the story of surfmen on Hatteras. In 1873, the United States Life Saving Service was established by Congress to assist poor souls caught in storms or grounded by sand bars and reefs. The treacherous Graveyard of the Atlantic was one of the areas most in need of such service. Chicamacomico was among the stations constructed at seven-mile intervals along this portion of the North Carolina coast. Crews patrolled the beaches by foot and on horseback. They used Lyle guns to fire rescue lines to sinking ships. At other times, they had to row out to rescue endangered crews. A bigger, improved Chicamacomico station was built in 1911.

The most famous rescue by the men at Chicamacomico occurred in 1918, when the English tanker *Mirlo* was torpedoed by a German U-boat. Captain John Allen Midgett, Jr., and his crew of five braved the surf and flames to save 47 of the 57 men aboard the ship. They were awarded medals by the British government in 1921 and were later recognized by the United States government.

Chicamacomico Life Saving Station now serves as a museum. Visitors enjoy the shipwreck exhibit with actual artifacts from, and pieces of, the wrecks themselves.

Chicamacomico Life Saving Station
PHOTOGRAPH BY ARTIE SPARROW

Lifesaving equipment is also on display. On Thursdays in summer, active-duty Coast Guard personnel perform a beach apparatus drill, a demonstration of the techniques used to rescue stranded sailors. The station is open Monday through Friday from noon to 5 P.M. Easter to Thanksgiving. The grounds are open year-round. For information, call 252-987-1552 or visit www.chicamacomico.net.

The ***United States Weather Bureau Station***, located at the corner of Saxon Cut and Kohler roads in Hatteras Village, was one of 11 dedicated weather bureaus built at the turn of the 20th century. Forecasting was crucial, due to the severe weather in the area and the large number of ships that passed through the waters offshore. The National Park Service has restored the building using the original plans, so its appearance—including the yellow exterior—is authentic. In addition to the exhibits of weather instruments, the station features a welcome center operated by the Outer Banks Visitors Bureau. For more information, call 252-986-2203 or visit www.nps.gov/caha/historyculture/weatherbureau.htm.

Cape Hatteras Lighthouse is located at 46379 N.C. 12 at Cape Point in Buxton (27920). This 208-foot lighthouse is the tallest and perhaps the most famous in the

United States. Over the years, it has come to be the unofficial emblem of the Outer Banks.

Like the other lighthouses along the Banks, the Cape Hatteras Light has a long and complicated history. Built in 1803 over a mile from the shoreline, the first version was poorly constructed and gave out a weak signal to passing ships. The lighthouse was damaged by Union naval shells in 1861. Shortly thereafter, the Confederate army removed its lamp altogether.

The lighthouse was rebuilt in 1870 more than 1,000 yards from the sea. It rested on a floating foundation this time, meaning that it sat on yellow pine timbers in fresh water on compacted sand, with a brick-and-granite foundation on top. As long as the sands held steady and no salt water seeped into the foundation, the lighthouse was safe. But what the engineers did not account for was that Hatteras Island itself was moving westward. The federal government abandoned the lighthouse in 1935 due to the constant erosion. The following year, it set up a temporary skeletal steel light tower. Once the 1870 lighthouse was abandoned, vandals damaged its lens.

It wasn't until 1950 that the light was moved back to the 1870 lighthouse, after extensive repairs. But beach erosion continued. In 1980, a storm washed away the foundation of the original 1803 lighthouse, which until then had stood more than 600 feet from the shore. That storm reinforced the idea that something had to be done to save the existing lighthouse. In 1989, after much debate, the National Park Service decided to move the aged structure.

Nearly a decade later, the move was finally approved by Congress. The 1870 lighthouse closed its doors on November 22, 1998, as the National Park Service readied for the move. Engineers lifted the lighthouse from its foundation, sunk eight feet deep into the sand. They moved it 2,900 feet and reanchored it in a safer spot, leaving it about the same distance from the sea as back in 1870. After being closed for 550 days, the lighthouse reopened for visitors on May 26, 2000. The beam again lights the night sky to a distance of 20 miles offshore.

Also on the grounds are the double keepers' quarters, which house a museum and visitor center, the principal keeper's quarters, and the Hatteras Island Visitor Center. Admission to the grounds is free, though a fee is charged to climb the lighthouse. The grounds are traditionally open year-round from 9 A.M. to 4:30 P.M. except for Christmas; hours are extended in the summer. The lighthouse is open for climbing from Easter weekend to Columbus Day weekend, weather permitting. Keep in mind that the climb is equivalent to trekking up a 12-story building—without air conditioning. For more information, call 252-473-2111 or 252-995-4474 or visit www.nps.gov/caha.

Museums and Science Centers

Museums and exhibits where visitors can learn about the life of the early colonists dot the Outer Banks. But the *Frisco Native American Museum and Natural History Center*, at 53536 N.C. 12 in Frisco (27936), is one of the few places to learn about the people who inhabited the area hundreds of years before the English arrived. Founded and operated by Carl and Joyce Bornfriend, this nonprofit educational foundation displays collections of authentic Native American artifacts and explores the origins of different tribes, their tools, their religions, and their ways of surviving. Also on the grounds are nature trails, a pavilion, a gift shop, and a bookstore. The annual Inter-Tribal PowWow, held in the spring, features dancers and drummers from all over the country. The museum is open year-round Tuesday through Sunday from 11 A.M. to 5 P.M. and Monday by appointment. A nominal admission fee is charged. For information, call 252-995-4440 or visit www.nativeamericanmuseum. org.

Graveyard of the Atlantic Museum, at 59200 Museum Drive in Hatteras (27943), is dedicated to the preservation of maritime history and the shipwrecks of the Outer Banks from the mid-1500s to today. More than 1,500 ships, including Civil War blockade runners and German U-boats, have sunk off the treacherous North Carolina coast since settlement efforts began over 400 years ago. The museum chronicles the stories of these ill-fated ships—along with those of such vessels as Blackbeard's *Adventure*, which safely navigated the area's sand bars and shoals—through artifacts, models, and exhibits. It features artifacts from the *Carroll A. Deering,* the legendary ghost ship of the Diamond Shoals, a five-mast schooner whose crew vanished without a trace in January 1921. The museum offers regular author appearances and book signings during the summer as part of its heritage series, which is free and open to the public. The hours are subject to change, so call ahead. Admission is free, but donations are accepted. For more information, call 252-986-2996 or visit www. graveyardoftheatlantic.com.

Recreation

Though the sportfishing and surfing are legendary here, visitors should use common sense while exploring the waters of the island, as the weather can change at a moment's notice. Riptides and strong currents can surprise even the hardiest swimmers.

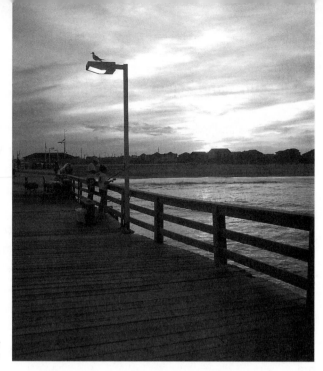

Avon Golf and Fishing Pier
PHOTOGRAPH BY ARTIE SPARROW

For fishermen, the places to go include *Hatteras Island Fishing Pier* (252-987-2323; www.hatterasislandresort.com) in Rodanthe, *Avon Golf and Fishing Pier* (252-995-5480; www.avonpier.com) in Avon, and *Cape Hatteras Fishing Pier* (252-986-2533) in Frisco. All offer about the same amenities, including bait, tackle, ice, and snacks. They are open seasonally.

For those interested in Gulf Stream fishing, several marinas in Hatteras offer charter boats. These include *Hatteras Landing Marina* (800-551-8478 or 252-986-2077; www.hatteraslanding.com), *Hatteras Harbor Marina* (800-676-4939 or 252-986-2166; www.hatterasharbor.com), *Oden's Dock* (888-544-8115 or 252-986-2555; www.odensdock.com), and *Teach's Lair Marina* (888-868-2460 or 252-986-2460; www.teachslair.com).

Surfers, windsurfers, and kite boarders can turn to *Hatteras Island Sail Shop* (252-987-2292; www.hiss-waves.com) in Waves, *Fox Watersports* (252-995-4372) in Buxton, and *Carolina Outdoors* (252-986-1446) in Hatteras. *Canadian Hole* in Pamlico Sound has been called "the Windsurfing Capital of the East Coast," thanks to its calm waters and steady breezes.

Pea Island National Wildlife Refuge is located at the northern tip of Hatteras Island between Oregon Inlet and Rodanthe; the visitor center is just off N.C. 12 five miles south of the Bonner Bridge. The refuge is known as a birder's paradise, as it is the feeding and resting area for more than 365 species of migratory birds. Estab-

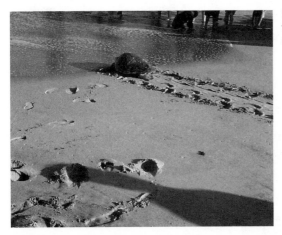

Rehabilitated loggerhead turtle returning to the sea near Buxton
PHOTOGRAPH BY ARTIE SPARROW

lished in 1937 by an act of Congress, the refuge covers 5,834 acres of Hatteras Island and 25,700 acres of Pamlico Sound. No migratory waterfowl hunting is allowed here, but visitors may canoe, kayak, surf, fish, meander the beaches, and participate in interpretive programs.

The name Pea Island comes from the acres of "dune peas" covering the refuge. These beans, packed with protein, are a source of energy for the birds on their long flights. Birds spotted here include piping plovers, peregrine falcons, Canada and snow geese, tundra swans, herons, egrets, ibises, bald eagles, and over 25 species of ducks. Observation decks and nature trails enable visitors to view all the different winged visitors. Pea Island is also home to river otters, muskrats, rabbits, and raccoons. In addition, loggerhead turtles use the refuge as their northernmost nesting ground. The temperature at which the eggs incubate determines the sex of loggerheads; this northern nesting ground produces many members of the male loggerhead population.

The refuge's visitor center offers wildlife exhibits and a gift store; it is open daily from 9 A.M. to 5 P.M. in the summer and from 9 A.M. to 4 P.M. the rest of the year. The refuge is administered by Alligator River National Wildlife Refuge. Admission is free. For more information, call 252-473-1131 or visit www.peaisland.fws.gov.

Buxton Woods Reserve is a 1,725-acre maritime forest, the largest in North Carolina. It features interdune ponds, live oak and red cedar forests, and freshwater marshes that are home to a variety of water-loving plants, including ferns, saw grass, cattails, and wild rice. Over 135 species of migratory birds make this a stopping place on their long annual journeys. Visitors can enjoy a day of hiking, birding, and picnicking. The reserve is located between Cape Hatteras National Seashore and N.C. 12 in Buxton. The trails may be accessed from the intersection of N.C. 12 and

Old Doctor's Road. For more information, call 252-995-4474 or visit www.nature. org/wherewework/northamerica/states/northcarolina/preserves/art5593.html.

Places to Stay

It used to be that the majority of hostelries on Hatteras Island were no-frills hotels and motels that catered to fishermen and those on a budget. Those places are still here, but as the area's popularity has surged, so have the options in accommodations. Now, road-weary travelers can choose from several bed-and-breakfasts and even a resort. Everyone visiting Hatteras Island should be able to find a place to suit their needs and tastes.

Resorts, Hotels, and Motels

Comfort Inn—Hatteras Island. Deluxe. 46745 N.C. 12 in Buxton, 27920 (877-424-6423 or 252-995-6100; www.outerbankscomfortinn.com). This is one of the few chain hotels on Hatteras Island.

Hatteras Landing. Deluxe/Expensive. N.C. 12 next to the ferry landing in Hatteras (866-348-8819; www.hatteraslanding.com). This resort offers 10 rooftop residences ranging in size from 1,400 to 2,200 square feet, ample room for a family to spread out. Guests feel like they're staying in a home, thanks to the granite countertops, maple cabinets, and state-of-the-art appliances. The residences sit atop shops and restaurants. When not downstairs shopping or visiting the local bakery, guests can enjoy the large decks with nearly 360-degree views of the ocean and sound. The resort will assist with reservations for charter boats, scooters, bikes, and beach equipment.

Avon Motel. Moderate. 40279 Younce Road in Avon, 27915 (252-995-5774; www.avonmotel.com). This ocean-side motel has been family owned and operated since 1954. Its 45 units include the basics, like air conditioning, phones, and televisions; some have fully equipped kitchens. A guest laundry and a lighted fish-cleaning station are available. The motel is open from March to December.

Cape Hatteras Motel. Moderate. 46556 N.C. 12 in Buxton, 27920 (800-995-0711 or 252-995-5611; www.capehatterasmotel.com). Offering 11 rooms, two efficiencies, and 21 apartments, this motel has much to choose from. All rooms have a television, a microwave, a small refrigerator, and a coffee maker. Fully equipped kitchens and linens are provided in the efficiencies and apartments. All guests have access to a pool, a Jacuzzi, and a freezer for the day's catch. This motel is one of the closest accommodations to Canadian Hole and is only a 20-minute walk from the lighthouse. It is open year-round.

Hatteras Harbor Marina & Efficiencies. Moderate. 58058 N.C. 12 in Hatteras, 27943 (800-676-4939; www.hatterasharbor.com/efficiencies.html). Hatteras Harbor's five one-bedroom efficiencies are located on the second floor of a marina building, making this the perfect place for sincere fishermen. Some rooms can accommodate up to five people and include full kitchens with linens and dishes. Each room has a balcony, from which guests can enjoy watching the boats come in and the sunset over the sound.

Lighthouse View Motel and Cottages. Moderate. 46677 N.C. 12 in Buxton, 27920 (800-225-7651 or 252-995-5680; www.lighthouseview.com). Guests here are almost at the foot of the lighthouse. This large complex offers over 85 units ranging from single rooms to efficiencies and villas. The amenities include coffee makers, microwaves, refrigerators, cable television, private porches and decks, washers and dryers, a pool, and a hot tub.

Sea Gull Motel. Moderate. 56883 N.C. 12 in Hatteras, 27943 (252-986-2550; www.seagullhatteras.com). This motel, located within a mile of Hatteras Fishing Center, offers 45 oceanfront apartments and efficiencies, all with televisions, phones, refrigerators, coffee makers, and microwaves. It also has cottages for rent. A fish-cleaning area and outdoor showers are provided for fishermen. Kids love the outdoor pool and the private beach. The motel is open March through November.

Inns and Bed-and-Breakfasts

The Inn on Pamlico Sound. Deluxe/Expensive. 49684 N.C. 12 in Buxton, 27920 (866-995-7030 or 252-995-7030; www.innonpamlicosound.com). The dozen suites in this lovely inn offer stunning views of the sound and the innkeepers' well-tended garden; many of the rooms are in fact named after the flowers growing there. All suites offer king- or queen-sized beds, private baths, phones, TVs with DVD/VCR players, and high-speed Internet connections. Many have whirlpool tubs as well. The innkeepers pride themselves on the sumptuous homemade three-course breakfasts served here, which include selections such as Belgian waffles and raspberry-stuffed French toast. In the afternoons, guests can treat themselves to fresh baked goods and beverages. The inn features a 14-seat home theater. Guests can also borrow kayaks and bicycles.

Cape Hatteras Bed-and-Breakfast. Expensive/Moderate. 46223 Old Lighthouse Road in Buxton, 27920 (800-252-3316 or 252-995-3002; www.capehatterasbandb.com). The address lets you in on how close this bed-and-breakfast is to the lighthouse. It is only 500 feet from the ocean as well. Its seven rooms and two suites include basic amenities like private baths, refrigerators, and cable television. Guests can also take advantage of the inn's sun deck, surfboard and sailboard storage, bicycles, beach chairs, coolers, and beach bags. A hearty breakfast is served each morning. The inn is open from April to December.

Places to Eat

You'll discover a surprising number of restaurants on Hatteras Island. Most are located on the sound side near the lighthouse. You'll find everything here, from gourmet fare to a quick bite on the run. Most people are also surprised and pleased at the lack of chain eateries.

Sandbar & Grille. Expensive. 49250 N.C. 12 in Buxton, 27920 (252-995-3413; www.sandbarandgrille.com). This sound-side restaurant is a favorite among locals. Its second-floor dining room and deck provide great views of Pamlico Sound. It offers a variety of steaks, seafood choices, pasta dishes, soups, salads, and sandwiches. In addition to food, you'll find live music and karaoke here, as well as a large game room downstairs to keep the children entertained. The restaurant opened in Hatteras Village in 1997 but was blown north to Buxton by Hurricane Isabel in September 2003. It is open for lunch and dinner daily in summer.

The Breakwater Restaurant. Expensive/Moderate. N.C. 12 at Oden's Dock in Hatteras, 27943 (www.odensdock.com; 252-986-2733). The second-story dining room, deck, and bar of this restaurant overlook Pamlico Sound, affording great views of the sunset and of boats on their way to dock for the evening. The specialties include seafood, prime rib, veal, and pasta. Just try not to fill up on the freshly baked bread and appetizers before your meal! Dinner is served Thursday through Monday from March to December.

The Dolphin Den. Moderate. 40126 N.C. 12 in Avon, 27915 (252-995-7717; www.dolphinrestaurant.com). If you're looking for good North Carolina seafood, this is an excellent place to try. From traditional fried seafood platters to soft-shell crab sandwiches, The Dolphin Den revels in its prime location by the ocean. Angus steaks, pasta dishes, and burgers are offered as well. In addition, the restaurant has a smoker for ribs and chicken wings. Lunch and dinner are served daily.

Hatteras Harbor Deli. Moderate. 58058 N.C. 12 in Hatteras, 27943 (252-986-2500; www.hatterasharbor.com/deli.html). Located adjacent to Hatteras Harbor Marina, this eatery offers a menu heavy on seafood. Try the scallop burger or the shrimp pasta salad. The porch is a nice place to go in the afternoon to enjoy hand-dipped ice cream and to watch the boats come in. If you're a fisherman, you'll appreciate the deli's prepacked breakfasts and lunches for those all-day trips; call a day ahead to request what you want. Breakfast and lunch are served daily year-round.

Orange Blossom Bakery & Café. Inexpensive. 47028 N.C. 12 in Buxton, 27920 (252-995-4109; http://orangeblossombakery.com). The Orange Blossom Bakery is famous for its "Apple Uglies," the tastiest fritters you'll ever experience. It also sells a variety of pastries, doughnuts, and breakfast sandwiches. Breakfast is served daily.

A Well-Weathered Past

Excerpted from *Hatteras Journal* by Jan DeBlieu

Theodore Stockton Midgett was the son of a commercial fisherman. His wife, Ersie, a short, red-haired, and jovial woman, was the daughter of Efrica and Jethro Anderson Midgett, who ran a business delivering food and dry goods that they brought to the island by sailboat. At the time Stockton and Ersie built the white house, Hatteras Island was still little more than a sparsely vegetated bar of sand. There were no paved roads, no running water, no electricity, no dunes. Construction on the Oregon Inlet bridge was forty years away. With no reliable weather forecasting system, the island's residents stayed continually prepared for major blows. . . .

. . . When the Civilian Conservation Corps set up a base camp in Rodanthe to headquarter their dune-building project, Stockton realized the crews of men needed a source of food and supplies. In 1936 he built a general store just west of the white house. At first he intended to turn the store's operation over to his sons, Harold, Anderson, and Stockton, Jr. But the boys soon tired of staying inside to clerk and put up stock. Within two years the storekeeping had been delegated to Ersie, who was quick at figuring prices and balancing books. Stockton had other plans for his sons. In the fall of 1938 he went to Baltimore and came back with a franchise for the island's first transportation system, a bus line from Hatteras village to Manteo. . . .

. . . Harold and Anderson were determined to start running their new business as soon as they could. To help drive their first "bus"—a brand-new Ford station wagon—they recruited their young brother, Stocky. Once a day the station wagon made its way from Hatteras village to a ferry at Oregon Inlet, then on to Manteo and back. "We called the route one-O-one—a hundred and one different ways," Stocky recalled. "At low tide we drove the beach. At high tide we drove the bank—the top of the beach, where the dunes are now—or the inside road, which consisted of several different tracks. There were always more people than we had room for; most of the time we'd put 'em on the running boards and in each other's laps, and sometimes on the hood. If we got stuck, which we often did, everybody got out and pushed."

The modern world had begun to discover Hatteras Island. In addition to the debut of public transportation, 1938 brought electricity to Hatteras village with the formation of a municipal cooperative. Electricity meant running water, indoor toilets, refrigeration. Slowly residents began to enjoy more luxuries and to have more contact with the outside world. Occasionally a hurricane or a strong wind blow would disrupt the island's development, but storms were accepted as sporadic, shortlived dangers, like tornados in the Midwest. In 1944 a major hurricane pushed eight feet of water through Rodanthe. As Ersie, Joyce, and Anderson sat in the wood-frame house, a sudden blast of wind twisted the structure and sent it sliding twelve feet off its foundation. When the eye passed overhead, the family rushed

Cape Hatteras Lighthouse
PHOTOGRAPH BY ARTIE SPARROW

to the home of a relative—only to have that house picked up beneath them by a surge and floated fifty yards, tossing and lurching in the waves. The receding tide left the relative's house perched on top of Anderson's brand-new Ford.

And still the pace of progress quickened. In 1948 the electric cooperative extended its service to the north section of Hatteras Island, and the state paved the first portion of Highway 12, a twenty-mile stretch between Hatteras village and Avon. In 1952 the surfaced road reached the length of the island. Although easier to drive than the beach, it was frequently overwashed or covered with sand, and the Midgett brothers' vehicles continued to get stuck. One evening as Stocky was driving back from Manteo in a school bus loaded with people, he suddenly found himself driving through water. "The sea had backed up right behind the dunes, and one of the dunes broke through," he

says. "Water came rushing through like a funnel. I had on a pair of leather boots, so I climbed around on the fenders trying to get the hood up without getting my feet wet. By the time I dried off the engine, the front wheels of the bus had settled down through the highway. And before we could do anything else, the rear wheels fell through. The bus started settling down just like you'd put a casket in a grave."

Passengers piled out of the vehicle and climbed a dune while Stockton started north, walking and swimming toward the nearest Coast Guard station. An hour later when he returned with help, the bus had disappeared. "When the tide fell, the highest point of the bus was the left front corner. It was about eighteen inches above the surface of the road. I called my brother to tell him I'd lost the bus. He wanted to know if I'd been off drinking someplace."

The Ocracoke-Swan Quarter Ferry
PHOTOGRAPH BY ARTIE SPARROW

Ocracoke Island

The last of the barrier islands that make up the thin, long, wind-swept Outer Banks, Ocracoke has long been known for its seclusion. Over the centuries, it has been the haunt of wild ponies, pirates, and German U-boats. Tourism didn't develop on the island until after World War II; it was only then that electricity, telephone lines, and paved roads were installed here. Even today, the 16-mile-long island is accessible only by ferry or plane. This seclusion and the slow pace of life attract people looking to get away from it all. Regulars have made Ocracoke their vacation destination for generations.

Ocracoke Village, the only town on the island, wraps around the beautiful Silver Lake. The island has only one major road; walking and biking are the ways most people get around.

You definitely don't want to miss a thing Ocracoke has to offer.

Historic Places, Gardens, and Tours

When many people think of the island, the ***Ocracoke Lighthouse*** comes to mind. Built in 1823, it is the oldest lighthouse in operation in North Carolina and the

JUST THE FACTS

Ocracoke is accessible by water or air. A free ferry crosses from Hatteras Island to Ocracoke about every half-hour in the summer. Reservations are not accepted; passengers cross on a first-come, first-served basis. Two ferries operate between Ocracoke and mainland North Carolina, one to the west from Swan Quarter in Hyde County and the other to the south from Cedar Island in Carteret County. Reservations are accepted for these ferries, and a fee is charged. For information on ferry schedules, fees, and crossing times, call 800-BY-FERRY or visit www.ncferry.org.

The only major road is N.C. 12; in Ocracoke, its official name is Irvin Garrish Highway.

The Greater Hyde County Chamber of Commerce, located on the mainland in Swan Quarter, is a good source for information about Ocracoke; call 888-493-3826 or 252-926-9171 or visit www.hydecounty.org.

Ocracoke Lighthouse
PHOTOGRAPH BY ARTIE SPARROW

second-oldest in the United States. It's the shortest on the North Carolina coast, too, standing only 75 feet in height. Its beam penetrates 14 miles out to sea. The lighthouse was first given its distinctive whitewash in 1868; the wash was a brew of lime, a peck of salt, a half-pound of powdered Spanish whiting, three pounds of ground rice, a pound of glue, and enough boiling water to hold it all together. The builders of the lighthouse had the good sense to situate it on the island's highest point, so it has been spared from flooding several times. When a hurricane in 1944 flooded many of the island's homes with as much as two and a half feet of water, the waves merely lapped at the lighthouse's doorstep. Now fully automated, the lighthouse is administered by the United States Coast Guard. Guests can tour the grounds, but the lighthouse is not open for climbing. For more information, visit www.nps.gov/caha/ocracokelh.htm.

Some people strolling Ocracoke are surprised to find a British flag flying here. The **British Cemetery**, located not far from Silver Lake, is a memorial to the men of the HMS *Bedfordshire*, a British antisubmarine ship torpedoed and sunk off Cape

Lookout by a German U-boat in May 1942. All aboard perished. Four bodies washed ashore on Ocracoke and were given a burial befitting men serving their country and helping to protect the United States. The graveyard, surrounded by a white picket fence and maintained by the Coast Guard, contains concrete crosses with bronze plaques. One features the words of Rupert Brooke: "If I should die, think only this of me; / That there's some corner of a foreign field / That is for ever England."

Another British legacy on the island may be the ***wild ponies of Ocracoke***. Legend has it that on at least one of Sir Walter Raleigh's expeditions to the New World, his colonists left ponies on Roanoke Island. The ponies spread throughout the Outer Banks, as the islands used to be connected by land bridges until various hurricanes and nor'easters shifted the sands and created channels. A second theory postulates that the ponies may be descended from mustangs that swam ashore from Spanish galleons that met their watery end in the Atlantic. In either case, hundreds of wild ponies roamed the Banks until the advent of development and tourism after World War II. In 1959, those on Ocracoke were corralled into a 180-acre pasture near the northern end of the island. The Boy Scouts took over the care of the ponies around that time, becoming the nation's only mounted troop. The National Park Service stepped in to care for the ponies in the early 1960s and continues in that role today. While viewing the ponies, you can conjecture about whether they are descended from shipwreck survivors or Raleigh's brood. Visit www.nps.gov/caha/oc_ponies.htm for more information.

Museums and Science Centers

Though Ocracoke isn't large, it is steeped in history and legend. The Native Americans of the area called the island Wokokon. Legend has it that the infamous Edward Teach, better known as the pirate Blackbeard, renamed the island on his final night. Anxious to do battle against the British who were trying to capture him, he cried out, "O Crow Cock!" beckoning the morning to appear. You can find out the complete history of the island at the ***Ocracoke Visitor Center***, located in Ocracoke Village by Silver Lake. The entire village was placed on the National Register of Historic Places in July 1990. The visitor center offers exhibits detailing the important events in the island's history. The National Park Service administers the site. Rangers are on hand to answer questions and to guide you to good books in the book shop. The center is open from 9 A.M. to 5 P.M. year-round except Christmas; longer hours are offered in summer. To contact the visitor center for information, including docking fees, visit www.nps.gov/caha/planyourvisit/visitor-centers.htm or call 252-928-4531.

Ocracoke Preservation Society Museum, at 49 Water Plant Road (27960) near the ferry docks off N.C. 12, is another excellent resource for information on the island's history. The society is dedicated to honoring Ocracoke's unique cultural, environmental, and architectural history. It was instrumental in getting many of the area's homes and businesses recognized on the National Register. The society opened its museum in 1992 in the circa-1900 Captain David Williams House, home to the island's first Coast Guard station chief. During summer, the society hosts art shows and museum porch talks on the village's history. Admission is free. For information, call 252-928-7375 or visit www.ocracokemuseum.org.

Special Shopping

Ocracoke offers a number of distinctive shops where visitors can find anything from the basic necessities to souvenirs to commemorate their trip.

Deepwater Pottery, at 62 School Road (27960), offers pottery, hand-blown glass, candles, and jewelry, much of it either by local artisans or certified by the Fair Trade Federation. It is housed in a historic home set amid a grove of live oaks and cedars, so the exterior is as charming as what you'll find inside. Call 252-928-7472 or visit www.deepwaterpottery.com.

Books to Be Red, next door to Deepwater Pottery at 34 School Road (27960), is an excellent shop offering new and used books ranging from local history to the latest fiction. For more information, call 252-928-3936.

Ocracoke Variety Store, at 950 Irvin Garrish Highway/N.C. 12 (27960), offers exactly what its name implies—a variety of everything. You'll find grocery items, T-shirts, tools, books, postcards, and just about everything in between. Call 252-928-4911.

Natural Selections, at 35 School Road (27960), is also known as "the Hemp Shop." When it opened in 1998, its focus was on selling products made from industrial hemp. It has now expanded to offer a variety of products made from bamboo, soy, organic cotton, flax linen, silk, and wool. The emphasis is on items made from the most environmentally friendly products possible. Call 252-928-4367 or visit www.ocracokeislandhemp.com.

Teach's Hole is located at 935 Irvin Garrish Highway/N.C. 12 (27960). This essential stopping place is a "Blackbeard Exhibit and Pirate Specialty Shop." A short film tells shoppers about Blackbeard's connection to the island, his supposed haunts, and how he met his bloody end. History buffs will enjoy the displays of weapons, bottles, maps, coins, and flags of Blackbeard's day. Visitors can select from over 1,000 pirate-related items, including books, maps, music, and even party supplies. Call 252-928-1718 or visit www.teachshole.com.

Recreation

One of the best ways to take in the natural bounty of Ocracoke is through the kayak ecotours offered by ***Ride the Wind Surf & Kayak***. Several options are available, including a sunrise tour, a sunset tour, and a full-moon tour. Be sure to bring bug spray so the pests won't enjoy the tour more than you do. Surf camps for kids and surf lessons for all ages are offered as well. Call 252-928-6311 or visit www.surfocracoke.com for more information.

Fishermen will want to make ***Anchorage Marina*** one of their first stops. Only 18 miles from the Gulf Stream, this marina is one of the closest jumping-off places for those in search of yellowfin tuna, wahoo, amberjack, and bluefish. The marina offers charter boats, dockage, gas and diesel, water and power hookups, showers, and

Fishing boat in the harbor at Ocracoke
PHOTOGRAPH BY ARTIE SPARROW

even bikes for touring the island. A café on the premises sells drinks, lunches, and fishing supplies. Call 252-928-6661 or visit www.theanchorageinn.com/marina.htm for more information.

Seasonal Events

The annual *Ocrafolk Music and Storytelling Festival*, held in early June along School Road, features a variety of local artists and performers. The festival includes a cookoff, a parade, a fund-raising auction, and boat-building demonstrations. Admission is free. For more information, visit www.ocrafolkfestival.org.

Those who can't make it to town for the festival should visit *Deepwater Theater*, located on School Road off N.C. 12. During the summer, the theater is home to Molasses Creek (a local bluegrass band of national acclaim) and the Ocrafolk Opry. General-admission tickets are sold 30 minutes prior to showtime; times vary, so call ahead. Call 252-928-4280 or visit www.deepwatertheater.com.

Places to Stay

Many Ocracoke regulars have a certain hotel or bed-and-breakfast they come back to time and again. You're sure to find your favorite spot, too. Be sure to book early, since lots of new "regulars" discover Ocracoke each season.

Resorts, Hotels, and Motels

Captain's Landing. Deluxe/Expensive. 324 Irvin Garrish Highway/N.C. 12, 27960 (252-928-1999; www.thecaptainslanding.com). This luxury hotel was named to honor the many captains in the proprietors' families, including hometown hero Horatio Williams, a noted sailor who evaded the Yankees during the Civil War. The hotel's comfortable waterfront suites overlook Silver Lake and feature queen beds, full kitchens, and private decks. The top-of-the-line penthouse offers a master suite, a guest room, a gourmet kitchen, and a laundry room. If neither of these options suits you, you can book the Captain's Cottage for the ultimate in private, spacious relaxation—two bedrooms with private bathrooms, a full kitchen, a living room, a dining room, and a private patio. The hotel also provides bicycles and a grilling area.

Silver Lake
PHOTOGRAPH BY ARTIE SPARROW

Blackbeard's Lodge. Expensive/Moderate. 111 Back Road, 27960 (800-892-5314 or 252-928-3421; www.blackbeardslodge.com). The friendly staff, the second-story sun deck, and the front desk made of a ship's prow have made this place a favorite for many visitors. The lodge, which has been around since 1936 and touts itself as the island's oldest hotel, offers 38 rooms and apartments. Guests may choose from a variety of rooms, some of which have full kitchens and whirlpool tubs. Kids enjoy the heated pool and the game room. Blackbeard's Lodge is open March through November.

Anchorage Inn. Moderate. 205 Irvin Garrish Highway/N.C. 12, 27960 (252-928-1101; www.theanchorageinn.com/inn.htm). The Anchorage Inn has five floors with 35 rooms and suites, many offering excellent views of the ocean and sound. The suites have full kitchens and private decks. A café, a pool, and grills are among the popular features here. Because of the Anchorage's proximity to the marina, guests can charter boats from the inn.

Inns and Bed-and-Breakfasts

Ocracoke Harbor Inn. Deluxe. 144 Silver Lake Drive, 27960 (888-456-1998 or 252-928-5731; www.ocracokeharborinn.com). Overlooking Silver Lake, the Ocracoke Harbor Inn offers 16 rooms and seven suites, most of which feature a private porch that provides a stunning view of the village and the harbor. The inn features a continental breakfast on its waterfront deck and has grills available for use. All rooms and suites have televisions, telephones with modem ports, coffee makers, and refrigerators; the suites include kitchenettes and Jacuzzis. Guests can enjoy the luxury of strolling to dinner or biking to nearby shops. The inn is open from mid-March through the Monday after Thanksgiving.

Castle Bed-and-Breakfast and Courtyard Villas. Deluxe/Expensive. 155 Silver Lake Drive, 27960 (800-471-8848 or 252-928-3505; www.thecastlebb.com). This bed-and-breakfast offers two types of accommodations. Those looking for traditional lodging will like the 11 guest rooms, which have paneled walls, big, comfy beds, and private baths. Those looking for more spacious digs can enjoy one of the 22 villas, which have fully equipped kitchens and washers and dryers. A full buffet breakfast is offered for all guests. Other treats include a masseuse, a heated pool, and a sauna. Outdoor lovers will appreciate the on-site marina and the complimentary bicycles. Boat owners have access to complimentary dockage with power hookups at the Castle's docks.

The Cove Bed-and-Breakfast. Deluxe/Expensive. 21 Loop Road, 27960 (252-928-4192; www.thecovebb.com). Nestled near the foot of the lighthouse, this charming establishment has four guest rooms and three suites, each with queen-sized beds and private baths and balconies. The great views of the sound may inspire guests to lounge on the wraparound porch after breakfast or to borrow the inn's bicycles. Continental breakfast and an evening wine reception are offered. The Cove is open year-round except for most of January.

Pelican Lodge. Expensive/Moderate. 1021 Irvin Garrish Highway/N.C. 12, 27960 (888-773-5422 or 252-928-1661; www.bbonline.com/nc/pelican). This rustic-looking lodge, split into Pelican Lodge East and Pelican Lodge West, prides itself on its attention to guests' needs and desires. A registered dietitian supervises breakfast. A car-rental service and the lodge's own air service, Pelican Airways, provide transportation; aerial sightseeing tours are available. The five guest rooms have private baths and cable television. Complimentary bicycles are available for those who would like to explore the island. The lodge is open year-round.

Thurston House Inn. Expensive/Moderate. 671 Irvin Garrish Highway/N.C. 12, 27960 (252-928-6037; www.thurstonhouseinn.com). The Thurston House Inn was

Pamlico Sound between Ocracoke and Swan Quarter
PHOTOGRAPH BY ARTIE SPARROW

built in the 1920s by Captain Tony Thurston Gaskill. It offers six guest rooms, all with private baths, hot tubs, and televisions; some rooms have private decks and entrances. An expanded continental breakfast greets guests before the day's activities, all of which are easily accessible from the inn's large, breezy front porch. The inn is open March through mid-December.

Places to Eat

You really can't go wrong with any of the eateries on Ocracoke Island, so be adventurous and try a new one each opportunity you get. The variety—fresh-off-the-boat seafood, good old meat and potatoes, Italian, gourmet, casual—is enough to satisfy any palate. If you haven't been to Ocracoke lately, you should note that restaurants are now allowed to have full ABC permits. As with every place on the Outer Banks, hours are seasonal, so it's best to call ahead to make sure your restaurant of choice is serving.

The Back Porch. Expensive. 110 Back Road, 27960 (252-928-6401). This restaurant prides itself on being out of the way on the already out-of-the-way Ocracoke.

Secluded from N.C. 12 by trees and cacti, The Back Porch does indeed feature a lovely back porch. Or you can select the indoor dining room. From the first bite, it is obvious that all the sauces, condiments, and breads are made on-site. Freshly ground coffee and homemade desserts round out the evening. If you'd like to try your hand at any of The Back Porch's unique dishes, a cookbook is available at the hostesses' station. Dinner is served nightly in season.

Creekside Café. Moderate. 621 Irvin Garrish Highway/N.C. 12, 27960 (252-928-3606; www.ocracokeisland.com/creekside_cafe.htm). Creekside Café, overlooking Silver Lake, is a nice place to take a rest from your island explorations and get a cool drink and a bite to eat. Light fare like soups, salads, and sandwiches is offered. The truly hungry can choose from the seafood and burger selections. Try to get a seat on the porch to enjoy the breeze and the great view. Lunch and dinner are served daily.

A view of the Ocracoke Lighthouse from Silver Lake
PHOTOGRAPH BY ARTIE SPARROW

Ocracoke Lighthouse
PHOTOGRAPH BY ARTIE SPARROW

Flying Melon. Moderate. 804 Irvin Garish Highway/N.C. 12, 27960 (252-928-2533). Don't let the humble façade fool you. Inside, you'll find some of the best food on the island. The Flying Melon combines fresh seafood with a New Orleans mentality. Its sweet potato pancakes are already legendary, even though the restaurant is relatively new. Lunch is served Tuesday to Sunday and dinner Tuesday to Saturday. The restaurant is closed from mid-November to mid-March.

Howard's Pub and Raw Bar. Moderate. 1175 Irvin Garrish Highway/N.C. 12, 27960 (252-928-4441; www.howardspub.com). Open 365 days a year, this is a popular hangout for locals and visitors alike. The only raw bar on the island, Howard's features more than 200 imported, domestic, and microbrew beers. So it follows that it's famous for things like the spicy "Ocracoke Oyster Shooter." The dishes most in demand include steaks, barbecued ribs, blackened tuna, and marinated mahi-mahi. The hand-shaped half-pound burgers, the hand-cut fries, the homemade salsa, the chili, the chowder, and the desserts are popular, too. The screened-in porch invites visitors to sit back, relax, and slip into an "Ocracoma," an altered state caused by the sense of contentment the surroundings induce.

Island Inn Restaurant. Moderate. At the Island Inn on Lighthouse Road, 27960 (877-456-3466 or 252-928-4351; www.ocracokeislandinn.com/dining.htm). You don't have to be a guest of the Island Inn to enjoy this appealing restaurant; you just have to be hungry for a great meal. One of the oldest restaurants on Ocracoke, it uses china like you'd find at Grandma's house. The cooking, though, is definitely not Grandma's, unless she serves shrimp and oysters in the morning. And you won't be disappointed by the homemade fish cakes or the paella. Guests who would like to take part of their dining experience home can purchase Chardonnay bottled specially for the restaurant. Breakfast and dinner are served daily.

Thai Moon. Moderate. In Spencer's Market at 589C Irvin Garrish Highway/ N.C. 12, 27960 (252-928-5100). This takeout-only restaurant had its praises sung by a *Gourmet* magazine writer for having some of the best Thai food he'd tasted anywhere. If you're looking for a spicy diversion from traditional seafood, then you're at the right place. Thai Moon doesn't accept credit cards, though. And be sure to call ahead if you're catching the ferry. Lunch and dinner are served Tuesday to Sunday.

Marsh area at Ocracoke
PHOTOGRAPH BY ARTIE SPARROW

The beach at Ocracoke
PHOTOGRAPH BY ARTIE SPARROW

The Gallivantin' Outer Banks

Excerpted from *Ocracoke* by Carl Goerch

This old world of ours, after having gone through many geological changes, is pretty well established.

If you're a resident of Charlotte, if you were to pull up stakes and move out to California, and if you should return in thirty years or more, you'd be pretty sure that Charlotte would be exactly where it was when you left it. Of course the city might have grown a lot but this growth would be in the nature of expansion in all directions.

The same thing is true of practically every other place—except the outer banks, of which Ocracoke is a part.

Throughout the years there have been many changes along this strip of narrow islands along the coast of North Carolina. The beach has been built up at some points,

it has been washed away at others. Sand dunes move slowly up the coast, the sand being blown up one side and deposited on the other. It was because of this that the memorial to the Wright brothers on Kill Devil Hill couldn't be built until it had been "anchored" by planting grass on its slopes. Prior to that it kept inching up toward the north.

Inlets appear after a severe storm while others vanish. The same is true of channels. Many years ago someone may have left a worn-out automobile on the sand-flats: today it may be a sizable sand dune.

These changes have been recognized as one of the nation's major geographic curiosities. They are fascinating to the layman and expert alike.

The present shoreline has been built

up by wave action on what originally were shoals situated farther to the east. The outer banks are now being pushed toward the mainland by wave action, which washes the sand to the beach, and by wind action, which carries the sand inland. The winds are constantly moving the sand, building dunes and ridges in some places and tearing them down in others. This movement will continue as long as the sea remains at its present level.

Some 20,000 years ago, the shoreline was far back on the mainland. Let's say that it was where Washington, New Bern, Columbia and Elizabeth City are now located. The water level was 25 feet above its present level. Then came the last glaciation and the water level dropped 50 feet, or 25 feet lower than at present. That meant that such shallow areas as Diamond Shoals were completely out of water. As a matter of fact, I've heard Frank Kugler of Washington say that even in recent years he has jumped out of a boat at Diamond Shoals and has walked on dry sand. The final step was when the continental ice sheet melted and the sea level rose to its present height. This meant that many low areas, formerly out of the water, became submerged again.

It's an interesting study. And don't think for a moment that the changes are at an end. Not by a long shot; they will continue as long as the waves wash on the beach and as long as the wind blows the sand around.

Alligator from the Cape Fear River seen at Orton Plantation
PHOTOGRAPH BY ANGELA HARWOOD

The Coastal Plain

Albemarle Region
Elizabeth City
Edenton
Bath

Neuse River Region
New Bern
Morehead City
Beaufort
Bogue Banks

Cape Fear Coast
Topsail Island
Wilmington
Wrightsville Beach
Pleasure Island
Southport and Brunswick Islands

By Artie Sparrow and Angela Harwood

S preading out across the eastern third of the state is North Carolina's vast coastal plain.

Inland are small river towns known for their manufacturing—and, more importantly, their barbecue—and countless farming communities that produce the majority of the state's agricultural products, as well as a politician or two. Much like the Mississippi Delta, the flat landscape can be monotonous, but a closer look reveals lush, fertile fields that yield such crops as tobacco, corn, and peanuts.

Along the coast, a series of seven sounds gives North Carolina one of the longest shorelines in the United States. Dotting it are quite possibly the state's most beautiful, historic, and fascinating destinations.

In the north, the region surrounding Albemarle Sound is home to the state's oldest towns, Edenton and Bath, as well as one of the area's most vibrant communities, Elizabeth City. Also here is the Great Dismal Swamp, the continent's only live peat bog.

In the coastal plain's midsection, the Neuse River region encompasses some of the state's premier beaches, collectively called "the Crystal Coast," as well as picturesque fishing and sailing villages such as Beaufort and Oriental. Pirates were fond of the protected coves within the enormous Pamlico Sound, and legends of their antics abound. At the North Carolina Maritime Museum in Beaufort, artifacts from Blackbeard's ship *Queen Anne's Revenge* are on display. Upriver, along the banks of the Neuse River, historic New Bern and its impeccably reconstructed governor's mansion, Tryon Palace, should not be missed.

Farther south, the Cape Fear River region and its crown jewel, Wilmington, are among the state's fastest-growing areas. Among those drawn to this fair metropolis are filmmakers, who since the 1980s have given Wilmington the distinction of being "the Hollywood of the East." A visit to the area is not complete without a stop at the sparkling sands of Topsail Island, Pleasure Island, and the legendary Wrightsville Beach. South of Wilmington, the hamlet of Southport and the pristine Brunswick County beaches round out the lower Cape Fear region. As the midway point along the bustling Intracoastal Waterway, Southport is a port of call for all manner of pleasure boats. If golf is your game, you'll be pleased to learn of the 35-plus public courses in the vicinity. Or if your idea of a vacation is lounging on an uncrowded beach, then enjoy a sumptuous meal of fresh Calabash-style seafood and head for Oak Island, Holden Beach, or Sunset Beach.

Albemarle Region

By Artie Sparrow

Albemarle Sound, located in the northeast corner of North Carolina, is the largest freshwater sound in the United States. Some of the state's oldest communities, including North Carolina's first town, are located here. And Washington, North Carolina, is considered the "original" Washington—by locals, at least.

In the Albemarle region, you'll find historic sites maintained by the Colonial Dames of America. Unlike other Southerners, when these ladies speak of "the war," they're referring to the Revolutionary War, not the Civil War. History and heritage are a large part of the culture of the Albemarle region, and the extraordinarily gracious people of the area are happy to share them with you. The area is known for its wild naturalness. Passing along tar-patched, winding country roads by gum-tree swamps, old tobacco barns falling in on themselves, and fields of corn that go on forever will remind you that there are still parts of the world "progress" hasn't visited, and that leaving land as untamed as your great-grandfather knew it is far better than putting a mini-mart at every crossroads. The people of the Albemarle know that the beauty of the woods and swamps is easily superior to anything we could replace it with. If you visit the Albemarle region, remember to soak up the stories and local histories you're sure to hear from the proud residents. And be sure to enjoy the journey as much as you expect to love your destination.

Elizabeth City waterfront
COURTESY OF ELIZABETH CITY AREA CONVENTION AND VISITORS BUREAU

Elizabeth City

A self-proclaimed "Main Street Waterfront Community," Elizabeth City sits on the banks of the Pasquotank River, whose Indian name means "Where the Current of the Stream Divides." Water played a major role in the development of Elizabeth City. The area was first explored and navigated in the late 1500s. Settlements started appearing along the river the following century, and Elizabeth City was settled in the 1650s. The Dismal Swamp Canal is the oldest canal still in operation in the United States. Legend has it that George Washington and Patrick Henry traveled through the canal to Pasquotank County in the 18th century to survey for rich farmland and good hunting and fishing. Planters used the port to trade with the East Indies. During the Civil War, the Union navy captured Elizabeth City, the southern terminus of the Dismal Swamp Canal, thereby halting shipments of goods into the interior of the Confederacy.

Though not the important trading center it used to be, Elizabeth City is now home to the largest Coast Guard command complex in the lower 48 states. The Pasquotank River serves as an alternate route to the Intracoastal Waterway between Chesapeake Bay and Albemarle Sound. Elizabeth City takes great pride in this nautical heritage. Most of its cultural activities are centered around the river. Here, you'll find Southern hospitality in its highest form. For example, boats are given free dockage for two days at Mariners' Wharf; members of a volunteer group, the Rose Buddies, greet each disembarking newcomer with a rose and an invitation to a wine-and-cheese party. The town boasts museums, galleries, parks, and six historic districts listed on the National Register. It's no wonder that Elizabeth City was named in Norm Crampton's *The 100 Best Small Towns in America*.

JUST THE FACTS

Elizabeth City is accessible by land, water, and air.

U.S. 17 leads into town from the north and south. U.S. 158 leads into town from the west.

The Intracoastal Waterway and the Pasquotank River give access to the city's docks at Mariners' Wharf, where visitors receive free dockage for 48 hours.

The nearest large commercial airport is 50 miles north in Norfolk, Virginia. Elizabeth City Regional Airport, at 1028 Consolidated Road, shares runways with the Coast Guard, so it can accommodate aircraft ranging from private jets to Boeing 747s, should you happen to have one. For information, call 252-335-5634 or visit http://elizabethcity. ncflyports.com.

The Greyhound bus station is at 1900 North Road Street (27909). Call 252-335-5183 or visit www.greyhound.com for information.

The Elizabeth City Area Convention and Visitors Bureau, at 400 South Water Street (27909), is a great resource for learning about the area. For information, visit www. discoverelizabethcity.org or call 252-335-5330. You also can learn about local businesses through the Elizabeth City Chamber of Commerce, at 502 East Ehringhaus Street (27909). Call 252-335-4356 or visit www.elizabethcitychamber.org.

Things to Do

Historic Places, Gardens, and Tours

The best way to begin your sightseeing is to stop by the Elizabeth City Area Convention and Visitors Bureau to pick up a self-guided tour brochure. One of the most popular tours covers the *Elizabeth City commercial district* on Main Street. The commercial district sites let you see what eastern North Carolina downtowns looked liked before the Civil War. This area includes the largest number of brick antebellum commercial buildings in the state. Restaurants, antique shops, galleries, and boutiques perfect for browsing occupy the storefronts today. Elizabeth City is also home to six historic districts on the National Register, so you can spend an enjoyable hour or two casually wandering the charming downtown neighborhoods admiring the architecture and gardens. You'll likely notice many songbirds along the way, since the city is a recognized bird sanctuary.

Episcopal Cemetery and *Christ Episcopal Church*, at 200 South McMorrine Street (27909), are listed on the National Register of Historic Places. The graves in the Episcopal Cemetery date back to 1724. Many of eastern North Carolina's most prominent citizens have been laid to rest here, including John C. B. Ehringhaus, the state's governor from 1933 to 1937. In the southeastern corner of the cemetery is a plot containing the remains of at least four unknown Confederate soldiers. The church was completed in 1857, during the ministry of the Reverend Edward M. Forbes, a well-known local Civil War hero. According to legend, Forbes met the invading Union troops on the bank of the river and asked them to spare the town. Since he was a man of God, they honored his request. The church's 18 large stained-glass windows, added in 1947, depict the life of Christ. In addition to exploring the cemetery, which is open year-round during daylight hours, be sure to visit the lovely memorial garden between the church and the parish house. Admission is free for both the cemetery and the church, though donations are accepted. For information, call 252-338-1686 or visit www.christchurch-ecity.org.

Museums and Science Centers

The *Museum of the Albemarle*, at 501 South Water Street (27909), is a regional branch of the North Carolina Museum of History. The 50,000-square-foot museum explores the history of the Albemarle through exhibits chronicling the work, culture, and folklore of the area over the past 400 years. Included are Native American artifacts, antique duck decoys, hand-carved boats, lumber-camp supplies, and early-20th-century farm equipment. The museum is open Tuesday through Saturday from 9 A.M. to 5 P.M. and Sunday from 2 P.M. to 5 P.M.; it is closed state holidays. Admission is free. For information, call 252-335-1453 or visit www.museumofthealbemarle.com.

The *Elizabeth City State University Planetarium*, at 1704 Weeksville Road (27909), is open Monday through Friday from 8 A.M. to 5 P.M. year-round for those who wish to learn about space exploration and astronomy. Admission is free, though advance reservations are required. One of the 16 campuses in the University of North Carolina system, Elizabeth City State was established in 1891 as a two-year institution serving African-American students. By 1937, it had grown into a four-year teachers' college. It still concentrates on turning out some of the state's best teachers. For information, call 252-335-3759 or visit www.ecsuplanetarium.org.

Port Discover, located at 613 East Main Street (27909), is geared toward children and families. It encourages hands-on and self-directed science exploration. Each

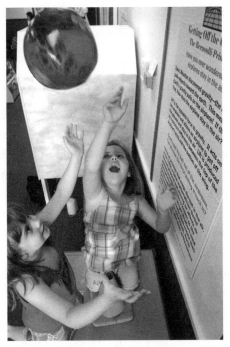

Port Discover
COURTESY OF ELIZABETH CITY AREA CONVENTION
AND VISITORS BUREAU

month, Port Discover features "Make-It" programs highlighting a different scientific theme. A wide range of programs is available to school and youth groups. Port Discover is open Tuesday through Saturday from 1 P.M. to 5 P.M. Admission is free, but donations are welcome. For more information, call 252-338-6117 or visit www.portdiscover.com.

Special Shopping

The Center, located at 516 East Main Street (27909), houses the Arts of Albemarle, the Jaquelin Jenkins Gallery, and the Maguire Theatre. The three-story brick commercial building was erected in 1897 and renovated in 2009. The Center provides opportunities to view and purchase local artwork from more than 200 artists. The gallery is open Monday through Saturday from 10 A.M. to 5 P.M. Admission is free. Call 252-338-6445 or visit www.artsofalbemarle.com.

The Weeksville Vineyard, at 1630 Salem Church Road (27909), is housed in a restored 1930s farmhouse that has a rustic charm. Here, you can taste a variety of fine wines, take in sweeping views of working farms, immerse yourself in the calm quiet of the country, listen to singing birds, and enjoy the gentle breezes, the walking paths, and the pond. This unique blend of vineyards, tasting rooms, and a gift shop will transport you to a bygone era. Hours vary by season. For information, call 252-330-2622 or 252-339-0077 or visit www.weeksvillevineyards.com.

Recreation

Elizabeth City boasts an impressive list of activities and recreational opportunities. The town's parks are a nice place to spend a lazy afternoon. *Waterfront Park, Moth Boat Park, Mariners' Wharf*, and *Dog Corner Park* provide visitors with great views of the Pasquotank River and chances to fish, boat, grill, play volleyball, or just fall asleep while reading a good book. Admission is free to all parks. For more information, call 252-335-1424.

Fun Junktion, at 983 Simpson Ditch Road (27909), is a 133-acre park built on land originally slated for landfill expansion. Once the county leaders decided to use it for purposes other than garbage, they came up with plans for an area that would bring people together and provide them with opportunities for relaxation and—as the name says—fun. Visitors will find a handicapped-accessible playground, bas-

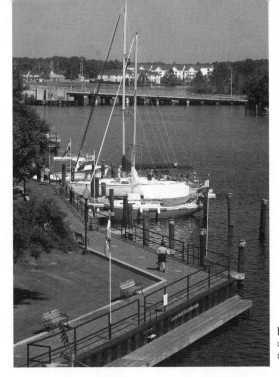

Mariners' Wharf
COURTESY OF ELIZABETH CITY AREA
CONVENTION AND VISITORS BUREAU

ketball courts, picnic areas, walking and biking trails, a skateboard park, and an 18-hole Frisbee golf course. If being in the water is more your idea of fun, you'll enjoy the several lakes, including a catch-and-release fishing pond, a man-made swimming lake, and a 20-acre competition skiing lake. Canoe and paddleboat rentals are available. Admission is free. For more information, call 252-337-6600 or visit www.co.pasquotank.nc.us/funjunktion.htm.

Seasonal Events

Just as you'd expect, the festivals and celebrations in Elizabeth City center around the river.

Perhaps the biggest draw is the annual *Moth Boat Regatta*, sponsored by the Pasquotank River Yacht Club and the Museum of the Albemarle on the third weekend in September. The regatta honors the tiny moth boat, a one-person sailboat created in Pasquotank County in 1929. As the story goes, Captain Joel Van Sant stopped in Elizabeth City on his way from Atlantic City to Florida to have some work done on his yacht, the *Siesta*. He met with Ernest Sanders of Elizabeth City to design a boat that could be raced on rivers and lakes. They came up with the moth boat, so named because it looked like a quick-winged moth floating over the water. The moth boat quickly caught on because of its speed and relative inexpensiveness. The regatta celebrates this heritage of boat racing and Elizabeth City's role in the creation of the

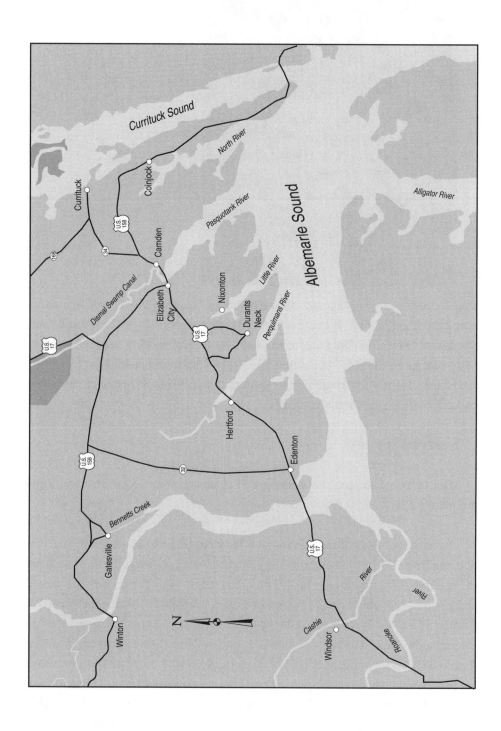

Currituck Sound

North River

Coinjock

Currituck

U.S. 158

158

34

Camden

Pasquotank River

Albemarle Sound

Alligator River

Little River

Nixonton

Durants Neck

Dismal Swamp Canal

Elizabeth City

U.S. 17

Perquimans River

U.S. 17

Hertford

Edenton

U.S. 158

32

Bennetts Creek

U.S. 17

Gatesville

River

River

N

Roanoke

Winton

Cashie

Windsor

boat. Visitors to the festival can enjoy harbor tours, live music, arts, and lots of food and crafts. For more information, call 252-335-5330.

Thousands attend the *North Carolina Potato Festival*, a family outdoor gathering that showcases "the Hometown Spirit of Fun and Excitement in the Harbor of Hospitality." This annual event is held on the downtown waterfront the third Saturday in May. Activities include live music, a potato-peeling contest, and water and children's activities. Food and craft vendors offer their wares for sale. The festival is sponsored by Elizabeth City Downtown, Inc. Call 252-338-4104 or visit www.ncpotatofestival. com for more information.

In early October, the Elizabeth City Historic Neighborhood Association sponsors the annual *Elizabeth City Historic Ghost Walk*. In addition to enjoying an insider's tour of several beautiful homes, participants learn some of the colorful history behind the ghoulish figures who can't quite seem to let go of this town. All proceeds go to historic preservation efforts. For more information, call 888-936-7387.

Places to Stay

Resorts, Hotels, and Motels

The majority of hotels and motels in Elizabeth City are of the chain variety and are located on Halstead Boulevard and South Hughes Boulevard. They include *Hampton Inn* at 402 Halstead Boulevard, 27909 (800-HAMPTON or 252-333-1800; www.hamptoninn.com), *Quality Inn* at 522 South Hughes Boulevard, 27909 (252-338-3951; www.qualityinn.com), *Holiday Inn Express* at 306 South Hughes Boulevard, 27909 (877-863-4780; www.hixpress.com), *Days Inn* at 308 South Hughes Boulevard, 27909 (252-335-4316; www.daysinn.com), *Fairfield Inn and Suites* at 1640 City Center Boulevard, 27909 (252-333-1155; www.marriott.com/orfec), and *Microtel Inn & Suites* at 848 Halstead Boulevard, 27909 (www.microtelinn.com; 252-331-7751).

Inns and Bed-and-Breakfasts

Pond House Inn. Deluxe/Expensive. 916 Rivershore Road, 27909 (888-335-9834 or 252-335-9834; www.thepondhouseinn.com). As the name suggests, this inn is surrounded by water, the Pasquotank River and Waters Pond gently lapping along its six acres. The bucolic environment is a fitting backdrop to the stunning 1941 manor house, which features a winding staircase, a cozy library, and a sunroom. The inn offers three rooms and a suite with king- or queen-sized beds, private bathrooms, plush robes, and conveniences like televisions, phones, and high-speed Internet access. A full breakfast and afternoon tea and wine are offered.

Grice-Fearing House Bed and Breakfast. Expensive. 200 South Broad Street, 27909 (252-333-1792; www.gricefearinghouse.com). Situated in the downtown historic district five blocks from the waterfront, the Grice-Fearing House, built around 1798, is the oldest home in Elizabeth City and is listed on the National Register. It offers two deluxe three-room suites, each with a color-coordinated bedroom, an adjoining sitting room with a TV and a DVD player, and a ceramic-tiled bathroom with a Jacuzzi. Luxurious amenities include high-thread-count linens, plush robes, hair dryers, ceiling fans, and wireless Internet. Breakfast in the elegant dining room features sterling silver, china, starched linens, and Waterford crystal. A three-course homemade gourmet breakfast is served, as are freshly baked cookies at bedtime. Guests are welcome to use the parlor, the library, and the sunroom, which opens to the enclosed brick patio and the koi pond.

The Culpepper Inn. Expensive/Moderate. 609 West Main Street, 27909 (252-335-9235; www.culpepperinn.com). This 1930s Colonial Revival inn, located in the heart of one of the city's historic districts, offers 11 guest rooms individually decorated with antiques. Each room features a king- or queen-sized bed with high-thread-count linens, a claw-foot tub, cable television, a phone, and high-speed Internet access. Some have gas fireplaces, and one is handicapped-accessible. The Tavern Room offers all guests a great place to gather to watch TV and play games. A full breakfast is served every morning, and an afternoon social gives guests the opportunity to mix and mingle. A meeting room is available. Government and corporate rates are offered.

Elizabeth City Bed-and-Breakfast. Expensive/Moderate. 108 East Fearing Street, 27909 (877-324-8922 or 252-338-2177; www.elizabethcitybb.com). This homey establishment offers guest rooms swathed in relaxing colors, comfortable linens, and soft light. Each room has a private bathroom. You'll feel like you're staying in an old friend's home, particularly when you smell the delightful scents of breakfast. Many guests choose to take their morning repast in the flower-filled courtyard, which is only a few blocks from downtown and the water. Several guest packages are available.

Places to Eat

Though Elizabeth City has many chain restaurants, you'll also find a good number of independently owned eateries downtown and near the waterfront. Choices range from light fare to casual gourmet to down-home Southern cooking.

Cypress Creek Grill. Expensive/Moderate. 113 South Water Street, 27909 (252-334-9915; www.cypresscreekgrill.com). Located downtown, this restaurant serves an inclusive American menu—seafood, chicken, steaks, pasta, sandwiches, and vegetarian dishes. The atmosphere is relaxed but upscale, making this exactly the kind of place locals recommend. Check out the grill's famous "SOBs," which come with the seafood combination platter. Regulars swear by these shrimp-and-oyster appetizers, wrapped in bacon and lightly fried. Lunch is served Monday through Friday and dinner Monday through Saturday.

Grouper's Waterfront Seafood Grille. Expensive/Moderate. 400 South Water Street, 27909 (252-331-2431). Located on the Pasquotank River, this is an excellent place to enjoy an outdoor table while watching the boats sail by. The fare includes chicken, beef, veal, lamb, and pasta, though everyone knows the real reason to come here is the delicious seafood. The portions are generous; try to save at least a little room for dessert. Lunch and dinner are served daily.

Montero's Restaurant. Expensive/Moderate. 414 McArthur Drive, 27909 (252-331-1067; www.monterosrestaurant.com). Montero's is housed in a quaint early-1900s farmhouse. This local favorite serves up American, Spanish, French, and Asian cuisine. Guests love the five small dining areas and take advantage of the two large banquet areas that seat 80 to 100 each. Montero's serves lunch and dinner Tuesday through Saturday and brunch on Sunday.

Carolina Theatre and Grille. Moderate. 115 Poindexter Street, 27909 (252-337-7600). Dinner and a movie are the specialties at the Carolina, where patrons can enjoy burgers, sandwiches, salads, and even steaks while catching the latest Hollywood flicks. This is a fun way to spend a relaxing evening without having to worry if the waiter is going to get you out of the restaurant in time to catch your movie. Lunch is offered Monday through Friday and dinner Monday through Saturday.

City Wine Seller Bakery and Deli. Moderate/Inexpensive. 102 North Water Street, 27909 (252-335-1163). Just try to walk past without getting drawn in by the homemade breads, pastries, and desserts. This New York–style deli serves sandwiches made with Boar's Head meats and cheeses on delicious homemade bread. Soups, salads, and quiches are available as well. Live local and regional musicians entertain every Friday evening. The deli serves breakfast and dinner Monday through Friday and lunch daily.

Nearby

The Albemarle region was the cradle of colonial North Carolina. Today, it abounds with small towns that, like Elizabeth City, boast rich histories and interesting attractions. Any one of the following would make a wonderful day trip.

Historic *Halifax*, the legal and administrative seat of Halifax County, is located near N.C. 125 and U.S. 301 about an hour and a half west of Elizabeth City. This is where the Fourth Provincial Congress met to declare independence from England, making North Carolina one of the first states to do so. The county also has provided the state with more governors, congressional representatives, attorneys general, and brigadier generals than any other county in North Carolina. A visitor center and a guided tour of several downtown historic structures are offered. *Lake Gaston*, located slightly northwest of Halifax, has more than 20,000 acres of water bordered by 350 miles of shoreline in North Carolina and Virginia. Boating and fishing are permitted with the appropriate licenses. For more information, call 800-522-4282 or 252-583-1687 or visit www.visithalifax.com.

Historic *Jackson* in Northampton County is about an hour west of Elizabeth City near N.C. 305 and U.S. 158. It is home to several historic structures, including antebellum homes that are open for viewing on a walking tour. The ***Northampton County Museum*** offers interesting exhibits on local Native American and African-American history. The Meherrin and Roanoke rivers are close by. Visit www.northamptonchamber.org for more information.

Historic *Murfreesboro*, about a 45-minute drive from Elizabeth City on U.S. 158 West, features a 12-block national historic district containing homes from the 18th and 19th centuries. A guided tour is available from the *Roberts-Vaughan Village Center*. The *Brady C. Jefcoat Museum of Americana* is home to the largest collection of washing machines, irons, and dairy items in the United States. Those interested in the decorative arts will enjoy the *Wheeler House*, a lovely two-story brick mansion constructed in 1810. The home features a classic white portico and columns and is authentically furnished with several original pieces. For information, call 252-398-5922 or visit www.murfreesboronc.org.

Located south of Elizabeth City almost halfway to Edenton is the small town of *Hertford* in Perquimans County. Recently declared a North Carolina "Main Street" community, Hertford was settled by Pennsylvania Quakers in the late 17th century and owes much of its history to that group. Here, you'll find a downtown of antique shops, cafés, and Queen Anne and Colonial Revival houses. Hertford was home to one of baseball's most storied players, Hall of Famer Jim "Catfish" Hunter, who won the Cy Young Award in 1974 while with the Kansas City Athletics and later led the New York Yankees to three pennants in the late 1970s. Call 252-426-5657 or visit www.visitperquimans.com to learn more.

The *Newbold-White House*, located off U.S. 17 Bypass on the Perquimans River in Hertford, was built in 1730 by Quakers Abraham and Judith Sanders. It is the oldest brick home in the state. Period pieces on display show what life was like during North Carolina's pioneer days. A nominal admission fee is charged for a 45-minute tour of the house, which is open Tuesday through Saturday from 10 A.M. to 4 P.M. and Sunday from 2 P.M. to 5 P.M. from March to Thanksgiving. Also on the six-acre grounds are a museum shop, an herb garden, and a picnic area. The *Periauger*, a double-masted 30-foot replica of the most common style of colonial workboat in the area, is docked on the river nearby. Visit www.newboldwhitehouse.com or call 252-426-7567 for more information.

The *Great Dismal Swamp* begins just north of Elizabeth City and covers almost 600 square miles of North Carolina and Virginia. The only live peat bog on the continent, it contains some of the wildest and most untamed land on the East Coast. Colonel William Byrd II gave the area its name in 1728, when he stated that the place was so dismal that no one could or would want to inhabit it.

President George Washington and Virginia governor Patrick Henry thought differently, however, seeing the economic potential that canals connecting Chesapeake Bay and Albemarle Sound could have on the nation. Canal construction began in 1793. By 1810, both the 22-mile Dismal Swamp Canal and the Jericho Canal were ready for boats. With ease of transportation, though, came greater deforestation during the 19th and early 20th centuries. Fortunately, the swamp recovered. Most of it is now covered by thick bogs, murky waters, and dense forests. As part of today's Intracoastal Waterway, the Dismal Swamp Canal remains a vital transportation route for folks boating between Chesapeake Bay and points south, making it the oldest continuously operating man-made canal in the United States. It is listed on the National Register of Historic Places.

In 1973, the Union Camp Corporation donated 49,100 acres of the swamp to the Nature Conservancy, which in turn handed the land over to the federal government. That tract has since grown to over 111,000 acres, including the 3,100-acre Lake Drummond. The facility is operated as the Great Dismal Swamp National Wildlife Refuge. For more information, call 757-986-3705 or visit www.fws.gov/northeast/greatdismalswamp.

The Dismal Swamp Canal Welcome Center, located a few miles north of Elizabeth City on U.S. 17, offers film and slide programs, information on the history and wildlife of the swamp, hiking and biking trails, fishing, and boating. Among the wildlife you may be able to spot in the swamp are 209 species of birds, 21 varieties of reptiles, skunks, bears, bobcats, minks, otters, muskrats, foxes, and deer. From Memorial Day to the end of October, the center is open daily from 9 A.M. to 5 P.M.; from November to Memorial Day, it operates Tuesday to Saturday from 9 A.M. to 5 P.M. For more information, call 877-771-8333 or visit www.dismalswamp.com.

Merchants Millpond State Park, located at 71 U.S. 158 near Gatesville (27938), about 30 miles northwest of Elizabeth City, is one of North Carolina's ecological treasures. The 3,252-acre park is home to a mingling of coastal-pond and swamp-forest habitats, one of the most diverse ecosystems on the East Coast. Over 160 species of birds have been spotted here, along with a wide variety of reptiles, amphibians, and mammals such as otters, beavers, minks, deer, and bears. The 760-acre millpond is home to 800-year-old bald cypresses and forests of tupelo gums draped with Spanish moss and resurrection ferns. The tupelo gums' trunks have been twisted into wild shapes by the creeping mistletoe, giving rise to a forest that is a sight to behold. Pine and hardwood forests stand nearby as well.

Because so much is available to see and explore at Merchants Millpond, many people choose to camp here. The park offers both primitive campgrounds and family campsites for tents and trailers. No water or electrical hookups are available. Canoe rentals are offered. Fees are charged for camping and canoe rentals. The park is open daily year-round with the exception of Christmas. For more information, call 252-357-1191 or visit www.ncparks.gov/Visit/parks/memi/main.php.

All Good Things

Excerpted from *A Historian's Coast: Adventures into the Tidewater Past* by David Cecelski

Even our wildest swamps have a natural history—sometimes gradual, other times cataclysmic—that has been influenced by settlement, exploitation, and other human practices. Most of this past has never been written down and is often not apparent, but you can find traces of it in the land itself if you spend the time and look closely. . . .

. . . A tar pit or rosin mound indicates a site where naval stores were produced, hence where a longleaf pine forest once stood. A tangle of narrow-gauge railroad track reveals that the swamp forest was timbered, most likely between 1880 and 1920, when Northern lumber companies moved into the old-growth forests of the South. Coils of copper wire and rusted barrels are of course evidence of the moonshine liquor industry that thrived on the Carolina coast during Prohibition. The East Lake and "CCC" (Craven County Corn) brands of homemade whiskey were famous in speakeasies from Norfolk to Boston. And when we stumble upon a sunken shad boat on a creek off the Alligator River or a hand-hewn bow net hidden along the White Oak River, we know that we have discovered traces of the springtime fishery that was the largest in the state in the late nineteenth century.

Other times, when we run up against cypress pilings on the waterfronts of tiny river communities like Rockyhock and Colerain, we are reminded of the great herring fisheries that flourished in the Albemarle Sound vicinity before the Civil War. Using seines that were often a mile and a half in length, thousands of slaves and free black fishermen caught the herring as they migrated out of the Atlantic to spawn in tidewater rivers. The pilings mark the old sheds where the laborers headed and salted the herring by the millions.

The canals that pass through coastal swamps also reveal a great deal about the past. Sometimes, all you notice is a narrow, all-too-straight line of visibility through a cypress swamp, but you can bet that it is an old canal once used to float white oak timbers, cypress shingles, and cedar staves to a mill. Along intertidal marshes, I have inadvertently paddled into a labyrinth of intersecting, narrow canals, a sign of rice cultivation in the slavery era, when large gangs of men and women in bondage cultivated the "golden grain" along the Lower Cape Fear. In places like Lake Phelps and Lake Mattamuskeet, I have followed other, larger canals that date to the late eighteenth and early nineteenth centuries, when slaves dug canals to drain swampland for agriculture and to raft crops and lumber to market.

In my travels, I have floated down even larger passages, known as "ships' canals," that bring to life the golden age of canal building between the American Revolution and the Civil War. During that period, many political leaders believed that ships' canals held the greatest promise for overcoming the navigational hazards of North Carolina's shallow sounds and dangerous, shifting inlets. Between 1794 and 1805, for example, slaves dug the twenty-two-mile-long Dismal Swamp Canal to serve as a shipping route between Albemarle Sound and Chesapeake Bay and to skirt the dangerous swash and bar at Ocracoke Inlet.

Though it was antiquated by the opening of the Albemarle and Chesapeake Canal in 1859, the Dismal Swamp Canal had lasting consequences that had nothing to do with shipping. The canal blocked the Great Dismal Swamp's natural water flow from west to east, which eventually dried up the vast wetlands east of the canal and opened them for agriculture. The canal also lowered water levels throughout the moister parts of the Great Dismal, drying out the highly combustible upper layers of peat during summer droughts. Even as early as 1860, unprecedentedly hot peat fires burned much of the old-growth forests of cypress, juniper, and gum in the Great Dismal.

Millponds also have a story to tell. Quite often, [my brother] Richard and I stumble upon old millponds along remote blackwater creeks. We frequently discover relics of the mills' dams and foundations. When on a millpond, I find it easy to imagine what much of our coastal landscape looked like from the Revolutionary War well into the twentieth century, when millponds could be found in practically every tidewater community. Local people dammed creeks and harnessed the water's flow to power sawmills and gristmills. . . .

Millponds, like all wetlands, are an example of what ecologists refer to as an ecotone, a transitional zone between two diverse ecological communities. Ecotones support life native to each of the two communities (woods and river, for instance), as well as plants and animals endemic to only the ecotone. The heightened diversity and density of life in these transitional zones—a phenomenon known as the "edge effect"—is what makes millponds so remarkably rich in life. . . .

Sometimes when I am staying overnight in a coastal swamp, I get a glimpse of an even more distant past. It is often not easy to find a dry campsite in a swamp forest. A few times, I have had to paddle well into the night before finding a place to rest my head. More than once on waking the next morning, I have discovered clusters of arrowheads and shards of pottery around my camp, letting me know that I was hardly the first person who found shelter on that knoll or hammock. The coastal Algonquians—or their ancestors—used these same places for fishing camps long before European contact in the sixteenth century. . . .

Above all, I am haunted by the fragility of these freshwater wetlands—our most endangered and underappreciated coastal habitats. Everybody admires the beauty of ocean beaches and salt marshes, and I think most people understand their importance for tourism and the seafood industry. But far fewer people have had the chance to fall in love with the natural beauty and ecological uniqueness of these coastal wetlands—the cypress swamps, blackwater creeks, river bottom lands, pine savannas, pocosins, and Carolina bays.

Sailboats in Edenton Bay
COURTESY OF EDENTON-CHOWAN COUNTY TOURISM DEVELOPMENT AUTHORITY

Edenton

One of the oldest communities in the state, Edenton proudly proclaims itself "the South's prettiest small town." Some say it's the profusion of well-maintained colonial and antebellum homes that justifies that claim. The long, tree-lined streets boast 18th- and 19th-century homes that once belonged to governors, aristocrats, and shipping magnates. South King Street is dotted with homes that predate the Civil War, with the exception of two "newcomers" built shortly thereafter. Others attribute Edenton's charm to the perfectly manicured lawns and the abundance of flowers and trees—roses, tulips, lilies, magnolias, and crape myrtles—along the blue waters of Edenton Bay and Albemarle Sound. Still others say Edenton is so beautiful because of the warm people living and working here. Edenton's fiercely proud residents will stop whatever they're doing to give you a history lesson and welcome you to their small piece of paradise.

When it was incorporated in 1722 as "the Towne on Queen Anne's Creek," this area became the first permanent settlement in North Carolina. A few years and a few name changes later, it came to be called Edenton in honor of the Royal governor who made his home here, Charles Eden. The town was designated the first capital of the colony.

But good feelings toward Britain did not last. By August 1774, the citizens of Edenton decided they had suffered enough of England's infamous taxation without representation. Daniel Earle, the rector of St. Paul's Church, rallied citizens by the courthouse and publicly denounced the Boston Port Act, signifying support of the revolutionaries in Massachusetts. That October, the ladies of Edenton decided to do their part to support the cause. Vowing not to purchase or drink any more tea or to wear clothes or fabrics from England until the unfair taxation stopped, the ladies disrupted trade with Britain and proved themselves a force in the battle for independence. A colonial teapot now standing atop one of the Revolutionary War cannons on the courthouse green celebrates the ladies' contribution.

Among Edenton's notable citizens were two signers of the most important documents in the establishment of our country. Joseph Hewes, a ship owner and merchant, signed the Declaration of Independence, while Hugh Williamson, surgeon general of the state's colonial troops, signed the Constitution in 1787. Both assisted the cause by donating and outfitting ships for the burgeoning United States Navy. Samuel Johnston, another Edenton patriot, was the first United States senator from North Carolina. Johnston's brother-in-law, James Iredell, was appointed to the United States Supreme Court by President George Washington.

Thanks to its many influential and powerful residents and its favorable location as an inland port, Edenton developed into an important commercial center around the time of the American Revolution. But following the construction of various canals in the area at the beginning of the 19th century, it fell out of favor as a trading post. Ever since then, the citizens have worked to maintain Edenton's heritage as the home of the revolutionary spirit of North Carolina.

JUST THE FACTS

Edenton is located on Albemarle Sound at the mouth of the Chowan River. You can reach the town from the east or west via U.S. 17 and from the north or south via N.C. 32.

Edenton Marina, at 607 West Queen Street (27932), offers full-service dockage for boaters passing by on Albemarle Sound. Call 252-482-7421 or visit www.edentonmarina.com for information.

The nearest large commercial airport is in Norfolk, Virginia. Northeastern Regional Airport, at 113 Airport Drive in Edenton (27932), accepts small charter flights; call 252-482-4664 for more information.

Edenton's bus station is located at 711 North Broad Street (27932); call 252-482-4117.

Edenton Harbor has transient slips where boaters can stay for free two nights per month. For information, visit www.townofedenton.com or call 252-482-2832.

Historic Edenton State Historic Site, at 108 North Broad Street (27932), offers written information, guided walking tours, and trolley tours; call 252-482-2637 or visit www.nchistoricsites.org/iredell. The Edenton–Chowan County Tourism Development Authority, at 116 East King Street (27932), offers a great deal of written information on the area; call 800-775-0111 or 252-482-3400 or visit www.visitedenton.com.

Things to Do

Historic Places, Gardens, and Tours

The draw for most people coming to Edenton is the state's largest collection of 18th-century homes. Most are listed on the National Register, and a few are national historic landmarks. You can wander the streets on your own, soaking up the Georgian, Federal, Jacobean, Greek Revival, and Victorian architecture, or you can take a guided tour on foot or by trolley.

Historic Edenton State Historic Site, also known as the Historic Edenton Visitors Center, is located at 108 North Broad Street (27932). Regardless of which way you choose to see the town, your first stop should be here. You can pick up maps and pamphlets detailing the architecture and history of each building for exploration on your own, or you can sign up for a guided tour that includes many of the historic sites listed below. Tours are given Monday through Saturday from 9 A.M. to 5 P.M. and Sunday from 1 P.M. to 4 P.M. A fee is charged; students and school groups receive discounted rates. Trolley tours are offered Tuesday through Saturday. The historic site is open daily year-round except for major winter holidays. For information, call 252-482-2637 or visit www.nchistoricsites.org/iredell.

St. Paul's Episcopal Church, located across the street from Historic Edenton State Historic Site at 102 West Church Street (27932), is a must-see stop. St. Paul's Parish was formed in 1701 on Hayes Plantation. Construction on St. Paul's Church—sometimes called "the Westminster Abbey of North Carolina"—started in 1736. It was here, at the second-oldest church in North Carolina, that Edenton's Revolutionary War effort had its beginnings. The membership log at St. Paul's is a who's who of the state's most important colonial leaders. An active congregation still worships here. For information, call 252-482-2279 or visit www.stpauls-edenton.org.

Cupola House is located at 408 South Broad Street (27932). This Jacobean-style home, built in 1758 by Francis Corbin, a land agent of Lord Granville, is the oldest house still standing in Edenton. Its formal gardens include an herb garden, parterres, an orchard, and an arbor with plants believed to have grown in the original gardens. Tours are coordinated by the Historic Edenton Visitors Center. For more information, visit www.cupolahouse.org.

The *Barker-Moore House*, located near Edenton Bay at 505 South Broad Street (27932), was the home of Penelope Barker, who initiated the Edenton Tea Party in 1774. Her husband, Thomas, was the London agent for the colony. Dating to 1782, the Barker-Moore House features an extensive collection of books on the history of the area. Admission is free, and visitors are welcome year-round. The house is open Monday through Saturday from 10 A.M. to 4 P.M. and Sunday from 1 P.M. to 4 P.M. For information, call 252-482-7800.

Cupola House
COURTESY OF NORTH CAROLINA DEPARTMENT OF CULTURAL RESOURCES

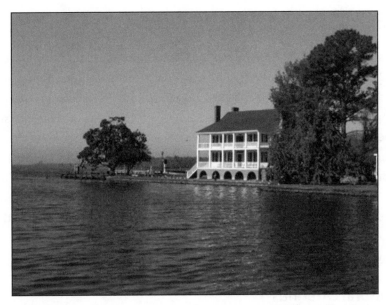

The Barker-Moore House
COURTESY OF EDENTON-CHOWAN COUNTY TOURISM DEVELOPMENT AUTHORITY

The ***Chowan County Courthouse*** is located at 117 East King Street (27932). This 1767 structure at the water's edge is where you'll see cannons and the famous teapot commemorating the bold actions of the town's ladies during the Edenton Tea Party. A national historic landmark, this is the oldest courthouse in North Carolina and one of the best examples of Georgian architecture in the nation. For information, call 252-482-2637 or visit www.edenton.com/history/court.htm.

The ***Chowan County Jail***, the oldest working jail in the nation, is located next to the courthouse.

Iredell House is located at 107 East Church Street (27932). Built in 1773, this was the home of James Iredell, United States Supreme Court appointee of President George Washington. Tours are coordinated by the Historic Edenton Visitors Center. For information, call 252-482-2637 or visit www.nchistoricsites.org/iredell.

The last and grandest of 15 screw pile light stations on North Carolina's sounds and rivers, the ***Roanoke River Lighthouse*** was built in 1886 to illuminate Albemarle Sound. It was decommissioned in 1955 and used as a private residence until the Edenton Historical Commission purchased it in May 2007. It is currently located in Edenton's Colonial Park and is in the process of being restored.

Museums and Science Centers

Established in 1898, **Edenton National Fish Hatchery**, at 1104 West Queen Street (27932), is one of the oldest of the 69 federal fish hatcheries spread throughout the United States. In its time, it has bred a wide assortment of warm-water fish, including largemouth bass, striped bass, channel catfish, bluegill, redear sunfish, shad, and herring. The hatchery currently produces striped bass, Cape Fear shiners, and American shad. The nearly 5 million fish hatched here every year are used to stock the sounds, lakes, and coastal rivers of North Carolina, South Carolina, and Virginia. Visitors are welcome to take self-guided tours of the hatchery's aquarium and grounds. They can also call ahead to arrange for a staff member to show them the facility. Admission is free. The hatchery is open daily from 7 A.M. to 3:30 P.M. For information, call 252-482-4118 or visit www.edenton.fws.gov.

Cultural Offerings

The **Chowan Arts Council Gallery and Gallery Shop**, at 200 East Church Street (27932), features the work of local and national artists. The eclectic mix ranges from commissioned portraits to folk art. A permanent exhibit entitled "A Century of Chowan through Photographs" traces life in the county from 1850 to 1954; it includes portraits of many of the area's most important figures and chronicles events significant in the county's history. You might consider this look at post–Revolutionary War Chowan County as an extension of your tour of colonial-era Edenton homes. The Gallery Shop sells original art and reproductions of some of the works displayed throughout the facility. Admission is free. The gallery and shop are open Monday through Saturday from 10 A.M. to 5 P.M. year-round. For information, call 252-482-8005 or visit www.chowanarts.org.

Recreation

Kayak, canoe, and paddleboat rentals are available at Edenton Harbor for visitors who wish to explore the local creeks and Edenton Bay. For those who enjoy a little adventure, **camping platforms** are offered at John's Island, located across the bay from Edenton, and at Holladay's Island, located on the Chowan River.

Chowan Golf and Country Club is located at 1101 West Sound Shore Drive (27932). If walking around Edenton to view the lush lawns puts you in the mood for some golf, try this semiprivate club. Driving and putting greens are available, in addition to the 18-hole course. Those not interested in golf can enjoy the pool and the tennis courts. Call 252-482-3606 or visit www.chowangolfandcountryclub.com.

Seasonal Events

The *Biennial Pilgrimage Tour of Homes and Countryside in Edenton and Chowan County* takes place on a Friday and Saturday in mid-April every two years. A number of buildings of historic merit, including private homes usually not open to the public, are made available to visitors wanting to satisfy their curiosity as to exactly what lies behind those doors. A single ticket is good for the entire weekend. All proceeds go to the preservation and promotion of the area's historic sites. For more information or to buy advance tickets, call the Edenton-Chowan Chamber of Commerce at 800-775-0111 or 252-482-7800.

The *Annual Peanut Festival* occurs at the beginning of October and honors one of American's favorite snacks with a parade, a band competition, arts and crafts, and a variety of foods, many of which contain the star of the day. Call 252-482-8426 or visit www.visitedenton.com for more information.

Edenton is especially lovely when its historic homes and sites are decorated for the holidays.

The *Candlelight Christmas Tour*, sponsored by the Edenton Historical Commission, features free town-wide festivities during the second weekend in December. This is a must-see if you're in town.

The *Iredell House Groaning Board*, a dessert showcase said to make the table boards "groan" from overabundance, is held at the 1773 home of former United States Supreme Court justice James Iredell. Guests can listen to harpsichord music and admire the 18th-century-style Christmas decorations while enjoying their desserts.

Just down the street is the *Cupola House Wassail Bowl*, where visitors can enjoy a cup of wassail, a traditional holiday drink.

Guests can partake of more holiday refreshments and a bit of art at the Chowan Arts Council's *Candlelight Confection Perfection*. Call 800-775-0111 for more information.

Places to Stay

Inns and Bed-and-Breakfasts

A couple of motels are located outside Edenton's historic district, but since you're here to see the beautiful buildings downtown, the best places to stay are the inns and bed-and-breakfasts. The rates are so reasonable at many of these establishments that you'll pay no more than what a room at a hotel would cost you. And the inns offer more personal attention, better locations, and prettier surroundings.

Granville Queen Inn. Expensive. 108 South Granville Street, 27932 (866-482-8534 or 252-482-5296; www.granvillequeen.com). Guests have a hard time choosing which of the seven bedrooms they'd like to try in this lovely 1907 mansion with a double-decker wraparound porch. Each room has its own style, ranging from Renaissance Revival to Art Deco. Nearly all of the rooms have a fireplace and a private balcony, and all include a private bathroom, cable television, and a phone. Guests are treated each morning to a large gourmet breakfast.

Trestle House Inn at Willow Tree Farm. Expensive. 632 Soundside Road, 27932 (800-645-8466 or 252-482-2282; www.trestlehouseinn.com). This bed-and-breakfast, nestled on a private five-acre lot five miles outside town, is named after the Southern Railway trestles used as exposed support beams in the ceiling and roof. Its five guest rooms, named after birds known to frequent this part of the country, feature private baths, ceiling fans, and central air. Guests can canoe from the pond behind the inn to Albemarle Sound and into Edenton. Both canoes and bikes are available for rent. A homemade breakfast is served daily.

Captain's Quarters Inn. Expensive/Moderate. 202 West Queen Street, 27932 (800-482-8945 or 252-482-8945; www.captainsquartersinn.com). Located in a 1907 Colonial Revival home, the Captain's Quarters offers eight individually decorated and nautically themed guest rooms, each with a private bath, a sitting room, a telephone, cable television, and Internet access. The 65-foot wraparound porch puts guests within walking distance of Edenton's major attractions and waterfront. A full breakfast, morning coffee service, and afternoon refreshments are included in the price of the stay. Sailing, golf, mystery weekends, and wine-and-dine packages featuring gourmet dinners are available.

Places to Eat

For a small Southern town, Edenton has an excellent selection of local, independently owned restaurants that serve tasty, creative meals. You might need to make a second trip to try all the culinary delights the community has to offer.

Sean's Market & Restaurant. Expensive. 309 South Broad Street, 27932 (252-482-8002; www.seansrestaurant.com). This new restaurant, already considered by many travelers and locals to be the best in town, offers a variety of entrées sure to please any palate. It's open for lunch Monday through Saturday and dinner Wednesday through Saturday.

Waterman's Grill. Expensive/Moderate. 427 South Broad Street, 27932 (252-482-7733; www.watermansgrill.com). Located in a historic building a block from Edenton Bay and within walking distance of the town's major sites, this restaurant specializes in good, fresh seafood and thick, juicy steaks. Wine connoisseurs and beer lovers will appreciate the wine shop and bar. Dinner is served Monday through Saturday.

Nixon Family Restaurant. Moderate. 327 River Road, 27932 (252-221-2244). Don't let the casual atmosphere fool you into thinking that food is taken lightly around here. The big draws are the oyster bar and the large variety of just-off-the-boat seafood. The generous buffet is also popular, particularly at lunchtime. Breakfast, lunch, and dinner are served Tuesday through Sunday.

Chero's Market Café and Catering. Moderate/Inexpensive. 112 West Water Street, 27932 (252-482-5525). This charming restaurant, located in a large brick building overlooking Albemarle Sound, serves gourmet fare that is both delicious and affordable. Fresh daily specials are offered, including many sandwiches with imported cheeses and tender meats. Vegetarians will find selections to please their palates as well. Lunch is offered Monday through Saturday and dinner Wednesday through Saturday. Chero's also serves Sunday brunch.

Nothin Fancy Café & Market. Moderate/Inexpensive. 701 North Broad Street, 27932 (252-482-1909). Visitors to this establishment can satisfy two hungers—for food and shopping—at once. The café features good, homemade down-home foods like cornbread, casseroles, and scalloped potatoes that will stick to your ribs. After catching a bite of lunch, head over to the antique store to satisfy your craving for beautiful things. Lunch is served daily and dinner Tuesday through Saturday. Breakfast is offered on Saturday.

Edenton Coffee House. Inexpensive. 302 South Broad Street, 27932 (252-482-7465; www.edentoncoffeehouse.com). For those looking for an exceptional cup of joe and freshly baked brownies, muffins, and pastries, Edenton Coffee is the perfect spot. Many regulars attend the live Saturday-night sessions featuring talented local musicians playing everything from bluegrass to gospel. The music starts around 6:30 P.M., and the shop fills up quickly. Patrons can also take advantage of the free Internet service. The coffee shop is open Monday through Saturday for breakfast and lunch, with extended hours on Saturday for the music.

Nearby

Somerset Place State Historic Site is about 45 minutes south of Edenton at 2572 Lake Shore Drive in the town of Creswell (27928). Located down an oak- and cypress-lined lane near Lake Phelps, Somerset Place was one of the four largest plantations in North Carolina. Home to several generations of the Josiah Collins family beginning in 1785, the plantation once encompassed 100,000 acres. More than 200 slaves worked the property at any given time, digging irrigation and transport canals, building sawmills, gristmills, and other structures, and cultivating rice, wheat, and corn. When the Civil War ended, the Collinses were unable to maintain Somerset Place without their unpaid labor, and the plantation ceased operation.

Archaeological research has been under way since the early 1950s to uncover facts about Somerset Place's many residents. Today, visitors can see what life was like for both the Collinses and their slaves through educational programs and tours of the mansion, the detached kitchen, the smokehouse, the dairy, and the Colony House, which was the Collinses' home before the completion of the plantation house. The historic site is open Monday through Saturday from 9 A.M. to 5 P.M. and Sunday from 1 P.M. to 5 P.M. from April through October. From November through March, it is open Tuesday through Saturday from 10 A.M. to 4 P.M. and Sunday from 1 P.M. to 4 P.M. Admission is free. For more information, call 252-797-4560 or visit www.nchistoricsites.org/somerset/somerset.htm.

Somerset Place State Historic Site
COURTESY OF NORTH CAROLINA DEPARTMENT OF CULTURAL RESOURCES

The crown jewel of *Pettigrew State Park*, located at 2252 Lake Shore Drive in Creswell (27928), is the 16,600-acre Lake Phelps. The second-largest natural lake in the state, Lake Phelps is remarkably shallow, averaging only four and a half feet deep. Its waters are clear, too, making it an anomaly among the area's brackish bodies of water. Visitors can fish or boat on the lake. While motorboats are welcome, the lake is really a canoeist's paradise. Those looking for dry recreation can camp, picnic, hike, and bird-watch on the park's 1,300 acres of land. Park rangers offer educational programs on the area's history, including the rich Native American legacy of eastern North Carolina. Humans are known to have frequented the region as early as 8000 B.C. Artifacts more than 4,000 years old—among them arrowheads, pottery, and dugout canoes—have been found. Admission is free, though a fee is charged for camping. The park is open daily with the exception of Christmas; extended hours are offered in the summer. For information, call 252-797-4475 or visit www.ncparks.gov/Visit/parks/pett/main.php.

Pocosin Lakes National Wildlife Refuge, at 205 South Ludington Drive in Columbia (27925), is located off N.C. 94 to the east and N.C. 45 to the west. It shares Lake Phelps with Pettigrew State Park. The 110,106-acre refuge was established in 1990, when it absorbed Alligator Lake and the 12,000-acre Pungo National Wildlife Refuge, home of Pungo Lake. It's named after the distinctive pocosin shrub bogs native to the area, which are comprised of fire-tolerant, dense broadleaf evergreen shrubs and pond pines. The refuge serves as a wetland- and wildlife-restoration site for species such as the Atlantic white cedar and the red wolf, which nearly went extinct in the 20th century. Visitors to the refuge occasionally see one or two of these shy creatures, in addition to black bears, red-cockaded woodpeckers, hooded merganser ducks, wood ducks, snow geese, tundra swans, and raptors. Fishing and hunting are allowed in the refuge with proper permits. The Scuppernong River Interpretive Boardwalk, listed as a national recreation trail by the National Park Service, is located behind the Walter B. Jones, Sr., Center for the Sounds. It offers a great way to see the area's natural beauty. The boardwalk connects to the downtown area of nearby Columbia. The refuge is open year-round except for federal holidays. Admission is free. For information, call 252-796-3004 or visit www.fws.gov/pocosinlakes.

Historic **Windsor**, near N.C. 308 and U.S. 17 about 20 minutes west of Edenton, was established in 1768 when William Gray offered 100 acres for a town. That original land is now recognized as a national historic district. Call the chamber of commerce at 252-794-4277 or visit www.albemarle-nc.com/windsor for more information.

While you're in Windsor, be sure to check out the **Sans Souci Ferry**, which crosses the Cashie River. It's a rustic, diesel-powered, one- to two-car vessel not affiliated with the state's ferry system. Instead, this independently run operation represents the important lifeline that local ferrymen provided to rural farmers, doctors, and other residents who needed to cross the river to get to town. Located off S.R. 1500, the ferry cuts the driving distance from riverbank to riverbank by nearly 20 miles. The system is quite informal. When you arrive, honk your horn; the ferry captain will chug across the river to pick you up for the 10-minute ride.

Historic Hope Plantation is located four miles outside Windsor at 132 Hope House Road/N.C. 308 (27983). The former home of North Carolina governor David Stone, the 1803 buff-colored, two-story Georgian- and Federal-style plantation house is authentically furnished with period antiques. Also on the grounds is the 1763 **King-Bazemore House**, one of only two remaining gambrel-roofed homes built with handmade brick end walls. It is also significant because it is representative of the classic mid-18th-century "hall and parlor" design. Originally situated five miles away, the King-Bazemore House was constructed by William King, a successful planter and cooper. In 1840, it was purchased by Stephen Bazemore. In 1974, the Bazemore family donated the house to the Historic Hope Foundation. Both homes are listed on the National Register. Hope Plantation is open Monday through Saturday from 10 A.M. to 5 P.M. and Sunday from 2 P.M. to 4 P.M. The plantation is closed Thanksgiving and the last two weeks of December. An admission fee is charged. For information, call 252-794-3140 or visit www.hopeplantation.org.

Roanoke River National Wildlife Refuge, headquartered at 114 West Water Street in Windsor (27983), is located a little less than an hour southwest of Edenton in Bertie County. It covers more than 17,000 acres scattered along 70 miles of the Roanoke River. Two large satellite tracts encompass nearly 200 acres; one is located near the town of Hamilton and the other near the mouth of the Roanoke, which flows into the western portion of Albemarle Sound. Hunting, fishing, boating, and hiking are permitted in the refuge. Bird watchers may see dozens of species, including bald eagles, at any given time. The refuge, in fact, is the largest inland heron rookery in the state. It is open year-round with the exception of federal holidays. Admission is free. For information, call 252-794-5326 or visit www.fws.gov/roanokeriver.

Historic *Williamston* is 45 minutes west of Edenton near U.S. 64 and U.S. 17. Its two national historic districts feature homes and buildings from the 19th and early 20th centuries. Railroad and tobacco money helped build the town, including the outstanding former county courthouse, constructed in the Italianate style in 1885. Annual events of interest in Williamston include the *North Carolina Country Stampede* in late September, run in conjunction with the Colgate Country Showdown, a national country-music talent contest akin to *American Idol*. The *Roanoke Arts and Crafts Guild Holiday Fair*, held in November, is also a big draw. For more information, call 252-792-5142 or visit www.townofwilliamston.com.

Historic *Plymouth*, south of Edenton near N.C. 32 and U.S. 64, is one of the top Civil War destinations in North Carolina. During three days in 1864, Union and Confederate soldiers fought the state's second-largest Civil War battle here at the mouth of the Roanoke River, one of Robert E. Lee's supply lines for the Confederate army in Virginia. Visitors can relive that heated fight—the last Confederate victory of the war—at the *Port O' Plymouth Civil War Museum*. Call 252-793-1377 or visit www.livinghistoryweekend.com/port_o.htm for more information. To learn about the town, try www.visitplymouthnc.com.

Historic Bath
COURTESY OF NORTH CAROLINA DEPARTMENT OF CULTURAL RESOURCES

Bath

Established in 1705, Bath is North Carolina's oldest town. As such, it is home to many of the state's "firsts," including the first church, the first public library, the first port of entry, and the first shipyard, among others. Thanks to its advantageous location near Pamlico Sound, Bath became a major port for naval stores, tobacco, and furs only a few years after French Protestants founded the town. The area was home to such notable personages as John Lawson, the surveyor general of the colony and the author of the first history of Carolina, published in 1709, and Edward Teach, better known as the pirate Blackbeard, who is rumored to have taken a wife here for a short time in 1716. Stories still circulate that some of Blackbeard's treasure is buried around Bath, though none has ever been found.

Problems started to beleaguer the town early on. Despite Bath's status as the first town in the state, it failed to grow. In 1711, Cary's Rebellion, a local struggle over religion and politics, turned violent. That same year, the town was ravaged by a drought and an outbreak of yellow fever. The Tuscarora War further debilitated Bath. When neighboring towns like Edenton and Washington were founded, many people moved from Bath to pursue economic and political opportunities.

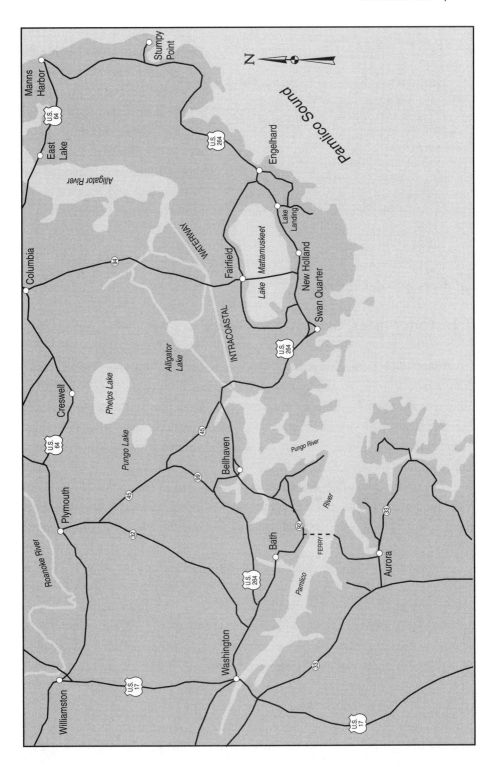

Today, Bath is a small community measuring only a few blocks. The original town limits survive as the boundaries for a national historic district that includes four buildings connecting Bath to its once-prosperous past. Visitors can enjoy an afternoon exploring the town on foot and learning about the old homes and church.

Things to Do

Historic Places, Gardens, and Tours

Historic Bath State Historic Site is headquartered at 207 Carteret Street (27808). Stop here to learn about the four historic buildings from colonial and antebellum times that are open for visitors. You can view a short film and pick up maps and pamphlets on the history of the town. The visitor center is open Tuesday through Saturday from 9 A.M. to 5 P.M. Call 252-923-3971 or visit www.nchistoricsites.org/bath/bath.htm.

The visitor center offers guided tours of two homes in the national historic district—the Bonner House and the Palmer-Marsh House. A modest admission fee is charged. You should plan on spending about an hour and a half going through the homes.

The *Bonner House*, a two-story white frame home built on the water in 1830, is representative of what daily life was like for a prosperous eastern North Carolina family between the Revolutionary War and the Civil War. It was home to Joseph Bonner, a local businessman who operated an expansive farm, a steam sawmill, and a turpentine distillery. Its most interesting features include blown-glass windowpanes, hand-carved mantels, and decorative paint treatments considered extravagant at the time. For further information, visit www.nchistoricsites.org/bath/bonner.htm.

The 1751 *Palmer-Marsh House* is the oldest home in Bath. It served as the residence of Robert Palmer, a wealthy and influential colonial customs collector and general-assembly member, and his troubled son, William, who could not decide between loyalty to his father's homeland (England) or his native Carolina. His inde-cision and resulting drinking problem drove the Palmers deep into debt. The family's estate was seized by the new Revolutionary War government. The home eventually came into the hands of brother merchants Jonathan and Daniel Marsh, whose de-scendants kept it in the Marsh family for more than 120 years. The home's signifi-cant features include an imposing double chimney and many 18th- and 19th-century antiques and reproductions representative of the house's style when important visi-tors like Royal Governor William Tryon and the Marquis de Lafayette called. For more information, visit www.nchistoricsites.org/bath/palmer-marsh.htm.

The 1790 ***Van der Veer House***, located just down the street, was purchased in 1824 by Jacob Van der Veer, a partner with Joseph Bonner in his sawmill and one of the founders of the nearby Bank of Washington. The house features a gambrel room and double-shouldered Flemish bond chimneys. It now operates as a museum and is open the same hours as the visitor center. Admission is free. For more information, visit www.nchistoricsites.org/bath/vanderveer.htm.

St. Thomas Episcopal Church, on Craven Street near the visitor center, rounds out Bath's roster of historic structures open for visitation. This is the oldest church in North Carolina. It houses the state's first public library, donated to St. Thomas Par-ish in 1701, four years before Bath was incorporated. No admission fee is charged, though donations are accepted. Tours here are self-guided. For further information, visit www.nchistoricsites.org/bath/st-thomas.htm.

Nearby

Aurora Fossil Museum is located at 400 Main Street in Aurora (27806), a free ferry ride over the Pamlico River from Bath. The museum, which grew out of dis-coveries made by the PCS Phosphate Company during mining operations in the 1950s and 1960s, uses fossil research and an 18-minute video presentation to explain the formation of the coastal plain. The area around Aurora and much of the rest of eastern North Carolina once lay under the ocean. As time passed, calcium phos-phate collected on the seabed and preserved the remains of many of the creatures that had lived in the water. After millions of year, the sea finally receded, leaving a thick layer of phosphate buried underneath sand and clay. It was in this fashion that coastal animals from eons ago were preserved.

Swan Quarter National Wildlife Refuge
PHOTOGRAPH BY ARTIE SPARROW

Visitors to the museum learn about the history of these sea creatures through exhibits that show what ocean life was like millions of years ago and through displays of fossilized bones, teeth, shells, and coral. Kids love the small phosphate yard near the museum, where they can search for their own fossils. The museum is open Monday through Saturday from 9 A.M. to 4:30 P.M. From March 1 through Labor Day, it is also open Sunday from 12:30 P.M. to 4:30 P.M. Admission is free, though donations are accepted. For more information, visit www.aurorafossilmuseum.com or call 252-322-4238

Bennett Vineyards is located half an hour south of Bath and three miles from the Aurora ferry at 6832 Old Sandhill Road in the community of Edward (27821). The largest muscadine and scuppernong vineyard in the Carolinas, it is situated between the Pamlico and Neuse rivers on a 138-acre parcel of colonial land-grant soil. The grapes this winery uses are indigenous to only the Southeast and are what the colonists picked for their wines. Tours are given daily by appointment. For information, call 877-762-9463 or 252-322-7154 or visit www.bennettvineyard.com.

Belhaven Memorial Museum is located in the old town hall at 210 East Main Street in Belhaven (27810), within easy driving distance of Bath on N.C. 99. Started as a collection of buttons by Mary Eva Blount Way, the holdings quickly grew to include all kinds of antiques and artifacts of life in Beaufort County, eastern North Carolina, and the South in general. "Miss Eva" decided to open her home to visitors in 1940 in order to share her collection—which by then included over 10,000 items—in an effort to aid the American Red Cross. After her death in 1962, a group of citizens purchased the collection to keep Miss Eva's memory and work alive. The group reopened the museum in the town hall three years later. Today, visitors will find war memorabilia, toys, household utensils, clothing, tools, and other items relating to the culture and people of the area dating back to the beginning of the 19th century. The museum is open Thursday through Tuesday from 1 P.M. to 5 P.M. Admission is free, but donations are accepted. For more information, call 252-943-6817 or visit www.beaufort-county.com/Belhaven/museum/Belhaven.htm.

Visitors to Belhaven can stay at a noteworthy inn. *River Forest Manor*, a Victorian mansion built in 1899 by John Aaron Wilkinson, has hosted the likes of James Cagney, Tallulah Bankhead, Twiggy, and Walter Cronkite over the years. It includes a marina, a shipyard, and a restaurant. For information, call 800-346-2151 or 252-943-2151 or visit www.riverforestmanor.com.

Historic *Washington*, the self-proclaimed "Heart of the Inner Banks," is located about 15 minutes from Bath near U.S. 17 and U.S. 264. Founded in 1775 as the first town in the United States named for George Washington, it quickly became a major port on the Pamlico River. When the Beaufort County seat was moved from Bath to Washington in 1785, Washington started to eclipse Bath in importance. Though the War for Independence was a major factor in the development of Washington, the War Between the States proved devastating. Union troops captured the city in 1864 and pillaged and burned it before their departure. The town was rebuilt, but flames destroyed much of the downtown area again in 1900, when a faulty stove flue caught a building on fire. Washington was rebuilt a second time. Today, the town's national historic district includes about 11 blocks of 19th- and early-20th-century buildings, including Gothic churches. Visit www.visitwashingtonnc.com or call 800-546-0162 for more information.

Overnight visitors to Washington might consider staying at the *Carolina House Bed-and-Breakfast*, located at 227 East Second Street (27889). This 1880 home, only two blocks from the Pamlico River, is listed on the National Register. Call 252-975-1382 or visit www.carolinahousebnb.com.

Another good option is *The Moss House*, at 129 Van Norden Street (27889). This 1902 Victorian home in the downtown historic district was recently awarded a Three Diamond rating by AAA. Call 252-975-3967 or visit www.themosshouse.com.

The *North Carolina Estuarium*, located on the Pamlico River in downtown Washington at 223 East Water Street (27889), is the only such facility in the state. It is dedicated to educating visitors about the Albemarle-Pamlico estuarine system, the second-largest in the nation. Estuaries, which are aquatic areas made up of both fresh and salt water, line the state's shoreline and are a vital part of the area's ecology. Visitors to the estuarium can enjoy a guided river tour, an aquarium, artifacts like boats and fishing equipment from local estuaries, and an audiovisual presentation concerning humans' effects on the estuarine system and the system's effects on man. A gift shop is on the premises. The estuarium is open Tuesday through Saturday from 10 A.M. to 4 P.M. For information, call 242-948-0000 or visit www.partnershipforthesounds.org/NorthCarolinaEstuarium.aspx.

Goose Creek State Park, headquartered at 2190 Camp Leach Road in Washington (27889), is located six miles west of Bath off N.C. 92. It's well known for its many recreational offerings, including a swim beach, hiking and canoeing trails, and camping and picnicking sites. Sailing and windsurfing are popular activities here. Interpretive and educational programs on the area's natural resources and wildlife are offered by rangers at the Environmental Education and Visitor Center. The park is open year-round during daylight hours with the exception of Christmas. Admission is free, though a small fee is charged for camping. For more information, call 252-923-2191 or visit www.ncparks.gov/Visit/parks/gocr/main.php.

Lake Mattamuskeet is located at 38 Mattamuskeet Road in Swan Quarter (27885), an hour east of Bath off U.S. 264. This is the largest natural lake in North Carolina, covering more than 40,000 acres and stretching for 18 miles at a width of five to six miles. But the water is surprisingly shallow, averaging a depth of only two feet. The massive lake is a bird watcher's paradise; thousands of tundra swans winter here every year.

It comes as a surprise to some that Lake Mattamuskeet has not always been here. *Mattamuskeet* is, in fact, Algonquian for "dry dust." Some conjecture that the lake came into existence only when wildfires burned deep into the peat soil, transforming the flat, dry land into a lake bed.

A group of investors tried to drain the lake in 1914. They renamed the area New Holland, after similar drainage projects in Holland. A network of canals, a model community, and the largest pumping station in the world—capable of pumping 1.2 million gallons of water a minute—were built. When the investors found the project too expensive, however, they abandoned New Holland.

The United States government bought the lake in 1934 and established Mattamuskeet National Wildlife Refuge. The pumping station was converted into a lodge, and the nearby smokestack was transformed into a 100-foot-tall observation tower. The lodge closed in 1974 and was added to the National Register in 1980.

Today's visitors to Lake Mattamuskeet and Mattamuskeet National Wildlife Refuge enjoy crabbing, fishing, bird-watching, and hunting. The refuge is open during daylight hours year-round with the exception of federal holidays. For more information, call 252-926-4021 or visit www.fws.gov/mattamuskeet.

A significant sanctuary just south of Lake Mattamuskeet is ***Swan Quarter National Wildlife Refuge***. Those taking the toll ferry between Swan Quarter and Ocracoke Island will travel through the refuge and get a unique view of the area's natural beauty. Created in 1932, the refuge covers more than 16,000 acres of salt-marsh islands and forested wetlands. Like Lake Mattamuskeet, it is a vital wintering and breeding ground for waterfowl including ospreys and canvasback and black ducks. Many visitors come to the refuge to fish from the 1,000-foot-long Bell Island Pier. Boating, hunting, and hiking are permitted as well. The refuge is open year-round during daylight hours with the exception of federal holidays. Call 252-926-4021 or visit www.fws.gov/swanquarter for more information.

New Bern clock tower
COURTESY OF NEW BERN/CRAVEN COUNTY CONVENTION AND VISITORS CENTER

Neuse River Region

By Angela Harwood

This area encompasses some of North Carolina's most fascinating historical and natural sites. The towns and villages that populate the Neuse River region— named for the Neusiok Indians, who once inhabited the river's shores—date primarily to the 18th century.

Among these is New Bern, the state's colonial capital. Overlooking the point where the Neuse and Trent rivers converge, New Bern is home to the magnificent Tryon Palace, which has secured the town a premier spot on the state's heritage trail. This year-round destination is not only for those interested in Revolutionary War history, however. Over the course of time, New Bern's downtown has undergone a renaissance, as more and more interesting shops and excellent restaurants have opened to serve the tourist trade. One of the town's most recent additions is a convention center on the banks of the Neuse.

Forty-five minutes east of New Bern is Morehead City, where world-class fishing tournaments attract anglers from far and wide. Be sure to plan a meal here, as the town's bustling waterfront restaurants serve up some of the area's best seafood. Morehead City is also the jumping-off point for the stunning sands of Bogue Banks.

Historic Beaufort is nothing less than idyllic. Overlooking Taylor Creek, this former pirates' hideout now quietly greets sailors of a different ilk. The first-class North Carolina Maritime Museum is headquartered amid the picturesque inns and bed-and-breakfasts. Some of the area's most innovative and best restaurants are located here as well.

Situated on the Intracoastal Waterway is another quaint fishing hamlet, Oriental. Regarded by many as the East Coast's premier yachting destination, Oriental offers a sailing school that serves both beginners and experienced sailors wishing to hone their skills.

Among outdoor enthusiasts, Croatan National Forest is an oasis for bird-watching, hiking, camping, and boating. Hunting and fishing are also permitted for visitors holding the proper permits. Indigenous insect-eating plants thrive here, including pitcher plants, sundews, and Venus flytraps. This vast 159,000-acre park is surrounded by water and has several lakes within its borders.

And of course, there are the beaches. Atlantic Beach, Pine Knoll Shores, and Emerald Isle—all on Bogue Banks—are among the state's most popular seaside resorts. Fort Macon State Park at Atlantic Beach offers a history lesson and a day at the beach all in one. Or if you'd rather escape the masses, you can ferry over to the incomparable Cape Lookout National Seashore, where a diamond-painted lighthouse continues in service 150 years after it was built. Another ferry ride away is pristine Hammocks Beach State Park, perhaps the land of buried treasure.

Whether you intend to tour the historic sites, to fish or boat, or to hang out on the beach, the Neuse River region is sure to please.

New Bern

New Bern is located 35 miles from the Atlantic Ocean at the confluence of the Neuse and Trent rivers. North Carolina's second-oldest town, it was named by its Swiss founder, Christophe von Graffenried, in honor of his home capital, Berne. Throughout the city, you will see New Bern's symbol, the black bear, which it shares with its European mother city.

In 1710—the same year that North and South Carolina were divided—von Graffenried

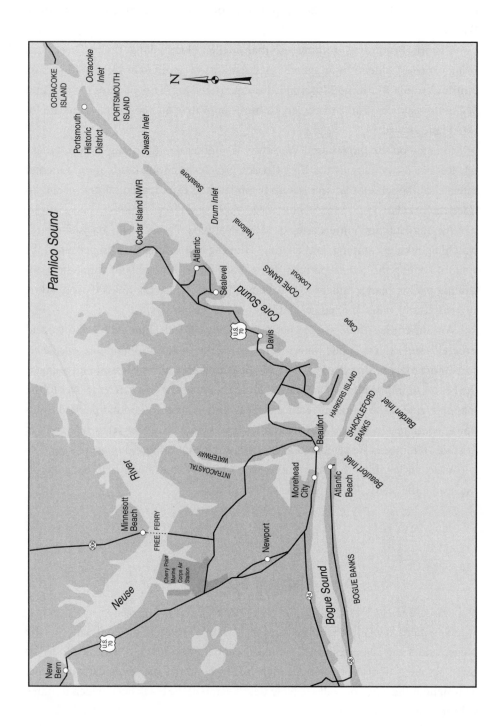

and two partners purchased an 18,750-acre parcel for a colony of German and Swiss emigrants. The purchase was inspired by colonial surveyor general John Lawson, who had returned to London extolling the virtues of the New World in his book, *A New Voyage to Carolina*. Subsequently dispatched by von Graffenried to select a site for the colony, Lawson laid out a town plan in the form of a crucifix, which served the dual purposes of religious expression and defense against Indians.

The newcomers also had to defend themselves outside the town boundaries, however. Although King Taylor of the Tuscaroras had been paid for the land where New Bern was settled, the influx of immigrants proved too much for him to stand. In September 1711, Lawson and von Graffenried embarked on a canoe trip up the Neuse River. A few days into the journey, they were captured by the Tuscaroras. Von Graffenried managed to save himself by persuading the Tuscaroras that his connections to the English Crown would serve them well should he live. Lawson wasn't so fortunate. The Tuscaroras supposedly pierced him with wood splinters, then lit him and burned him to death.

The three years of fighting that followed drove von Graffenried back to Europe, which left New Bern in the hands of Colonel Thomas Pollock. With the help of some of the Tuscaroras' traditional enemies, the colonists eventually vanquished the tribe. The Indians who survived migrated north, where they gave their new land the name of their Carolina home—Chattawka, now Chautauqua, New York.

Downtown New Bern
COURTESY OF NEW BERN/CRAVEN COUNTY CONVENTION AND VISITORS CENTER

Once the Indian threat was removed, white settlers flocked to New Bern, which prospered as a port for shipping tar, pitch, and turpentine. In 1723, it was incorporated and made the seat of Craven County, which it remains today. By the time the colonial assembly convened here in 1737, New Bern was well established as the most vital city between Virginia and Charleston, South Carolina.

In 1776, North Carolina's first governor, Richard Caswell, was heralded into office in New Bern, the state's first capital. When the capital was moved to Raleigh in 1794, New Bern's political role diminished, but the city continued to thrive as a shipping center. It was during this period that many of its lovely homes and buildings were constructed.

In 1862, New Bern was captured by Union forces under General Ambrose Burnside. The city remained a Union outpost for the rest of the Civil War.

During Reconstruction, lumber mills and the seafood industry kept the city going. After World War II, manufacturing and the military were at the heart of New Bern's development. Nearby Cherry Point remains the nation's largest Marine Corps air station.

Since the reconstruction of Tryon Palace in the 1950s, New Bern has seen a steady increase in tourism. Today, the city boasts a collection of National Register buildings second in number only to Charleston. In and around the historic district, dozens of antique and specialty shops, art galleries, and restaurants have sprouted up, making a trip to New Bern a delight.

JUST THE FACTS

New Bern is accessible by land, water, and air.

Car travelers can follow either U.S. 70, U.S. 17, or N.C. 55 to reach town. Those planning to take the bus should contact the Trailways station, located at 504 Guion Street (28560); the number is 252-633-3100.

Portions of the Neuse River double as the Intracoastal Waterway. Those arriving by water can stay at any of the private marinas along the river.

For those flying, US Airways offers seven commuter flights daily into Craven County Regional Airport. Fuel and maintenance are available here. Call 252-638-8591 or visit www.newbernairport.com for more information.

The New Bern/Craven County Convention and Visitors Center, located at the new convention center at 203 South Front Street (28563), offers an abundance of material on the area. For information, call 800-437-5767 or 252-637-9400 or visit www.visitnewbern.com.

The *New Bern Sun Journal* is the local daily newspaper.

Things to Do

Historic Places, Gardens, and Tours

For a self-guided tour of New Bern, pick up a free *Heritage Tour* guide at the New Bern/Craven County Convention and Visitors Center. You can also get maps to New Bern's numerous African-American heritage sites, Civil War sites, and historic homes, churches, and cemeteries, all of which are within walking distance of downtown. If you prefer to ride, check out the trolley tour offered by *New Bern Tours*; call 800-849-7316 or 252-637-7316 or visit www.newberntours.com. You can also tour historic New Bern the old-fashioned way—by horse-drawn carriage. *Springbrook Farms, Inc.*, uses only rescued horses; for information, call 910-251-8889, visit www. horsedrawntours.com, or e-mail horsedrawntours@bellsouth.net.

Tryon Palace Historic Sites and Gardens, the cornerstone of historic New Bern, is located at 610 Pollock Street (28563), one block south of U.S. 17 and U.S. 70 Business. The complex consists of Tryon Palace, its surrounding 14 acres of gardens and grounds, and four other historic landmarks—the John Wright Stanly House, the George W. Dixon House, the Robert Hay House, and the New Bern Academy Museum.

Tryon Palace is a reconstruction of North Carolina's first State Capitol, built before the population shifted west and before Raleigh became the capital city in 1794.

In 1765, Royal Governor William Tryon commissioned English architect John Hawkes to design and supervise the construction of Tryon Palace, an elegant Georgian mansion containing public rooms for government functions on the ground floor and family living quarters upstairs. Cooking and laundry facilities were in a wing on the left, while livery stables were in a wing to the right. In 1771, just 13 months after moving his family into the home, Tryon was appointed governor of New York. His successor, Josiah Martin, subsequently moved into Tryon Palace with much fanfare. Martin commissioned Hawkes to add a poultry house, a smokehouse, and a pigeon house. Martin spent four years lavishly furnishing his abode, impervious to the growing resentment around him. In 1775, patriots forced Martin to flee the house. He left all his possessions behind.

In 1777, the first North Carolina General Assembly convened at Tryon Palace, the newly designated State Capitol. By 1798, however, when fire destroyed the main building, Raleigh was the capital, and the role of New Bern and Tryon Palace was

Tryon Palace
COURTESY OF NEW BERN/CRAVEN COUNTY CONVENTION AND VISITORS CENTER

Latham Garden at Tryon Palace
PHOTOGRAPH BY ANGELA HARWOOD

greatly diminished. Through the years, portions of the grounds were sold. Tryon Palace languished, only the west wing remaining intact. Recovery began in 1939, when the original architectural plans were discovered in New York. A restoration trust fund was established by Mrs. Maude Moore Latham, a New Bern native whose dedication to the project and philanthropy were largely responsible for its success. Noted architect William G. Perry of the Boston firm that restored Colonial Williamsburg began his work in New Bern in 1951. Mrs. Latham died that same year but passed along her legacy to her daughter, Mrs. John A. Kellerman, who headed the state commission in charge of the project. On April 8, 1959, Tryon Palace opened its doors to the public.

Tours of Tryon Place begin in the visitor center, located across Pollock Street from the north side of the building. Following a 20-minute orientation film, you'll make your way along the Entrance Allée; don't be surprised if you are cheerfully met along the way by one of the many historical interpreters, busy with his or her chores. A costumed guide will greet you at the door and lead you into the marble entrance hall, through the public rooms downstairs, and up the pegged mahogany staircase to the private rooms. Thanks to an inventory of William Tryon's original furnishings, the palace contains some 7,000 pieces of art and 18th- and 19th-century American and English antiques that reflect the opulent world of the Royal governor. Among his personal possessions remaining at Tryon Palace is a library of 400 books.

After your tour of Tryon Palace, take time to stroll the formal ***Colonial Revival Gardens***, designed by Morley Jeffers Williams, an expert in 18th-century landscaping. The Latham Garden takes the style of cutwork parterre. Hedges define the beds, creating ornate patterns. Nearby is the private Green Garden, designed to be viewed from the palace. The Kellenberger Garden illustrates how ornamentals were grown for their decorative qualities. The wonderful Kitchen Garden produces heirloom varieties of herbs and vegetables grown for cooking, fragrance, and medicinal purposes.

The ***John Wright Stanly House***, an elegant 1779 Georgian home at 307 George Street, is one of the properties that are part of Tryon Palace Historic Sites and Gardens. On his Southern tour in 1791, President George Washington dined and danced at Tryon Palace, but he laid his head to rest at the John Wright Stanly House, which he described as "exceedingly good lodgings." The house is named for a powerful New Bern citizen who aided the American cause by raiding British vessels. Ironically, John Wright Stanly traced his lineage to King Edward I of England. The home served as General Ambrose Burnside's headquarters while Union forces occupied

John Wright Stanly House
COURTESY OF NEW BERN/CRAVEN COUNTY CONVENTION AND VISITORS CENTER

the city. The house's interior is noted for its intricate woodwork, especially its Chippendale staircase.

Built between 1826 and 1833, the *George W. Dixon House*, at 609 Pollock Street, is a fine example of Neoclassical architecture. Constructed on a lot that was originally part of Tryon Palace's gardens, it was the home of George W. Dixon, a merchant, tailor, and one-time mayor of New Bern. During the Union occupation, the house was used as a regimental hospital. Inside, you'll find hand-carved woodwork and antiques of the Federal and Empire periods.

The *Robert Hay House*, on Eden Street next to the Tryon Palace Museum Shop, was home to a Scottish wagon maker and a founding member of First Presbyterian Church in New Bern.

The *New Bern Academy Museum* is located four blocks from Tryon Palace at the corner of New and Hancock streets. Completed in 1809, it was the first chartered school in North Carolina. The museum contains four rooms, each focusing on an aspect of local history: the founding and early history of New Bern, the architecture of the city, the Civil War and Reconstruction, and education in New Bern. This is a great place to get a broad overview of the city. Thanks to its dedicated staff of volunteers, the museum is open daily from 1 P.M. to 4:30 P.M. Admission is included with your ticket to the Tryon Palace complex or can be purchased separately.

Tryon Palace Historic Sites and Gardens is open Monday through Saturday

New Bern Academy Museum
COURTESY OF NEW BERN/CRAVEN COUNTY CONVENTION AND VISITORS CENTER

from 9 A.M. to 5 P.M. and Sunday from 1 P.M. to 5 P.M. It is closed Thanksgiving, December 24, 25, and 26, and New Year's. An admission fee is charged. Special events include garden tours in April and October and Christmas tours in December. Its two gift shops—the Tryon Palace Museum Shop and the Crafts and Garden Shop—are open daily. For more information, call 800-767-1560 or 252-514-4900 or visit www.tryonpalace.org.

The *Attmore-Oliver House*, at 512 Pollock Street (28563), is another museum house well worth visiting. Now home to the New Bern Historical Society, the house was constructed in 1790 and enlarged in 1834. It is furnished with 18th- and 19th-century antiques and features Civil War artifacts and a doll collection. The home is open by reservation only. An admission fee is charged. For information, call 252-638-8558 or visit www.newbernhistorical.org/attmore.html.

The *North Carolina History Education Center* is scheduled to open in 2010, in time to celebrate New Bern's 300th anniversary. The 48,000-square-foot learning center is being built adjacent to the Tryon Palace gardens on the Trent River. Visitors will be able to experience the past by utilizing hand-held and other digital devices of the 21st century. Adults and children will have a variety of interactive options, such as becoming crew members trying to sail a ship along the treacherous North Carolina coast. To invest in the center, call the Making History Office at 252-514-4956 or visit www.tryonpalace.org/historyeducationcenter/index.html, where you can view floor designs and photographs of the groundbreaking ceremony and construction.

Museums and Science Centers

Firemen's Museum, at 408 Hancock Street (28563), honors New Bern's firefighting outfits through the years. It houses an array of 19th-century man- and horse-drawn fire engines, 20th-century steam and motorized fire engines, sundry firefighting equipment, and Civil War relics. Children enjoy learning about Fred the fire horse, whose mounted head hangs near equipment he once pulled. Fred joined the Atlantic Company in 1908 and valiantly served until his death in 1925, long after motorized fire engines came into use. The museum and gift shop are open Monday through Saturday from 10 A.M. to 4 P.M. The museum is closed Thanksgiving, Christmas, and New Year's. An admission fee is charged. For more information, call 252-636-4087 or visit www.newbernmuseums.com.

Cultural Offerings

Bank of the Arts, home of the Craven County Arts Council and Gallery, is located at 317 Middle Street (28560) in a 1913 granite Neoclassical Revival building that was once the Peoples Bank. This gallery displays an array of pottery, sculpture, paintings, photography, and fiber art by southeastern artists. It is open Tuesday through Saturday from 10 A.M. to 6 P.M. Admission is free. For information, call 252-638-2577 or visit www.cravenarts.org.

The *New Bern Civic Theatre*, at 412 Pollock Street (28563), features professional and local actors performing a variety of dramas, comedies, musicals, and even sign-language productions. Visit www.newberncivictheatre.org or call 800-634-9058 or 252-634-9057 for information.

Firemen's Museum
COURTESY OF NEW BERN/CRAVEN COUNTY CONVENTION
AND VISITORS CENTER

Special Shopping

The *Farmers' Market*, at 421 South Front Street (28560), offers fresh produce, homemade jams and jellies, and local artwork. It is open every Saturday from 8 A.M. to 1 P.M. Call 252-633-0043 or visit www.newbernfarmersmarket.com for information.

Visitors to New Bern can cool off with an ice-cold glass of "Brad's Drink" at the *Birthplace of Pepsi-Cola*, a souvenir shop at 256 Middle Street (28560) at the corner of Pollock. It was here that pharmacist Caleb "Doc" Bradham formulated his famous soft drink behind his soda fountain in the 1890s. Unfortunately, Bradham was forced into bankruptcy by the collapse of the sugar market following World War I, and the rights to the drink were purchased by a New York company. Bradham died in 1934, never having realized any of the profits his drink produced. Bradham's old pharmacy is open Monday through Saturday from 10 A.M. to 6 P.M. For information, call 252-636-5898 or visit www.pepsistore.com.

Carolina Creations, at 317-A Pollock Street (28560), sells an array of wonderful handcrafted pottery, sculpture, jewelry, cards, and prints by local and nationally known artists. It is open Monday, Tuesday, Wednesday, Thursday, and Saturday from 10 A.M. to 6 P.M.; Friday from 10 A.M. to 8 P.M.; and Sunday from 11 A.M. to 4 P.M. For information, call 252-633-4369 or visit www.carolinacreationsnewbern.com.

Mitchell Hardware, at 215 Craven Street (28560), is an authentic turn-of-the-20th-century hardware store complete with enamelware, crockery, pottery, and more. For information, call 252-638-4261 or visit www.mitchellhardwareonline.com.

Weavers Web Gallery, at 602 Pollock Street (28560), sells hand-woven textiles, skeins of beautiful yarn, and all manner of patterns for cross-stitch, weaving, and needlepoint. For information, call 252-514-2681.

Middle Street is peppered with antique shops. Check out *A Shopping Guide to the Governor's Walk*, available at the New Bern/Craven County Convention and Visitors Center, for a list of these and other shops.

Recreation

One of four national forests in North Carolina, *Croatan National Forest* is the only true coastal forest east of the Mississippi. Spreading over 161,000 acres south from New Bern to Bogue Sound, it encompasses ecosystems ranging from upland hardwoods to pocosins (swamps on a hill). It provides habitat for a variety of flora and fauna, including such endangered species as Venus flytraps, alligators, and red-cockaded woodpeckers. The forest offers numerous boating access areas and hiking trails, including the 26-mile Neusiok Trail, which stretches from the Neuse River to the Newport River. Primitive camping is permitted except in developed day-use areas and actively managed sites. Other outdoor recreational opportunities include bird-watching, camping, and picnicking. Fishing, hunting, and trapping are regulated by the North Carolina Wildlife Resources Commission; information is available where licenses are sold. The ranger's office, located at 141 East Fisher Avenue in New Bern (28560), is open Monday through Friday from 8 A.M. to 4:30 P.M.; an information kiosk is outside. For further information, call 252-638-5628 or visit www.cs.unca.edu/nfsnc/recreation/croatan.pdf.

Seasonal Events

The *Spring Historic Homes and Gardens Tour*, headquartered at 512 Pollock Street (28560), is held every April, when the azaleas and dogwoods are in full bloom. Cosponsored by the New Bern Historical Society and the New Bern Preservation Foundation, the tour includes many private houses usually closed to the public, as well as churches and other historically significant buildings. A fee is charged. For information, call 252-638-8558 or visit www.newbernhistorical.org/hhngt.html.

The annual *Mumfest* street festival is held downtown in mid-October. Food, entertainment, and an antiques-and-crafts show are offered. For information, call 252-638-5781 or visit www.mumfest.com.

The local historical society organizes a *New Bern Ghostwalk* around Halloween to benefit preservation and education programs. A candlelight tour of a cemetery, a presentation about ghosts from the Gilded Age, and a vaudeville show at the Masonic Theatre are just a few of the ticketed events. For more information, contact the New Bern Historical Society (252-638-8558; www.newbernhistorical.org) or the

New Bern/Craven County Convention and Visitors Center (800-437-5767; www. newbernhistorical.org/ghostwalk.html).

Places to Stay

Not surprisingly, a number of bed-and-breakfasts operate in New Bern's elegant historic houses. At the other end of the spectrum are newly constructed, well-known chains situated on the waterfront; most of these have marinas.

Resorts, Hotels, and Motels

Comfort Suites Riverfront Park. Deluxe/Expensive. 218 East Front Street, 28560 (877-424-6423 or 252-636-0022; www.comfortsuites.com/hotel-new_bern-north_ carolina-NC246). Comfort Suites is situated next to Union Point Park along the banks of the Neuse. Some suites have waterfront balconies and whirlpool baths. A fitness room and an outdoor swimming pool are available to guests. Complimentary continental breakfast is offered.

Hilton New Bern Riverfront Hotel. Expensive. 100 Middle Street, 28560 (800-445-8667 or 252-638-3585). At least half the rooms here offer a view of the Trent and Neuse rivers. The hotel has 156 boat slips for mariners. Its restaurant overlooks the marina and pool. Senior-citizen discounts are offered.

BridgePointe Hotel and Marina. Moderate. 101 Howell Road, 28562, at the junction of U.S. 70 and U.S. 70E Bypass (www.bridgepointehotel.com; 877-283-7713 or 252-636-3637;). All of the newly renovated rooms here have river views. Amenities include in-room coffee makers, cable television, a swimming pool, and a marina. Nikola's Restaurant, a Morehead City favorite, has a location here. Senior-citizen, military, and business rates are offered.

Inns and Bed-and-Breakfasts

The Aerie. Deluxe/Expensive. 509 Pollock Street, 28562 (800-849-5553 or 252-636-5553; www.aeriebedandbreakfast.com). Located a block from Tryon Palace, this charming 1880s bed-and-breakfast features a player piano. Each of its seven individually appointed guest rooms has a private bath, cable television, high-speed Internet access, and a telephone. A full breakfast with a choice of three entrées is served daily in the dining room.

Howard House. Deluxe/Expensive. 207 Pollock Street, 28560 (800-705-5261 or 252-514-6709; www.howardhousebnb.com). This lovely Victorian bed-and-breakfast features period antiques in its six guest rooms. Each has a private bath. Complimentary bicycles, terry-cloth robes, chocolates, and fresh flowers add to the experience. The full gourmet breakfast served each morning in the formal dining room may include orange French toast, "Bacon Omelet Baskets," or apple-pecan pancakes.

The Meadows Inn. Expensive. 212 Pollock Street, 28560 (877-551-1776 or 252-634-1776; www.meadowsinn-nc.com). Built in 1847, this antebellum home turned inn is located in the heart of the downtown historic district. It offers a two-room suite and six guest rooms with fireplaces and private baths. Breakfast and a morning newspaper are brought to guests' rooms.

Hanna House. Expensive/Moderate. 218 Pollock Street, 28560 (866-830-4371 or 252-635-3209; www.hannahousenc.net). The Rudolph Ulrich House was built in 1896 and served as the home of one of New Bern's grocery suppliers. Now revived as the Hanna House, it offers four rooms and a luxury suite, each with a private bath. Homemade breads, muffins, and unique breakfast entrées are served each morning in the formal dining room. Refreshments and snacks are offered during the afternoon in the dining room and on the front porch.

Harmony House Inn. Expensive/Moderate. 215 Pollock Street, 28560 (800-636-3113 or 252-636-3810; www.harmonyhouseinn.com). Housed in a handsome 1850s Greek Revival structure with a broad front porch, this friendly inn offers seven spacious guest rooms and three suites decorated with antiques and locally crafted reproductions. All have private baths. A full breakfast is served.

Places to Eat

The Harvey Mansion Historic Inn & Restaurant. Expensive. 221 South Front Street, 28560 (252-635-3232; www.harveymansion.attractionsbook.com). The Harvey Mansion has six formal dining rooms, where it serves award-winning duck, veal, lamb, and seafood. All dining rooms have a fireplace and showcase local art. The cellar pub offers an equally delicious but more casual menu. The mansion overlooks the Trent River and is listed on the National Register. It is open for dinner Tuesday through Sunday.

The Chelsea. Expensive/Moderate. 335 Middle Street, 28560 (252-637-5469; www.thechelsea.com). This restaurant and "publick house" serves up a smorgasbord of cuisines: French, German, Italian, Cajun, and American. The Chelsea is housed in the second drugstore operated by Caleb Bradham, the inventor of Pepsi-Cola. Lunch and dinner are served Monday through Saturday.

Morgan's Tavern & Grill. Moderate. 235 Craven Street, 28560 (252-636-2430; www.morganstavernnewbern.com). This convenient restaurant serves a wide range of salads, soups, entrées, pasta dishes, and sandwiches that will suit any palate. The wine list includes selections from over seven countries. Lunch and dinner are served daily; brunch is offered on Sunday.

Captain Ratty's. Moderate/Inexpensive. 202 Middle Street, 28560 (252-633-2088; www.captainrattys.com). This restaurant is housed in a handsome space with wood floors and a pressed-tin ceiling. Although it has a bar, it is nonetheless a good option for families with children. The menu is child-friendly, too. Be sure to try the tasty crab cake sandwich. Lunch and dinner are served daily.

Amy's Coffee and Confections. Inexpensive. 1706 U.S. 70E, 28560 (252-635-2697). This non-downtown coffee shop offers pastries and desserts from morning to mid-afternoon Monday through Saturday.

Cow Café. Inexpensive. 319 Middle Street, 28560 (252-672-9269). This whimsical spot is owned by Maola Dairy employees. The kids can enjoy a "Moonilla" ice-cream cone while you relax over a "Cowpuccino." You can browse the café's "Bovine Bazaar," which has more than 300 cow gift items, or visit "The Farm" if you have "calves in your herd." Lunch and dinner are served Monday through Saturday.

Bayard Wootten
COURTESY OF NORTH CAROLINA COLLECTION,
UNIVERSITY OF NORTH CAROLINA LIBRARY AT CHAPEL HILL

Bayard Wootten, Pictorial Photographer

by Anne Holcomb Waters

Mary Bayard Morgan was born in her grandparents' antebellum home on East Front Street in New Bern on December 17, 1875. The elder of two children of Mary Devereaux Clarke and Rufus Morgan was to become one of North Carolina's most illustrious photographers and a woman with an indomitable spirit of adventure.

Like her well-bred mother before her, Bayard (pronounced By-ard) studied drawing and painting as a child. It was a number of years before the camera became her chosen art form. A devotee of the pictorial style of photography, she would be well served by her classical training.

When Bayard was 17, she left New Bern to study at the North Carolina State Normal and Industrial School in Greensboro, now the University of North Carolina at Greensboro. In a letter to the school's president, she wrote, "I am determined to make my own living, and if I cannot do it by teaching I shall have to do it by sewing, and therefore am very anxious for an education."

Bayard left the school after a year and a half to teach art at the Arkansas Deaf-Mute Institute in Little Rock. From there, she went on to teach at the state school for the deaf in Cave City, Georgia, where she met and married Charles Thomas Wootten. The marriage failed following an unhappy incident involving a hot rent check. Barred from entering their apartment by the landlord while her husband was out of town on business, Bayard and son Charles traveled to New Bern on borrowed money. Nine months later, her second son, Rufus, was born.

Since she had children to provide for, Bayard worked with her mother decorating small items such as fans for the tourist trade. According to her son Charles, the first patented label for Pepsi-Cola was Bayard's handiwork.

In 1904, she began to explore camera work at Garrett Gerock's photography studio. He allowed her free reign of his darkroom until he began to see her emerging talent as a threat to his business. Having decided to go into photography, Bayard took a trip to Asheville to study with Ignatius "Nace" Brock, her friend and would-be mentor.

Early in her career, Bayard made her living doing routine trade photography. Beginning in 1898, the United States Post Office permitted privately made postcards to go through the mail at a one-cent rate. These penny postcards became enormously popular and gave Bayard her first taste of success as a photographer. From there, she insinuated her way into the North Carolina National Guard, becoming its first woman member. She was named chief of publicity.

Following a failed attempt at opening a studio in New York, Bayard found solid itinerant work at North Carolina's college and university campuses. In 1928, she moved to Chapel Hill, where she and her half-brother, George Moulton, opened a studio to accommodate their newfound business. It was during this period that she hit her artistic stride and created the timeless portraits for which she is famous.

A trip to the Penland School in the North Carolina mountains in 1927 to shoot photographs for the school's catalog was a catalyst for change in Bayard's career. With her boys raised and well educated at the United States Naval Academy and Harvard, and with her business rock-solid under the guidance of George Moulton, she finally had the freedom to pursue her artistic vision with vigor. Often traveling with young men from the Chapel Hill studio, Bayard hit the road with her eight-by-10-inch camera.

Cabins in the Laurel was the first of Bayard's six books to be published. She was well established in the South Carolina Low Country by the time her favorite book—*Charleston: Azaleas and Old Bricks*—was released. The last of the books she illustrated, *From My Highest Hill: Carolina Mountain Folks*, was published in 1941. Then in her 60s, she was undaunted by the journey for her work on that book, though she needed a team of oxen to extricate her auto from the mire on four separate occasions. Her return to the mountains brought her much acclaim but also ushered in the twilight years of her career.

In 1947, Bayard suffered a hemorrhage in her eye, which effectively ended her serious camera work. In 1954, she sold the Chapel Hill studio and moved back to her grandparents' home on East Front Street with 2,000 of her favorite negatives. She died there on April 6, 1959.

"I have always been chasing something," she wrote her friend Nace Brock, "but one of the surprises that life has held for me is that I am happier as an old woman than I ever was as a young one. Perhaps the reason for this is that I realize now it does not matter whether we arrive. The joy is in the going."

A Day at the Farm
COURTESY OF NEW BERN/CRAVEN COUNTY CONVENTION AND VISITORS CENTER

Nearby

A Day at the Farm is located 15 miles west of New Bern at 183 Woodrow Mc-Coy Road in Cove City (28523). This historic dairy farm provides a nice outing for the young at heart. It features old dairy barns, milking equipment, and period antiques, as well as farm animals, hayrides, a seasonal pumpkin patch and corn maze, a walking trail, and a picnic area. It also has an ice-cream parlor and gift shop. The farm is open Monday through Saturday from 9 A.M. to noon, but please call 252-514-9494 before coming. For more information, visit www.adayatthefarm.com.

Settled in the 1700s at the gateway to Pamlico Sound, *Oriental* is the sailing capital of North Carolina. Its name was inspired by the USS *Oriental*, which sank off the Outer Banks in 1862. This quaint fishing village beckons sailors of all skills, from yachtsmen on the nearby Intracoastal Waterway to novices who want to learn the skills at one of Oriental's sailing schools. Hunting, kayaking, canoeing, birding, cycling, and horseback riding are just a few recreational activities the town has to offer. To reach Oriental, take U.S. 17 North from New Bern, then follow N.C. 55; it's about a 25-mile drive.

If you are interested in sailing lessons, contact *Oriental School of Sailing* (252-249-0960; www.sailingschooloriental.com) or *Carolina Sailing Unlimited* (252-249-0850).

The *Circle 10 Art Gallery*, at 1103 Broad Street (28571), is an artists' cooperative with local artwork for sale. Call 252-249-0298 for hours of operation.

If you decide to stay in Oriental, you're sure to find a welcome at the *Cartwright House* (888-726-9384 or 252-249-1337; www.cartwrighthouse.com), *The Inn at Oriental* (252-249-1078; www.innatoriental.com), or *Oriental Marina Motel* (252-249-1818; www.orientalmarina.com), all of which are within easy walking distance of the harbor.

CSS Neuse State Historic Site and the ***Richard Caswell Memorial*** are located north of New Bern on U.S. 70 just within the city limits of Kinston. An audiovisual program and a statue at the Richard Caswell Memorial honor North Carolina's first governor. Under a shelter outside lie the remains of the last ironclad built by the Confederacy, the CSS *Neuse*. In 1865, its crew sank the vessel to keep it from enemy hands. It remained embedded in mud for nearly 100 years before it was extracted and put on display. The sites are open Tuesday through Saturday from 9 A.M. to 5 P.M. Admission is free. For information, visit www.nchistoricsites.org/neuse/neuse.htm or call 252-522-2091.

Minnesott Beach is located a free 20-minute ferry ride across the Neuse. Take the Cherry Branch ferry to U.S. 306; you can check the ferry schedule by visiting www.pamlico-nc.com/ferry.

Neuse River Recreation Area is approximately 11 miles southeast of New Bern on U.S. 70. Camping, hiking, fishing, and swimming are the main activities here. Call 252-638-5628 or visit www.cs.unca.edu/nfsnc/recreation/neuse_river.pdf for information. The ranger station is located at 141 East Fisher Avenue in New Bern (28560).

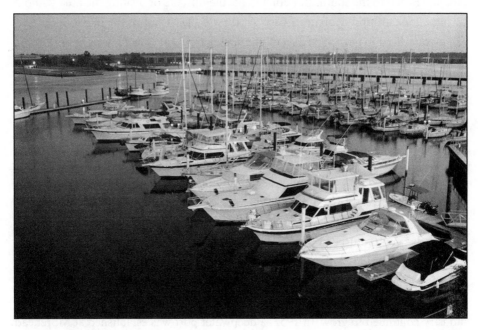

New Bern Grand Marina
COURTESY OF NEW BERN/CRAVEN COUNTY CONVENTION AND VISITORS CENTER

Scuba diving at Morehead City
COURTESY OF OLYMPUS DIVE CENTER, MOREHEAD CITY

Morehead City

Morehead City is for fishermen what Oriental is for sailors: a mecca. It is also the gateway to two alluring destinations—charming Beaufort to the east and lively Atlantic Beach to the south. But don't make the mistake of visiting the area without taking a look around Morehead City. At the very least, make the trip to its picturesque waterfront to gaze at its fleet of charter boats, to eat at its famous boat-to-shore seafood restaurants, and to shop at its fish markets and gift and antique shops.

Morehead City is the product of the ambitions of John Motley Morehead, governor of North Carolina from 1841 to 1845. Together with an associate, Silas Webb, Morehead purchased a 600-acre tract in 1853. He dreamed of developing it into a deepwater port that would eventually be linked by rail to the Piedmont and to cities on the Ohio and Mississippi rivers. That town, Carolina City, met an early demise when Morehead decided to subdivide his holdings. He subsequently planned a new town just to the east of the original, sketching out 50-by-100-foot lots that he put up for sale in November 1857. Two months later, excursion trains were bringing regular crowds from Goldsboro. By May 1858, every new lot in town had sold, earning Morehead $1 million. A post office was established here on February 28, 1859.

Morehead City was occupied during the Civil War. It rebounded at the turn of the 20th century to become a fashionable summer resort. Meanwhile, the fishing industry continued to grow. In 1952, a deepwater port was established at Morehead City, fulfilling John Motley Morehead's dream. The town has since become known as a port for shipping bulk cargo, particularly coal and phosphate.

Today, Morehead City is renowned for its fishing waters, fed by the Gulf Stream. Fishermen come to test their skills against marlin, amberjack, mackerel, tarpon, and bluefish. The town is also becoming known as a diving destination among those in search of shipwrecks and buried treasure.

JUST THE FACTS

Morehead City is on U.S. 70. It is accessible from the north via N.C. 101, from the west via N.C. 24, and from the south via N.C. 58.

Three airports serve the area. Craven County Regional Airport in New Bern offers US Airways express and charter flights; call 252-638-8591 for information. To the west in Jacksonville, Albert J. Ellis Airport offers US Airways commuter flights; call 910-324-1100. Michael J. Smith Airport, located in Beaufort, offers private and charter services; call 252-728-2323.

The bus station is located at 105 North 13th Street (28557); call 252-726-3029.

The best source for information on the area is the Crystal Coast Tourism Authority, at 3409 Arendell Street (28557); call 800-786-6962 or 252-726-8148 or visit www.crystalcoastnc.org.

The *Carteret County News Times* is the local newspaper.

Things to Do

Museums and Science Centers

The *History Place*, at 1008 Arendell Street (28557), is a 12,000-square-foot facility that houses the Rodney B. Kemp Museum Gallery, the Jack Spencer Goodwin Research Library, the Les A. Ewen Auditorium, and the Museum Store. It is also the new home of the Carteret County Historical Society. The History Place contains an interesting collection of artifacts and memorabilia reflecting the county's Native American, military, and maritime past. Visitors can walk through exhibits such as an old general store, an early school room, and a Victorian parlor. The History Place is open Tuesday through Saturday from 10 A.M. to 4 P.M. year-round except major holidays. The museum is run by volunteer docents. Admission is free. For more information, call 252-247-7533 or visit www.thehistoryplace.org.

The Museum Store features gifts reflecting the past and present of Carteret County. It offers a selection of publications, many produced by the Carteret County

Historical Society, as well as nautical ornaments, paintings, jewelry, locally carved birds, and other souvenirs.

The *Jack Spencer Goodwin Research Library* houses more than 8,000 publications and an extensive picture file documenting the history of Carteret County. Especially notable are the genealogy materials and the Civil War history collection.

Recreation

Fishing is the reason most people visit Morehead City. Opportunities to test your skills abound. Onshore and offshore fishing trips are available, as are charter rigs. Or you can bring your own boat or rent one at the waterfront. A list of charters and head boats is available from the Crystal Coast Tourism Authority.

Scuba-diving adventures can be booked through a number of outfits. You might try *Olympus Dive Center*, on the waterfront at 713 Shepard Street (28557). Call 252-726-9432 or visit www.olympusdiving.com.

Seasonal Events

The *Big Rock Blue Marlin Tournament*, held the second week in June, is part of the World Billfish Series. Blue marlin fishermen come from near and far to compete for cash prizes totaling over $1 million; the winner takes home nearly $500,000. For information, call 252-247-3575 or visit www.thebigrock.com. For a list of all area fishing tournaments and for information on obtaining tournament licenses, call the North Carolina Division of Marine Fisheries at 252-726-7021 or visit www.ncdmf. net.

The *North Carolina Seafood Festival* is held the first weekend in October on the Morehead City waterfront. Thousands flock to the festival to enjoy the music, to admire the arts and crafts, and, of course, to sample the delicious seafood. For information, call 252-726-6273 or visit www.ncseafoodfestival.org.

The *Bald Is Beautiful Convention and Contest* originally sought to gather at Bald Head Island, off the Cape Fear coast. But Morehead City, which has a sense of humor about its name, is glad the convention opted to meet here instead. On the second Saturday in September, the bald and the proud compete for such titles as "Most Kissable" and "Shiniest Head." For information, call 252-726-1855 or visit www.2camels.com/bald-is-beautiful-convention.php.

Places to Stay

Resorts, Hotels, and Motels

Accommodations in Morehead City tend to be less expensive than in Beaufort and Atlantic Beach, especially in the high season. Chain hotels and motels have secured the market here.

Hampton Inn Morehead City. Deluxe/Expensive. 4035 Arendell Street, 28557 (800-538-6338 or 252-240-2300; www.hamptoninn.com). This hotel overlooks Bogue Sound. It offers a complimentary continental breakfast, free in-room movies, an exercise room, and an outdoor pool. Its suites have living rooms, microwaves, refrigerators, and wet bars.

Quality Inn. Expensive/Moderate. 3100 Arendell Street, 28557 (800-422-5404 or 252-247-3434; www.moreheadhotels.com). This motel offers comfortable rooms, cable television, complimentary continental breakfast, a newspaper delivered to your door, a pool, a fitness room, and golf packages.

Buccaneer Inn Magnuson Hotel. Moderate. 2806 Arendell Street, 28557 (www.magnusonhotels.com/buccaneer-inn-magnuson-hotel; 877-747-8713 or 252-726-3115;). The Buccaneer Inn offers a complimentary breakfast and newspaper, cable television, a pool, and golf and fishing packages. Rooms with king-sized beds and Jacuzzis are available.

Econo Lodge. Moderate. 3410 Bridges Street, 28557 (877-424-6423 or 252-247-2940; www.econolodge.com). A motor inn with a colonial theme, the Econo Lodge offers free continental breakfast, cable television, a pool, and golf and fishing packages.

Places to Eat

William's. Expensive. 711-B Evans Street, 28557 (www.williamsfinedining.com; 252-240-1755). William's opened in 2001 and has been a local favorite ever since. Executive chef Jason Foster concentrates on the bounty of local seafood, along with fresh vegetables and fruits. The "Hoisin-Glazed Sea Scallops" are a great starter, as are the fried oysters. The pan-seared grouper and the grilled tuna are also delicious. Dinner is served Tuesday through Saturday.

Mrs. Willis' Restaurant. Expensive/Moderate. Behind Morehead Plaza at 3114 Bridges Street, 28557 (252-726-3741; www.mrswillisrestaurant.com). Mrs. Willis began cooking barbecue, chicken, and pies in 1949. Her family carries on the tradition today. Lunch is served Sunday through Friday; dinner is offered daily.

Sanitary Fish Market. Expensive/Moderate. 501 Evans Street, 28557 (252-247-3111; www.sanitaryfishmarket.com). A Tar Heel institution, the Sanitary Fish Market has been serving fresh seafood on the Morehead City waterfront since 1938. This vast, 600-seat restaurant offers broiled and fried seafood, steaks, lobster, homemade soups, chowder, and hush puppies. It is open daily for lunch and dinner from February through November.

Trateotu. Expensive/Moderate. 506 Arendell Street, 28557 (252-240-3380). Trateotu specializes in Caribbean-style cuisine with an emphasis on seafood. Its menu changes frequently. When you visit, the entrées may include "Panko Shrimp and Scallops with Wasabi Aioli" and "Chicken Breast Stuffed with Prosciutto and Havarti." Lunch is served Tuesday through Friday and dinner Monday through Saturday.

Windansea. Expensive/Moderate. 708 Evans Street, 28557 (252-247-3000). This bright restaurant on the waterfront offers a nice mixture of entrées, including seafood, lamb, and wood-oven pizzas. Dinner is served Wednesday through Sunday.

Bistro by the Sea. Moderate/Inexpensive. 4031 Arendell Street, 28557 (252-247-2777; www.bistro-by-the-sea.com). The specialty here is seafood, but the other entrées, including the "Bistro Burger," are also tasty. Start with a cup of shrimp bisque before moving on to the "Almond-Encrusted Chicken Breast with Hazelnut Cream

Sauce." The piano-and-cigar bar offers specialty martinis. Dinner is served Tuesday through Saturday; a "Bistro Lite" menu is offered from 5 P.M. to 6 P.M. Tuesday through Thursday. The restaurant is closed during January.

Raps Grill and Bar. Moderate/Inexpensive. 715 Arendell Street, 28557 (252-240-1213; www.rapsgrillandbar.com). Housed in a lovingly renovated 19th-century structure that boasts a 35-foot oak bar, Raps offers seafood, pasta, chicken, burritos, burgers, and Maryland-style crab. Lunch is served Monday through Saturday; dinner is offered daily.

Beaufort waterfront
PHOTOGRAPH BY ANGELA HARWOOD

Beaufort

Beaufort is a lovely old fishing village that has the distinction of being North Carolina's third-oldest town. At the time of the American Revolution, it was the third-largest port in the state. Today, it boasts a 12-block national historic district on the original "Plan of Beaufort Towne," platted by Henry Somerset in 1713.

When French Huguenots and immigrants from Germany, Sweden, England, Scotland, and Ireland arrived here around 1708, the place was known to the Indians as Wareiock, or "Fish Town." It was renamed Beaufort for the duke of Beaufort, one of the Lords Proprietors.

Beaufort was an important military port during the War of 1812, when much privateering occurred here. One of the most famous and successful privateers was Otway Burns, captain of the *Snap Dragon*, who between 1812 and 1814 captured cargoes worth millions of dollars. After the war, he stayed in Beaufort and became a successful shipbuilder, merchant, and politician.

In the 19th century, Beaufort continued to prosper as a port and as an agricultural, commercial, and governmental center. Wealthy planters and their families sought its pleasant and healthful environment.

Early in the Civil War, Beaufort was again called to military duty, this time aiding blockade runners bringing supplies to the Confederacy. On March 25, 1862, the town was occupied by Union forces. It was from Beaufort that the Federals launched the formidable fleet that helped conquer the South.

After the war, Beaufort was a seasonal resort town, its economic importance diminished. Fishing became its major industry. The harvesting and processing of menhaden—used for fish meal and industrial oils—proved particularly important.

By the 1970s, Beaufort's waterfront was in serious decline. Residents embarked upon a mission to save the old village. The result of their efforts is one of the most attractive and appealing destinations in the entire state.

JUST THE FACTS

From the north or south, drivers can take U.S. 17 to U.S. 70 to reach Beaufort.

Craven County Regional Airport in New Bern offers express and charter flights via US Airways and Midway Airlines; call 252-638-8591 for information. Michael J. Smith Airport, named in honor of the Beaufort son who perished in the *Challenger* space shuttle accident, offers private and charter service; call 252-728-1777 or 252-728-2323.

The nearest bus station is located at 206 North 15th Street in Morehead City; call 252-726-3029.

Boaters can stop at the Beaufort Municipal Docks (252-728-2503) or Town Creek Marina (252-728-6111; www.towncreekmarina.com).

A good source for information on the area is the Crystal Coast Tourism Authority, located at 3409 Arendell Street in Morehead City (28557); call 800-786-6962 or 252-726-8148 or visit www.crystalcoastnc.org. For information on Beaufort, visit www.historicbeaufort.com.

Things to Do

Historic Places, Gardens, and Tours

Beaufort Historic Site, located at 130 Turner Street (28516), includes three restored homes built between 1767 and 1825; the Carteret County Courthouse, constructed in 1796; the Carteret County Jail, built in 1829; and the Apothecary Shop and Doctor's Office, erected in 1859. From March through November, it is open 9:30 A.M. to 5 P.M. Monday through Saturday; from June through August, it is also open Sunday from 1 P.M. to 4 P.M. From December through February, it is open 10 A.M. to 4 P.M. Monday through Saturday. For more information, call 800-575-7483 or 252-728-5225 or visit www.beauforthistoricsite.org.

While you're at the site, be sure to browse the books, hand-carved decoys, dolls, fine porcelain, and silver in *The Old Beaufort Shop*, the museum store in the Safrit Historical Center, where tickets for various tours may be purchased. You'll also want to check out the *Mattie King Davis Art Gallery*, which features the works of over 100 local and regional artists. The gallery, located in the historic Rustell House on the grounds of the historic site, is open 10 A.M. to 4 P.M. Monday through Saturday.

The *Old Burying Ground*, on Ann Street, is the site of graves from the Revolutionary War and Civil War eras. The cemetery, administered by the historic site, is listed on the National Register. Shaded by majestic live oaks entwined with ancient wisteria vines, it has many tales to tell. Among those interred here are Otway Burns, privateer hero of the War of 1812, and a 13-year-old girl buried in a rum barrel.

Guided tours of the historic site are offered daily at 10 A.M., 11:30 A.M., 1 P.M., and 3 P.M. Tours of the cemetery are conducted June through September on Tuesday, Wednesday, and Thursday at 2:30 P.M. The site also offers English double-decker bus tours, operated by the Beaufort Historical Association (http://historicbeaufort. com/bhaindex.htm). These entertaining tours, available April through October, run about 45 minutes; they are offered Monday, Wednesday, Friday, and Saturday at 11 A.M. and 1:30 P.M. Fees are charged for all three tours.

Museums and Science Centers

A visit to the *North Carolina Maritime Museum*, at 315 Front Street (28516), is a wonderful way to learn about coastal and maritime history. This bustling museum offers exhibits on the United States Life Saving Service and its historic lighthouses, coastal and marine life, watercraft, decoys, and artifacts recently recovered from an 18th-century shipwreck thought to be Blackbeard's flagship, the *Queen Anne's Revenge*. Highlights include a miniature submarine-like "life car," an "observation bell" reminiscent of *Twenty Thousand Leagues under the Sea*, and an amazingly primitive, basket-like boat called a "bamboo coracle." Beyond its fascinating exhibits, the museum offers a broad range of educational programs for children and adults. These programs range from boat-building and sailing classes to environmental studies at the museum's Cape Lookout facility. Quarterly calendars are available.

To watch boatbuilders in action, visit the **Harvey W. Smith Watercraft Center**, located across the street from the museum. The center also houses the **John S. MacCormack Model Shop**, where scale models of watercraft are constructed.

The museum's gift shop stocks a great selection of books on maritime and natural history. Its library is available for research. The North Carolina Maritime Museum is open Monday through Friday from 9 A.M. to 5 P.M., Saturday from 10 A.M. to 5 P.M., and Sunday from 1 P.M. to 5 P.M. Admission is free, though donations are welcome. Call 252-728-7317 or visit www.ncmaritime.org.

Recreation

Island Ferry Adventures, at 610 Front Street (28516), is a convenient water-taxi service that provides transportation and scenic tours to Cape Lookout, Shackleford Banks, and the Rachel Carson Estuarine Research Reserve. For information, call 252-728-7555 or visit www.islandferryadventures.com.

Lookout Cruises, located on the Beaufort waterfront on Front Street, sails to Cape Lookout twice daily. You can also try a morning dolphin watch or a sunset or moonlight cruise aboard the company's 42-passenger catamaran. Call 252-504-SAIL or visit www.lookoutcruises.com for information.

If you want to go snorkeling or diving in search of shipwrecks, you might try **Discovery Diving** at 414 Orange Street (28516). If you're an experienced diver and would like to join up with others, Discovery can help out, too. Call 252-728-2265 or visit www.discoverydiving.com for information.

For information on ecology tours, contact the North Carolina Maritime Museum's *Cape Lookout Studies Program*, headquartered at 315 Front Street (28516); call 252-504-2452 or visit www.capelookoutstudies.org. Another excellent option is *Coastal Ecology Sails* (252-241-6866 or 252-247-3860; www.goodfortunesails.com).

Seasonal Events

Sponsored by the Beaufort Historical Society, the *Beaufort Old Homes and Gardens Tour* and the *Antiques Show and Sale* are held the last full weekend in June. Visitors enjoy tours of historic homes, churches, gardens, and the Old Burying Ground. Antiques are shown at the Morehead City Civic Center. Double-decker bus tours are conducted throughout the weekend, and entertainment is provided. For more information, call 800-575-7483 or 252-728-5225 or visit www.beauforthistoricsite. org/oldhomestourintro.htm.

Beaufort Historic Site celebrates the holidays with two annual events. Visitors can enjoy Thanksgiving dinner served on the grounds of the historic site at the *Community Thanksgiving Feast*, hosted the Sunday before Thanksgiving. The *Coastal Carolina Christmas Walk*, held the second weekend in December, is a festive open house and self-guided walking tour of the historic site and Beaufort's bed-and-breakfasts, all decorated for the holiday season.

The *Beaufort Wine and Food Weekend* is held annually the last full weekend in April. The festival showcases great wineries and winemakers from around the world, pairing their products with food prepared by local, regional, and visiting chefs. Events such as the Celebrity Gala and Auction; Beer, Bubbles & BBQ; the Champagne Celebration Brunch; and Cool Art, Hot Wine are spread over five days. Tickets can be purchases in advance or on-site. Funds raised from the events go directly to nonprofits that excel in drawing tourism to Carteret County. For more information, e-mail info@beaufortwineandfood.com or visit www.beaufortwineandfood.com.

Places to Stay

Inns and Bed-and-Breakfasts

Beaufort Inn. Deluxe/Expensive. 101 Ann Street, 28516 (800-726-0321 or 252-728-2600; www.beaufort-inn.com). Beaufort Inn offers 44 well-appointed waterfront rooms overlooking Taylor Creek. It provides boat slips, an exercise room, an outdoor hot tub, and bicycles upon request.

The Cedars Inn. Deluxe/Expensive. 305 Front Street, 28516 (252-728-7036; www.cedarsinn.com). Located in the heart of the historic district, The Cedars is comprised of two elegant historic houses, one of them a former shipwright's 1768 home. All 11 guest rooms have private baths. The inn offers a full breakfast, a wine bar, a deck, and bicycles.

Langdon House Bed-and-Breakfast. Deluxe/Expensive. 135 Craven Street, 28516 (252-728-5499; www.langdonhouse.com). This hospitable inn has four guest rooms, each with a private bath. The rooms are decorated in a simple 18th-century style. A full breakfast is included.

Pecan Tree Inn. Deluxe/Expensive. 116 Queen Street, 28516 (800-728-7871 or 252-728-6733; www.pecantree.com). This inn offers seven guest rooms and three suites, all with private baths. Two of the suites have king-sized canopy beds and Jacuzzis, while the third consists of two adjoining rooms. Pecan Tree also has a lovely flower and herb garden. Continental breakfast is provided.

Otway House Bed-and-Breakfast. Expensive. 368 U.S. 70 in Otway, 28516 (252-728-5636 or 252-342-5636; www.otwayhouse.com). For a pet-friendly option, stay a few miles outside Beaufort in Otway. The Otway House has four rooms, each with a private bath. It is located on six acres with walking trails. Indoor and outdoor kennels are offered, and well-behaved dogs may stay in the room when their owners are present. Guests may board their dogs at the Otway House while they set out to explore the Crystal Coast.

Captain's Quarters. Expensive/Moderate. 315 Ann Street, 28516 (800-659-7111 or 252-728-7711; www.captainsquarters.us). Captain's Quarters, a charming Victorian inn with a wraparound porch, is located a block from the waterfront. Its three guest rooms have private baths. Continental breakfast is provided. Children under 12 are not allowed.

Inlet Inn. Expensive/Moderate. 601 Front Street, 28516 (800-554-5466 or 252-728-3600; www.inlet-inn.com). Each harbor-front room here includes a seating area, a refrigerator, a bar, and cable television. Many have private porches with rocking chairs, while others have fireplaces or window seats with a view of Cape Lookout. Continental breakfast is provided. Boat slips are available.

Old Seaport Inn. Expensive/Moderate. 217 Turner Street, 28516 (800-349-5823 or 252-728-4300; www.oldseaportinn.com). This 1866 inn offers three guest rooms furnished with antiques. Each has a private bath. The gracious hosts will provide beach chairs and bicycles if asked. Refreshments are served in the afternoon. The inn is open year-round.

Places to Eat

The Spouter Inn. Expensive. 218 Front Street, 28516 (252-728-5190; www.thespouterinn.com). For over 20 years, The Spouter Inn has served up fresh seafood in a relaxed setting overlooking Taylor Creek. Lunch features a variety of sandwich-and-soup combos, while much of the dinner menu celebrates the fruits of the sea. Lunch and dinner are served Tuesday through Sunday.

Beaufort Grocery. Expensive/Moderate. 117 Queen Street, 28516 (252-728-3899; www.beaufortgrocery.com). Charles and Wendy Park, executive chef and pastry chef, respectively, have been serving delicious homemade soups, breads, desserts, and Mediterranean-style specialties at this popular deli-by-day, bistro-by-night since 1991. It is open daily for lunch and dinner. Sunday brunch is also served. And Beaufort Grocery will gladly pack you a picnic. Reservations are recommended for dinner.

Blue Moon Bistro. Expensive/Moderate. 119 Queen Street, 28516 (252-728-5800; www.bluemoonbistro.biz). "The Moon" is a welcome addition to the fine-dining establishments of Beaufort. Creative appetizers include a shrimp-and-grits "martini" served in—you guessed it—a martini glass. Rib-eye steak, roast chicken, and other entrées come with deliciously fresh vegetables. Dinner is served Tuesday through Saturday. Reservations are recommended.

Front Street Grill at Stillwater. Expensive/Moderate. 300 Front Street, 28516 (252-728-4956; www.frontstreetgrillatstillwater.com). With its spacious deck and tasteful dining room overlooking Taylor Creek, Front Street Grill is hard to beat for watching the sunset while enjoying appetizers and a glass of wine. Try the tasty coconut fried shrimp or grilled portobello mushroom and asparagus appetizers, but be sure to leave room for dinner. Lunch and dinner are served Tuesday through Sunday; Sunday brunch is also offered. Reservations are accepted.

The Net House. Expensive/Moderate. 133 Turner Street, 28516 (252-728-2002). The steamed and lightly battered seafood served here has earned The Net House bragging rights for years. The nightly specials and creamy seafood bisque are favorites, too. Dinner is served nightly.

The Royal James Café. Inexpensive. 117 Turner Street, 28516 (252-728-4573). This local landmark is the oldest continuously operating business in Beaufort. Visitors can enjoy the signature burgers and secret sauce before a game of pool on one of the nearly 50-year-old tables. Lunch is served daily and dinner Monday through Saturday.

Nearby

Directly across Taylor Creek from the Beaufort waterfront is the **Rachel Carson Estuarine Research Reserve**, a series of small islands. A half-mile interpretive trail winds through the islands' mud flats, uplands, and salt marshes, illustrating the various environments found in estuarine systems. A small herd of feral horses roams the islands, and over 200 bird species have been recorded here. Access is by boat only, but the islands' proximity to Beaufort makes this a good destination for beginning kayakers to enjoy a day of shelling and swimming. The reserve includes restricted areas, including nesting areas and freshwater sources for the horses. A trail guide is available over the Internet or from the North Carolina Maritime Museum or the sanctuary office, located at 135 Duke Marine Lab Road (28516). For information, call 252-728-2170 or visit www.nerrs.noaa.gov/NorthCarolina/Component_Rachel.html, then go to the Rachel Carson link.

Cape Lookout National Seashore is comprised of 56 miles of pristine barrier islands including North Core Banks, punctuated by historic Portsmouth Village at its northern tip; South Core Banks and its famed Cape Lookout Lighthouse; and Shackleford Banks, home of a herd of wild horses. The seashore's visitor center is located at Shell Point on Harkers Island, a sound island lying behind the string of barrier islands.

This is truly a national treasure that should not be missed. Cape Lookout is home to myriad bird life and is a protected breeding ground for endangered loggerhead turtles and other marine turtles. A visit can be enjoyed as a day trip to the lighthouse or a week-long vacation for hardy souls desiring rustic accommodations and solitude. With the exception of two cabin-rental agencies, no garbage pickup is offered on the islands; visitors are expected to take their trash away with them. Likewise, no concessions are available, so plan to take water, snacks, sunscreen, and insect repellent with you. Cape Lookout's fishing camp is *Morris Marina Kabin Kamps and Ferry Service* (252-225-4261).

From Beaufort, take U.S. 70 East to Otway and follow the signs for the *Harkers Island Visitor Center*, at 131 Charles Street (28531). The visitor center is a good place to gather information about the seashore's attractions, and it's one of several locations where parking and camping permits can be obtained. Call 252-728-2250 or visit www.nps.gov/calo.

The seashore is accessible only by water. Private and toll ferries depart from the following towns, ranging from north to south: Ocracoke, Atlantic, Davis, Harkers Island, Beaufort, and Morehead City. Only the ferries from Atlantic and Davis accommodate vehicles, and only four-wheel-drive vehicles are appropriate. The visitor center offers a list of ferry services. *Calico Jacks Inn & Marina* provides ferry service to Cape Lookout and Shackleford Banks, as well as truck service to Cape Lookout Village and to Cape Point for shelling; for more information, call 252-728-3575. And while it is possible to paddle to the islands, doing so is not recommended for novices. Experienced paddlers can file their float plans at the visitor center. Private watercraft can also be used to reach the seashore.

Portsmouth Village was established in 1753 to encourage development of a port at Ocracoke Inlet. In 1842, more than 500 people lived in Portsmouth, at that time the state's premier port. Successive hurricanes beginning in 1846 drove inhabitants away, however. The surviving structures reflect a sleepy 1930s fishing village, not a lively 19th-century seaport. You can reach Portsmouth Village by making private ferry arrangements on Ocracoke Island.

The current *Cape Lookout Lighthouse* was built in 1859 to replace a previous structure erected in 1812 that was deemed too short. Its distinctive black and white diamond "daymarks" give directions to sailors; the black diamonds are oriented east-west and the white diamonds north-south. In June 2003, the lighthouse was transferred from the Coast Guard to the National Park Service, which currently opens it to the public only on special occasions. The *Innkeepers House*, located adjacent to the lighthouse, operates as a small museum and information center.

Many of the ferry services offer shuttle access to *Cape Point* and *Cape Lookout Village Historic District*. The opportunity for gathering seashells at Cape Point is unsurpassed. Among the several interesting buildings in the historic village is a former Coast Guard station, where the North Carolina Maritime Museum conducts educational tours. You can reach this portion of the island from Harkers Island or Beaufort.

On the ride to the lighthouse, one sight you're likely to see is the famous *wild horses of Shackleford Banks*. If Shackleford is your destination, you can embark from Harkers Island, Beaufort, or Morehead City. If you visit Shackleford, use caution regarding the horses, as they are wild animals.

Wild horses on Shackleford Banks
PHOTOGRAPH BY ANGELA HARWOOD

The *Core Sound Waterfowl Museum* is located at 1785 Island Road on Harkers Island (28531). Like the decoys that inspired its creation, the museum has been a labor of love since its inception in 1987. Located adjacent to Cape Lookout's headquarters, the museum's beautiful new facility houses a large collection of antique and contemporary decoys and pays homage to the area's hunting and fishing traditions. The educational portion of the building opened in 2003. Fund-raising is ongoing to complete the galleries, a research library, and a tower. Situated on 16 acres of maritime forest, the facility includes a four-acre freshwater waterfowl habitat, hiking trails, and viewing platforms. The museum is open from 10 A.M. to 5 P.M. Monday through Saturday and from 2 P.M. to 5 P.M. on Sunday. Admission is free. For more information, call 252-728-1500 or visit www.coresound.com.

About 24 miles from Beaufort on U.S. 70 is *Cedar Island National Wildlife Refuge*, which was authorized by the Migratory Bird Act of 1964. Over 270 species of birds can be spotted here, the peak months being December and January. Since approximately 11,000 of the refuge's 14,480 acres are under shallow water, kayaks and canoes are the best way to explore the area. A boat ramp is provided at the end of Lola Road.

Bogue Banks

Bogue Banks is a 29-mile-long barrier island that stretches from Beaufort Inlet on the east to Bogue Inlet on the west. Until the 1950s, Bogue Banks was virtually undeveloped. But once people came to recognize it among the state's longest, most accessible barrier islands, its beautiful, expansive white beach became one of the most popular vacation destinations on the coast. After several decades of development, much of the native landscape has been supplanted by condominiums, beach houses, hotels, and resorts. However, Bogue Banks still boasts one of the prettiest beaches in the state.

The eastern end of the island is dominated by Atlantic Beach, the oldest town on Bogue Banks. Its bustling commercial area includes shops, restaurants, and entertainment parks; children and teenagers love it. Adjacent to Atlantic Beach is Fort Macon State Park, the most-visited state park in North Carolina, attracting 1.24 million guests a year.

Midway down the island, at Salter Path and Pine Knoll Shores, beach cottages are the norm. Pine Knoll Shores was developed by Theodore Roosevelt's children, who were heirs of his distant cousin Alice Hoffman, the owner of most of the island from 1918 to 1953. The Roosevelt family donated 322 acres of local land, including 2,700 feet of beachfront, to the state. Pine Knoll Shores was incorporated in 1973. It is now home to Theodore Roosevelt State Natural Area.

Past Indian Beach at the island's western end is the town of Emerald Isle. Things are slower and quieter here. Few of the local buildings reach over two stories.

JUST THE FACTS
‖‖

Bogue Banks is a barrier island sandwiched between Bogue Sound and the Atlantic Ocean. N.C. 58 runs almost the entire length of the island. Visitors coming from the north can connect to N.C. 58 from U.S. 70. Those coming from the south can take U.S. 17 to N.C. 24 in Jacksonville or connect directly to N.C. 58 from U.S. 17 near Croatan National Forest.

Air access is via Craven County Regional Airport (252-638-8591) in New Bern, Albert J. Ellis Airport (910-324-1100) in Jacksonville, or Michael J. Smith Airport (252-728-1777 or 252-728-2323) in Beaufort.

The best source for information on the area is the Crystal Coast Tourism Authority, at 3409 Arendell Street in Morehead City (28557); call 800-786-6962 or 252-726-8148 or visit www.crystalcoastnc.com.

Things to Do

Historic Places, Gardens, and Tours
‖‖

The top historical draw on Bogue Banks is without a doubt *Fort Macon State Park*, located east of Atlantic Beach at the tip of the island at 2300 East Fort Macon Road (28512). The War of 1812 demonstrated the coastline's vulnerability to enemy attack. By 1865, some 38 permanent forts had been built from Maine to the Gulf Coast and in California.

For over 150 years, Fort Macon has stood guard over Beaufort Inlet. The pentagon-shaped fortress, completed in 1834, was named to honor Nathaniel Macon, a former speaker of the House of Representatives and United States senator. Not long after it was garrisoned, Fort Macon began to give way to erosion and storms, so the

United States Army sent one of its young West Point engineers, Robert E. Lee, to rectify the problem. The stone jetties designed by Captain Lee are still in use today. During the Civil War, the 500 Confederate troops at Fort Macon were forced to surrender to Union general Ambrose Burnside following an 11-hour bombardment. The fort was garrisoned again during the Spanish-American War and World War II. Between conflicts, it was often occupied by a single caretaker.

A self-guided tour with audiovisual displays provides historical background on the fort for visitors of all ages. From mid-April through mid-October, fort tours are offered daily on the hour from 10 A.M. to 3 P.M. The museum on the premises exhibits tools, weapons, and artifacts and offers a slide presentation. The bookstore has a variety of historical material.

The 385-acre park is a favorite spot for bird-watching, sportfishing, and shelling. In the summer, the lifeguard-protected swimming area, the bathhouses, and the picnic areas are popular with visitors. Events here include Civil War reenactments, musket-firing and cannon-firing demonstrations, and nature tours and talks. You can pick up a schedule at the Carteret County Tourism Bureau or visit www.clis.com/friends for more information.

Fort Macon State Park is open from 9 A.M. to 5:30 P.M. daily except Christmas. Admission is free. For information, call 252-726-3775 or visit www.ncparks.gov/visit/parks/foma/main.php.

Museums and Science Centers

The *North Carolina Aquarium at Pine Knoll Shores* is one of the island's most popular attractions. Its 16-tank viewing gallery, exhibits, touch tank, and two nature trails are designed to educate visitors about North Carolina's fragile and fascinating marine life. Included are the 200-gallon Precious Waters exhibit, a salt-marsh tank, and a riverbank display featuring live alligators. The Loggerhead Odyssey exhibit includes a nursery for injured turtles. The aquarium is located five miles west of Atlantic Beach near Milepost 7 on N.C. 58 at 1 Roosevelt Drive (28512). It is open from 9 A.M. to 5 P.M. daily year-round; the hours are extended to 9 P.M. every other Thursday in summer. An admission fee is charged. Call 866-294-3477 or 252-247-4003 or visit www.ncaquariums.com/pine-knoll-shores for information.

Recreation

Theodore Roosevelt State Natural Area is a 265-acre nature preserve located next to the aquarium at 1 Roosevelt Drive in Pine Knoll Shores (28512). This is the perfect place to observe local wildlife and get a glimpse of the island in its native state. Few amenities are offered here. Call 252-247-4003 for information.

Oceanana Fishing Pier is located at 700 East Fort Macon Road in Atlantic Beach (28512). A fee is charged. For information, visit www.oceanana.com or call 252-726-4111.

Places to Stay

Resorts, Hotels, and Motels

Sheraton Atlantic Beach. Deluxe. 2717 West Fort Macon Road in Atlantic Beach, 28512 (800-624-8875 or 252-240-1155; www.sheratonatlanticbeach.com). The Sheraton offers 200 ocean-view rooms and suites. Among its amenities are indoor and outdoor pools, a game room, an exercise room, a spa, a restaurant, and a 600-foot fishing pier.

Atlantis Lodge. Deluxe/Expensive. Milepost 5 on N.C. 58 at 123 Salter Path Road in Pine Knoll Shores, 28512 (252-726-5168; www.atlantislodge.com). The Atlantis is a golden oldie nestled amid the maritime woods. Most of its accommodations are suites that come complete with kitchens and dining areas. All rooms have a patio or a deck facing the ocean. Kids will adore the swimming pool.

Clamdigger Ramada Inn. Deluxe/Expensive. 511 Salter Path Road in Atlantic Beach, 28512 (800-338-1533 or 252-247-4155; www.clamdiggerinn.com). Each room here has a private balcony overlooking the beach, a microwave, a mini refrigerator, a coffee maker, an iron, an ironing board, and cable television. A pool, a restaurant, and a lounge round out the amenities.

Oceanana. Expensive/Moderate. 700 East Fort Macon Road in Atlantic Beach, 28512 (252-726-4111; www.oceanana.com). Located near Fort Macon, Oceanana is an old-fashioned beach place for the whole family. It offers a pool, a playground, a pier, and a lifeguard on the beach during the summer.

The Seahawk Motor Lodge and Villas. Moderate. Milepost 4¾ on N.C. 58 at 105

Salter Path Road in Pine Knoll Shores, 28512 (800-682-6898 or 252-726-4146; www. ncbeach-motel.com). This charming motor lodge has been pleasing visitors for generations. Its friendly atmosphere is fostered by seaside hammocks and swings. All of its 38 oceanfront rooms have a balcony or patio. Bikes, fishing rods, and grills are yours for the asking. A pool is on the premises.

Caribbe Inn. Moderate/Inexpensive. 309 East Fort Macon Road in Atlantic Beach, 28512 (252-726-0051; www.caribbe-inn.com). Located two and a half blocks from the ocean, this fanciful little motel offers 12 rooms, each with a refrigerator and a microwave. It is pet-friendly, too.

Places to Eat

The Crab's Claw Restaurant and Oyster Bar. Expensive. 201 West Atlantic Beach Boulevard in Atlantic Beach, 28512 (252-726-8222; www.crabsclaw.com). Fresh from the sea is what The Crab's Claw is all about. Situated on the boardwalk in the thick of things, it serves a variety of steamer pots and a terrific roasted corn and clam chowder. Members of the under-12 crowd can enjoy "Chicken Dinosaur" or a PBJ, if they prefer. Lunch and dinner are served daily.

Amos Mosquito's Restaurant and Bar. Expensive/Moderate. 703 East Fort Macon Road in Atlantic Beach, 28512 (252-247-6222; www.amosmosquitos.com). Recently transplanted from Morehead City, this café offers an array of fresh salads, sandwiches, pastas, and seafood entrées, some bearing Asian and southwestern influences. Dockside dining is available. Guests love the table-side hibachis, where they can make their own s'mores. Dinner is served daily.

Channel Marker. Expensive/Moderate. 718 Atlantic Beach Causeway in Atlantic Beach, 28512 (252-247-2344; www.thechannelmarker.com/cam.html). Channel Marker offers outdoor dining overlooking Bogue Sound. Dinner specialties include fresh seafood, served steamed or grilled, and Angus beef. Ample boat dockage is available. Dinner is served daily.

Kathryn's Bistro & Martini Bar. Expensive/Moderate. 8002 Emerald Drive in Emerald Isle, 28594 (252-354-6200; www.kathrynsbistro.com). This recent upscale addition to Emerald Isle was highly needed. It features seafood, steak, and chicken entrées prepared on a wood-fired grill. The pastas and the "She-Crab & Corn Soup" are also among the favorites. But the real specialty here is the massive variety of martinis. Visitors can try a "Black Martini," a "Chocolate Kiss," and many more. A designated driver is recommended! Kathryn's is open daily for dinner.

Ballyhoo's Island Sports Grill. Moderate/Inexpensive. 140 Fairview Drive in Emerald Isle, 28594 (252-354-9397; www.ballyhoos.net). Opened in 2007, Ballyhoos has quickly risen to the top of Emerald Isle's restaurant list. It offers a wide variety of dishes featuring Angus beef and local seafood, along with soups, salads, and more. Ballyhoo's has the largest selection of ales on the island; guests can choose from over 50 varieties. This family- and kid-friendly restaurant also features late-night entertainment starting around 10 P.M. for adults only; local and regional acoustical musical acts perform. Dinner is served daily.

Emerald Grill. Inexpensive. 301 Mangrove Drive in Emerald Isle, 28594 (252-354-9700). Standard breakfast and lunch fare is served here—omelets, burgers, wings, wraps, and salads—but be sure to try the nontypical items like the popular shrimp burger and the sweet-potato fries. Breakfast, lunch, and dinner are served daily.

Nearby

Swansboro is a pretty, historic fishing village on the White Oak River, just over the Emerald Isle bridge on N.C. 24. This "Friendly City by the Sea," as locals like to refer to it, has been greeting visitors for over 250 years. Among its historic structures are the *William Pugh Ferrand Store*, erected in 1839, and the *Jonathan Green, Jr., House*, built in the mid-18th century and thought to be the town's oldest home. Swansboro offers a picture-perfect look at coastal North Carolina life in days gone by. It's a great place to browse antique and craft shops.

If you're looking for a bite to eat while you're in town, you're sure to enjoy *Yana's Ye Olde Drugstore and Restaurant*, located at 9 Front Street (28584). Yana's is popular, so be prepared to wait. The "Bradburger," a hamburger with egg, cheese, bacon, lettuce, and tomato, will make it worth your while. Yana's serves traditional breakfasts daily at 7 A.M. and a variety of sandwiches and fried fruit pies for lunch until 4 P.M.; call 910-326-5501 or visit www.yanamamas.com.

Barrier Island Kayaks, at 160 Cedar Point Boulevard (28584), offers rentals and tours to area destinations including Bear Island and Hammocks Beach. Call 252-393-6457 or visit www.barrierislandkayaks.com.

Hammocks Beach State Park is one of the most beautiful and unspoiled beaches on the East Coast. Ironically, our nation's ugly segregationist past is largely the reason. In 1914, Dr. William Sharpe, a pioneer in brain surgery, bought the island. Shortly thereafter, he named a black couple, John and Gertrude Hurst, as caretakers. When Sharpe began to receive unsigned letters stating that a black man was unfit to manage the property, he bought an ad in the local paper offering $5,000 for information leading to the arrest and conviction of anyone damaging the island or its occupants. The threats ended.

In the 1940s, when he was an old man, Sharpe decided to leave the island to the Hursts. Mrs. Hurst persuaded him to instead leave it to the North Carolina Teachers Association, a black teachers' alliance. His beloved Hammocks Beach thus fulfilled Sharpe's dream of being a "refuge and a place for enjoyment for some of the people whom America treated so badly."

On May 3, 1961, at the dawn of the civil-rights movement, the property was presented to the state. Visitors to Hammocks Beach today enjoy swimming, primitive camping, picnicking, shelling, surf fishing, and nature programs.

To get to Hammocks Beach State Park, catch the ferry at the visitor center on Hammocks Beach Road (S.R. 1511), located off N.C. 24. A nominal fee is charged. For information, call 910-326-4881 or visit www.ncparks.gov/visit/habe/main.php.

Historic Wilmington river front
COURTESY OF WILMINGTON/CAPE FEAR COAST CONVENTION AND VISITORS BUREAU

Cape Fear Coast

By Angela Harwood

The name will probably draw you in, just as it did Hollywood. Since the 1980s, the Cape Fear coast has been the location of such feature films as *Billy Bathgate, The Hudsucker Proxy*, and *Blue Velvet*. It was the film location of the popular television series *Dawson's Creek* and is now the location for *One Tree Hill*. Wilmington, the area's thriving city, has become known as "the Hollywood of the East." It ranks third to Los Angeles and New York in cinematic productivity.

But this is much more than a pretty, inexpensive place to make movies. The southernmost promontory of North Carolina's coast gets its name from the deadly shoals at the mouth of its like-named river, the Cape Fear. At the northern edge of the region is Topsail Island, whose name honors its legacy of crafty pirates. Next comes the exclusive Figure Eight Island, where former vice president Al Gore and family have been among those seeking its isolated beauty. Wilmington, the largest deepwater port in the Southeast, is situated on the banks of the Cape Fear River, as is the quaint port town of Southport, a popular stopover for boaters cruising the Intracoastal Waterway. Along the Atlantic coast east and south of Wilmington are some of the state's premier beaches, including Kure Beach, Carolina Beach, and the fabled Wrightsville Beach. Off Southport is the selectively developed Bald Head

Island, accessible only by boat. Stretching from Southport to the South Carolina line are the lovely, uncrowded beaches of Brunswick County.

While summer is certainly the most popular time to visit the Cape Fear coast, the area's mild climate makes it an inviting destination any time of year. In the spring, Wilmington is at its showiest during the annual Azalea Festival. In the fall, when the king mackerel are running, fishing tournaments abound. And in winter, Wilmington's vibrant cultural scene heats up the chilly nights. Whenever you choose to visit, the area's abundant recreational opportunities and cultural diversions will make it an ideal destination.

Topsail Island

Midway between Cape Lookout and Cape Fear is the 26-mile barrier island known as Topsail. Although the name sounds like the product of 21st-century resort marketing, legend has it that it dates to the golden age of piracy, when marauding pirates would moor their vessels in the sound behind the island, waiting to spring on unsuspecting ships. It wasn't long before word spread among ship pilots to keep an eye out for the pirate ships' topsails over the dunes—hence the name. Chances are the infamous pirates Blackbeard and Stede Bonnet roamed these shores. Treasure hunters still flock here with their metal detectors and scuba gear to search for loot.

Written records describing Topsail date from the 1500s, when early European explorers ventured into its protected inland waterways. Artifacts from the Tuscaroras and other Native Americans reveal that the island was a favorite hunting and fishing spot long before white settlers came along.

Interestingly, Topsail Island played an important role in both the Civil War and World War II. During the Civil War, it was the site of a Confederate saltworks. In World War II, Camp Davis, an enormous antiaircraft training center, was constructed on Topsail. Following the war, Camp Davis was deactivated. The island was subsequently selected as a testing ground for missiles, and Operation Bumblebee was thus born. The 200 missiles that were launched here paved the way for the development of the ramjet engine, which enabled aircraft to break the sound barrier. Concrete observation towers from that era still dot the landscape.

When the military left in 1948, civilians moved in. The island has grown steadily as a resort destination since then. The town of Surf City was incorporated in

Jolly Roger Pier
PHOTOGRAPH BY VICKI McALLISTER

1949, followed by Topsail Beach in 1963 and North Topsail Beach in 1990. In 1954, Hurricane Hazel leveled nearly all the buildings on the island. Two more hurricanes, Donna and Diane, later wreaked more havoc. The most recent catastrophic weather came in 1998, but the tenacious islanders rebuilt and are once again ready to welcome visitors to their lovely stretch of sand and surf.

JUST THE FACTS

The island can be reached from U.S. 17 via bridges at North Topsail Beach and Surf City.

The nearest airports are at Wilmington, to the southwest, and Jacksonville, to the north. Nearby Holly Ridge also has a public airstrip.

The Greater Topsail Island Chamber of Commerce is located at Treasure Coast Landing at 13775 N.C. 50, Suite 101, in Surf City (28445). For information, call 800-626-2780 or 910-329-4446 or visit www.topsailcoc.com.

Things to Do

Museums and Science Centers

Topsail Island Museum: Missiles and More, at 720 Channel Boulevard in Topsail

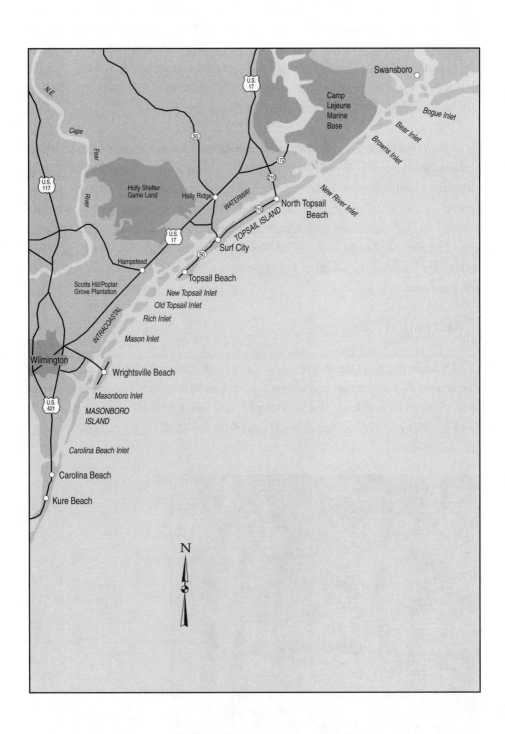

Beach (28445), offers Indian artifacts and displays on pirate activity and World War II operations. From mid-May to early September, it is open Monday through Saturday from 2 P.M. to 4 P.M. From early April to mid-May and from early September to mid-October, it is open Monday through Friday from 2 P.M. to 4 P.M. Admission is free, though donations are accepted. Call 800-626-2780 or 910-328-8663 or visit www.topsailmissilesmuseum.org for information.

The **Karen Beasley Sea Turtle Rescue and Rehabilitation Center** is located at 822 Carolina Boulevard in Topsail Beach (28445). Topsail and the other barrier islands along the North Carolina coast are a breeding ground for several different marine turtles, including the endangered loggerhead. The dedicated volunteers at the turtle hospital rescue and rehabilitate scores of injured animals annually. The center is open for tours from 2 P.M. to 4 P.M. on Monday, Tuesday, Thursday, Friday, and Saturday; it is closed during winter. For information, call 910-328-3377 or visit www.seaturtlehospital.org.

Recreation

Three fishing piers are on the island. Located in the heart of Surf City, **Surf City Pier** is open 24 hours a day, seven days a week; call 910-328-3521. **Jolly Roger Pier** is located at 803 Ocean Boulevard in North Topsail Beach (28445); call 910-328-4616. **Sea View Pier** is in North Topsail Beach; call 910-328-3172.

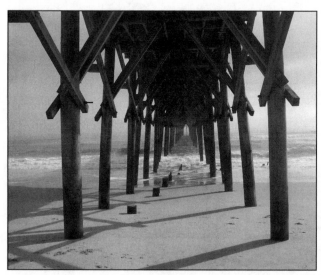

Beneath the Surf City Pier
PHOTOGRAPH BY VICKI McALLISTER

Visitors can rent kayaks from *Herrings Outdoor Sports*, located at 701 New River Drive in Surf City (28445). Call 910-328-3291 or visit www.herringsoutdoorsports. com.

Five public golf courses are located within 15 miles of Topsail Island. Call the chamber of commerce at 800-626-2780 or 910-329-4446 for a list.

Places to Stay

Though cottage and condominium rentals dominate Topsail Island's accommodations, visitors have a few other options as well.

Resorts, Hotels, and Motels

Sea Vista Motel. Expensive/Moderate. 1521 Ocean Boulevard in Topsail Beach, 28445 (800-SEA-VISTA or 910-328-2171; www.seavistamotel.com). Located on the ocean at the southern end of N.C. 50, Sea Vista offers 33 oceanfront rooms, efficiencies, and mini efficiencies. Pets are allowed for a surcharge.

Breezeway Motel. Moderate. 636 Channel Boulevard in Topsail Beach, 28445 (800-548-4694 or 910-328-7751; www.breezewaymotel.com). Located on Topsail Sound, Breezeway offers spacious rooms, a pool, balconies, boat docks, a fishing pier, and a waterfront restaurant.

Inns and Bed-and-Breakfasts

The Pink Palace Bed-and-Breakfast. Expensive/Moderate. 1222 South Shore Road in Surf City, 28445 (910-328-5114). This is the only oceanfront bed-and-breakfast on Topsail Island. Each suite has access to a screened porch and three open-air decks. The Pink Palace offers all the amenities, including a hot tub. Weekly rentals are available in summer. The Pink Palace returns to a bed-and-breakfast in mid-August.

Places to Eat

Indigo Marsh. Expensive. 602-B Roland Avenue in Surf City, 28445 (910-328-2580; www.indigomarsh.com). Guests here enjoy chophouse-style steaks and creatively prepared fresh local seafood whether dining inside or taking in the view of the Intracoastal Waterway from the back deck. Homemade breads and pastries are also available. Dinner is served Monday through Saturday. Reservations are recommended.

The Breezeway Restaurant. Moderate. 634 Channel Boulevard in Topsail Beach, 28445 (910-328-4302). The Breezeway enjoys a solid reputation for its fresh seafood and steaks. In business since 1949, it offers waterfront dining. Dinner is served daily.

Mollie's Restaurant. Moderate/Inexpensive. 107 North Shore Drive in Surf City, 28445 (910-328-0505; www.molliesrestaurant.com). This friendly restaurant serves breakfast, lunch, and dinner daily. Off-season hours may vary. Its specialties include seafood, steaks, pasta dishes, salads, and sandwiches.

Nearby

Sneads Ferry is a busy fishing community located on the New River near the northern tip of Topsail Island on N.C. 172. Every August since 1971, the *Sneads Ferry Shrimp Festival* has attracted seafood lovers from all over. Proceeds from the festival have enabled the town to construct the Shrimp Festival Community Building and acquire a 14-acre park. For information, call 910-327-3335 or visit www.sneadsferrynorthcarolina.com.

If you're looking for a bite to eat in Sneads Ferry, try the *Riverview Café*, located at Fulcher's Landing at 119 Hall Point Road (28460). The Riverview has been offering fresh local seafood since 1946. For information, call 910-327-2011.

Mayberry by the Sea

Excerpted from *Topsail Island: Mayberry by the Sea*
by Ray McAllister

Topsail Island is a small barrier island off the North Carolina coast south of the Outer Banks and north of Wilmington and Wrightsville Beach. The map shows Topsail—pronounced "TOP-sul" by those who have been here more than once—to be pencil thin. Indeed, it is not much more. There are only 15 square miles on this 26-mile-long strip of sand. The width is rarely much more than a half-mile and sometimes only 200 yards, providing a splendor of almost incomprehensible logistics: morning sunrises over water followed, nearby, by evening sunsets over water. Did the Great Island Creator make a mistake? Was Topsail supposed to get both?

The map also shows Topsail divided among three towns: Topsail Beach at the south, Surf City in the middle, and the newcomer, North Topsail Beach, above them. The relative few residents who live on the island year-round will tell you the three are very much distinctive, that sometimes the towns are at odds politically, one town snubbing another that seeks cooperation, though the snubs seem to be lessening, and that—here their voices drop almost to a whisper—somehow folks who live in the other two towns are, well, different. It is true, they insist, but they say it with a smile, as if describing a slightly daft aunt or a cousin you just can't help loving anyway.

Visitors do not see the distinctions among the towns—not at first, anyway—nor do they necessarily care. The island is intoxicating. So what does it matter? Everyone is friendly.

Small shop owners—and there are no other kind on Topsail—are supposed to be friendly. But why the requirement that the man you meet walking the other way will not only say hello but will stop to say it? Who has decreed that the woman in the grocery store, whether one of the tiny mom-and-pops on the island or a supermarket just off, will ask how you're doing as if she cares how you are doing?

Who does that anymore?

People search for a way to describe the allure of Topsail. Allan Libby, director of the island's chamber of commerce, calls it simply "The Magic." The Magic, he says, is whatever draws a person to the island. The Magic is different things to different people.

Doug Medlin, who moved with his family to Surf City in 1952, when the number of island families could be counted on one hand, or surely on two, has a ready answer. "I think the quaint family atmosphere," he says. "When you think of Myrtle Beach, you think of all the shows, the rides. This is just a great family atmosphere."

Family is a part of it, to be sure. Quaintness is a part of it, too.

But isn't it odd that so many describe what Topsail has by enumerating what it doesn't have?

The island is always spoken about in those terms. It has a family atmosphere, someone will tell you. Even teenagers like the island, they will say—and then immediately launch into a laundry list of the things a teen would want that the island does *not* have. There is no shopping mall, of course, or anything like it. The nearest movie theater, well, that's the better part of an hour away. And so forth.

What sort of place is this?

"It's like you're back in time, this island is," says Jeffrey Stewart Price, who moved to Topsail Beach to take over the Beach Shop and Grill before the summer of 2002. "It's not a Myrtle Beach. It's not commercialized. People like that. It's for families." Even at the height of the season, the island is not what any new arrivals would call crowded.

The island does seem caught in a time warp, not yet overtaken by the commercial development of Virginia Beach, Nags Head, Wrightsville Beach, or Myrtle Beach. Nor is it likely to be. Topsail now is what those resorts were decades ago, even a half-century ago, or perhaps what we only thought they once were. Call it "the Little Island That Time Forgot." Many do. The moniker is intended as more endearing than demeaning. Topsail has a small-town feel of beach shops and cafés, a slow pace, and residents who know one another, as their parents and grandparents knew one another. Throw in the sea breezes, dunes, sea oats, and sea gulls and you have a Mayberry by the Sea. More than one smitten visitor has called it that. You can't help feeling that the residents of the fictional North Carolina town in

The Andy Griffith Show would recognize these islanders. Is it coincidence that Griffith himself has spent much of his life on the North Carolina coast, even keeping a home on Figure Eight Island, just south of Topsail?

Even the Topsail Island police departments, rarely troubled by serious crime, specialize in community relations, just as in the fictional town of . . . well, you know.

That step back in time is part of The Magic. So, too, is the ocean setting. The surf, the breeze, the mist. And the fishing. The surfing. The diving and even nearby parasailing, for those inclined. And no doubt the isolation factors in. You can't get here from there, they say. Sometimes, it seems you can't get here from anywhere, so maybe the difficulty of the journey is part of what makes the destination more rewarding.

But who is in a hurry?

No one, at least not for very long.

The main road down the narrow island—in places, there is room for only one road—rarely carries a speed limit of more than 45 miles an hour; often it is 35 and sometimes 25. And yet the speed limit seems too high. Most drivers go 10 miles an hour under the limit. Who goes 10 miles an hour *under* anymore? "Slow Down," reads one island bumper sticker. "This Ain't the Mainland." Indeed. Vacationers invariably find themselves riding the bumpers of the cars in front when they arrive. By the end of the week, they are the ones slowing down the next week's arrivals.

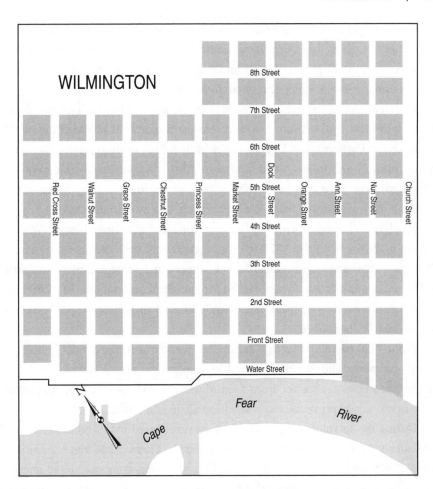

Wilmington

Until the turn of the 20th century, Wilmington was North Carolina's largest city. Today, it remains one of its most vibrant and interesting.

Thanks to the city's preservation efforts, a large section of downtown spreading out from the banks of the Cape Fear River is recorded on the National Register of Historic Places. Down along the river's edge are Riverfront Park and Riverwalk, a lovely pedestrian path that runs alongside Water Street, a mostly brick-and-cobblestone lane lined with antique lamps. Also along the water are cozy specialty shops and restaurants at Chandler's Wharf and the Cotton Exchange. Many of the city's tour operators are based at the foot of Water Street.

Wilmington's historic and cultural attractions include an array of stunning colonial- and antebellum-era homes, such as the Burgwin-Wright House and Bellamy Mansion, as well as splendid museums like the Louise Wells Cameron Museum of Art and the Cape Fear Museum. Boasting more than 200 houses of worship, Wilmington is a showcase of church architecture.

The city's charm has not been lost to popular culture. Over the past two decades, Wilmington has evolved into the third-busiest movie mill in the country. What began in 1983 when Dino DeLaurentiis built a $1.5 million studio has evolved into a multimillion-dollar industry. Star-spotting is a favorite pastime here. Some Wilmingtonians have caught the acting bug, appearing as extras in the 400-plus films and television shows that have been shot in and around the city.

Much of Wilmington's appeal lies in its long and illustrious history. White settlement in the area came in 1725 at Brunswick Town, south of the city. Founded in 1732, the city was originally called New Liverpool and subsequently New Carthage and Newton before it was finally named for Spencer Compton, earl of Wilmington. Wilmington proved to be more strategically located than Brunswick Town, which was ultimately abandoned.

From 1720 to 1870, North Carolina led the world in the production of naval stores—tar, pitch, and turpentine—and Wilmington was the primary export center. Its protected position upriver from the turbulent storms and marauding pirates of the Atlantic would prove the city's salvation again and again.

During the Revolutionary War, the area was spared major bloodshed save for the battle at Moores Creek Bridge, 20 miles north. There, 1,060 clever patriots outwitted 1,600 loyalists by tricking them into attacking their evacuated camps by leaving the fires burning. When the Tories attempted to cross the bridge in pursuit, they discovered that only two logs remained—two logs slathered with grease. On April 12, 1781, Lord Cornwallis and company occupied the city following their costly victory at Guilford Courthouse near Greensboro. The troops reconnoitered here for two weeks before their fateful march to Yorktown, Virginia.

Wilmington grew slowly for the next 50 years, until the Wilmington and Weldon Railroad arrived in 1840. By 1850, Wilmington was the largest city in the state. Over the decade that followed, many of its most impressive buildings—including Thalian Hall, the Zebulon Latimer House, and Bellamy Mansion—were constructed.

In the latter stages of the Civil War, the city became the lifeline of the Confederacy before the fall of Fort Fisher, which overlooks the mouth of the Cape Fear River to the south. Under the fort's protection, stealthy and daring blockade runners played cat and mouse with the formidable Union navy to provide much-needed supplies to the Confederates and to maintain the city's economy. It took the largest war fleet ever assembled to bring down the fort on January 15, 1865. Six months later, Lee surrendered at Appomattox.

After the war, Wilmington endured a brief depression until the export of cotton helped the economy rebound. Expansion continued into the 20th century. During World Wars I and II, Wilmington flourished as a shipbuilder. In 1952, the North Carolina Ports Authority opened here. Economic decline followed in 1960 when the Atlantic Coast Line Railroad, one of the area's chief employers, moved its corporate headquarters. About the same time, recognition of the city's treasure trove of historic architecture spurred a preservation movement. In 1974, much of Wilmington's downtown was recorded on the National Register.

Today, the population of Wilmington is 100,000 and growing. Also growing more numerous are the golf and other resort communities that lure thousands of retirees to the area to bask in its temperate climate and enjoy the dynamic cultural scene. Those who come to stay and visitors here for the historic sites can testify that another heyday has arrived in Wilmington.

JUST THE FACTS

Wilmington can be reached via Interstate 40 and U.S. 421 from the northwest, U.S. 74/76 from the west, and U.S. 17 from the south.

Wilmington International Airport is served by US Airways, United Express, and A.S.A. Atlantic Southeast, the Delta connection. Call 910-341-4125 for information.

The Trailways bus station is at 201 Harnett Street (28401); call 910-762-6073. The Wilmington Transit Authority provides local bus service; call 910-343-0106.

The Wilmington/Cape Fear Coast Convention and Visitors Bureau is located in the 19th-century courthouse at 24 North Third Street (28401); for information, call 800-222-4757 or 910-341-4030 or visit www.cape-fear.nc.us. The Riverfront Information Booth, at the foot of Market and Water streets, also provides information; its hours vary seasonally.

The local newspaper is the *Wilmington Star News*, the state's oldest daily. Its entertainment guide, *Currents*, and the free weekly newspaper *Encore* provide up-to-date event listings.

Things to Do

Historic Places, Gardens, and Tours

Sightseeing in Wilmington is a treat, especially in the spring and autumn. Although its historic district is one of the largest in the country—over 200 blocks—many of the most interesting sites are concentrated near the Cape Fear River and can easily be seen on foot. However, if you'd prefer a nostalgic ride aboard a horse-drawn carriage, a trolley, or a riverboat, opportunities abound.

For a self-guided walking tour, pick up a *Cape Fear Coast Attractions Guide Map* from the Wilmington/Cape Fear Coast Convention and Visitors Bureau. Another option is a self-guided driving tour that takes about two hours, including the ferry ride from Fort Fisher to Southport. Optional sites along the way include the Battleship *North Carolina*, Orton Plantation, Brunswick Town, Southport, Fort Fisher, and the North Carolina Aquarium at Fort Fisher.

Engaging guides lead *Wilmington Adventure Walking Tours* from the corner of Market and Water streets at the Cape Fear River. Tours are offered daily April through October from 10 A.M. to 2 P.M. A fee is charged. Call 910-763-1785.

Horse-Drawn Carriage and Trolley Tours, based at Market and Water streets, offers narrated tours between 10 A.M. and 10 P.M. daily from April to October and between 11 A.M. and 4 P.M. Sunday through Thursday from November to March. A fee is charged. Call 910-251-8889 or visit www.horsedrawntours.com.

Wilmington Trolley Company, based at Dock and Water streets, offers an eight-mile, 45-minute open-air narrated trolley tour daily from June to August. For the off-season schedule, call 910-763-4483 or visit www.wilmingtontrolley.com. The tour includes mansions, homes, museums, historic sites, movie locations, and more. A fee is charged.

Cape Fear River Boats conducts sightseeing and dinner dance cruises and offers water-taxi service to the Battleship *North Carolina*. A fee is charged. Call 800-676-0162 or 910-343-1611 or visit www.cfrboats.com.

The 67 acres of *Airlie Gardens*, at 300 Airlie Road (28403), are what remain of a vast estate that dates back to 1886, when Pembroke and Sarah Jones bought the property and commissioned German landscape architect Rudolph Topel to reshape Airlie House, the 155 acres along Airlie Road, and the lodge at Pembroke Park, with its 1,300-acre hunting preserve. The Joneses' parties were legendary, as they were the

The 450-year-old Airlie Oak at Airlie Gardens
PHOTOGRAPH BY ANGELA HARWOOD

The Bottle House, a tribute to artist Minnie Evans at Airlie Gardens
PHOTOGRAPH BY ANGELA HARWOOD

toast of New York and the Newport society set.

The gardens and lakes date to 1901. Over a half-million azaleas and 5,000 camellias were added in the 1920s. Visitors can set their own pace in the self-guided walking tour, stand in the shade of the 450-year-old Airlie live oak, and enjoy the natural maritime forest of live oaks, pines, cedars, hollies, wax myrtles, and unusual hardy tropicals. Golf-cart tours are available for those who have difficulty walking. This unique environment is one of the last major undeveloped tracts of land along the Bradley Creek watershed.

Airlie Gardens is also an important African-American heritage site. Be sure to visit the Minnie Evans Sculpture Garden and Bottle House, a tribute to Evans's "outsider" art. Local artists and area schoolchildren have paid homage to Evans by interpreting her work through metal sculptures, mosaics, and ceramics.

The gardens are open daily from 9 A.M. to 5 P.M. from late March through December; extended hours are offered during peak azalea season and special events. The gardens are closed on Sunday during winter. An admission fee is charged. For more information, call 910-798-7700 or visit www.airliegardens.org.

At the ***New Hanover County Arboretum***, located at 6206 Oleander Drive (28403), visitors can explore seven acres containing over 4,000 species of native plants. A children's cottage, a Japanese teahouse, a gazebo, the Ability Garden, and various changing displays are open for touring seven days a week from sunup to sundown. Admission is free. For more information, call 910-798-7670 or visit www.gardeningnhc.org.

Thalian Hall, at 310 Chestnut Street (28401), is a historic 1858 Italianate theater designed by John M. Trimble, whose credits include the New York Opera House.

In 1788, the Thalian Association, the oldest amateur theatrical group in the United States, was formed in Wilmington. At the beginning of the 19th century, the group used an auditorium where Thalian Hall now stands. By the time the city acquired that land and announced plans for a new city hall, the Thalians were so entrenched in the cultural scene that citizens demanded the new building also house a theater for the players. Among the luminaries who performed or lectured here were

New Hanover County Arboretum
COURTESY OF WILMINGTON/CAPE FEAR COAST CONVENTION AND VISITORS BUREAU

Oscar Wilde, Marian Anderson, Charles Dickens, and William Jennings Bryan.

Today, Thalian Hall is a multiuse facility that houses city hall and Thalian Hall Center for the Performing Arts, Inc. Self-guided tours are available for a fee Monday through Friday from noon to 6 P.M. and Saturday from 2 P.M. to 5 P.M. Guided tours are offered by appointment; call 910-343-3660 or visit www.thalianhall.com. To reach the box office, call 800-523-2820 or 910-343-3664.

Burgwin-Wright Museum House and Gardens is located at 224 Market Street (28401). The home was built in 1770 on a foundation of stone from an old jail. The lovely Georgian-style structure features 18th- and early-19th-century furnishings and is surrounded by three gardens and an orchard. Visitors can take a peek into the 18th-century dungeon. Behind the house is a freestanding building that houses the kitchen and a craft room. Open-hearth cooking demonstrations are presented the second Saturday of each month. The house is open for tours Tuesday through Saturday from 10 A.M. to 4 P.M. An admission fee is charged. For information, call 910-762-0570 or visit www.geocities.com/picketfence/garden/4354.

The *Latimer House Museum*, at 126 South Third Street (28401), was built in 1852 for a prosperous merchant who had migrated to Wilmington from Connecticut in the 1830s. An elegant four-story Italianate house, it is a wonderful example of the

Burgwin-Wright Museum House and Gardens
COURTESY OF WILMINGTON/CAPE FEAR COAST CONVENTION AND VISITORS BUREAU

ornate style so popular in the city at that time. It serves as the headquarters of the Lower Cape Fear Historical Society, which purchased the house and its furnishings from the Latimer family in 1963. Family portraits still adorn the walls. Be sure to view the archives, the library, the Victorian garden, and the servants' quarters. The house is open Monday through Friday from 10 A.M. to 4 P.M. and Saturday from noon to 5 P.M. Two-hour "Walk and Talk" tours are given Wednesday and Saturday at 10 A.M. An admission fee is charged. For more information, call 910-762-0492 or visit www.latimerhouse.org.

Bellamy Mansion, at 503 Market Street (28401), is a magnificent home constructed in 1859 by free black and slave artisans. Designed by James F. Post, it was the residence of Dr. John D. Bellamy and family, who moved in on the eve of the Civil War. Fear of the Union army and a yellow-fever epidemic forced the Bellamys to flee until after the war. The house remained in the family until 1946, when the last surviving daughter, Ellen Bellamy, died. Since then, it has been under the stewardship of Preservation North Carolina. The restored mansion and Victorian gardens are open for tours. The carriage house serves as the visitor center. Plans are under way for restoration of the slave quarters. The home is open Tuesday through Saturday from 10 A.M. to 5 P.M. and Sunday from 1 P.M. to 5 P.M. Admission is charged. For more information, call 910-251-3700 or visit www.bellamymansion.org.

Bellamy Mansion and Kenan Fountain
PHOTOGRAPH BY LYNN SELDON, WILMINGTON/CAPE FEAR COAST CONVENTION AND VISITORS BUREAU

Battleship *North Carolina*
COURTESY OF BATTLESHIP *NORTH CAROLINA*

The **Battleship *North Carolina***, moored across the Cape Fear River at Eagles Island (28401), was arguably the mightiest sea fighter in World War II. In 1941, as the ship was undergoing sea trials, it passed in and out of New York Harbor so frequently that journalist Walter Winchell dubbed it "the Show Boat," a tribute to the Edna Ferber novel and subsequent musical. During the war, it earned 15 battle stars and participated in every major offensive in the Pacific. Decommissioned in 1960, the battleship was relegated to the mothball fleet until North Carolina's citizens—most notably its schoolchildren—raised the money to bring it to the state.

The self-guided tour of the ship takes about two hours. The battleship's visitor center offers exhibits and an orientation film that illustrate the boat's history. It also has bathrooms, a snack bar, and a picnic area. The site is open daily from 8 A.M. to 8 P.M. Admission is charged. To reach the ship, drive over the Cape Fear Memorial Bridge from Wilmington or take a water taxi from the bottom of Market Street. For more information, call 910-251-5797 or visit www.battleshipnc.com.

Oakdale Cemetery is a special place often overlooked by visitors. Canopied by tremendous live oak trees, it is a garden oasis whose stone monuments chronicle the lives of Wilmington's citizenry. It is located on 15th Street (28401) off Market Street. The cemetery gates are open 365 days a year from 8 A.M. to 5 P.M. For more information, call 910-762-5682 or visit www.oakdalecemetery.org.

Museums and Science Centers

The *Cape Fear Museum*, at 814 Market Street (28401), features exhibits and photographs tracing Wilmington's history, science, and culture. It includes a model of 1863 Wilmington, a diorama of the Battle of Fort Fisher, and the Michael Jordan Discovery Gallery, an interactive natural-history exhibit designed for children. Kids will also marvel at the reproduction of a giant ground sloth skeleton. From Memorial Day to Labor Day, the museum is open Monday through Saturday from 9 A.M. to 5 P.M. and Sunday from 1 P.M. to 5 P.M.; it is closed on Monday the rest of the year. Admission is charged. Call 910-798-4350 or visit www.capefearmuseum.com.

The *Cape Fear Serpentarium*, at 20 Orange Street (28401), boasts the largest collection of venomous snakes in the world. From March to November, it is open weekdays from 11 A.M. to 5 P.M. and weekends from 11 A.M. to 6 P.M. Winter hours vary. Admission is charged. Call 910-762-1669 or visit www.capefearserpentarium.com for information.

The *Louise Wells Cameron Art Museum*, at 3201 South 17th Street (28412), occupies an impressive 42,000-square-foot structure designed by noted architect Charles Gwathmey. It has a fine collection of North Carolina and American art from the 18th century to the present. African-American artists Minnie Evans and Romare Bearden are represented, and there is a gallery dedicated to the work of Claude Howell. Visitors also enjoy the color prints by Mary Cassatt, the glass cases filled with historic and contemporary North Carolina pottery, and the Bruce B. Cameron Decoy Collection. Civil War enthusiasts will be interested in the recently restored Confederate defense mounds from the Battle of Forks Road, which are located on the museum's 10-acre campus.

The museum's café serves fresh salads, sandwiches, and light entrées such as crab cakes. The gift shop sells upscale collectibles and other art-related items. The museum is open Tuesday through Friday from 11 A.M. to 2 P.M. and

Louise Wells Cameron Art Museum sculpture court
COURTESY OF LOUISE WELLS CAMERON ART MUSEUM,
WILMINGTON/CAPE FEAR COAST CONVENTION AND VISITORS BUREAU

Saturday and Sunday from 11 A.M. to 5 P.M. Admission is charged except on the first Sunday of each month. For more information, call 910-395-5999 or visit www.CameronArtMuseum.com.

The *Wilmington Railroad Museum* is located at the corner of Water and Red Cross streets at 505 Nutt Street (28401) in downtown Wilmington. In 1840, the Wilmington and Weldon Railroad was the longest continuous rail line in the world, measuring 161 miles. Several years later, it merged with other railways to form the Atlantic Coast Line Railroad, one of the city's largest employers until its move to Jacksonville, Florida, in 1960. The museum is dedicated to preserving the railroad history of the Southeast, the Atlantic Coast Line in particular. Its gift shop stocks T-shirts, books, and railroad memorabilia. From April 1 to September 30, the museum is open Monday to Saturday from 10 A.M. to 5 P.M. and Sunday from 1 P.M. to 5 P.M.; the rest of the year, it is open Monday to Saturday from 10 A.M. to 4 P.M. Admission is charged. Call 910-763-2634 or visit www.wilmingtonrailroadmuseum.org.

The *Children's Museum of Wilmington*, located at 116 Orange Street (28401) at the corner of Second Street downtown, is a place where kids can learn about geography, discover the properties of sand, build bridges made of Legos, and create their own puppet shows. Admission is charged. From Memorial Day through Labor Day, the museum is open Monday to Saturday from 10 A.M. to 5 P.M. and Sunday from 1 P.M. to 5 P.M. The rest of the year, it is open Tuesday to Saturday from 9 A.M. to

5 P.M. and Sunday from 1 P.M. to 5 P.M. For more information, call 910-254-3534 or visit www.playwilmington.org.

Cultural Offerings

Opera House Theatre Company, at 2011 Carolina Beach Road (28401), is a non-profit organization that presents professional productions featuring guest artists. Call 910-762-4234 or visit www.operahousetheatrecompany.net for more information.

Thalian Hall Center for the Performing Arts hosts a film series and excellent local theater productions. For box office information, call 800-523-2820 or 910-343-3664 or visit www.thalianhall.com.

Students and locals give outstanding performances at *Kenan Auditorium* on the campus of the University of North Carolina at Wilmington (28403). For information, call 800-732-3643 or 910-962-3500 or visit www.uncwil.edu/kenan.

Special Shopping

Thanks to its long history and its continuing appeal to artistic spirits, Wilmington has antique shops and art galleries galore. You can pick up copies of *A Guide to Greater Wilmington Antique Shops* and *Gallery Guide* at the Riverfront Information Booth.

To meet artists and craftspeople, go to the *Old Wilmington City Market* on South Water Street, where you'll find hand-woven baskets, handmade soaps, eclectic gift shops, and even a masseuse.

The *Cotton Exchange*, located in the 300 block of Front Street, houses a variety of specialty shops and restaurants in several turn-of-the-20th-century buildings, many of which were cotton warehouses. Most of the shops are open Monday through Saturday from 10 A.M. to 5:30 P.M. and Sunday from noon to 4 P.M. Visit www.shopcottonexchange.com for more information.

Chandler's Wharf is located on the waterfront at the corner of Water and Ann streets. Its boutiques and restaurants offer a wide range of choices.

Recreation

Greenfield Park & Gardens, located at 1510 South Third Street (28401), features a 150-acre cypress-studded lake, paddleboats, and a playground. A path for walking or biking winds around the park, whose 20 acres of gardens are a showplace during the North Carolina Azalea Festival. A five-mile scenic drive circles the 250-acre city park. Tours are offered on Saturday and Sunday at 11 A.M. and 1 P.M. from May through August. Reservations are required for tours, and a fee is charged. In summer, the amphitheater is filled with music. Call 910-341-7852.

Some 39 golf clubs dot the Cape Fear coast, a number that is growing annually. Contact the Wilmington/Cape Fear Coast Convention and Visitors Bureau to ask

Cotton Exchange shops
COURTESY OF WILMINGTON/CAPE FEAR COAST CONVENTION AND VISITORS BUREAU

Horse-drawn carriage at Chandler's Wharf
COURTESY OF WILMINGTON/CAPE FEAR COAST CONVENTION AND VISITORS BUREAU

for a free *Area Golf Guide*. Some notable course designers who have worked in the area include George Cobb, Willard Byrd, Tom Fazio, and Dan Maples.

Seasonal Events

The *North Carolina Azalea Festival* lures thousands of visitors to Wilmington each April, just when the city is looking its best. Guests enjoy the annual corona-tion of Queen Azalea, a variety show, a parade, a street fair, a circus, and a concert. The main attraction, of course, is the gardens bursting with dogwood trees and the South's signature azaleas. Tickets for the Azalea Garden Tour and the Azalea Home Tour can be purchased in advance or at the garden sites. Call 910-794-4650 or visit www.ncazaleafestival.org.

The *Cape Fear Blues Festival* is a three-day draw for blues lovers each July. Call 910-350-8822 or visit www.CapeFearBlues.org.

Riverfest is held each October in Riverfront Park. Boat races, a raft regatta, mu-sic, dancing, and booths offering arts, crafts, and deep-fried foods attract visitors and locals alike to the banks of the Cape Fear River. Call 910-452-6862 or visit www. wilmingtonriverfest.com.

Places to Stay

Resorts, Hotels, and Motels

Hilton Wilmington Riverside. Deluxe. 301 North Water Street, 28401 (910-763-5900; www.wilmingtonhilton.com). Located downtown, the Hilton has a com-manding view of the river. It offers an outdoor pool, an outdoor whirlpool, exercise facilities, two ballrooms, a gift shop, a restaurant and lounge, and a boat dock for those arriving by water. Children stay free with their parents.

Best Western Coastline Inn. Deluxe/Expensive. 503 Nutt Street, 28401 (800-617-7732 or 910-763-2800; www.coastlineinn.com). Though this is a standard Best West-ern hotel, its downtown location makes it worthy of note. All 53 rooms overlook the river. In-room coffee service, phones with data ports, and fax and copier service are offered. A complimentary continental breakfast is served at your door.

Inns and Bed-and-Breakfasts

The Front Street Inn. Deluxe. 215 South Front Street, 28401 (800-336-8184 or 910-762-6442; www.frontstreetinn.com). Built in 1923 and once home to the Salvation Army of the Carolinas, this great little inn has airy rooms with patios and balconies and names like the Molly Brown Suite. The place is vibrantly decorated with American art gathered from galleries, fairs, auctions, and attics. Guests can enjoy a glass of champagne in the Sol y Sombra Bar and Breakfast Room upon arrival or have a tasty breakfast there the next morning.

The Graystone Inn. Deluxe. 100 South Third Street, 28401 (888-763-4773 or 910-763-2000; www.graystoneinn.com). The elegant Graystone Inn has appeared in several films and has also played host to many talented actors and actresses who came here to make them. Originally the Bridgers Mansion, completed for Elizabeth Haywood Bridgers in 1906, the inn has been returned to its turn-of-the-20th-century grandeur. The Graystone features a spacious parlor, a baby grand piano, an elegantly set dining room, and a lovely mahogany-paneled library. Many of its rooms have fireplaces and claw-foot tubs.

The Verandas. Deluxe. 202 Nun Street, 28401 (910-251-2212; www.verandas.com). Built in 1853, The Verandas was devastated by fire in 1992. In 1995, current owners Dennis Madsen and Charles Pennington completely refurbished the home, returning it to its Italianate elegance. Each of the eight large corner guest rooms has it own luxurious bath equipped with Caswell-Massey toiletries. Guests can venture up the spiral staircase to the cupola for a panoramic view of the city.

The Worth House. Deluxe. 412 South Third Street, 28401 (800-340-8559 or 910-762-8562; www.worthhouse.com). This turreted 1893 Queen Anne–style home is located a short stroll from the river. Antiques and period art grace its seven guest rooms, some of which have fireplaces. Complimentary breakfast is served.

Blue Heaven Bed-and-Breakfast. Expensive. 517 Orange Street, 28401 (910-772-9929 or 910-471-9929; www.bbonline.com/nc/blueheaven). This lovely 1897 Victorian retains many of its original features, including seven fireplaces with mantels and some lovely stained-glass windows. All the rooms have private baths, fireplaces, phones, cable television, DVD players, and air conditioning.

Places to Eat

The restaurant scene in Wilmington is vibrant and eclectic. Many of the hot spots are located downtown within easy walking distance of the river.

Deluxe Café. Expensive. 114 Market Street, 28401 (www.deluxenc.com; 910-251-0333). The Deluxe serves delicious local seafood, premium all-natural meats, and locally grown organic produce. Try the "Lemon- and Sage-Roasted Grouper," served with a savory onion-Parmesan bread pudding. The café is open for dinner nightly and for brunch on Sunday.

Caffè Phoenix. Expensive/Moderate. 9 South Front Street, 28401 (910-343-1395; www.thecaffephoenix.com). Caffè Phoenix offers a variety of Mediterranean-influenced dishes like chicken Marsala and tuna niçoise salad. This has been a downtown favorite for years. Al fresco dining is available. Lunch and dinner are served Monday through Saturday; brunch is offered on Sunday.

Elijah's Restaurant. Expensive/Moderate. 2 Ann Street, 28401, in Chandler's Wharf (910-343-1448; www.elijahs.com). Located on the banks of the Cape Fear River, this grill serves delicious local seafood. Guests enjoy dining al fresco here and at Elijah's parent restaurant, the Pilot House. Lunch and dinner are served daily.

Pilot House Restaurant. Expensive/Moderate. 2 Ann Street, 28401, in Chandler's Wharf (910-343-0200; www.pilothouserest.com). The venerable Pilot House has been serving fresh seafood for many years. It overlooks the river and offers outdoor dining. Lunch and dinner are served daily.

Caprice Bistro. Moderate. 10 Market Street, 28401 (www.capricebistro.com; 910-815-0810). This traditional French bistro with a mirrored wall and white tablecloths offers outstanding food at a reasonable price. Dinner is served nightly; a three-course prix fixe menu is offered from Sunday to Thursday. Upstairs is a sofa bar where guests can enjoy a nightcap or a specialty martini.

Circa 1922. Moderate. 8 North Front Street, 28401 (www.circa1922.com; 910-762-1922). This is a fun tapas bar that serves Asian-style treats in addition to continental European items. It also has an extensive wine list. Dinner is served nightly.

Genki. Moderate. 4724 New Centre Drive, 28405 (910-796-8687). This Japanese restaurant and sushi bar features maki sushi, sashimi, beef curry, vegetarian entrées, and homemade sauces. Its sushi has been voted the best in the city by *Encore* magazine. It is open nightly for dinner.

Le Catalan. Moderate. 224 South Water Street, 28401 (910-815-0200; www.lecatalan.com). This French café, wine bar, and shop in downtown Wilmington offers wine by the glass or bottle, to be enjoyed as you view the Cape Fear River from Riverwalk. Note Le Catalan's custom woodwork and French café decor. Lunch and dinner are served Tuesday to Sunday from May through August and Tuesday to Saturday the rest of the year.

K38 Baja Grill. Moderate/Inexpensive. 5410 Oleander Drive, 28403 (910-395-6040), and 8211 Market Street, 28405 (910-686-8211). The flavors of the Southwest and the Pacific Rim are captured in the "Baja Fresh" cuisine at K38's two Wilmington locations. Try the delicious "Takoshimi" or the shrimp and goat cheese quesadilla. In fact, try anything on the menu—you can't go wrong. Lunch and dinner are served daily. For information, visit www.k38baja.com.

Nikki's Fresh Gourmet. Moderate/Inexpensive. 16 South Front Street, 28401 (910-772-9151). Vegetarians will delight at the variety of vegetable wraps and tasty tofu offerings at Nikki's, which serves great sushi spring rolls, too. The choices for carnivores include the spicy Asian chicken salad and even a Philly cheese steak. Lunch is served Monday through Saturday and dinner Thursday through Saturday.

Flaming Amy's Burrito Barn. Inexpensive. 4002 Oleander Drive, 28403 (910-799-2919; www.flamingamysburritobarn.com). This is not your Old El Paso kind of place. Although Amy's signature burrito is pretty standard, some of the other choices—like the "Thai Me Up," the "Wok on the Beach," and the "Big Jerk"—let you know what you're in for. Lunch and dinner are served daily.

Nearby

Poplar Grove Historic Plantation is located nine miles north of Wilmington on U.S. 17 at Scotts Hill (28411). James Foy, Jr., purchased the estate from Joseph Mumford in 1795. Its 628-acre farm produced peas, corn, and beans and held 64 slaves. In 1849, the manor house was destroyed by fire. It was rebuilt on its present site in 1850. Relying on peanuts as its staple crop, Poplar Grove remained a focal point of the community under the ownership of the Foy family until its sale in 1971. Renovated and opened to the public in 1980, the estate now serves as a museum complex consisting of the house, its outbuildings, and 16 acres of grounds. A host of craftspeople demonstrate traditional skills such as weaving, spinning, basket making, and blacksmithing. The plantation is open Monday through Saturday from 9 A.M. to 5 P.M. and Sunday from noon to 5 P.M. A fee is charged. For more information, call 910-686-9518 or visit www.poplargrove.com.

On the Cape Fear River 18 miles south of Wilmington is *Orton Plantation Gardens*, located off U.S. 133 at 9149 Orton Road SE in Winnabow (28479). Orton was the rice-plantation home of Roger Moore, who came in 1725 from South Carolina and founded the town of Brunswick with his brothers. Roger Moore's son, George Moore, was one of the leaders of the first armed resistance to British rule in the colonies. The tombs of Roger Moore and members of his family are located in the gardens. After the fall of the Confederate stronghold of Fort Fisher in 1865, Orton was occupied by Union troops and used as a hospital, sparing it the fate of many homes in the South. The beautiful gardens were the inspiration of Luola Murchison Sprunt and her husband, James, who in 1910 inherited the property and began constructing terraces overlooking the river and planting avenues of live oak trees. In 1916, Dr. Sprunt erected the quaint Luola's Chapel as a memorial to his wife. The gardens were greatly expanded by the Sprunts' son and daughter-in-law under the supervision of landscape architect Robert Swann Sturtevant.

The impressive house is not open for tours. A tour of the gardens takes about an hour, but many choose to stretch a visit into a full morning or afternoon. The gardens are open daily from 8 A.M. to 6 P.M. from March to August and from 10 A.M. to 5 P.M. from September to November. Admission is charged. For more information, call 910-371-6851 or visit www.ortongardens.com.

Duplin Winery is located 40 miles north of Wilmington at 505 North Sycamore

Orton Plantation
PHOTOGRAPH BY ANGELA HARWOOD

Street/U.S. 117 in Rose Hill (28458). The oldest winery in North Carolina, it follows traditional recipes and methods passed down from the Swiss and German immigrants who settled this part of North Carolina in the 1700s.

Free tastings of Duplin's award-winning scuppernong and muscadine wines are offered. Production tours are available; a fee is charged for custom tours. The winery is open from 9 A.M. to 6 P.M. Monday, Wednesday, and Saturday and from 9 A.M. to 9 P.M. Thursday and Friday. It is closed on major holidays. *The Bistro Restaurant*, located on the grounds, is open for lunch from Monday through Saturday and for dinner on Thursday and Friday. Dinner comes with a show. The winery also has a gift shop and museum. For more information, call 800-774-9634 or visit www.duplinwinery.com.

Wrightsville Beach

Wrightsville Beach consists of two islands: the inland Harbor Island, connected to the mainland by a drawbridge, and outlying Wrightsville Beach, a four-mile barrier island located across Banks Channel. In recent years, resort and golf communities here have become permanent homes for retirees and others drawn to Wrightsville Beach's beauty and climate. Year-round residents number about 3,200, but when summer rolls around, the number explodes to approximately 25,000. Although Wrightsville Beach is heavily developed, it is still an exquisite destination. If you

Wrightsville Beach aerial view
COURTESY OF WILMINGTON/CAPE FEAR COAST CONVENTION AND VISITORS BUREAU

don't mind the crowds, head here in the summer. If you do, wait until the off-season, when you can share this bit of coastal paradise with the few who call it home.

Wrightsville Beach is one of the oldest resorts in North Carolina. "The Banks," as the community was originally known, was developed in 1853 by a group of enterprising businessmen who erected a clubhouse they called the Carolina Yacht Club. The club remains one of the oldest of its kind in the country. In 1888, the Wilmington Sea Coast Railway accessed Harbor Island. Shortly thereafter, two bathhouses and a restaurant were built, establishing the island as a resort. After the place was advertised as Ocean View for a time, Wrightsville Beach became the official name in 1900.

In 1905, electric trolleys began to bring passengers to Wrightsville Beach, ushering in its most romantic period. Hoping to entice Wilmingtonians and others to ride the trolleys out to the island, the Tidewater Power Company built several attractions, the foremost of which was the now-legendary Lumina Pavilion, so called for the thousands of incandescent lights that made it sparkle. In the daytime, the Lumina provided bathers with amusement options including bowling alleys, snack bars, and slot machines. In the evening, it shone so brightly that it served as an aid to mariners. Wilmingtonians and visitors from all over the South danced the nights away to the music of Tommy Dorsey, Guy Lombardo, Cab Calloway, and Louis Armstrong in the Lumina's grand ballroom. Outside, silent pictures projected on a large movie screen entertained people on the beach. Sadly, the Lumina fell to the wrecking ball in 1973. But its legend lives on in memory and lore.

Like Pleasure Island and the Brunswick County beaches, Wrightsville Beach was practically demolished by Hurricane Hazel in 1954. Few buildings that stood before Hazel remain today. Luckily, one of them is the 1907 Myers Cottage, which houses Wrightsville Beach's small but alluring museum. Other attractions here include world-class fishing, great shopping, fine dining, and, of course, the seashore and all its pleasures.

JUST THE FACTS

Wrightsville Beach is about 10 miles east of Wilmington on U.S. 74/76. A small drawbridge separates the island from the mainland.

Air service is available through Wilmington International Airport; call 910-341-4333.

A good source of information about the area is the Wilmington/Cape Fear Coast Convention and Visitors Bureau, at 24 North Third Street in Wilmington (28401); call 800-222-4757 or 910-341-4030 or visit www.cape-fear.nc.us. To contact the Wrightsville Beach Chamber of Commerce, call 800-232-2469 or visit www.wrightsville.com.

The local newspaper is the *Wilmington Star News*. Its entertainment guide, *Currents*, and the free weekly newspaper *Encore* provide event listings.

Things to Do

Museums and Science Centers

The ***Wrightsville Beach Museum of History*** is housed in the island's second-oldest cottage, Myers Cottage, which dates to about 1907. In addition to a collection of artifacts and archival photographs, the museum has a scale model of Wrightsville Beach as it looked around that same year. The museum also hosts traveling exhibits.

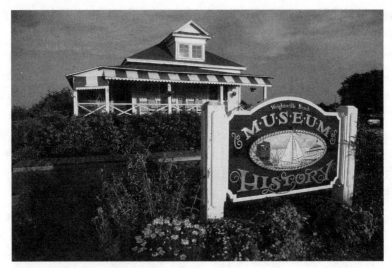

Wrightsville Beach Museum of History
COURTESY OF WILMINGTON/CAPE FEAR COAST CONVENTION AND VISITORS BUREAU

Located at 303 West Salisbury Street (28480), it is open from 10 A.M. to 4 P.M. Tuesday through Friday, from noon to 5 P.M. on Saturday, and from 1 P.M. to 5 P.M. on Sunday. A modest admission fee is charged. For information, call 910-256-2569 or visit www.WBMuseum.com.

Special Shopping

Roberts Market, at 32 North Lumina Avenue (28480), has been providing beach residents and visitors with the necessities since 1919. Call 910-256-2641.

Recreation

This area has one of the largest recreational fishing fleets north of Florida. Numerous charter boats and head boats are available for hire. For information, call 800-232-2469 or visit www.wrightsville.com.

The landmark *Johnny Mercer's Pier* is back in business. Devastated by Hurricanes Bertha and Fran in 1996, the pier has been completely rebuilt and is the only

Johnny Mercer's Pier
COURTESY OF WILMINGTON/CAPE FEAR COAST CONVENTION AND VISITORS BUREAU

all-concrete, steel-reinforced fishing pier in North Carolina. Open 24 hours a day, it offers a snack bar, a game area, and bathrooms. A small fee is charged to walk on the pier and a larger one to fish. Rods are available for rent. Call 910-256-2743.

Wrightsville Beach Park has 13 acres of tennis courts, basketball courts, softball fields, football fields, soccer fields, sand volleyball courts, playground equipment, and fitness trails. It is located in the middle of Harbor Island.

The Loop is a popular 2.5-mile path that runs from downtown to Wrightsville Beach Park. If you're tired of running on the sand, this is an ideal morning outing, as long as you don't mind sharing the path with others walking, jogging, biking, and skating.

Seasonal Events

King mackerel is indeed king around here. The *Wrightsville Beach King Mackerel Tournament* is held in September. For information, call the North Carolina Marine Fisheries Department at 910-395-3900 or visit www.wbkmt.com.

Places to Stay

Resorts, Hotels, and Motels

Blockade Runner Resort Hotel. Deluxe. 275 Waynick Boulevard, 28480 (800-541-1161 or 910-256-2251; www.blockade-runner.com). The Blockade Runner offers an excellent stay at the beach. Celebrating more than 30 years in business, this well-managed establishment has one of the prettiest, best-maintained stretches of sand on the island. Amenities include an outdoor pool, a beach-side bar, a spa, and outdoor patio dining. A two-night minimum stay on weekends is required in the summer. Children under 12 stay free with their parents.

Silver Gull Oceanfront Resort Motel. Deluxe/Expensive. 20 East Salisbury Street, 28480 (800-842-8894 or 910-256-3728). Every room at this motel has a kitchenette and a private balcony with an ocean view. A lifeguard is on duty during the summer.

Carolina Temple Apartments. Expensive. 550 Waynick Boulevard, 28480 (910-256-2773; www.carolinatempleislandinn.com). This historic inn consists of two large Plantation-style buildings—the oceanfront Carolina Cottage and the sound-front Temple Cottage. Each two-story structure contains eight efficiency apartments. The apartments rent by the week in the summer; a two-night minimum stay is in effect otherwise. The facility is closed in winter.

Places to Eat

Oceanic Restaurant. Expensive/Moderate. 703 South Lumina Avenue, 28480 (910-256-5551; www.oceanicrestaurant.com). Oceanic's local awards include Best Water View, Best Grilled Seafood, and Best Restaurant. In addition to seafood, it offers superb steaks and fresh pasta dishes. Outdoor dining is available on the pier. Lunch and dinner are served daily.

Southbeach Grill. Moderate. 100 South Lumina Avenue, 28480 (910-256-4646; www.southbeachgrillwb.com). This grill offers outdoor dining overlooking Banks

Channel. Its creative beach cuisine centers around fresh seafood and innovative seasonal entrées. Lunch and dinner are served daily.

The Sandwich Pail Seaside Grill. Moderate/Inexpensive. 1 Stone Street, 28480 (910-256-8225). This sandwich shop offers hand-pattied Cuban burgers, fresh homemade salads, and more. Kids can order their lunch in a pail and keep the pail! Free beach delivery is available Monday through Friday with a $20 minimum. The grill is open daily for lunch and dinner during summer; call for winter hours.

Nearby

Masonboro Island is the largest undisturbed barrier island along the coast of southern North Carolina. The island's nature trails offer the possibility of spotting endangered loggerhead sea turtles and shorebirds. Located off the southern tip of Wrightsville Beach, Masonboro is accessible only by boat. **Cape Fear Kayaks** (910-798-9922), **Carolina Coastal Adventures** (910-458-9111), and **Island Style Adventure Company** (910-509-9726) are a few of the companies that offer excursions to the island.

Masonboro Island
COURTESY OF WILMINGTON/CAPE FEAR COAST CONVENTION AND VISITORS BUREAU

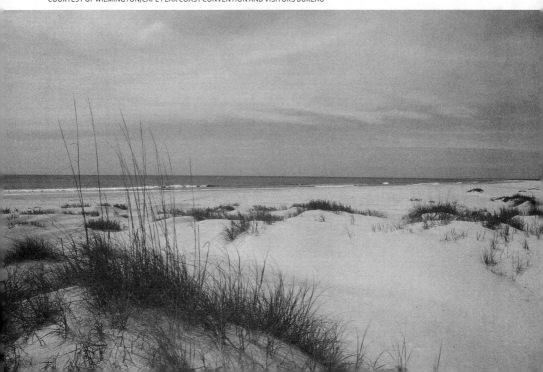

Pleasure Island

Carolina Beach, Kure Beach, and Fort Fisher make up Pleasure Island. This area prides itself on its clean, uncrowded beaches, reasonably priced accommodations, and friendly atmosphere. Don't be discouraged by the commercial nature of the drive in on U.S. 421. The beaches on the other side of all the buildings are well worth the visit.

Carolina Beach occupies the northern end of the island, while Kure is located at its southern end, next to Fort Fisher. Both beaches are characterized by cottages, family-owned motels and restaurants, and a small-town air. Carolina Beach is the livelier and more developed of the two.

Carolina Beach dates to the late 19th century, when Joseph L. Winner, a Wilmington merchant, purchased 108 acres to develop into a resort town. Although his town, which he called St. Joseph, never took off, other developers followed his lead. By 1915, Carolina Beach had both electricity and a paved road leading to Wilmington. In 1954, Hurricane Hazel devastated the town, leveling some 362 cottages and other buildings and damaging that many again.

Today, Carolina Beach takes pride in its post-Hazel renaissance. With its boardwalk, piers, Ferris wheel, merry-go-round, gazebo, and arcade, it is a slice of coastal

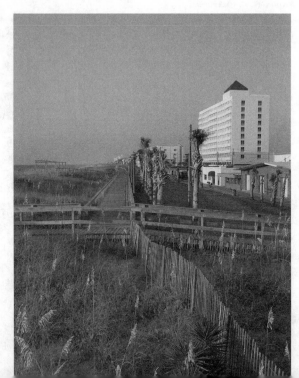

Carolina Beach boardwalk
COURTESY OF WILMINGTON/CAPE FEAR COAST
CONVENTION AND VISITORS BUREAU

Americana. And of course, it wouldn't be "the beach" without the requisite water slides and miniature golf courses. Fishing is also a major activity here; anglers can test their skills on the piers, in the surf, and on deep-sea charters. Carolina Beach State Park invites hikers, picnickers, and campers to explore the area's vegetation.

As you drive across the island to Kure Beach, you'll no doubt notice the devices along the road that look like solar panels. For decades, the federal government has been conducting an experiment here to determine the corrosive effects of salty sea air on various types of metals.

Kure Beach is a small, family-oriented community dominated by vacation cottages that by law cannot exceed 30 feet in height. It is named for its founder, Hans Kure, who acquired land here in 1891. In the 1930s, Kure Beach was the site of the world's first facility designed to extract bromine from seawater. (Years ago, ethylene dibromide was the ingredient that made leaded gasoline safe—or so it was thought.) Among other riches discovered while testing the seawater were gold, silver, copper, and aluminum. During World War II, a German U-boat fired—actually, misfired—on the plant, despite heavy security. Shortly after the war, the laboratory closed.

Popular pastimes here today include fishing, strolling the 711-foot Kure Beach Fishing Pier, picnicking at nearby Fort Fisher, and enjoying the sand and surf.

JUST THE FACTS

Pleasure Island is about 12 miles south of Wilmington on U.S. 421. It can also be reached via the Southport–Fort Fisher toll ferry.

Air travelers will need to make arrangements through Wilmington International Airport; call 910-341-4333.

The main source for information on the area is the Pleasure Island Chamber of Commerce, at 1121 North Lake Park Boulevard in Carolina Beach (28428); call 910-458-8434 or visit www.pleasureislandchamber.org.

The weekly newspapers of Pleasure Island are the *Island Gazette* and the *Weekly News*.

Things to Do

Historic Places, Gardens, and Tours

Fort Fisher State Historic Site is located on U.S. 421 south of Kure Beach (28449) at 1610 Fort Fisher Boulevard South. Named for Colonel Charles Fisher, a North

Fort Fisher State Historic Site mounds
COURTESY OF WILMINGTON/CAPE FEAR COAST CONVENTION AND VISITORS BUREAU

Carolina hero who died at First Manassas, Fort Fisher was the Civil War's largest earthen fortress, built to protect the port of Wilmington. In January 1865, some 10,000 Federal troops and history's heaviest naval bombardment to that date finally brought down the fort, signaling the end of the Civil War. What remains of the fort today is slowly eroding, despite efforts to protect it. The state has seeded the mounds that survive; a trail leads around them and offer views of the Cape Fear River.

A trip to the visitor center will give you an idea of the fort's role in protecting Wilmington and the daring blockade runners that smuggled supplies for the Confederacy. You can enjoy a slide show, dioramas, artifacts, and a complete model of Fort Fisher that was studied in classrooms at West Point following the Civil War. The grounds include a picnic area. From April to September, the site is open Monday through Saturday from 9 A.M. to 5 P.M. and Sunday from 1 P.M. to 5 P.M. From October to March, it is open Tuesday to Saturday from 10 A.M. to 4 P.M. It is closed Christmas and New Year's. Admission is free. Visit www.nchistoricsites.org/fisher/fisher.htm or call 910-458-5538.

Museums and Science Centers

The *North Carolina Aquarium at Fort Fisher*, located off U.S. 421 across the road from Fort Fisher State Historic Site at 900 Loggerhead Road in Kure Beach (28449), reopened in a fantastic new facility in 2002. In the Cape Fear Freshwater Conservatory, you'll meander along a path past plant life and tanks filled with freshwater fish. The alligator and turtle tank is filled with small alligators floating limply with only

North Carolina Aquarium at Fort Fisher atrium
COURTESY OF WILMINGTON/CAPE FEAR COAST CONVENTION AND VISITORS BUREAU

their heads breaking the water. One of the main attractions is the magnificent two-story aquarium filled with sharks, stingrays, and other creatures. Also mesmerizing is the black-lit jellyfish tank. For more information, call 910-458-8257 or visit www.ncaquariums.com.

Recreation

Carolina Beach State Park, 10 miles south of Wilmington on U.S. 421 at 1010 State Park Road in Carolina Beach (28428), has one of the few public campgrounds on this part of the coast. Located inland on the Intracoastal Waterway, it boasts 1,773 acres encompassing a variety of ecosystems, including dune ridges of longleaf pine and turkey oak, longleaf and evergreen savannas, pocosins, and brackish tidal marshes. It is home to the indigenous carnivorous Venus flytrap, red sundew, and pitcher plant. The park offers five hiking trails and a full-service marina with two boat ramps. The campground has shower facilities and 82 drive-up spots available on a first-come, first-served basis. All are shaded, so the heat probably won't bother you. The insects might, though, so pack your bug balm. During summer, nature programs are offered in the park's amphitheater. For more information, call 910-458-8206 or visit www.ncparks.gov/visit/parks/cabe/main.php.

Carolina Beach State Park paddleboats
COURTESY OF WILMINGTON/CAPE FEAR COAST CONVENTION AND VISITORS BUREAU

At *Fort Fisher State Recreation Area*, located near Fort Fisher State Historic Site at 1000 Loggerhead Road in Kure Beach (28449), visitors can picnic in the shade of lovely live oaks after enjoying a morning on the four-mile stretch of undeveloped beach. Restrooms, showers, and a snack bar are provided. Call 910-458-8206 or visit www.ncparks.gov/visit/parks/fofi/main.php.

Kayak Carolina, located at 103 Winner Avenue in Carolina Beach (28428), offers a two-hour introduction to the sport, as well as an interpretive nature tour. For information, call 910-458-9111 or visit www.kayakcarolina.com.

The convergence of the Cape Fear River, the Intracoastal Waterway, and the Atlantic Ocean makes Pleasure Island one of the premier bottom-, pier-, and surf-fishing destinations on the East Coast. The *Carolina Beach yacht basin* is a center for boating activities. A number of charter boats (limited to six passengers) and head boats (up to 150 passengers) are based there.

Seasonal Events

Pleasure Island hosts two fishing tournaments a year—the *East Coast Classic King Mackerel Tournament* in July and the *Carolina Beach Surf-Fishing Tournament* in October. Call the chamber of commerce at 910-458-8434 for information.

The second weekend of October ushers in the annual *Pleasure Island Seafood,*

Blues, and Jazz Festival. The event takes place overlooking the Cape Fear River at the Fort Fisher Air Force Base Recreation Area. Call 910-458-8434 for information.

Places to Stay

Pleasure Island is thick with accommodations; the following list is by no means inclusive. Be mindful that rates vary greatly according to the season. Many places have a two-day minimum, particularly on weekends. In summer, some even have a week's minimum. The chamber of commerce can provide a list of rental cottages and condominiums; call 910-458-8434.

Resorts, Hotels, and Motels

Golden Sands. Deluxe. 1211 South Lake Park Boulevard in Carolina Beach, 28428 (888-458-8334 or 910-458-8334; www.goldensandscarolinabeach.com). This place has 88 rooms and efficiencies, two swimming pools, and a private pier. Complimentary coffee is served in the lobby.

Savannah Inn. Deluxe/Expensive. 316 Carolina Beach Avenue North in Carolina Beach, 28449 (800-334-8533 or 910-458-6555; www.thesavannahinn.com). This inn offers clean oceanfront rooms and efficiencies individually decorated with a beach theme. A three-night minimum is required during summer.

Admiral's Quarters Motel. Expensive/Moderate. U.S. 421 in Kure Beach, 28449 (800-535-4984 or 910-458-5050; www.admiralsquartersmotel.com). Admiral's Quarters has 37 rooms, all but three of which overlook the ocean. All have private porches or balconies with rocking chairs. The motel offers two pools, a gazebo, and a sandy playground for the kids.

Sand Dunes Motel. Expensive/Moderate. 133 Fort Fisher Boulevard in Kure Beach, 28449 (800-535-4984 or 910-458-5470; www.thesanddunes.com). Sand Dunes has 39 rooms and efficiencies, 27 of which overlook the ocean. A lifeguard is on duty during summer. The motel offers beach-side Adirondack chairs for relaxing.

Places To Eat

Barnacles. Expensive. 300 North Lake Park Boulevard in Carolina Beach, 28428 (910-458-6001). For seafood lovers, Barnacles offers fresh fish, lobster, and a raw bar. For the rest, it has plenty of chicken and steak entrées. Lunch and dinner are served daily.

The Cottage Restaurant. Expensive/Moderate. 1 North Lake Park Boulevard in Carolina Beach, 28428 (910-458-4383). The Cottage is, in fact, housed in a renovated 1916 beach cottage. It serves terrific seafood dishes, such as a lobster-and-shrimp torte appetizer, as well as an array of fresh alternatives like a chicken salad wrap and a grilled portobello sandwich. The pasta dishes are great, too. You may dine indoors or outside on the covered deck. Lunch and dinner are served Monday through Saturday year-round.

Deck House. Moderate. 205 Charlotte Avenue in Carolina Beach, 28428 (910-458-1026). Housed in a former church, the Deck House specializes in seafood but also offers lots of chicken, pasta, and steak options. All are served with a choice of salad, grouper chowder, or Manhattan clam chowder and—unless the entrée is served over pasta—a choice of baked potato, house potato, rice pilaf, fries, or mixed vegetables. Dinner is served nightly in season; the restaurant is closed on Mondays in winter.

Michael's Seafood Restaurant and Catering. Moderate/Inexpensive. 1206 North Lake Park Boulevard in Carolina Beach, 28428 (910-458-7761; www.mikescfood. com). This restaurant is celebrated for its seafood chowder, which it ships around the country. At Michael's, you can have your seafood grilled, broiled, or sautéed, but you can't have it fried. You may dine inside with the 700-gallon fish tank or outside on the deck. Lunch and dinner are served daily.

Southport and the Brunswick Islands

Located midway between New York and Miami along the Intracoastal Waterway is the quiet town of Southport, which caters to boaters sailing north and south. Southport is listed on the National Register of Historic Places. Originally named Smithville for Benjamin Smith, a Continental Army general who later became governor of North Carolina, Southport was renamed in 1887 to reflect its geography. In recent years, it has become an appealing destination for non-seafaring travelers drawn to its antique shops, historic homes, restaurants, art galleries, and live-oak-shaded parks. Since the town is surrounded by water, it is not surprising that the most popular spot in Southport is Waterfront Park. From there, visitors can watch ocean ships pass on their way up the Cape Fear River to Wilmington, a remarkable photographic opportunity. Southport itself is so photogenic that a number of motion pictures and television films have been made here.

A good place to begin is Southport's visitor center, on West Moore Street. Here, you can pick up maps, brochures, and information about Southport and the Brunswick County beaches. Just around the corner is the North Carolina Maritime Museum at Southport. Take time to enjoy the town's historic business district, especially the many antique shops along Howe and Moore streets. Also, be sure to stroll the Southport Riverwalk and to visit the shops around the yacht basin and near the marina. Finally, take time to enjoy some local seafood.

Wind-swept live oak and yaupon trees grace Oak Island, a 10-mile stretch of beach with quiet surf and moderate tides. This family-oriented community offers water activities for all ages. Its three piers, marina, and public launch facilities make it popular with fishermen, especially those looking for king mackerel. Oak Island grew from a few prewar cottages to a community of over 300 homes after World War II. In 1954, Hurricane Hazel destroyed all but five houses here. Incorporated in July 1999, the town of Oak Island consists of the communities once known as Long Beach and Yaupon Beach.

Named after historic Fort Caswell, located at the top of the island, Caswell Beach is home to the brightest lighthouse in the United States. It also boasts a Coast Guard station reminiscent of the old lifesaving stations. Deep dunes and sprawling beach cottages line the ocean. On the marsh side, cottages on pilings overlook the Cape Fear River's shipping channel. The only souvenirs available at Caswell Beach are the shells waiting to be collected on quiet low-tide walks along the beautiful shore.

Holden Beach is an 11-mile-long south-facing island. It, too, was devastated by Hurricane Hazel in 1954, but developers lost no time in rebuilding ample rental space for its numerous visitors. The western end of Holden overlooks Shallotte Inlet, a shrimp-boat harbor said to possess water with curative powers. At Windy Point, the story goes, people have been mysteriously cured of infections. The most plausible reason is a type of reed that grows here but nowhere else. Although the water's curative power is unsubstantiated by scientists, people have come here from as far away as Canada to put it to the test.

Ocean Isle Beach and Sunset Beach round out the Brunswick County beaches. An exciting addition to Ocean Isle is the Silver Coast Winery. Ocean Isle also boasts the terrific Museum of Coastal Carolina. Sunset Beach is considered by many to be the most beautiful of North Carolina's southern islands.

Things to Do

Historic Places, Gardens, and Tours

Southport Trail is a self-guided tour map available from the Southport 2000 Visitors Center or the Southport Historical Society (910-457-0579). This one-mile walk through town visits many interesting historical sites. A few are described below.

JUST THE FACTS

Southport, located about 25 miles south of Wilmington, can be reached via N.C. 133 or N.C. 87. For a more scenic approach, take the Southport–Fort Fisher ferry from Pleasure Island. Oak Island can be reached via N.C. 133. The three southern Brunswick islands are connected to U.S. 17 by small state roads.

Several agencies supply information about the area. The Southport–Oak Island Chamber of Commerce is located at 4841 Long Beach Road Southeast in Southport (28461); call 800-457-6964 or visit www.southport-oakisland.com. The Southport 2000 Visitors Center is headquartered at 113 West Moore Street in Southport (28461); call 910-457-7927 or visit www.oak-island.com. For information on Holden Beach, Ocean Isle Beach, and Sunset Beach, contact the South Brunswick Islands Chamber of Commerce in Shallotte by calling 800-426-6644 or 910-754-6644 or visiting www.nebrunswick.com.

The *State Port Pilot* and the *Brunswick Beacon* are the local weekly papers.

Southport–Fort Fisher ferry
COURTESY OF WILMINGTON/CAPE FEAR COAST CONVENTION AND VISITORS BUREAU

The *Adkins-Ruark House* is where author and journalist Robert Ruark spent his childhood summers. His book *The Old Man and the Boy* is an account of his time in Southport.

Keziah Memorial Park, on Moore Street, is the home of the 800-year-old Indian Trail Tree. This live oak was deliberately bent by Native Americans to create a landmark to guide them.

Stede Bonnet, nicknamed "the Gentleman Pirate," was making repairs to his ship, *The Revenge*, when Colonel William Rhett caught up with him at what is now called *Bonnet's Creek*. A one-time wealthy planter, Bonnet is said to have taken to piracy for a bit of adventure and to get away from his shrewish wife.

Museums and Science Centers

The *North Carolina Maritime Museum at Southport*, at 116 North Howe Street (28461), houses materials pertaining to the nautical history of the lower Cape Fear. A self-guided tour leads among 12 exhibits linked to each other through a story line. Shipwrecks, navigational aids, and fishing are covered, as is the history of Southport. The museum is open Tuesday through Saturday from 9 A.M. to 5 P.M. Admission is free. For more information, call 910-457-0003 or visit www.ncmaritime.org/branches/southport_default.htm.

The *Museum of Coastal Carolina*, at 21 East Second Street in Ocean Isle Beach (28467), is a handsome 7,500-square-foot building constructed in 1991. A hands-on interactive museum, it explores the natural history and heritage of the area and has a touch tank with live sea animals. During the high season, it is open Wednesday and Thursday from 10 A.M. to 8:30 P.M. and Monday, Tuesday, Friday, and Saturday from 10 A.M. to 5 P.M. Call for hours the rest of the year. Admission is charged. Call 910-579-1016 or visit www.museumofcc.org.

Cultural Offerings

Housed in a 1904 schoolhouse that subsequently became Southport's city hall, then its library, the *Franklin Square Art Gallery* features the products of local artists working in a variety of media. Legend has it that if you drink from the hand pump in Franklin Square Park, you're sure to return to the town. The gallery is located at 130 East West Street (28461), behind the park. It is open Monday through Saturday from 10 A.M. to 4 P.M. For more information, call 910-457-5450 or visit www.franklinsquaregallery.org.

Special Shopping

Southport is noted for its antique shops. More than 15 shops and 75 dealers trade here. Head for Howe and Moore streets to visit a concentration of them.

Olde Southport Village, at 1102 North Howe Street (28461), is a growing assemblage of painted cottages that are being salvaged and collected by Phil Hemphill. Gift and craft outlets dominate, but a seamstress and a beautician also tend shop here. Most of the shops are open Tuesday through Saturday from 10 A.M. to 5 P.M. For more information, call 910-448-1088 or visit www.oldesouthportvillage.com.

Silver Coast Winery, at 6680 Barbecue Road in Ocean Isle Beach (28469), is one of the many fine wineries that have cropped up in the state in recent years. Located in a lovely wooded setting, this is an ideal place to share a peaceful picnic with friends. In addition to its tasty Barbera and Chardonnay wines, it offers an art gallery, a gift shop, and a monthly wine festival. It is open Monday through Saturday from 11 A.M. to 6 P.M. and Sunday from noon to 5 P.M. For more information, call 910-287-2800 or visit www.silvercoastwinery.com.

Recreation

Oak Island Nature Center and *Register Park* overlook the Intracoastal Waterway and the marsh at the end of 52nd Street in Oak Island (28465). Among the wide range of activities for adults and children here are various mineral, rock, and animal exhibits, including a large touch tank. Adjacent to the nature center is a park with trails, a picnic shelter, bathrooms, and opportunities for fishing. *Talking Trees Walking Trail* is an interactive trail where dogwoods, red cedars, Southern magnolias, black gums, and other trees talk to you as you walk. Admission is free. The hours are seasonal; call 910-278-5518 or visit www.oakislandnc.com/Recreation/nature_center.htm.

Scuba South Diving Company is located at 222 South River Drive in Southport (28461). Owner and skipper Wayne Strickland leads shipwreck scuba tours amid Frying Pan Shoals. For information, call 910-520-2809 or visit www.scubasouthdiving.com.

Seasonal Events

Southport hosts the official *North Carolina Fourth of July Festival*. The town has been observing Independence Day since 1795. Call 800-457-6964 or 910-457-6964 or visit www.nc4thofjuly.com for information.

Two annual fishing tournaments—the *U.S. Open King Mackerel Tournament* (800-457-6964; www.usopenkmt.com), based at Southport Marina, and the *South Brunswick Islands King Mackerel Classic*, based at Holden Beach Marina—offer $100,000 in prizes each. Call 800-426-6644 for details.

Places to Stay

Resorts, Hotels, and Motels

The Winds Resort Beach Club. Deluxe. 310 East First Street in Ocean Isle Beach, 28469 (800-334-3581 or 910-579-6275; www.TheWinds.com). The Winds offers a complimentary breakfast buffet, three pools, a garden bar and restaurant, and golf packages.

Blue Water Point Motel and Marina. Moderate. 5710 West Beach Place on Oak Island, 28465 (888-634-9005 or 910-278-1230; www.bluewaterpointmotel.com). This motel offers rooms with a view of the water, cable television, mini refrigerators, coffee pots, a restaurant, and free sunset cruises during summer.

Inns and Bed-and-Breakfasts

The Brunswick Inn. Deluxe. 301 East Bay Street in Southport, 28461 (910-457-5278; www.brunswickinn.com). This lovely Federal-style inn overlooking the Cape Fear River offers three spacious rooms. A two-night minimum stay is required for holiday and in-season weekends.

Lois Jane's Riverview Inn. Deluxe/Expensive. 106 West Bay Street in Southport, 28461 (910-457-6701; www.loisjanes.com). This 1890s home was built by Lois Jane's grandfather and restored by her children in 1995. The inn is furnished with period antiques, many of them family heirlooms. It offers three rooms with private baths and two with a shared bath. Breakfast is included in the room rate.

Places to Eat

Giggling Mackerel. Expensive/Moderate. 65 Causeway Drive in Ocean Isle Beach, 28469 (910-575-0902; www.gigglingmackerel.com). The Giggling Mackerel offers lunch and dinner seven days a week. Try the steamed platter of crab legs, shrimp, and clams, and be sure to visit the rooftop tiki bar, where you can enjoy cold beer while watching the sunset.

The Pharmacy. Expensive/Moderate. 110 East Moore Street in Southport, 28461 (910-457-5577). At lunchtime, The Pharmacy serves chicken salad, ham-and-cheese strudel with sweet potato chips, and a quiche of the day. For dinner, it turns to more sophisticated fare. Try the bouillabaisse or the gravlax for a change of pace. Lunch is served daily and dinner Thursday through Sunday.

Betty's Waterfront Restaurant. Moderate. 1045 Varnamtown Road SW in Holden Beach, 28462 (910-842-3381). Betty's offers fresh seafood any way you want it:

grilled, fried, blackened, or broiled. Chicken and steak are also on the menu. Dinner is served daily.

Jones' Seafood House. Moderate. 6404 East Oak Island Drive on Oak Island, 28465 (910-278-5231). This family-owned restaurant specializing in Calabash-style seafood has been a local favorite since it opened its doors in 1964. Dinner is served daily.

Crabby-Oddwaters Restaurant. Moderate/Inexpensive. 310 Sunset Boulevard North in Sunset Beach, 28468 (910-579-6372). This place is located upstairs from Bill's Seafood Market, the source of its fare. To get fresher seafood, you'd have to catch it yourself. Dinner is served daily.

Sugar Shack. Moderate/Inexpensive. 1609 Hale Beach Road in Ocean Isle Beach, 28469 (910-579-3844). The Sugar Shack serves Jamaican fare prepared by a Jamaican chef. Try the jerk chicken or pork or the coconut shrimp with mango-chutney salsa. If you're feeling adventurous, try the curried goat! Dinner is served Tuesday through Saturday. Reservations are recommended.

Thai Peppers. Moderate/Inexpensive. 115 East Moore Street in Southport, 28461 (910-457-0095; www.thaipeppersnc.com). Curries, "Pad Thai," and hot-and-sour seafood are served here. Guests can enjoy them indoors or out with an ice-cold beer to cool off the fiery heat—of the day and of the food. Lunch is served Monday through Friday and dinner Monday through Saturday. Hours are seasonal.

Yacht Basin Provision Company. Inexpensive. 130 Yacht Basin Drive in South-port, 28461 (910-457-0654; www.provisioncompany.com). Don't miss eating at this place. Check your preconceptions at the door, grab the beverage of your choice, stand in line, and place your order, then go outside and wait for one of the cheerful servers to bring you the freshest basket of steamed clams or grilled fish you've ever eaten. The burgers are out of this world, too. The restaurant is open daily for lunch and dinner.

Nearby

Once a haven for pirates, ***Bald Head Island*** is now a pristine triangle of land south of Wilmington accessible only by water. Visitors can ferry over to the island from Southport or pilot their own boats to the harbor. Among the favorite pastimes here are glimpsing the island's famous loggerhead turtles and enjoying a pleasant tour that includes a hike into Bald Head's remaining patch of maritime forest and a climb up Old Baldy, the oldest lighthouse in the state. Old Baldy is privately owned, so access is restricted.

Aside from a handful of utility vehicles, automobiles are not allowed on the island, so the speediest way to get around is by golf cart. Since 1986, the state's 10,000-acre portion of the island has been designated a day-use state park. The remaining land is privately owned and under careful development. The upscale resort here consists of the Marsh Harbour Inn and Conference Center, a championship golf course, and a variety of rental cottages and condominiums. Accommodations at the inn include round-trip ferry passage and use of the club and a golf cart. For more information, call 800-432-RENT or visit www.baldheadisland.com.

Museum artifacts, crumbling foundations, and the walls of St. Philip's Church are all that remain of historic ***Brunswick Town***, located 18 miles south of Wilmington off N.C. 133 at 8884 St. Philip's Road in Winnabow (28479). Co-founded in 1726 by Maurice Moore, one of the enterprising sons of a former South Carolina governor, Brunswick Town was the site of the first colonial rebellion against British rule. In 1766, eight years before the Boston Tea Party, some 150 armed citizens known as the Sons of Liberty encircled customs officials and forced them to take an oath that they would issue no more stamped paper.

Brunswick Town initially flourished as a port for shipping tar, pitch, and turpentine. But despite its early promise, it was abandoned soon after New Bern took over as the state capital and Wilmington assumed prominence. After decades of calm, the site again took on a historic role in 1861, when an earthen fortress, ***Fort Anderson***, was constructed to protect Confederate blockade runners against the Union navy. In 1865, following the fall of Fort Fisher at the mouth of the Cape Fear River, Union forces attacked Fort Anderson by land and water. After three days of fighting, the Confederates evacuated the fort in the dark of night.

Now a state historic site, Brunswick Town is open Tuesday through Saturday from 9 A.M. to 5 P.M. year-round. Admission is free. For information, call 910-371-6613 or visit www.nchistoricsites.org/Brunswic/brunswic.htm.

For 50 years, seafood lovers have flocked to the small town of *Calabash*, located off U.S. 17 just north of the South Carolina line, for some original "Calabash-style" seafood, lightly battered and fried. Estimates suggest there is one restaurant for every 75 of Calabash's 1,300 citizens. Try the *Boundary House Restaurant* (910-579-8888), at 1045 Riverview Road (28467); *Dockside Seafood House* (910-579-6775), on the Calabash River at 9955 Nance Street (28467); or any of the restaurants along N.C. 179. Be prepared for a wait in summer.

In mid-October, the *North Carolina Oyster Festival* is held in Shallotte, located on N.C. 130 off U.S. 17. What began as a tiny oyster roast in 1979 has grown into the state's official oyster celebration. The highlight is an oyster-shucking championship. Visit www.brunswickcountychamber.org/OF-nc-oyster-festival.cfm or call 910-754-6644 for information.

The Blockade Takes the Life of a Rebel Spy

Excerpted from *Gray Phantoms of the Cape Fear* by Dawson Carr

Rose O'Neal Greenhow's brief career as a Southern spy had already exposed her to danger. Her husband, Dr. Robert Greenhow, had been a native Virginian whose position in the State Department had brought him to Washington. There, Rose quickly endeared herself to members of government and the city's elite. After her husband's death, she continued to reside in Washington, although her heart was in the South.

When the war broke out, she resolved to do all in her power to help the Rebels. Upon learning details of the North's plan to attack at Manassas in July 1861, she passed the word to Confederate general P. G. T. Beauregard. Some say this information allowed the Rebels to make advance preparations that led to a major triumph.

Greenhow was later held under arrest in Washington and nearly thrown in prison for passing information to Southern military leaders. At her trial, she was given the option of swearing allegiance to the United States, but she haughtily declined. Uncertain what to do with such a woman, the Union eventually agreed to pardon her if she would at least swear to leave the North and never return. To this, she agreed.

But that did not mean she would abandon the cause. Greenhow understood the importance of good relations between England and the South. She decided to try her hand at being a Confederate agent in Europe. . . .

Her trip to Europe proved more successful than even she had hoped. Honored by high officials in both England and France, Greenhow also won popularity among the residents of those two nations, especially the British. While in England, she published her memoirs, entitled *My Imprisonment and the First Year of Abolition Rule at Washington*. The book was well received all over England, helping further her goal of influencing public opinion in favor of the Confederacy. Copies were snatched up eagerly by people anxious to read a firsthand account of the war across the Atlantic—and especially to hear the story of such an attractive and popular spy.

Now, as she prepared to travel back to Wilmington, Greenhow carried several thousand dollars in gold coins, her share of the profits from the book's sales. Of all the Southern patriots who came across the sea to win over the English, it's unlikely that any was as well liked as she, and it was with some regret that she was leaving. Yet she missed her friends back across the Atlantic and wanted to see them again in spite of the dangers of the forthcoming voyage. Also, it was rumored that she carried secret dispatches for President Jefferson Davis.

She stepped aboard the new blockade runner *Condor*—a magnificent gray behemoth with three stacks and remarkable speed—as the vessel prepared to leave Scotland in September 1864. The captain was a furloughed British naval officer using the alias Samuel Ridge. . . .

It was the first week of October when the *Condor* reached the vicinity of New Inlet. Guiding her was Thomas Brinkman, one of the small cadre of Smithville pilots who helped blockade runners reach the Cape Fear River through the maze of sand bars and shoals. Brinkman directed the shadowy vessel along the shoreline, taking advantage of her seven-foot draft to cruise at the very edge of the surf. The skies were stormy that night, and although waves rocked the ship, the crewmen were thankful for the additional cover. . . .

In the darkest part of the night, just before dawn, the *Condor* increased speed as she approached the mound battery at Fort Fisher, now faintly visible a couple of miles ahead. Unfortunately,

the omnipresent [Union vessel] *Niphon* was waiting. . . .

Rose O'Neal Greenhow was desperate, believing that the enemy would board the *Condor* momentarily and that she would be arrested. She pleaded with Captain Ridge to take her to shore, but he tried to reassure her that once daylight arrived, they could make it to the beach safely. He explained that the stormy weather made the sea too dangerous for an attempt in the dark. Still, she begged him until he finally relented.

The captain asked three of his most experienced crewmen to launch a lifeboat and deliver her to shore. As soon as they were aboard the small craft, a monstrous wave overturned it, and all aboard were tossed into the swirling waters. The men all surfaced and made their way to land. But Greenhow was never seen alive again, as the heavy gold coins she carried in her garments pulled her to the bottom. . . .

Greenhow [is] . . . buried in Oakdale Cemetery in the heart of [Wilmington].

The Piedmont

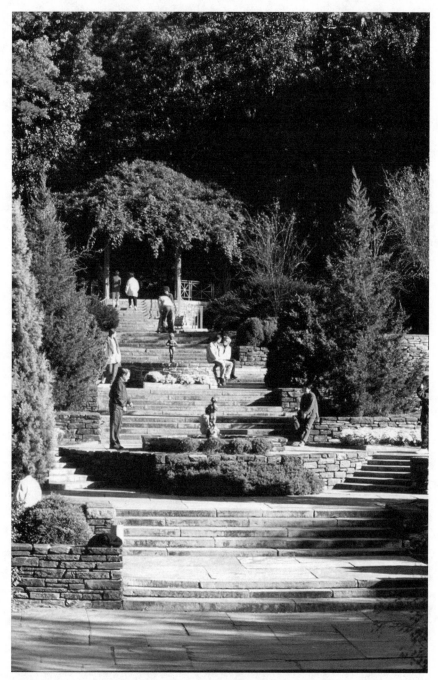

The terraces at Sarah P. Duke Gardens

PHOTOGRAPH BY BRUCE R. FEELEY, COURTESY DURHAM CONVENTION AND VISITORS BUREAU

(Photograph on page 213 Courtesy Visit Charlotte)

The Triangle

Raleigh

Durham

Chapel Hill and Carrboro

Research Triangle Park

Triangle Nearby

By Steve Kirk

T
he Triangle is one of North Carolina's best-known regions, though outsiders might be hard-pressed to distinguish the six counties (or eight counties, depending on who's counting), the three major cities, and the myriad
small towns that comprise it. Many know it as the home of the most heated basketball rivalry in the nation. While Duke University and the University of North
Carolina have the most storied basketball programs, they are only two of the seven
major universities nearby. The Triangle claims one of the highest concentrations
of Ph.D.'s in the nation.

Raleigh, the area's largest city, is home to over 385,000 residents. The capital of North Carolina, it's also a thriving center of education, art, and sports.
The Carolina Hurricanes, the 2006 Stanley Cup winners, play here. The locals are
equally comfortable in seats by the ice, watching movies on the lawn at the North
Carolina Museum of Art, or enjoying their favorite snack at one of Raleigh's
many restaurants and watering holes.

Durham, though richly steeped in tobacco history, is now called "the City of
Medicine." Thanks to the relationship between Duke University and companies
in nearby Research Triangle Park, this area is the center for some of the world's
most important medical and pharmaceutical research, as well as groundbreaking work in microelectronics, textiles, telecommunications, and instrumentation

technology. Duke also brings some of the world's best theater, art exhibits, speakers, dancers, and musicians to its hometown.

Chapel Hill, the third corner of the Triangle, is defined by its historic school—the University of North Carolina at Chapel Hill, the first state-supported university in the nation. Chapel Hill is the definition of a college town. Years ago, when funding for a state zoo was first discussed, conservatives quipped that proponents could simply build a fence around Chapel Hill. Chapel Hill's history of tolerance may be due to the fact that academia is a fairly steady business, so the area has long been spared many of the economic woes affecting other parts of the state. Its small population enjoys a good standard of living and a strong sense of community.

Neighboring towns such as Carrboro and Hillsborough have their own special qualities. The heavy concentration of artists and writers in Carrboro has prompted some to call this former mill town "the Paris of the Piedmont." Hillsborough, known for its grand old houses, boasts some of the best architecture in the state.

Collectively, the Triangle is a powerhouse. Real-estate prices and employment opportunities have attracted a large population of transplants from all over the country, but the area also retains many of its born-and-bred natives.

The wide span of significant area history deserves a look. From the Native American tribes that converged at the Great Indian Trading Path to the colonial settlement of Raleigh to Martin Luther King's famous civil-rights speech in Durham, history is lodged in every corner of the Triangle.

Visitors enjoy the hundreds of award-winning restaurants, the dozens of first-rate theaters, and the half-dozen lakes; the gardens, museums, and shopping malls; the fairs, flea markets, and antique shops; the sports arenas, golf courses, and greenways; and the nightclubs, comedy clubs, and walking tours.

The people here are educated. They enjoy a broad range of activities, from kayaking on Lake Crabtree to listening to music at the Cat's Cradle. Natives are fiercely loyal to their hometowns. Transplants rave about the climate and the laid-back, affable spirit of their neighbors. In recent years, telling the two groups apart has become increasingly difficult. So visit the Triangle for the people-watching, if nothing else. Then have fun choosing from the area's countless activities. Just try not to let the options overwhelm you.

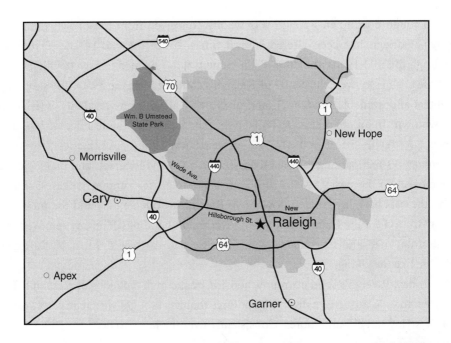

Raleigh

If the streets of downtown Raleigh seem unnaturally gridlike, it's because North Carolina's capital is the only one in the country built on land bought for the sole purpose of establishing the state seat. What's more, it's one of only three state capitals planned out on paper before the cornerstone was laid.

In 1788, a group of commissioners was sent in search of a centrally located section of land suitable for setting up the legislature. A few older and more distinguished North Carolina towns, including Fayetteville, felt they were entitled to the honor and objected, to no avail. The delegation pushed on until it came upon a local watering hole owned by Isaac Hunter. After spending some time there, the commissioners found his land to be almost exactly what they were looking for, proclaiming that Hunter's property was within 10 miles of precisely where the capital needed to be. They continued to study the area. During their travels, the thirsty bunch came upon another well-known tavern, owned by a Revolutionary War colonel named Joel Lane. Local lore claims that Colonel Lane brewed a stout concoction called Cherry Bounce that finally swayed their votes. After purchasing 1,000 acres, the city's forefathers began drawing up plans. By 1792, the town was up and running.

Though downtown Raleigh was wholly conceived from the outset, the city's original design has been altered several times. From the end of the Civil War through the mid-1970s, the door of the State Capitol opened to Fayetteville Street, whose businesses were the center of Raleigh's commerce. In the 1950s, the shopping centers and available residential land of North Raleigh drew residents away from downtown. In an attempt at revitalization, the city council built a pedestrian mall over Fayetteville Street in 1976. The effort achieved the opposite effect; the mall eliminated street parking for the businesses on Fayetteville Street, and many closed or moved. In the past 15 years, residential buildings, restaurants, galleries, shops, and theaters have invigorated downtown Raleigh by opening around the mall and away from the State Capitol and other government buildings. The city removed the pedestrian mall and reopened Fayetteville Street to car traffic. Most of Raleigh's people like the change.

Today, Raleigh's solid economy, boosted by the high-tech jobs of Research Triangle Park, has attracted a diverse labor force that has brought with it an eclectic mix of lifestyles and cultural mores. Consistently over the last two decades, Raleigh has won recognition as one of the nation's most desirable places to live and work. And the Joel Lane House is still open, though you won't find a drop of Cherry Bounce there now.

JUST THE FACTS

Interstate 40 is one of Raleigh's main thoroughfares. The Interstate 440 Beltline (divided into the mystifying-to-newcomers Inner Beltline and Outer Beltline) provides access to the Capital City, Research Triangle Park, and the surrounding communities. Interstate 95 and Interstate 85 run within 25 miles of the city.

Raleigh-Durham International Airport is a 15-minute drive from downtown Raleigh. It offers more than 300 daily departures, including international flights to London, Toronto, Ottawa, and the Bahamas.

The Greyhound bus terminal is located at 314 West Jones Street (27603); call 919-834-8275 for information. Within greater Raleigh, the Capital Area Transit (CAT) bus system and CAT Connectors (vans) provide riders with an extensive network of routes. The hours of operation are 6 A.M. to 10 P.M. Monday through Saturday and 8 A.M. to 8 P.M. Sunday.

Raleigh is accessible by Amtrak train. The station is located at 320 West Cabarrus Street (27601). For information, call 919-833-7594.

One of the best sources of information about Raleigh is Capital Area Visitor Services, located in the lobby of the North Carolina Museum of History at 5 East Edenton Street (27601). For preplanned itineraries, maps, and other

Peace College

Peace

William
Thomas
House

Johnson

Tucker

Capital Blvd.

Polk

Oakwood
Inn

BLOUNT
STREET
HISTORIC
DISTRICT

North

North
Capital Area
Visitor Center

HISTORIC
OAKWOOD
DISTRICT

Lane

Glenwood

Lane

State Archives
State Library

Executive
Mansion

State
Legislative
Building

Jones

West

Harrington

Dawson

McDowell

Salisbury

Wilmington

Blount

Person

Bloodworth

Edenton

NC State
Capitol

Hillsborough

Morgan

Explorus
& IMAX

Hargett

FAYETTEVILLE

Martin

City
Market

Artspace

Davie

Cabarrus

Raleigh
Convention &
Conference
Center

Lenoir

South

BTI Center for the
Performing Arts &
Memorial
Auditorium

Shaw
University

Western Blvd.

Martin Luther King Jr. Blvd.

information, call 919-807-7950 or visit http://ncmuseumofhistory.org. The Greater Raleigh Convention and Visitors Bureau, located at 421 Fayetteville Street (27601), is another source. Call 800-849-8499 or 919-834-5900 or visit www.visitraleigh.com. For information about the Historic Raleigh Trolley Tour, call 919-857-4364.

Raleigh's morning newspaper is the *News & Observer*, one of the largest in the state. The *Independent Weekly* (www.Indyweek.com) covers the entire Triangle; it is a good source of information about local activities, entertainment, dining, and shopping.

Things to Do

Historic Places, Gardens, and Tours

The ***North Carolina State Capitol*** is located at 1 East Edenton Street (27601) on Capitol Square. Entering from Wilmington Street brings you up the front lawn and past a bronze sculpture depicting the three United States presidents with North Carolina origins—Andrew Jackson is on horseback, James Polk is seated and holding a map, and Andrew Johnson is seated and holding the United States Constitution. The current State Capitol is the second to occupy the square. The original,

The State Capitol
PHOTOGRAPH BY ELIZABETH KIRK

simple two-story brick structure was built between 1792 and 1796. A fire caused by an unattended smelting pot (which, ironically, was being used to melt zinc to fire-proof the roof) destroyed it in 1831. In 1833, plans for a new building were drafted. By 1840, the current State Capitol was completed. Considered a fine example of Greek Revival architecture, the building is a national historic landmark. It currently houses the offices of the governor and lieutenant governor. Free tours allow visitors to see the old Senate and House chambers, complete with their original furniture and fireplaces. You may also spy a ghost. Local lore has it that the spirit of a Confederate soldier roams the building's second floor. Over the years, staff members have reported hearing strange noises and witnessing odd occurrences. Sound intriguing? Check it out for yourself. The State Capitol is open to visitors from 9 A.M. to 5 P.M. Monday through Saturday and from 1 P.M. to 4 P.M. on Sunday. Public tours are offered at 11 A.M. and 2 P.M. on Saturday and at 2 P.M. on Sunday; self-guided tours are available Monday through Friday. The building is closed most state holidays. For information, call 919-733-4994 or visit www.nchistoricsites.org/capitol; to arrange a group tour, call 866-724-8687 or 919-807-7950.

The *Executive Mansion*, at 210 North Blount Street (27601), is the official residence of the governor. Built solely of materials from within the state, it is considered one of the finest examples of Queen Anne cottage-style architecture in North Carolina. Franklin D. Roosevelt described its interior as the most beautiful of any governor's residence in America. Construction on the house began in 1885. To keep

The Executive Mansion
PHOTOGRAPH BY ELIZABETH KIRK

costs down, prisoners from the state penitentiary made bricks and did much of the labor; the initials of several prisoners are visible in sidewalk pavers. Still, the final price spiraled to an unheard-of $58,000 by the time the house was completed in 1890. Tours are available; admission is free. For tour times, call Capital Area Visitor Services at 919-807-7950.

The *Historic Oakwood District*, located off North Person Street between Jones and Boundary streets, is the only intact 19th-century neighborhood in Raleigh. Built after the Civil War in the dense woods of the Mordecai Grove at the northwestern corner of the city, the district showcases a variety of Victorian architectural styles and reflects the middle-class tastes of its founding fathers and the refined craftsmanship of local architects and builders. Listed on the National Register of Historic Places, Oakwood is a reminder of Southern urban life during the 19th and 20th centuries. Some homes still retain the blue porch ceilings of the period, painted to resemble the sky and, according to Southern folklore, to scare away flies. Sidewalk strolls are free, but please respect the privacy of the homeowners. For information about Oakwood and the annual Oakwood Garden Tour, visit www.historicoakwood.org.

The *Joel Lane House*, located at the corner of St. Marys and West Hargett streets, is the oldest dwelling in Raleigh. Built in the early 1770s, it was the site of numerous historic events, including general assembly sessions during the Revolutionary War. According to local lore, Colonel Joel Lane opened his home to six state commissioners on their way to Isaac Hunter's home, a popular meeting place that was already under consideration for the site of the new state capital. Like Hunter, Lane operated an inn and tavern out of his house. Plying the commissioners with his famous Cherry Bounce, Lane persuaded them to buy 1,000 acres from him rather than from Hunter, with the added agreement that one of the streets in the new city would carry his name. Joel Lane has been called "the Father of Raleigh." Today, costumed guides lead tours through his fully restored house and formal gardens. From March to December, tours are offered Wednesday through Friday from 10 A.M. to 1 P.M. and Saturday from 1 P.M. to 3 P.M. During January and February, they are available on Saturday only. Appointments for Sunday group tours may be made year-round. A small admission fee is charged. For more information, call 919-833-3431 or visit www.joellane.org.

Mordecai Historic Park, located at 1 Mimosa Street (27604), is a five-acre historic site managed by the city of Raleigh. The grounds once anchored a 5,000-acre plantation. Mordecai House, constructed in 1785 by Joel Lane, is one of the oldest in the city. It takes its name from Moses Mordecai, who twice married into the Lane family. An 1820s addition by William Nichols transformed the home into a Greek Revival mansion. Among the several outbuildings open for touring are a kitchen, a law office, a chapel, a post office, and the humble birthplace of Andrew Johnson. Tavern worker and church sexton Jacob Johnson died when the future 17th president was barely four years old, upon which the family fell into hard times. Andrew was later apprenticed to a tailor and settled in Tennessee. The park is open Tuesday through Saturday from 9 A.M. to 4 P.M. and Sunday from 1 P.M. to 4 P.M. Docent-led tours are offered on the hour from 10 A.M. to 3 P.M. except on Sunday. A fee is charged. Mordecai Historic Park is also the departure point for the narrated Historic Raleigh Trolley Tour, which operates on Saturdays from March through December. For more information, call 919-857-4364 or visit www.raleighnc.gov/mordecai.

The *J. C. Raulston Arboretum* at North Carolina State University, located on Beryl Road off the Interstate 440 Beltline near the fairgrounds, is a nationally acclaimed garden containing one of the most diverse collections of landscape plants in North America. As part of the Department of Horticultural Science at the university, the arboretum is primarily a research and teaching garden that focuses on the

The Bell Tower at N.C. State
PHOTOGRAPH BY ELIZABETH KIRK

evaluation, selection, and display of plant material from around the world. Named in honor of its late founder and director, this eight-acre masterpiece includes such wonders as the Klein-Pringle White Garden, a Japanese garden meditation space, the Paradise Garden (designed to delight all five senses in the fashion of the ancient Persian gardens), and, famously, the 300-foot Perennial Border, based on the color scheme used by Gertrude Jekyll in the long border at her home, Munstead Wood. The gardens are open from 8 A.M. to 8 P.M. from April through October and from 8 A.M. to 5 P.M. from November through March. Guided tours are offered on Sunday at 2 P.M. from March through October. The facility is closed the first Sunday in May. Admission is free, but leave your pets at home. For more information, call 919-515-3132 or visit www.ncsu.edu/jcraulstonarboretum.

Museums and Science Centers

The *North Carolina Museum of Art*, at 2110 Blue Ridge Road (27607), began in 1947. North Carolina was the first state in the nation to appropriate public funds to purchase art, making this one of the earliest state-supported art museums in the country. It showcases an enviable collection of national and international works. The European gallery contains paintings and sculpture from the Renaissance through the Impressionist period. The gallery of American art features works by John Singleton Copley, Thomas Cole, and Winslow Homer, while the modern and contemporary galleries highlight art by the likes of Georgia O'Keeffe and John Biggers. More than 5,000 years of artwork from ancient Egypt to the present are on display to the public. Lectures and workshops are available, and films and concerts are regularly held in the museum's park and its outdoor cinema. Prices and times for special exhibits and programs vary, so call the box office at 919-715-5923 for information. The museum is open Tuesday, Wednesday, Thursday, and Saturday from 9 A.M. to 5 P.M., Friday from 9 A.M. to 9 P.M., and Sunday from 10 A.M. to 5 P.M. It is closed major holidays. Admission is free, as are guided tours, offered Tuesday through Sunday at 1:30 P.M. The museum was undergoing renovations at the time of this writing. For more information, call 919-839-6262 or visit www.ncartmuseum.org.

The *North Carolina Museum of History*, at 5 East Edenton Street (27601) on Bicentennial Plaza, contains more than 150,000 artifacts representative of North Carolina's rich heritage. Housing both long-term and changing exhibits, the museum focuses on seven broad categories of the state's history: agriculture and industry, community history, costumes and textiles, folk life, furnishings and decorative arts, military history, and political and socioeconomic history. It is also home to the North Carolina Sports Hall of Fame. Guided tours are available. Admission is free. The museum is open Monday through Saturday from 9 A.M. to 5 P.M. and Sunday from noon to 5 P.M. For information, visit www.ncmuseumofhistory.org or call 919-807-7900.

The *North Carolina Museum of Natural Sciences*, at 11 West Jones Street (27601), offers hands-on programs every day. Visitors can touch a flying squirrel, make lightning, or step inside a room filled with butterflies. Featuring over 3,000 live animals in four floors of exhibits, it has something to excite everyone in your group. Be sure to check out the four enormous whale skeletons on display. One hangs from the ceiling in the mezzanine. You can't miss it; it's 50 feet long. And if staring at the belly of a whale doesn't astound you, then take a look at the fossilized heart of the 66-million-year-old plant-eating Thescelosaurus nicknamed "Willo." It's the only one in the world! And it's on permanent display here, at the largest natural-history museum in the Southeast. The museum is open free of charge Monday through Saturday from 9 A.M. to 5 P.M. and Sunday from noon to 5 P.M. For more information, call 919-733-7450 or visit www.naturalsciences.org.

Marbles Kids Museum, at 201 East Hargett Street (27601), is a 2008 Parents' Picks winner. This interactive global learning center with hands-on exhibits boasts a popular IMAX theater that allows kids of all ages to travel to distant places and

North Carolina Museum of Natural Sciences
PHOTOGRAPH BY ELIZABETH KIRK

meet people from around the globe. State-of-the-art images on a screen seven stories high and a 12,000-watt surround-sound stereo system take movie watching to a whole new level, making viewers feel as if they've truly gone on an adventure. The museum is open Tuesday through Saturday from 9 A.M. to 5 P.M. and Sunday from noon to 5 P.M. Admission is charged. For information, call 919-834-4040 or visit www.marbleskidsmuseum.org. You can learn the showtimes for the IMAX theater by calling 919-822-IMAX.

The *Raleigh City Museum*, at 220 Fayetteville Street (27601), is a private, non-profit organization dedicated to preserving over 200 years of Capital City history. It is open Tuesday through Friday from 10 A.M. to 4 P.M. and Saturday from 1 P.M. to 4 P.M. Admission is free. For information, visit www.raleighcitymuseum.org or call 919-832-3775.

The *Olivia Raney Local History Library* is located at 4016 Carya Drive (27610), just outside the beltline in Wake County Office Park. If you're a genealogist or a history buff who likes digging through old records, this is the place for you. Students and researchers will find a plethora of historical material pertaining to Wake County and the surrounding area, as well as information about the Revolutionary War, the Civil War, North Carolina history, United States history, and African-American history. If you can, attend one of the lectures or ask about joining the Wake County Genealogical Society. Or you can just have fun tracing your family lineage by perusing the many historical journals and marriage, census, and tax records. The library is open Monday and Thursday from 10 A.M. to 8 P.M., Tuesday and Wednesday from 10 A.M. to 6 P.M., and Saturday from 10 A.M. to 5 P.M. For information, call 919-250-1196 or visit www.wakegov.com/locations/libraries/oliviaraneyhistorylibrary.htm.

Cultural Offerings

Artspace, located downtown at 201 East Davie Street (27601), promotes visual and performing art by allowing visitors to watch the creative process. You can interact with over 30 regional, national, and international artists while they work in open studios. You can also stroll through the many public exhibitions, catch one of the art talks, sit in on a lecture or demonstration, or, better yet, take a class. Admission is free. The center is open Tuesday through Saturday from 10 A.M. to 6 P.M. On the first Friday of each month, the hours are 10 A.M. to 10 P.M. Individual studio hours vary. For information, call 919-821-2787 or visit www.artspacenc.org.

The ***Progress Energy Center for the Performing Arts***, on the corner of Wilmington and South streets, is a multi-theater complex offering an extensive array of live shows. Three new theaters have been added to the original performing-arts arena, Raleigh Memorial Auditorium. You'll find everything from Broadway hits, musicals, and operas to experimental plays, original dance numbers, and stand-up comedy. Meymandi Concert Hall, home of the ***North Carolina Symphony*** (919-733-2750; www.ncsymphony.org), is located on the west side of the center. To the east is Fletcher Opera Theater, a more intimate setting. Performances by the ***Carolina Ballet*** (919-719-0800; www.carolinaballet.com), the ***National Opera Company***, and the ***A. J. Fletcher Institute***, a division of the University of North Carolina School of the Arts, are offered at Raleigh Memorial Auditorium and Fletcher Opera Theater. For something avant-garde, check out the Kennedy Theatre, a 40-by-60-foot black-box theater where you can usually find an edgy production by ***Burning Coal Theatre Company*** (919-834-4001; www.burningcoal.org) or ***Hot Summer Nights*** (919-633-6038; www. hotsummernightsatthekennedy.org). For tickets, call Ticketmaster at 919-834-4000. For general information, call 919-831-6060 or visit www.progressenergycenter.com.

Gallery C, located at 3522 Wade Avenue (27607) in Ridgewood Shopping Center, is the best known of Raleigh's many galleries and one of the leading galleries in the Southeast. The gallery represents more than 30 artists from all over the country working in a variety of media. It also has an impressive collection of Asian and Haitian art and jewelry. Gallery C hosts at least eight special exhibitions or solo shows per year; the exhibitions run from four to six weeks. If you happen to be in town during an opening reception, check out the art and experience one of the most popular social events in Raleigh. For more information, call 919-828-3165 or visit www.galleryc.net.

North Carolina Theatre, at 1 East South Street (27601), offers Broadway-series musicals. Combining talent from New York, North Carolina, and across the country, the group has staged productions of such shows as *Jesus Christ Superstar, The Sound of Music*, and *Good Ol' Girls*, a musical based on the stories of Hillsborough novelist Lee Smith and Lumberton native and writer Jill McCorkle. For ticket information, call 919-831-6950 or visit www.nctheatre.com.

Sertoma Arts Center, located in Sertoma Park, a wooded setting adjacent to Shelley Lake, offers classes for children and adults in the visual and performing arts, as well as concerts, workshops, and gallery space for local artists. Operated by Raleigh

Parks and Recreation, it is open Monday through Thursday from 9 A.M. to 10 P.M., Friday from 9 A.M. to 5 P.M., Saturday from 9 A.M. to 3 P.M., and Sunday from 1 P.M. to 5 P.M. For information, call 919-420-2329.

Special Shopping

Citysearch.com voted *Fairgrounds Flea Market*, located on the North Carolina State Fairgrounds at 1025 Blue Ridge Road (27607), "Best Free Attraction" two years in a row. That's understandable, since it's the largest indoor and outdoor flea market in the state and one of the largest in the entire Southeast. For over 30 years, bargain shoppers have bought antiques, handmade crafts, homemade fudge, vintage clothing, furniture, rare books, and just about anything else you can imagine from the nearly 300 permanent dealers and the 200 to 300 temporary dealers who peddle their wares here every weekend. The flea market is open Saturday and Sunday from 9 A.M. to 6 P.M. except in October during the North Carolina State Fair. For information, call 919-899-3532 or visit www.raleighfleamarket.net.

Historic City Market, located at 303 Blake Street (27601) at the intersection of Blount and Martin streets in downtown Raleigh, opened in 1914. Thanks to revitalization efforts in the 1980s, the Spanish Mission–style marketplace with cobblestone streets is bustling with art galleries, restaurants, and specialty shops that sell antiques, pottery, jewelry, and gourmet foods, among other things. The live bands, the Old World ambiance, and the site just three blocks off Fayetteville Street make City Market an attractive and convenient option for visitors to the city's major attractions. Among the noteworthy businesses here are *Rum Runners Dueling Piano Bar and Grill* (919-755-6436) and *Visual Art Exchange* (919-828-7834). Individual hours vary.

North Carolina State Farmers Market is located at 1201 Agriculture Street (27603); take the Lake Wheeler Road exit (Exit 297) off Interstate 40/440. This is the largest of the five farmers' markets owned by the state of North Carolina. It offers shoppers 75 acres of indoor and outdoor specialty shops, restaurants, a garden center, and fruits and vegetables from all over North Carolina. Growers sell in excess of 300 different items, including locally grown plants, Christmas trees, and handmade crafts. Busy shoppers can grab lunch at the Farmers Market Restaurant or the North Carolina Seafood Restaurant, located on the grounds. The market is open Monday through Saturday from 5 A.M. to 6 P.M. and Sunday from 8 A.M.

to 6 P.M. For information, call 919-733-7417 or visit www.agr.state.nc.us/markets/facilit/farmark/raleigh.

Recreation

The *Capital Area Greenway* is a nationally acclaimed system of natural multiuse trails spanning 63 miles along Raleigh's three primary waterways—the Neuse River, Walnut Creek, and Crabtree Creek—and their tributaries. Sponsored by Raleigh Parks and Recreation, the greenway project is quickly realizing its goal of building interconnecting trails to many of the city's 150 parks to facilitate activities such as biking, hiking, and jogging. For information about access or for a free map, call 919-996-4786 or 919-996-4115 or visit www.raleigh-nc.org/parks&rec/index.asp.

Lake Wheeler Metropolitan Park, at 6404 Lake Wheeler Road (27603), is a 650-acre lake managed by Raleigh Parks and Recreation. In addition to offering kayak, canoe, johnboat, and sailboat rentals, the park is open to all types of private boating. Superb fishing and picnicking opportunities are also available. Although swimming is not allowed, visitors may indulge in other water-related activities such as windsurfing and water-skiing. The award-winning Waterfront Program Center overlooks the lake; it boasts a popular lakeside conference room and a huge, open deck with rocking chairs and picnic tables. Cited as a favorite getaway by the *News & Observer*, Lake Wheeler is open year-round seven days a week from sunrise to sunset. It hosts a variety of special events and offers classes in windsurfing, water-skiing, and boating. For information, call 919-662-5704 or visit parks.raleighnc.gov.

Lake Wheeler is only one of many park options; the area boasts 4,300 acres of parkland and 1,400 acres of water. Check out www.visitraleigh.com for information about *William B. Umstead State Park, Durant Nature Park, Jordan Lake, Falls Lake, Johnson Lake, Shelley Lake*, and many others.

Raleigh Parks and Recreation operates five locations for *Neuse River canoe launches*. Gravel driveways allow year-round access to Falls Dam Access, located off Falls of the Neuse Road; Buffaloe Road Access, located off Elizabeth Drive; Milburnie Dam Access, located at Old Milburnie Road off U.S. 64 East; Anderson Point Access, located off Anderson Point Drive; and Poole Road Access. There is no charge. For information, call 919-831-6855.

Pullen Park and Aquatic Center, located in the downtown area at 520 Ashe Avenue

(27606), became the first public park in North Carolina when it was founded in 1887. According to the National Amusement Park Association, it is the 14th-oldest amusement park in the world. Pullen Park is named in honor of Richard Stanhope Pullen, who donated the land to the city. Today, the park offers a variety of recreational opportunities, including amusement rides, swimming, playground facilities, picnic shelters, lighted tennis courts, fitness programs, workshops, and art classes. The park's magnificent carousel dates to around 1900 and is one of only 14 Dentzel menageries still in operation in North America. The C. P. Huntington Train, a miniature replica of a locomotive built in 1863, attracts kids of all ages for a ride around the park's perimeter. The park is open year-round, but hours of operation vary by season. For information, call 919-831-6468.

The *RBC Center*, located at 1400 Edwards Mill Road (27607), is a 700,000-square-foot entertainment and sports arena with a seating capacity of 21,500. NCAA men's basketball featuring Raleigh's own *North Carolina State Wolfpack* begins in November and lasts until March. NHL hockey fans will find the *Carolina Hurricanes* on the ice from October to April. And AFL football fans can catch *Carolina Cobras* games from January through May in this $158 million state-of-the-art facility. The center also hosts special events like circuses and monster truck shows. To contact the box office, call 919-861-2323. For other information, call 919-861-2300 or visit www.rbccenter.com.

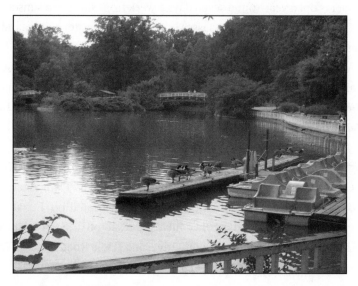

The lake at Pullen Park
PHOTOGRAPH BY ELIZABETH KIRK

The *North Carolina State women's basketball team* plays at Reynolds Coliseum, located at 103 Dunn Avenue on the university campus; for ticket information, call 919-865-1510 or visit www.gopack.com.

The *Capital City Bicycle Motocross Race Track*, located in Lions Park at 516 Dennis Avenue (27603), offers BMX races organized according to age group and skill level. Admission is free to spectators. Hours of operation vary; call 919-834-4269 for information.

Two locations for *Frisbee golf* are Cedar Hills Park, at 5600 Sweetbriar Street (27609), and Kentwood Park, at 4531 Kaplan Drive (27606). Each facility offers 18 holes. Professional and amateur tournaments are held monthly. Both parks are open daily from sunrise to sunset. For information about Frisbee golf at Cedar Hills Park, call 919-870-2880; for information about Frisbee golf at Kentwood Park, call 919-303-5328 or visit www.kentwooddiscgolf.com. For general information, visit www.raleighdiscgolf.com.

Seasonal Events

The *North Carolina State Fair*, held on the fairgrounds at 1025 Blue Ridge Road (27607), is the largest annual event in the state. It takes place in mid-October. Proud vegetable growers enter carefully selected specimens (watermelons the size of wheelbarrows, for example) in the Agricultural Fair Showcase, while producers bet the farm that their sheep or goats will win the livestock judging. For over 150 years, the coveted blue ribbon has been a symbol of North Carolina agricultural pride. Artisans in the Village of Yesteryear dress in period costume. Appearances and performances by celebrities and artists such as Bobby Flay and Bucky Covington are offered. An admission fee is charged. For information, call 919-821-7400 or visit www.ncstatefair.org.

The *Oakwood Candlelight Tour*, offered each December, includes a holiday sleigh ride through the Historic Oakwood District, where luminaries light the path and Christmas trees illustrate traditions from around the world. Select private residences and bed-and-breakfasts are open to the public for self-guided tours. Tours run from 1 P.M. until 7 P.M. A fee is charged. For information, call 919-832-9712 or visit www.historicoakwood.org.

The ***Storytelling Festival*** takes place at Historic Oak View County Park at 4028 Carya Drive (27610). Sponsored by the Wake County Public Libraries, it is held one Friday and Saturday during September. Talented professional storytellers from across the state and the country entertain area schoolchildren with tall tales, legends, folk tales, and ghost stories. Over 4,000 students usually attend. Special story times for adults, young adults, and older children are offered. Admission is free. For information, call 919-250-1200 or 919-250-1013 or visit www.wakegov.com/libraries.

The* Amistad *Saga: Reflections is presented in July at the African American Cultural Complex, located at 119 Sunnybrook Road (27610). The state's only outdoor drama written, produced, and directed by African-Americans, it tells the harrowing story of mutiny aboard the slave ship *Amistad* and dramatizes the plight of the ship's slaves, from their capture to their heroic battle for freedom. The African American Cultural Complex also offers other shows and a museum open by appointment. For information, call 919-250-9336 or visit www.aaccmuseum.org.

Artsplosure Spring Art Festival is held downtown the third weekend in May. This city-sponsored free outdoor festival features regional, national, and local jazz, blues, country, and pop musicians in continuous shows. Included are 150 artists' booths and lots of interactive and educational activities for children. For information, call 919-832-8699 or visit www.artsplosure.org.

First Night Raleigh is an alcohol-free New Year's Eve celebration of the arts held at various locations downtown. Throughout the afternoon and evening, participants enjoy art exhibits, music, dance, comedy, theater, and children's activities. The event culminates in a countdown to midnight, when "the City of Oaks," as Raleigh is sometimes called, holds its traditional "Acorn Drop" just as the new year is ushered in with a spectacular fireworks display. For information, call 919-832-8699 or visit www.firstnightraleigh.com.

La Fiesta del Pueblo takes place in August at the fairgrounds. Local citizens gather to celebrate Latin American art, music, food, and tradition. This weekend event boasts an attendance estimated at 35,000 to 40,000. A modest admission fee is charged. For information, visit www.elpueblo.org or www.ncstatefair.org.

Places to Stay

Resorts, Hotels, Motels

Sheraton Raleigh Hotel. Deluxe. 421 South Salisbury Street, 27601 (800-325-3535 or 919-834-9900; www.sheraton.com). This elegant hotel offers first-rate service and amenities including an indoor pool and Jacuzzi, a workout facility, room service, coffee makers, hair dryers, irons, high-speed Internet access, and complimentary breakfast. Express check-in and checkout are available. For an added level of service, guests can stay in one of the concierge-level rooms. As with most hotels, making reservations in advance will significantly lower the rate.

Courtyard by Marriott at Crabtree Valley. Deluxe/Expensive. 3908 Arrow Drive, 27612 (919-782-6868; www.marriott.com). This European-style hotel is a jewel. Located near Crabtree Valley Mall, it has 84 rooms, including deluxe rooms and several suites. Each room and suite has high-speed Internet access, a refrigerator, a hair dryer, luxurious bathrobes, special bath amenities, a coffee maker, an iron, and an ironing board. A breakfast buffet is offered every day. A restaurant, a lounge, an outdoor pool, and an exercise room are on the premises. Pets are welcome, with some restrictions.

Inns and Bed-and-Breakfasts

The Oakwood Inn. Deluxe. 411 North Bloodworth Street, 27604 (919-832-9712; www.oakwoodinnbb.com). This AAA Three Diamond inn is listed on the National Register as the Raynor-Stronach House. Built in 1871, it is one of four surviving homes of the original 11 that started what is now known as the Historic Oakwood District. In 1984, the house was converted into Raleigh's first bed-and-breakfast. The six guest rooms have period antiques, private baths, cable television, fireplaces, and modern amenities like computer ports. A full breakfast is served daily; complimentary snacks and beverages are offered 24 hours. Dinner-and-theater packages are available; each package includes a night's stay at The Oakwood Inn, dinner at a selected area restaurant, and tickets to a play produced by one of Raleigh's many theaters.

The Cameron Park Inn. Deluxe/Expensive. 211 Groveland Avenue, 27605

(888-257-2171 or 919-835-2171; www.cameronparkinn.com). Located just off Hillsborough Street at the North Carolina State Bell Tower, The Cameron Park Inn offers easy access to the university, Cameron Village, Raleigh Little Theatre, downtown, the City Market, Mordecai Historic Park, the Historic Oakwood District, the fairgrounds, the RBC Center, and Glenwood Avenue's restaurants and shops. Built in 1916 on a prominent corner lot in Cameron Park, the inn was one of the first 150 homes constructed in Raleigh's earliest planned subdivision. Owners Jon and Nikki D'Ambrose have gone for a Victorian feel in the inn's five guest rooms, which include private baths, ceiling fans, flat-screen TVs, DVD players, and wireless high-speed Internet access. The inn serves gourmet breakfasts. It is a 2008–9 BedandBreakfast. com Award winner for "Best of the South."

Places to Eat

Angus Barn. Expensive. 9401 Glenwood Avenue/U.S. 70 West, 27612, at Aviation Parkway (919-781-2444; www.angusbarn.com). This homey steakhouse with its blue-and-white gingham tablecloths has been a Capital City staple for over 40 years. The restaurant's four dining rooms, which can accommodate a whopping 600 hungry diners, serve 245,000 customers each year. A beef eater's haven, the Angus Barn is famed for—what else?—its Angus beef, which the staff ages for 28 days in the restaurant's own aging room. Not surprisingly, the menu is dominated by steaks, prime rib, rack of lamb, and a good assortment of seafood such as Alaskan king crab claws. But vegetarians do have a couple of choices. The 81-page wine list is considered one of the top 100 wine lists in the world; the wine cellar holds over 25,000 bottles. Dinner is served seven days a week; lunch is served for private functions of 25 people or more. The Wild Turkey Lounge offers a full bar and live entertainment; it opens at 4 P.M. on weekends and 4:30 P.M. on weekdays.

Second Empire Restaurant and Tavern. Expensive. 330 Hillsborough Street, 27603 (919-829-3663; www.second-empire.com). This restaurant is located in the elegantly restored Dodd-Hinsdale House, built around 1879. Second Empire's menu changes every month; it features creations from the freshest seasonal ingredients. Entrées may include grilled marinated swordfish and roasted Australian lamb loin. The lighter and more casual alternatives on the tavern's menu range from hickory-smoked Maine lobster risotto to steamed "Icy Blue" mussels. Second Empire is a recipient of *Wine Spectator*'s Award of Excellence and a Four Diamond rating from

AAA. Dinner is served Monday through Saturday; the tavern is also open Monday through Saturday evenings.

42nd Street Oyster Bar. Expensive/Moderate. 508 West Jones Street, 27603 (919-831-2811; www.42ndstoysterbar.com). In 1931, J. C. Watson opened a grocery at the current location of 42nd Street Oyster Bar. A loyal patron, Dr. Louis "Tick" West, suggested that Watson start serving oysters to his customers. Two years later, after Prohibition ended, Watson's was the first business in Raleigh to offer draft beer in frosted mugs. The combination of steamed oysters and cold beer has made 42nd Street Oyster Bar a Raleigh favorite for over 70 years. Today, the restaurant offers a full range of seafood, as well as chicken, steak, and pasta. It is still a place where sophisticated patrons talk business and politics, just as Tick and his doctor colleagues must have done. Lunch is served Monday through Friday and dinner seven days a week. Live music and a full bar are offered.

Big Ed's City Market. Inexpensive. 220 Wolfe Street, 27601 (919-836-9909). Located in the historic City Market district, Big Ed's serves up traditional American fare with down-home Southern hospitality. Its breakfast has been voted one of the best in North Carolina by Citysearch.com; Big Ed's offers homemade flapjacks, red-eye gravy, grits, biscuits, and fried squash. The lunch menu includes steaks, crab cakes, burgers, and fried chicken. Breakfast is served Monday through Saturday and lunch Monday through Friday.

Roast Grill. Inexpensive. 7 South West Street, 27603 (www.roastgrill.com; 919-832-8292). The menu here is famously limited. In fact, there really isn't one. Since 1940, the Roast Grill has served only grilled hot dogs (diners choose the "degree of burn") with a choice of mustard, onions, slaw, and amazing homemade chili. Ketchup and mayonnaise are sacrilege here. Homemade pound cake and baklava for dessert round out the offerings. Visitors will find no better place for a taste of Raleigh the way it used to be. Lunch is served Monday through Saturday.

The Most Interesting Man in the World: Capital Edition

Sir Walter Raleigh
COURTESY OF NORTH CAROLINA STATE ARCHIVES

If you think Sir Walter Raleigh was just an Elizabethan poet in a frilly collar, think again. It's not easy getting a state capital named after you when you never set foot in North America. Try it sometime.

Raleigh was born around 1552 in Devonshire and briefly attended Oxford. Around age 20, he helped quell the Desmond Rebellions in Ireland, during which he oversaw the slaughter of Spanish and Italian soldiers after their surrender at Smerwick. His good looks and quick wit won him favors from Queen Elizabeth I beyond the norm for his military service. He was granted two Irish towns and 40,000 local acres, Durham House in London, and various other properties, leases, and licenses. He was knighted in 1584.

The 1580s saw Raleigh's sponsorship of the colonization expeditions to Roanoke Island, culminating in the Lost Colony of 1587. The lessons learned from his failure helped pave the way for success at Jamestown.

He also undertook explorations of his own, the most famous of which brought him to what is now Venezuela in 1595. He subsequently contributed to the El Dorado legend by publishing

The Discovery of Guiana, considered by many the greatest Elizabethan adventure narrative.

In his spare time, Raleigh introduced tobacco and potato cultivation to Ireland, though the latter claim is disputed. A noted scalawag and ladies' man, he was arrested on multiple occasions for dueling. His poetic *oeuvre* includes such nuggets as "If she seem not chaste to me,/ What care I how chaste she be?" He helped Edmund Spenser publish the first three books of *The Fairie Queene*, thereby earning the enmity of English students everywhere. He spelled his name dozens of ways, though he apparently never hit upon the version in use today.

Over the course of his life, Raleigh was both the most loved and the most hated man in England. He first ran afoul of Queen Elizabeth in 1591, when he secretly married one of her ladies-in-waiting, Elizabeth

"Bess" Throckmorton, pregnant at the time. Then in the mid-1590s came accusations of atheism. After the queen's death in 1603, Raleigh was charged with treason for his alleged role in a plot against King James. He was tried and imprisoned in the Tower of London. Upon his release in 1616, he undertook a second expedition in search of El Dorado, during which his men attacked a Spanish outpost. For that action, the Spanish ambassador asked King James to sentence Raleigh to death.

At his beheading in October 1618, Raleigh's skills as a wordsmith may have served him better than at any time in his 66 or so years. Upon seeing the ax, he said, "This is a sharp Medicine, but it is a Physician for all diseases and miseries." Waiting for the blow, he exclaimed, "Strike, man, strike!"

As was the custom, his body was buried and his head was embalmed and presented to his wife. In some accounts, she kept it in a red leather bag for 29 years until her death. In others, she stored it in a cupboard to show to Sir Walter's many admirers.

Durham

Durham owes its best-known nickname to a happy marketing accident. Tobacco magnate John Green of the Blackwell Tobacco Company admired the bull logo that Colman's Mustard used and mistakenly thought the mustard was produced in Durham, England. Green thus named his brand of tobacco Bull Durham. By 1890, Bull Durham was the most famous trademark in the world. The name even generated popular words and phrases like *bullpen* and *shoot the bull*. After James B. Duke bought the company, he packaged "cigarette cards" in his tobacco; their popularity led to the creation of baseball cards. The famous image of John Green's bull was painted on barns and other sites around the world. The tobacco-and-baseball tie-in lasted well into the 20th century.

Durham's other successes are the result of more concerted efforts. In 1898, the same year James B. Duke bought the Blackwell Tobacco Company, John Merrick founded North Carolina Mutual, the nation's largest and oldest African-American-owned life insurance company. In 1907, the Mechanics and Farmers Bank opened in North Carolina Mutual's neighborhood near Parrish Street. It subsequently became one of the largest African-American-owned banks in the United States. When other successful businesses began operations nearby, the bustling neighborhood became known as "the Black Wall Street."

Trying in recent years to change its image from that of a tobacco town, Durham launched a "City of Medicine" campaign, based on the town's hospitals and pharmaceutical companies. The invention of BC Headache Powder in Durham back in 1910 is thought to have been the city's first step in that direction. When Duke University Medical School opened in 1930, Durham extended its reach into medicine. Now, the city boasts a renowned diet center and five major hospitals. And Research Triangle Park, home to many pharmaceutical and biomedical engineering companies, is surrounded on three sides by the city.

Durham offers great accommodations and restaurants and some of the best attractions and cultural events in the region. In fact, it has two symphony orchestras; 15 art centers and performance halls; over 20 annual festivals and events; more than 60 parks, trails, and waterways; 12 science and nature centers; lots of nightclubs; several professional sports teams; and numerous historic sites and shopping centers.

JUST THE FACTS

Durham sits at the northern point of the Triangle; Raleigh lies southeast and Chapel Hill southwest. Durham can be reached via Interstate 85, Interstate 40, U.S. 15/501, and U.S. 70.

Raleigh-Durham International Airport is less than 20 minutes away; it is accessible via the Durham Expressway leading to Interstate 40 East.

The Amtrak station is at 400 West Chapel Hill Street (27701); for information, call 800-872-7245.

The Triangle Transit Authority runs buses from Duke University Medical Center to the airport and Chapel Hill; call 919-549-9999 or visit www.triangle-transit.org for information. Duke University Transit sends buses between the school's East and West campuses; call 919-684-2218. The Greyhound bus station is located at 820 West Morgan Street (27701); call 919-687-4800.

The daily newspaper is the *Durham Herald-Sun*. The *Raleigh News & Observer* has a special Durham section every day. Comprehensive listings of local events can be found in the *Independent Weekly*, a free paper that covers the entire Triangle.

The Durham Convention and Visitors Bureau is located at 101 East Morgan Street (27701). For information, call 800-446-8604 or 919-687-0288 or visit www.durham-nc.com.

Things to Do

Historic Places, Gardens, and Tours

Duke University was created in 1924 by James B. Duke as a memorial to his father, Washington Duke. The Dukes had long felt an interest in Trinity College. In December 1924, the college's trustees gratefully accepted an endowment from James B. Duke that provided in part for the expansion of Trinity College into Duke University. After undergoing a massive expansion in the Georgian style, the original Durham campus of Trinity became known as the East Campus. The West Campus, which has an English Gothic style fashioned after the Ivy League, opened in 1930. Since then, Duke has achieved an outstanding record of academic excellence. It is now home to several renowned schools, Duke University Medical Center, the Terry Sanford Center, and the Nasher Museum of Art. For information, visit www.duke.edu.

Duke Chapel, located on Chapel Drive on the West Campus, is the university's most recognizable landmark. Its 210-foot tower is visible for miles. This awe-inspiring

Duke Chapel
COURTESY OF DURHAM CONVENTION AND VISITORS BUREAU

structure was constructed of stone from the Duke Quarry near Hillsborough, as was the rest of the impressive West Campus. The chapel was one of the country's last great collegiate Gothic projects. Founding father James B. Duke envisioned a "great towering church" in the center of the campus that would have a "profound influence on the spiritual life of the young men and women" who came here. One of the chapel's designers, Julian Abele, was America's first black architect of renown. He and fellow designer Horace Trumbauer turned James B. Duke's vision into a reality. Upon entering the chapel, visitors are immediately drawn to the great chancel window at the end of the center aisle. Altogether, a total of 77 stained-glass renderings containing 800 to 900 figures made from over a million pieces of glass tell stories from the Old and New testaments. The chapel also holds a massive pipe organ and a 50-bell carillon housed in an impressive structure of intricately detailed stone, wood, and stained glass. Visitors are welcome to tour the chapel and to participate in the interdenominational services held on Sunday at 11 A.M. Afternoon visits on weekends are not recommended without checking ahead to see if a wedding is scheduled; call 919-681-9414. For more information, call 919-681-1704 or visit www.chapel.duke.edu.

Cameron Crazies
COURTESY OF DURHAM CONVENTION AND VISITORS BUREAU

Sarah P. Duke Gardens, at 426 Anderson Street (27708) on the West Campus, encompasses 55 acres of stunning landscaped and wooded gardens in the midst of the university. Five miles of walks and pathways wind in and around the Blomquist Garden of native North Carolina plants, the Culberson Asiatic Arboretum, a lily pond, waterfalls, and a variety of flower beds that change with the seasons. These magnificent gardens also serve as a backdrop to live music and dance performances. They are open to the public every day until sunset. Guided tours are available but must be prearranged; a fee is charged. For information, call 919-684-3698 or visit www.hr.duke.edu/dukegardens.

The *Duke Homestead and Tobacco Museum*, located at 2828 Duke Homestead Road (27705), is a national historic landmark and a living-history archive that chronicles the humble beginnings of tobacco magnate Washington Duke. The homestead and museum showcase his 19th-century house and the farm and factories where he first grew and processed tobacco. Later, his sons founded the American Tobacco Company, the largest tobacco company in the world. Museum exhibits trace the history of tobacco from Native American times to the present. The Duke Homestead and Tobacco Museum is currently open Tuesday through Saturday from 9 A.M. to 5 P.M. Admission and tours are free. Groups are asked to schedule visits in advance. For information, call 919-477-5498 or visit www.ibiblio.org/dukehome.

Bennett Place State Historic Site is a small farmhouse at 4409 Bennett Memorial Road (27705). In April 1865, Generals Joseph E. Johnston and William T. Sherman gathered under a flag of truce to discuss a peaceful resolution to the Civil War. They and their escorts met on the Hillsborough Road midway between the opposing lines. Needing a place for a conference, Johnston suggested a simple farmhouse nearby. On three separate occasions, the Union and Confederate generals struggled to achieve equitable terms for surrender at the home of James and Nancy Bennett (or Bennitt). On April 26, the Bennett dwelling became the site of the largest troop surrender of the Civil War.

The original buildings were destroyed by fire in 1921, but the present structures were carefully reconstructed in the 1960s using sketches and early photographs. Today, the farmhouse, kitchen, and smokehouse give visitors a glimpse into the life of an ordinary Southern farm family during the Civil War. Bennett Place is currently open Tuesday through Saturday from 9 A.M. to 5 P.M. Free tours are offered through the visitor center. For the current schedule, visit www.nchistoricsites.org/bennett or call 919-383-4345.

Reenactors at Bennett Place
COURTESY OF DURHAM CONVENTION AND VISITORS BUREAU

Historic Stagville, located at 5828 Old Oxford Highway (27712), is a state his-toric site featuring 18th- and 19th-century buildings dedicated to African-American cultural and historic studies. The 71-acre site occupies the remnants of one of the largest plantations of the pre–Civil War South. It belonged to the Bennehan and Cameron families, whose combined holdings totaled approximately 900 slaves and almost 30,000 acres by 1860. Historic Stagville is currently open Tuesday through Saturday from 10 A.M. to 4 P.M., but the hours of operation may change; call ahead to confirm. Admission and guided tours are free. Since you'll be doing some walk-ing, it's a good idea to wear comfortable shoes and carry bottled water; no food or drinks are available at the site. For information, call 919-620-0120 or visit www.historicstagvillefoundation.org.

North Carolina Mutual Life Insurance Company, formerly located at 114–116 West Parrish Street, was once the home of the Mechanics and Farmers Bank, known as "the World's Largest Negro Business." It helped win Durham a reputation as "the Capital of the Black Middle Class." The white-brick structure, erected in 1921 on the site of the company's first office building, is listed on the National Register and is a national historic landmark. The company's current headquarters is at 411 West Chapel Hill Street (27701).

West Point on the Eno City Park, at 5101 North Roxboro Road (27704) in northern Durham, is a 388-acre natural and historical park along the Eno River. It features a reconstructed, working 1778 gristmill and part of the community that surrounded it, including a re-created blacksmith shop. The park also offers the *Hugh Mangum Museum of Photography* and an amphitheater. It is the site of the Festival for the Eno in early July. The park facilities are open daily from sunrise to sunset, but the buildings are open only from 1 P.M. to 5 P.M. on weekends. Admission is free. The entire Eno River State Park encompasses over 2,000 undeveloped acres along the river. It offers opportunities for hiking, picnicking, camping (by permit only), canoeing, and rafting. For information about West Point on the Eno, call 919-471-1623 or visit www.enoriver.org. For camping, hiking, and canoeing regulations, call 919-383-1686 or e-mail eno.river@ncmail.net.

Museums and Science Centers

The *North Carolina Museum of Life and Science*, at 433 West Murray Avenue (27704), is more fun than kids of any age ought to have. Featuring a 13-foot tornado, a percussion hut, dozens of interactive exhibits, over 100 live animal species from owls to wolves, the Magic Wings Butterfly House, an insectarium, an aerospace exhibit, the News Channel 11 Accu-Weather Station, an outdoor nature park, and the Ellerbee Creek Railway, this place is guaranteed to entertain for hours. It is one of only 35 institutions in the world accorded full member status by the Association of Science-Technology Centers. The museum is open Monday through Saturday from 10 A.M. to 5 P.M. and Sunday from noon to 5 P.M.; it is closed on Monday from September 14 to December 21. An admission fee is charged. For information, call 919-220-5429 or visit www.ncmls.org.

The *Nasher Museum of Art at Duke University* is located adjacent to the Sarah P. Duke Gardens at 2001 Campus Drive (27708). Uruguayan architect Rafael Viñoly designed the building, made up of five pavilions arranged around a pentagonal central hall with a dramatic glass-and-steel canopy. The pavilions hold three gallery spaces, a 173-seat auditorium, and an education wing. The education wing is home to the Nasher Museum Café and a museum shop. The museum's permanent holdings include the Brummer Collection of Medieval and Renaissance Art, a pre-Columbian collection from Central and South America, the George Harley Memorial Collection of African Art, and numerous classical pieces. Temporary exhibitions that reflect the museum's increasing focus on modern and contemporary art are offered throughout

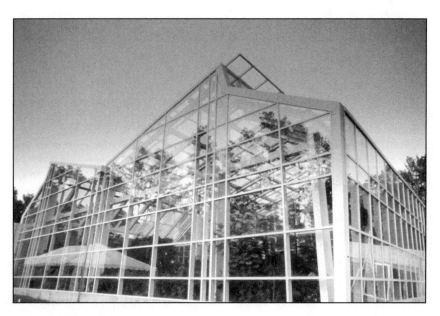

Magic Wings Butterfly House
COURTESY OF DURHAM CONVENTION AND VISITORS BUREAU

the year. The museum is open Tuesday, Wednesday, Friday, and Saturday from 10 A.M. to 5 P.M.; Thursday from 10 A.M. to 9 P.M.; and Sunday from noon to 5 P.M. An admission fee is charged. For information, call 919-684-5135 or visit www.nasher. duke.edu.

The *Duke University Lemur Center*, located at 3705 Erwin Road (27705), is the world's leading facility dedicated to prosimian primates. Approximately 250 animals, including 233 lemurs encompassing 15 species, are housed here, among them lemurs from Madagascar, loris from Asia, galagos from Africa, and tarsiers from the islands of eastern Asia. Located about a quarter-mile from the Duke campus, this facility provides an extraordinary opportunity to see and appreciate these increasingly endangered creatures. The center is open for tours Monday through Friday from 9 A.M. to 4:30 P.M. Saturday hours vary by season. Visitors are allowed access by appointment only. Due to an increase in tour requests, be sure to call at least two weeks in advance. In accordance with United States Department of Agriculture regulations, all visitors must be accompanied by a trained docent or staff member while on the premises. Large groups with children should be accompanied by several adult chaperones. For information, call 919-489-3364 or visit www.lemur.duke.edu.

The Triumvirate

First came John Merrick, born a slave in Clinton, North Carolina, in 1859. After moving to the Raleigh area in his teens, Merrick worked as a brick mason and then as a shoeshine boy and barber. In 1880, a friend asked him to help open a barbershop in Durham. Merrick soon bought a share in the shop, then the entire shop, then a total of eight barbershops, some catering to blacks and the others to whites. He got his education cutting hair and absorbing the wisdom of the professors, businessmen, and occasional luminaries like William Jennings Bryan who were his clients. Upon venturing into real estate, he became one of the largest landowners in Durham's Hayti section.

Second came Aaron Moore, born in 1863 into a tradition of free mixed-race farmers in Columbus County. Educated in Lumberton and Fayetteville, Moore taught for a time before enrolling in medical school at Shaw University in Raleigh, where John Merrick had laid bricks just a few years earlier. Moore finished the four-year program in three years and moved to Durham, becoming the city's first black physician.

Third came C. C. Spaulding, Dr. Moore's nephew, born in 1874 into the same Columbus County enclave. In 1894, Spaulding moved to Durham, where he worked traditional black jobs—waiter, bellhop, office boy—before becoming manager of a black cooperative grocery.

In 1900, the three coalesced into what became known as Durham's "Triumvirate." Merrick had a business interest in the Royal Knights of King David, a black fraternal organization that was one of the few concerns selling insurance to African-Americans. Real-izing the shortcomings of that system, Merrick joined with several partners in 1898 to found North Carolina Mutual Provident Life. Within six months, he bought out his partners and brought in Dr. Moore. Within two years, they changed the name to North Carolina Mutual Insurance Company and hired Spaulding as general manager.

The combination clicked. In the early days, Merrick and Moore ran the business without pay while Spaulding was on the road peddling policies and collecting commissions. By 1910, the company claimed status as "the World's Largest Negro Business."

Married to the daughter of a black political leader, Dr. Moore ran for county coroner on at least one occasion. In fact, all three men likely had political aspirations. But sensing white hostility toward any such efforts, they adopted the Booker T. Washington philosophy of social progress through advancement in business. Merrick established the *Durham Negro Observer* and helped found Mechanics and Farmers Bank. During World War II, the United States Navy commissioned the SS *John Merrick*, a merchant ship. With Merrick's fund-raising help, Dr. Moore founded Lincoln Hospital and the Durham Colored Library and otherwise devoted himself to the education of rural blacks. Spaulding outlived his partners by many years and witnessed the dawn of a new political era. He worked for the Urban League and other social organizations and influenced Franklin Roosevelt's appointments to the "black cabinet."

Many others were part of the story, of course, but the Triumvirate was front and center in Durham's rise to becoming "the Capital of the Black Middle Class."

Cultural Offerings

The *Carolina Theatre* is located at 309 West Morgan Street (27701). The last remaining of the city's original 13 theaters, this 1926 performance hall is a rich part of Durham history. Lovingly restored in 1992, it is the only historic theater in the country with two fully operating state-of-the-art cinemas. Part of the Durham Civic Center complex, the main auditorium, Fletcher Hall, and the Connie Moses Ballroom are nothing short of gorgeous, and the events that take place here are a thrill. Visitors can sit back in the renovated glory of this Beaux-Arts structure and enjoy first-run art shows; live music by such artists as George Jones, John Berry, and Susan Tedeschi; performances by the Durham Symphony; and live theater and opera. For tickets, call 919-560-3030. For information, call 919-560-3040 or visit www.carolinatheatre.org.

Hayti Heritage Center, at 804 Old Fayetteville Street (27701), is located in Durham's historic Hayti community. The center is an integral part of the Triangle's cultural landscape. The 1890s church that houses the complex is a national historic landmark. The center offers innovative programming and exhibitions featuring local, regional, and national artists in its effort to educate the entire population about African-American life, history, and culture, as viewed through many artistic perspectives. Among the programs the Hayti Heritage Center coordinates are the Black Film Diaspora, the Bull Durham Blues Fest, and the Martin Luther King Festival. It is also the home of the Lyda Moore Merrick Gallery. From September to May, the center is open Monday through Friday from 10 A.M. to 5 P.M. and Saturday from 10 A.M. to 3 P.M. From June to August, it is open Monday from 5 P.M. to 8 P.M., Tuesday through Friday from 10 A.M. to 5 P.M., and Saturday from 10 A.M. to 3 P.M. For information, call 800-845-9835 or 919-683-1709 or visit www.hayti.org.

Manbites Dog Theater, at 703 Foster Street (27701), is a professional nonprofit theater company founded in Durham in 1987. This plucky group takes on controversial issues that leave audiences talking for days. Noteworthy productions have included the first North Carolina performances of Arlene Hutton's *Last Train to Nibroc*, Diana Son's *Stop Kiss*, and Paula Vogel's Pulitzer Prize–winning *How I Learned to Drive*. Original productions have included the 2003 world premiere of *Bucknaked: A Love Story*. For information or tickets, visit www.manbitesdogtheater.org or call 919-682-4974.

The four galleries at the **Center for Documentary Studies at Duke University**, at 1317 West Pettigrew Street (27705) near Duke's East Campus, show works by nationally known photographers and photojournalists and Duke faculty and students. The center also features audio and mixed-media projects. Visitors can check out the books and educational projects that the center produces. During the school year, the galleries are open Monday through Friday from 9 A.M. to 9 P.M., Saturday from 11 A.M. to 4 P.M., and Sunday from 1 P.M. to 5 P.M. During summer, they are open Monday through Thursday from 9 A.M. to 7 P.M. and Friday from 9 A.M. to 5 P.M.; call for summer weekend hours. For information, call 919-660-3663 or visit http://cds.aas.duke.edu.

Special Shopping

Brightleaf Square, at the corner of Main and Gregson streets in downtown Durham, is comprised of two former tobacco warehouses built between 1900 and 1904. In 2004, Brightleaf Square was extensively renovated. Many of the shops, restaurants, and galleries now face a central courtyard between the two buildings. For information, call 919-682-9229 or visit www.historicbrightleaf.com.

Ninth Street, near Duke's East Campus, offers an eclectic row of boutiques, galleries, cafés, a great bookstore, and a toy store that just begs kids to pop inside.

Patterson's Mill Country Store, at 5109 Farrington Road (27707) between N.C. 54 and Old Chapel Hill Road, is an authentic country store and pharmacy with hundreds of pieces of historical memorabilia. A collector or amateur pharmaceutical historian could spend a day in this quaint shop. The store includes a furnished early-20th-century doctor's office. Antiques, collectibles, and North Carolina crafts and gifts are for sale. The store is open Tuesday through Saturday from 10 A.M. to 5 P.M. and Sunday from 2 P.M. to 5 P.M. For information, call 919-493-8149.

The Streets at Southpoint, located at 6910 Fayetteville Road (27713), is a super-mall featuring a 200,000-square-foot outdoor cityscape called "Main Street." It offers 1.3 million square feet of retail space and over 150 shops and restaurants. Shoppers can find anything here. The hours are Monday through Saturday from 10 A.M. to 9 P.M. and Sunday from noon to 7 P.M. For information, call 919-572-8808 or visit www.thestreetsatsouthpoint.com.

The *Tuba Exchange*, at 1825 Chapel Hill Road (27707), is a unique clearing-house for new and used tubas, euphoniums, and sousaphones. This store is truly the only one of its kind in the nation! While you're here, take a look at what is among the largest privately held collections of low brass instruments in the world. The Tuba Exchange is open Monday through Friday from 9 A.M. to 5 P.M. by appointment. For information, call 800-869-TUBA or 919-493-2200 or visit www.tubaexchange.com.

The *Music Explorium*, at 5314 N.C. 55, Suite 107 (27713), specializes in percussion instruments, including unusual drums. In the spirit of community and self-expression, it offers rhythm parties and drum-and-dance circles; little or no musical expertise is needed. Even non-musicians will find the Music Explorium fascinating. It is open during events and by appointment. For information, call 919-484-9090 or visit www.musicexplorium.com.

Recreation

Durham Bulls Athletic Park, on Willard Street (27701) between Mangum and Blackwell streets, is the nationally acclaimed, 10,000-seat downtown home of the Durham Bulls class AAA baseball club. The park includes skyboxes and the year-round Ball Park Corner, which sells Bulls memorabilia. For tickets or information, call 919-687-6500 or visit www.durhambulls.com. Historic *Durham Athletic*

Durham Bulls Athletic Park
COURTESY OF DURHAM CONVENTION AND VISITORS BUREAU

Park, at the corner of Morris and Corporation streets, is the old site where generations of fans gathered to watch the Bulls play and where the movie *Bull Durham*,
starring Kevin Costner and Susan Sarandon, was filmed.

Duke Forest encompasses over 7,000 acres in six principal tracts in Durham, Orange,
and Alamance counties. The forest was organized in 1931 under the direction of Clar-
ence Korstian, the dean of Duke University's School of Forestry. Hiking, biking,
and horseback riding are popular on the property's network of roads and fire trails,
as is fishing along New Hope Creek in the forest's Korstian Division. For information, call 919-613-8013 or visit www.dukeforest.duke.edu.

The *American Tobacco Trail* offers six miles of trails connecting downtown
Durham to N.C. 54. Bikers, hikers, and joggers take advantage of this greenway,
conveniently located in the heart of the city. For information, visit www.triangle-
trails.org/ATT.HTM.

Carolina Barnstormers, at 4340 East Geer Street (27704), offers "flightseeing"
tours from the open cockpit of Mike Ratty's red biplane. Guests can take a 25-min-
ute tour of the airport vicinity or opt for an hour-long tour and choose their own
destination. The tours, for one or two people at a time, are offered from September through mid-June. For information, call 919-608-0181 or 919-408-0370 or visit
www.carolinabarnstormers.com.

Seasonal Events

The *American Dance Festival* takes place in Page Auditorium on Duke's West
Campus, in the Reynolds Industries Theatre, and at other locations. The largest and
most influential modern-dance festival in the world, it boasts more than two dozen
dance companies, hundreds of choreographers and writers, and students who participate in classes, seminars, and performances. The festival runs from early June
to late July and attracts an audience from around the world. For information, call
919-684-6402 or visit www.americandancefestival.org.

The *Bull Durham Blues Festival* takes place in early September at historic Durham Athletic Park at the corner of Morris and Corporation streets. The state's largest blues celebration, it has drawn fans from all over North Carolina and from 25
different states and five countries. In 2000, the festival was awarded the "Keeping

Bull Durham Blues Festival
COURTESY OF DURHAM CONVENTION AND VISITORS BUREAU

the Blues Alive Award" by the Blues Foundation. It showcases national, regional, and local blues performed by contemporary artists including Taj Mahal, Etta James, Aaron Neville, Otis Rush, and Alberta Adams. For ticket information, call the Hayti Heritage Center at 919-683-1709 or visit www.bulldurhamblues.org.

The *Festival for the Eno*, held at West Point Park, is North Carolina's oldest and most prestigious environmental event. It draws over 100 artists and craftsmen and as many performers, who entertain audiences at five stages. This three-day festival on the Fourth of July weekend raises money for the purchase and protection of land in central North Carolina's Eno River Basin. Past performers have included Doc Watson, Ralph Stanley, and the African-American Dance Ensemble. For information or tickets, call 919-620-0900, ext. 203, or visit www.enoriver.org/Festival.

The *Full Frame Documentary Film Festival* takes place in April in the Carolina Theatre's Royal Center for the Arts. Formerly called the DoubleTake Festival, this international event is presented in association with the Center for Documentary Studies at Duke University, the *New York Times*, the Museum of Modern Art in New York, the North Carolina Museum of Art in Raleigh, and the Hague Appeal for Peace in the Netherlands, among others. Touted by *Entertainment Weekly* as "the 'It' Documentary Film Festival," Full Frame now draws more submissions than

Sundance and has been endorsed by Martin Scorsese. For information, call 919-687-4100 or visit www.fullframefest.org.

Places to Stay

Resorts, Hotels, and Motels

The Washington Duke Inn and Golf Club. Deluxe. 3001 Cameron Boulevard, 27706 (800-443-3853 or 919-490-0999; www.washingtondukeinn.com). The Washington Duke was built in the style of an English country inn. The lobby and hallways are graced with Duke family treasures and art. Known for its exceptional service, this is a rare Mobil Four Star, AAA Four Diamond hotel in eastern North Carolina. It features 271 elegantly appointed guest rooms and suites, as well as the Four Diamond–rated *Fairview Restaurant* and a 300-acre golf course.

Inns and Bed-and-Breakfasts

Arrowhead Inn. Deluxe. 106 Mason Road, 27712 (800-528-2207 or 919-477-8430; www.arrowheadinn.com). Nestled on six acres of spectacular gardens and magnolia-shaded lawns, the Arrowhead is pure luxury in a historical plantation setting. This AAA Four Diamond bed-and-breakfast was built around 1775. It has been meticulously renovated down to its original moldings, mantelpieces, and heart-of-pine floors. The inn has been featured in *USA Today, Southern Living*, and *Food and Wine* for its historical importance and elegance. Innkeepers Phil and Gloria Teber leave no detail overlooked. Guests can expect to find Gloria's attentive touch in every nook and cranny of each of the seven beautifully appointed guest rooms and the private log cabin and garden cottage. Aside from the fine furnishings, the exquisite linens, and the whirlpool tubs, amenities include plush bathrobes, complimentary snacks, fresh-cut flowers, candles, and a small collection of romantic music. The guest journals in the rooms reveal that past honeymooners and others have been pampered with trails of rose petals and private gourmet dinners delivered to their doors. Treat yourself to even one night here and you'll never want to stay in a hotel again.

Morehead Manor Bed-and-Breakfast. Deluxe. 914 Vickers Avenue, 27701 (888-437-6333 or 919-687-4366; www.moreheadmanor.com). This 8,000-square-foot Colonial Revival beauty is located in the historic Morehead Hill neighborhood just south of downtown, near Brightleaf Square. Built in 1910 for the CEO of Liggett & Myers Tobacco Company, the Art Deco–furnished home features four distinct guest rooms. Complimentary beverages, scrumptious homemade desserts, and a full breakfast are just some of the pleasures afforded here. Fun options include a "Murder Mystery Weekend" package, a "Get Me to the Church on Time" package for bridesmaids, a "You Go, Girl" getaway, and a "Greta's PJ Party" package.

Blooming Garden Inn. Deluxe/Expensive. 513 Holloway Street, 27701 (888-687-0801 or 919-687-0801; www.bloominggardeninn.com). Located in the historic district and run by innkeepers Dolly and Frank Pokrass, this sunny Victorian inn features antique beds, goose-down pillows, stained-glass accent panels, Jacuzzis, and beautiful porcelain sinks. The wraparound porches offer stunning views of the azaleas in the garden.

Carol's Garden Inn. Expensive. 2412 South Alston Avenue, 27713 (877-922-6777; www.carolsgardeninn.com). Built in 1910, this two-story Craftsman-style farmhouse has been completely renovated. It features a wide, open staircase and corner fireplaces. The two-story front porch overlooks pecan trees, a beautiful water garden, and a large pond. Guest-room amenities include high-speed Ethernet connections and private baths with whirlpool tubs.

Old North Durham Inn. Expensive. 922 North Mangum Street, 27701 (919-683-1885; www.bbonline.com/nc/oldnorth). This restored early-1900s Colonial Revival home was the recipient of the Durham Historic Preservation Society's Architectural Conservation Citation. It features a rocker-lined wraparound porch, coffered ceilings, beautiful oak floors, period wall coverings and furnishings, and much more. Located across the street from the residence used in the movie *Bull Durham*, the inn is close to Duke University, Durham Bulls Athletic Park, and the Carolina Theatre. In 1992, innkeeper Jim Vickery won the name-the-mascot contest for the Bulls baseball team; he now offers guests free tickets to all home games.

Places to Eat

Four Square. Expensive. 2701 Chapel Hill Road, 27707 (919-401-9877; www.foursquarerestaurant.com). This Triangle standard is located in the 1908 Bartlett Mangum House, listed on the National Register. Having trained with superstars like

Emeril Lagasse and Charlie Trotter, executive chef Shane Ingram has in turn taught several of the chefs at Durham's other top eateries. But he saves his best for the romantic restaurant he owns with his wife and partner, Elizabeth Woodhouse. Four Square serves dinner Monday through Saturday.

Magnolia Grill. Expensive. 1002 Ninth Street, 27705 (www.magnoliagrill.net; 919-286-3609). The Magnolia Grill has received about every culinary accolade possible, making it a destination for foodies from all over the country. Chef-owners Ben and Karen Barker helped set the trend in Southern-inspired cuisine from Magnolia Grill's open kitchen. The grill is frequently packed, so reservations are almost essential. Dinner is served Tuesday through Saturday.

Nana's Restaurant. Expensive. 2514 University Drive, 27707 (919-493-8545; www.nanasdurham.com). This Durham favorite features an intimate dining area with smart white linens and art by local artists. Former Magnolia Grill chef Scott Howell studied at the Culinary Institute of America in New York before opening this popular mingling spot. His menu stresses craft. Some of Nana's best offerings include house-smoked or house-cured meats. Nana's wine list has won *Wine Spectator*'s Award of Excellence; the restaurant hosts some of the best wine dinners in the area. Dinner is served Monday through Saturday; you'll need reservations.

Vin Rouge. Expensive/Moderate. 2010 Hillsborough Road, 27705 (919-416-0466; www.vinrougerestaurant.com). An open kitchen greets you as you walk in the door of the simple but elegant Vin Rouge. The food here includes bistro standards like "Steak Frites." The bacon-spiked "Gratin de Macaroni" is the Mercedes of macaroni and cheese. The wine list is all French; staff members are more than capable of matching your preferred style of wine or grape with an appellation you didn't know you liked. Vin Rouge's patio is a great place for Sunday brunch. Dinner is served Tuesday through Sunday; brunch is offered on Sunday only. Reservations are necessary on weekend nights.

Pop's Italian Trattoria. Moderate. 810 West Peabody Street, 27701 (919-956-7677; www.pops-durham.com). Located next to Morgan Imports and across the street from Brightleaf Square, this upscale casual restaurant offers good food and a bright clientele. The cuisine is stylish, fresh Italian. The desserts and breads are baked on the premises. Dinner is served daily. Reservations are appreciated.

Hong Kong Chinese Restaurant. Moderate/Inexpensive. 3003 Guess Road, 27705 (919-479-8339). Though this place doesn't look particularly special, many proclaim it to be the best and most authentic Chinese restaurant in the state. Its overflowing parking lot and rainbow coalition of customers attest to its popularity. Here, you can go beyond familiar selections and try "Turnip Pudding," "Beef Tripe," or "Chicken Feet"—and those are just a few of the appetizer choices. People pour in at midday on weekends for the dim sum, wheeled among the tables on carts. Lunch and dinner are served Wednesday through Monday.

James Joyce and *The Federal.* Moderate/Inexpensive. 912 and 914 West Main Street, 27701. These sister establishments, located next door to one another across the street from Brightleaf Square, are under the same ownership. Both are wildly popular hangouts for Duke students and young professionals. James Joyce (919-683-3022; www.jamesjoyceirishpub.com) serves traditional pub fare and offers great specials. The Federal (919-680-8611; www.thefederal.net) is more bar than restaurant, but the quality of its food far exceeds what you might expect from the setting. Both serve lunch and dinner daily.

Bullock's BBQ. Inexpensive. 3330 Quebec Drive, 27705 (919-383-3211). Bullock's is a family-owned barbecue place with impressive staying power. Imitators have opened up on all sides of it, but Bullock's remains busy serving great BBQ, Brunswick stew, fried chicken, and other traditional Southern food. The crowd is a mixture of townies and transplants of all ages. Come hungry and bring cash! Lunch and dinner are served Tuesday through Saturday.

Foster's Market. Inexpensive. 2694 Durham–Chapel Hill Boulevard, 27707 (919-489-3944; www.fostersmarket.com). Sarah Foster, a caterer and former chef for Martha Stewart, converted this former lawn-mower repair shop into a gourmet market and sandwich shop in 1990. She furnished it with mismatched vintage chairs that complement the building's lived-in feel. Foster's is arguably the best place for lunch in Durham. Its sandwiches, salads, and prepared foods can be bought by the pound or by portion. For breakfast or a snack, the scones, muffins, crumb cakes, and breads are in a class by themselves. Pick up a jar of Sarah's "Seven Pepper Jelly" on your way out and invent a use for it when you get home. Breakfast, lunch, and dinner are served daily.

Toast Paninoteca. Inexpensive. 345 West Main Street, 27701 (919-683-2183; www.toast-fivepoints.com). Located in the heart of Durham at Five Points, Toast serves interesting and varied panini, tramezzini, bruschetta, and crostini choices. If you don't know what those are, the definitions on the wall will tell you. But suffice it to say they're far superior to the average sandwich. Bountiful salads, homemade soups, biscotti, and a selection of beers are also offered. Toast is open for lunch Monday through Saturday and for dinner Monday through Friday.

Chapel Hill and Carrboro

Chapel Hill residents used to refer to their town as "the southern part of heaven." Tar Heel fans liken their team's colors to the celestial shades. But the origin of the school's signature Carolina blue and white has actually been traced back to two campus literary societies whose members wore the separate colors to distinguish one group from the other. Beginning around 1800, the Dialectic and Philanthropic societies wore light blue and white, respectively. At commencements and other events, a student official or marshal wore the color of his society. Whenever a student leader represented the entire school, not just his society, he wore both colors. In 1888, the university began fielding its first intercollegiate athletic teams. Because the colors had already come to represent the university at large, the choice was easily settled; light blue and white became the official colors.

Authorized by the North Carolina Constitution in 1776, the university was chartered 12 years later when George Washington was inaugurated as president. Charter members looking for a central location agreed on New Hope Chapel Hill, the site where several colonial roads intersected. The cornerstone for the first state university building in the United States, Old East, was laid on October 12, 1793. A year and a half later, the first student was admitted. By the late 1800s, only Yale University had a larger enrollment.

In the antebellum era, slaves helped build some of the campus's first buildings. Since those early days, the university has trained many state officials (including about

Franklin Street
COURTESY OF CHAPEL HILL/ORANGE COUNTY VISITORS BUREAU

half of North Carolina's governors), as well as leaders in virtually every profession. One of its early graduates was future United States president James K. Polk. Vice presidential candidate John Edwards graduated from the university's law school.

In the early 1800s, students and faculty at UNC were the first in the country to make systematic astronomical observations. Their recorded notes date from 1827 to 1831. A year later, they built the first university-run observatory in North America. In the 1820s, university faculty members conducted the nation's first state geological survey. Though Carolina was one of the few Southern universities to remain open during the Civil War, Reconstruction forced it to close from 1871 to 1875—the only time in its history. As the university moved into the 20th century, growth in student enrollment, programs, and intellectual influence brought more prominence.

Since the 1950s, Chapel Hill has become known for more than just the university. The town boasts several independent theater companies, a pioneering record label, regionally and nationally regarded restaurants, and a community of artists working in a variety of media. Neighboring Carrboro is a center for unique galleries and festivals.

Ample bike parking is available in downtown Chapel Hill and Carrboro; bike trails weave across both towns. A good map of Chapel Hill's greenways and bike trails is available at www.chapelhillparks.org.

JUST THE FACTS

Chapel Hill, in Orange County, is accessible via N.C. 54, U.S. 15/501, and Interstate 40, which connects Chapel Hill, Durham, Research Triangle Park, and Raleigh. Hillsborough, the county seat, is just to the north; it can be reached from Interstate 40 or by heading north on N.C. 86.

The nearest major airport is Raleigh-Durham International, about a half-hour away. Small planes can land just north of town at Horace Williams Airport, which has a 4,500-foot lighted landing strip; call 919-962-1337 for information.

The Greyhound/Trailways bus station is at 311 West Franklin Street (27516); call 919-942-3356. Intercity bus service is offered in Chapel Hill, Durham, and Raleigh by the Triangle Transit Authority; call 919-549-9999.

Finding free parking in Chapel Hill and Carrboro can be a challenge, so strapping a bike onto your bumper is highly recommended. If that's not an option, metered parking spaces are available on the university campus at Morehead Planetarium, Country Club Road, South Road, Ridge Road, Raleigh Street, West Drive, and the student union. Meters are also located on Franklin, Rosemary, Henderson, and Columbia streets. Parking at metered spaces on campus and in town is usually limited to one or two hours and is monitored closely. The parking deck at 150 East Rosemary Street, a block north of Franklin Street, and the lot at the corner of North Columbia and Rosemary streets operate on an hourly basis. Those who park in the lots at the corner of Church and West Rosemary streets and at 415 West Franklin Street from 8 A.M. to 6 P.M. Monday through Saturday must feed the meters; otherwise, parking there is free.

The Chapel Hill/Orange County Visitors Bureau is located at 501 West Franklin Street, Suite 104 (27516); call 888-968-2060 or 919-968-2060 or visit www.chocvb.org.

The local newspapers are the *Chapel Hill News*, the *Chapel Hill Herald*, the *Daily Tar Heel*, and the *News & Observer* of Raleigh. The free *Independent Weekly* offers in-depth reporting and listings of activities.

Things to Do

Historic Places, Gardens, and Tours

The *University of North Carolina at Chapel Hill*, flanked primarily by Franklin Street, Hillsborough Street, Raleigh Road, and Columbia Street, continues to spread. The main historic campus lies between Franklin Street and Cameron Avenue. Visitors can enjoy a campus walking tour between those two streets.

Silent Sam, located between Franklin Street and Cameron Avenue near the campus visitor center, is a Civil War monument erected in 1913 to honor the 321 alumni who died in Confederate service. Although the soldier holds a rifle, it is useless because he wears no cartridge box for ammunition.

The ***Davie Poplar*** marks the spot where, legend has it, William R. Davie selected the site for the campus in 1792. It sits in McCorkle Place, the large green separating Franklin Street from the campus.

At the heart of the campus on Cameron Avenue stands the visual symbol of the university, the ***Old Well***. For many years, it served as the sole water supply for Old East and Old West dormitories. In 1897, it was given its present decorative form at the direction of university president Edwin A. Alderman, who based his beautification on the Temple of Love in the Garden of Versailles. Though local custom has it that a sip from the well brings wisdom and good luck, frequent nocturnal visits by students from nearby North Carolina State University generally render a drink from the well unwise.

The first building on the campus—indeed, the only building for two years—was the three-story brick structure that came to be called ***Old East***, located on what is

The Old Well
COURTESY OF CHAPEL HILL / ORANGE COUNTY VISITORS BUREAU

now Cameron Avenue. A national historic landmark, it is the oldest state-university building in America. The college opened to students on January 15, 1795, but its first and only professor had to wait as student Hinton James of New Hanover County walked from home, arriving on February 12. By March, two professors and 41 students were present. Old East now serves as a coed dorm.

Visitors enjoy the gardens and the prominent wisteria-laden pergola at the *Coker Arboretum*, on East Cameron Avenue. The original arbor was constructed in 1913 of black locust, a decay-resistant wood that was again chosen when the arbor was renovated in 1996–97. A gift of the UNC class of 1997, the entryway and stone circle commemorate students in the class who did not survive to graduate. In the circle's center, a large stone tulip-poplar leaf points toward the Davie Poplar a few hundred yards west.

PlayMakers Theatre, on Cameron Avenue, is considered by some to be the most beautiful building on campus. This 1851 Greek Revival temple is one of the masterworks of New York architect Alexander Jackson Davis, who designed it as an unlikely combination library and ballroom. During the Civil War, Union troops stabled their horses in it. Years later, it became the theater for the Carolina PlayMakers, who, under the leadership of "Proff" Fred Koch and playwright Paul Green, were largely responsible for developing folk and outdoor drama in the United States.

Forest Theatre, on Country Club Road, sits on what was once Battle Park. The site was first utilized for a theatrical presentation in 1916, on the tricentennial of Shakespeare's death. W. C. Coker, the faculty botanist who developed the nearby arboretum, chose the location. Several years later, when Fred Koch came to the university, it was developed into a permanent theater. The outdoor amphitheater, dedicated to Koch, still serves as a performance space for local groups, including the Open Door Theatre Company.

The *North Carolina Botanical Garden* is administered by the university, though it is located off the main campus at 100 Old Mason Farm Road (27517) near N.C. 54. The garden encompasses nearly 600 acres of native plants and herbs. The indigenous southeastern plants around the Trotten Center are arranged in natural-habitat gardens of the Sandhills, the coastal plain, and the mountains. At the Mercer Reeves Hubbard Herb Garden is a renowned collection of carnivorous plants. Self-guided tours are available year-round. Trained volunteer docents lead tours for groups of 10 to 60. The garden is open weekdays from 8 A.M. to 5 P.M.; weekend hours vary by season. For more information or to schedule a tour, call 919-962-0522 or visit www. ncbg.unc.edu.

Museums and Science Centers

The *Ackland Art Museum*, at 101 South Columbia Street (27599) on the university campus, was founded through the bequest of William Hayes Ackland, a Nashville, Tennessee, native who, as the words on his tomb suggest, "wanted the people of his native South to know and love the fine arts." The permanent collection includes more

Bottle tree at North Carolina Botanical Garden
COURTESY OF CHAPEL HILL / ORANGE COUNTY VISITORS BUREAU

than 14,000 works of art from around the world. The Ackland is rich in paintings and sculptures by artists such as Degas, Rubens, and Pissarro; Indian miniatures; Japanese paintings; North Carolina folk art; and prints, drawings, and photographs. It also hosts four to six temporary loan exhibitions annually. The museum is open Wednesday through Saturday from 10 A.M. to 5 P.M. and Sunday from 1 P.M. to 5 P.M. It remains open until 9 P.M. the second Friday of each month. Admission is free, but donations are welcome. For information, call 919-966-5736 or visit www. ackland.org.

Morehead Planetarium, at 250 East Franklin Street (27599), has become a land-mark since its construction in the late 1940s. It has far exceeded its modest origi-nal purpose of educating a single community. As the American space effort took wing, the planetarium was used to train astronauts from the Mercury program to the Apollo-Soyuz program. The first planetarium owned by a university, it still serves as an educational and instructional training ground, as well as a program- and educa-tion-oriented facility. It is home to one of the most spectacular pieces of equipment on the East Coast—the magnificent Zeiss Model VI projector, which is capable of showing nearly 9,000 stars in the 68-foot dome. The complex also houses exhibits, an art gallery, a rose garden with a sundial, a gift shop, and banquet facilities. Public planetarium shows and live sky shows narrated by staff members teach the public about the night sky, lunar landings, the travels of the *Voyager* spacecraft, black holes, weather tracking, the Big Bang, and more. On occasion, music laser shows are offered. An admission fee is charged. The planetarium is open Sunday from 12:30 P.M. to 5 P.M. and Tuesday through Saturday from 10 A.M. to 3:30 P.M. It reopens on Friday and

Morehead Planetarium
COURTESY OF CHAPEL HILL /
ORANGE COUNTY VISITORS BUREAU

Saturday nights from 6:30 P.M. to 8:45 P.M. For information, call 919-549-6863 or 919-962-1236 or visit www.moreheadplanetarium.org.

The *North Carolina Collection Gallery*, located on the second floor of the Louis Round Wilson Library on the UNC campus, offers exhibits of material from among the 250,000 books and pamphlets, 400,000 photographic images, and 15,000 museum objects in the collection. Long-term exhibits interpret the exploration and settlement of Roanoke Island and depict the native Algonquian culture of that region. An exhibit on the gold rush in North Carolina includes rare Bechtler pioneer gold coins. Other exhibits are devoted to university history, the North Carolina Collection's rare Audubon bird prints, and Eng and Chang Bunker (the original Siamese twins, who lived in Surry County from 1811 to 1874). Guided tours are available. Admission is free. For information, call 919-962-1172 or visit www.lib.unc.edu/ncc/.

The *Chapel Hill Museum*, located at 523 East Franklin Street (27514) at the intersection with Boundary Street, has two main exhibit halls that showcase fine-art photography, crafts, and architecture and host events that document the character and people of Chapel Hill. The museum is open Wednesday through Saturday from 10 A.M. to 4 P.M. and Sunday from 1 P.M. to 4 P.M. For information, call 919-967-1400 or visit www.chapelhillmuseum.org.

Cultural Offerings

The *ArtsCenter*, at 300-G East Main Street in Carrboro (27510), offers a year-round calendar of community-centered art classes, live theater and jazz productions, and art exhibits. On weekends, musicians from the Appalachians to the Andes perform in the Earl Wynn Theater. The world-music concert series highlights emerging and established artists. The center also hosts a nationally recognized jazz series featuring regional and national performers. Family entertainment at the center encompasses drama, musical theater, puppetry, storytelling, and music of all kinds. Theatrical programs include the ArtsCenter Community Theater, a venue that encourages actors of all skill levels to explore and develop their craft. The West End Project series provides informal theater space for artists performing new material or learning new skills. The ArtsCenter also hosts productions by some of the Triangle's many professional theater companies. For a catalog or a monthly calendar of events, call 919-929-2787 or visit http://www.artscenterlive.org.

Meet the Author Teas have been held at the Chapel Hill Public Library since 1968, when the library moved from makeshift quarters to its official home at 100 Library Drive (27514). Sponsored by the Friends of the Chapel Hill Public Library, the teas have provided the community with numerous opportunities to meet writers who are now household names. A faithful committee makes the arrangements, prepares the room, makes the tea, and arranges flowers. Refreshments are served at 3:30 P.M. The programs run from 4 P.M. to 5 P.M. For information or a schedule of speakers and dates, visit http://www.friendschpl.org/activities/meettheauthorteas/ or call 919-968-2779.

PlayMakers Repertory Company, an offshoot of the original Carolina PlayMakers, is a professional regional theater troupe offering up to six productions per year (including original works) in the Paul Green Theatre on the university campus. The Carolina PlayMakers, founded by Fred Koch, launched many of the school's alumni and associates into the arts. Among these were Thomas Wolfe, who performed the title role in his student-written play, *The Return of Buck Gavin*; Pulitzer Prize–winning playwright Paul Green; comedian Andy Griffith; bandleader Kay Kyser; and composer and lyricist Richard Adler. Visit www.playmakersrep.org or call 919-962-PLAY or for information.

Deep Dish Theater Company produces four plays each year in Chapel Hill's University Mall. Deep Dish specializes in new or rarely seen plays and interesting productions of long-loved favorites. Its versatility is impressive; the company has produced *The Misanthrope, Hedda Gabler*, new works by Triangle playwright Adam Sobsey, and southeastern premieres of several contemporary plays. For information, call 919-968-1515 or visit www.deepdishtheater.org.

The *Chelsea Theatre*, at 1129 Weaver Dairy Road (27514), offers a great selection of foreign and independent films. Locals suggest arriving early for parking and seats. The selection of movies is stellar. For information, call 919-968-3005 or visit www.chelseavarsity.com.

Special Shopping

Don't miss the scene on *East Franklin Street*, the main artery that runs beside the university. You'll see saxophone players, accordion players, bagpipe players, rappers, college students, professors, lawyers, record stores, bars, galleries, cafés, old churches, trees, shops, and the Morehead Planetarium—all within the space of about a quarter-mile. Go down to *West Franklin Street* and you'll find bakeries, art shops, antiquarian bookstores, vintage clothiers, designer boutiques, a wine bar, a teahouse, and sporting-goods stores. These days, the action extends all the way to *Main Street in Carrboro*, where you'll find more galleries, the ArtsCenter, an army surplus store, and on and on and on; just keep following Franklin Street westward.

The *Carrboro Farmers' Market* is held at the town commons, located next to the town hall at 301 West Main Street (27510). For 25 years, it has provided the people of Carrboro with fresh produce, prepared foods, flowers, crafts, and special events such as tastings and cooking demonstrations. The market is open Saturday from 7 A.M. to noon and Wednesday from 3:30 P.M. to 6:30 P.M. The *Southern Village Farmers' Market* is located across from the Lumina Theatre on Market Street (27516) in Chapel Hill. It is open on Thursday from 3:30 P.M. to 6:30 P.M. For information about both markets, call 919-280-3326 or visit www.carrborofarmersmarket.com.

Carr Mill Mall, located behind the Weaver Street Market and Café at 200 North Greensboro Street in Carrboro (27510), was built in 1890 as the historic Alberta Cotton Mill, which closed in the 1930s. Opened in 1977 at the insistence of community members, Carr Mill Mall houses a number of specialty stores, boutiques, and restaurants with vaulted ceilings, hardwood floors, and exposed-brick walls. Individual store hours vary. Free parking is available. For information, call 919-942-8669 or visit www.carrmillmall.com.

The *Last Unicorn*, at 536 Edwards Ridge Road (27514), is a unique garden center specializing in wrought-iron gates and fences, antique stained glass, and other interesting items. The showroom, unlike any other, stretches across five acres of wooded trails. Wrought-iron gates lead to hidden paths lined with ornate fences and garden art. You'll walk through acres of forest and gardens before coming across the *Unicorn Shoppe*, which houses a collection of precious antique stained glass, and the *Ole Log Cabin*, which showcases one-of-a-kind home-and-garden collectibles. The Last Unicorn offers one of the largest collections of wrought-iron gates in the Southeast. For information, call 919-968-8440 or visit www.thelastunicorn.com.

The *North Carolina Crafts Gallery*, located in the building known as "the Point" at 212 West Main Street in Carrboro (27510), features work by artists from across the state. A variety of pottery, turned wood, jewelry, blown glass, sun catchers, quilts, wind chimes, garden sculptures, steppingstones, and other handmade pieces make unique gifts. When it opened in 1989, this was the first crafts gallery in Carrboro to carry work by North Carolina artists. It is open Monday through Saturday from 10 A.M. to 6 P.M. and Sunday from 1 P.M. to 4 P.M. For information, call 919-942-4048 or visit www.nccraftsgallery.com.

One of the first gourmet stores in the area, *A Southern Season*, located off U.S. 15/501 at 201 South Estes Drive (27514), has been offering Southern and European specialties since 1975. Opened originally as a tiny coffee "roastery," it is now a 28,000-square-foot market that offers a full-service restaurant called *The Weathervane*, a coffee-and-wine bar, and an impressive schedule of cooking classes. Store hours are Monday through Saturday from 10 A.M. to 7 P.M. and Sunday from 11 A.M. to 6 P.M. The Weathervane serves lunch daily and dinner Monday through Saturday; it also offers brunch on Sunday. Make sure you take a good look at the weathervane—the arrow always points south, no matter the wind direction. For information, call 919-929-7133 or visit www.southernseason.com.

Recreation

The *University of North Carolina Tar Heels* are a subject sure to get a strong reaction from almost anyone on the street in Chapel Hill. Calling the 22,000-seat Dean Smith Center home has put the university's men's basketball team a little farther away from many of its fans but has done little to hinder its success. ACC basketball is one of the most exciting spectator sports around, and you're right at the heart of it. For information, call the Dean Dome at 919-962-7777 or visit www.tarheelblue. com. To reach the box office, call 919-962-2296.

Hard-core fans will want to check out the *Carolina Basketball Museum*, housed on the first floor of the Ernie Williamson Athletics Center, adjacent to the Dean Dome. It is open Tuesday through Friday from 10 A.M. to 4 P.M. and Saturday from 9 A.M. to 1 P.M. Admission is free. Call 919-843-9921 or visit http://tarheelblue.cstv. com/museum/.

If you enjoy *cycling*, you'll be pleased to learn that Chapel Hill and Carrboro are extraordinarily bicycle friendly. The two towns have a well-developed system of bike trails and lanes and a commitment (through the Chapel Hill Greenway Commis-

Carolina Basketball Museum
COURTESY OF CHAPEL HILL / ORANGE COUNTY VISITORS BUREAU

sion) to eventually develop over 40 miles of pathways. Several good trails are already available. For information, call 919-968-2784.

The *Cat's Cradle*—that monster of a nightclub, that giant bus stop on the rock-'n'-roll route from Atlanta to New York, that incubator of musical movers—is located at 300 East Main Street (27516). This music club is known far and wide. Though it has moved around a bit in its 20 or 30 (who's counting?) years, it still brings in big-name acts that actually *ask* to play here. R.E.M. performed here, as did the Riders in the Sky, Brave Combo, and even Nirvana. What a club! Call 919-967-9053 or visit www.catscradle.com to get the lowdown, or check the *Independent Weekly* for listings.

Music and Movies on Market Street is a program periodically offered on the green at the Lumina Theatre, located at 620 Market Street (27516) in Southern Village at Chapel Hill. Concerts start at 7 P.M. and are free to the public. Movies begin at dusk; a small fee is charged. Bring a lawn chair. For information, call 919-969-8049.

Golf opportunities include *Twin Lakes Golf Course* (919-933-1024), at 648 Willow Way (27516), six miles south of Chapel Hill, and the university's *Finley Golf Course* (919-962-2349), located two miles from Interstate 40 on N.C. 54. In 1999, Finley Golf Course underwent an $8 million renovation by architect Tom Fazio. It has since been called a masterpiece. The 18-hole, par-72 course offers reduced rates to students and faculty of the university.

Seasonal Events

FestiFall, an annual street fair, takes place on Franklin Street in October. Sponsored by the Chapel Hill Parks and Recreation Department, it offers live music and other entertainment, a variety of foods, and lots of vendor stalls for a Sunday of fun. For information, call 919-968-2784 or visit www.festifall.com.

Carrboro Music Festival takes place in "the Paris of the Piedmont" the last Saturday in September. The event brings every available musician to the microphone and every able-bodied Carrboro citizen to the ranks of celebrants. For information, visit www.carrboromusicfestival.com.

Places to Stay

Resorts, Hotels, and Motels

Carolina Inn. Deluxe. 211 Pittsboro Street, 27516 (800-962-8519 or 919-933-2001; www.carolinainn.com). This historic Four Diamond hotel is the grand old lady of Chapel Hill. It offers elegant, magnolia-clad Southern hospitality in a location that is unbeatable by Tar Heel standards. From its site on the corner of the university campus, guests can easily walk to the arboretum, the planetarium, the PlayMakers Theatre, the Forest Theatre, and the Wilson Library. The inn is listed on the National Register of Historic Places. It is indeed rich in history, as the walls and the staff will be glad to explain. Visitors will need to book ahead, since the inn is such a favorite for wedding parties and alumni gatherings. All 184 rooms are nicely decorated. Guests enjoy complimentary coffee and freshly baked chocolate chip cookies on arrival. And yes, a ghost is in residence, but you'll have to wheedle the staff into telling you about it.

Governors Club. Deluxe. 10100 Governors Drive, 27514 (800-925-0085 or 919-968-8500; www.governorsclub.com). At the Governors Club, guests will find a group of cottages situated in a hilly setting on a Jack Nicklaus golf course. Each cottage has four to seven comfortable suites, a large living area, and a fully equipped kitchen. Suites can be individually contained for single travelers, or they can access the adjoining living area for groups and families, allowing for mixing and mingling in ways not possible in standard hotel settings. The Governors Club is popular for conferences, parties, and retreats. Tennis courts are available for those who don't enjoy golf.

Siena Hotel. Deluxe. 1505 East Franklin Street, 27514 (800-223-7379 or 919-929-4000; www.sienahotel.com). An individually owned and operated boutique hotel inspired by the romantic villas of Tuscany, the Siena is the picture of opulence. It boasts a Four Diamond rating from AAA and a Condé Nast Johansens recommendation. The 79 guest rooms are individually appointed with hand-selected European antiques, specially commissioned armoires, rich fabrics, and French doors leading to European balconies. They also offer the latest technology and luxury amenities such as nightly turn-down service, fine Belgian chocolates, and marble bathrooms with European toiletries. A morning newspaper, a complimentary health-club membership, and a full buffet breakfast are included. During your stay, you can dine at *Il Palio Ristorante*, a Four Diamond establishment. You can even spend the day behind the scenes in the kitchen. The "Day As the Chef" package lets you create your own four-course menu, shop for fresh ingredients, and work alongside executive chef Adam Rose. For restaurant reservations, call 919-918-2545.

Inns and Bed-and-Breakfasts

The Inn at Bingham School. Expensive. On N.C. 54 at Mebane Oaks Road (800-566-5583; www.chapel-hill-inn.com). Opened in 1845 as a prep school for boys seeking entrance to the nearby university, this quiet inn seems far removed from the ever-increasing crowd of the Triangle. Though it has been renovated, the inn retains its historical authenticity in its original wood and masonry and its period antiques in every room. The five guest rooms include a 1790s log cabin; depending on your choice of room, you may enjoy a fireplace, a whirlpool, or a canopy bed.

Places to Eat

Carolina Crossroads. Expensive. In the Carolina Inn at 211 Pittsboro Street, 27516 (919-918-2777; www.carolinainn). Carolina Crossroads offers the elegant cuisine of a world-class executive chef and the hospitable atmosphere of Chapel Hill's most beloved inn. Breakfast and dinner are served daily; lunch is served Monday through Saturday; brunch is offered on Sunday.

Elaine's on Franklin. Expensive. 454 West Franklin Street, 27516 (919-960-2770; www.elainesonfranklin.com). Elaine's signature culinary style of sophistication-meets-farmers'-market has made it a Chapel Hill staple. Since its opening in 1999 under chef-owner Bret Jennings, Elaine's has garnered awards from *Wine Spectator* and accolades from *Southern Living*. Dinner is served Tuesday through Saturday. Reservations are recommended.

Provence. Expensive. 203 Weaver Street in Carrboro, 27510 (919-967-5008; www. provenceofcarrboro.com). Chef-owner Felix Roux has turned a 1920s mill house into one of the area's trendiest eateries. Roux specializes in seafood. Every dish is prepared with a Mediterranean flair. Guests have a choice of traditional French and Italian specialties and an array of French wines. Dinner is served Monday through Saturday.

Crook's Corner Café and Bar. Moderate. 610 West Franklin Street, 27516 (919-929-7643; www.crookscorner.com). Crook's Corner is Southern dining at its best. You'll find barbecue on the menu here. You'll also find grits served in one of their finer settings—alongside shrimp. This is a great place to check out the work of local artists, whose pieces hang on the walls and even in the restrooms. You can see the works of Clyde Jones anytime you stop by; they're here permanently, hanging from the eaves and rafters. And of course, Bob Gaston's signature pink pig proudly adorns the roof. Garden dining is available in season. If you're lucky, you'll catch sight of everybody's favorite, Bill Smith, head chef *extraordinaire* and modest but unforgettable town historian. Dinner is served Tuesday through Sunday; brunch is offered on Sunday.

The Spotted Dog Restaurant & Bar. Moderate. 111 East Main Street in Carrboro, 27510 (919-933-1117). The menu here is vegetarian-friendly, and the atmosphere is artsy casual. Over 50 varieties of draft and bottled beer are available, as is a wine list featuring more than 40 selections. Artwork is on display; a portion of all art sales goes toward local charities. And the place recycles. What more can you ask for? Lunch and dinner are served Tuesday through Saturday; a late-night menu is available from 11 P.M. until midnight.

Top of the Hill Restaurant & Brewery. Moderate. 100 East Franklin Street, 27514 (919-929-8676; www.topofthehillrestaurant.com). This casual upscale restaurant overlooks downtown Chapel Hill from a large third-floor patio. The winner of over

20 "Best of" awards, including Best Restaurant in Chapel Hill, Best Microbrew, and Best Outdoor Deck, Top of the Hill caters to a mature, sophisticated clientele that some will find a bit stuffy. Though beer is brewed on the premises, serious beer enthusiasts may consider Top of the Hill more restaurant than bar. The menu includes appetizers, sandwiches, specialty pizzas, and entrées. Lunch and dinner are served daily.

Allen and Son Pit-Cooked Bar-B-Q. Inexpensive. 6203 Millhouse Road, 27514, at N.C. 86 North (919-942-7576). This is a bastion of hickory-cooked chopped barbecue. Order up a platter with fries, slaw, hush puppies, and Brunswick stew and you'll be ready for a tailgating party Chapel Hill–style. And don't forget the sweetened iced tea. If it's a football weekend, you'd better call ahead because Allen and Son is sure to be busy. There's another location on U.S. 15/501 near Pittsboro if you're headed south and you've just gotta have it. Lunch and dinner are served Tuesday through Saturday.

Flying Burrito. Inexpensive. 746 Martin Luther King Jr. Boulevard, 27514 (919-960-2922; www.originalflyingburrito.com). The folks at the Flying Burrito serve up the biggest, greatest burritos and the most delicious margaritas; they have a great nonalcoholic margarita, too! Fresh fish, great salsa, a friendly bar, a colorful atmosphere, and a lively crowd are what you'll find here. Lunch and dinner are served daily; brunch is offered on Saturday and Sunday.

Mama Dip's Kitchen. Inexpensive. 408 West Rosemary Street, 27516 (919-942-5837; www.mamadips.com). This Southern-style restaurant is owned by—you guessed it—Mama Dip. Though she has been acclaimed by such notables as Craig Claiborne of the *New York Times* and has had her own book published, she will likely be working in the kitchen when you eat here. She is deservedly famous for, among other things, her barbecue sauce, her sweet potato pie, her chicken and dumplings, and, yes, her chitlins. Southern-cooked vegetables are also a specialty. Breakfast, lunch, and dinner are served daily.

Sutton's Drugstore. Inexpensive. 159 East Franklin Street, 27514 (919-942-5161). This is a comforting sight for returning Tar Heels who have seen lots of spots come and go. They can sit at the counter and order a good, old-fashioned cheeseburger, crispy crinkle-cut fries, and a chocolate milk shake or an orangeade. Guests are served under a broad-bladed ceiling fan within walls filled with pictures of students, athletes, cheerleaders, local kids, and townspeople. They can enjoy a chat with the cook (or the pharmacist, who'll take over if the cook steps out) and a taste of the village. Breakfast and lunch are served daily.

Weaver Street Market and Café. Inexpensive. 101 East Weaver Street in Carrboro, 27510 (919-929-0100; www.weaverstreetmarket.com). This is a happening place. Part of Carrboro's artsy downtown, Weaver Street Market and Café is not your typical restaurant. People come here to be part of the action, not to sit and chat in dark corners. They mill around all over the place—in the co-op grocery store, outside on the patio and under the trees, and around the café's hot and cold bars loaded with healthy foods. If you're a vegetarian, this place is right up your alley, but it also has good chicken and fish. Weaver Street offers an excellent assortment of cooked fresh vegetables, soups, and ready-made cold salads such as tabouli, spicy Szechuan noodle, and "Aioli Farfalle." If none of these strikes your fancy, you can fashion your own creation from the salad bar. Live music, gourmet cooking classes, and art shows are also offered. Breakfast, lunch, and dinner are served daily.

The Lady Who Saved the University

You likely know many UNC heroes. William R. Davie, he of the outsized poplar. Thomas Wolfe, literary man-child from the mountains. Liberal educator Frank Porter Graham. TV star Andy Griffith. Coach Dean Smith. Michael Jordan and Mia Hamm. Even Anoop Desai, who couldn't stop talking about his beloved Chapel Hill on *American Idol*.

But what about the lady with no formal education who rescued the university in its darkest hour, decades before it began admitting women?

Cornelia Phillips was born in Harlem but moved as an infant to Chapel Hill, where her father chaired the Mathematics Department. In 1851, she met law student James Spencer. They married in 1855, settled in Alabama, and had a child before James took ill and died in 1861. The following year, Cornelia moved back to her father's in Chapel Hill.

She arrived to find UNC disintegrating before her eyes. Though President David Swain successfully appealed to Jefferson Davis to exempt students from military service, the young men of Chapel Hill departed campus in droves to don Confederate gray. A student body of 300 to 400 dwindled to 50. Boardinghouses closed. Food grew scarce. Union forces under General Smith D. Atkins arrived on campus in mid-April 1865. By the ninth day of their occupation, the student population was down to one senior and one junior, according to an eyewitness.

Matters worsened after the war. New university president Solomon Pool submitted a plan to the trustees to put the campus up for lease. In early 1871, UNC closed. Trees had been felled for firewood. Windows were broken. Doors, carpets, and furniture had been stripped from buildings. The place was ruined.

Enter Cornelia Phillips Spencer and other university supporters like Zebulon Vance and Kemp Battle. Using letter writing in part to fight her tendency toward depression, Spencer lambasted Solomon Pool: "The President is a little formal arrogant prig, without two clear ideas in his brains beyond his own selfish aggrandizement." His fellow administrators, she opined, busied themselves "cutting down shade trees . . . as if oaks grew every year like pea-vines." She extolled the beauty of the campus and wrote of the traditions she feared might

pass. She tirelessly exhorted North Carolinians to reopen their university.

In 1875, the state legislature finally passed a bill allowing the university to reorganize and pledging financial support. Spencer penned a hymn to celebrate the reopening. During the ceremony, she climbed to the attic of South Building, grabbed the rope to the campus bell, and pulled for all she was worth.

Spencer also wrote a couple of books and edited the *Chapel Hill Ledger*. In recent years, a divergent view of her role in "saving" UNC has emerged. It paints her as a kind of flip-flopping foremother to presidential candidate John Kerry, on the grounds that her fear of racial equality led her to be *for* the closing of the university before she was *against* it. But that interpretation has yet to gain much traction. Spencer Hall and the Cornelia Phillips Spencer Bell Award continue to honor her memory.

Research Triangle Park

Research Triangle Park was created in 1959. Now, this 7,000-acre area, one of the largest research parks in the world, is home to more than 170 companies employing 45,000 people. The concept for the park is credited to University of North Carolina sociology professor Howard Odum, but it was Romeo Guest who coined the name *Research Triangle*. His idea came from the park's proximity to, and affiliation with, the area's three major universities. Together, Odum and Guest solicited the assistance of investor Karl Robbins, who agreed to fund the project by purchasing large tracts of land in the southeastern corner of Durham County. Today, the park encompasses an area eight miles long and two miles wide, with room to develop an additional 1,300 acres. Drawing on the expertise of the three universities, research-and-development companies conduct studies in biotechnology, biopharmaceuticals,

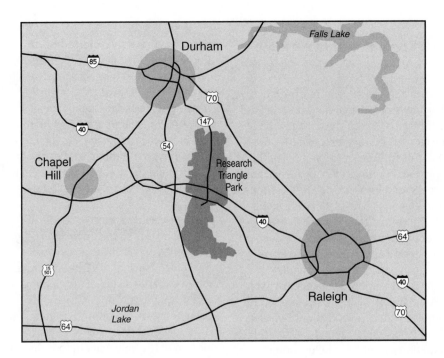

computer applications, chemicals, environmental science, information technology, microelectronics, instrumentation, and telecommunications. And those are only a few of the fields being researched.

Visitors will find little to do in RTP itself. For Triangle residents, it is primarily a place to work, though the thirst for convenience has placed a few residential areas and strip malls here in recent years. The area has some hotels and restaurants, but many eateries are open only Monday through Friday during work hours. Most business travelers in RTP will do well to stay in Raleigh or Durham to enjoy the area's best dining and nightlife.

JUST THE FACTS

Research Triangle Park is northwest of Raleigh and southeast of Durham on Interstate 40 near the intersection of N.C. 54 and N.C. 55.

Raleigh-Durham International Airport is conveniently located several miles to the east.

The major papers in the area are the *News & Observer* of Raleigh and the *Durham Herald-Sun*. Dining and events information is available in the free *Independent Weekly*.

Things to Do

Recreation

Lake Crabtree County Park, at 1400 Aviation Parkway in Morrisville (27560), is located about 10 minutes northwest of Raleigh. Visitors can hike or bike the park's network of trails and take a break at any of its numerous picnic areas. Small sailboats and canoes are available for rent from mid-April through October. Sailing classes and guided wildlife tours are also offered. The park is open from 8 A.M. to dusk every day. Entry is free. For information and a schedule of tours and educational programs, call 919-460-3390 or visit www.wakegov.com/parks/lakecrabtree/default.htm.

Places to Stay

Resorts, Hotels, and Motels

Sheraton Imperial Hotel and Conference Center. Deluxe. 4700 Emperor Boulevard in Durham, 27703 (800-325-3535 or 919-941-5050; www.sheratonrtp.com). This Mobil Three Star, AAA Three Diamond hotel has 331 guest rooms, including 62 club-level rooms with a concierge on duty. Complimentary continental breakfast is served in the morning and hors d'oeuvres and beverages in the evening in the private club-level lounge. Each room has a coffee maker, an iron, an ironing board, on-demand movies, voice mail, and computer data ports.

Radisson Governor's Inn. Deluxe/Expensive. 150 Park Drive in Research Triangle Park, 27709 (919-549-8631; www.radisson.com). This 198-room facility at Exit 280 off Interstate 40 is the only hotel actually within RTP. Its business rate includes breakfast, a complimentary drink, and an in-room movie. Each room has a coffeepot and a desk with a data port and voice mail. A swimming pool and a fitness center are on the premises. Off-site laundry service is available.

Places to Eat

Carmen's Cuban Café. Expensive/Moderate. 108D Factory Shops Road in Morrisville, 27560 (919-467-8080; www.carmenscubancafe.com). Carmen's reverses the Triangle's normal traffic pattern, as patrons from Raleigh, Durham, and Chapel Hill drive to the first and only Cuban restaurant in the area for some of the best food and Latin dancing around. The "Pan-Latin" menu features Cuban specialties like "Ropa Vieja" alongside empanadas and a mammoth seafood paella that two or three people can share. And then they can wash it all down with the best mojitos anywhere. After 10 P.M. Tuesday through Saturday, Carmen's becomes the Touch Night Club, and the dancing begins. Lunch and dinner are served daily.

Piper's in the Park. Inexpensive. 2945 South Miami Boulevard in Durham, 27703 (919-572-9767; www.pipersinthepark.com). Piper Lunsford's old sandwich shop in Durham was a neighborhood favorite, and her new restaurant has many of the same superlative deli sandwiches she served there. Pastas, wraps, and fresh salads are also available. Try a "Papa Sweeney's Pimento Cheese Sandwich," followed by some of "Mama Windham's Fruit Cobbler" for dessert! Lunch is served daily.

TRIANGLE NEARBY

Many people know *Cary* only as a faux acronym—the town is said to be the Containment Area for Relocated Yankees. But that is decidedly uncharitable. For years now, Cary has been a fixture on the lists of America's best places to live and fastest-growing communities. It currently ranks as North Carolina's seventh-largest municipality and is still climbing. Though not a destination just yet, it is likely to be in the not-too-distant future.

If you're staying in the area, you can't do better than the *Umstead Hotel and Spa*, located at 100 Woodland Pond (27513). This Mobil Five Star and AAA Five Diamond facility is the creation of Jim Goodnight, founder of the SAS business software company, and his wife, Ann. It features 150 oversized rooms and suites, a 14,500-square-foot spa and health club, a conference center, 12 acres of gardens and lake, and the outstanding *Herons* restaurant, the province of executive chef Scott Crawford. If you bump into major-league athletes or big-name acts staying at the Umstead while in town to play or perform at the nearby RBC Center, be classy enough to allow them their privacy. For information, call 866-877-4141 or 919-447-4000 or visit www.theumstead.com.

Another can't-miss dining choice in Cary is *Ân*, at 2800 Renaissance Park Place (27513). Jim and Ann Goodnight can also take credit for bringing executive chef Michael Chuong to the area. Chuong's New World cuisine is a fusion of Vietnamese, French, and other influences, and his restaurant is a showcase for beautiful art and antiques. For information, call 919-677-9229 or visit www.ancuisines.com.

Historic Hillsborough is home to more than 100 sites listed on the National Register, some dating back to pre–Revolutionary War times. Visitors can take a self-guided walking tour or arrange for tours led by costumed docents. Information on all sites open to the public is available at 150 East King Street (27278) at the office of the Alliance for Historic Hillsborough, housed in the late-18th-century Alexander Dickson House. Visitors can also get information about the *Christmas Candlelight Tour* and the biennial *Spring Historic Home and Garden Tour*. In the gardens on the premises are traditional 18th- and 19th-century plants used for cooking, dyeing, and making medicines. For information, call 919-732-7741 or visit www.historichillsborough. org.

Ayr Mount, at 376 St. Mary's Road (27278), is one of North Carolina's finest Federal-period plantation houses. Built in 1815 by William Kirkland of Scotland, the brick house sits on 265 acres overlooking the Eno River Valley. Tours are offered Wednesday at 11 A.M., Thursday through Saturday at 11 A.M. and 2 P.M., and Sunday at 2 P.M.; a small admission fee is charged, but the daily Poet's Walk around the grounds is free. The grounds are open from 9 A.M. to 6 P.M. For information, call 919-732-6886 or visit www.classsicalamericanhomes.com.

Occaneechi Indian Village is located along the Eno River on South Cameron Avenue (27278) in the downtown area. The village—reconstructed to look as it did in the late 17th century—includes a palisade, huts, a cooking area, and a sweat lodge. It is open to the public during daylight hours. For information, call the tribal office of the Eno-Occaneechi Indian Association at 919-304-3723.

The *Triangle SportsPlex*, located at One Dan Way (27278), is Orange County's largest sports and recreation facility. The 80,000-square-foot complex features an NHL-sized ice rink, three indoor pools, a fitness center, a café, and a pro shop. Public ice skating, swimming lessons, and personal fitness training are just a few examples of what it has to offer. For information, call 919-644-0339 or visit www. trianglesportsplex.com.

The *Vietri Outlet Store* is located at 343 Elizabeth Brady Road (27278). Vietri imports handcrafted Italian products and wholesales them to the finest specialty stores, department stores, and catalog companies in North America. The outlet store in Hillsborough offers an incredible array of one-of-a-kind overstocks and slightly flawed samples and seconds, and the prices are unbeatable. The store is open two days a week only—Friday from noon to 6 P.M. and Saturday from 9 A.M. to 1 P.M. For information, call 800-277-5933 or 919-732-5933 or visit www.vietri.com.

A great place to stay is the *Inn at Teardrops*, at 175 West King Street (27278). The old building, which dates to 1768, is beautifully decorated with exotic antiques and memorabilia. No televisions or telephones are in the six rooms, but wireless Internet access is available. For information, call 919-732-1120 or visit www.innatteardrops.com.

Located at 101 North Churton Street (27278) is *Tupelo's*. Here, you'll find Creole classics such as jambalaya and crawfish ravioli, as well as a few surprises. Who can resist "Bayou Voodoo Shrimp"? If you're not up for a full meal, check out the tavern next door. It has a more casual atmosphere and serves a variety of soups and sandwiches. Lunch and dinner are served Monday through Saturday. For information, call the restaurant at 919-643-7722 or the tavern at 919-643-2223 or visit www.tupelos.com.

Maple View Farm Country Store lies south of Hillsborough (27278) at 6900 Rocky Ridge Road, at the intersection with Dairyland Road; it is about 3.5 miles west of the Orange County community of Calvander. Maple View offers a year-round ice-cream menu. Favorites include milk shakes, floats, sundaes, banana splits, and ice-cream cakes. Flavors include butter pecan, honey-toasted almond, double chocolate, coffee, cookies-and-cream, cookie dough, cherry vanilla, maple, mocha, blueberry, peach, coconut, and cheesecake. Sugar-free choices are offered, too. The store is perched on a hill looking west over the farm and adjacent fields; the covered front porch, furnished with rocking chairs, is strategically positioned for a sweeping view of the rolling countryside. Picnic tables are available on the hill, a perfect spot for watching the sunset. The store is open seven days a week from noon to 10 P.M. For information, call 919-960-5535 or visit www.mapleviewfarm.com.

The drive down U.S. 15/501 into Chatham County features great scenery. The communities here host many artists, sculptors, and craftspeople. *Pittsboro* is home to a variety of sites listed on the National Register. Nearby *Moncure* offers a number of unique things to see and do. *Siler City*, the site of Mount Vernon Mineral Springs, plays host to several interesting Latino celebrations, including the annual Stations of the Cross procession, conducted in both Spanish and English. For information on Chatham County, call 800-316-3829 or 919-542-8296 or check out www.visitchathamcounty.com.

Antiquing is a popular pastime in downtown Pittsboro. Visitors can meander through a variety of shops that offer vintage pieces, fine furniture and accessories, collectibles, estate jewelry, clothing, rare books, and more. Then they can have lunch in the old-fashioned *S & T Soda Shop* or one of the cafés nearby. Visit www.pittsboroshops.com for information about stores and a vendor/street map.

Beggars and Choosers, at 38 Hillsboro Street in Pittsboro (27312), is a vintage store and collectibles shop deluxe. But don't go in if you haven't the time to do it right! You'll want to loaf here for hours. The shop is open Thursday through Saturday from 10:30 A.M. to 5 P.M. and the first Sunday of every month from 1 P.M. to 5 P.M. For information, call 919-542-5884.

Anyone in Pittsboro will gladly tell you about the *Piedmont Farm Tour*, which takes place in April. You can visit more than 30 farms for $25; if you buy tickets early, you can get them for five bucks less. You'll enjoy a close look at the work done at dairies, apiaries, nurseries, vegetable farms, and horse farms. The tour is an extremely kid-friendly event. For information, call 919-542-2402 or visit www.carolinafarmstewards.org.

Fearrington Village is located on U.S. 15/501 between Pittsboro and Chapel Hill. Some years ago, a portion of this 200-year-old farm was converted into a world-class restaurant that has come to be known for its prix fixe menu and charming country setting. The village has now grown to include an entire community of specialty shops, a market, a medical center, a bookstore, a flower-and-plant shop, and, perhaps most recognizably, a dairy barn and silo. *McIntyre's*, the outstanding independent bookstore at Fearrington, is known for bringing in distinguished authors such as Jimmy Carter for autographing events. The *Fearrington House Restaurant and Country Hotel* is a member of the international organization Relais & Châteaux and is the recipient of AAA Five Diamond and Mobil Five Star ratings. Distinctive touches include ecclesiastical doors used as headboards and pine flooring from a workhouse along the Thames. For information about Fearrington or to make reservations at the inn, call 919-542-2121 or visit www.fearringtonvillage.com.

Rosemary House Bed-and-Breakfast is a 1912 Colonial Revival home at 76 West Street in the heart of Pittsboro (27312). It offers five comfortable guest rooms with private baths, data ports, cable television, fireplaces, and two-person whirlpools. The inn serves a full gourmet breakfast. For information, call 888-643-2017 or 919-542-5515 or visit www.rosemary-bb.com.

The *General Store Café*, at 39 West Street in Pittsboro (27312), is a great place to visit neighbors and catch up on Chatham County news. It's also the ideal spot to pick up herbal elixirs, teas, a few groceries, and breakfast or lunch. Vegetarians will be pleased with the "Tofu Eggless Salad Sandwich" and other such offerings, and everybody will be happy with the homemade desserts and scones. In addition, visitors can get a map of the 50-plus studios and galleries in Pittsboro and the surrounding area. Local artists—potters, sculptors, painters, jewelers, glass workers and blowers, ironworkers, and others—can be accessed through the *Chatham County Arts Council*. Those who attend the grand studio tour in December will be able to do some holiday shopping that will make everyone on their list happy. For information about the arts council, call 919-542-0394 or visit www.chathamarts.org; for information about the General Store Café, call 919-542-2432 or visit www.thegeneralstorecafe.com.

For a good hike or an afternoon outdoors, visit *White Pines Nature Preserve*, on River Fork Road south of Pittsboro. The preserve is the jewel of the Triangle Land Conservancy. The Rocky River and the Deep River border the preserve and provide a cool microclimate for the white pines and other mountain plant populations that thrive here. Five trails offer hours of hiking and beautiful views of the rivers and the preserve. The Triangle Land Conservancy also owns and maintains four other preserves in the area that are open to the public; for information, call 919-833-3662 or visit www.tlc-nc.org.

Be sure to visit Pittsboro's neighbor Moncure. *The Rocks*, at 535-A Old Sanford Road (27559), offers the chance to experience the thrills of gemstone mining and gold panning. If you're lucky, you'll strike it rich. But don't worry if you're having a dry spell; just check out the on-site gift shop, where you can purchase mineral specimens, custom jewelry, and more. The Rocks is open Tuesday through Saturday from 10 A.M. to 5 P.M.; call 919-542-6112 or visit www.ncgems.com.

You can round out your visit to Chatham County with a trip to Siler City. While you're there, be sure to visit the *grave site of Aunt Bee*. *The Andy Griffith Show* was a long-running sitcom based on the North Carolina town of Mount Airy. One of the country's most endearing character actors, Frances E. Bavier played Aunt Bee until the show ended in 1968. In 1972, she retired to a two-story brick home on West Elk Street in Siler City, a town she had often visited. After her death in 1989, the Emmy-winning actress was buried in Oakwood Cemetery. For information, call 800-316-3829.

Mount Vernon Springs, located on S.R. 1134 in Siler City, is the 122-acre site of a once-active health spa and hotel. Between 1881 and 1920, visitors flocked to the 50-room resort for a regenerative dip in one of the twin springs, named "Health" and

"Beauty." Later, the mineral water was bottled and sold around the country. Today, Mount Vernon Springs is listed on the National Register. Clear drinking water still flows from the sister springs. For information, call 800-316-3829.

Weary travelers shouldn't miss the *Inn at Celebrity Dairy*, located at 144 Celebrity Dairy Way in Siler City (27344). This inn, which dates to the 1820s, offers eight rooms and a suite. Sheltered on a gentle knoll under 250-year-old oak trees, it actually encompasses two buildings—a modern Greek Revival farmhouse skirted by wide porches and the original settlers' 1800 log cabin. The surrounding outbuildings include the original log hay barn and granary, an 1880s smokehouse, 1940s tobacco barns, and a goat dairy. The famous goats here provide cheese to many of the finest stores and restaurants in the Triangle. Guests are served a hearty breakfast—fresh goat cheese, homemade preserves, fresh eggs, and seasonal fruits and vegetables. For information, call 877-742-5176 or 919-742-5176 or visit www.celebritydairy.com.

For the best of the Triangle's class AA baseball, check out the *Carolina Mudcats*, who swing into action from April to September at Five County Stadium in Zebulon; call 919-269-2287 or visit www.gomudcats.com.

Lovers of fine crafts will enjoy a short trip north of the Triangle to Granville County, where they'll find the *Cedar Creek Gallery*, located at 1150 Fleming Road in Creedmoor (27522). This gallery, owned and operated by craftspeople, is a winner of the North Carolina Governor's Award for Excellence in the Arts and Humanities. Cedar Creek draws pilgrims from all over, who come to see the work of over 200 artists, many of whom have work displayed in permanent national collections such as the Smithsonian and the Chrysler Museum. On display are stoneware, quilts, baskets, jewelry, furniture, candles, wind chimes, musical instruments, and other items. The gallery is open seven days a week from 10 A.M. to 6 P.M. For information, call 919-528-1041 or visit www.cedarcreekgallery.com.

Falls Lake State Recreation Area has its headquarters at 13304 Creedmoor Road in the community of Wake Forest (27587), located 10 miles north of Raleigh. Falls Lake offers outdoor recreation at seven facilities on its 38,000 acres of woodlands and lake in Wake and Durham counties. RV and tent sites, primitive sites, and sites for group camping are available year-round. Visitors also come for the swimming, the picnic facilities, the hiking trails, and the interpretative programs. A privately managed concessionaire, *Rollingview Marina*, offers boat launching, slips, mooring, rentals, and supplies. The recreation area is open from 8 A.M. to 6 P.M. November through February; from 8 A.M. to 8 P.M. during March, April, September, and October; and from 8 A.M. to 9 P.M. May through August. For information, call 919-676-1027 or visit http://ils.unc.edu/parkproject/visit/fala/home.html.

The *North Carolina Renaissance Faire* is held each spring at 13239 Capital Boulevard in Wake Forest (27587). This 16th-century festival includes numerous booths where artisans display their wares, as well as multiple staging areas where actors in period dress bring to life the pageantry of the year 1573. Patrons are encouraged to wear costumes like those of Queen Elizabeth's royal court. Jousts are held in the Queen's Tiltyard. Attendees also see hand-fasting ceremonies, knightings, singing, juggling, dancing, puppetry, fencing, sword fighting, and a quest for the Holy Grail. Pets are welcome. The fair runs from 10 A.M. to 6:30 P.M. An admission fee is charged except for children five and under. For information, call the Historical Enrichment Society of North Carolina at 919-755-8004 or visit www.ncrenfaire.com.

The Sandhills

Fayetteville

Pinehurst and Southern Pines

By Steve Kirk

The Cape Fear River helps create the temperate conditions that have long drawn tourists to the Sandhills. In the late 19th century, the Sandhills were a retreat for those seeking wellness through a change of climate. Now, the area is a haven for golfers from all over the country. Pinehurst and Southern Pines boast more than 40 championship courses woven among the area's longleaf forests. Large tracts of farmland have also made the area a site for equestrian shows and competitions of all kinds. Even in the winter, visitors will spot trotters and pacers training on some of the stately farms. Come spring, the big shows are at full canter.

In the 19th century, nearby Fayetteville was an inland port and a hub of the system of plank roads used for overland travel. It was here that Congress later established an artillery training facility called Camp Bragg, where it could lengthen the training season during World War I. Today, Fort Bragg and Pope Air Force Base make up one of the world's largest military installations. Fort Bragg is the home of the 82nd Airborne and Special Operations units, while the 43rd Airlift Wing calls Pope Air Force Base its headquarters. For military enthusiasts, this town is a dream come true, offering a number of museums dedicated to telling the story of the American fighting man. Fayetteville, which narrowly lost out to Raleigh when the state capital was named, has much to offer history aficionados. And the promise of good weather means a walking tour won't be rained out.

Fayetteville

By Sheryl Monks

The most recent push to soften Fayetteville's image from that of a town full of roughneck GIs has resulted in a new community slogan: "History, Heroes, a Hometown Feeling!" This resident-led effort aims to develop a stronger sense of community pride and a more harmonious relationship with the area's two military bases—Fort Bragg and Pope Air Force Base. This time, the town may have hit its mark.

History of all kinds is easy to spot in Fayetteville. The city boasts nearly 60 structures listed on the National Register, including houses, railroad stations, taverns, churches, and even a university; Fayetteville State University is the second-oldest school in the state, after the University of North Carolina at Chapel Hill. This is also a community rich in both Native American culture and African-American culture.

The city has a long military history. During the Revolutionary War, Lord Cornwallis camped outside what is now Fayetteville on his way to meet George Washington's army at Yorktown. In fact, the city was named after the French hero of the Revolution, the Marquis de Lafayette, who visited the area in 1825, long after the conflict. From that point, Fayetteville's military history has only grown richer.

Fort Bragg was established in 1918, and what is now Pope Air Force Base was organized the following year.

But Fayetteville's legacy extends beyond its military ties. The city boasts some of the oldest architecture in North Carolina, even though two large fires swept through the town and destroyed over 600 of its buildings. The historic Market House was constructed in 1832 on the site of the old statehouse, where several landmark events—including the ratification of the United States Constitution in 1789 and the chartering of the country's first state-funded university, the University of North Carolina—took place.

Fayetteville's fondness for its heroes is apparent. A life-sized bronze statue of

"Iron Mike"
COURTESY OF FAYETTEVILLE AREA CONVENTION AND VISITORS BUREAU

the Marquis de Lafayette stands in Cross Creek Park on Green Street. Not far away, at the corner of Randolph and Armistead, is a heroic effigy affectionately known as "Iron Mike," a giant monument to American paratroopers dropped in desolate places worlds away. One of the primary functions of the Airborne and Special Operations Museum is to glorify the men and women of those elite units. As a mark of respect for another group of brave men, the 35 who earned the Victory Cross, the JFK Special Warfare Museum has a Hall of Heroes. The museum honors Special Operations units from World War II to the present and focuses heavily on Vietnam and the development of the Green Berets.

If Fayetteville doesn't strike you as a place imbued with hometown feeling, maybe you should look again. Its special events include all-American activities such as fishing and horseback riding. Or maybe you'll prefer the parades and street festivals that capture the same esprit de corps. One such festival honors North Carolina's state flower, the dogwood, and another contributes its proceeds to the North Carolina Burn Center, truly exemplifying a community spirit.

So try to look beyond Fayetteville's battle-hardened surface. You'll start to see the thinking behind the town's new slogan. Enjoy your stay. A trip to Fayetteville promises a slew of things to see and do, from touring historic landmarks to shopping for antiques and fine pottery to museum-hopping. With the right attitude, you'll come away with a greater appreciation for the city and quite likely a renewed sense of patriotism.

JUST THE FACTS

Fayetteville is located just east of Interstate 95 roughly 26 miles south of Interstate 40. It can be reached via U.S. 401, N.C. 24, or N.C. 87.

Fayetteville Regional Airport is south of the city, off Interstate 95 Business. For information, call 910-433-1160.

The Greyhound/Trailways bus station is located at 324 Person Street (28301). Call 910-483-2580.

Over 300,000 residents live in Cumberland County, about 170,000 of them in Fayetteville, the county seat. Fayetteville is the sixth-largest city in North Carolina. About 50,000 Cumberland County residents are members of the armed forces stationed at Fort Bragg or Pope Air Force Base.

The daily newspaper is the *Fayetteville Observer-Times. Paraglide* is the official newspaper of Fort Bragg and Pope Air Force Base. You can find information and show times in the free publication *Up and Coming*.

The Fayetteville Area Convention and Visitors Bureau is located at 245 Person Street (28301). Signs provide clear directions from Interstate 95; once you're there, you can use the convenient drive-through window. The bureau is open Monday through Friday from 8 A.M. to 5 P.M. For information, call 800-255-8217 or 910-483-5311 or check out www.visitfayettevillenc.com.

Things to Do

Historic Places, Gardens, and Tours

The *Market House*, at the intersection of Green, Gillespie, Person, and Hay streets, was built in 1832 on the foundation of the old statehouse, which burned in the fire of 1831. Within the walls of the statehouse, North Carolina ratified the United States Constitution in 1789 and chartered the University of North Carolina. It was also here that the state ceded its western lands to form Tennessee. The Market House is listed on the National Register. Its ground floor was used as a market for many years, and its upper level housed the town hall. The clock still chimes at 7:30 A.M. for

LEFT: Market House
PHOTOGRAPH BY TIM SCIANDRA, COURTESY OF
FAYETTEVILLE AREA CONVENTION AND VISITORS BUREAU

ABOVE: Liberty Point
COURTESY OF FAYETTEVILLE AREA CONVENTION
AND VISITORS BUREAU

breakfast, at 1 P.M. for dinner, at sundown, and at 9 P.M., which was once the local curfew.

Liberty Point, at Bow and Person streets, is the site where, on June 20, 1775, some 55 patriots signed what is generally known as the Liberty Point Resolves, a petition declaring independence from Great Britain. A granite stone notes the names of the patriots and their pledge to their country at that historic meeting: "We stand ready to sacrifice our lives to secure her freedom." The building at the site, constructed between 1791 and 1800, is one of the oldest in Fayetteville. For information, call 910-433-1612.

Cool Spring Tavern, at 119 North Cool Spring Street (28301), is thought to have been built in 1788. It is one of the few remaining Federal-style buildings in Fayetteville. Having survived the fire of 1831, it is believed to be the oldest structure in the city. The tavern was built in a failed attempt to entice the men deliberating the location of the new state capital. The decision fell to Raleigh, of course. For information about the tavern, call 910-433-1612.

Cape Fear Botanical Garden, at 536 North Eastern Boulevard/U.S. 301/Interstate 95 Business (28301), sits at the confluence of the Cape Fear River and Cross

Creek. The 85-acre garden contains an old-growth forest and over 2,000 specimens of ornamental plants, making it a beautiful attraction year-round. The signature camellia garden boasts over 200 named varieties. It and other formal gardens are marked with signs that provide both historical and horticultural information. A restored 100-year-old farmhouse and its outbuildings help illustrate the local lifestyle of a century past. An admission fee is charged except for children under five; reduced rates are offered for military personnel, retired persons, and children ages six to 12. The garden is open from 10 A.M. to 5 P.M. Monday through Saturday and from noon to 5 P.M. on Sunday; it is closed on Sunday from mid-December to February. For information, call 910-486-0221 or visit www.capefearbg.org.

The **Atlantic Coast Line Railroad Station**, at 472 Hay Street (28301), is a rare example of Dutch Colonial architecture. Parts of the station date to World War I. Today, the Amtrak passenger station and the Atlantic Coast Line Depot Railroad Historical Center are housed at the site. For information, call 910-433-1612.

Cross Creek Cemetery #1, on Cool Spring Street, is one of the few cemeteries in the country listed on the National Register. It contains some of the remarkable masonry of famed Scottish artist George Lauder and the graves of many Confederate and Union soldiers, as well as that of Lauder himself. For information, call 910-433-1612.

Evans Metropolitan AME Zion Church, at 301 North Cool Spring Street (28301), was established around 1800 by the Reverend Henry Evans, a free black shoemaker and preacher who was passing through Fayetteville on his way to Charleston and decided to stay. His ministry served both black and white members until the founding of the predominantly white Hay Street Methodist Episcopal Church in the early 1830s. The current Gothic-style building, which dates to 1893–94, is a monument to the craftsmanship of African-American artisans James Williams and Joseph Steward. The church is open by appointment. For information, call 910-483-2862 or 910-483-2270 or visit www.evansmetropolitan.org.

St. John's Episcopal Church, at 302 Green Street (28301), was rebuilt after the 1831 fire in basically the same design as the original structure, with a big exception—10 pyramidal spires replaced the single spire that had topped the church. The extraordinary stained-glass windows, imported from Munich, Germany, are said to have been carried by oxcart from New York; they were installed around the turn of the 20th century. For information, visit www.stjohnsfayetteville.com or call 910-483-7405.

St. Joseph's Episcopal Church, at 509 Ramsey Street (28301), was established in 1873 by the black members of St. John's Episcopal Church with the assistance of that church's rector, the Reverend Joseph Caldwell Huske. Built in the Shingle style with Gothic and Spanish influences, it is notable for the five exquisite "Resurrection windows" by Tiffany and for its pipe organ, built in 1857 by Henry Erben of New York. The organ, purchased from St. John's for $100, has been powered by hand, water, gas, and now electricity. It is one of the oldest still in use in the country. The church is open by appointment. For information, call 910-323-0161 or visit www.stjoseph-episcopal.org.

Museums and Science Centers

The ***Airborne and Special Operations Museum***, at 100 Bragg Boulevard (28301), opened in 2000 and is one of the area's premier attractions. Its state-of-the-art educational facilities house exhibits highlighting the feats of Airborne and Special Operations units from 1940 to the present. The museum features graphic coverage of combat missions; extensive displays of uniforms, insignia, and weapons;

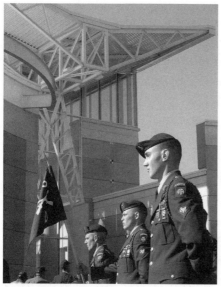

Military reunion outside the Airborne and Special Operations Museum
COURTESY OF FAYETTEVILLE AREA CONVENTION AND VISITORS BUREAU

and information on Airborne songs, marches, and customs. It includes a 250-seat Vistascope theater, a 24-seat Vista-Dome simulator, the Hall of Honors, and a main exhibit gallery. Admission is free, though guests must purchase tickets for the theater and the simulator. The museum is open Tuesday through Saturday from 10 A.M. to 5 P.M. and Sunday from noon to 5 P.M. For information, call 910-643-2766 or visit www.asomf.org.

The **JFK Special Warfare Museum**, located in Building D-2502 at Ardennes and Marion streets, offers a behind-the-scenes look at unconventional warfare. The museum houses weapons, military art, and international cultural items with an emphasis on Special Operations units from World War II to the present. Visitors will find displays covering the evolution of the unconventional warrior, beginning with the Indian scouts of the American West. Exhibits from World War II, Korea, and Vietnam explain the development of the Green Berets. Most exhibits pertain to Vietnam. The heart of the collection is a model of the Son Tay prisoner-of-war camp. In 1970, Colonel Arthur D. "Bull" Simons organized and led a daring attempt to rescue 107 POWs held there. Sadly, the prisoners had been moved before the rescuers arrived. The display explains that the attempt was not in vain, though; the prisoners were still years away from freedom, but their living conditions did improve after the raid. A gift shop is on the premises. Admission to the museum is free. It is open from 11 A.M. to 4 P.M. Tuesday through Sunday, as well as on federal holidays that fall on Monday. For information, call 910-432-4272 or visit www.jfkwebstore.com.

The **82nd Airborne Division War Memorial Museum**, at Ardennes and Gela streets, houses over 3,000 artifacts from World War I through Operation Desert Storm. The exhibits include weapons, helmets, uniforms, photographs, aircraft, parachutes, and other items. A film is shown each hour. The gift shop sells out-of-the-ordinary keepsakes. Admission to the museum is free. It is open Tuesday through Saturday from 10 A.M. to 4:30 P.M., as well as on federal holidays that fall on Sunday and Monday. For information, call 910-432-3443 or 910-436-1735 or visit www.bragg.army. mil/18abn/museums.htm.

Fascinate-U Children's Museum is located at 116 Green Street (28301), next to the Market House. This fun interactive museum allows kids to explore the world around them through creative role-playing. Exhibits include a grocery store, a bank, and a newsroom. The museum is open Tuesday, Thursday, and Friday from 9 A.M. to 5 P.M., Wednesday from 9 A.M. to 7 P.M., Saturday from 10 A.M. to 5 P.M., and Sunday from noon to 5 P.M. An admission fee is charged. For information, call 910-829-9171 or visit www.fascinate-u.com.

The *Fayetteville Museum of Art*, at 839 Stamper Road (28303), was founded in 1971. Originally housed in the Market House, it moved in 1978 to its present facility, which has the distinction of being the first building in North Carolina designed and built as an art museum. The museum includes two galleries, classrooms, studio space, a library that lends art reference materials and slides, and a museum store. The 5.8-acre grounds and pond offer visitors a place to relax. This parklike setting, an oasis in the midst of a heavily trafficked area, is the site of large-scale sculpture displays, art festivals, and public concerts. Admission is free, though donations are appreciated. The museum is open from 10 A.M. to 5 P.M. on weekdays and from 1 P.M. to 5 P.M. on Saturday and Sunday. For information, call 910-485-5121 or visit www.fayettevillemuseumart.org.

The *Museum of the Cape Fear Historical Complex*, at 801 Arsenal Avenue (28305), combines a modern museum building, the 1897 Poe House (yes, that's E. A. Poe, but this Poe was a potter), and the eerie remains of the Fayetteville Arsenal. The museum and the arsenal site are open for self-guided tours; visitors receive a guided tour of the Poe House upon arrival. A gift shop is located in the museum proper. Admission is free. The complex is open from 10 A.M. to 5 P.M. Tuesday through Saturday and from 1 P.M. to 5 P.M. on Sunday. For information, call 910-486-1330 or visit www.ncmuseumofhistory.org/osm/mcf.html.

The *Fayetteville Area Transportation Museum* is located at 325 Franklin Street (28301) in the former Cape Fear and Yadkin Valley Railway Depot, built around 1890. Its focus is on the area's evolving means of transportation, from Native American watercraft to plank roads to river steamboats to trains to cars. The museum is open Tuesday through Saturday from 10 A.M. to 4 P.M. Admission is free. For information, visit www.fcpr.us/FayettevilleAreaTransportationMuseum.php or call 910-433-1455.

Cultural Offerings

Cameo Art House Theatre, at 225 Hay Street (28301), shows a variety of classic, independent, and foreign films in a beautifully restored 1920s theater open seven

Cape Fear Regional Theatre
COURTESY OF FAYETTEVILLE AREA CONVENTION
AND VISITORS BUREAU

nights a week. For show times, call 910-486-6633 or visit www.cameoarthouse. com.

The award-winning *Cape Fear Regional Theatre*, at 1209 Hay Street (28305), has been around for nearly four decades. Local, regional, and national performers present premieres, musicals, classic dramas, comedies, and children's favorites in an intimate 325-seat theater. The group's Studio Performing Arts Program offers courses in acting, voice, and audition techniques for ages eight through adult. For a list of upcoming shows, call 910-323-4233 or visit www.cfrt.org.

The *Gilbert Theater* is located at 116 Green Street (28301). For over a decade, it has provided quality theatrical productions for children, the elderly, minorities, and the economically disadvantaged while at the same time giving local artists a venue for displaying their diverse talents. The company has produced classics, thought-pro-voking works such as *How I Learned to Drive*, children's puppet shows, and original local and regional plays. The theater involves students whenever possible, both on stage and off. For information, call 910-678-7186 or visit www.gilberttheater.com.

The *Fayetteville Symphony Orchestra* performs several concerts a year at Reeves Auditorium, Crown Theatre, and Seabrook Auditorium. For information, call 910-433-4690 or visit www.fayettevillesymphony.org.

Special Shopping

What's a visit to a military town without reconnoitering an army surplus store? Try *Old Sarge's Surplus*, at 240 South Bragg Boulevard/N.C. 87 at the southern edge of Spring Lake (28390), just beyond Fort Bragg's northern border. This place is so well disguised that it might as well be wearing camouflage. It's on the west side of South Bragg between Main and Lake Avenue, hidden behind—surprise!—a tattoo parlor and a used-car lot. Turn in where the old army truck and trailer are parked beside the road. Aside from the bin of Rambo-style knives, Old Sarge's stock is largely non-lethal. For information, call 910-497-5335.

Cape Fear Studios, at 148-1 Maxwell Street (28301) in the downtown area, is a nonprofit art gallery and studio where local artists and craftsmen sell original work such as fine jewelry, pottery, watercolor paintings, pastels, and many other items. For information, call 910-433-2986 or visit www.capefearstudios.com.

David R. Walters Antiques, at 1110 Hay Street (28305), specializes in early-20th-century furniture. Antiques and other collectibles are also available. For information, call 910-483-5832.

Angels & Antiques, at 1213 Hay Street (28305), serves all your angel needs—paintings, tree ornaments, statues, figurines, clocks, lamps, dolls, plates, cards, candleholders, nightlights, etc. It also has general antiques. For information, call 910-433-4454 or visit www.angelsandantiques.com.

"Antiques with an attitude" describes *Not Quite Antiques*, at 2829 Raeford Road (28303). The shop specializes in antiques, mid-20th-century items, works by local artists and craftspeople, and unique modern pieces other antique shops may not carry. For information, call 910-323-0300.

Recreation

Docks at the Capitol defies easy description. Housed in an old theater at 126 Hay Street (28301), it encompasses a bowling alley, a video-game parlor, a sports bar and pool hall, a dance venue, a cocktail lounge, a café, a gift shop, a shoe store, a skateboard shop, an ice-cream parlor, and a spa. As a kids' party spot, it's Chuck E. Cheese on steroids. For information, visit www.docksatthecapitol.com or call 910-42DOCKS.

The *Crown Center*, at 1960 Coliseum Drive (28306), offers a wide array of entertainment, from concerts, theater productions, and family shows to amateur and professional sports. The *Crown Coliseum* is the home of the *Fayetteville FireAntz* (910-321-0123; www.fireantzhockey.com/home.aspx) of the Southern Professional Hockey League and the *Fayetteville Guard* (910-202-4753; www.fayettevilleguard.com) of the American Indoor Football Association. For a list of upcoming events at the Crown Center, call 910-438-4100 or visit www.crowncoliseum.com.

J. P. Riddle Stadium on Legion Road hosts games of the *Fayetteville SwampDogs* baseball team of the Coastal Plain League. For information, call 910-426-5900 or visit http://goswampdogs.com.

Fishermen should check out the 500-foot pier at *Lakeview Park Fishing Pier and Campground*, located at 377 Waldos Beach Road (28306); for information, call 910-424-4814. A couple of boat ramps are located along the Cape Fear River, one at the junction of U.S. 301 and Old N.C. 87 and the other at *Riverside Sports Center*, at 1122 Person Street (28301). Fort Bragg has 13 lakes that are open to the public, including *Muddy Lake, Little Muddy Lake*, and *Mott Lake*; for information, call 910-396-7506.

Smith Lake Riding Stables, located on Smith Lake Road on the Fort Bragg property, offers pony rides, riding lessons, trail rides, and hayrides. Advance notice is required for groups of 10 or more. For information, call 910-396-4510 or visit www.fortbraggmwr.com/stables.php.

Smith Lake Recreation Area, at 1129 Smith Lake Road (28302), offers swimming, picnicking, mountain biking, camping, volleyball and basketball courts, sandy beaches, paintball games, paddleboats, and a water-ski shop. For information, call 910-396-5979 or visit www.fortbraggmwr.com/sportsrec/smithlake/smithlake.htm.

Seasonal Events

The *Dogwood Festival*, held at 145 Person Street (28301) every April, includes an array of activities, the premier event being a drive along the 18-mile *Dogwood Trail*, which winds through the downtown historic district and among beautiful residential areas. Symphony performances, rodeos, and street dancing take place all around Fayetteville to celebrate the thousands of blooming dogwoods, azaleas, daffodils, and camellias. For information, visit www.fayettevilledogwoodfestival.com or call 910-323-1934.

The *Blues 'n Brews Festival* is held on a Saturday in late spring at Festival Park, located downtown on Ray Avenue between Rowan Street and Maiden Lane. Around 15 breweries participate, as do lots of down-home blues performers. Be sure to bring lawn chairs or a blanket. For information, call 910-323-4233 or visit www.cfrt.org/bluesnbrews.php.

Where better to celebrate the Fourth of July than the mother of all military installations? *Operation Celebrate Freedom*, held on the main parade field at Fort Bragg, is free and open to the public. Visitors enjoy live music, parachuting demonstrations, a flag ceremony, food, and fireworks. For information, call 910-396-9126 or visit www.fortbraggmwr.com/julyfourth.php.

The *International Folk Festival* has been named one of the top 20 events in the

Operation Celebrate Freedom
COURTESY OF FAYETTEVILLE AREA CONVENTION AND VISITORS BUREAU

southeastern United States by the Southeast Tourism Society. Held each September on Hay Street in downtown Fayetteville, it pays homage to the region's diverse cultures. Visitors enjoy a smorgasbord of international foods, an eclectic array of world entertainment, and the highlight—the Parade of Nations. For information, call the Arts Council of Fayetteville/Cumberland County at 910-323-1776 or visit www.theartscouncil.com/International_Folk_Festival.html.

The *Holly Day Fair*, held in late November at the Crown Center, is a one-stop holiday shopping event that draws about 21,000 visitors. Sponsored by the Junior League of Fayetteville, this is the largest holiday gift-and-craft show in eastern North Carolina. Shoppers can choose from an extensive selection of unique handcrafted and manufactured gifts such as Christmas decorations, jewelry, clothes, toys, food specialties, household accents, and more. For information, call 910-323-5509 or visit www.hollydayfair.com.

Places to Stay

Resorts, Hotels, and Motels

Comfort Inn Cross Creek. Expensive/Moderate. 1922 Skibo Road, 28314 (910-867-1777). Located near the mall, the Comfort Inn offers 123 rooms and suites, Jacuzzis, an outdoor pool, and complimentary breakfast. It has been awarded a Two Diamond rating by AAA.

Holiday Inn Bordeaux. Moderate. 1707 Owen Drive, 28304 (877-863-4780 or 910-323-0111; http://hibordeaux.com/). This hotel has 298 rooms. Children stay free. Amenities include 30,000 square feet of meeting space; a concierge; dry-cleaning service; complimentary shuttle service to the airport, the bus station, and the train station; a full-service restaurant; a sports bar; a nightclub; and an outdoor pool.

Hotel Prince Charles. Moderate. 450 Hay Street, 28301 (www.450hay.com; 910-433-4444). If you want to stay downtown, your choice is pretty much limited to the Prince Charles. Built in 1924, this beautiful building is listed on the National Register and is a member of the Historic Hotels of America. It's just around the corner from many of the city's historic sites and is a good base if you're interested in a walking tour. Considered one of the finest Colonial Revival structures in Fayetteville, it features exquisite marble floors and staircases, arched Palladian windows and doorways, and beautiful brass railings. Twenty-six oversized guest rooms and 57 luxurious two-room suites are available, all filled with custom period furniture. This is as close to a bed-and-breakfast as you'll find in Fayetteville. A full-service restaurant and an exercise room are on the premises.

Places to Eat

The Barn of Fayetteville. Expensive. 1021 Bragg Boulevard, 28301 (910-678-0686). This fine-dining restaurant specializes in traditional and unique Italian dishes. It offers a full menu of veal, pasta entrées, steaks, chicken, and fresh seafood. It is open for dinner Monday through Saturday.

Hilltop House Restaurant. Expensive. 1240 Fort Bragg Road, 28305 (910-484-6699; www.hilltophousenc.com). This beautiful old restaurant is located in the historic Haymount district right across from the Cape Fear Regional Theatre. For 70 years, it has served up steaks, seafood, and Greek specialties at a reasonable rate. Lunch and dinner are served Tuesday through Saturday; brunch is served on Sunday; wine tastings are offered on Tuesday nights.

Mash House Restaurant & Brewery. Expensive/Moderate. 4150 Sycamore Dairy Road, 28303 (910-867-9223; www.themashhouse.com). This microbrewery has won medals at some of the largest beer festivals in the world. And its Kobe beef burgers, wood-fired pizzas, lunch specials, and late-night munchies are great accessories to the beer. The Mash House is open daily for lunch and dinner.

Highlander Café & Pub. Moderate. 1217 Hay Street, 28305 (910-485-4777; www.highlander-of-haymount.com). This Scottish establishment offers traditional pub dishes. It is open daily for lunch and dinner.

Huske Hardware House. Moderate/Inexpensive. 405 Hay Street, 28301 (910-437-9905; http://huskehardware.com). This place is worth the trip just to see the building. The 100-year-old structure holds rich significance for Fayetteville. At the time it was built, it was called "Major Huske's Folly" because it was so far from the Market House. Proving his critics wrong, the major went on to open six hardware stores, all bearing the initials *HHH*. Now a brewery and restaurant, Huske Hardware House sits in a prime location for visitors to the Airborne and Special Operations Museum. It offers such dishes as "Filet Tips" and "Tomato-Basil Shrimp," as well as some vegetarian fare, preferably served alongside its signature Airborne Ale. Live music is offered. Lunch is served daily and dinner Monday through Saturday.

Nearby

Bentonville Battleground is located approximately an hour northeast of Fayetteville; take U.S. 701 to S.R. 1008. Bentonville was the site of the last great Confederate charge of the Civil War and the largest battle ever fought in North Carolina. The Battle of Bentonville, which took place in March 1865 between General Joseph Johnston's Confederate troops and General William T. Sherman's Union men, ended with 2,500 casualties for the South and 1,500 for the North. The battlefield is now a state historic site that includes a Confederate cemetery, Union trenches, monuments, and a visitor center. It is open Monday through Saturday from 9 A.M. to 5 P.M. Admission is free. For information, visit www.nchistoricsites.org/bentonvi or call 910-594-0789.

The **National Hollerin' Contest** is held the third Saturday in June at the volunteer fire department in Spivey's Corner, located northeast of Fayetteville at the junction of U.S. 13 and U.S. 421. Hollerin' is an old custom of fieldworkers in the rural South, handed down from generation to generation. The contest is a living celebration of Sampson County, its history, and its people. Admission is free. For information, call 910-567-2600 or visit www.hollerincontest.com.

Not Your Average Summer Camp

If you've ever visited the Sandhills in summer, you know how oppressive it is just to cross the parking lot to an air-conditioned grocery store. But consider for a moment what some local soldiers put themselves through to defend our country.

The army's Special Forces qualifying program evaluates tactical skill, leadership, motivation, and ability to cope with stress. Among the program's components are "Psychology Tests," "Physical Fitness Tests," "Swim Tests," "Runs," "Obstacle Courses," "Rucksack Marches," "Small Unit Tactics," and "Military Orienteering." That sounds like good, clean fun—kind of like the Boy Scouts.

Trainees might tell a different story, in the unlikely event you could get them to talk.

The army's Level-C SERE (Survival, Evasion, Resistance, and Escape) training is conducted at Camp Mackall, part of the Fort Bragg complex. The program is designed for Special Forces operating behind enemy lines—the very people who merit a hefty al Qaeda bounty if killed or captured. At the core is what is blandly called "stress inoculation." The army says little about it, so as to maximize the anxiety of future trainees. That's the whole point, after all.

Trainees must learn to live off the land and evade capture if separated from their mates. They must also learn how to resist if imprisoned and tortured.

First, they're placed in a wilderness setting without food, water, or weapons and hunted down by armed "enemies." Trainees set about fashioning crude but lethal weapons. They conquer their food aversions by eating turtles, snakes, insects, and worms—whatever they can catch using whatever traps or lures they scavenge or make. Actually, since hunger is looked upon as a stressor to be overcome, any food at all is considered a "crutch." Most trainees lose 15 or more pounds during the three-week course—and these are people who didn't carry much fat entering the program.

Next, they're captured, hooded, roped together, and marched to a mock POW camp complete with guard towers, barbed wire, cages, concrete cells, fake graves, and Third World latrines—but no toilet paper, of course. They're further starved and subjected to sleep deprivation. Details of the physical and mental abuse aren't made public—again, in order to keep the stress sky-high for future campers.

The SERE program at Camp Mackall has produced some interesting data. Trainees' hormonal measurements indicate some of the highest stress levels ever recorded. For example, they encounter stress 25 percent greater than patients facing major surgery and 100 percent greater than first-time sky divers. The data also shows that Special Forces have higher adrenaline levels during stress than do normal soldiers, and that they recover normal adrenaline levels much faster after stress testing is completed. In other words, Special Forces have a superior ability to manage themselves under extreme circumstances.

If you encounter any Special Forces personnel around Fayetteville, give them a nod, ask how long they'll be in the area, and offer to buy their coffee. But be wary of hitting them up for a tour of Camp Mackall.

Pinehurst and Southern Pines
Introduction by Sheryl Monks

Sometime in the mid- to late 1800s, a collective hysteria formed in the minds of the upper middle class. They came to think their health was failing. What followed was a preoccupation with sicknesses, both real and imagined, that led to a search for radical detoxification. People looked to Mother Nature for antidotes—sea salt, mineral water, clean mountain mists. During this "Great Age of Inland Spas," savvy land developers sought to tap into the health craze by promoting some tracts of land as having the power to heal whatever ailed a body.

One such visionary saw the Sandhills as just the sort of place where the infirm might spend a few days recovering from the pollutants of Northern city life. After all, the area's sandy pine bluffs didn't seem fit for much else. Only the most resilient Scottish farmers took on the challenge of cultivating the nutrient-poor soil of Moore County, often called "the Pine Barrens" back then. Longleaf pines were truly the only things that seemed to thrive here—perhaps a fact not wasted on John Patrick, the state's commissioner of immigration, who bought 675 acres in 1883 for less than two dollars an acre in hopes of opening a health resort.

Some called his investment folly. Undeterred, Patrick laid out a town in square blocks and named the streets for Northern states to try to attract visitors from that part of the country. Then he sought the endorsements of doctors on the health bene-

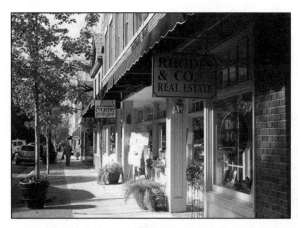

Broad Street in Southern Pines
COURTESY OF CONVENTION AND VISITORS
BUREAU, PINEHURST / SOUTHERN PINES /
ABERDEEN AREA

fits of air purified by trees. He advertised in Northern newspapers and brochures, praising the pine-scented air. New York physician G. H. Saddelson wrote this statement for Patrick: "Where the long leaf pine exists, ozone is generated largely and it has been demonstrated that persons suffering with throat and pulmonary diseases are much benefited when living in an atmosphere impregnated with this gas." Once the seed was planted, Patrick's concept of a health resort took hold, and the town of Southern Pines grew quickly.

John Patrick's health resort brought entrepreneur James Tufts to the Sandhills. He and his son Leonard introduced the Scottish game of golf to sanitarium residents as a cure for boredom. Tufts's purchase of 5,000 or so acres led to the development of Pinehurst Country Club, and the rest is history.

Today, the area maintains its legacy as a place of tranquility. Despite the cosmopolitan features of the sister towns of Pinehurst and Southern Pines—the lively shops, restaurants, and cultural centers—there remains something therapeutic about the pine-scented air. Just look at the lasting popularity of activities such as golf and equestrian events and you'll see that people still prefer the outdoors to the stale, refrigerated air of the modern indoors.

But you'll discover more to do in Pinehurst and Southern Pines than just play golf and ride horses. Folks here love the arts. You're sure to find a long list of high-caliber cultural events going on at any given time. Residents also support the preservation of local architecture. While you're in the area, take a guided tour through the historic districts. Landmark sites include private homes, churches, and a historic horse track. And don't forget the nearby Indian village of Town Creek. You'll also find shopping opportunities that range from pottery outlets and antique galleries to unique gift shops and sprawling malls. And everyone knows that shopping is regenerative to the spirit.

JUST THE FACTS

Southern Pines is approximately four miles south of the intersection of U.S. 1 and U.S. 15/501. Pinehurst is four miles to the west, close to the intersection of N.C. 5 and N.C. 2.

Moore County Regional Airport, located at Airport Road and N.C. 22 near Sandhills Community College, offers commuter air service, including daily connecting flights to Charlotte. For information, call 910-692-3212.

Amtrak reservations may be made by calling 800-872-7245. The train stops right in the middle of Southern Pines.

The twice-weekly newspaper in Southern Pines is *The Pilot*. The local magazine is *Pinehurst: The Magazine of the Sandhills*.

The number for the local chamber of commerce is 910-692-3926. The Pinehurst, Southern Pines, Aberdeen Area Convention and Visitors Bureau is located at 10677 U.S. 15/501 in Southern Pines (28388); call 800-346-5362 or visit www.homeofgolf.com.

Things to Do

Historic Places, Gardens, and Tours

Pinehurst Harness Track, at 200 Beulah Hill Road South/N.C. 5 (28374), is listed on the National Register of Historic Places. Horses have long been a feature of the Sandhills. In the early days of the resort, they helped in the construction and care of the golf course and in ferrying guests from the nearby railroad station. Constructed around 1915, the track was the winter home of polo ponies, hunter horses, racehorses, and Standardbreds. Owners, trainers, and resort guests enjoyed friendly competition during the Wednesday matinee programs. Today, Standardbred training occurs from October to May. Track events include spring races, horse shows, and polo matches. The track is operated by the village of Pinehurst. It is open daily year-round from 8 A.M. to dusk. Guided tours are available. For information, visit www.villageofpinehurst.org/VillageGovernment/Departments/HarnessTrack/tabid/126/Default.aspx call 800-644-TROT or call 910-295-4446.

The *Shaw House properties* are located at 110 Morganton Road in Southern Pines

Pinehurst Harness Track
COURTESY OF CONVENTION AND VISITORS BUREAU, PINEHURST / SOUTHERN PINES / ABERDEEN AREA

Shaw House
COURTESY OF CONVENTION AND VISITORS BUREAU, PINEHURST / SOUTHERN PINES / ABERDEEN AREA

(28387). Listed on the National Register, this trio of early structures depicts the daily life of the area's first settlers. The Shaw House, built around 1840 by Charles Shaw, is nothing like the antebellum plantation homes that usually come to mind. Much less extravagant, it exemplifies sturdy simplicity. The Garner House, built around 1830, is a log structure boasting wide-board heart-pine paneling, original hand-forged hinges, and board doors. The Britt-Sanders Cabin (also known as "the

Loom House") is a simple one-room pioneer home with a loft. The latter two houses were restored and moved to their present locations by the Moore County Historical Society. All three homes are open Tuesday through Friday from 1 P.M. to 4 P.M. Admission is free, though donations are welcome. For information, call 910-692-2051 or visit www.moorehistory.com.

Museums and Science Centers

Weymouth Woods–Sandhills Nature Preserve, at 1024 Fort Bragg Road in Southern Pines (28387), tells visitors about the importance of longleaf pine forests. Its interactive hands-on exhibits cover topics from prescribed burning to the naval-stores industry in the Sandhills. Built in 1978, the exhibit hall was renovated in 2001 and again in 2006. Located in the park's visitor center, it is open from 9 A.M. to 5 P.M. daily. Interpretive programs are held in the auditorium at the visitor center every Sunday at 3 P.M. from April through November. Outside, hikers may observe nearly 500 plant species and a number of animal species along more than four miles of well-marked, easy-to-hike trails in the wooded nature preserve. Guided tours are offered. The nature preserve is open from 8 A.M. to 8 P.M. March through October and from 8 A.M. to 6 P.M. November through February. Admission is free. For information, call 910-692-2167 or visit www.ncparks.gov/Visit/parks/wewo/main.php.

Cultural Offerings

The *Weymouth Center for the Arts and Humanities*, at 555 East Connecticut Avenue in Southern Pines (28387), has flourished as a cultural center since 1979. Once the home of North Carolina author James Boyd and his wife, Katharine Lamont Boyd, the center is a portion of the house built by the author's grandfather. Upon the elder Boyd's death, grandsons James and Jackson split the house in two. They hauled the main portion by mule across the road, where it became the Jackson Boyd House; now known as the Campbell House, it serves as the home of the Arts Council of Moore County. The portion that became the Weymouth Center was redesigned and enlarged in the 1920s by Aymar Embury II, a friend of the Boyds who went on to become the official architect of Princeton. Then as now, the building served as a center for literary activity, hosting visits from such friends as F. Scott Fitzgerald, Thomas Wolfe, Paul Green, and Sherwood Anderson. Today, the center has a writers-in-residence program that offers writers and composers stays of up to two weeks to pursue their work. Over 600 artists have taken advantage of the oppor-

The Weymouth Center
COURTESY OF CONVENTION AND VISITORS BUREAU, PINEHURST /
SOUTHERN PINES / ABERDEEN AREA

tunity; many testify that they accomplished their most creative work in the tranquil, inspiring atmosphere of the Boyds' former home. All phases of the arts and humanities are included in the Weymouth Center's programs. The concerts offered by the center feature artists from North Carolina universities, supplemented by nationally and internationally known chamber musicians; local youths are provided an opportunity to participate in a young musicians' competition. The center hosts frequent readings by acclaimed North Carolina writers and a lecture series that brings in a diverse group of speakers. For information, visit www.weymouthcenter.org or call 910-692-6261.

Campbell House Galleries, at 482 East Connecticut Avenue in Southern Pines (28387), is the home of the Arts Council of Moore County. The galleries provide three spacious exhibit areas featuring paintings and pottery for sale by local artists. In addition, tennis and basketball courts and a fitness area are available for public use. The galleries are open from 9 A.M. to 5 P.M. Monday through Friday and from 2 P.M. to 4 P.M. on the third Saturday and Sunday of each month. Admission is free. For information, call 910-692-4356.

Special Shopping

Sandhills Woman's Exchange, at 15 Azalea Road in Pinehurst (28374), is a co-op shop in a historic log cabin. It offers early-American crafts and baked goods for sale. The store is open September to mid-May. The hours are 10 A.M. to 4 P.M. on weekdays and 11 A.M. to 3 P.M. on Saturday. The tearoom on the premises serves lunch Monday through Friday. For information, call 910-295-4677 or visit www. sandhillsonline.com/history/womans.htm.

Recreation

Moore County, known as "the Golf Capital of the World," has over 720 golf holes (with many more on the drawing board), covering in excess of 270,000 yards. That's over 153 miles (or 2,700 football fields) of fairways, which are in constant use by the thousands of visitors who come to follow the little white ball. The density of golf-related activities here is said to be the highest in the world. Indeed, the village of Pinehurst and the Pinehurst Resort have been awarded national historic landmark status for their significant role in golf history—the only golf-related designation of its kind in the United States.

Tradition abounds in the land where legends like Jack Nicklaus, Arnold Palmer, Ben Hogan, Sam Snead, and Babe Didrikson Zaharias tested their skills on the finest courses in the world. Nearly 40 championship courses are located in the Sandhills; visitors will find a course suitable for every golfer, regardless of handicap. The courses were laid out by people like Donald Ross (who designed seven local courses), Tom Fazio (who designed four), Robert Trent Jones, Jack Nicklaus, Arnold Palmer, and Gary Player. The area has hosted dozens of major competitions, including the U.S. Women's Open, the U.S. Open, the PGA Championship, the Ryder Cup, and the World Open. Most major competitions are staged at Pinehurst No. 2.

What follows is a brief overview of a few of the finest courses. For more extensive information, visit www.homeofgolf.com.

Pinehurst Country Club, at 80 Carolina Vista Drive (28374), features eight premier courses. The mecca has long been Pinehurst No. 2, built by golf master Donald Ross. Ross, who always considered Pinehurst his home course, once called it "the fairest test of championship golf I have ever designed." Recently, this course hosted the U.S. Open in 1999 and 2005. Access is restricted to members and their guests. For information, call 800-ITS-GOLF or 910-295-6811 or visit www.pinehurst.com.

Pine Needles Lodge and Golf Club, at 1005 Midland Road in Southern Pines (28387), opened in 1927. It, too, was designed by Donald Ross. This was the site of the U.S. Women's Open in 1996, 2001, and 2007. The course is open to the public, based on availability. For information, call 800-747-7272 or 910-692-7111 or visit www.pineneedles-midpines.com.

The Carolina, at 277 Avenue of the Carolinas in nearby Whispering Pines

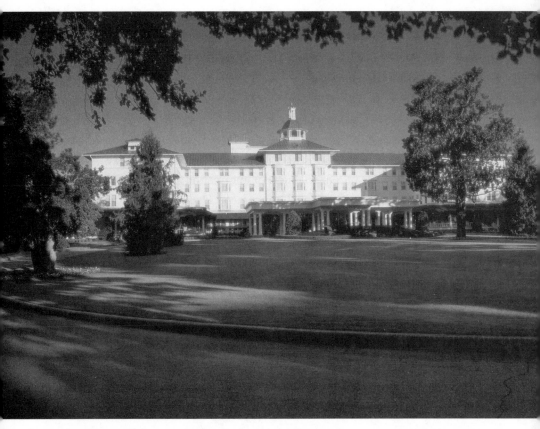

Pinehurst Country Club
COURTESY OF CONVENTION AND VISITORS BUREAU, PINEHURST / SOUTHERN PINES / ABERDEEN AREA

(28327), is an 18-hole course designed by Arnold Palmer. It opened in 1997 and is available to the public. For information, call 888-725-6372 or 910-949-2811 or visit www.thecarolina.com.

Though golf reigns supreme in the Sandhills, it isn't the only thing to do. Equestrian activities come in a close second. Between rounds of golf, try *Carriage Tours of Pinehurst Village*, which will let you explore the quaint town via horse-drawn carriage while learning local history. From Tuesday through Sunday, day and evening tours depart from the Carolina Hotel and the Magnolia Inn; tours last approximately 30 minutes. For information, call 910-235-8456. The *McLendon Hills Equestrian Center*, located at 275 McLendon Hills Drive/N.C. 211 in nearby West End (27376), offers horseback riding for adults and children eight years and older. Call 910-673-4971.

Seasonal Events

One of the first things you'll notice in visiting the area is the abundance of horse farms. Green fields and fences serve as a backdrop to creamy Arabians and grazing, gleaming thoroughbreds. For years, Moore County has been a center for the training of the country's best Standardbred harness horses, trotters, and pacers, in addition to thoroughbreds. The county has been home to five Olympic equestrian champions.

The *Carolina Carriage Classic* is held at the Pinehurst track in May. A parade takes place on the Sunday after the classic. For information, call 910-295-4446 or visit www.villageofpinehurst.org/VillageGovernment/Departments/HarnessTrack/tabid/126/Default.aspx.

The *Carolina Horse Park at Five Points*, located at 2814 Montrose Road in Raeford (28376), is a premier equestrian center offering national and international competitions, including the popular *Stoneybrook Festival and Steeplechase* in April. Situated on what was 250 acres of beautiful farmland, the horse park is approximately 12 miles south of Southern Pines. It offers flat fields perfect for show jumping, dressage, and racing, as well as expansive wooded areas that serve as cross-country courses. Gorgeous hardwoods and longleaf pines have been carefully preserved as part of the development plan. For information, visit www.carolinahorsepark.com or call 910-875-2074.

The entire Moore County area, with its beautiful greenery and rolling terrain, is wonderful for cycling. It has been used to qualify and train Olympic bicycle teams and is the site of the *Tour de Moore Century Ride*, which draws cyclists from around the world each Labor Day. The feature race, as the name suggests, is 100 miles around Moore County. Several levels of competition are offered. For information or a map of the course, call 910-692-4494 or visit www.rainbowcycles.com.

Places to Stay

Resorts, Hotels, and Motels

Pine Needles Lodge and Golf Club. Deluxe. 1005 Midland Road in Southern Pines, 28387 (800-747-7272 or 910-692-7111; www.pineneedles-midpines.com). For three generations, the legendary Peggy Kirk Bell and her family have been welcoming guests to Pine Needles Lodge and Golf Club. Here, you'll find the ideal atmos-

Thanksgiving Day fox hunt, Sandhills-style
COURTESY OF CONVENTION AND VISITORS BUREAU, PINEHURST / SOUTHERN PINES / ABERDEEN AREA

phere in which to improve your golf game, vacation with family and friends, or hold a business function. *Golf Digest* has awarded this resort a Four Star rating. You'll play on a Donald Ross course that has been the site of the U.S. Women's Open multiple times. And when you're not on the course, you'll enjoy the at-home feeling of one of the 11 rustic cabins. The resort offers a bed-and-breakfast option at the 1920s Georgian-style *Mid Pines Inn*; to reserve a room there, call 910-692-2114.

Pinehurst Resort Hotel. Deluxe. 80 Carolina Vista Drive in Pinehurst, 28374 (800-487-4653 or 910-235-8507). This is where it all began in Pinehurst, and it doesn't get any more luxurious. The resort encompasses *The Carolina, The Holly Inn, The Manor*, and *The Villas*. It offers a total of 530 rooms, all of which have nightly turndown service, in-room mini-bars, room service, express checkout, and data ports. Each has access to the concierge desk at The Carolina, which can arrange a host of services. Handicapped-accessible and nonsmoking rooms are available. The resort offers meeting space and health-and-fitness facilities. Recreation options include swimming, fishing, windsurfing, and canoeing. The *Pinehurst Post*, issued weekly to all guests, gives a rundown of the many activities and services at the resort.

Residence Inn by Marriott. Deluxe/Expensive. 105 Bruce Wood Road off U.S. 15/501 in Southern Pines, 28387 (910-693-3400; www.marriott.com). This friendly all-suites hotel is just right for the casually inclined. Its quiet, comfortable suites include living rooms and fully equipped kitchens. The inn offers an outdoor pool, a fitness center, complimentary continental breakfast, and packages at over 40 local golf courses. It is centrally located between Southern Pines and Pinehurst.

Inns and Bed-and-Breakfasts

The Knollwood House. Deluxe. 1495 West Connecticut Avenue in Southern Pines, 28387 (910-692-9390; www.knollwoodhouse.com). This gracious and stately home, built in 1927 as a holiday retreat for a wealthy Philadelphia family, was renovated and restored in 1992. Since then, it has become one of the area's premier bed-and-breakfasts. Set on five acres amid azaleas, holly trees, longleaf pines, and towering magnolias, the English manor–style home is beautifully decorated. The sunlit garden room, filled with flowering plants and wicker furniture, offers a view of the back lawn and gazebo and a glimpse of the 14th and 15th fairways of the famous Donald Ross course at Mid Pines. The Knollwood House is within easy walking distance of the lovely Southern Pines shopping district. Special golf packages are available.

Magnolia Inn. Deluxe/Expensive. 65 Magnolia Avenue in Pinehurst, 28374 (800-526-5562 or 910-295-6900; www.themagnoliainn.com). This century-old mansion has 11 guest rooms furnished with period antiques. It offers an English pub, a more formal restaurant, and an outdoor pool. The location is perfect for a downtown stroll. Golf packages are available.

Old Buggy Bed-and-Breakfast Inn. Expensive. 301 McReynolds Street in Carthage, 28327 (800-553-5247 or 910-947-1901; www.oldbuggyinn.com). This lovingly restored Victorian bed-and-breakfast lies in the heart of the Sandhills. W. T. Jones, president of the Tyson-Jones Buggy Manufacturing Company, built the 6,000-square-foot home for his wife, Florence, in 1897. Today, it stands at the entrance to Carthage's beautiful historic district, only minutes from the Pinehurst and Southern Pines golf resorts. Guests enjoy the inn's fanciful gingerbread trim, extravagant woodwork, old-fashioned wraparound porch, private swimming pool, verandas, and gardens. A gourmet breakfast and afternoon refreshments are provided. The inn offers special Murder Mystery Weekends and Romance Weekends.

Places to Eat

As you might expect, the area offers top-notch dining establishments. Each of the resorts has its own first-class restaurant; if you have the wherewithal and the proper attire, you will find excellent food and service at any of them.

Ashten's Restaurant & Pub. Expensive. 140 East New Hampshire Avenue in Southern Pines, 28387 (910-246-3510; www.ashtens.com). This restaurant's globally inspired cuisine encompasses Japanese, Italian, English, Indian, and other influences. Ashten's was a 2009 finalist in the "Best Dish NC" contest, sponsored by the North Carolina Department of Agriculture. It serves brunch on Sunday and dinner Tuesday through Sunday.

Chef Warren's. Expensive. 215 Northeast Broad Street in Southern Pines, 28387 (910-692-5240; www.chefwarrens.com). Chef Warren's has a cozy, open kitchen and a mouth-watering menu. This upscale restaurant offers nightly specials, a seasonal menu, and an extensive wine list. It serves locally grown organic products whenever possible. Dinner is served Monday through Saturday.

Dugan's Pub. Moderate. 2 Market Square in Pinehurst, 28374 (910-295-3400; www.duganspub.net). This full-service restaurant and pub boasts the largest selection of imported drafts in Pinehurst, as well as a complete wine list. Located in the Village Shops area, Dugan's has a traditional Irish pub upstairs and a second pub downstairs. Live entertainment is offered on Friday and Saturday nights. Lunch and dinner are served daily.

Squire's Pub. Moderate/Inexpensive. 1720 U.S. 1 South in Southern Pines, 28387 (910-695-1161; www.thesquirespub.com). A tradition in Southern Pines, Squire's serves Irish fare in a casual pub atmosphere. It offers the usual entrées—shepherd's pie and corned beef and cabbage. It also has a delicious, light trifle. Lunch and dinner are served Monday through Saturday.

Nearby

Bethesda Church and Cemetery, on N.C. 5/Bethesda Road in Aberdeen (28315), was built around 1790. Among its points of interest are "the Old Slave Gallery," bullet holes from a Civil War battle, and graves of area pioneer settlers. Listed on the National Register, Bethesda Church and Cemetery hosts an annual homecoming the last weekend in September. Guided tours for groups are available by appointment. Admission is free, though donations are welcome. For information, call 910-944-1319.

The **Bryant House** and the **McLendon Cabin**, located at 3361 Mount Carmel Road west of Carthage (28327) in the Harris Crossroads area, are two unaltered historic properties that depict early Moore County life. Built around 1820, the Bryant House has two fine mantels and handmade doors. The McLendon Cabin, constructed around 1760, is the county's oldest structure in its original location. The site is about a 15-minute drive from Pinehurst. Guided tours are available. The structures are open from 2 P.M. to 4 P.M. on the second and fourth Sundays from May through October. Admission is free, though donations are welcome. For information, call 910-947-3995 or visit www.moorehistory.com.

If you have time, make the short drive north to **Sanford** in Lee County. Each spring, over 150 potters and 50 artisans and craftsmen converge at the Dennis A. Wicker Civic Center complex at 1801 Nash Street (27330) to participate in the **Sanford Pottery Festival**. You'll marvel at the hundreds of exhibits and demonstrations and have a chance to buy some of the finest pottery in the world. For information, call 800-789-2241 or 919-776-0345 or visit www.sanfordpottery.org.

The **House in the Horseshoe**, at 288 Alston House Road west of Sanford (27330), is so named because of its location in a bend of the Deep River. Now a state historic site, it was built by Philip Alston in 1772, becoming one of the first big houses along North Carolina's frontier. During the American Revolution, irregular warfare was waged in the back country between bands of Whigs and Tories. Two of the Piedmont's more notable adversaries were Whig colonel Alston and Tory guerrilla David Fanning. One altercation between their followers left Fanning compatriot Kenneth Black beaten to death. At his friend's deathbed, Fanning heard Black name Alston as the man responsible. On Sunday, August 5, 1781, Fanning and his men surrounded Alston's house, trapping the colonel, his family, and a couple dozen of Alston's militia. When a British officer in the company of Fanning tried to lead a charge, he was shot dead. The direct approach having proved fatal, Fanning's men remained well covered. Shots were fired back and forth for hours, neither side gaining an advantage. As the day wore on, Fanning tried another approach. His men pushed a cart filled with hay to the side of the house, the intent being to set the hay on fire and burn Alston's home down around him. Alston's men frantically debated how they might surrender without being shot in the process. Mrs. Alston, confident that no one would fire upon a woman, took matters into her own hands. Bravely stepping into the yard, she told Fanning that the men inside would lay down their arms if Fanning agreed not to harm them or the house. Fanning agreed after receiving a promise that Alston and his men would not again take up arms in support of the American Revolution.

The house is still riddled with bullet holes today. A reenactment of the skirmish is conducted the first weekend in August. The site is open from 9 A.M. to 5 P.M. Tuesday through Saturday year-round. Admission is free. For information, call 910-947-2051 or visit www.ah.dcr.state.nc.us/sections/hs/horsesho/horsesho.htm.

Town Creek Indian Mound, at 509 Town Creek Mound Road in Mount Gilead (27306), is about an hour west of Pinehurst on N.C. 731 off N.C. 73. One of the best reconstructions of pre-white civilization in the country, Town Creek is also North Carolina's oldest state historic site. Visitors get a glimpse of pre-Columbian life in the Piedmont. The visitor center offers interpretive exhibits and audiovisual programs that bring alive a rich cultural heritage from the buried past. Self-guided tours allow guests to examine the rebuilt structures and mound. The site includes a museum, two temples, a burial house, and a reconstructed palisade wall. Town Creek is open Tuesday through Saturday from 9 A.M. to 4 P.M. and Sunday from 1 P.M. to 5 P.M. Admission is free. For information, call 910-439-6802 or visit www.ah.dcr.state.nc.us/sections/hs/town/town.htm.

Old Salem Museums and Gardens
COURTESY OF WINSTON-SALEM CONVENTION AND VISITORS BUREAU

The Triad

Winston-Salem
Greensboro
High Point
Triad Nearby

By Anne Holcomb Waters and Carolyn Sakowski

T o people who are not North Carolina residents, it can be confusing to keep the Triad and the Triangle straight. The Piedmont Triad actually covers an area greater than the three cities—Greensboro, High Point, and Winston-Salem—that are usually associated with the name. Technically, the Triad encompasses a 12-county area that runs from the Yadkin River on the west to the Haw River on the east and from the Virginia border on the north to the start of the Sandhills to the south.

The concept of a Triad region came to light in the mid-1960s, when elected officials from the area's county and municipal governments met to discuss common concerns. They adopted the name Piedmont Triad Committee. As best as can be determined, this was the first time the word *Triad* was used to describe the area. In 1987, the name of the airport was changed to Piedmont Triad International Airport.

Although local governments and chambers of commerce try to work together on issues of mutual concern, old rivalries die hard. The cities have been pitted against each other in recruiting wars for too long. So much friction exists between

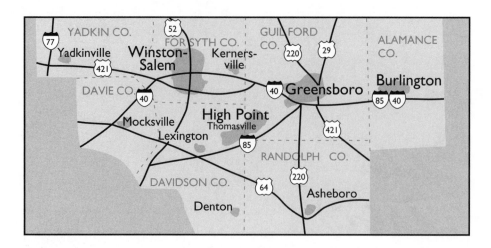

Greensboro and High Point that at one point High Point wanted to secede from Guilford County and form a new county. Fortunately, the newcomers arriving in the area in droves don't know about the old battle lines, so cooperation among the communities seems to be on the rise. Thousands of Triad couples have one partner working in one city and the other in another, further diminishing the old lines.

Today, due to the state's increased visibility in technology-related industries, the Piedmont Triad is drawing more and more people and businesses. Greensboro, its largest city, has a population of over 251,000. A city that owes much of its economic base to textiles, it is now home to several colleges and universities. Boasting a population of over 224,000, Winston-Salem is the second-largest city in the region. Although it owes much of its prosperity to tobacco, Winston-Salem has now become a leader in the medical field. The home of both the country's first arts council and the University of North Carolina School of the Arts, it is known as "the City of the Arts." High Point has a population of over 102,000. Known internationally as a furniture capital, it attracts thousands of people to its showrooms. Altogether, the 12-county area claims a population of approximately a million.

With the mountains less than two hours distant and the beaches only four hours away, this region becomes more attractive with each passing year.

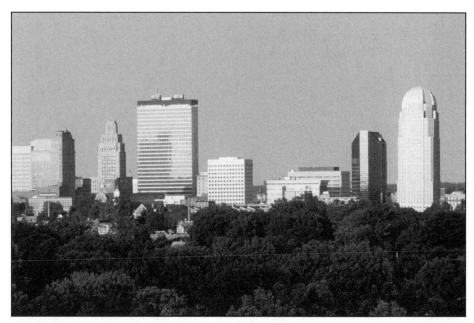

Downtown Winston-Salem
© WACHOVIA CORPORATION

Winston-Salem

By Anne Holcomb Waters

As is reflected in its hyphenated name, Winston-Salem has always been a city that throws together opposites and comes out stronger as a result. In other words, you take pious Salem, throw in raw Winston, and get a city remarkable for its civility, its commitment to education, and its culture both classical and folk.

The Moravians who came to the area they named *Die Wachau* (later Latinized to Wachovia) in 1753 were sober, thrifty, disciplined, and peaceful. After establishing the villages of Bethabara and Bethania, they began building their main city, Salem, in 1766.

The Salem Moravians belonged to one of the first Protestant sects. They came mostly from German-speaking areas of Bohemia, Poland, and, of course, Moravia. Arriving in America to escape persecution, they settled first in Pennsylvania, then sent colonists into their new land in the back country of North Carolina. They organized themselves—they were nothing if not organized—into congregational towns in which just about everything was owned and controlled by the church. No non-Moravians were allowed to live in Bethabara or, later, in Salem.

The Moravians were frequently envied and mistrusted by their neighbors, most of whom were small farmers leading hardscrabble lives on the frontier. These farmers struggled all their lives just to eat. By contrast, the Moravians essentially finished building Salem—complete with church, meeting house, and a water system—in five years.

Despite this mistrust, Salem quickly became the trading center of northwestern North Carolina and southwestern Virginia. Nearby was the only safe place to cross the Yadkin River for 50 miles, so all the major thoroughfares in the area (including the Great Wagon Road from Pennsylvania) ran by Salem.

When Forsyth County was created out of Stokes County in 1849, Salem was the logical choice for the county seat. The Moravian leaders, however, wanted no truck with the rabble that came with a county courthouse, so they agreed to sell the new county 51 acres for a town a mile north of Salem Square. For almost two years, the Forsyth County seat was known as "that place north of Salem." In 1851, the North

Carolina General Assembly named the town after a local Revolutionary War hero, and Winston was born.

While Salem built textile mills, Winston was known for selling dried berries. Not until after the Civil War and Reconstruction did it begin to capitalize on the area's major crop and pledge fealty to King Tobacco. Factories for making plug tobacco and tobacco auction houses and warehouses sprang up around the young town, but those were lemonade stands compared to what a 24-year-old former traveling tobacco salesman had in mind.

Just as his statue outside city hall suggests, Richard Joshua Reynolds arrived in Winston on horseback. He was drawn from his Virginia home in 1874 by Winston's new rail line, by which the young Reynolds realized he could ship his tobacco anywhere and permanently retire his salesman's wagon.

Reynolds built his tobacco company and Winston at the same time. He was phenomenally hardworking and uncommonly canny. A decent man, he was also one of the first industrialists to realize how closely his own fortunes were tied to his workers'. He paid his (mostly black) employees well by the day's standard, instituted profit-sharing plans, and provided drinking water, lunchrooms, day nurseries, and a medical department. His wife, Katharine, encouraged and continued his philanthropy, and the leaders who followed him at R. J. Reynolds Tobacco Company and elsewhere placed a high value on giving back to the community.

Winston officially merged with Salem in 1913, although they had been called "the Twin City" for years. The two combined, in the words of longtime *Winston-Salem Journal* writer Chester Davis, "the Salem conscience with the Winston purse."

Most of the 20th century was a heyday for Winston-Salem. Reynolds tobacco and Hanes hosiery were sold around the world. Piedmont Airlines, started at what would become Z. Smith Reynolds Airport, grew into one of the best-run airlines in the country. In the 1950s, Wake Forest College moved from its home near Raleigh to a new campus in Winston-Salem donated by R. J. Reynolds's daughter and son-in-law. A new limited-access highway was designed to relieve downtown traffic; the planned east-west expressway became, before its completion, part of Interstate 40. Winston-Salem boasted the first municipal arts council in the nation. In the 1960s, the Twin City beat out several other communities to become the home of what is now the University of North Carolina School of the Arts.

As the century drew to a close, however, so did Winston-Salem's period of startling growth. Population declined in the 1980s, the first time since Salem's founding. Piedmont Airlines was bought by USAir. The AT&T plant on Lexington Road shut down in 1988. Most devastating of all was the move of the headquarters of

R. J. Reynolds Tobacco—now RJR Nabisco—to Atlanta. RJR Nabisco president and CEO F. Ross Johnson became the most hated man in town when he justified the move by calling Winston-Salem too "bucolic."

But as the poet noted, "Tho' much is taken, much abides." The misfortunes that beset Reynolds and other local giants forced the city to diversify its economy. And the sudden absence of patriarchal industry captains led the city to learn how to run itself. Winston-Salem still has the cultural legacy left by its forebears. Wake Forest University, Winston-Salem State University, Salem College, and the University of North Carolina School of the Arts call the city home. So do two major art museums—Reynolda House Museum of American Art (housed in the former country estate of R. J. Reynolds) and the Southeastern Center for Contemporary Art. The Stevens Center for the Performing Arts plays host to outstanding productions of dance, music, film, and drama. Throw in its thriving Downtown Arts District and Winston-Salem can truly claim to be "the City of the Arts."

Just as the Moravians learned to coexist with their rural neighbors, and staid Salem with boisterous Winston, high culture in Winston-Salem coexists with the rowdy working-class legacy of the city's industrial past. Many of the happenings in the revitalized downtown, for example, make use of Winston-Salem's tradition of mountain bluegrass, gospel, and Piedmont blues, the music of the farmers and sharecroppers who brought their crops to town and the workers who labored in the mills and factories.

Winston-Salem boasts as much culture as any city in the state, while retaining a blue-collar earthiness that has been glossed over elsewhere beneath tides of transplants and slick prosperity. It's a Jeffersonian combination that reflects the industriousness, piety, and simplicity of the Moravian pioneers. It's a combination that has helped make Winston-Salem thrive again.

JUST THE FACTS

Winston-Salem is the county seat of Forsyth County, which has a population of more than 343,028. The Winston-Salem Visitors Center, in the historic Brookstown Mill at 200 Brookstown Road (27101), can provide information on the city; call 866-728-4200 or visit www.visitwinstonsalem.com.

Located in the northwestern corner of the North Carolina Piedmont, Winston-Salem is less than two hours from the heart of the Blue Ridge Mountains and less than an hour from the Virginia border. Interstate 40 runs east and west just south of town; Interstate 40 Business cuts straight through downtown. U.S. 52 connects Winston-Salem with the Virginia mountains and the Blue Ridge Parkway to the north and with the Yadkin River Valley to the south. In the near future, U.S. 52 is slated to become part of Interstate 73/74, which will run between Detroit and Charleston, South Carolina.

The city's Greyhound bus station is at 250 Greyhound Court (27101); call 800-231-2222 or 336-724-1429. The nearest Amtrak station is in Greensboro, but a connector is available; call 800-872-7245 for information.

Piedmont Triad International Airport, located off Interstate 40 just across the Guilford County line, is the major airport for Winston-Salem. Seven carriers provide flights daily. Call 336-721-0088 or visit www.ptia.org for general airport information. Smith Reynolds Airport, 10 minutes north of downtown Winston-Salem at 3801 North Liberty Street (27105), is a base for commuter and corporate aircraft; call 336-767-6361 or visit www.smithreynolds.org.

Things to Do

Historic Places, Gardens, and Tours

Old Salem Museums and Gardens, at 900 Old Salem Road (27101) near the intersection of Academy and Main streets, is where most visitors will want to begin—where Winston-Salem itself began. The Moravian town has been carefully restored into a living-history community. Costumed interpreters lead tours, demonstrate traditional crafts, and chat with visitors as if the 19th century, rather than the 21st, has just turned.

Though visitors can stroll the old streets free of charge, tickets are required for admission to some of the restored buildings. They may be purchased at the visitor center, located across the street from Old Salem. The visitor center is open Tuesday through Saturday from 9 A.M. to 5 P.M. and Sunday from 12:30 P.M. to 5 P.M. The hours for various buildings and shops within Old Salem may vary slightly. Old Salem is closed Easter, Thanksgiving, Christmas Eve, and Christmas. Most shops—including the Moravian Book and Gift Shop, T. Bagge Merchant, A. Butner Hat Shop, and the highly aromatic Winkler Bakery—do not require tickets. Nor does the Salem Tavern, described in the "Places to Eat" section below. Nor does God's Acre, the burial ground used by original settlers and modern-day Moravians alike; it is to God's Acre that worshipers march from Salem Square at dawn during the traditional Easter Sunrise Service, celebrated since 1773. A ticket gains the purchaser unlimited one- or two-day admission to all gardens and restorations, including the

Single Brothers House, where visitors can see early trades demonstrated; the Miksch House and Manufactory; the Vierling House, home of an early physician; the Boys School; the Schultz Shoemaker Shop; the Tavern Museum Barn; the St. Philips log and brick churches; and the John Vogler House. At each stop, interpreters tell about the building, the town, and the orderly, pious life of the Moravians. The ticket also includes admission to the Museum of Early Southern Decorative Arts (MESDA) and the Old Salem Toy Museum, which are covered in the "Museums and Science Centers" section. It takes at least a half-day to see Old Salem thoroughly. Visitors should enjoy it at a leisurely 18th-century pace anyway. For more information, call 888-653-7253 or 336-721-7350 or visit www.oldsalem.org.

The most recent happenings at Old Salem include the return of the 1821 Herbst House to its original site, the unearthing of archaeological remains of the Reich-Hege House, and, most notably, the restoration of St. Philips. Originally known as "the African Moravian Church," St. Philips serves as an interpretive center for the story of the African-Americans of Salem. A special walking tour called "African-Americans in Salem" is offered, as is an audiovisual presentation. The Moravians were uncomfortable with slavery—but not uncomfortable enough to end the practice.

Old Salem adjoins the campuses of Salem College and Salem Academy, which are among the oldest women's institutions in the country and a testament to the Moravians' belief that both sexes deserved an education.

Historic Bethabara Park, at 2147 Bethabara Road (27106), is a restoration of the Moravians' first settlement in Wachovia. The men who came to scout the site spent their first night in an abandoned trappers' cabin. The town was never intended to be a permanent settlement; in fact, its name means "House of Passage." Bethabara soon became a trading center for the region. A palisade was built to protect against raiding parties during the French and Indian War. The town, however, was largely abandoned when Salem was established in 1772.

The palisade, the Potter's House, and the Gemeinhaus (or Congregation House) are still standing and are open to the public. Several foundations unearthed at the town site have been studied by archaeologists, and gardens have been re-created. The restored site is surrounded by a 175-acre park and nature preserve that includes trails to the site of Bethabara's mill, a beaver pond, and a picnic ground overlooking the village.

Bethabara does not take as long to explore as Old Salem, but a visit here should certainly not be rushed. A visitor center is located across Bethabara Road. The

Two Sweet Piedmont Originals

by Anne Holcomb Waters

Two famous North Carolina originals have their roots in the Piedmont, and, boy, are they sweet!

Although technically started in Paducah, Kentucky, Krispy Kreme Doughnuts (www.krispykreme.com) has been based in Winston-Salem since founder Vernon Rudolph opened his doughnut shop in 1937.

With two assistants, a 1936 Pontiac, a few pieces of doughnut-making machinery, and $25 in cash, Rudolph rented a building on South Main Street in the middle of what is now Old Salem. After spending his little money, he had to convince a nearby grocer to loan him the ingredients for his first batch of doughnuts, which he delivered in his Pontiac outfitted with a baking rack.

Although Rudolph originally established himself as a wholesaler, the alluring aroma of his yeast-raised doughnuts created such demand that he responded by cutting a hole in the shop's wall in order to sell directly to customers. Thus, he created the company's successful model for drive-through windows and open viewing of the doughnut-making process.

In 1997, Krispy Kreme artifacts were placed in the Smithsonian Institution, forever securing the company's place as an American icon. "Hot Doughnuts Now" signs currently shine from the Piedmont to the Philippines. If you see one lit up, stop in for a melt-in-your-mouth morsel worth every fat-filled calorie.

Cheerwine (www.cheerwine.com) is a cherry-flavored cola created in Salisbury in 1917. While its appeal isn't quite as far-reaching as Krispy Kreme's—yet—it is a much-loved soda throughout the Southeast.

Curiously, Cheerwine can also be traced to Kentucky, where company founder L. D. Peeler and some other investors bought stock in a regional branch of the maker of MintCola. In 1917, they bought out the company, changed the name to Carolina Beverage Corporation, and purchased Cheerwine's unique flavoring from a "flavor salesman" from St. Louis.

When L. D. Peeler died in 1931, his son Clifford took over, serving as president until 1992 and chairman until his death in 2000 at the age of 96. The company, still family-owned, is thriving under the leadership of L. D. Peeler's great-grandsons, Mark and Cliff Ritchie, who have steadily increased sales.

For those who don't have a taste for sweets, both companies sell an array of cool paraphernalia featuring their nostalgic, retro logos.

exhibit buildings are open for guided tours from April 1 through December 16 except for Thanksgiving and Sundays in December. Tours run Monday through Friday from 10:30 A.M. to 4:30 P.M. and Saturday and Sunday from 1:30 P.M. to 4:30 P.M. A modest admission fee is charged. The grounds are open all day, every day. For more information, call 336-924-8191 or visit www.bethabarapark.org.

Reynolda Gardens of Wake Forest University occupies most of the land adjacent to Reynolda House on Reynolda Road. Owned by the university, the property includes greenhouses, four acres of formal flower and vegetable gardens, and 125 acres of woods and streams with marked trails. The grounds are open free of charge during daylight hours year-round. The greenhouses are open free of charge from 10 A.M. to 4 P.M. Monday through Saturday except for Saturdays in January. For more information, call 336-758-5593 or visit www.reynoldagardens.org.

Adjacent to the gardens at 2201 Reynolda Road (27106) is *Reynolda Village*, created to house and educate the workers on the Reynolds estate. Katharine Reynolds planned the green-roofed, whitewashed village as a model farm where area farmers could learn the latest agricultural techniques. The village has been renovated to house upscale shops, galleries, and restaurants. For more information, call 336-758-5584 or visit www.reynoldavillage.org.

Museums and Science Centers

Reynolda House Museum of American Art, at 2250 Reynolda Road (27106), was the country home of tobacco magnate R. J. Reynolds. Devoted to building his tobacco company, Reynolds married late. He took as his bride his distant cousin Katharine. She was many years his junior, but he had long admired her intelligence and bearing. For most of their married lives, they lived in a mansion on Fifth Street, where they had four children: Richard Jr., Mary, Nancy, and Zachary Smith.

In 1912, they began work on what they called a "bungalow" on their country estate about three miles north of town. The house was designed by Philadelphia architect Charles Barton Keen. But the driving force behind the development of the estate was unquestionably Katharine. That it was called *Reynolda*, the female Latin version of the family name, was no accident.

By the time the house was finished in 1917, R. J. was near death. Katherine did not long outlive him. The house was left to the children, who tended to use it as a holiday house as they grew older. In 1936, however, Mary and her husband, Charles Babcock, renovated the property for use as their family home.

In 1964, Charles Babcock donated the house and 20 surrounding acres to be used as a nonprofit institution dedicated to the arts and education. His daughter, art historian Barbara Babcock Millhouse, and then–executive director Nicholas Bragg set about turning Reynolda House Museum of American Art into one of the country's finest facilities for the study of American art, architecture, and design. Thomas Cole, Georgia O'Keeffe, Grant Wood, Frederic Remington, Mary Cassatt, Thomas Hart Benton, Alexander Calder, Jacob Lawrence, and Jasper Johns are all represented in the museum's permanent collection. Visitors will also find a number of quietly magnificent works by lesser-known artists, including *The Old Hunting Ground* by Worthington Whittredge. A collection of vintage clothing from the Reynolds family is housed in the attic.

Reynolda House is itself a museum. It is a classic of the Arts and Crafts movement of the late 19th and early 20th centuries, which encouraged simplicity and rustic craftsmanship in design and decor. The most impressive feature is an Aeolian organ with 2,566 pipes, some of which are visible from the second-floor gallery and in the attic. All rooms are furnished with period pieces, including many Reynolds family originals. Children and adults also enjoy seeing the bungalow's indoor swimming pool, bowling alley, shooting range, squash court, and mirrored Art Deco bar.

A wing added in recent years houses an auditorium, the visitor center, the mu-

Reynolda House Museum of American Art
COURTESY OF REYNOLDA HOUSE AND WINSTON-SALEM CONVENTION AND VISITORS BUREAU

seum shop, exhibition space, classrooms, studios, and a library.

Reynolda House is open from 9:30 A.M. to 4:30 P.M. Tuesday through Saturday and from 1:30 P.M. to 4:30 P.M. on Sunday. It is closed Thanksgiving, Christmas, and New Year's. Admission is charged. Students with valid identification are admitted free. For more information, visit www.reynoldahouse.org or call 888-663-1149 or 336-758-5150.

The *Southeastern Center for Contemporary Art* (SECCA), not far from Reynolda House at 750 Marguerite Drive (27106), is housed in the 1929 English-style home of Hanes Hosiery industrialist James G. Hanes. Twenty thousand square feet of exhibit space have been added to the original house. None of this space is used for a permanent collection; instead, SECCA hosts as many temporary exhibits as possible, bringing some of the Southeast's most impressive and up-to-the-minute work to Winston-Salem. Like Reynolda House, SECCA hosts a variety of programs and performances in the house and on the grounds.

Readers of a certain age may recall the dustup in 1989 surrounding Andres Serrano's "Piss Christ," which won SECCA's "Awards in the Visual Arts" competition. A Google search 20 years later lists 15,600 hits—a testament to the ongoing interest in the controversy.

SECCA is currently undergoing major renovations and is scheduled to reopen in January 2010. Since new hours of operation are under consideration, contact the museum before planning your visit. Admission is charged except for children under 17 and SECCA members. For more information, call 336-725-1904 or visit www.secca.org.

The *Museum of Anthropology of Wake Forest University* is located behind Kentner Stadium on Wake Forest's main campus. Founded in 1963 by the faculty of the school's Department of Anthropology, it was originally intended for Wake students but is now a favorite of Triad residents and visitors.

The permanent collection features artifacts from the Americas, Africa, Asia, and Oceania. Some of the most interesting pieces, however, are prehistoric artifacts found here in the Yadkin River Valley. The museum also hosts a wide range of special exhibits and programs.

The museum and its gift shop are open from 10:30 A.M. to 4:30 P.M. Tuesday through Saturday except for holidays and WFU intersession. Admission is free. For more information, call 336-758-5282 or visit www.wfu.edu/MOA.

While you're here, the university campus is well worth a quick stroll. Wake

Forest College was founded by Baptist ministers in the town of Wake Forest, just north of Raleigh, in 1834. In the 1940s, the Reynolds family invited the college to move to Winston-Salem, offering land on R. J. Reynolds's country estate and a sizable endowment. In 1953, President Harry Truman turned the first shovelful at the groundbreaking ceremony. Five years later, classes began on the new campus.

Built of local red bricks in the Colonial Revival style, the campus is dominated by Wait Chapel, located at the northern end of the quad. The sanctuary for Wake Forest Baptist Church and a popular site for weddings and the annual Christmas Lovefeast, Wait Chapel was host to presidential debates in 1988 and 2000.

SciWorks, at 400 West Hanes Mill Road (27106), focuses on earth and physical sciences. Kids love the interactive exhibits and programs at this venerable children's museum. SciWorks boasts 25,000 square feet of attractions including a Foucault pendulum, a 15-acre environmental park, and a 119-seat planetarium. Kids can see mounted animals from around the world, walk inside a 20-foot tree to check out its age, and, best of all, strum a stringless harp and play "Happy Birthday" on the floor piano. SciWorks also offers nature trails, habitats for river otter, deer, and waterfowl, and a small collection of farmyard animals.

From June 1 through Labor Day, the facility is open Monday through Saturday from 10 A.M. to 5 P.M. The rest of the year, it is open Monday through Friday from 10 A.M. to 4 P.M. and Saturday from 11 A.M. to 5 P.M. Admission is charged; the price includes a planetarium show. For more information, call 336-767-6730 or visit www.sciworks.org.

SciWorks' Millennium Fountain
COURTESY OF SCIWORKS AND WINSTON-SALEM CONVENTION AND VISITORS BUREAU

The *Museum of Early Southern Decorative Art* (MESDA), at 924 South Main Street (27101) in Old Salem, is dedicated to preserving, exhibiting, and researching regional decorative arts. Covering the years from colonization to 1820, MESDA exhibits furniture, paintings, textiles, ceramics, and silver in 24 period rooms and seven galleries.

Visitors will note the marked cultural differences in the Colonial and early Federal Southeast; the region was anything but a "Solid South." The Scots-Irish settlers on the frontier lived very different lives from their German neighbors, who in turn existed a world apart from the Englishmen and French Huguenots in the cities of the coastal plain. MESDA takes as its geographical area a region that includes the Chesapeake, the Low Country, and the back country. This encompasses all of the Carolinas and Virginia and wide swaths of Maryland, Kentucky, Tennessee, Georgia, and what is now West Virginia.

MESDA is open Monday through Saturday from 10 A.M. to 5 P.M. and Sunday from 1 P.M. to 5 P.M. Guided tours are offered on the hour. Visitors have to buy an all-in-one ticket to Old Salem to get into MESDA. For more information, call 888-348-5420 or 336-721-7300 or visit www.mesda.org.

MESDA shares the Frank L. Horton Museum Center with the *Old Salem Toy Museum*. The latter houses a permanent collection of more than 1,200 antique toys dating from 225 A.D. to the 1920s. Here, you can see third-century toys dredged from the Thames River, as well as a plethora of 19th-century German toys enjoyed by the children of Salem. As with MESDA, an Old Salem ticket is required to enter the museum. The hours are Tuesday through Saturday from 9:30 A.M. to 4:30 P.M. and Sunday from 1 P.M. to 4:30 P.M.

Cultural Offerings

Diggs Gallery, on the campus of Winston-Salem State University at 601 Martin Luther King, Jr. Drive (27110), brings in traveling exhibits and artists of national renown. It features a sculpture garden, a pair of noteworthy murals by John Biggers, and a permanent collection focusing on traditional and contemporary African-American art. The gallery also houses an impressive collection of works on paper by well-known European and American artists including Jean-François Millet, Joan Miro, and Robert Rauschenberg. The gallery is open Tuesday through Saturday from 11 A.M. to 5 P.M. Admission is free. For information, call 336-750-2458 or visit www.wssu.edu/WSSU and select "Diggs Gallery" under "featured links".

The *Delta Arts Center*, located at 2611 New Walkertown Road (27101), is the attractive new gallery space of Winston-Salem Delta Fine Arts, Inc., established in 1972 to promote cultural arts by African-Americans. That same year, it started a permanent collection at Winston-Salem State University that remains housed in the O'Kelly Library. The gallery features fine art, crafts, and performance art by Hispanic and African-American artists. The hours are Tuesday through Friday from 10 A.M. to 5 P.M. and Saturday from 11 A.M. to 3 P.M.; the center is closed major holidays. For information, call 336-722-2625 or visit www.deltafinearts.org.

The *North Carolina Black Repertory Company* has its offices at 610 Coliseum Drive, Suite 1 (27105). The company sponsors the week-long National Black Theatre Festival every other year. Professional theater groups from around the world come to Winston-Salem for the festival, as do celebrities from theater and film. Call 336-723-2266 or visit www.nbtf.org for more information.

The *Stevens Center for the Performing Arts*, at 405 West Fourth Street (27101), was a vacant 1920s movie theater until the early 1980s, when what is now the University of North Carolina School of the Arts (UNCSA) turned it into one of the finest performance venues in the Southeast.

The center has a seating capacity of 1,400. It hosts year-round events ranging from UNCSA student productions to performances by such local and regional groups as the Piedmont Triad Symphony, the Piedmont Opera Theatre, the North Carolina Dance Theatre, and the North Carolina Shakespeare Festival. It also brings in national acts, touring productions of Broadway shows, and children's performances, including that perennial holiday favorite, *The Nutcracker*. In recent years, the Stevens Center has returned to its cinematic roots, playing host to the Films on Fourth series (which brings independent, foreign, and limited-release films to Winston-Salem) and to screenings during the RiverRun International Film Festival.

Call 336-721-1945 or visit www.ncarts.edu/stevenscenter for information about ticket prices and upcoming events.

Special Shopping

A gallery hop is held the first Friday of every month in Winston-Salem's *Downtown Arts District*, centered along Fifth, Seventh, and Trade streets. Sponsored by the Downtown Arts District Association, this is one of the best free social and cultural activities the city offers. Two of the premier shops are almost directly across Trade

Street from one another: the *Piedmont Craftsmen* shop and *Urban Artware*. Their respective websites are www.piedmontcraftsmen.org and www.urbanartware.com.

Recreation

Winston-Salem sponsors downtown parties every Thursday, Friday, and Saturday night from April to October. *Alive after Five*, held Thursday from 5:30 P.M. to 8:30 P.M. at Corpening Plaza, brings in pop and alternative acts aimed at young professionals. *Downtown Jazz*, held every Friday from 5:30 P.M. to 8:30 P.M. in the revitalized Fourth Street area, offers funk and soul in addition to jazz and blues. *Summer on Trade*, billed as "Winston's Roots Revival," is held in the Downtown Arts District on Trade and Sixth streets on Saturday from 7 P.M. to 10 P.M. It draws on the musical heritage of the Piedmont and the Blue Ridge and has featured performers such as Doc Watson. For more information, call the Downtown Winston-Salem Partnership at 336-354-1500 or visit www.dwsp.org.

At the time of this writing, the swanky new downtown baseball park for the newly minted *Winston-Salem Dash* (named for the Camel City's hyphen) stood three-quarters built at First Street and Peters Creek Parkway. Stalled by the recession, construction should soon resume thanks to the unanimous support of Winston-Salem city officials and an additional allocation of $12.7 million. When completed sometime in 2010, the stadium promises to be a first-class sports arena that also encompasses specialty shopping and fine dining. For information, call 336-714-BATS or visit www.wsdash.com.

Seasonal Events

The *Dixie Classic Fair*, the regional exposition for northwestern North Carolina, is the last big fair before the North Carolina State Fair in Raleigh. Originally a chance for local farmers to show off their crops and livestock, the Dixie Classic still shows its agricultural and community roots. Concession stands are operated by local nonprofit organizations such as Boy Scout troops, Little Leagues, and the Kiwanis Club; prizewinning student artwork is displayed in the exhibit hall; and one of the most popular events is the pig race. A re-created folk village offers demonstrations of blacksmithing and woodcarving; bluegrass bands play on the front porch of one of the log cabins. The mile-long midway, meanwhile, is filled with ample opportunities to lose money on games of skill and chance. Rides are available for all ages and courage levels. The fairgrounds are behind Lawrence Joel Veteran's Memorial Coliseum, which is on the corner of University Parkway and Deacon Boulevard. The fair is held in late September or early October. Call 336-727-2236 or visit www.dcfair.org for more information.

The *Piedmont Crafts Fair*, held each November in the M. C. Benton Convention Center downtown, brings in more than 100 regional craftsmen to display and (they hope) sell their wares. The fair is sponsored by the Piedmont Craftsmen organization, which operates a gallery at 601 North Trade Street year-round. You can reach the gallery at 336-725-1516 or learn about it by visiting www.piedmontcraftsmen. org.

Old Salem is renowned for its Moravian Christmas celebrations. *A Salem Christmas*, which includes strolling brass bands and seasonal decorations, is capped by the *Christmas Candle Tea*, in which a Lovefeast of buns, coffee, and hymns is held by candlelight in the Single Brothers House.

The *RiverRun International Film Festival* began in Brevard but moved to Winston-Salem in 2003. Founded by Gennario D'Onofrio, father of *Full Metal Jacket* and *Law & Order: Criminal Intent* star Vincent D'Onofrio, RiverRun uses the facilities of the University of North Carolina School of the Arts, the Stevens Center, and other downtown venues to showcase the best new films by independent, international, and student filmmakers. Among its many noteworthy screenings have been *The Baker*, *Crazy Love*, *The Notebook*, and the Christopher Guest "mockumentary" *A Mighty Wind*. Call 336-724-1502 or visit www.riverrunfilm.com for more information.

Places to Stay

Resorts, Hotels, and Motels

In earlier times, Winston-Salem boasted two of the finest hotels in the South: the Hotel Zinzendorf and the Hotel Robert E. Lee. The Zinzendorf stood on the hill overlooking the West End neighborhood, near what is now the intersection of Fourth and Glade streets. It burned in its prime on Thanksgiving Day in 1892; among the diners who had to be evacuated were R. J. Reynolds and William A. Blair, whose son John founded the company that publishes this book. The Hotel

Robert E. Lee suffered a long period of decline after World War II. It was imploded in 1972 to make way for a succession of fine hotels.

Most of Winston-Salem's hotels are representatives of national chains. The following, however, feature distinctive accommodations with a definite local flavor.

Brookstown Inn. Deluxe. 200 Brookstown Avenue, 27101 (800-845-4262 or 336-725-1120; www.brookstowninn.com). Located in the historic Brookstown Mill area on the edge of the even more historic Old Salem, Brookstown Inn is listed on the National Register. It is housed in what was one of Salem's first textile mills. Each of the 71 guest rooms and suites is furnished with what the inn says are "authentic early-American pieces," including poster beds and handmade quilts. A complimentary continental breakfast is served every morning; a complimentary wine-and-cheese reception is offered each evening. Complete business services (fax, copiers, etc.), an exercise room, meeting space, and banquet facilities are available.

The Hawthorne Inn and Conference Center. Expensive/Moderate. 420 High Street, 27101 (877-777-3099 or 336-777-3000; www.hawthorneinn.com). Located just off Interstate 40 Business, The 155-room Hawthorne is convenient to downtown, Old Salem, and Wake Forest University Baptist Medical Center. In fact, the inn is owned and operated by North Carolina Baptist Hospitals, Inc., which means that those in town because of the medical center receive especially good rates. Particularly suited to business travelers, The Hawthorne combines the cozy comfort of an inn with the facilities of a business hotel. It offers a fitness center, meeting space, an amphitheater, and the Bayberry Restaurant.

Wingate Inn. Moderate. 125 South Main Street, 27101 (800-228-1000 or 336-714-2800; www.wingateinns.com). The first franchise of the Wingate chain in the Triad, this inn is considered a key part of the effort to revitalize downtown Winston-Salem. Designed to attract business travelers, the Wingate employs the latest technology in its 24-hour business center and its rooms, which have cordless keyboards for Web TV, free high-speed Internet access, and cordless phones. The lobby features a mural of Old Salem. Valet parking and a breakfast buffet are included in the room rate. The Twin City Chop House opened next to the inn in 2001.

Inns and Bed-and-Breakfasts

Henry F. Shaffner House. Deluxe/Expensive. 150 South Marshall Street, 27101 (800-952-2256 or 336-777-0052; www.shaffnerhouse.com). In the shadow of Winston-Salem's skyscrapers and just off Interstate 40 Business sits the expansive Henry F. Shaffner House. Built for one of the city's early industrialists, the home is located on what was once called Millionaire's Row, the stretch of fine houses constructed just south of Winston during the post–Civil War boom. Each of the nine guest rooms has a different decorative theme and a name taken from Winston-Salem's history. All rooms have cable television, high-speed Internet access, and phones. A hot breakfast is included. The inn serves dinner nightly.

The Augustus T. Zevely Inn. Expensive. 803 South Main Street, 27101 (800-928-9299 or 336-748-9299; www.winston-salem-inn.com). Not to be confused with the Zevely House restaurant in the West End neighborhood, the Zevely Inn, built in 1842, sits in the heart of Old Salem. Some of its 12 rooms have original fireplaces. All are decorated with period antiques and reproductions and have lovely views of Old Salem. Rates include a "continental-plus" breakfast during the week and a full gourmet breakfast on weekends, nonalcoholic drinks throughout the day, and wine and cheese at night. Pets can be accommodated if arrangements are made at the time of reservation.

Summit Street Bed-and-Breakfast Inns. Expensive/Moderate. 420 and 434 Summit Street, 27101 (336-777-1887; www.bbinn.com). Comprised of the 1887 Jacob Lott Ludlow House and the 1895 Benjamin Joseph Sheppard House, the Summit Street Bed-and-Breakfast Inns are located in the historic West End neighborhood. These two large, adjacent 100-year-old Victorian houses offer a range of amenities including two-person Jacuzzis, in-room gourmet breakfasts, an exercise room with Nautilus equipment, and a billiards room.

Places to Eat

Salem Tavern. Expensive. 736 South Main Street, 27101 (336-748-8585; www.oldsalem.org/visit/dining). The restaurant known as the Salem Tavern is actually located in the Salem Tavern Annex. The original Salem Tavern burned in 1784 but was rebuilt that same year; the brick structure located next to the annex, it hosted a visit from President George Washington in 1791 and serves as a museum today. The highlight of the restaurant's menu is the authentic Moravian chicken pie, though more contemporary food is also served. The restaurant is open for lunch daily and for dinner Monday through Saturday. Reservations are recommended.

Bleu Restaurant & Bar. Expensive/Moderate. 3425 Frontis Street, 27103 (336-760-2026; www.bleurestaurantandbar.com). The food at Bleu is fresh and dependable and the atmosphere hip. The menu includes inventive tapas, pizzas, pasta dishes, salads, sandwiches (at lunch), and a full array of grilled meat and seafood—yep, something for everyone. Lunch and dinner are served daily.

Downtown Thai. Expensive/Moderate. 219 West Fourth Street, 27101 (336-777-1472). If you want to save a buck, eat lunch here. If $24 Thai entrees don't bother you, go for dinner. From good, old, comfortable "Pad Thai" to "Pet Nam Prik Pow," everything is fresh, delicious, and lovingly prepared. Lunch and dinner are served daily.

Miss Annie's. Expensive/Moderate. 3064 Healy Drive, 27103 (336-774-0922; www.missannies.com). Don't be discouraged by the somewhat dilapidated shopping center where Miss Annie's is located. The Caribbean-inspired food served here is excellent. Chef Jean Spence Eubank is a native of Jamaica who cut her culinary teeth cooking for United Nations dignitaries before opening her own four-star restaurant in New Jersey. Luckily, she decided to move south. In addition to her Jerk chicken and seafood dishes, her specials are highly recommended. Miss Annie's serves lunch on Thursday and dinner Tuesday though Saturday.

Noble's Grill. Expensive/Moderate. 380 Knollwood Street, 27103 (336-777-8477; www.noblesrestaurants.com). Chef and restaurateur Jim Noble has built a solid reputation for his "clean and natural cooking." In other words, he prepares food in the tradition of the legendary Alice Waters. His wood-fired pizzas, delectable soups and salads, and roasted meat entrées are all first-rate. Noble's serves lunch Monday through Saturday and dinner all week.

Xia Asian Fusion. Expensive/Moderate. 134 North Spruce Street, 27101 (336-723-1400). This restaurant serves delectable appetizers, including a fresh summer roll filled with mint and shrimp, as well as an array of Japanese and Thai dishes such as "Spicy Lemon Grass Chicken and Asparagus." Guests can dine in the sleek red-and-black dining room with its peaceful wall fountain. Or if the weather is fair, they can enjoy the patio out front. Lunch and dinner are served Monday though Saturday.

Sweet Potatoes. Moderate. 529 Trade Street, 27101 (www.sweetpotatoes-arestaurant. com; 336-727-4844). Sweet Potatoes offers the best casual dining experience in the city, in the opinion of many. Located in the heart of the Downtown Arts District, it serves delicious Southern food. And yes, as the name implies, many recipes include sweet potatoes. You might start with the "Red and White Fries," follow that with "Catfish Nola," and finish with the sweet potato cheesecake. Of course, you may then need to fast for a week. Sweet Potatoes is open for lunch Monday through Saturday and for dinner Thursday through Saturday.

Athena Greek Taverna. Moderate/Inexpensive. 680 South Stratford Road, 27103 (336-794-3069). In a town where many restaurants are owned by Greeks but few actually specialize in Greek food, this small, bright eatery was a welcome addition when it opened several years ago. Try the roasted chicken with lemon potatoes. If you order the "Horiatiki"—a country Greek salad—plan on sharing because it's enough to feed a small village. Lunch and dinner are served Monday through Saturday.

Foothills Brewing Company. Moderate/Inexpensive. 838 West Fourth Street, 27101 (336-777-3348). Though folks definitely come to Foothills for the beer, the food is surprisingly good, too. The inventive offerings include "Pear and Arugula Salad" and "Fried Cashew-Encrusted Chevre and Bibb Lettuce Salad." Foothills also offers the requisite quarter-pound burger. It serves lunch and dinner daily.

Ichiban. Moderate/Inexpensive. In Thruway Shopping Center at 270 South Stratford Road, 27103 (336-725-3050). This small storefront restaurant serves the best sushi in town, and its Japanese fare is pretty good, too. The front dining room is very brightly lit, so head for the sushi bar in the back for more intimate dining. Ichiban serves lunch and dinner daily but is closed during midafternoon.

NOMA. Moderate/Inexpensive. 321 West Fourth Street, 27101 (336-703-5112). NOMA (short for nearby *No*rth *Ma*rshall Street) offers an inventive Sunday brunch menu that includes "Bloody Mary Benedict" and "Orange Dreamsicle Crepes," among other fare. Since NOMA stays open late on weeknights, it's a good bet after a show at the Stephens Center, located across the street. The owners, husband-and-wife team Chris and Kathleen Barnes, are also the talent behind 6th & Vine. Lunch and dinner are served daily; brunch is offered on Sunday.

6th & Vine Wine Bar & Café. Moderate/Inexpensive. In the Downtown Arts District at 209 West Sixth Street, 27101 (336-725-5577). This establishment sells over 40 wines by the glass and more than 300 by the bottle, as well as fine fare including tapas, salads, paninis, and flatbread pizzas. In addition, 6th & Vine offers a full bar and live music on Friday and Saturday evenings. Lunch and dinner are served Tuesday through Saturday; brunch is offered on Sunday.

Village Tavern. Moderate/Inexpensive. 221 Reynolda Village, 27106 (336-748-0221) and 2000 Griffith Road, 27103 (336-760-8686). The Village Tavern began in Reynolda Village and has spread across the state and the Southeast and into Colorado and Arizona. The patio in the original location has become famous; the atmosphere is upscale but relaxed enough for college students. The second Winston-Salem location is just off Hanes Mall Boulevard at the intersection with Stratford Road; it offers a snazzier ambiance and is more spacious. Both locations serve lunch and dinner daily and brunch on Sunday. For information, visit www.villagetavern.com.

West End Café. Moderate/Inexpensive. 926 West Fourth Street, 27101 (336-723-4774; www.westendcafe.com). West End Café is always bustling, and for good reason. It serves fresh, delicious food in a pleasant atmosphere; businessmen, families with small children, and young people are all comfortable here. The ambiance is rivaled only by the setting, in the West End neighborhood just across from beautiful Grace Court. Lunch and dinner are served Monday through Saturday.

Krankie's Coffee and *Camino Bakery*. Inexpensive. 211 East Third Street, 27101 (336-722-3016). Krankie's and Camino Bakery stretch the restaurant definition but are too unique not to mention. Both are housed in the Wherehouse, a multiuse performance and gallery space downtown. Here, you can get delicious coffee, baked goods, and even wine and beer.

Little Richard's Barbecue. Inexpensive. 4885 Country Club Road, 27104 (336-

760-3457). Like its renowned neighbors to the south, Little Richard's serves "Lexington-style" barbecue, which means that it has a tomato base. It gets high praise from Mr. Barbecue himself, Bob Garner, for being one of the few stalwarts still using a wood-fired pit. Don't miss the hush puppies. And if you don't like pork, you'll be pleased to know that the barbecued chicken is outstanding as well. Lunch and dinner are served Monday through Saturday.

Ollie's Bakery. Inexpensive. 200 South Marshall Street, 27101 (336-727-0404). Although Ollie's is primarily a European-style bakery, it is such an asset to the city that it merits mention here. With its proximity to Old Salem and its outdoor tables for enjoying scones in the morning and focaccia in the afternoon, it is a perfect spot for a light meal. It is open Tuesday through Saturday from morning to late afternoon and Sunday from morning to early afternoon.

North Carolina Gets a "Toe-Dancin' School"

by Ed Southern

"A faith in our youth and the talent of our youth. A realization of the place art has in our civilization."

This was the answer Vittorio Giannini gave whenever he was asked what characteristics a city should have to be home to the North Carolina School of the Arts (now the University of North Carolina School of the Arts). This was in the early 1960s, when the question of the School of the Arts' existence, much less its location, was far from settled. Giannini, an internationally renowned composer from Philadelphia who had long spent his summers in the North Carolina mountains, was an early advocate who would become the school's first president.

The School of the Arts was the brainchild of novelist and Asheville native John Ehle. In 1961, Ehle wrote an article for the *News & Observer* of Raleigh entitled "What's the Matter with Chapel Hill?" The article was a wide-ranging critique of the failure of the University of North Carolina at Chapel Hill, and liberal-arts colleges in general, to provide the proper environment and training for creative and performing artists.

The article caught the eye of Governor Terry Sanford. Sanford made education a cornerstone of his administration, going so far as to bring Ehle on board his staff as special assistant for new projects. Ehle and Sanford accomplished a number of initiatives, including the Governor's School and the North Carolina Film Board, but the School of the Arts was by far their most original, unorthodox, and controversial project.

Unlike liberal-arts colleges, the school gives students at both the high school and college levels an intensive and rigorous program in their chosen art. Unlike traditional conservatories, it also provides a solid general education.

The School of the Arts met with opposition from two sides. One side consisted of proponents of traditional liberal-arts colleges and their existing music, art, and drama programs. The second consisted of those who objected to spending tax dollars on a "toe-dancin' school."

Ehle argued, as he had in his 1961 article, that while liberal-arts colleges were superbly equipped to teach the study of the arts, they were inadequate for teaching the techniques of creation and performance.

The second argument was finally defeated on the floor of the North Carolina General Assembly by Representative John Kerr, who took to task for their shortsightedness those who opposed government support of the arts. Kerr closed his speech with this: "Now, some of you have ridiculed this legislation as a toe-dancin' bill. Well, if there's going to be toe-dancin', I want to be there." At that, he assumed a ballet pose, which was photographed for the state's newspapers.

Once the bill for the creation of the

School of the Arts passed, the work of selecting a site began in earnest. Biltmore House in Asheville and Reynolda House and Graylyn in Winston-Salem were considered. Several cities expressed some degree of interest, but in the end, only three were judged to have viable claims to being the best location: Raleigh, Charlotte, and Winston-Salem.

Winston-Salem had a tradition of supporting the arts that went back to its founding. The Moravians who built Salem made music an integral part of their worship and culture. The industrialists who built Winston had long supported education. Winston-Salem was the first city in the country to have an arts council. It had at its disposal the facilities of Salem College, Wake Forest College, and Winston-Salem State University.

Tradition, however, was not going to bring the School of the Arts to Winston-Salem. Two city leaders, Smith Bagley and Philip Hanes, spearheaded a drive to prove the Twin City's eagerness and worthiness to host the school. More than 200 volunteers worked the phones in a "Dial for Dollars" campaign that raised nearly $600,000 in two days. A plan was drawn up to convert Gray High School into a campus for the School of the Arts.

But according to Leslie Banner's *A Passionate Preference: The Story of the North Carolina School of the Arts*, the deciding factor was not just that Winston-Salem had better-laid plans and a more successful fund drive. Winston-Salem simply wanted the school more than the other cities did.

John Ehle had a strange thought: to start a school, far from the world's cultural centers, that would teach students to be professional artists of the highest caliber. Unimaginable to most, scoffed at, and threatened with extinction, the University of North Carolina School of the Arts is now known around the world for the quality of its training, faculty, students, and alumni.

Greensboro skyline
PHOTOGRAPH BY CAROLYN SAKOWSKI

Greensboro

By Carolyn Sakowski

Greensboro and Guilford County have a long tradition of valuing education. Prior to the formation of the county, a staunchly religious group of settlers arrived around 1750. These settlers were members of the Religious Society of Friends, a group commonly known as Quakers. The Quakers named their first settlement New Garden. These settlers would have a lasting influence on educational standards and moral decisions in the area.

In 1767, David Caldwell started a local school known as the Log College. Serving as a Presbyterian minister in what was then the wilderness, Caldwell established the school to educate young men for the ministry. Five of his students went on to become governors of their states; one of them, John Motley Morehead, was governor of North Carolina from 1841 to 1845.

In 1771, North Carolina's colonial assembly created Guilford County in order to gain more administrative control over the growing Piedmont population. Named after the earl of Guilford, a friend of King George III, the county had a sparse population of about 10,000. By 1774, a log courthouse and jail were built at a place known as Guilford Courthouse.

On March 15, 1780, Guilford Courthouse played an important role in the Revolutionary War. The battle that raged in the woods and over the fields proved the beginning of the end for Lord Cornwallis's campaign to squelch patriot forces in the South. When the county courthouse was ready in 1809, the new town needed a name. The commissioners chose to honor Nathanael Greene, the leader of the American forces at the Battle of Guilford Courthouse. Somehow, the final *e* on the name got lost, so the town was named Greensborough.

In 1837, the Society of Friends opened New Garden Boarding School to train teachers. In 1887, this school became Guilford College, the first coeducational institution in the South. In 1863, the Methodist Church founded a school for girls named Greensboro Female College, which came to be called Greensboro College. In 1905, its new leader, Lucy H. Robertson, became the first woman to serve as a college president in North Carolina. In 1873, the Freedmen's Aid Society established Bennett Seminary, a normal school. In 1889, the Methodist Church began to support the school, which eventually became Bennett College.

In the 1820s, young John Motley Morehead, who augmented his law practice with a dry-goods and grocery business, began to push for a railroad to come to Greensboro. He became the first president of the North Carolina Railroad. By July 1851, construction began on the railroad, which was to have its western terminus in Charlotte and its eastern terminus in Goldsboro. Thanks to Morehead, the railroad would pass through Greensboro. The line was completed in 1856.

When war clouds threatened, Morehead and other powerful men in Greensboro did not readily embrace secession. These conservative businessmen realized what war would do to economic progress. In 1861, the citizens of Guilford, including the antislavery Quakers, defeated a proposal to call a convention to consider secession; the margin was 2,771 to 113.

But Guilford benefited from the war when the Confederate government built the Piedmont Railroad to connect Greensboro with Danville, Virginia. The railroad proved the missing link in the supply line from Columbia, South Carolina, to the Army of Northern Virginia.

After the war, industrialization reached Greensboro in a big way when Moses and Ceasar Cone began construction on their Proximity Mill. It was in 1891 that the Cone brothers decided to enter the textile business. Previously, they had been whole-sale grocery and tobacco distributors. Oftentimes, they were paid in bolts of cloth from small local mills; they then turned around and sold that cloth. They thought they could produce a better-quality product and create a strong marketing organization. By the mid-1890s, the Cones' company was offering services to 90 percent of the South's textile-mill owners and getting about five cents on each dollar of the gross receipts. This company would evolve into Cone Mills.

In 1896, the first denim rolled off the looms of the Proximity Mill. Four years later, the Cones joined the Sternberger brothers in building the first flannel mill in the South. The Revolution Cotton Mill's production allowed the owners to boast that they were the world's leader in flannel production. In 1905, the White Oak plant began to produce denim. Cone Mills combined with other textile companies to make Greensboro one of the nation's leading textile-manufacturing centers.

In the 1890s, the city's leaders again showed their enthusiasm for education when the state announced plans to establish two new colleges—one for women and one for African-Americans. In 1891, the state selected Greensboro as the location for the Agricultural and Mechanical College for the Negro Race; to win the bid, the city came up with $8,000 in cash and a suitable site. This college would go on to become North Carolina A & T State University. Also in 1891, Greensboro was selected as the site for the Normal and Industrial School for Women, which would become the University of North Carolina at Greensboro. To finance this bid, the city raised $30,000 through a bond issue and donated a suitable location.

Thanks to the vision of its forefathers, Greensboro is a thriving business and educational center for the vibrant North Carolina Piedmont today. Its revitalization efforts in the Old Greensborough & Downtown Historic District and its well-planned Cultural District are tributes to the continued vision of its leaders.

JUST THE FACTS

Greensboro is located at the intersection of Interstate 40 and Interstate 85, which skirt the southeastern section of town.

Piedmont Triad International Airport, which is served by carriers including US Airways, Delta, Continental, American, Allegiant, and United, is centrally located among Greensboro, High Point, and Winston-Salem. Many hotels offer free transportation to and from the airport.

The Amtrak station is located at 236 East Washington Street (27401). Call 336-272-6755 for information.

The Greyhound/Trailways bus terminal is located in the restored train depot near Old Greensborough at 234-A Washington Street (27401). Call 336-272-8950 for information.

The best source for local information is the Greensboro Area Convention and Visitors Bureau, at 2200 Pinecroft Road, Suite 200 (27407). Call 800-344-2282 or 336-274-2282 or visit www.visitgreensboro.com.

The city's daily newspaper is the *Greensboro News and Record*, which also publishes *GoTriad*, a free weekly tabloid that tells about activities in the area; visit www.gotriad.com.

Things to Do

Historic Places, Gardens, and Tours

Guilford Courthouse National Military Park is six miles north of downtown off U.S. 220 (Battleground Avenue) at 2332 New Garden Road (27410).

After a three-year standoff in the North, Lord Cornwallis, the British commander, decided to conquer the South. By 1780, the British controlled Georgia and South Carolina. After Cornwallis suffered a setback in October 1780 at Kings Mountain, he moved to Charlotte just as Nathanael Greene took command of the Americans' Southern forces.

Greene divided his troops into two segments. To counter, Cornwallis divided his men into three columns. In January 1781, the British were defeated at Cowpens, but Cornwallis pursued Greene's forces into North Carolina. By March, Greene had received reinforcements that brought his strength to 4,400 men. He chose Guilford Courthouse as the site for a battle. Greene wanted a location that would be easy for the militia to find, where the British would have to move through woods and make their final assault up a hill across a clearing, and where the Americans would not be trapped by water as they departed.

Cornwallis led his force of 1,900 men into the trap on March 15, 1781. The first exchange came just after one o'clock in the afternoon. The militiamen waiting in the woods were under orders to fire three rounds before retreating. A second line of militia deeper in the woods was reinforced with cannons and cavalry. A third line was on a rise above the clearing. After two hours of fighting, the British drove the Americans from the field and claimed the day. But it was a Pyrrhic victory. Cornwallis lost one-fourth of his men. And nearly 30 percent of his officer corps was down. He later said, "I never saw such fighting since God made me. The fighting was furious."

Too weak to pursue the rebels, Cornwallis began his seven-month journey that would end with the British surrender at Yorktown.

In 1886, David Schenck, a Greensboro-based attorney for the Richmond and

Nathanael Greene statue at Guilford Courthouse National Military Park
PHOTOGRAPH BY CAROLYN SAKOWSKI

Danville Railroad, wrote that he was going to "save the battlefield." He helped form the Guilford Battleground Company, which purchased more than 125 acres where the battle was fought. In 1911, Congress appropriated $30,000 to erect an equestrian monument to General Greene; the statue was dedicated on July 3, 1915. Two years later, on March 2, 1917, the Guilford Battleground Company ceded the battleground to the United States government. Today, the park preserves 220 acres of historic fields and forests and 28 monuments.

Among the interesting statues is one of Kerenhappuch Turner, a woman who rode on horseback from Maryland to care for her son, who was wounded in the battle. Another interesting participant is memorialized at the battlefield. Peter Francisco stood six-foot-six when he joined the Continental Army at age 16. He was a foot taller and 100 pounds heavier than the average American soldier. The story goes that Francisco earned fame at Guilford Courthouse when he slew 11 soldiers with his sword in one brief encounter. A tablet that pays tribute to Francisco stands next to the Cavalry Monument. Guests can also see one of Francisco's immense shoes on display in the visitor center. The battlefield is home to the graves of William Hopper and John Penn, signers of the Declaration of Independence, and Joseph Winston, the Revolutionary War hero for whom the town of Winston (now part of Winston-Salem) was named.

Guests can tour the park on foot, by bicycle, or by automobile. The visitor center includes exhibits, military memorabilia, films, and a bookstore. The battlefield is open from 8:30 A.M. to 5 P.M. daily except for Thanksgiving, Christmas, and New Year's. Admission is free. For more information, call 336-288-1776 or visit www.nps.gov/guco.

Adjacent to the Guilford Courthouse battlefield at 2200 New Garden Road (27410) is *Tannenbaum Historic Park*. This eight-acre park is the site of the restored 1778 *Hoskins House*. During the Battle of Guilford Courthouse, the house served as a staging area for British troops under Cornwallis. The *North Carolina Colonial Heritage Center* is also located at the park; there, guests can enjoy a diorama of the battle, a gallery of original maps, a museum store, and hand-on exhibits depicting colonial life. They can also stand in a pillory and feel the weight of a musket. The park is open Friday through Sunday from 8:30 A.M. to 5 P.M. year-round. Regular tours of the Hoskins House are available. Admission is free. For more information, call 336-545-5315 or visit http://www.colonialmuseum.com.

Museums and Science Centers

The city planners have done an excellent job of putting many of Greensboro's museums and other cultural offerings together in a compact few blocks identified by street signs as the "Cultural District." Here, you'll find the Greensboro Historical Museum, the Greensboro Children's Museum, the central branch of the Greensboro Public Library, the Greensboro Cultural Center at Festival Park (discussed in the "Cultural Offerings" section below), and the downtown branch of the YWCA.

The *Greensboro Historical Museum*, at 130 Summit Avenue (27401), has exhibits that focus on early settlement, military history (there's an interesting display of weapons used during the Civil War), Native Americans, and transportation. Located in a building that dates to the turn of the 20th century, the museum is listed on the National Register of Historic Places. Some of the more popular displays show items—a snuffbox, a collection of fine china, French gowns—once owned by Greensboro native Dolley Madison, the wife of President James Madison. Another display features items owned by Greensboro native William Sydney Porter, better known as O. Henry. These items include photographs, letters, and early editions of his books, as well as sketches he made when he worked at his uncle's drugstore. A reproduction of that drugstore is also featured. One exhibit highlighting a more recent historical event includes stools and the countertop from the local Woolworth's where four college students staged a sit-in demonstration that sparked the nation. Behind the museum, visitors can walk through a small cemetery where several Revo-

Greensboro Historical Museum
PHOTOGRAPH BY CAROLYN SAKOWSKI

lutionary War soldiers rest. They can also see examples of early Guilford County homes and a bust commemorating another local native, Edward R. Murrow. The museum is open from 10 A.M. to 5 P.M. Tuesday through Saturday and from 2 P.M. to 5 P.M. on Sunday. Admission is free. For more information, call 336-373-2043 or visit www.greensborohistory.org.

Across from the new Greensboro Public Library at 220 North Church Street (27401) is the *Greensboro Children's Museum*. This active place offers hands-on exhibits and activities for children ages one to 10. The "Our Town" section has a grocery store complete with checkout registers, a bank, a theater, a media studio, a house under construction, and a post office. A craft room and exhibits about the continents, the furniture industry, and the textile industry are also on the premises. But the section that excites children the most is the transportation area. Here, they can climb into the cockpit of an airliner and sit in a NASCAR automobile, a police car, and a fire truck. They can also place objects on a Bernoulli blower, which demonstrates how an airplane flies; although the blower teaches the four forces of aerodynamics and Newton's Third Law, most children have a ball just watching the air pressure shoot objects toward the ceiling. The museum is open from 9 A.M. to 5 P.M. Tuesday through Saturday, with extended hours to 8 P.M. on Friday; it is also open from 9 A.M. to noon on Monday for members only and from 1 P.M. to 5 P.M. on Sunday. Hours vary during the summers and holidays, so it's a good idea to check the website for exact times. An admission fee is charged; discounted rates are available for groups of 10 or more. Teachers are admitted free with a valid identification. For more information, call 336-574-2898 or visit www.gcmuseum.com.

The *Natural Science Center* is located at 4301 Lawndale Drive (27544), northeast of the downtown area. This is a hands-on museum, zoo, and planetarium. Visitors can come face to face with a 36-foot model of a *Tyrannosaurus rex*, see endangered lemurs, look directly at sunspots over 200,000 miles across, pet a variety of small wildlife including merecats, tigers, and an anteater in the 30-acre zoo, and tour the herpetarium and the gem-and-mineral gallery. The center is open from 9 A.M. to 5 P.M. Monday through Saturday and from 12:30 P.M. to 5 P.M. on Sunday. The zoo has shorter hours; call for planetarium show times. An admission fee is charged. For more information, call 336-288-3769 or visit www.natsci.org.

Cultural Offerings

The *Greensboro Cultural Center at Festival Park*, at 200 North Davie Street

Guilford County's Quaker Heritage

Much of Guilford County's heritage is tied to the Religious Society of Friends, more commonly known as the Quakers.

In 1740, Quaker pioneers from Pennsylvania, Virginia, and Nantucket Island began to settle in northwestern Guilford County. By 1754, they established the New Garden Meeting, which quickly became a center for Quakerism in North Carolina. The Battle of Guilford Courthouse, which raged around Quaker homes and farms in New Garden in 1781, saw the meeting house turned into a hospital for soldiers from both sides. Many of the dead were laid to rest in the Friends' burial ground. Even the leader of the American forces at the battle, Nathanael Greene, was a Quaker. One historical figure from Guilford County with a Quaker connection was Dolley Madison, born in 1768 to parents who were members of the New Garden Meeting.

In 1818, some young people from the New Garden Meeting organized a "Sabbath School House." By 1821, Levi Coffin, Jr., was teaching slaves to read the Bible there. Levi and his wife, Catherine, became leaders in giving assistance to fugitive slaves. In 1826, they moved to a settlement in Indiana, where their efforts to hide runaway slaves earned Levi the title of "president of the Underground Railroad."

Since fugitive-slave laws provided severe penalties for anyone who interfered with the recovery of slaves, the efforts of such men and women had to be secretive. The Underground Railroad helped slaves escape to the Northern states and Canada by setting up "sta-

False-bottomed wagon believed to have been used on the Underground Railroad
COURTESY OF HIGH POINT CONVENTION AND VISITORS BUREAU

tions" every 10 to 20 miles along the way. The wagons and carriages used to transport the slaves were called "trains." The runaway slaves usually traveled at night in groups of two or three. The drivers who assisted them were called "conductors." One Quaker couple who proved a vital link in the North Carolina segment of the Underground Railroad was Joshua and Abigail Stanley, who lived in the Centre community. Levi Coffin and Abigail Stanley had grown up together in New Garden.

Today, a wagon with a false bottom used to transport fugitive slaves on the Underground Railroad is on display at the Mendenhall Plantation in Jamestown. A nearly identical wagon is housed at the Levi Coffin House and Museum in Fountain City, Indiana. At both the Mendenhall Plantation and the nearby Museum of Old Domestic Life, visitors can see artifacts left by the Quakers.

The New Garden Friends Meeting still holds worship services at 801 New Garden Road (27410) near Guilford College, which also has its roots in the Society of Friends.

(27401) in the Cultural District, comes close to providing one-stop shopping for the city's visual and performing arts. All told, the center includes four levels of galleries, studios, classrooms, and rehearsal halls. It has a sculpture garden, a privately operated restaurant with outdoor café-style seating, and the Price Bryan Performance Place, an outdoor amphitheater. The complex houses offices for many of the city's cultural organizations, as well as exhibit space for the *Green Hill Center of North Carolina Art*, the *Guilford Native American Art Gallery*, the *African American Atelier*, *Art Alliance*, the *Center for Visual Artists*, and the *United Arts Council*. For information, call 336-373-2712 or visit www.greensboro-nc.gov/Departments/Executive/events/hosting/culturalcenter.

The *Eastern Music Festival* is an internationally acclaimed classical music event founded in 1962. From late June to early August, 200 exceptionally talented students between the ages of 14 and 20 combine with a faculty of outstanding musicians from leading symphony orchestras and music schools for an intensive training program on the campus of Guilford College. They stage more than 50 orchestral concerts and chamber-music performances during the festival. These concerts, especially the ones featuring the faculty orchestra, offer some of the best classical performances available for the money. Top guest artists are brought in to perform with the professional ensembles. In recent years, the festival has added the *EMF Fringe Series*, which features diverse musical acts ranging from Americana to Latin, roots to rock, country to bluegrass, and gospel to rhythm-and-blues. For more information, call 336-333-7450 or visit www.easternmusicfestival.org.

Although Guilford College, Greensboro College, and North Carolina A & T State University all have galleries that host touring exhibits, the *Weatherspoon Art Gallery* at the University of North Carolina at Greensboro is special, primarily because of Etta Cone's donation in 1949. Miss Cone was a part of the intellectual scene in Paris that included Gertrude Stein. Her bequest of a remarkable collection of lithographs and bronzes by Henri Matisse helped form the core of this collection. Today, the Weatherspoon boasts one of the best university collections of 20th-century American art. Located at the corner of Spring Garden and Tate streets on the university campus, it is housed in a building that won architectural awards for its design. The structure contains six galleries and a sculpture courtyard. The gallery is open from 10 A.M. to 5 P.M. on Tuesday, Wednesday, and Friday; from 10 A.M. to 9 P.M. on Thursday; and from 1 P.M. to 5 P.M. on Saturday and Sunday. For more information, call 336-334-5770 or visit http://weatherspoon.uncg.edu/.

One of Greensboro's enduring landmarks is the *Carolina Theatre*. Since its opening in 1927 as a vaudeville theater, it has survived as one of the city's principal performing-arts centers, offering theater, dance, concerts, and films. The impressive structure, listed on the National Register, is downtown at 310 South Greene Street (27401). For more information, call 336-333-2605 or visit www.carolinatheatre. com.

If you're looking for live theater, check what's scheduled at *Triad Stage*. Founded by two men who met as graduate students at the Yale School of Drama, Triad Stage has been called "one of the best regional theaters in America" by New York's Drama League. Its 300-seat performance space offers an intimate setting for original productions as well as classical plays. The theater is located downtown at 232 South Elm Street (27401). For more information, call 336-272-0160 or visit www. triadstage.org.

Special Shopping

In recent years, the *Old Greensborough & Downtown Historic District* has become a revitalized turn-of-the-20th-century commercial area. The district is located in and around South Elm Street from the 100 block to the 600 block. It also includes blocks of South Davie, South Greene, and East and West Washington streets. The area is alive with antique shops, antiquarian book dealers, chic restaurants, bars, and art galleries.

State Street Station, located north of downtown between Church and Elm streets a block south of Cornwallis Drive, is a group of unique boutiques and restaurants that cater to a decidedly upscale clientele. The buildings were once part of a small mill community, so the shops have the feel of a village within a city. For information, call 336-282-1450.

The major shopping centers are *Four Seasons Town Centre*, located at the High Point Road exit off Interstate 40, and *Friendly Center* and the newly opened neighboring *Shops at Friendly Center*, located on Friendly Avenue off Wendover Avenue. For information, visit www.shopfourseasons.com and www.friendlycenter.com.

For something entirely different, check out *Replacements, Ltd.*, the world's larg-

Elm Street in Old Greensborough
COURTESY OF HIGH POINT CONVENTION AND VISITORS BUREAU

est retailer of old and new china, crystal, flatware, and collectibles. Founded in 1981, the warehouse has over 3 million pieces, all of which are entered in its state-of-the-art computer system. The 225,000-square-foot gift facility includes new stock and over 2,000 unique pieces of china, crystal, and silver. It is located just east of Greensboro at 1089 Knox Road in McLeansville (27301); from Interstate 85/40, take the Mount Hope Church Road exit (Exit 132). It is open from 9 A.M. to 7 P.M. daily. Complimentary tours are offered every 30 minutes. For information, call 800-737-5223 or 336-697-3000 or visit www.replacements.com.

Recreation

Greensboro has a wide variety of public parks. Couple these with the more than 200 acres available for walking, running, or biking at Guilford Courthouse National Military Park and you have a lot of green space. A complete list is available by contacting the Greensboro Area Convention and Visitors Bureau or by visiting http://www.greensboro-nc.gov/Departments/Parks/default.htm.

If you like golf, you'll feel you've died and gone to heaven. The Greensboro area offers over 20 public golf courses. For a complete list, contact the Greensboro Area Convention and Visitors Bureau by calling 800-334-2282 or 336-274-2282 or visiting www.visitgreensboro.com.

Entrance to First Horizon Park, home of the Greensboro Grasshoppers
PHOTOGRAPH BY CAROLYN SAKOWSKI

The **Bryan Park Complex** and **Lake Townsend** offer two 18-hole championship courses. The Players Course, designed by George Cobb and modified by Rees Jones, opened in 1974. The Champions Course, which opened in 1990, was designed by Rees Jones; seven of its holes border scenic Lake Townsend. The park also offers a conference center, horseshoe pits, picnic shelters, tennis and volleyball courts, and an 11-field soccer complex. Sailing, boating, and fishing are popular on Lake Townsend. Located off U.S. 29 North at 6275 Bryan Park Road in Browns Summit (27214), the park is open daily from 8 A.M. to sunset; the golf courses have seasonal hours. For more information, call 336-375-2200 or visit www.bryanpark.com.

If you like minor-league baseball, you'll enjoy the **Greensboro Grasshoppers**, a class A farm club for the Florida Marlins. Affiliated with the South Atlantic League, the Grasshoppers play in the state-of-the-art First Horizon Park, located near Old Greensborough on the corner of Bellmeade and Edgeworth streets. For information, call 336-268-BALL or visit www.gsohoppers.com.

Seasonal Events

A **reenactment of the Battle of Guilford Courthouse** is held every year at Country Park, located at 3905 Nathanael Greene Drive (27455). The event takes place on the weekend closest to the March 15 anniversary of the conflict. Hundreds of reenactors portray British and American soldiers fighting in the American Revolution. The battle is staged at 2 P.M. Admission is free. Call 336-373-3648 for information.

The ***Wyndham Championship***, part of the FedEx Cup, is the third-oldest event on the PGA tour. The tournament is currently played at Sedgefield Country Club. For dates and ticket prices, contact the tournament office at 401 North Greene Street (27401), call 336-379-1570, or visit www.wyndhamchampionship.com.

Resorts, Hotels, and Motels

Every major chain is represented somewhere in the Greensboro area. Most hotels are grouped at the various exits off Interstates 85 and 40. The greatest concentration is at the N.C. 68 exit off Interstate 40 west of town; this is the exit for Piedmont Triad International Airport, so the crowd of hotels makes sense. Many of the accommodations listed below are deluxe or expensive. If you are looking for a more moderate price, the budget chains are your best bet.

Grandover Resort and Conference Center. Deluxe. 1000 Club Road, 27407 (800-472-6301 or 336-294-1800; www.grandover.com). Located just southwest of town, this resort is nestled among 1,500 acres of land. One big draw is its two 18-hole golf courses just outside the lobby. The lobby evokes an Old World feel, with contrasting floor patterns of Italian travertine, Tasmanian gold limestone, and black granite. Several types of guest rooms are available. Basic rooms include cable television, two dual-line telephones with voice mail, a data jack, a refrigerator, a wet bar, and a complimentary newspaper. The resort offers a spa, tennis and racquetball courts, a whirlpool, a pool, a fitness center with sauna and steam room, and restaurants.

O. Henry Hotel. Deluxe. 624 Green Valley Road, 27408 (800-965-8259 or 336-854-2000; www.ohenryhotel.com). Located off Wendover Avenue at Benjamin Parkway near Friendly Center, this 131-room grand hotel has an intimate feel. The O. Henry earned a Four Diamond rating from AAA in its first year, and you'll see why the minute you enter the wood-paneled lobby. The regular room amenities include color television, high-speed Internet access, a dressing room with two vanities, a safe, in-room movies and video games, a microwave, a refrigerator, a makeup mirror, a complimentary newspaper, and voice mail. In the suites, you get all these amenities plus a gas-burning fireplace in the separate sitting area, a stereo, a DVD, and a huge dressing room. The hotel offers a fine restaurant, afternoon tea and cocktails in the lobby, a business center, an exercise facility, and an outdoor pool. A complimentary home-cooked breakfast buffet is served daily. And of course, each room has a collection of O. Henry short stories to remind guests of a local boy who made good.

Proximity Hotel. Deluxe. 706 Green Valley Road, 27408 (800-379-8200 or 336-379-8200). This hotel, designed to look like a remodeled textile factory, was the first in America to be awarded LEED Platinum certification by the U.S. Green Building Council. The 147-room, AAA Four Diamond hotel offers stylish loft-like guest rooms with such amenities as flat-panel TVs, microwaves, CD players with MP3 connections, high-speed Internet, and WiFi. The hotel has a fitness studio, a spa, and an outdoor pool.

Greensboro Marriott Downtown. Expensive. 304 North Greene Street, 27401 (336-379-8000; www.marriott.com). This is the only full-service hotel in the downtown area. It has 281 guest rooms, including seven suites. You'll find the usual Marriott amenities. The hotel offers meeting space for conferences.

Sheraton Greensboro Hotel at Four Seasons. Expensive. 3121 High Point Road,

Entrance to the Proximity Hotel
PHOTOGRAPH BY CAROLYN SAKOWSKI

27407 (800-242-6556 or 336-292-9161; www.kourycenter.com). The Joseph S. Koury Convention Center, which connects with this hotel, calls itself the largest hotel and convention center in the Carolinas. Located at the High Point Road exit off Interstate 40, the hotel has over 1,000 guest rooms and access to 250,000 square feet of meeting and banquet space. As a result, it attracts numerous conventions. Amenities include cable television, high-speed Internet access, hair dryers, and voice mail. It offers a full-scale business center, a health club, a pool, a whirlpool, a sauna, and a racquetball court. Because the same developers own the Grandover Resort, the Sheraton staff can make reservations for you at the Grandover spa or tennis and golf courses. Greensboro's major shopping mall, Four Seasons Town Centre, is next door.

Inns and Bed-and-Breakfasts

Andrea's Troy-Bumpas Inn. Expensive. 114 South Mendenhall Street, 27403 (800-370-9070 or 336-370-1660; www.troy-bumpasinn.com). Built in 1847, this home is listed on the National Register. Close to the campuses of the University of North Carolina at Greensboro and Greensboro College, it offers four rooms with telephones, private baths, hair dryers, cable TV with DVD players, and robes. All are furnished with antiques or antique reproductions.

The Biltmore Greensboro Hotel. Expensive. 111 West Washington Street, 27401 (800-332-0303 or 336-272-3474; www.thebiltmoregreensboro.com). This hotel, which bills itself as "a unique European boutique hostelry," is located in the Old Greensborough & Downtown Historic District. Guests enter the elegant walnut-paneled lobby through crystal front doors. In the morning, a deluxe continental breakfast is served; in the evening, a reception featuring an informal wine tasting and hors d'oeuvres is offered. The rooms have king-sized four-poster canopy beds and 16-foot ceilings. Amenities include cable televisions, telephones with data ports, refrigerators, hair dryers, DVD players, coffee makers, and irons and ironing boards. Free parking is provided.

Greenwood Bed-and-Breakfast. Expensive. 205 North Park Drive, 27401 (866-374-5456 or 336-274-6350; www.greenwoodbb.com). The Greenwood is a turn-of-the-20th-century Craftsman-style home located just off Elm Street in the historic Fisher Park neighborhood. Each of the five guest rooms has a private bath and wireless Internet.

Places to Eat

Because of space constraints, some excellent restaurants are not mentioned here. Despite an effort to balance the offerings in each price category, most of the exceptional restaurants in Greensboro fall within the expensive and moderate ranges. Also included below are restaurants that continually appear on everyone's list of favorites.

Bistro Sofia. Expensive. 616 Dolley Madison Road, 27410 (336-855-1313; www. bistrosofia.com). The cuisine here is European and New American, influenced by Eastern Europe—hence the name Sofia, in honor of the Bulgarian capital. The chef, who graduated from nearby Guilford College, trained at the New England Culinary Institute. The restaurant offers prix fixe menus on certain weekdays and before certain times, so check the website. Dinner is served Tuesday through Sunday.

Marisol. Expensive. 5834-E High Point Road, 27407 (336-852-3303; www.the-marisol.com). Although this is one of the most expensive restaurants in the Triad, it also makes all the lists of the top places to dine. It's the sort of place where people celebrate special occasions. The main dining room has a café ambiance; Marisol also has a separate piano bar with leather seating. The printed menu lists first courses only; the servers recite the entrée descriptions orally. Each entrée is part of a complete conception including vegetable portions. Lunch is served Tuesday through Friday and dinner Tuesday through Saturday.

Undercurrent Restaurant. Expensive/Moderate. 327 Battleground Avenue, 27401 (336-370-1266; www.undercurrentrestaurant.com). Located near the stadium where the Grasshoppers play baseball, this restaurant features New American and classical cuisine with Asian influences. The *New York Times* called this a "smart restaurant." Lunch is served Monday through Friday and dinner Tuesday through Saturday.

Green Valley Grill. Moderate. 624 Green Valley Road, 27408 (336-854-2015; www.greenvalleygrill.com). This grill is the restaurant wing of the O. Henry Hotel. Green Valley's owners have established a reputation for developing relationships with local farms and dairies and for presenting innovative food programs to the public. The restaurant uses a wood-fired oven for pizzas and a wood-fired grill to roast chicken and beef on a spit. Lunch and dinner are served daily.

Liberty Oak. Moderate. 100-D Washington Street, 27401 (336-273-7057; www. libertyoakrestaurant.com). Liberty Oak has been around for over two decades, which says a lot in this business. Its relocation to downtown helped jump-start the area's revival. Reasonable prices combine with quality ingredients to make the dishes here probably the best value in the area. The blue-plate entrées are especially enticing. Liberty Oak was one of 11 restaurants chosen for *Southern Living*'s "Top Food Finds" in the "Uptown Food" category. Lunch and dinner are served Monday through Saturday.

Solaris Tapas Restaurant and Bar. Moderate. 125 Summit Avenue, 27401 (336-378-0198; www.gettapas.com). A tapas menu offers a wide variety of smaller-than-usual servings, priced accordingly. This style of dining allows guests to select several dishes that can be shared for the same price as a normal entrée. The wine list at Solaris features Spanish vintages; a martini list is offered as well. Lunch is served Tuesday through Friday and dinner Tuesday through Saturday.

Southern Lights. Moderate. 105 North Smyres Place, 27403 (336-379-9414). In business since 1986, this restaurant offers an informal ambiance and reasonably priced dishes prepared with fresh ingredients. On weeknights, the featured entrées are quite a bargain. Guests can order sandwiches and burgers as well as creative chicken, beef, and seafood dishes. Lunch is served Monday through Friday and dinner Monday through Saturday.

Stamey's Barbecue. Inexpensive. Across from the Greensboro Coliseum at 2206 High Point Road, 27401 (336-299-9888), and at 2812 Battleground Avenue, 27408 (336-288-9275). You can't come to North Carolina and not try the barbecue. Stamey's serves what is called Lexington-style barbecue, which has a vinegar-and-tomato sauce. Its dining rooms are large and busy, but you can also use the drive-through lanes. Both places serve barbecue cooked the old-fashioned way in a smokehouse behind the High Point Road location. Lunch and dinner are served Monday through Saturday. For information, visit www.stameys.com.

The Greensboro Four

On February 1, 1960, four students from North Carolina A & T State University—David Richmond, Franklin McCain, Jibreel Khazan (Ezell Blair, Jr., before his conversion to Islam), and Joseph McNeil—paid a visit to the F. W. Woolworth store in downtown Greensboro that would change the world. Though they knew that Jim Crow laws prohibited an integrated lunch counter, the four men took seats and politely requested coffee around 4:30 P.M. After being told that "coloreds" were not served at the counter, the four remained seated in silence until the store closed at 5:30.

They returned the next day around 10:30 A.M. with a group of 20 students. The students made small purchases elsewhere in the store, then sat at the lunch counter in groups of three or four as spaces became available. They sat there until noon without being waited on, while white customers were served.

Sit-in demonstrations had been tried previously in other cities. No one knows exactly why the spontaneous actions of four students in Greensboro sparked a movement. They were soon joined by more students from A & T, as well as students from Bennett College and from what is now the University of North Carolina at Greensboro. Within two weeks, sit-ins were staged in 11 other cities. Eventually, 54 cities in nine states saw similar demonstrations.

It took the Greensboro students six months before Woolworth's relented on its policy of respecting "local custom." The actions of these young students played a vital role in the early days of the civil-rights movement, which changed our nation's policies and laws regarding racial segregation.

When the F. W. Woolworth Company announced the closing of the Elm Street location in 1993, a group of citizens organized to preserve the architecturally significant Art Deco building and its historically significant lunch counter. The seemingly never-ending project has been marked by controversy, but progress is being made to convert the building into the International Civil Rights Center and Museum.

In 1998, the Greensboro Public Library and the online division of the *Greensboro News and Record* joined forces to launch an impressive website about the sit-ins. By visiting www.sitins.com, you can hear nearly 100 audio clips in which the participants themselves describe what happened. You can also read the original news articles and see historic photographs.

A portion of the lunch counter and four of the original stools are currently on display at the Greensboro Historical Museum. The faded Formica lunch counter and four 1950s stools are featured in the Smithsonian in Washington, D.C.

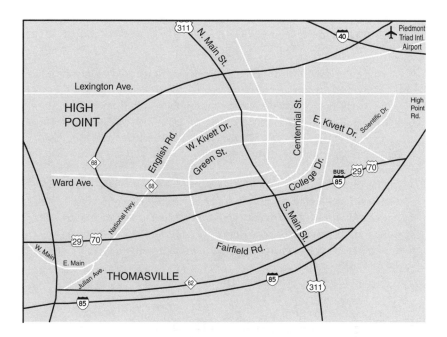

High Point

By Carolyn Sakowski

When John Motley Morehead brought the North Carolina Railroad to Guilford County, a survey revealed that the tracks would intersect with the existing plank road that connected Fayetteville to Salem. That intersection, located 912 feet above sea level, would be the highest point on the rail line. It was obvious that this new transportation hub would draw speculators. By 1859, the village at that site had 525 people, two hotels, two churches, and seven stores. In May of that year, the two-mile-square town was chartered under the name High Point.

High Point has been linked to the furniture industry since the 1880s. Today, its residents are proud to call their city "the Home Furnishings Capital of the World."

If you're looking for a fun photo opportunity, check out "the World's Second-Largest Chest of Drawers," located two blocks east of Main Street at the corner of Westwood and North Hamilton. Built in 1926 and restored in 1996, it is actually the facade of a building shaped like an 18th-century chest of drawers. The socks hanging out of one of the drawers represent the city's hosiery industry. The honor of having the largest chest of drawers is claimed by Furnitureland South, which built an 85-foot-tall replica as a facade for its showroom.

JUST THE FACTS

High Point is southwest of Greensboro. It may be reached via Interstate 85 Business or U.S. 311.

Piedmont Triad International Airport is centrally located among High Point, Greensboro, and Winston-Salem. Its carriers include US Airways, Delta, Continental, United, American, Allegiant, and Northwest. Some local hotels offer free transportation from the airport. Call 336-454-3213 or 336-665-5600 for airport information.

The Amtrak station is located at 100 West High Street (27260), off Main Street near the center of downtown. A pedestrian walkway connects the renovated historic depot to the city's bus transfer center. For information, call 336-841-7245 or visit www.amtrak.com.

The Trailways bus station is located at 100 Lindsay Street (27262). Call 336-882-2000.

A good source for information is the High Point Convention and Visitors Bureau, at 300 South Main Street (27260). Call 800-720-5255 or 336-884-5255 or visit www.highpoint.org.

The city's daily newspaper is the *High Point Enterprise*. You can also check out *GoTriad*, a free weekly tabloid. Its website is www.gotriad.com.

Things to Do

Historic Places, Gardens, and Tours

Tours of furniture manufacturers' market showrooms are available to groups of 15 or more. Reservations must be made in advance by calling the High Point Convention and Visitors Bureau at 800-720-5255 or by visiting www.highpoint.org. No tours are available when the furniture markets are held.

Mendenhall Plantation is located at 603 West Main Street/U.S. 70 Alternate in neighboring Jamestown (27282). James Mendenhall, a Pennsylvania Quaker, received a land grant in 1762. The settlement that grew up around his farm was called Jamestown in his honor. In 1811, his grandson Richard built the original part of what is now known as Mendenhall Plantation.

This wonderful example of early-19th-century Quaker architecture has been enlarged several times but retains its simple character. The grounds feature a "bank barn" built into a hillside, in the tradition of the Pennsylvania settlers. One of the nation's few surviving false-bottomed wagons, used to help slaves to freedom on the

Underground Railroad, is on the site. The house and grounds are open from 11 A.M. to 3 P.M. Tuesday through Friday, from 1 P.M. to 4 P.M. on Saturday, and from 2 P.M. to 4 P.M. most Sundays. An admission fee is charged. For information, call 336-454-3819 or visit www.mendenhallplantation.org.

Museums and Science Centers

High Point Museum and Historical Park is located at 1859 East Lexington Avenue (27262). The park contains the 1786 Haley House, listed on the National Register of Historic Places, as well as a blacksmith shop and a weaving house from the mid-1700s. The renovated museum has furniture displays, military artifacts including rifles made in Jamestown, pottery, and more. It is open Tuesday through Saturday from 10 A.M. to 4:30 P.M. and Sunday from 1 P.M. to 4:30 P.M. The historical structures in the park are open only on weekends. For information, call 336-885-1859 or visit www.highpointmuseum.org.

Cultural Offerings

The *North Carolina Shakespeare Festival* is headquartered in the High Point Theatre, at 220 East Commerce Avenue (27262). This professional troupe performs plays—most of them by Shakespeare—at different venues in the Triad during the late summer and fall. It also stages *A Christmas Carol* in December. To learn more, contact the festival at P.O. Box 6066 (27262), call 336-841-2273, or visit www.nc-shakes.org.

Special Shopping

Although High Point has dozens of retail stores that feature a vast array of home furnishings to suit every taste and budget, one special outlet is described below. The High Point Convention and Visitors Bureau offers free furniture-shopping directories. The best deals are usually to be found in August and right after the furniture markets in April and October.

The phenomenal *Furnitureland South* is located at 5635 Riverdale Drive in Jamestown (27282), just off Interstate 85 Business between High Point and Greensboro. It bills itself as "the World's Largest Home Furnishings Showplace." The complex is over 800,000 square feet and still growing. From the moment you see the 85-foot-tall chest of drawers from the highway, you'll know this is not an ordinary furniture

The "World's Largest Chest of Drawers" (*left*) is an 85-foot-tall replica at the entrance of Furnitureland South. The "World's Second Largest Chest of Drawers" is a façade of a building located two blocks east of Main Street.
PHOTOGRAPHS BY CAROLYN SAKOWSKI

store. It's so big that you'll even be given a map. You are free to browse the several buildings, where furniture is shown in gallery settings and grouped according to type and style. When you need assistance, just pick up the nearest telephone. The showrooms are open Monday through Thursday and Saturday from 8:30 A.M. to 5:30 P.M. and Friday from 8:30 A.M. to 8:30 P.M. For information, call 336-436-8056 or visit www.furniturelandsouth.com.

Recreation

Oak Hollow Lake Park and Marina, at 3431 North Centennial Street, has an 18-hole Pete Dye–designed golf course with a practice range and a clubhouse. The 1,500-acre park offers boating, water-skiing, and sailing; small sailboats can be rented for use on the lake. It also includes tennis courts and 90 campsites with full hookups. The administrative office is at 136 Northpoint Avenue (27262); call 336-883-3494 or visit http://www.high-point.net/pr/marina.cfm.

City Lake Park, at 602 West Main Street in Jamestown (27282), is a 969-acre site with a 340-acre lake. Visitors enjoy the fishing, the paddleboats, and the fishing-boat and canoe rentals. The park has amusement rides, a train, a water slide, the largest outdoor swimming pool in the state, a miniature golf course, a gymnasium, a playground, and an excursion boat. Call 336-883-3498 or visit www.high-point.net.

Piedmont Environmental Center was founded in 1972 to provide environmental education through outdoor experiences. Located at 1220 Penny Road (27265) adjacent to High Point Lake, its 376 acres of protected land offer 11 miles of trails for jogging and hiking. The *Bicentennial Greenway*, a 10-foot-wide, 6.5-mile-long paved trail, also runs through the site. The center's educational building is a study in recycled-materials construction—beverage cans were used for the red roof, newspapers for the gray roof, ketchup bottles for office carpeting, and car windshields for the bathroom tiles. The center has a nature preserve; a nature store; animal exhibits including a red fox, a white-tailed deer, hawks, raccoons, and owls; and a large "walk-on" relief map of North Carolina that demonstrates the state's geology, geography, and physiography. It is open Monday through Saturday from 9 A.M. to 5 P.M. and Sunday from 1 P.M. to 5 P.M. The trails are open from sunrise to sunset seven days a week. Admission is free. For information, visit www.piedmontenvironmental.com or call 336-883-8531.

Seasonal Events

Say no more—the big events in town are the two *High Point Markets*, held in the spring and fall (see page 365).

Places to Stay

Good locally owned accommodations are few in High Point. Most of the major chains are represented around the intersections of Interstate 40 and N.C. 68 (the airport exit) and Interstate 40 and High Point Road. Both areas are within a quick drive of downtown. Also see the Greensboro listings, since the two cities have virtually run together.

Resorts, Hotels, and Motels

Best Western High Point Hotel. Expensive. 135 South Main Street, 27260 (336-889-8888; www.hotelhighpoint.com). Located next to the largest of the furniture showroom buildings, this hotel is the best in downtown High Point. It has over 200 rooms, a restaurant, a bar, a fitness room, an indoor pool, and meeting space. The hotel provides free airport transportation.

J. H. Adams Inn
PHOTOGRAPH BY CAROLYN SAKOWSKI

Inns and Bed-and-Breakfasts

J. H. Adams Inn. Deluxe. 1108 North Main Street, 27262 (888-256-1289 or 336-882-3267; www.jhadamsinn.com). When built in 1918, this place was the home of a family that made its fortune in the local hosiery business that for decades was the only North Carolina company on the New York Stock Exchange. Now listed on the National Register, the home was renovated and opened as an inn in 2001. Each of the 31 rooms and suites showcases a distinct furniture collection from the best manufacturers in the world. The amenities are comparable to those in world-class inns.

Places to Eat

Blue Water Grille. Expensive. 126 East State Avenue, 27262 (336-886-1010; www.bluewatergrillenc.net). The cuisine here is an interesting fusion of French, Asian, Caribbean, and Low Country influences. Although you can expect excellent seafood entrées, as the name suggests, you can also enjoy a variety of other offerings. Dinner is served Monday through Saturday.

Gullah Gullah Cuisine. Expensive. 2801 North Main Street, Suite 113, 27265 (336-883-2009; www.tastegullah.com). A graduate of Johnson & Wales, owner-chef Carlos Brown brings a classic French sensibility to his Low Country–inspired cuisine. Lunch is served Tuesday through Saturday and dinner Tuesday through Sunday.

Southern Roots. Expensive. In the J. H. Adams Inn at 1108 North Main Street, 27262 (336-882-3267; www.jhadamsinn.com/southern.html). As the name implies, much of this restaurant's menu derives its inspiration from Southern tradition. For example, Southern Roots offers pan-seared sea scallops served on ham-braised cabbage and kale over creamy cheese grits. Lunch is served Monday through Friday and dinner Monday through Saturday; brunch is offered on Sunday.

Emerywood Fine Foods. Moderate/Inexpensive. 130 West Lexington Avenue, 27262 (336-882-6971; www.emerywood.com). Emerywood serves a large variety of classic and gourmet sandwiches and salads, as well as outstanding entrées in the evening. It also runs a popular catering service. Lunch is served Monday through Saturday and dinner Tuesday through Saturday.

The Furniture Industry and High Point

Drawing on the nearby hardwood forests, local furniture factories owned and run by Northern industrialists were shipping their products out of High Point by the trainload in the 1880s. In 1889, High Point Furniture Company became the first locally owned furniture manufacturer. Others soon followed. Local entrepreneurs realized that the quality of their furniture exceeded that produced in the North. They just needed to come up with some way to display their wares. In 1905, the High Point Exposition Company opened its first furniture show. In 1909, the city's furniture manufacturers began hosting biannual expositions, but they couldn't compete with the ones held in the North.

In 1911, J. J. Farris, editor of the *High Point Enterprise*, suggested that High Point construct a large display building. The Southern Furniture Manu-facturers' Association led the movement to create a display building that would make High Point the center for Southern furniture. In June 1919, construction began on a 10-story, $1 million structure that would have 261,000 square feet of exhibit space. When the building opened in 1921, more than 700 furniture buyers showed up to view the 149 exhibits. By 1924, the building's exhibit space was completely rented. Over the years, the Southern Exposition Building underwent repeated expansions. When the first postwar market was held in January 1947, some 5,147 retail furniture buyers came to town. By 1955, the display area increased to 500,000 square feet.

Now known as the International Home Furnishings Center, the showrooms have completely taken over downtown High Point. The city boasts 12 million square feet of display space.

It plays host to "the market" twice a year—in the spring and fall. The market attracts over 2,000 manufacturers, as well as more than 85,000 visitors from every state and 110 countries. Because accommodations are scarce during these times, many local residents rent their homes to market attendees and use the money to go on vacation.

Although the markets are not open to the public, the city's huge furniture retailers are. People from all over the country come to High Point to take advantage of prices 40 to 50 percent off retail. When you're shopping, remember that these retailers do not have huge warehouses stocked with ready-to-ship furniture. Rather, the retailers place orders with the manufacturers; it usually takes eight to 12 weeks for customers to receive their shipments. Some manufacturers require local retailers to exhibit complete collections in order to get volume discounts. This means that customers have a better selection in High Point than in traditional stores.

In addition to full-service stores, several clearance centers are located in High Point. The area around South Main Street near Interstate 85 Business could be called "Clearance Row." These stores stock unclaimed merchandise, discontinued items, and pieces moved out of the galleries to make room for new collections. Items that were originally 40 to 50 percent off retail in the main stores are discounted even further.

When you come to High Point, you will see that this is indeed "the Home Furnishings Capital of the World."

Elephants cooling off at North Carolina Zoological Park
COURTESY OF NORTH CAROLINA ZOOLOGICAL PARK

TRIAD NEARBY

By Anne Holcomb Waters and Carolyn Sakowski

North Carolina Zoological Park, centrally located at 4401 Zoo Parkway in Asheboro (27205), is the largest walk-through natural-habitat zoo in the country. Designed to display animals and plants in settings as similar to their native habitats as possible, the zoo offers five miles of meandering trails through indoor exhibits and two vast "continental regions"—North America and Africa. In all, the park covers more than 500 acres in the Uwharrie Mountains, with over 900 acres available for expansion. Because of the zoo's size, officials recommend spending five hours for a visit, though the highlights can be seen in just a couple of hours.

You can start your visit at either the North America or the Africa entrance, where you'll find lockers, ATMs, and wheelchairs and strollers for rent. Be sure to check out the animal status boards outside the admissions windows; the boards state times for animal feedings and keeper talks and indicate which animals may be off exhibit. Although the zoo has a tram, walking is the best way to see the animals, so wear comfortable shoes. The habitats range from wide-open fields like the "African Plains and Prairie" exhibit, where spotting antelope and bison can be challenging, to indoor-outdoor exhibits like the "Rocky Coast," where you can watch polar bears and sea lions dipping and diving underwater. You'll see alligators in the "Cypress Swamp" and gorillas in the "Forest Glade." In short, the wild, wonderful world of animals awaits.

The zoo has three restaurants, seasonal snack shops, several picnic areas, and two gift shops. Buses will take visitors back to their cars at the end of their visits. The zoo is open every day except Christmas; it closes during severe weather. It is open 9 A.M. to 5 P.M. from April through October and 9 A.M. to 4 P.M. from November to April. Admission is charged; no rain checks are given. To reach the zoo, take U.S. 220 South from Asheboro and follow the signs. For more information, call 800-488-0444 or visit www.nczoo.org.

The unique hamlet of *Seagrove* is the pottery center of North Carolina. Located 30 miles south of the Triad at the north end of the Uwharries, it is home to scores of potters who practice their craft in the tiny town and its environs. While some carry on family traditions over 200 years old, others are relative newcomers who have congregated in this artists' community, thus making the pottery available here richly diverse. Along with traditional face jugs and salt-glazed jugs, you'll find fine raku and museum-quality porcelain.

Start your visit at the North Carolina Pottery Center, at 233 East Avenue (27341), where you can pick up a free map with brief descriptions of potteries even if the center is closed. However, this interpretive and educational facility is well worth a visit if you're interested in the history of North Carolina pottery. It is open Tuesday through Saturday from 10 A.M. to 4 P.M. Admission is charged. Call 336-873-8430 or visit www.ncpotterycenter.com for more information. Two marketing associations also offer websites; visit www.discoverseagrove.com and www.seagroveheritage.com. Many, though not all, of the potteries are closed on Sunday.

Tanglewood Park is the former estate of William Neal Reynolds, brother of tobacco entrepreneur R. J. Reynolds. Perched on the banks of the Yadkin River, this

Mark Heywood of Whynot Pottery at work
PHOTOGRAPH BY MEREDITH HEYWOOD

Tanglewood Park Manor House
COURTESY OF TANGLEWOOD PARK AND WINSTON-SALEM CONVENTION AND VISITORS BUREAU

lush 1,100-acre park has been turned into northwestern North Carolina's premier recreation area. In addition to lovely gardens, a riding stable, a small lake with paddleboats, and miles of trails for riding and biking, Tanglewood boasts the Championship Course, designed by Robert Trent Jones, Jr., as well as another 18-hole golf course and a par-three course. More recent enhancements include the splendid Pete S. Brunstetter Aquatic Center and lighted clay and hard-surface tennis courts. Picnic facilities abound, including several shelters that can be reserved for large parties. Tanglewood also offers accommodations at the lovely *Manor House Bed-and-Breakfast*, Reynolds's former home; for information, call 336-778-6370.

Tanglewood hosts special events throughout the year, including the *Independence Day Fireworks Celebration*, the *North Carolina Wine Festival* in the spring, and the *Festival of Lights* during the holiday season.

The entrance to Tanglewood is about 10 miles southwest of Winston-Salem at 4061 Clemmons Road in the village of Clemmons (27012); it is easily accessible from Interstate 40. The park is open daily from 7 A.M. to sunset except on Christmas. Admission is charged. Call 336-778-6300 or check www.co.forsyth.nc.us/Tanglewood for more information.

Alamance Battleground State Historic Site is located at 5803 N.C. 62 South (27215) near Burlington, east of Greensboro. This is the site of a 1771 battle between Royal Governor William Tryon's militia and the rebellious back-country farmers known as Regulators. The Regulators objected to the control exercised over the colonial government by the merchants and planters to the east; their dissatisfaction eventually led to the short-lived War of Regulation. They were crushed by Tryon here at Alamance, which ended the Regulator Movement. On the other hand, many interpret the battle and the Regulators' grievances as a warmup for the American Revolution.

The battleground is currently open from 9 A.M. to 5 P.M. Monday through Saturday. Admission is free. Be sure to call ahead; the number is 336-227-4785. The website is www.nchistoricsites.org.

Charlotte Hawkins Brown Memorial State Historic Site was North Carolina's first state historic site honoring the contributions of an African-American citizen. Located about 10 miles east of Greensboro at 6136 Burlington Road in Sedalia (27249), this was also the first state historic site to honor a woman. To reach it, take Exit 135 (Rock Creek Dairy Road) off Interstate 85, follow the signs to U.S. 70, turn left, and travel 1.5 miles to the site.

Charlotte Hawkins Brown was born in North Carolina but grew up in Cambridge, Massachusetts. Dissatisfied with the lack of educational opportunities for blacks in the Jim Crow South, she returned to North Carolina in 1901 to teach African-American youths in Sedalia. When the school where she was working closed after she had taught only one term, she raised money in New England to found her own school, which she named Palmer Memorial Institute. In its early years, the day and boarding school emphasized agricultural and industrial education for rural living. During her 50-year presidency, Dr. Brown saw more than 1,000 students graduate from her school.

The historic site focuses not only on Palmer Memorial Institute but on the educational and social history of North Carolina as well. It offers exhibits, tours of historic structures, and audiovisual presentations. It is open Monday through Saturday from 9 A.M. to 5 P.M. Admission is free. Be sure to call ahead; the number is 336-449-4846. The website is www.nchistoricsites.org.

Horne Creek Living Historical Farm is located north of Winston-Salem off U.S. 52 at 308 Horne Creek Road in Pinnacle (27043). This state historic site interprets everyday farm life on a typical middle-class North Carolina farm during the early 1900s. It is open Tuesday through Saturday from 9 A.M. to 5 P.M. It is closed on major holidays. Admission is free except for special events. Call 336-325-2298 or visit www.nchistoricsites.org/horne/horne.htm for more information.

A Time of Trains

The Southern Crescent chugs by Barbour Station at
the North Carolina Transportation Museum
COURTESY OF NORTH CAROLINA TRANSPORTATION MUSEUM

Midway between the Triad and Charlotte off Interstate 85 are the towns of Salisbury and Spencer, which lie only minutes from the interstate but a century from its congestion, thanks to the legacy of the railroad. The older of the two, Salisbury, was established before the American Revolution, but it took the arrival of the North Carolina Railroad in 1855 to rejuvenate the century-old town. Spencer owes its very existence to the railroad.

If you're approaching from the north, take the Spencer exit (Exit 82, a left-hand exit), which will bring you over the Yadkin River on U.S. 29. Here, in April 1865, a band of Confederates (with the help of some Union prisoners turned Confederate sympathizers) thwarted the efforts of Union major general George Stoneman and his men to burn the railroad bridge. Continue on U.S. 29

to arrive in Spencer, then Salisbury.

In the 1890s, Southern Railway's president, Samuel Spencer, decided to establish a locomotive repair facility at the midpoint between Atlanta and Washington, D.C. And so the town of Spencer was born. Incorporated in 1905, it thrived until the 1950s and 1960s, when the Spencer Repair Shops began to be phased out.

The North Carolina Transportation Museum and Historic Spencer Shops are located at 411 South Salisbury Avenue in Spencer (28159) on the site of what was once Southern Railway's largest steam-locomotive repair facility. The site features an authentic train depot, antique automobiles, and a 37-bay roundhouse that includes 25 locomotives, dozens of rail cars, and other exhibit areas. The museum offers seasonal train rides, guided tours for scheduled groups, and special events throughout the year. Included among these is the semi-annual appearance of Thomas the Tank Engine—a must for tiny tykes. Admission is free, but donations are appreciated; admission may be charged for special events. Small fees are charged for the train and turntable rides. From May through October, the facilities are open from 9 A.M. to 5 P.M. Monday to Saturday and from 1 P.M. to 5 P.M. on Sunday. From November through April, the hours are 9 A.M. to 4 P.M. Tuesday to Saturday and 1 P.M. to 4 P.M. on Sunday. For more information, call the museum at 877-NCTM-FUN or 704-636-2889 or visit www.nctrans.org.

Continue on U.S. 29, which becomes Salisbury Avenue, then Main Street as you approach downtown Salisbury. Chartered in 1755, Salisbury is steeped in history and is devoted to preserving it, as evidenced by its 10 historic districts encompassing 30 blocks. Throughout the town are lovely 19th- and 20th-century homes, churches, and businesses where you can still buy homemade ice cream and get Mary Janes and Bit-O-Honeys out of bins.

Start your visit at the Rowan County Convention and Visitors Bureau (800-332-2343 or 704-638-3100; www.visitsalisburync.com), located at 204 East Innes Street (28144). To get there, turn left off Main Street onto Innes and go two blocks; the bureau is on the left.

Here, you can pick up information for self-guided walking and driving tours and trolley tours. Among the sites are the following.

The Rowan Museum, at 202 North Main Street (28144), occupies the 1854 courthouse, a fine example of Greek Revival architecture from before the Civil War. Among its holdings are Civil War–era artifacts and memorabilia of Salisbury native and author Frances Fisher Tiernan, who penned her works under the name Christian Reid.

The handsome Josephus Hall House, at 226 South Jackson Street (28144), was built in 1820 as an academy for young women. Later converted into a private residence, it was owned by the Hall family for generations before being purchased by the Historic Salisbury Foundation, which operates it as a museum. It is open Saturday and Sunday from 1 P.M. to 4 P.M. Admission is charged.

Historic National Cemetery and Confederate Prison Site, at 202 Government Road (28144), was established in 1865 to honor the thousands of Union soldiers who died at the Salisbury prison during the Civil War. Today, the cemetery is a burial ground for veterans of all of America's wars. For information, call 704-636-2661.

And last but certainly not least is the Salisbury Railway Passenger Station, at 215 Depot Street (28144). A fine example of the Spanish Mission style, it was designed by noted architect Frank Milburn in 1906. Two Amtrak trains, the Piedmont and the Carolinian, pass through daily between Charlotte and New York, continuing a century-old tradition. Indeed, Norfolk Southern and Amtrak trains rumble through town with such regularity that a former loading dock along the rails has become an informal train-spotting platform. Each weekend, (mostly) men come out and set up their lawn chairs to watch. Some residents refer to them affectionately as "train nuts," since trains pass so frequently here that they are regarded more as noisy nuisances then objects of fascination.

Lexington, approximately 25 miles south of Winston-Salem on U.S. 52, is the county seat of Davidson County and the undisputed "Barbecue Capital of North Carolina." Home to more than 20 barbecue restaurants, Lexington is known for its western-style (or Lexington-style) barbecue, which features pork shoulders with a vinegar sauce that includes tomato. This distinguishes it from eastern-style barbecue, which involves roasting the whole hog and using a zestier vinegar-only sauce. If this seems a small distinction, you're wrong. The relative merits of the two styles are hotly debated in the state. Lexington's famous **Barbecue Festival** takes place each October. Call 336-956-1880 or visit www.barbecuefestival.com for information.

Lexington's favorite son is Bob Timberlake, a gifted and extraordinarily successful painter. Inspired to take up painting as an adult by an article about Andrew Wyeth, Timberlake has since branched out into furniture making, clothing design, and, most recently, architecture. Almost everything Timberlake puts his name on sells like hot cakes and can be found at the **Bob Timberlake Gallery**, located at 1714 East Center Street Extension (27242). Visit www.bobtimberlake.com or call 800-244-0095 for more information.

The quaint town of **Mount Airy** is a must for those who love *The Andy Griffith Show*. If you're a fan, you probably already know that Mount Airy is Griffith's hometown and the model for Mayberry. Located on U.S. 52 about 30 miles northwest of Winston-Salem, Mount Airy is a living monument to Griffith and the popular television show, boasting Floyd's Barber Shop, the Old Mayberry Jail, and Griffith's childhood home. If you visit at mealtime, be sure to try a porkchop sandwich at the Snappy Lunch, Mount Airy's oldest restaurant. The visitor center is located at 200 North Main Street (27030). For information, call 800-948-0949 or visit www.visitmayberry.com.

Each September, Mount Airy commemorates *The Andy Griffith Show* with its Mayberry Days festival, which attracts fans worldwide. Call the Surry Arts Council at 800-286-6193 or visit www.mayberrydays.org for information.

Speaking of Mayberry, **Pilot Mountain State Park** is right next to the town of Pilot Mountain, the basis for Mount Pilot on *The Andy Griffith Show*. The park is located off U.S. 52 at 1792 Pilot Knob Park Road in the Surry County community of Pinnacle (27043). Though many visitors think Mount Pilot is the correct name, it's not. And don't go looking for any "fun girls" here either. Pilot Mountain is the most distinctive peak in the Sauratown range and a well-known landmark of the Triad. The state park offers picnic grounds, campsites, bridle paths, and plenty of hiking trails. The quartzite dome atop Pilot Mountain, however, is a fragile ecosystem unto itself; climbing it is not allowed. Call 336-325-2355 or visit http://www.ncparks. gov/Visit/main.phd for more information.

Hanging Rock State Park, located about 15 miles east of Pilot Mountain off N.C. 89 at 2015 Hanging Rock Park Road near Danbury (27016), is the largest state park in the Piedmont. Three sheer rockfaces—Cooks Wall, Moores Knob, and Hanging Rock itself—dominate the park. Climbing is popular on the first two but not on Hanging Rock. Campsites, cabins, picnic areas, swimming, fishing, and 20 miles of hiking trails are the attractions here. Many visitors like to canoe the Dan River, a gentle, slow-moving river except after storms. Call 336-593-8480 or visit http:// www.ncparks.gov/Visit/main.phd for more information.

Nestled in the foothills of the Blue Ridge, Wilkes County comes alive the last weekend in April thanks to *Merlefest*, an annual celebration of Americana music. Held to honor the late son of flat-picking legend Doc Watson, this four-day music festival grew from a few of Doc and Merle's musician friends playing on the back of a flatbed truck for 4,000 people in 1988 to a crowd of over 40,000 fans who come to see some of the best bluegrass, Celtic, and Cajun musicians in the business. Numerous stages are spread over the hillsides of the campus of Wilkes Community College. What makes this festival so special is the magic that often occurs when musicians who rarely play together team up for intimate jam sessions at some of the smaller venues. You can learn more by writing Merlefest at P.O. Box 120 in Wilkesboro (28697), calling 800-343-7857, or visiting www.merlefest.org.

Doc Watson performing
COURTESY OF BOONE CONVENTION AND VISITORS BUREAU

The Yadkin Valley: North Carolina's Wine Country

by Anne Holcomb Waters

Westbend Vineyards
COURTESY OF WESTBEND VINEYARDS AND WINSTON-SALEM CONVENTION AND VISITORS BUREAU

Situated in the heart of the North Carolina Piedmont, the Yadkin River Valley has emerged as the state's premier wine region. Spurring this wine revolution is the gradual decline of the tobacco industry. Since the 1990s, area farmers have been planting former tobacco fields with grapevines and other alternative crops. The cultivation of vinifera and European varietal grapes has been so successful here, in fact, that the region was recognized in 2003 as North Carolina's first American Viticultural Area, or "appellation."

For wine enthusiasts, a tour of the Yadkin Valley wineries offers the chance not only to sip some award-winning Chardonnays and Cabernets but also to travel the rolling valleys and picturesque foothills of the Piedmont. The valley boasts 23 vineyards and wineries, with more on the horizon. The following tour follows a roughly circular route to visit four wineries of distinction. I strongly urge you to expand your tour of the wine country if you have time.

In the 1970s, the pioneering efforts of the late Jack Kroustalis and his wife, Lillian, at Westbend Vineyards proved that vinifera grapes could grow in the Piedmont. Named for a western bend in the Yadkin River, Westbend began as a vineyard only, growing grapes for other wineries, before becoming a bonded winery in 1988. Its first wines were released in 1990, and the awards have flowed in ever since. It is open for wine tastings Tuesday through Saturday from 11 A.M. to 5 P.M. and Sunday from noon to 5 P.M.; the hours may vary in winter. Wine tours cost three dollars. For more information, call 336-945-5032 or visit www.westbendvineyards.com. Westbend is located at 5394 Williams Road in Lewisville (27023) on the western outskirts of Winston-Salem. From Winston-Salem, take U.S. 421 North to Shallowford Road (Exit 246). Turn left, go 2.4 miles, and turn left onto Williams Road. Westbend is the fourth drive on the left.

RayLen Vineyards and Winery is located at 3577 U.S. 158 in Mocksville (27028). Joe and Joyce Neely received a big boost when Westbend Vineyards' longtime winemaker, Steve Shepard, decided to join their fledgling vineyard in the late 1990s. Every one of RayLen's initial releases in 2000 earned medals in competitions. Named for the Neelys' two daughters, Rachel and Len, the vineyard has a spacious tasting room with tables and chairs and a wraparound porch with rocking chairs for use in fair weather. A full-flight wine-tasting costs eight dollars, while a red- or white-flight only is five. The winery is open year-round from 11 A.M. to 6 P.M. Monday through Saturday. For information, visit www.raylenvineyards.com or call 336-998-3100. To reach RayLen from Winston-Salem, head west on Interstate 40 to Exit 180 and turn left on N.C. 801 South. The entrance is four miles on the right.

Shelton Vineyards, at 286 Cabernet Lane in Dobson (27017), is owned by brothers Ed and Charlie Shelton, who first planted 60 acres of European varietals on an old dairy farm in 1999. By 2001, that acreage had expanded to more than 200, making this the largest family-owned estate winery in North Carolina. In addition to investing in their own state-of-the-art facility, the Shelton brothers sponsored the application for the area's appellation designation and started the viticulture and oenology program at Surry Community College in Dobson. The vineyard is open from 10 A.M. to 6 P.M. Monday through Saturday and from 1 P.M. to 6 P.M. on Sunday during daylight saving time. The winter hours are 10 A.M. to 5 P.M. Monday through Saturday and 1 P.M. to 5 P.M. on Sunday. The cost is five dollars per person. Guests receive a guided tour of the 33,000-square-foot winery, an overview of the art of winemaking, a tasting of five wines, and a souvenir glass. For information, call 336-998-3100 or visit www.sheltonvineyards.com. To reach Shelton Vineyards from Mocksville, take U.S. 601 North to Dobson.

Named for a prizewinning Holstein cow, RagApple Lassie Vineyards & Winery is located at 3824 RagApple Lassie Lane in Boonville (27011). When the winery was honored as one of two finalists for the distinction of being the "Best New Winery in the United States," owners Frank and Lenna Hobson were quick to credit the Yadkin Valley appellation. Winemaker Linda King also deserves some of the praise for RagApple Lassie's early, heady success. Tastings, available daily, cost $12 dollars to sample 13 wines or six dollars to sample five of the reds, whites, or dessert wines; participants receive a souvenir glass. If you want a tour, just ask. Call 866-724-2775 or visit www.ragapplelassie.com. To reach the winery from Dobson, go east on N.C. 67 off U.S. 601 and look for the sign.

For additional information about North Carolina's vineyards and wineries, visit www.ncwine.com or call 877-3NC-WINE. For a member list of the Yadkin Valley Wine Growers Association and an interactive map, call 336-366-4734 or visit www.yadkinvalleywineries.com.

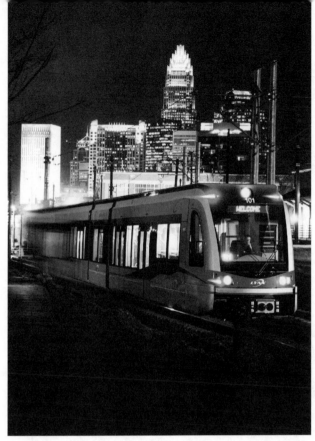

Charlotte light rail
COURTESY OF VISIT CHARLOTTE

Charlotte

By Anne Holcomb Waters

There is no reason on God's green earth for Charlotte to be here.

Charlotte has no advantage of nature to justify its location, its geographical presence. It has no port like New York or New Orleans, no confluence of rivers like Charleston or Pittsburgh, no navigable river like Wilmington, no commanding heights like Memphis.

So as the first white men moved west from the coast and south down the Great Wagon Road, why did they stop here? When Thomas Spratt, the first European to settle in the area, walked into what is now the heart of Uptown Charlotte, what made him decide to stay and (literally) set up shop?

The land Spratt saw was unquestionably beautiful. Green hills swelled gently from ridge to red-clay field to ridge; pines grew in stands thick as jungles with brush and briars and berries; and throughout ran clear, fast creeks that fed the Catawba River to the west.

But the land that would be Charlotte and Mecklenburg County had more going for it than just beauty. The soil was more fertile than that in the Uwharries to the east or the Blue Ridge to the west. Close at hand were several of the best fords for crossing the Catawba. For centuries, the Cherokee and Catawba tribes had directed their trading routes toward these fords, so that two main paths had developed, one running northeast and southwest, the other northwest and southeast.

So when Thomas Spratt made his way to the top of the low hill where Trade Street now crosses Tryon Street, the thought that has occurred to thousands since when gazing upon Charlotte may have come to his mind: *I could do all right for myself here.*

Stand at Trade and Tryon on any weekday and picture the courthouse here at the corner, which is where it stood until the mid-19th century (and which is why the intersection is still referred to as "the Square," as in Courthouse Square). Look up at the steel and glass around you and imagine the fine Victorian houses that once lined both streets as far as the city limits. Now watch the traffic speed by and try to see the

One of the four Raymond Kraskey bronze sculptures
at Trade and Tryon Streets
PHOTOGRAPH BY ED SOUTHERN

intersection of two dusty Indian trading paths, traveled by foot or mule or horse.

Spratt opened a trading post here in 1753. Small farms already dotted the area, farms that would coalesce into townships mostly remembered now by street names: Providence, Sharon, Berryhill, Mallard Creek. Charlotte has been growing since the very beginning, and growing aggressively. As one longtime resident has said, "Charlotte's always been a chamber-of-commerce town." The colonial-era city fathers built a courthouse and jail before their community was named the county seat, then used the finished construction as proof that Charlotte deserved to be the county seat.

The new county—Mecklenburg—and Charlotte itself took their names from the German queen of King George III of England, a rather blatant attempt to curry favor. This proved ironic, since Mecklenburg County was one of the earliest places to call for independence from Great Britain, and since guerrilla opposition was so fierce when Cornwallis came through that he called Charlotte "a damned hornet's nest of rebellion," inadvertently naming the city's original NBA basketball team.

The boom really began when the railroad came through in 1852. Suddenly, the cotton grown in all those surrounding townships no longer needed to be hauled in wagons all the way to Cheraw or Camden in South Carolina for boats to take it to market in Charleston. Now, farmers could have their crops weighed, graded, and loaded onto rail cars right in Charlotte. Business prospects and population growth took flight in the county seat.

The Civil War left Charlotte safely tucked away in the back country, surprisingly intact. The town subsequently experienced another boom in wealth and population. Country boys and newly freed blacks rushed in to take advantage of the opportunities created first by the railroads and then by that emblem and icon of the New South: the textile mill.

Charlotte and the rest of the South built mills during the 1880s. The first local operation, Robert Oates's Charlotte Cotton Mill, opened in 1880 just a block off West Trade Street in the Fourth Ward. Three more mills—the Alpha, the Ada, and the Victor—opened within the city limits by the end of the decade. As the railroads had done a generation earlier, the mills lured thousands to Charlotte, some seeking opportunity, some just a steady paycheck.

Textile mills were trumpeted by men like Charlotte's D. A. Tompkins as the means by which the New South would rise. Looking at Charlotte, which is more of a New South city than even Atlanta, one would have to agree. By 1930, mills and the industries they brought with them made Charlotte once and for all the largest city in the Carolinas, laying the groundwork for the prosperity Charlotteans enjoy today.

But they also indirectly hardened barriers of race and class. Read the letters to the editor in the *Charlotte Observer* today, with their concerns over busing, unequal opportunity, and Uptown versus the suburbs, and you find the long-term effects of sudden industrialization.

Economically, the cotton mills carried Charlotte through the onset of the 20th century, World War I, and World War II. The spun and woven cotton from the mills had to be transported. Luckily, Charlotte sat astride "the Main Street of the South"—J. P. Morgan's Southern Railway line from Washington, D.C., to New Orleans. By the second decade of the 20th century, three more major railroads ran through Charlotte, making the Queen City the center of the Piedmont's vast network of textile mills. Rather than simply shipping Mecklenburg's own cotton crop, Charlotte brought crops in by rail from as far away as Mississippi and Alabama. The railroads continued to grow until after World War II, when new highways and then the Eisenhower Interstate System—specifically, Interstates 77 and 85—brought the trucking industry up to speed.

The opening of the 20th century saw tobacco magnate James B. Duke ready to experiment with the newfangled science of harnessing electrical power. Charlotte, having a strong industrial base and having the Catawba River nearby, seemed the logical place for the project's headquarters. In 1904, Duke sent engineer Bill Lee to

Charlotte to form the Catawba Power Company, the forerunner of Duke Energy.

In contrast to their counterparts in other areas of the South, Charlotte's business leaders did a remarkable job of diversifying industry while riding the crest of the cotton wave. Everything from cars to crackers was made here. Historian Thomas Hanchett, in his book *Sorting Out the New South City*, said that by the 1920s, "if you went to a movie or wrote a check or bought a bottle of cough syrup anywhere from Charleston to Raleigh, you were probably doing business indirectly with some resident of the Queen City."

Which was a good thing, because the mills were slowly dying by the postwar years, vulnerable as they were to foreign production. But although no one knew it at the time, the mills had left Charlotte in position for another economic and population boom, one greater and richer and grander than even D. A. Tompkins, much less Thomas Spratt, could have imagined.

All the money that the mills generated, you see, had to be managed, had to be kept and nurtured and used wisely. Banks sprang up around town to receive the deposits of mill owners and mill hands alike. The Federal Reserve opened a regional master bank in Charlotte. In the 1890s, textile men from the North joined with local magnates and formed Charlotte National Bank, which in time became North Carolina National Bank, which in time became NationsBank, which in 1999 became Bank of America, the first coast-to-coast bank.

It should be mentioned that Charlotte, ranked second after New York City among the nation's banking centers, has been hit hard by the current financial crisis. Ironically, a decade after Hugh McColl masterminded the takeover of San Francisco–based Bank of America, rival Wachovia was purchased by the City by the Bay's giant Wells Fargo corporation. No one yet knows how many jobs might be lost to consolidation, but as the Queen City's mayor put it, "Charlotte does have very strong resilience, and I anticipate that a lot of the talent that's moving out of the banks will stay."

Charlotte's current leaders are different from their predecessors in looking beyond the bottom line. Having built their companies, they are now working to build their community into all that the word *city* implies. Charlotte has seen not only an economic boom, but a cultural one as well. The downtown area, which most Charlotteans call "Uptown" because they like the sound better, has undergone an extensive revitalization that has brought in restaurants, nightclubs, and facilities such as Spirit Square, the McColl Center for the Visual Arts, Discovery Place, the Mint Museum of Craft + Design, and, most recently, The EpiCentre. Charlotte has even recognized and mostly stopped what was once its most pernicious habit—tearing down anything old, regardless of its historic value, to make way for the new. Finally interested in more than doing well, Charlotte concentrates today on doing good.

JUST THE FACTS

Charlotte sits just this side of the North Carolina–South Carolina border in the Piedmont region. It has more than 700,000 people within its city limits, 1.5 million within its metro area, and 6 million within a 100-mile radius.

Having experienced most of its growth in the late 20th century, Charlotte is easy to get to and around by car. Interstates 85 and 77, which intersect in northern Charlotte, are major thoroughfares through the west side of Charlotte and Mecklenburg County. U.S. 74 runs east and west to connect Charlotte to the coast and the mountains, while N.C. 16 runs north and south through the city along the Catawba River Valley. Interstate 485 provides an inner loop connecting Uptown to the surrounding areas.

Charlotte is served by Greyhound buses and Amtrak trains. The bus station is at 601 West Trade Street (28202); call 704-372-0456 for information. The train station is at 1914 North Tryon Street (28202); call 800-USA-RAIL or 704-376-4416 or visit www.amtrak.com.

The new LYNX Blue Line Light Rail is the first rapid transit system in North Carolina. So far, it connects only a 10-mile stretch from southern Charlotte to Uptown, but more connections are in the planning stages. Call 704-336-RIDE or visit www.charmeck.org/deparments/CATS/LYNX. The free Gold Rush trolley-like buses offer jaunts up and down Tryon and Trade streets from 7 A.M. until 10 P.M. Call 704-336-RIDE or visit www.charmeck.org/deparments/CATS.

Charlotte/Douglas International Airport sees more than 500 flights daily and offers nonstop service to 160 cities; visit www.charlotteairport.com for information or call 704-359-4910.

Please note that you must include the area code when making local calls in Charlotte. Currently, the area code for Charlotte is 704, with the exception of its public schools, which use the 980 area code.

For more facts on Charlotte, contact the Visit Charlotte Visitor Information Center, run by the Charlotte Convention and Visitors Bureau. The bureau is located at 330 South Tryon Street (28202) in the city's center. Call 800-231-4636 or visit www.charlottecvb.org.

Things to Do

Historic Places, Gardens, and Tours

The Charlotte Convention and Visitors Bureau publishes a brochure for the *Cen-*

ter City Walking Tour, which leads visitors to many of the sites listed below, plus places for shopping, Thomas Polk Park, Settlers Cemetery, the Victorian Fourth Ward neighborhood, and Ericsson Stadium, home of the NFL's Carolina Panthers. Go to www.charlottesgotalot.com to download a PDF of the tour or call the bureau at 800-231-4636 for more information.

The Arts and Science Council offers the *Public Art Walking Tour*; to learn about it, see the "Seen on the Streets of Charlotte" sidebar.

For those who prefer to ride, the *Charlotte Trolley* provides visitors the opportunity to step back in time as they step into one of the renovated vintage trolley cars that run from historic South End to Uptown. Along the way, conductors entertain riders with stories of old Charlotte. The trolley is headquartered at the *Powerhouse Museum*, located at 1507 Camden Road (28203). Tokens for one-way, round trip, and one-day unlimited rides are available. A fee is charged. Call 704-375-0850 or visit www.charlottetrolley.org for more information.

The *Charlotte Museum of History* and the *Hezekiah Alexander Homesite*, both at 3500 Shamrock Drive (28215), together tell Charlotte's story from its earliest pioneers to its boom as a manufacturing center to its current heyday as a banking powerhouse.

The Charlotte Museum of History is housed in a handsome, four-wing, multi-gallery structure that replaced the cramped quarters it had occupied since 1976. Its displays include artifacts from pre-colonial times, historic flags, a re-created gold mine, a replica of the original Mecklenburg County Courthouse, and household items from throughout Charlotte's history that were either found by historians or donated by Mecklenburg families. The museum also houses a research library and an archive.

Located atop a small hill behind the museum, the Hezekiah Alexander Home-

Hezekiah Alexander Homesite
at Trade and Tryon streets
PHOTOGRAPH BY ANNE HOLCOMB WATERS

site is Mecklenburg County's oldest surviving structure. A member of one of the area's earliest and most prominent families, Hezekiah Alexander supposedly signed the Mecklenburg Declaration of Independence; he also co-founded Queens College and helped frame North Carolina's first state constitution. His rock house is three miles from what was then the hilltop village of Charlotte; the area in between was so wild that Alexander's brother always carried two loaded pistols whenever he came to visit. A re-created log kitchen sits behind the house, and a reconstructed stone springhouse is alongside the creek at the bottom of the hill, which makes for a cool spot to picnic.

The Charlotte Museum of History and the Hezekiah Alexander Homesite are open Tuesday through Saturday from 10 A.M. to 5 P.M. and Sunday from 1 P.M. to 5 P.M. Admission is charged. Try to plan a visit to coincide with the guided tours scheduled at 1:15 P.M. and 3:15 P.M. daily. Visit www.charlottemuseum.org or call 704-568-1774 for more information.

Historic Latta Plantation, at 5225 Sample Road in neighboring Huntersville (28078), is the 1800 Catawba River plantation home of merchant and planter James Latta. The house and immediate grounds are now a living-history farm owned and run by the Mecklenburg County Department of Parks and Recreation. The house is furnished with antiques dating from 1790 to 1840, roughly the period when the Latta family occupied the property. The grounds contain 13 outbuildings used as interpretive centers to tell about work on the site and the lives of the plantation's slaves and the area's yeoman farmers. The fields are planted with crops appropriate to the period and place, and farm animals roam the barnyard. Volunteer docents dressed in period costumes assist with the self-guided tours through the house, fields, and grounds. The house and grounds are open Tuesday through Saturday from 10 A.M. to 5 P.M. and Sunday from 1 P.M. to 5 P.M., with guided tours offered on the hour. They are closed Thanksgiving, Christmas, and New Year's. Admission is charged. For information, call 704-875-2312 or visit www.lattaplantation.org.

Historic Rosedale Plantation, at 3427 North Tryon Street (28206), is one of the finest examples of Federal architecture in North Carolina. Built in 1815 by merchant Archibald Frew, it was referred to as "Frew's Folly" by neighbors, who possibly took issue with its chrome yellow trim. Rosedale was the plantation home of Dr. D. T. Caldwell and his family in the 1830s. Located three miles from what is now Uptown Charlotte, Rosedale was part of the farming community known as Sugaw Creek, from which present-day Sugar Creek Road gets its name.

Rosedale hosts special events including lectures and exhibits. Along with the Hezekiah Alexander Homesite, it is one of the last places in Charlotte to celebrate Mecklenburg Declaration of Independence ("Meck Dec") Day. Guided tours of the home, gardens, and grounds are given at 1:30 P.M. and 3 P.M. Thursday through Sunday. Groups of 12 or more need to call in advance. Rosedale also offers specially scheduled tours that examine the lives of children and slaves on antebellum plantations. Admission is charged for anyone over eight. Call 704-335-0325 or visit www.historicrosedale.org for more information.

The *James K. Polk Memorial*, at 308 South Polk Street in nearby Pineville (28134), marks the birthplace of the United States' 11th president. Born in 1795, Polk spent most of his childhood in Mecklenburg County before moving with his family to Tennessee. He later returned to North Carolina to study at the university in Chapel Hill. Polk accomplished more in his single term as president than many others have in two. His tenure saw the creation of an independent treasury, the creation of the Department of the Interior, the settlement of the Oregon boundary, the annexation of Texas, and the acquisition of California, which provoked the unpopular Mexican War. Polk had promised not to seek a second term, and he kept his word. He died in 1849 three months after leaving the presidency.

The farm where he was born is now a state historic site. The log cabin and farm buildings and their furnishings are not Polk family originals, but period pieces from the early 1800s that create an impression of what life must have been like for the young Polk. Mecklenburg County was still the back country in those days, and the memorial accurately depicts the work required to succeed on the frontier.

The James K. Polk Memorial is currently open year-round from 10 A.M. to 5 P.M. Tuesday through Saturday except for major holidays. Admission is free, but donations are welcome. For more information, visit www.nchistoricsites.org/polk/polk.htm or call 704-889-7145.

The *UNCC Botanical Gardens*, on the campus of the University of North Carolina at Charlotte, offer a green respite from the traffic and development of the surrounding University City area. The property is comprised of three main attractions: the McMillan Greenhouse, which features orchids, cacti, carnivorous plants, and a small rain forest; the three-acre Susie Harwood Garden; and Van Landingham Glen, a woodland retreat filled with native plants and the most diverse collection of rhododendrons in the state. The gardens are open daily; the greenhouse is open Monday through Saturday from 10 A.M. to 3 P.M. and Sunday from 1 P.M. to 4 P.M.

Call 704-687-2364 or visit http://gardens.uncc.edu for more information.

The University of North Carolina at Charlotte was founded in 1947 to handle the sudden increase in college applicants created by the GI Bill. UNCC has since grown into a premier regional university. It has a nationally recognized faculty and students from all over the country. The university is located at 9201 University City Boulevard (28223).

Wing Haven Gardens and Bird Sanctuary is one of Charlotte's very own love stories, written in birds, bushes, and bricks. Before Eddie Clarkson brought his new bride, Elizabeth, to Charlotte in 1927, he built a house to the specifications she had outlined in her many letters from Texas. Included was a raised brick terrace where her piano could be relocated from the living room through French doors. The couple entertained near the reflecting pond, where Elizabeth would attach hummingbird feeders to the backs of guests' chairs.

Located at 248 Ridgewood Avenue (28209), Wing Haven offers four acres of woodlands and formal gardens in Myers Park, one of Charlotte's most genteel neighborhoods. Pools, fountains, and baths are available for birds and classes, special events, and an upscale gift shop for humans. The sanctuary is open Tuesday and Wednesday from 3 P.M. to 5 P.M. and Saturday from 10 A.M. to 5 P.M. Admission is charged. Call 704-331-0664 or visit www.winghavengardens.com for more information.

Museums and Science Centers

If you're going to make a day of visiting Charlotte's Uptown museums, look into an *Uptown Museum Pass*, which offers discounted admission to the Levine Museum of the New South, Discovery Place, and the Mint Museum of Craft + Design. Call or visit any of the participating museums for information.

The *Levine Museum of the New South*, at 200 East Seventh Street (28202), is the only museum in the country that concentrates on the New South period (1865 to the present). It features hands-on activities and displays that not only tell the history of the New South but also put it in the context of national and world history. The concentration, of course, is on Charlotte and the Piedmont region of the Carolinas. The permanent exhibit called "Cotton Fields to Skyscrapers" allows visitors to step inside replicas of a sharecropper's cabin, a textile mill, a mill-village house, an early Belk department store, a civil-rights-era lunch counter, and a 21st-century Latino bakery. The museum also houses several lecture halls and galleries for changing exhibits. It is open from 10 A.M. to 5 P.M. Monday through Saturday and from noon to 5 P.M. on Sunday. Admission is charged except for children under six. For more information, call 704-333-1887 or visit www.museumofthenewsouth.org. It is worth noting that visitors to the museum can park free for up to 90 minutes at the adjacent Seventh Street Station, the only parking deck in Charlotte that laughs (at you or with you, depending on your self-esteem). It also lights up as pedestrians pass.

Discovery Place, at 301 North Tryon Street (28202), is a must-see if you have children or even if you don't. Its permanent exhibits include a range of interactive science and natural-history displays where kids can experience everything from touching a simulated tornado to broadcasting their own weather reports. Young children will enjoy the fish, snakes, and birds throughout the aquarium and rainforest exhibits, whereas older kids will get a charge out of orbiting the International Space Station in a motion simulator. Discovery Place also has a planetarium and the *Charlotte Observer* OMNIMAX theater for IMAX films.

Discovery Place is currently undergoing a $31.6 million transformation, which is anticipated to be completed in June 2010. The museum will remain open during the process, but certain displays will be closed while new ones appear in their place. In the words of the museum's literature, the intent is to "re-invent the visitor experience at Discovery Place, filling the Museum with all new science and technology exhibits and interactive displays that present science in a topical and contemporary way."

Discovery Place operates daily except for Thanksgiving and Christmas. The exhibit halls are open from 9 A.M. to 5 P.M. Monday through Friday, from 10 A.M. to 6 P.M. on Saturday, and from noon to 5 P.M. on Sunday. Admission is charged except for children under two. Times and ticket prices for the planetarium and OMNIMAX shows

Discovery Place
COURTESY OF VISIT CHARLOTTE

vary. For more information, call 704-372-6261 or visit www.discoveryplace.org.

A component of Discovery Place is the **Charlotte Nature Museum**, at 1658 Sterling Road (28209). This small nature center is located adjacent to Freedom Park. Recently expanded and refurbished, it features a live-animal room, a butterfly pavilion, a nature trail, and a puppet theater. It is open Tuesday through Friday from 9 A.M. to 5 P.M., Saturday from 10 A.M. to 5 P.M., and Sunday from noon to 5 P.M. It is closed Thanksgiving, Christmas Eve, Christmas, New Year's, and Easter. An admission fee is charged for those over age three. Call 704-372-6261 or visit www.discoveryplace. org/naturemuseum.asp for more information.

The **Mint Museum of Craft + Design** is currently located at 220 North Tryon Street (28202) in the old Montaldo's department store building; however, in February 2010, it will close to the public in anticipation of its metamorphosis into the **Mint Museum Uptown**, scheduled to open in October 2010. In addition to its focus on international studio craft and design, including a spectacular Dale Chihuly chandelier and countless other outstanding contemporary works in metal, clay, wood, and other media, the Mint Museum Uptown will spotlight collections of contemporary, American, and European art.

The Mint Museum of Craft + Design is open from 10 A.M. to 5 P.M. Tuesday through Saturday; on the third Thursday of the month, the hours are from 10 A.M. to 8 P.M. Admission is charged except for Tuesday from 10 A.M. to 2 P.M. and the third Thursday of the month from 5 P.M. to 8 P.M. Children under five are admitted free. If used on the same day, one ticket covers admission to both the Mint Museum of Craft + Design and the Mint Museum of Art, unless otherwise noted. The new facility will be located in the Wells Fargo Cultural Campus, located at First Street and South Tryon. For more information, visit www.mintmuseum.org or call 704-337-2000.

The **Mint Museum of Art**, at 2730 Randolph Road (28207), is the oldest art museum in North Carolina. The story of how it came to be is an unusual one. In 1799, a 12-year-old found a shiny rock on his father's farm 25 miles east of Charlotte. Gold miners from as far as Europe flocked to the area. To take advantage of the ready gold supply, the United States Mint built a Charlotte branch in 1837. The mint thrived until Charlotte's gold rush was overshadowed by California's in 1849. The mint closed in 1913. By 1933, the building was slated for demolition. Instead, it was merely dismantled and moved brick by brick to its present location in the Eastover neighborhood. In 1936, the Mint Museum of Art opened.

The museum's permanent collection focuses on American art from pre-Columbian to contemporary. It includes not only works by masters such as Andrew Wyeth and Thomas Eakins, but also pottery from nearby Seagrove, ceramics, and even some of the gold coins made during the building's former life. Also in the permanent collection are works from Europe and Africa, including ceremonial masks. The museum hosts impressive traveling exhibits year-round.

It is open Tuesday from 10 A.M. to 9 P.M. and Wednesday through Saturday from 10 A.M. to 5 P.M. Admission is charged except on Tuesday from 5 P.M. to 9 P.M. Children under four are admitted free. For more information, call 704-337-2000 or visit www.mintmuseum.org.

The *Carolina Raptor Center*, located on the grounds of Latta Plantation Park and Nature Preserve at 6000 Sample Road in Huntersville (28078), is dedicated to environmental education and the conservation of birds of prey through public education, the rehabilitation of injured raptors, and research. The only eagle aviary in the Carolinas, it has a nature trail on which visitors can view the eagles, falcons, owls, vultures, and hawks that the facility has treated but cannot release into the wild. Try to time your visit to catch one of the volunteer presentations, which are both informative and fun. You'll be every bit as enraptured (sorry) as your kids by being in the proximity of peregrine falcons, barn owls, and even vultures. The center is open Monday through Saturday from 10 A.M. to 5 P.M. and Sunday from noon to 5 P.M. Presentations are offered on Saturday at 11 A.M., 1 P.M., and 3 P.M. and on Sunday at 1 P.M. and 3 P.M. Admission is charged except for children four and under. The center is closed on major holidays. For more information, call 704-875-6521 or visit www.carolinaraptorcenter.org.

The *Carolinas Aviation Museum* is located at 4108 Airport Drive (28208) near Charlotte/Douglas International Airport, a World War II training field that has become one of the busiest hubs in the country. Housed in an old hangar, the museum offers guided tours and aviation "artifacts" from the early days of flight. Most people come for the aircraft, including a "Top Gun" F-14D Super Tomcat, an F-102 Delta Dart, an A-7E Corsair, and a DC-3 built in 1942 and restored to flight-ready condition in 1987. The museum is open Tuesday through Saturday from 10 A.M. to 4 P.M. and Sunday from 1 P.M. to 5 P.M. Tuesdays and Thursdays are work days, so plan to visit then if you want to meet or see people restoring old aircraft. Admission is charged except for children under six. For more information, call 704-359-8442 or visit www.carolinasaviation.org.

ImaginOn: The Joe and
Joan Martin Center
COURTESY OF VISIT CHARLOTTE

Cultural Offerings

ImaginOn: The Joe and Joan Martin Center, at 300 East Seventh Street (28202), is a wonderful, whimsical building that encompasses an entire city block in the heart of Uptown. The facility includes the *Spangler Children's Library* and the *Children's Theatre of Charlotte*. There is no charge to use the library, to explore the building and use its StoryLab, or to participate in drop-in programming. The Children's Theatre, now in its 62nd season, has received numerous accolades through the years and prompted the *Charlotte Observer*'s theater critic to refer to it as "the city's leading professional troupe." Make sure to stop by *Reid's Grocery* next door for lunch or a quick snack; eat outside so the kids (of all ages) can play with the giant chimes set into the building. For box-office and ticket information, call 704-793-2828 or visit www.imaginon.org.

The *North Carolina Blumenthal Performing Arts Center*, at 130 North Tryon Street (28202), opened in 1992 adjacent to the Bank of America Corporate Center and Founders Hall. The Blumenthal Center is now the umbrella organization that oversees the Belk Theater and Booth Playhouse, both of which are located here, as well as the Duke Energy Theatre, Knight Theater, the McGlohon Theater, Ovens Auditorium, and Stage Door Theater, located elsewhere in the city. National touring productions of Broadway shows and performances by the Charlotte Symphony Or-

North Carolina Blumenthal Performing Arts Center
COURTESY OF VISIT CHARLOTTE

chestra, the Charlotte Repertory Theatre, Opera Carolina, and the North Carolina Dance Theatre are all staged at the Belk Theater, while the other venues showcase a sweeping variety of music, dance, and contemporary theater. For information on ticket prices and upcoming performances, visit www.blumenthalcenter.org or call 704-372-1000.

Adjoining the Blumenthal Center is the massive ***Bank of America Corporate Center***, the tallest skyscraper in the Carolinas, at 100 North Tryon Street (28255). Designed by renowned architect Cesar Pelli (who also designed the Blumenthal Center), the tower is a welcome break from the glass-and-steel boxes that dominated the Charlotte skyline for decades. In its lobby are three frescoes by world-famous artist and North Carolina native Ben Long.

Spirit Square Center for Arts and Education
PHOTOGRAPH BY ED SOUTHERN

Finishing up the city block is *Founders Hall*, also at 100 North Tryon Street, a two-story indoor plaza offering upscale shopping and dining and a box office for the Blumenthal Center.

Spirit Square Center for Arts and Education, at 345 North College Street (28202), came under the auspices of the Blumenthal Center in 1997. It was built in 1909 as First Baptist Church; the facade facing Tryon Street still features the church's Byzantine design and stained-glass windows. The church moved in the 1970s, at which time the property was turned into a community arts center. The former sanctuary is now the McGlohon Theatre, named after Charlotte native and jazz composer and pianist Loonis McGlohon. Spirit Square also houses the Duke Energy Theatre and five galleries devoted to visual arts. The focus, however, is education; Spirit Square hosts numerous workshops and programs sponsored by Charlotte's cultural institutions. For more information, call 704-372-1000 or visit www.performingartsctr.org.

The *McColl Center for Visual Art*, at 721 North Tryon Street (28202), is housed in a former Associate Reformed Presbyterian church built in 1926. Vacated in the 1950s when its congregation dissolved, the church was heavily damaged by fire in 1985 and stood as a charred remnant of urban flight until it was purchased by Bank of America in 1995. In 1999, the McColl Center opened its doors to the public and to its artists-in-residence and affiliated artists, all of whom enjoy the lovely, airy studio space. The *Dickson Gallery* and *Gallery 115* are located on the first floor, but visitors are encouraged to explore all three floors and to interact with artists in their studios. Gallery hours are from 11 A.M. to 4 P.M. Tuesday through Saturday. Admission is free. Call 704-332-5535 or visit www.mccollcenter.org for more information.

Like Spirit Square and the McColl Center, the *Afro-American Cultural Center*, at 401 North Myers Street (28202), is housed in a former church. It takes a multidisciplinary approach to education and programming, hosting art exhibits, film series, and performances of music, drama, and dance to preserve Charlotte's rich African-American heritage. It maintains a visual-arts gallery, an outdoor amphitheater, a 200-seat indoor theater, and classroom space. As with the Mint Museum of Craft + Design, the center is scheduled to relocate to the Wells Fargo Cultural Campus in fall 2010. For more information, call 704-374-1565 or visit www.aacc-charlotte.org.

Slated for completion in fall 2010, the *Wells Fargo Cultural Campus*, at First Street and South Tryon, will exemplify the ongoing commitment to the arts in Charlotte. The new facility will house the *Mint Museum Uptown* (currently the Mint Museum of Craft + Design), the *Knight Theater*, the *Harvey B. Gantt Center for African-American Arts and Culture* (currently the Afro-American Cultural Center), and, last but not least, the new *Bechtler Museum of Modern Art*.

Named for the family of Andreas Bechtler, a Charlotte resident and native of Switzerland who assembled and inherited a collection of more than 1,400 artworks by major figures of 20th-century modernism, the Bechtler Museum will showcase artworks by seminal figures such as Alberto Giacometti, Joan Miro, Jean Tinguely, Max Ernst, Andy Warhol, Le Corbusier, Sol Lewitt, Edgar Degas, Nicolas de Stael,

Artist's rendering of Bechtler Museum of Modern Art
COURTESY OF BECHTLER MUSEUM OF MODERN ART

Barbara Hepworth, and Picasso. Designed by Swiss architect Mario Botta, the museum will further Charlotte's transition from a regional to a national powerhouse. Its hours of operation are yet to be determined. The museum will be located at 420 South Tryon Street. For information, visit www.bechtler.org.

Special Shopping

As artists are wont to do, Ruth Ava Lyons and J. Paul Sires quietly started a revolution in Charlotte when they opened their now-famous *Center of the Earth Gallery* at 3204 North Davidson Street (28205) in 1985. Thus began the transformation of a former mill village into Charlotte's historic arts district, commonly referred to as *NoDa*. Home to numerous galleries and performance outlets, NoDa offers gallery crawls twice a month. Check out www.noda.org for more information. The Center of the Earth Gallery is open Tuesday to Friday from 11 P.M. to 5 P.M. and Saturday from noon to 7 P.M. Call 704-375-5756 or visit www.centeroftheearth.com for more information.

Concord Mills, at 8111 Concord Mills Boulevard in Concord (28027), is located at Exit 49 off Interstate 85 north of Charlotte. This place has managed to turn itself into a tourist destination as well as a shopping mall. Boasting over 200 retail and manufacturer's outlets, it offers a store for every taste, as well as a massive food court featuring a carousel. When their shopping is done, visitors can play at the NASCAR Speed Park or see a movie at the 24-screen AMC theater, which will soon sport an IMAX screen. Be sure to stop by the Bass Pro Shops' enormous fish tank, which is big enough for fishing demonstrations. Hours of operation are from 10 A.M. to 9 P.M. Monday through Saturday and from noon to 7 P.M. on Sunday. Concord Mills is closed on Easter, Thanksgiving, and Christmas. Visit www.concordmills.com or call 704-979-3000 for more information.

SouthPark, located at 4400 Sharon Road (28211), is both geographically and economically far removed from Concord Mills. Here, you'll find Nordstrom, Tiffany & Co., Kate Spade, Louis Vuitton, and more. Call 704-364-4411 for information. The mall is open Monday through Saturday from 10 A.M. to 9 P.M. and Sunday from noon to 6 P.M. Visit www.southpark.com for more information.

Charlotte's newest mall, *Northlake*, is located at 6801 Northlake Mall Drive

(28216), just north of the city at Exit 18 off Interstate 77. Its vibe is between those of Concord Mills and SouthPark. Northlake offers a nice variety of department stores, specialty stores, and restaurants, as well as a movie theater. Hours of operation are Monday through Saturday from 10 A.M. to 9 P.M. and Sunday from noon to 6 P.M. Call 704-599-6665 or visit www.shopnorthlake.com for more information.

Birkdale Village is located at 8712 Lindholm Drive in Huntersville (28078), just north of Charlotte at Exit 25 off Interstate 77. It offers open-air, upscale shopping in a village atmosphere. Shoppers can browse their favorite specialty shops and quirky gift shops and try a wide range of restaurants. Anchoring the center is Birkdale Theaters, where visitors can catch popular as well as indie films. A fountain in the middle of Birkdale Village invites kids of all ages to cool off in the summer. That area also serves as one of Santa's stops during the Christmas season; snow is scheduled (yes, scheduled) various evenings. The stores are open Monday through Thursday from 10 A.M. to 7 P.M., Friday and Saturday from 10 A.M. to 8 P.M., and Sunday from noon to 6 P.M. For more information, visit www.birkdalevillage.net.

EpiCentre, at 210 East Trade Street (28202) in Uptown, defies easy definition. It is an outdoor mall with shops, restaurants, and a movie theater. It is an entertainment complex with a bowling alley and nightclubs. It also offers accommodations at its hotel, Aloft. Going to a movie here is an experience. The theater offers plush, intimate seating and little tables where viewers can place their truffle fries and glass of wine or mixed drink. Movie tickets can be ordered in advance at www.epicentretheaters.com. And leave it to EpiCentre to take bowling to another level. StrikeCity encompasses bowling alleys, a first-class restaurant menu, a full bar featuring an extensive martini menu, over 75 super-large high-definition video screens, a 60-foot TV wall, and a dance floor. Strike City is open daily from 11 A.M. to 2 A.M. Visit www.strikecity.clickcom.com or call 704-716-9300 for more information.

Recreation

The property beyond the immediate grounds of Historic Latta Plantation is *Latta Plantation Nature Center and Preserve*. Picnic tables and shelters, nature trails, bridle paths, canoe rentals, and fishing on Mountain Island Lake are all available to visitors. The nature center is open Monday through Saturday from 9 A.M. to 5 P.M. and Sunday from 1 P.M. to 5 P.M. The preserve is open daily from 7 A.M. until sunset. Admission is free except during special events and at certain facilities within the preserve. For more information about the house and grounds, see Historic Latta Plantation under "Historic Places, Gardens, and Tours."

McDowell Nature Center and Preserve, at 15222 York Road (28278), is located on Lake Wylie south of town off N.C. 49. Visitors can camp, hike, fish, picnic, and boat on the facility's 1,000 acres. Lake Wylie, one of a series of lakes formed by the damming of the Catawba River, is the last before the river leaves North Carolina. The nature center is open Monday through Saturday from 9 A.M. to 5 P.M. and Sunday from 1 P.M. to 5 P.M. The preserve is open daily from 7 A.M. until sunset. An admission fee is charged. Call 704-588-5224 for the nature center or 704-583-1284 for the campground or visit www.charmeck.org/Departments/Park+and+Rec/Inside+The+Department/Divisions/Stewardship+Services/Nature+Preserves/McDowell.htm.

Located at 1900 East Boulevard (28277) across a wooden footbridge from the Charlotte Nature Museum is ***Freedom Park***, the largest public park within the city limits. Tennis courts, basketball courts, volleyball sand pits, baseball fields, soccer fields, playgrounds, picnic tables and shelters, an old locomotive for kids to play on, a pond, and a band shell for outdoor concerts are all located at the park. You might even discover a little solitude here, five minutes from Uptown. The outdoor facilities

The pond at Freedom Park
PHOTOGRAPH BY ED SOUTHERN

are open daily from dawn to dusk, while the indoor facilities are open from 7 A.M. to 11 P.M. unless otherwise specified.

Straddling the border between North and South Carolina, *Carowinds* is the largest theme park in the Carolinas. It has evolved far beyond the wooden Thunder Road roller coaster. Thrill seekers will adore the Borg Assimilator and Carolina Cyclone coasters. The more family-friendly attractions include Scooby Doo's Haunted Mansion and the new Boomerang Bay water park. Musical revues and concerts are held at the park. Visiting Carowinds can easily take an entire day; be sure to wear sunscreen. The park is located at 14523 Carowinds Boulevard (28273); take Exit 90 off Interstate 77. It is open from early spring to early fall. Boomerang Bay is open June 1 through Labor Day. For hours and admission prices, call 800-888-4386 or visit www.carowinds.com.

Ray's Splash Planet Waterpark, at 215 North Sycamore Street (28202), is a joint venture between the Mecklenburg County Department of Parks and Recreation and the Charlotte-Mecklenburg schools. Opened in 2002, the facility includes an indoor water park with a three-story water slide, a fitness center, an aerobics and dance room, a cardiovascular theater, a playground, and concessions. An admission fee is charged. The park is open from 9 A.M. to 8 P.M. Monday through Friday, from 9 A.M. to 7 P.M. on Saturday, and from 1 P.M. to 7 P.M. on Sunday. It is closed Thanksgiving and Christmas. Call 704-432-4RAY or visit http://www.charmeck. org/Departments/Park+and+Rec/Aquatics/Rays+Splash+Planet/Home.htm for additional information.

The *U.S. National Whitewater Center*, located at 5000 Whitewater Center Parkway (28214), is a much-heralded outdoor recreation and environmental education center just 10 minutes from Uptown. The park's best-known feature is its multi-channel customized whitewater river, where rafters, canoeists, and kayakers of all abilities are welcome. For those who want to stay dry, the park offers mountain biking and running trails and a climbing center and challenge course. And when you're ready to come inside, you can relax at the 300-seat *River's Edge Bar & Grill*. The main gate and trails are open 365 days a year from 6 A.M. to 10 P.M., weather permitting. If you want to ride the river—and who doesn't?—you have "family-style" and "adventure-style" options, depending on the water flow. Both are offered daily; mornings are usually designated for the family-style option. The schedule fluctuates, so call or visit the website before going. Likewise, the park urges visitors to check weather conditions in advance. Admission is charged; a variety of passes are available. Call 704-391-3900 or visit www.usnwc.org for more information.

Seasonal Events

The *Carolinas' Carrousel Parade* is a lot like an old small-town Christmas parade, only bigger. So much of Charlotte's history has been lost to development that holdovers like the Carrousel Parade have become more attractive through sheer nostalgia. Held on Thanksgiving Day, the parade proceeds down Tryon Street through Uptown. Onlookers enjoy the floats, the marching bands, and, of course, Santa and his sleigh bringing up the rear. For information, call 704-525-0250 or visit www.carrouselparade.org.

Festival in the Park has been bringing arts, crafts, music, food, and crowds together in Freedom Park since 1964. More than 200 artists and craftsmen from across the region and the nation display their work in tents set up around the pond. Nearly 1,000 entertainers perform in the band shell and at sites across the park. Workers string lights so activities can continue after dark. The festival is held over a weekend in September. For information, call 704-338-1060 or visit www.festivalinthepark. org.

The *Novello Festival of Reading*, sponsored by the Public Library of Charlotte and Mecklenburg County, brings in some of the most renowned authors in the world for lectures, readings, discussions, and signings. More than 20 authors and illustrators participate in events held throughout the city; a downtown street festival is also offered for families. Past guests have included the late Pulitzer Prize winner Frank McCourt and Nobel laureate Toni Morrison. Novello is held throughout October; call 704-336-2020 or visit www.plcmc.org/novello for more information.

The *Taste of Charlotte Festival*, held in Uptown every June, showcases the city's exciting variety of restaurants. Since its inception in 1999, the festival has expanded to offer kids' interactive activities, open-air shopping, and "Tavern at the Taste," which gives visitors the chance to try microbrews and wines while listening to live music. Admission is free, but festival coins must be purchased to sample food and beverages. For more information, call 704-947-6590 or visit www.tasteofcharlotte. com.

The *Southern Christmas Show*, the *Southern Spring Home & Garden Show*, the *Southern Ideal Home Show*, and the *Southern Women's Show* are held at various times during the year at The Park (formerly the Charlotte Merchandise Mart) at 2500 East Independence Boulevard (28205). Each features fashions, crafts, and tips on design and decorating appropriate to its theme and season. For exact dates and ticket prices, contact Southern Shows, Inc., by calling 704-376-6594 or visiting www.southernshows.com.

The *Loch Norman Highland Games*, sponsored by the Catawba Valley Scottish Society, are held each April at Rural Hill Farm, the former Davidson family plantation overlooking the Catawba River at 4431 Neck Road in Huntersville (28078). The site is rolling, grassy, and partially wooded. Given all the kilted lads strolling about, the more imaginative (or drunk) members of the crowd might come to believe they're actually in old Caledonia. Sanctioned competitions in Highland dancing, fife-and-drumming, and, of course, Scottish athletics like caber tossing are held. You'll also find dart throwing, archery, and demonstrations of Scottish crafts and artwork. The clans erect tents around the main competition field, so visitors can check to see if they're related to William Wallace or Robert the Bruce. A food-and-drink area is on the grounds. Yes, you can get haggis, but why would you want to? Admission is charged, as is a parking fee. For more information, call 704-875-3113 or visit www.ruralhillscottishfestivals.net.

Only at the *Carolina Renaissance Festival* can one attend a jousting tournament, see a sword swallower, belly dancers, and the occasional Klingon, and feast on a turkey leg—all in the same place. Located just north of Charlotte at 16445 Poplar Tent Road in Huntersville (28078), "RenFest" is held at a 20-acre medieval theme park open for seven weekends in October and November. As visitors pass through the gates, they are transported to a 16th-century village populated by artisans, circus performers, musicians, and a royal court. RenFest offers food, crafts, music and comedy shows, people-powered rides, games of skill, and costumed characters who entertain visitors with songs, tales, and tricks. The daily jousts by dashing knights at the King's Tournament Arena are the favorite events. Admission is charged, but parking is free. Visit www.royalfaires.com/carolina for more information.

The Legend of the Meck Dec

By Ed Southern

Despite naming their political subdivisions for King George III's queen, the people of Charlotte and Mecklenburg County were among the earliest supporters of the Continental Congress's effort to break free of Great Britain.

Exactly how early this support came has been a cause for debate for more than two centuries.

The crux of the debate is the Mecklenburg Declaration of Independence. Since seemingly everything in Charlotte has to have a perky nickname, this document has long been known as the "Meck Dec." The story goes that on May 20, 1775, the leading citizens of Mecklenburg County met at the county courthouse, just east of the Trade and Tryon intersection, to decide on a course of action in response to the British occupation of Boston Harbor. According to Meck Dec believers, this meeting ended with the writing and signing of a declaration of independence announcing that British law no longer held effect in Mecklenburg County, and that Mecklenburg's citizens would thenceforth be responsible for their own governance.

A copy of the document was given to someone recorded in history as "Captain Jack," the son of a local tavern keeper. Captain Jack was supposed to carry the Meck Dec to Philadelphia to present it to the Continental Congress. Records show that he stopped in Salisbury and Salem, but he never arrived in Philadelphia. What the good citizens of Mecklenburg learned from this was that a man called Captain Jack may be absolutely trusted to make popcorn shrimp, but that he should not be trusted with history-making political documents.

The original was kept in the home of one of the signers and was destroyed in a house fire. No other copies existed.

Many outside the Carolinas soon began to question the authenticity of the Meck Dec. One of these was Thomas Jefferson, who found the version of the Meck Dec pieced together from the signers' memories to be remarkably similar to his Declaration of Independence. Meck Dec supporters retorted that the similarities in language resulted from the strong influence of John Locke on both statements.

Regardless of whether or not the Meck Dec existed, or existed in the form its supporters claim, Mecklenburg County deserves recognition for being quick to take up the cause of liberty. Three weeks after the meeting that produced the Meck Dec, another such meeting indisputably produced the Mecklenburg Resolves, a less strongly worded denunciation of British injustices in America. And Mecklenburg men were present in April 1776 when North Carolina issued the Halifax Resolves, the first official recommendation by a colonial government that the colonies declare their independence from Great Britain.

Many in Charlotte and Mecklenburg County continue to insist on the authenticity of the Meck Dec. May 20, "Meck Dec Day," was an official county holiday until the 1960s, celebrated with parades and speeches by local and even national leaders. Some sites in Charlotte, such as the Hezekiah Alexander Homesite and Rosedale Plantation, still celebrate Meck Dec Day, though it draws much less attention than in times past.

Places to Stay

Resorts, Hotels, and Motels

While most of Charlotte's accommodations are national chains, almost all occasionally offer midweek, seasonal, and other types of promotions that make a stay pretty affordable.

Ballantyne Resort Hotel. Deluxe. 10000 Ballantyne Commons Parkway, 28277 (866-248-4824 or 704-248-4000; www.ballantyneresort.com). The area's first resort, Ballantyne completely reshaped southern Charlotte when it opened, causing new roads to be built and old roads to be renamed, rerouted, or closed. The resort offers 200 hotel rooms, each with 10-foot ceilings, custom furnishings, and original artwork; a 36-room lodge; and a four-bedroom cottage. It also has 20 suites, including two Presidential Suites for those who want to feel like the leader of the free world. Guests enjoy the 24-hour in-room dining menu. The hotel overlooks the 18th fairway of a golf course that is home to the Dana Rader Golf School; Rader, the author of *Rock Solid Golf*, has been ranked one of America's premier golf instructors by both *Golf Magazine* and *Golf Digest*. Ballantyne also offers accommodations at The Lodge at Ballantyne Resort, Staybridge Suites, and a Courtyard by Marriott location.

The Dunhill Hotel. Deluxe/Expensive. 237 North Tryon Street, 28202 (704-332-4141; www.dunhillhotel.com). Nestled among the towers of North Tryon Street, The Dunhill, built in 1929, offers elegant charm in the manner of a European hotel. The richly and traditionally decorated rooms include well-stocked refrigerators tucked into armoires. In the lobby are a comfortable seating area and the Monticello restaurant, which comes highly recommended.

Charlotte Marriott City Center. Expensive. 100 West Trade Street, 28202 (704-333-9000; www.marriott.com/property/propertypage/CLTCC). The Marriott boasts a heated indoor pool, an exercise room, valet parking, airport transportation, two restaurants, a wine bar, a cigar bar, a gift shop with Starbucks coffee, one of the biggest ballrooms in town, and an exceptional staff. It also lives up to the "City Center" in its name; guests are only steps from the intersection of Trade and Tryon.

Hilton at University Place. Expensive. 8629 J. M. Keynes Drive, 28262 (704-547-

7444; www.charlotteuniversity.hilton.com). This 12-story hotel is the most visible landmark of the University City area, off Interstate 85 at Harris Boulevard. The service here is exceptional. University Place offers distinctive shops and fine restaurants clustered around a picturesque lake.

Hilton Charlotte Center City. Expensive. 222 East Third Street, 28202 (704-377-1500; www.hilton.com). The Uptown location of the Hilton offers 407 rooms, each with two telephones and a refreshment center. The hotel completed a $30 million renovation in June 2008, resulting in a fresh, cosmopolitan feel to its rooms, suites, meeting spaces, restaurant, and lounge. Guests have access to the Uptown YMCA, an unusually large fitness center.

The Westin Charlotte. Expensive. 601 South College Street, 28202 (704-375-2600; www.westin.com/charlotte). Charlotte's new convention hotel boasts startling architecture, a fantastic location, outstanding service, and, lest anyone forget, the Westin chain's famous Heavenly Bed in each of its 700 guest rooms. It also has 32,000 square feet of meeting space, including a 16,000-square-foot grand ballroom. Guests have access to the hotel's spa, the Bar 10 outdoor café, and the Ember Grille gourmet restaurant. Located across the street from the convention center, The Westin is a stop on the trolley route running from the South End through the city's center.

Aloft Charlotte Uptown at the EpiCentre. Expensive/Moderate. 210 East Trade Street, 28202 (704-333-1919; www.starwoodhotels.com/alofthotels). Situated at Charlotte's hip new entertainment mecca, the EpiCentre, Aloft offers custom a-menities by Bliss Spa. Guests can enjoy wireless Internet and the large TVs in their rooms, then venture to the bar or lounge for a night out. Plus, the EpiCentre is right outside for nonstop shopping, dining, moviegoing, and dancing.

Charlotte Marriott SouthPark. Expensive/Moderate. 2200 Rexford Road, 28211 (704-364-8220; http://www.marriott.com/hotels/travel/cltph-charlotte-marriott-southpark). Located adjacent to the tony SouthPark shopping mall, this boutique hotel has 194 of Charlotte's most well-appointed rooms. Amenities include an outdoor pool, a health club, the Charles Grayson Day Spa, a putting green, and an ever-helpful concierge.

Great Wolf Lodge. Expensive/Moderate. 10175 Weddington Road in Concord, 28027 (704-549-8206; www.greatwolf.com). Just like the new EpiCentre, Great Wolf

Lodge refuses to be categorized. The lodge features thematic, family-friendly suites like "KidKamp" and "Wolf Den," where guests can relax after a full day at the lodge's water parks, which include the six-story "Howlin' Tornado," "Fort MacKenzie," and more. Age-appropriate programming (including story time for toddlers) is offered, as are miniature golf and arcade games for older kids. Adults will enjoy the fitness center and full-service spa; Great Wolf even has a spa for the 12-and-under set.

Inns and Bed-and-Breakfasts

The Duke Mansion. Deluxe. 400 Hermitage Road, 28207 (888-202-1009 or 704-714-4400; www.dukemansion.com). Built in 1915, this inn is James B. Duke's former estate in the tree-lined Myers Park neighborhood. Guests in its 20 rooms enjoy private baths, newspaper delivery, gourmet bedside treats, and all the modern conveniences. Breakfast is served daily, and other meals can be arranged with advance notice. The Duke Mansion offers an elegant, tranquil stay and also serves as a meeting and retreat facility.

Ms. Elsie's Caribbean Bed-and-Breakfast. Deluxe. 334 North Sharon Amity Road, 28211 (704-365-5189; www.mselsies.com). Ms. Elsie's offers authentic Caribbean charm in the Cotswold neighborhood, convenient to SouthPark and the Mint Museum of Art. It features four guest rooms and a three-course breakfast with fresh fruit and seafood.

The Morehead Inn. Deluxe/Expensive. 1122 East Morehead Street, 28204 (704-376-3357; www.moreheadinn.com). The 1917 Morehead Inn is located in the historic Dilworth neighborhood just minutes from Uptown. Updated in 1995, this popular spot for nuptials offers a full Southern breakfast, private baths, fluffy bathrobes, and loads of amenities such as privileges at the nearby Central YMCA. Meeting rooms are available.

Seen on the Streets of Charlotte

by Ed Southern

Southbound on Interstate 77, you'll see the Charlotte skyline rise slowly. Starting with the crown of the Bank of America Corporate Center, one skyscraper after another comes into view on the horizon. Like the new commerce seeping up the interstate—the car lots and hotels, the chain restaurants and fast-food joints—the skyscrapers are a boast of Charlotte's abundance. But a closer look shows that they are also a symbol of something more.

Charlotte is the only city in the Carolinas to make Skyscraper.com's list of the top 100 skylines in the world. More than just an outgrowth of economic boom times—for other Carolina metropolises have enjoyed similar fortunes—the appearance of Charlotte's Uptown is a visible sign of the commitment of business leaders to leavening the commercial with the cultural.

Long before "world-class city" became Charlotte's number-one cliché, ambition, or joke, depending on your point of view, the bankers and businessmen who built the most recent boom had made it clear that transforming Charlotte into a true city, with the variety of experiences the word implies, was a high priority. They had turned what was once a backwoods town into the second-largest financial center in America. Executives from New York City and San Francisco now answered to them, and they didn't want those big-city executives snickering or moaning about getting their marching orders from some burg out in the boondocks.

Rather than just reflexively associating *bigger* with *better* in the traditional American way, Charlotte's leaders sought to build with an eye for the eyes, a dedication to aesthetics that would make the city's core as alive and pleasing as the Carolina countryside.

The axis around which the skyline turns is North Tryon Street's Bank of America Corporate Center, the tallest building between Philadelphia and Atlanta. Designed by Cesar Pelli and opened in 1992, this postmodern tower is capped by concentric rings of spires that, particularly when lit at night, bear more than a passing resemblance to a crown. (Pelli reportedly swears he was not thinking of Charlotte's "Queen City" tag when he conceived his design.) Flanked by the performance halls of the Blumenthal Center and the upscale shopping and dining of Founders Hall, the Bank of America Corporate Center single-handedly began the transformation of urban Charlotte into something more cosmopolitan.

Charlotte's skyline grew with the economy of the 1990s. Bank of America funded two other skyscrapers on North Tryon Street, 1997's IJL Financial Center and 2002's Hearst Tower. The architect for both—Smallwood, Reynolds, Stewart, Stewart & Associates—designed the towers to complement the Bank of America Corporate Center. All three use similar materials. The IJL Financial Center has a crescent shape except on its sharp-angled west facade, which looks as if it is clinging to the hump of the semicircle. The Hearst Tower created a stir when its design became apparent. In contrast to the Bank of America tower, whose facade recedes as it rises— fulfilling the popular expectation of how a skyscraper should look—the Hearst Tower's facade expands as it nears its cowl-shaped top. Thanks to the Art Deco flourishes on the exterior (which are continued inside) and the fact that the tower's top is lit at night, the overall impression is that of an Olympic torch (or perhaps a scepter for the Queen City?).

Most of Charlotte's other skyscrapers have their own distinctive architectural offerings that add to the beauty of the whole. One Wachovia Center on College Street has glass spines running through its east and west facades that make the tower glow at sunrise and sunset. The Interstate Tower and the Carillon Tower, both on Trade Street, have imaginative and contrasting tops best seen when approaching Charlotte from the west. The Interstate Tower is capped by a postmodern cone straight out of the Space Age, while the Carillon Tower takes its central spire from the Neo-Gothic First Presbyterian Church across the street.

The Carillon Tower is also home to two of the finest examples of downtown Charlotte's public works of art, *Cascade* by Jean Tinguely and *The Garden* by Jerry Peart. The Arts and Science Council, whose offices are in the Carillon Tower, offers the Public Art Walking Tour in the city's center. The tour includes art by internationally renowned artists such as Peart, Tinguely, Romare Bearden, Ben Long, and Arnaldo Pomodoro. Visit www.artsandscience.org/index.asp?fuseaction=PublicArt.WalkingTour for information.

Places to Eat

Since the 2005 arrival of Johnson & Wales University, a culinary-arts school, Charlotte's already-thriving restaurant scene has only improved. The following list is an effort to showcase a mixture of cheap eats, elegant fare, ethnic restaurants, traditional home-style cooking, and Charlotte institutions. Likewise, it aims to guide you to some of Charlotte's most interesting neighborhoods.

Blue. Expensive. 214 North Tryon Street, 28202 (www.bluerestaurantandbar.com; 704-927-2583). Blue serves innovative Mediterranean cuisine that sparkles like the Aegean Sea. Guests can choose from a variety of appetizers such as prosciutto-wrapped scallops and crab-stuffed calamari or dive right into the delicious "Moroccan Lamb Tagine" or the pan-seared sea bass. Dinner is served Monday through Saturday; a late-night menu is offered Wednesday through Saturday.

Carpe Diem. Expensive. 1535 Elizabeth Avenue, 28204 (704-377-7976; www. carpediemrestaurant.com). Now in its third location in 15 years, Carpe Diem has staying power. Its elegant Art Nouveau setting is perfect for enjoying the amazingly light buttermilk-fried chicken breast or the spinach-and-cheese dumplings. And don't forget to follow your meal with the mango-pineapple sorbet. Dinner is served Monday through Saturday; brunch is offered on Sunday.

Cantina 1511. Expensive/Moderate. 1511 East Boulevard, 28203 (704-331-9222; www.cantina1511restaurant.com). A great way to begin your meal here is the "Top Shelf Guacamole," made fresh table-side, and a cool margarita. You can follow that with one of the fresh seafood appetizers or, if you're really hungry, the "Barbacoa de Puerco." Outdoor dining is available. Cantina 1511 is open for lunch Monday through Friday, for dinner nightly, and for brunch on Sunday.

Copper. Expensive/Moderate. 311 East Boulevard, 28203 (704-333-0063; www. copperrestaurant.com). Located in the historic Mayer House, where Carson Mc-Cullers began writing *The Heart Is a Lonely Hunter*, this lovely restaurant serves classic Indian cuisine with a modern twist. Traditionalists will appreciate the rich curries and tandoori-cooked meats, while more adventurous eaters may want to try the "Paneer Napoleon," a cheese-and-roasted-vegetable pie. Lunch is served weekdays and dinner Monday through Saturday.

Dolce Ristorante. Expensive/Moderate. 1710 Kenilworth Avenue, 28203 (704-332-7525; www.dolceristorante.net). Dolce is a charming Italian spot tucked into the Kenilworth Commons Shopping Center off East Boulevard. Originally a *gelateria*, this full-fledged trattoria now serves delicious traditional pastas and *secondi* such as "Linguini ai Frutti di Mare" and "Saltimbocca Trastevere." Be sure to leave room for a scrumptious gelato. Lunch is served weekdays and dinner Monday through Saturday.

Greek Isles, Expensive/Moderate. 200 East Bland Street, 28203 (704-444-9000; www.greekislesrestaurant.com). This is the real deal, folks—and as an ancient Greek major, your humble author has spent some time in Hellas. Here, you can get gorgeous fresh fish, grilled octopus, flaming *saganaki*, luscious *pastitsio*, *dolmades*, and baklava. *Opa!* Lunch is served Sunday through Friday and dinner Monday through Saturday.

Pewter Rose Bistro. Expensive/Moderate. 1820 South Boulevard, 28203 (704-332-8149; www.pewterrose.com). The Pewter Rose has long been one of the most exciting restaurants in Charlotte, offering a menu as imaginative as the decor. The entrées are outstanding, the wine list is expansive, and the adjacent Tutto Mondo nightclub accentuates the slightly eccentric ambiance. This is one of the best places in Charlotte to take a first date. The Pewter Rose is open daily for lunch and dinner and serves an enormously popular Sunday brunch.

Cabo Fish Taco Baja Seagrill. Moderate. 3201 North Davidson Street, 28205 (704-332-8868; www.cabofishtaco.com). Located in the heart of the artsy NoDa district, this casual place combines coastal Mexican cuisine with California flair. What this means, dude, is that it serves myriad wraps, tacos, and burritos stuffed with seafood, chicken, and other healthy things. You can also get a mean margarita. Cabo is open daily for lunch, dinner, and "late evenings."

Mert's Heart and Soul. Moderate/Inexpensive. 214 North College Street, 28202 (704-342-4222; www.mertsuptown.com). One bite of its greens landed Mert's an entry in this book, despite slow service due to a lost dining ticket. Stick with the fried chicken, porkchops, and Southern-style veggies and you can't go wrong. This noisy, bustling place located in the heart of Uptown offers darn good down-home food at reasonable prices. Mert's serves lunch daily and dinner Tuesday through Sunday; it also offers brunch on Saturday and Sunday.

NOFO on Liz. Moderate/Inexpensive.1609 Elizabeth Avenue, 28204 (704-444-9003; www.nofo.com). "What is it?" you may ask when you see this place. The answer is that it's a gift store *and* a food market *and* a café—a very lively café. NOFO serves an array of fresh salads, grilled "Pizzette," sandwiches, and heartier entrées including walnut-and-spinach ravioli and bacon-wrapped grouper. It's fun. It's funky. And it's on Elizabeth Avenue. Lunch and dinner are served Monday through Saturday; Sunday brunch is also offered.

Casablanca Café. Inexpensive. In the Terraces at University Place, 9609-I North Tryon Street, 28262 (704-503-4748; www.casablancacafecharlotte.com). Charlotte has become a veritable melting pot of international cuisines. The Casablanca Café offers Moroccan, Mediterranean, and Middle Eastern food that's as tasty as it is affordable. First-timers should try the "Casablanca Special," a combo platter of hummus, *babaghannouj*, tabbouleh, saffron rice, and a kebab each of chicken and beef. It's a bargain—and it can feed two people. The kids' menu includes a hamburger made with beef ground in the kitchen and grilled chicken tenders served on a skewer. For those attracted to the new hookah fad, the restaurant offers a variety of flavored tobaccos and water pipes after 8:30 P.M. Lunch and dinner are served daily.

Lupie's Café. Inexpensive. 2718 Monroe Road, 28205 (704-374-1232; www.lupiescafe.com). In a city full of bankers, Lupie's is the most economical spot you're likely to find. The quantity of food for the money is staggering. A different special is offered each night. The meat loaf on Monday is a favorite, but Lupie's is just as famous for its chili. The side dishes run the gamut and are meals unto themselves. Even the children's portions are huge. If physically possible, save room for the banana pudding. The atmosphere is loud but relaxed, and the wait staff is friendly and easygoing, making Lupie's a great place to bring kids. The walls are decorated with work by local artists and photographers; a big poster of John Wayne is near the kitchen. Lupie's does not take reservations, so be prepared to wait at lunchtime and on most weekend nights. Lunch and dinner are served Monday through Saturday. Lupie's also has a location on Old Statesville Road in Huntersville.

The Penguin. Inexpensive. 1921 Commonwealth Avenue, 28202 (704-375-6959). What began as an ice-cream parlor became a drive-in. Then the drive-in became a retro diner and bar boasting the best jukebox in the Southeast. Tucked a block off Central Avenue near the corner of Thomas Avenue, The Penguin is typical of the neighborhood's independent, offbeat feel. The kitchen closes at midnight, though the bar stays open later. Some advice: order your burger Southern-style, and ask for an appetizer of fried pickles. Lunch and dinner are served daily.

Price's Chicken Coop. Inexpensive. 1614 Camden Road, 28203 (704-333-9866; www.priceschickencoop.com). Fried chicken and fish from Price's Chicken Coop are as much a Charlotte tradition as bank takeovers. A little over a mile distant but a world away from the slick bistros of Uptown, Price's is as Southern as it gets. Call for directions if you're new to town. Otherwise, you'll likely get lost, but the chicken is worth the search. Lunch and dinner are prepared Tuesday through Saturday for takeout only.

Nearby

Waxhaw, a small town 13 miles south of Charlotte on N.C. 16, is known for its turn-of-the-20th-century architecture and its large number of antique outlets. Shopping here is leisurely; shopkeepers rarely keep to a set schedule. Each February, the Waxhaw Women's Club hosts an antique show at the American Legion hut. Waxhaw is where Andrew Jackson spent his childhood.

The **Reed Gold Mine**, at 9621 Reed Mine Road in the Cabarrus County town of Midland (28107) northeast of Charlotte, saw the beginning of the short-lived Charlotte gold rush, one of the first in the United States. It is now a state historic site. The mine and the legacy of the gold rush are preserved through a museum, a film, a guided underground tour, a stamp mill, and walking trails. For a small fee, you can even learn to pan for gold—but don't get your hopes up. The site is currently open Tuesday through Saturday from 9 A.M. to 5 P.M., but be sure to inquire ahead. Call 704-721-4653 or visit www.nchistoricsites.org/reed.

Morrow Mountain State Park, at 49104 Morrow Mountain Road east of Albemarle (28001), is a beautiful and tranquil piece of the Uwharrie Mountains only 45 minutes from Charlotte. A swimming pool served by a bathhouse from the Civilian Conservation Corps era, vacation cabins, and tent and trailer campsites are available. Visitors can also fish, picnic, and rent canoes and boats. The Kron House is the reconstructed cabin of one of the area's earliest doctors. The hiking trails here are challenging and scenic. A modest fee is charged to use the pool, as are rental fees for some activities. Hours vary by month; the park is closed Christmas. Call 704-982-4402 or visit http://ils.unc.edu/parkproject/visit/momo/home for more information.

Uwharrie National Forest lies just across the Pee Dee River from Morrow Mountain State Park at 789 N.C. 24/27 East near Troy (27371). Camping, horseback riding, mountain biking, and hiking are just some of the land-based activities at this 55,000-acre oasis, while canoeing, tubing, fishing, and swimming in popular ***Badin Lake*** help visitors cool off in summer. Call 910-576-6391 or visit www.cs.unca.edu/nf-snc/recreation/uwharrie for more information.

The ***Schiele Museum of Natural History***, at 1500 East Garrison Boulevard in Gastonia (28054), is the area's largest nature museum. The exhibition galleries showcase North American habitats and wildlife. The half-mile nature trail takes visitors through 16 acres of Piedmont forest to a re-created 18th-century backwoods farm and a Catawba Indian village. The Schiele Museum also houses a state-of-the-art planetarium. The museum is open Monday through Saturday from 9 A.M. to 5 P.M. and Sunday from 1 P.M. to 5 P.M. except on major holidays. Admission is charged. Call 704-866-6900 or visit www.schielemuseum.org for more information.

Crowders Mountain State Park lies just west of Gastonia near the South Carolina line and Kings Mountain National Military Park at 522 Park Office Lane in Kings Mountain (28086). In addition to hosting the normal state-park activities, Crowders Mountain is one of the best rock-climbing sites east of the Appalachians. An admission fee is charged. Call 704-853-5375 or visit www.crowdersmountain.com for information.

Davidson, a college town just off the banks of Lake Norman, is remarkable for its old-time Main Street, maintained in the face of Mecklenburg County's astounding growth. Main Street runs alongside the campus of ***Davidson College***, where future president Woodrow Wilson studied. It features a row of shops, coffee houses, and a soda shop, housed mainly in 19th-century buildings.

Lake Norman State Park, at 159 Inland Sea Lane in Troutman (28166), is on Lake Norman, the state's largest manmade lake. The park lays claim to the only public swimming area on the lake. Boating access is available along the park's 13 miles of shoreline. Out of the water, visitors can enjoy hiking trails, campgrounds, interpretive programs, and picnic areas. Fees are charged for canoe and paddleboat rentals and for the use of park facilities. Hours vary according to the season; the park is closed Christmas. For information, call 704-528-6350 or visit www.ncparks.gov/visit/lano.

The Heart of NASCAR: *A Race Fan's Tour of the Piedmont*

By Andrew Waters

"Racing was built here. Racing belongs here." Charlotte used this slogan in its successful bid to become the location for the NASCAR Hall of Fame. Like most slogans, this one is part truth and part hyperbole. Although stock-car racing has been a popular pastime all over the South for more than 50 years, and though its popularity stretches across the country today, Charlotte and the North Carolina Piedmont are home to some of the sport's most famous drivers, legends, and races. Racing is big business in the Piedmont. Despite the economic downturn that has hit the sport in the past several years, numerous NASCAR teams still have their headquarters here, creating high-paying jobs and tourist attractions across the region.

Start your tour northwest of Winston-Salem in Wilkes County, home to the sport's first great hero, Junior Johnson. Literary types can bone up on Junior's legacy by reading Tom Wolfe's famous profile of the driver, entitled "The Last American Hero." Wilkes is a gorgeous, sprawling county with picturesque mountains and rolling farmland, making it a pleasure to spend some time on the same back roads where Junior honed his driving skills running moonshine in the foothills of the Blue Ridge. You can enjoy trout fishing, hiking, and camping at *Stone Mountain State Park*, located at 3042 Frank Parkway in Roaring Gap (28668); call 336-957-8185 or visit www.ncparks.gov/Visit/parks/stmo/main.php. Or you can spend the afternoon boating at *W. Kerr Scott*

Reservoir, located at 499 Reservoir Road in Wilkesboro (28697); call 336-921-3390 or visit www.saw.usace.army.mil/WKScott. On your way south, be sure to drive by the **North Wilkesboro Speedway**, located on U.S. 421. Opened in 1947, the .625-mile oval quickly grew in prominence, eventually hosting two annual Winston Cup (now Sprint Cup) races. But the sport outgrew the track. In 1996, it was purchased by a group including NASCAR mogul Bruton Smith for the purpose of moving those races to larger markets. Though the track is now permanently closed, travelers can get a good view of this one-time racing mecca from the highway.

Continue south on U.S. 421 to Winston-Salem, home of another historic track in NASCAR history, **Bowman Gray Stadium**, located at 1250 South Martin Luther King Jr. Drive (27107). Bowman Gray has been hosting races for more than 50 years, making it the country's longest-operating NASCAR short track. Between 1958 and 1971, the track hosted 29 Grand National races. Still featuring NASCAR-sanctioned racing on Saturday nights during summer, Bowman Gray is a great place to catch the kind of action that made stock-car racing such a popular pastime in the South. The drivers here race for love of the sport, not fame or fortune. Visit www.bowmangrayracing.com or call 336-723-1819 for information about upcoming events.

For a glimpse of another side of NASCAR, drive south on U.S. 52 to the intersection with U.S. 64, where **Childress Vineyards** sprawls across the Piedmont foothills at 1000 Childress Vineyards Road in Lexington (27295). Vineyard owner Richard Childress turned a moderately successful career as a NASCAR driver into a spectacularly successful career as a NASCAR team owner, winning six championships with driver Dale Earnhardt in the 1980s and 1990s. Thanks to NASCAR's popularity, successful team owners and drivers now earn salaries that would astound those original bootleggers. To Childress's credit, he has invested part of his fortune in his hometown of Lexington, an area hit hard by the demise of the furniture and textile industries. The wine at Childress Vineyards has won several awards since its opening in 2004, and the Tuscan-style winery has become a popular destination for both locals and tourists. For information, call 336-236-9463 or visit www.childressvineyards.com.

From Lexington, continue south on U.S. 52 and merge with Interstate 85 headed toward **Kannapolis**. Seven-time Winston Cup champion Richard Petty is "the King" of North Carolina NASCAR drivers, but Dale Earnhardt, who died in the 2001 Daytona 500, is the state's patron saint of racing. Earnhardt's hard-charging style earned him the nickname "the Intimidator," and his legendary number 3 still can be seen on bumper stickers across the Piedmont. Kannapolis is proud of its favorite son and has developed "The Dale Trail" to celebrate his history here. Sites on the trail include the neighborhood where he grew up; Dale Earnhardt Plaza in the center of town, featuring a nine-foot statue of the Intimidator himself; and many other racing-related sites. For a map of "The Dale Trail," visit www.daletrail.com or stop by the Cabarrus County Visitor Center, located just north of Exit 60 off Interstate 85 on Dale Earnhardt Boulevard.

From Kannapolis, head south on U.S. 29 to **Charlotte Motor Speedway**, located at 5555 Concord Parkway South in Concord (28027). Currently home to three NASCAR Sprint Cup races—the Coca-Cola 600, the Bank of America 500, and the NASCAR Sprint All-Star Race—the speedway's 1.5-mile quad-oval track seats 167,000 people, with room for 50,000 more spectators in the infield. Constructed in 1959, it was the first speedway to host nighttime racing (in 1992) and to offer year-round residences (in 1984), with 52 condominiums. Many consider this track the epicenter of NASCAR, as 90 percent of all teams are based within 50 miles of the site. Tours of the facility are available on non-race days. To reach the ticket hot line, call 800-455-FANS. For information, call 704-455-3200.

Charlotte Motor Speedway is just a short drive from the sport's newest mecca, the NASCAR Hall of Fame, scheduled to open in May 2010 in the heart of Uptown Charlotte. From the speedway, head north on Bruton Smith Boulevard to Interstate 85, then follow Interstate 85 South to Interstate 77 South. From Interstate 77 South, take the exit for Interstate 277 East (John Belk Freeway) around downtown Charlotte. Leave Interstate 277 at the Caldwell Street/ South Boulevard exit. The NASCAR Hall of Fame, located at the intersection of Caldwell and Stonewall streets, is visible from the exit.

Boasting futuristic architecture that makes it resemble a racetrack, the **NASCAR Hall of Fame** is to be a 40,000-square-foot facility honoring all things NASCAR. It will include a Hall of Honor, where greats such as Richard Petty will be immortalized. Other attractions will include the Full Throttle Theater, where visitors can see a movie highlighting the sport's past, present, and future; a state-of-the-art racing simulator; the "Week in the Life" exhibit, where visitors will gain a behind-the-scenes look at how a NASCAR team prepares for race day; the "NASCAR Vault," featuring some of the sport's most historic artifacts; the "Heritage Speedway" exhibit, where individual galleries will tell the story of NASCAR's exciting 60-plus-year history; and much more. Admission prices and hours of operation were unavailable at the time of this writing. For the latest information, visit www.nascarhall.com.

Looking to experience a little Charlotte nightlife NASCAR-style? **Dale Earnhardt Jr.'s Whisky River** is located at 210 East Trade Street, seven blocks from the NASCAR Hall of Fame. Thanks to its unique blend of rock and country music, VIP tables, mechanical bull riding, live music, and electrifying DJs, Whisky River is quickly becoming one of Uptown's most popular nightspots. And there's always a chance you might see Junior sipping a brew. For more information, call 704-749-1097 or visit www.whiskyrivercharlotte.com.

The Mountains

Blue Ridge Parkway

1. Cumberland Knob
2. Doughton Park
3. E.B. Jeffress Park
4. Moses Cone Memorial Park
5. Julian Price Memorial Park
6. Linville Falls
7. Crabtree Meadows
8. Craggy Gardens
9. Folk Art Center
10. Mount Pisgah

The Blue Ridge Parkway

By Carolyn Sakowski

The Blue Ridge Parkway is an unusual part of the national parks system. It's really a linear park, stretching 469 miles from Shenandoah National Park in Virginia to Great Smoky Mountains National Park on the North Carolina–Tennessee border.

The parkway is refreshing. Regulations keep the signage to a minimum; what is there is informative and tasteful. A major purpose of the highway's construction was to give men jobs during the Depression. You'll see their clearly identifiable stonework all along the route. In recent years, the Blue Ridge Parkway Foundation and other parties have gone to great lengths to ensure that the pastoral feel of the land is preserved.

One thing you'll notice is that the speed limit is never over 45 miles per hour. The parkway is designed for leisurely driving, with plenty of overlooks along the way. If you're in a hurry, take the regular roads.

It is legal to pull onto the shoulder for a picnic, as long as you make sure your vehicle is completely off the road. On weekends in summer and fall, you'll see lots of people taking advantage of this opportunity.

This chapter provides a few details about some of the sites along the Blue

Ridge Parkway. The parkway actually begins near Charlottesville, Virginia; the markers start with Milepost 0 at Shenandoah National Park. The North Carolina section starts at Milepost 217 at the North Carolina–Virginia line. For information about the parkway, call 828-298-0298 or visit www.nps.gov/blri or www.blueridgeparkway. org. You can pick up a free publication called *Blue Ridge Parkway Trip Planner* at most of the parkway gift shops. It includes maps of all the trails at parkway sites, as well as information about facilities and fishing and bicycling regulations. Be sure to consult www.nps.gov.blri and click on "Closures" before making your trip, as short detours for construction are frequently in effect.

Milepost 217.5—Cumberland Knob is in Alleghany County. The boundary line that divides North Carolina and Virginia was surveyed in 1749 by a group that included Peter Jefferson, Thomas Jefferson's father. Just south of the line is Cumberland Knob Recreation Area, where restrooms, water fountains, picnic tables, and hiking trails are available. You can take a short walk to Cumberland Knob or a two-hour hike into Gully Creek Gorge.

Milepost 218.6—Fox Hunter's Paradise recalls a once-popular sport in the mountains. Men would turn loose their dogs to "run" foxes through the night. Catching one was rare—and not the point. Listening to the "music" of fox hounds calling through the deep woods was what mattered. A picnic table and a hiking trail are located at Fox Hunter's Paradise. You can contact the visitor center here by calling 828-657-8161.

Milepost 229—U.S. 21 intersects the parkway here. Sparta is seven miles west and Roaring Gap four miles east.

Milepost 230—Little Glade Mill Pond offers picnic tables and a short hike around the pond.

Milepost 232.5—Stone Mountain Overlook offers a good view of Stone Mountain State Park, which is covered in the "Recreation" section of the Alleghany County chapter.

Milepost 237.1—Air Bellows Gap is appropriately named; on a windy day, the wind sweeps up from the deep gorge below.

Milepost 238.5—Brinegar Cabin is an original mountain homestead that has been preserved. The farm of Martin and Caroline Joines Brinegar is located to the left. When it is open, you can get a glimpse of old-time life in the mountains. Craft demonstrations are offered at various times; check at Doughton Park for a schedule. Two trails—the 4.4-mile Cedar Rock Trail and the 7.5-mile Bluff Mountain Trail—begin at the far end of the parking lot.

Milepost 238.5–244.7—Doughton Park, named for Congressman Robert Doughton, is one of the parkway's treasures. The park offers the Bluffs Lodge and Coffee Shop, a campground, a gift shop, an excellent network of hiking trails, and wonderful views. The telephone number at the visitor center is 336-372-4499.

Milepost 242—The Alligator Back rest area has a 20-minute walking trail to Bluff Overlook.

Milepost 248.1—N.C. 18 intersects the parkway here. Laurel Springs is two miles west and North Wilkesboro 24 miles east.

Milepost 252.5—Jesse Sheets built a small cabin for his family at Sheets Gap

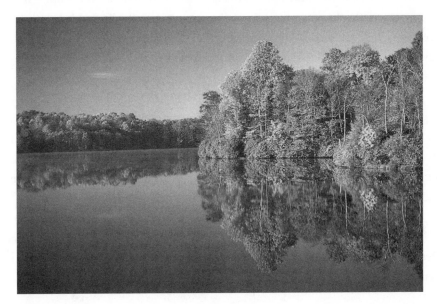

Julian Price Park
COURTESY OF BOONE CONVENTION AND VISITORS BUREAU

around 1815, making this one of the oldest surviving settlers' cabins. An overlook at Sheets Gap is 0.3 mile south; from there, a trail leads back to the cabin.

Milepost 259—Northwest Trading Post is described in the "Special Shopping" section of the Alleghany County chapter.

Milepost 260—At the end of the parking lot is an easy walking trail to Jumpinoff Rock. A small picnic area is also located here.

Milepost 261—N.C. 16 intersects the parkway here. Glendale Springs is five miles west and North Wilkesboro 20 miles east.

Milepost 264.4—The Lump provides sweeping views of the forested foothills below.

Milepost 267—This site overlooks Mount Jefferson State Park, which is covered in the "Recreation" section of the Ashe County chapter.

Milepost 271.9—The Cascades Nature Trail offers a brisk hike through rich pine forests. In late May, the mountain laurel is beautiful here. At the bottom of the trail, a waterfall rolls down the side of the mountain to the lowlands below. Hikers need to exercise caution on the rocks near the waterfall. Even in recent years, people have fallen to their deaths here. Restrooms, water fountains, and picnic tables are available at this site.

Milepost 272.6—E. B. Jeffress Park has plenty of hiking trails, a picnic area, and two historic buildings. One is the Jesse Brown Cabin, built in the mid-1800s. Nearby is Cool Spring Baptist Church, an open-air shelter that was already standing when the Civil War ended in 1865; it was typical of the earliest churches in the region. An overlook here offers a short trail to these structures.

Milepost 276.4—A bridge over the four-lane U.S. 421 graces the entrance to Deep Gap, which is the way into Watauga County from the east. A Civil War entrenchment once stood near where the parkway bridge is today.

Milepost 281.7—Grandview Overlook is exactly what its name implies.

Milepost 285.1—Daniel Boone Trace marks the place where Boone regularly camped and hunted in this area in the 1760s, before opening Kentucky to settlers. A roadside picnic table is located here.

Milepost 289–290—Raven Rocks and Thunder Hill are two exceptional over-looks near Blowing Rock. Raven Rocks offers views of the mountains surrounding the valley of the Watauga River. Thunder Hill's view looks over the valley of the Yadkin River stretching to Lenoir, Hickory, and beyond. Both are popular spots with locals and visitors alike.

Milepost 291.9—U.S. 221/321 intersects the parkway here. Boone is seven miles north and Blowing Rock two miles south.

Milepost 293–295—Moses H. Cone Memorial Park is described in the "Special Shopping" section of the Blowing Rock chapter.

Milepost 295–299—Julian Price Park offers a campground, an amphitheater, and canoe rentals on Price Lake, plus a host of trails to hike. The trail around 47-acre Price Lake is relatively level. The campground's 197 spaces are offered on a first-come, first-served basis. Cold water and grills are available, but electricity is not. A dump station is located near the office. The office is normally open from 8 A.M. to 8 P.M.; campers may self-register after hours and at times when no ranger is available. Price Lake offers excellent fishing. It is classified as "general trout waters"; fishermen may use natural or artificial baits but no fresh eggs or live or dead fish or amphibians. A state license is required, but a trout stamp is not.

Milepost 298–305—Grandfather Mountain is the crown jewel of the parkway. For over 50 years, owner Hugh Morton fought the government over the environmental impact its original road plans would have caused this landmark—and visitors are glad he did. The Linn Cove Viaduct, which almost rivals the mountain itself in beauty, was the compromise the two sides found. You can read more about Grandfather Mountain in the "Recreation" section of the Banner Elk, Beech Mountain, and Linville chapter.

Milepost 304.4—The Linn Cove Viaduct is one of the engineering marvels of our age, and the view from it is unmatched in the eastern United States. The Linn Cove Viaduct Trail leads beneath the viaduct and gives a true appreciation of this

Linn Cove Viaduct
PHOTOGRAPH BY CAROLYN SAKOWSKI

architectural masterpiece. The visitor center here has displays, books, videos, and restrooms.

Milepost 305.2—U.S. 221 intersects the parkway here. Linville is three miles west and the entrance to Grandfather Mountain one mile west.

Milepost 306—Grandfather Mountain Overlook offers a view of the mountain's southern side, which resembles a bird of prey. That explains why the Cherokees called it Tanawha, meaning "hawk." One of the best trails in the area is the Tanawha Trail, which extends from Milepost 305.5 for 13.5 miles toward Price Lake. If you can hike only a short part of the trail, try the section off the Rough Ridge parking area near Milepost 303.

Milepost 308.2—Flat Rock Overlook has a short nature trail that leads to a view of the Linville Valley and Grandfather Mountain.

Milepost 310—Lost Cove Cliffs Overlook offers one of the best vantage points for seeing the Brown Mountain Lights. In recent years, the haze that appears on most summer evenings has prevented visitors from witnessing the mysterious lights moving along the ridge in the distance. No one has ever explained what causes these lights, but the tales that have grown up around them make great campfire stories.

Milepost 312—N.C. 181 intersects the parkway here. Pineola is two miles north and Morganton 32 miles southeast.

Milepost 316.3—Linville Falls is covered in the "Recreation" section of the chapter on Banner Elk, Beech Mountain, and Linville. The Linville Falls Visitor Center has a gift shop, a picnic area, and a bridge from which you can fish in the Linville River; the number for the visitor center is 828-765-1045. The Linville Falls community is three miles south. Marion is 24 miles south via U.S. 221.

Milepost 320.7—Chestoa View offers a good view of Humpback Mountain.

Milepost 331—The Museum of North Carolina Minerals is described in the "Museums and Science Centers" section of the chapter on Spruce Pine and Burnsville. Spruce Pine is six miles north and Marion 14 miles south. The Overmountain Victory National Historic Trail crosses the parkway at Gillespie Gap, near the museum. This trail commemorates the campaign leading up to the American victory over the British at Kings Mountain in 1780.

Milepost 334—N.C. 226A intersects the parkway at Little Switzerland.

Milepost 339.5—Crabtree Meadows offers a 250-acre park that includes a picnic area and a comfort station. The focus of the park is the 40-minute hike to Crabtree Falls.

Milepost 344—N.C. 80 intersects the parkway at Buck Creek Gap. Burnsville is 16 miles north and Marion 16 miles south.

Milepost 355.4—N.C. 128 leads to Mount Mitchell State Park, described in the "Recreation" section of the chapter on Spruce Pine and Burnsville.

Milepost 364.4—The Craggy Gardens Visitor Center offers information, exhibits, a picnic area, a comfort station, and self-guided tours. In June, the rhododendron gardens here are spectacular.

Crabtree Falls at Crabtree Meadows
COURTESY OF BOONE CONVENTION AND VISITORS BUREAU

Milepost 377.4—N.C. 694 intersects the parkway here. Asheville is eight miles west.

Milepost 382—The Folk Art Center is described in the "Special Shopping" section of the Asheville chapter.

Milepost 382.6—U.S. 70 intersects the parkway here. It is one mile to Oteen, five miles to Asheville, and 10 miles to Black Mountain.

Milepost 384—The Blue Ridge Parkway Destination Center has museum-quality exhibits, a 22-foot interactive map, and a 24-minute film about the parkway.

Milepost 384.7—U.S. 74A intersects the parkway here. Asheville is three miles west. Chimney Rock, Bat Cave, and Lake Lure lie to the east.

Milepost 388.8—U.S. 25 intersects the parkway here. Asheville is five miles north and Hendersonville 17 miles south.

Milepost 393.6—N.C. 191 intersects the parkway here. Asheville is six miles north and Hendersonville 20 miles south.

Milepost 408.6—Mount Pisgah, which was part of the 100,000 acres donated from George Vanderbilt's Biltmore Estate, offers a campground, a picnic area, trails, an inn, a restaurant, and a service station. The 5,749-foot peak is visible in the distance.

Milepost 412—U.S. 276 intersects the parkway at Wagon Road Gap. Brevard is 18 miles south, Cruso eight miles north, and Waynesville 22 miles northwest. On the way to Brevard, you can visit the Cradle of Forestry in America.

Milepost 417—Looking Glass Rock is a 3,969-foot summit whose sheer cliffs give it its name.

Milepost 418.8—Graveyard Fields Overlook has a 2.3-mile loop trail to Yellowstone Falls.

Milepost 422.4—From the Devil's Courthouse parking area, a strenuous half-mile hike leads to the Devil's Courthouse itself. The Cherokees believe this 5,462-foot mountain was the location of the giant Judaculla's courtroom.

Milepost 423.2—N.C. 215 intersects the parkway at Beech Gap. Waynesville is 24 miles north and Rosman 17 miles south.

Milepost 431—At the Haywood-Jackson Overlook, a 1.5-mile self-guided loop trail leads to the summit of Richland Balsam, which is the highest point on the parkway, measuring 6,047 feet.

Milepost 431.4—Richland Balsam Overlook is located here.

Milepost 443.1—U.S. 74/23 intersects the parkway at Balsam Gap. Waynesville is seven miles east and Sylva 12 miles west.

Milepost 451.2—At Waterrock Knob Overlook, you'll find an information center, a comfort station, a trail to the knob, and a four-state view.

Milepost 455.7—U.S. 19 intersects the parkway at Soco Gap. Cherokee is 12 miles west and Maggie Valley five miles east.

Milepost 458.2—From here, Heintooga Ridge Road Spur goes 1.3 miles to

Mile High Overlook. It is 12 miles to the Great Smoky Mountains National Park Campground.

Milepost 461.9—Big Witch Overlook is located here.

Milepost 469.1—Great Smoky Mountains National Park begins at the junction with U.S. 441. Cherokee is two miles south and Gatlinburg, Tennessee, 29 miles north.

The High Country

Alleghany County

Ashe County

Boone

Blowing Rock

Banner Elk, Beech Mountain,
    and Linville

Spruce Pine and Burnsville

By Carolyn Sakowski

T his book's definition of the High Country differs slightly from that employed by the North Carolina High Country Host organization. This section covers Alleghany, Ashe, Watauga, Avery, Mitchell, and Yancey counties.

In this northern portion of North Carolina's Appalachian Mountains, you'll find the highest peaks not only in the state but in the entire eastern United States. You'll discover a booming tourism industry thanks to the cool summer temperatures, the vibrant fall foliage, and the winter skiing. All of the places mentioned here are within an easy day's drive of each other.

Although many of the top attractions—Grandfather Mountain, the New River, the Blowing Rock, Linville Falls—have remained the same for millions of years, the last three decades have brought dramatic changes to the rest of the area. When the tourists began to arrive, they liked what they saw so much that they bought mountain property and built summer or retirement homes. As a result, many of the natural vistas have disappeared. It's a double-edged sword. While longtime residents lament

Tweetsie Railroad
COURTESY OF BOONE CONVENTION AND VISITORS BUREAU

the influx of "outsiders," they now have amenities they could not have imagined a few decades ago. Residents not only don't have to drive 30 miles to buy groceries or an alcoholic beverage, they can now get espresso and the Sunday *New York Times*—on the same Sunday as in New York—a few minutes from almost anywhere.

Speaking of alcoholic beverages, the liquor laws in these mountain counties are highly inconsistent. Some resorts have been creative in procuring legislative exemptions that allow them to serve alcohol. Some townships have voted to allow it, while people are unable to purchase even beer or wine a few miles away. If having access to alcoholic beverages is important to your vacation, you might want to check on the liquor laws where you plan to stay and dine.

You should also know that, even though you may be leaving 90-degree temperatures to come to the mountains, you'll still need a jacket or sweater in the evenings. The rule of thumb is to expect a five-degree change in temperature for every 1,000 feet of change in elevation. You might also want to throw in rain gear. Many a clear, sunny day has a short late-afternoon shower here. These cool days and frequent showers ensure that the region's wildflowers and cultivated mountain gardens are prolific. You'll be struck by the abundance of vibrant colors.

The last few decades have brought an explosion of outdoor activities in the mountains. Skiing, golf, whitewater rafting, mountain biking, and hiking have all attracted thousands of people. For those who prefer less physical "exercise," the area has also seen a boom in shopping outlets, gourmet restaurants, first-rate resorts, and bed-and-breakfasts in wonderful restored homes. Although I recommend some specific places to stay, all of these counties have scores of individual cabins and condominiums for rent. Contact the appropriate chamber of commerce to be put in touch with realtors.

JUST THE FACTS

You can get visitor information from North Carolina High Country Host, at 1700 Blowing Rock Road/U.S. 321 in Boone (28607); call 800-438-7500 or 828-264-1299 or visit www.highcountryhost.com. This regional visitor center promotes tourism in Watauga, Ashe, Avery, Alleghany, Mitchell, and Wilkes counties. It is open Monday through Saturday from 9 A.M. to 5 P.M. and Sunday from 10 A.M. to 4 P.M.

In fall 2009, a new state-of-the-art visitor center featuring the latest in green technology opened near North Wilkesboro on the north side of U.S. 421 east of the Edgewood Road overpass. The center offers information for 10 counties in the region.

Stone Mountain
PHOTOGRAPH BY CAROLYN SAKOWSKI

Alleghany County

Alleghany County was once known as "the Lost Province" because of its early isolation. Even today, the county has a year-round population of only 10,000 people. But it is finally starting to reap the benefits of its former isolation. The local chamber of commerce now touts the county as "the Unspoiled Province," and that's exactly what it is. Here, you'll find scenic views still largely unmarred by progress. As you drive along Alleghany County's two-lane highways, you'll be struck by the number of two-story white clapboard farmhouses with wraparound porches sitting smack dab in the middle of large working farms. You won't see the clutter of billboards and the urban sprawl that come with national chain stores and gimmicky roadside gift shops.

Nestled among mountains that reach 3,000 to 4,000 feet, the county is surrounded by 20,000 acres of national and state parks, including Doughton Park, Stone Mountain State Park, New River State Park, and Grayson Highlands State Park in Virginia. The Blue Ridge Parkway weaves along the edge of the county for 30 miles.

If you want to see the mountains like they used to be, you'd better hurry to Alleghany County before the rest of the world discovers it.

JUST THE FACTS

To reach Alleghany County, you can travel on N.C. 18 or U.S. 21, which intersect in the county seat, Sparta. A short trip on U.S. 21 from Interstate 77 leads to Roaring Gap and Sparta. Interstate 77 offers quick access from Roanoke, Virginia, which is 115 miles away, and Charlotte, which is 105 miles away. To the east, Winston-Salem is 75 miles from Sparta.

For visitor information, write the Alleghany County Chamber of Commerce at 58 South Main Street (P.O. Box 1237) in Sparta (28675). Or you can call 800-372-5473 or 336-372-5473 or visit www.sparta-nc.com.

The *Alleghany News* is the area's weekly newspaper. Its website is www.alleghanynews.com.

Things to Do

Recreation

Stone Mountain State Park is located in Alleghany and Wilkes counties seven miles southwest of Roaring Gap. From U.S. 21, turn onto Traphill Road (S.R. 1002), which will take you to the John P. Frank Parkway. If you're coming from the west, take N.C. 18 North and turn right on N.C. 268 East. Go three miles, turn left on Airport Road, go six miles to Traphill Road, and turn left. Follow Traphill Road for 12 miles to the John P. Frank Parkway and turn left. The address is 3042 John P. Frank Parkway in Roaring Gap (28668).

Located on 14,100 acres, the park offers four easily accessed waterfalls, miles of trout streams, two handicapped-accessible fishing piers, hiking and horseback-riding trails, and a historic mountain homestead. However, the big attraction is Stone Mountain itself, a 600-foot granite dome. Climbing on the cliffs is permitted in designated areas, but all climbers must register and possess a valid rock-climbing permit.

Campsites are available for a fee. The campground has a wash house with hot showers; some sites have utility hookups. Campers cannot leave the park after the gates are closed. The park is open from 8 A.M. to 6 P.M. November through February, from 6 A.M. to 7 P.M. in March and October, from 8 A.M. to 8 P.M. in April, May, and September, and from 8 A.M. to 9 P.M. June through August. For information, call 336-957-8185 or visit www.ncparks.gov.

Doughton Park is part of the Blue Ridge Parkway. It has over 30 miles of hiking trails ranging from modest strolls to all-day outings. Horse trails, fishing, camping, and picnicking are all offered. See the chapter on the Blue Ridge Parkway for more information.

New River State Park is located in Ashe and Alleghany counties. The Alleghany County Access Area can be reached only by canoe. Camping and canoeing on the New are big draws here. For more information, see the chapter on Ashe County and the sidebar about the New River.

Two local operations bill themselves as canoe campgrounds. *River Camp USA* has sites for RVs and tents. It offers full hookups, picnic tables, a country store, a playground, a laundry, and hot showers. The proprietors rent canoes and inner tubes and provide shuttle service. For information, write the camp at P.O. Box 9 in Piney Creek (28663), call 800-RIVERCAMP or 336-359-CAMP, or visit www.rivercamp. net. *New River Canoe and Campground*, located at 628 U.S. 21 North six miles north of Sparta (28675), has grassy and shady spots along the river. All sites have a picnic table, a lantern post, and a fire ring. The campground offers RV hookups, cabins, a camp store, a restaurant, a playground, and pedal boats for rent. Guests can make arrangements for canoeing instruction and day or overnight canoe trips. For information, call 336-372-8793.

Two Alleghany County golf courses—*New River Country Club* (336-372-4869) in Sparta and *Olde Beau Golf Club* (336-363-3333) in Roaring Gap—allow nonmembers to play.

Nearby Virginia offers two exceptional opportunities for bicycling. The *Virginia Creeper Trail* and *New River Trail State Park* are both rails-to-trails venues that are perfect for inexperienced riders, children, and even experienced cyclists who want to test their stamina. Unfortunately, Sparta does not have any bike-rental establishments, but you can make arrangements in the Virginia community of Damascus. For information about the Virginia Creeper Trail, visit www.vacreepertrail.com.

Places to Stay

Resorts, Hotels, and Motels

Bluffs Lodge. Moderate. 45356 Blue Ridge Parkway in Laurel Springs, 28644

(336-372-4499; www.blueridgeresort.com, then click "Bluffs Lodge"). The draw at this rustic motel, located in Doughton Park at Milepost 241, is the sweeping views from the balconies and patios. In exchange, guests leave behind telephones and televisions. The lodge is open from May through October.

Freeborne's Eatery and Lodge. Moderate. Near Milepost 248 at 14300 N.C. 18 South in Laurel Springs, 28644 (877-528-7356 or 336-359-8008; www.freebornes. com). The intersection of N.C. 18 and the Blue Ridge Parkway has become a magnet for motorcyclists, but not the Hell's Angels variety. You're more likely to find yourself next to a doctor from Charlotte who rode up for the day on his BMW. Nearby Station's Inn has been a motorcyclists' favorite for years. In 2009, Freeborne's opened across the street. It has a renovated 1950s-style motel as well as a restaurant and bar. On weekends, live music is performed in the field behind the motel.

Station's Inn. Moderate. 14317 N.C. 18 in Laurel Springs, 28644 (336-359-2888; www.stationsinn.com). Located at Milepost 248 on the Blue Ridge Parkway, this motel offers wood-paneled rooms with 1950s-style furniture. A country store and restaurant are on the premises. The restaurant will cater all-you-can-eat cookouts for groups of 20 or more.

Note: Next to Freeborne's and across from Station's Inn is a store worth checking out. *Wild Woody's Store*, at 14234 N.C. 18 South in Laurel Springs (28644), has been owned and operated by Linda Woody since 1971. Her family has lived in this area for seven generations. The store has a collection of vintage albums for sale that will bring back memories to anyone alive in the 1960s and 1970s. Linda operates a small campground behind the store. For information, call 336-984-8088.

Inns and Bed-and-Breakfasts

Harmony Hill. Deluxe/Expensive. 1740 Halsey Knob Road in Sparta, 28675 (336-372-6868; harmonyhillbnb.com). Harmony Hill is eight miles from Sparta; a map is available on the website. This beautifully restored Victorian home has an incredible view of the surrounding countryside. It offers four bedrooms and a carriage house. Each bedroom is air-conditioned and has a private bath. Some rooms have Jacuzzis; most have fireplaces with gas logs; all have ceiling fans, televisions, and

Doughton-Hall Bed-and-Breakfast
PHOTOGRAPH BY CAROLYN SAKOWSKI

telephones. Breakfast is served in the dining room, in the gazebo, or on the porch. Pets and children under 12 are not allowed.

Doughton-Hall Bed-and-Breakfast. Expensive. 12668 N.C. 18 South in Laurel Springs, 28644 (336-359-2341; doughtonhall@hotmail.com). This is the historic residence of Robert L. Doughton, who served in the United States House of Representatives from 1911 to 1953, during which time he was the powerful head of the House Ways and Means Committee. Doughton was largely responsible for bringing the Blue Ridge Parkway to this area. Located 13 miles from Sparta and 1.7 miles from the intersection of the Blue Ridge Parkway and N.C. 18, his Queen Anne–style home dates to 1898. It is listed on the National Register of Historic Places. It has four guest rooms, three with private baths and Jacuzzis. Wine and hors d'oeuvres are served nightly, and a full country breakfast is offered each morning.

Mountain View Lodge & Cabins. Expensive. 164 Mountain View Lodge Drive in Glendale Springs, 28629 (336-207-7677; www.mtnviewlodge.com). One unusual thing about this establishment is that guests are allowed to bring pets if they are staying in one of the cabin buildings. Located near Milepost 256 on the Blue Ridge Parkway, Mountain View has two types of cabins—one features a bedroom and loft, the other two bedrooms and a loft. The cabins sleep four to eight people. The main lodge is available for large groups.

Places to Eat

Brown's Family Restaurant. Inexpensive. 115 Jones Street in Sparta, 28675 (336-372-3400). This family-owned restaurant offers steaks, seafood, and chicken dishes. Breakfast, lunch, and dinner are served Tuesday through Saturday.

The Pizzeria. Inexpensive. In the Trojan Village Shopping Center at 665 South Main Street in Sparta, 28675 (336-372-8885). This restaurant serves pizza, subs, and sandwiches, but it's also known for its great chicken pie, which comes with the luncheon buffet on Sunday and Wednesday. A lunch buffet and dinner are served Tuesday through Sunday.

The New River
PHOTOGRAPH BY CAROLYN SAKOWSKI

The New River—North Carolina's American Heritage River

The New River, which some say is 300 million years old, is supposedly the oldest river in North America. It begins in Watauga County and is the only river in the eastern United States that flows northward to the Midwest. The North Fork and South Fork of the river join a few miles south of the North Carolina–Virginia border. From there, the river continues through Virginia and West Virginia.

Archaeological investigations suggest that humans have been in the region for at least 10,000 years. Arrowheads, pottery shards, and stone axes indicate the Canawhay Indian tribe occupied the river valley during the precolonial period. Evidence also exists of hunting trails used by Creeks, Shawnees, and Cherokees moving north along the New River to the Ohio River.

The first European to see the river was probably Colonel Abraham Wood, who came seeking trade with the Indi-

ans in 1654. Before the 1770s, long hunters were probably the only white men to venture into the region. Originally known as Wood's River, it was renamed the New by Peter Jefferson, the father of Thomas Jefferson, when he surveyed the North Carolina–Virginia boundary in 1749.

In 1752, Bishop Augustus Spangenberg, an early traveler sent by the Moravian Church to find land for a settlement, wrote the following: "For several days we followed the river in the hope that it would lead us out, we found ourselves only deeper in the wilderness, for the river ran now north, now south, now east, now west, in short to all points of the compass! Finally, we decided to leave the river and take a course between east and south, crossing the mountains as best we could." If you look at the course of the river on a modern map, you'll see exactly why Bishop Spangenberg was so frustrated.

In 1965, the Appalachian Power Company applied for a license to dam the river. In response to unprecedented grass-roots opposition, the North Carolina General Assembly declared a 26.5-mile stretch from the river's confluence with Dog Creek to the Virginia line a state scenic river. In April 1976, the New was designated a national wild and scenic river, thus ensuring that it will remain untouched. On July 30, 1998, President Bill Clinton and Vice President Al Gore showed up with a group of dignitaries to proclaim the New an American heritage river.

The centerpiece of New River State Park, the river is a popular spot for camping, canoeing, picnicking, and fishing. The easy flow and mild rapids make it perfect for inexperienced paddlers. The best months for high water levels are May and June; August and September are usually the low-flow months.

Those wishing to canoe can leave their vehicles at the Wagoner Road Access Area, located at River Mile 26, eight miles southeast of Jefferson; the access area can be reached via S.R. 1590 off N.C. 88 some 1.2 miles east of the intersection of N.C. 16 and N.C. 88. A second parking area is at the U.S. 221 Access Area, located at River Mile 15, eight miles northeast of Jefferson; it

may be reached via U.S. 221. The third option is Kings Creek Access Area at River Mile 7. The directions to this access are complex; you can find them on the New River State Park website, listed below. Picnic areas and primitive campsites with tables and grills are located at the three access areas. The Wagoner Road Access Area offers bathrooms with hot showers. The U.S. 221 Access Area has 20 drive-in campsites, all with full hookups. It also offers a visitor center and a bathhouse with hot showers.

The Alleghany County Access Area can be reached only by canoe. It has canoe campsites, pit toilets, and a pump for drinking water. Canoes can also be launched from several bridges and roads that cross the river.

The South Fork and North Fork of the New offer excellent smallmouth and redeye bass fishing. Trout fishing is excellent in the small tributaries, most of which are stocked regularly with rainbow and brown trout. Make sure you get that fishing license!

For more information, contact the chambers of commerce in Ashe and Alleghany counties. You can write New River State Park at P.O. Box 48 in Jefferson (28640); call 336-982-2587 or visit www.ncsparks.net/neri.html.

Christmas tree farm
COURTESY OF BOONE CONVENTION
AND VISITORS BUREAU

Ashe County

The farther south you travel from the Virginia line, the more you'll witness tourism development and the proliferation of vacation homes. Ashe County lies between Alleghany and Watauga counties not only geographically but developmentally as well. Here, you'll see more chain motels and urban sprawl than in Alleghany, but it's nothing like in Watauga.

Thanks to its cheese factory and its frescoes, Ashe County has long been a great day trip from anywhere in the High Country. Because of its canoe access areas for New River State Park, it has also been a logical place for outfitters to spring up. This is one of the major areas for the growing of Fraser fir Christmas trees, so the landscape is dotted with uniform rows of evergreens along the hillsides.

The town of Jefferson, the county seat, was founded in 1800 at the base of Mount Jefferson. In 1917, a group of investors founded West Jefferson, which attracted the railroad. Jefferson subsequently went into decline, leaving West Jefferson as the economic center of the county.

JUST THE FACTS
|||||||||||||||||||||||||||||||||||||||||||||||||||||||||||||||

To reach Ashe County's twin cities of Jefferson and West Jefferson, take U.S. 221 from Deep Gap, U.S. 421 from the Blue Ridge Parkway, or N.C. 194 or N.C. 16 from Virginia.

For visitor information, contact the Ashe County Chamber of Commerce at One North Jefferson Avenue, Suite C (P.O. Box 31) in West Jefferson (28694). A separate visitor center is located at the corner of Main Street and Jefferson Avenue. Visit www.ashechamber.com or call 888-343-2743 or 336-846-9550.

The *Jefferson Post* is the area's weekly newspaper; its website is www.jeffersonpost.com. *Ashe Mountain Times*, a free weekly, is distributed throughout the county.

Things to Do

Historic Places, Gardens, and Tours
||||||||||||||||||||||||||||||||||||||||||||||||||||||||||||||||||||||||||||||||||||||||||||||||||||||||||

Located at 106 East Main on the corner of Fourth Street in downtown West Jefferson (28694) is North Carolina's only cheese manufacturer, **Ashe County Cheese Company**. This establishment has been producing cheese since 1930. You can see cheese being made; call ahead, since the cheese-making schedule is subject to change. Be sure to stop at the wine-and-cheese shop, too. The plant and store are open Monday through Saturday. For more information, call 336-246-2501 or visit www.ashecountycheese.com.

Cultural Offerings
|||||||||||||||||||||||||||||||||||||||||||||||||||||||||||

Just outside West Jefferson are signs for the frescoes at **St. Mary's Episcopal Church** in Beaver Creek. Less than 10 miles to the east on N.C. 16 in Glendale Springs is the larger fresco at **Holy Trinity Episcopal Church**. All were created by North Carolina native Ben Long and his helpers. While at Holy Trinity, be sure to see the columbarium, located downstairs. If you've ever wondered where your cremated ashes might be stored, the columbarium provides an interesting option. For more information, write the Parish of the Holy Communion at P.O. Box 177 in Glendale Springs (28629); call 336-982-3076 or visit www.churchofthefrescoes.com.

St. Mary's Episcopal Church
PHOTOGRAPH BY CAROLYN SAKOWSKI

Holy Trinity Episcopal Church
PHOTOGRAPH BY CAROLYN SAKOWSKI

Special Shopping

The *Northwest Trading Post*, at Milepost 259 on the Blue Ridge Parkway, is a gift shop whose mission is to keep alive the old mountain crafts. The shop sells handmade crafts from over 500 craftsmen from 11 northwestern North Carolina counties. You'll find woodcarvings, baskets, woven materials, handmade toys, pottery, baked goods, jellies, jams, musical instruments, bird feeders, and even country hams. The shop is open from 9:30 A.M. to 5:30 P.M. daily from May to October. For more information, write the gift shop at 414 Trading Post Road in Glendale Springs (28629) or call 336-982-2543.

The *New River General Store* is located at 10725 U.S. 221 North, where the highway crosses the New River between Jefferson and Sparta. This is the oldest continuously operating store in the area. Visitors can browse antiques, buy old-fashioned candies, and purchase gifts, groceries, and cheese. The store is open daily from 8:30 A.M. to 6 P.M. New River Outfitters runs its canoe trips out of this store. For information, write the store at P.O. Box 433 in Jefferson (28640). Or you can call 800-982-9190 or 336-982-9192 or visit www.canoethenew.com.

Recreation

Mount Jefferson State Natural Area, located on Mount Jefferson Road off U.S. 221 at West Jefferson, is a relatively undeveloped park covering 539 acres. It offers picnicking and a few short trails, but the big attraction is the view. Mount Jefferson rises abruptly more than 1,600 feet above the surrounding landscape. Visitors can see the farms and forests of a great part of the county from its summit. For information, write the natural area at P.O. Box 48 in Jefferson (28640). Or you can call 336-246-9653 or visit www.ncparks.gov.

The big pastimes in Ashe County are canoeing and tubing on the New River. Because the water flows so gently, the river is safe even for young children. Local outfitters give lessons and provide inner tubes, canoes, safety equipment, and shuttle service. Contact *Zaloo's Canoes* (800-535-4027; www.zaloos.com), at 3874 N.C. 16 South in Jefferson (28640); *New River Outfitters* (800-982-9190; www.canoethenew. com), headquartered in the New River General Store (see earlier entry); *River Camp USA* (800-748-3722 or 336-359-2267; www.rivercampusa.com), at P.O. Box 9 in Piney Creek (28663); or *Riverside Canoe* (336-982-9439; www.riversidecanoeing.com), at 2966 Garvey Bridge Road in Crumpler (28617).

See the sidebar about the New River for information on *New River State Park*.

Seasonal Events

Christmas in July is held in downtown West Jefferson during the weekend nearest the Fourth of July. Workers in the area's Christmas tree industry challenge each other for cash and prizes in a variety of competitions. Visitors can hear live music and purchase crafts and other items from the vendors lining the streets. Call 336-846-9196 or visit www.christmasinjuly.info.

Resorts, Hotels, and Motels

Jeremy's Lodge at Jefferson Landing. Deluxe/Expensive. Off N.C. 16 (P.O. Box 110) in Jefferson, 28640 (800-292-6274 or 336-982-4449; www.jeffersonlandingclub. com). All the rooms here have a balcony or deck with a view of the golf course and mountains. Also available are suites featuring a sitting area, a wet bar, and a stone fireplace. Guests may use the golf course, the club's dining facilities, the swimming pool, the fitness center, and the tennis courts.

Best Western Eldreth Inn. Moderate. 829 East Main Street in Jefferson, 28640 (800-221-8802 or 336-246-8845; www.bestwestern.com/eldrethinnatmtjefferson). Located at the intersection of U.S. 221 and N.C. 88, this locally owned motel offers the basic amenities, including free wireless Internet. Some chains are starting to come into the area, but this motel has been in Jefferson for years.

Inns and Bed-and-Breakfasts

River House Country Inn. Deluxe/Expensive. 1896 Old Field Creek Road in Grassy Creek, 28631 (336-982-2109; www.riverhousenc.com). This inn offers nine guest rooms, each with a private bath and a Jacuzzi. Most rooms have views of the mountains and/or the river; some have private porches. Two cabins beside the mill-pond are also available. The inn is situated on 170 acres with a mile of river front; the property includes two tennis courts. Coffee and tea are left by guests' doors in the morning. A full breakfast is served. The inn frequently hosts special culinary events and live music in the evenings.

Buffalo Tavern Bed-and-Breakfast. Expensive. 958 West Buffalo Road in West Jefferson, 28694 (877-615-9678 or 336-877-9080; www.buffalotavern.com). This Southern Colonial home, originally a tavern, was the place to go during the 1920s. Today, it offers three guest rooms, each with a private bath, a fireplace with gas logs, and a claw-foot tub. A guest refrigerator, complimentary beverages, and laundry service are available. Satellite TV and wireless Internet are provided. A full country breakfast is served each morning. A two-night minimum stay is required for some weekends and holidays. Children are not allowed.

Places to Eat

River House Inn and Restaurant. Expensive. 1896 Old Field Creek Road in Grassy Creek, 28631 (336-982-2109; www.riverhousenc.com). The River House Inn features country French cuisine and regional fare. Beer and wine are offered; reservations are required. Dinner is served Wednesday through Saturday from April through December. On Sunday afternoons, the inn's salon series offers a lecture, a film, or a performance of music or poetry, followed by a four-course chef's choice menu.

Matthew's 102 North. Expensive/Inexpensive. 102 North Jefferson Avenue in West Jefferson, 28694 (336-846-4102; www.matthews102north.com). Lunch at Matthew's features burgers, sandwiches, and salads. The dinner entrées lean more toward gourmet dining. Lunch and dinner are served from Tuesday through Saturday; a good brunch is offered on Sunday.

Fraser's. Moderate. 108 South Jefferson Avenue in West Jefferson, 28694 (336-246-5222; www.frasersrestaurant.com). For lunch, this establishment offers freshly made soups, sandwiches, and salads. For dinner, guests can order fresh seafood, steaks, pasta dishes, and nightly specials. Beer and wine are available. Lunch is served Thursday through Tuesday and dinner Thursday through Saturday.

Shatley Springs Inn. Moderate. 407 Shatley Springs Road in Crumpler, 28617 (336-982-2236; www.shatleysprings.com). Located off N.C. 16 five miles north of Jefferson, this is one of those all-the-home-cooking-you-can-eat places. Its fixed-price meals include fried chicken, country ham, tons of vegetables, and homemade cobbler. In summer and fall, you may have to wait for a table. Luckily, you can try one of the rocking chairs on the front porch. Breakfast, lunch, and dinner are served daily from April 15 through November 30.

The Last Supper at Holy Trinity Episcopal Church
COURTESY OF BOONE CONVENTION AND VISITORS BUREAU

The Frescoes

Though St. Mary's Episcopal Church now houses one of the area's main tourist attractions, it was not always the focus of community pride.

Milnor Jones was an Episcopal minister and missionary who organized the first Episcopal church in Ashe County, the Church of St. Simon the Zealot. On June 21, 1896, Bishop Joseph Blount Cheshire came from Raleigh to conduct services. He was met at the church by an unexpected greeting committee. Cheshire wrote, "I was assaulted and forcibly prevented from entering this building by a mob of between fifty and one hundred men which had been got-

ten together for the express purpose of preventing our service that day. And the reason they gave for this action was that they 'did not like Mr. Jones' doctrine' and they understood that I taught the same doctrine." Cheshire further noted that he "met with the most violent opposition, accompanied with bitter abuse from Methodists and Baptists, especially the latter."

Milnor Jones went on to organize a school at Beaver Creek. His quaint Church of St. Simon the Zealot was later renamed St. Mary's. It was eventually abandoned for lack of funds until a different sort of notoriety came its way.

The Mystery of Faith at St. Mary's Episcopal Church
PHOTOGRAPH BY CAROLYN SAKOWSKI

In the summer of 1980, artist Ben Long returned to the United States to train others in a dying art form. For seven years, he had studied fresco painting in Italy with a master of Renaissance technique. Long took on as many as 20 apprentices at one time in Ashe County and used two Episcopal churches in the area as his studios.

Fresco painting is a tedious and complicated process, which explains its rarity in today's world. Ground natural pigment is mixed with distilled water, thinned with lime, and painted on damp plaster. As the plaster dries, the lime and pigment bind chemically, so that the wall literally becomes the painting. This unusual technique produces an interesting effect—many say that fresco walls seem to glow. The drawback is that the pigment is absorbed the moment brush touches plaster, so a mistake can necessitate the removal of an entire section of wall.

Ben Long imported lime from the same site in Florence, Italy, that Michelangelo used when working on the Sistine Chapel. He mixed it with North Carolina sand to make his plaster. Local people served as models for the figures in his frescoes; Long himself took the role of Doubting Thomas. The results are so impressive that thousands of people a year visit the out-of-the-way chapels to view the frescoes. Those at St. Mary's are *Mary, Great with Child; John the Baptist;* and *The Mystery of Faith*. At Holy Trinity Episcopal Church is Long's interpretation of the Last Supper, which occupies the entire front wall. Despite frequent busloads of tourists, both churches are worthwhile stops.

Over the years, Long has continued to create frescoes throughout the state. An official Ben F. Long Fresco Trail includes frescoes in seven counties. For more information, visit www. benlongfrescotrail.com.

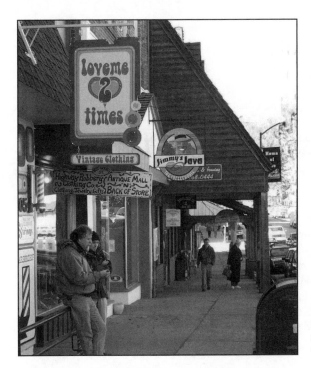

Downtown Boone
COURTESY OF BOONE CONVENTION AND
VISITORS BUREAU

Boone

Boone is home to Appalachian State University, a branch of the University of North Carolina that has seen amazing growth in recent years. If you haven't visited the campus in the last decade, you won't recognize it. Along with the growth of the university has come urban sprawl. Boone is where everyone who lives in the area does their regular shopping. The town has an indoor mall and several strip shopping centers, as well as all the usual chain motels and eateries. But it also boasts a lively downtown area that has been honored for its revitalization. It was recognized by the National Trust for Historic Preservation as a national Main Street center, a highly coveted honor.

This chapter also includes scenic Valle Crucis, a North Carolina rural historic district. In 1915, local historian John Preston Arthur wrote, "There is a dreamy spell which hangs over this little valley." Although many remember the spell as being stronger a few decades ago, the area still retains its mystique. Much of the history of Valle Crucis revolves around the work of the Episcopal Church. Visitors can still see the community's historic buildings—a cabin built by Bishop L. Silliman Ives, a conference center, and a small church. The other noteworthy places that draw tourists to Valle Crucis are the Mast Farm Inn and the Mast General Store complex. For more information, visit www.vallecrucis.com.

JUST THE FACTS

To get to Boone, you can take either U.S. 321 or U.S. 421. Both N.C. 105 and N.C. 194 terminate here. You can reach Valle Crucis by traveling N.C. 105 from Boone and turning onto S.R. 1112 (Broadstone Road).

For visitor information, contact the Boone Chamber of Commerce/Boone Convention and Visitors Bureau, at 208 Howard Street (28607); call 800-852-9506 or 828-264-3516 or visit www.VisitBooneNC.com. This office is not open on weekends, so a better source is North Carolina High Country Host, at 1700 Blowing Rock Road in Boone (28607); call 800-438-7500 or visit www.highcountryhost.com. Blowing Rock Road is U.S. 321, which leads to Blowing Rock. This stretch contains most of the franchise stores and restaurants.

The *Watauga Democrat*, published weekly, includes an entertainment section called the "Watauga Mountain Times." That insert is also available as a free handout at various locations. The newspaper's website is www.wataugademocrat.com.

Things to Do

Special Shopping

Shoppes at Farmers Hardware and Supply Company, located in an 80-year-old downtown landmark at 661 West King Street in Boone (28607), houses over 100 unique shops. The building still has its original tin ceilings and oiled wooden floors. It is open from 10 A.M. to 6 P.M. Monday through Saturday and from noon to 5 P.M. on Sunday. For information, call 828-264-8801.

Mast General Store, on N.C. 194 in Valle Crucis (28691), is the granddaddy of the area's restored general stores. It opened in 1883 and quickly gained a reputation for carrying everything from "cradles to caskets." Even today, you'll find goods ranging from hiking boots to reproductions of antique cooking utensils to mountain toys. The post office inside the store is still used by local residents, as is the huge potbelly stove you'll notice as soon as you enter. The *Mast Store Annex* is just down the road. Here, you'll find casual clothing and a complete outfitter's shop. The best part is the candy store, where you'll rediscover candies you haven't seen since childhood. Mast General Store is open from 7 A.M. to 6:30 P.M. Monday through Saturday and from noon to 5 P.M. on Sunday. For information, call 866-367-6278 or 828-963-6511 or visit www.maststoreonline.com.

Mast General Store
PHOTOGRAPH BY CAROLYN SAKOWSKI

You can also visit *Old Boone Mercantile*, a Mast outlet at 630 West King Street in downtown Boone (28607). The Boone store is open from 10 A.M. to 6 P.M. Monday through Saturday and from noon to 6 P.M. on Sunday. Call 828-262-0000.

A *Mast Store Candy Barrel* is located at 1087-3 Main Street in Blowing Rock (28605). Call 828-295-8733.

Todd General Store is 10 miles south of West Jefferson and 11 miles north of Boone off N.C. 194. It overlooks the South Fork of the New River from its location at 3866 Railroad Grade Road in Todd (28684). Railroad Grade Road has been turned into one of the most scenic bike routes in the area. Established in 1914, the store features jams, jellies, and antiques. It also has a deli. Its summer hours are as follows. The store is open from 10 A.M. to 5 P.M. Monday and Thursday. On Tuesday, it stays open from 10 A.M. until the storytelling session (which starts at 6 P.M.) is over. On Friday, it opens at 10 A.M.; dinner is served at 6:30 P.M., followed by live music from 7 P.M. until around 9 P.M. It is open from 9 A.M. to 5 P.M. on Saturday and from noon to 5 P.M. on Sunday. It is closed Wednesday. Call 336-877-1067 or visit www. toddgeneralstore.com.

In the past 10 years, the number of artists in the High Country has grown from a handful to over 200. These are not just your average mountain craftspeople; these artists work in all media in traditional, contemporary, and exploratory genres. An excellent brochure listing the craft and art galleries in Boone, Blowing Rock, Valle Crucis, and Foscoe is available by calling North Carolina High Country Host.

Recreation

Located on U.S. 321 about halfway between Boone and Blowing Rock, *Tweetsie Railroad* is one of North Carolina's oldest theme parks. The centerpiece of this

Tweetsie Railroad
PHOTOGRAPH BY JUDI SCHARNS, COURTESY OF BOONE CONVENTION AND VISITORS BUREAU

re-created Wild West town is a historic narrow-gauge, coal-fired steam locomotive that used to carry passengers on a daily 66-mile trip from Johnson City, Tennessee, to Boone. In addition to riding the train (and maybe getting attacked by robbers), you can take the chairlift up the mountain to pan for gold, pet friendly animals, try the amusement rides, and take in a show that includes music and clogging. From mid-May to mid-August, Tweetsie Railroad is open daily from 9 A.M. to 6 P.M.; from mid-August to the end of October, it is open the same hours but only on weekends; it is also open Labor Day. An admission fee is charged. The address is 300 Tweetsie Railroad Lane in Blowing Rock (28605); call 800-526-5740 or 828-264-9061 or visit www.tweetsie.com.

Next to Tweetsie is *Mystery Hill*, founded in 1949. A day pass gains you access to four different areas. The main attraction is a house in which you have to stand at a 45-degree angle to keep from falling over. You can also witness water flowing uphill and see a swing that defies gravity. In the Hall of Mystery are hands-on experiments that let you lose your shadow, stand inside a giant soap bubble, and see optical illusions. At the Appalachian Heritage Museum, you'll see antiques and artifacts showing how mountain families lived at the turn of the 20th century; the exhibit is housed in the Dougherty House, built by the brothers who were instrumental in the founding of Appalachian State University. The final section exhibits over 50,000 Native American artifacts. Mystery Hill is open daily all year; the hours vary with the season. An admission fee is charged. The address is 129 Mystery Hill Lane in Blowing Rock (28605); call 828-263-0507 or visit www.mysteryhill-nc.com.

The cool summer climate is perfect for *golfing*. This area has been a golf mecca since the first holes were built in Linville in 1895. Although the really famous mountain courses are private, some excellent facilities around Boone are open to the public. Among them are *Boone Golf Club* (828-264-8760), located off U.S. 221/321 heading toward Blowing Rock, and *Willow Creek Golf Course* (828-963-6865), located off N.C. 105 south of Boone at Willow Valley Resort.

A sport that has exploded on the High Country scene in recent years is *cycling*—whether mountain biking or road biking. *Rivergirl Fishing Company* (336-877-3099; www.rivergirlfishing.com) in Todd and *Boone Bike and Touring* (828-262-5750; www. boonebike.com) and *Magic Cycles* (828-265-2211; www.magiccycles.com), both in Boone, are three local shops that offer bike rentals.

Several outfitters offer *whitewater rafting* trips down the Nolichucky and Watauga rivers and Wilson Creek. Try *Cherokee Adventures* (800-445-7238; www. cherokeeadventures.com), *Edge of the World* (800-789-3343; www.edgeoworld. com), *High Mountain Expeditions* (www.highmountainexpeditions.com; 800-262-9036 or 828-264-7368), *Wahoo's Adventures* (800-444-RAFT or 828-262-5774; www. wahoosadventures.com), or *Watauga Kayak* (423-542-6777; www.wataugakayak. com).

One activity that doesn't require a guide is *hiking*. The area is flush with trails of all lengths and difficulties. For information about the Blue Ridge Parkway trails, see the chapter on the parkway. The Tanawha Trail and the trails at Julian Price Park and Moses H. Cone Memorial Park are all excellent choices. See the Banner Elk, Beech Mountain, and Linville chapter for information about trail maps.

Pisgah National Forest offers trails at Linville Gorge, Wilson Creek, Lost Cove Cliffs, and Harper Creek. For information about hiking in the national forest, contact the Grandfather Ranger District by writing 109 East Lawing Drive in Nebo (28761); the phone number is 828-652-2144. The office is located at Exit 90 off Interstate 40 near Nebo and Marion.

Seasonal Events

Since 1952, Kermit Hunter's outdoor drama, **Horn in the West**, has played on summer nights. The story is set during the American Revolution, when Daniel Boone and the mountain men struggled against the British. It's fun to sit outside under the stars and watch the drama unfold. Lots of whooping and gunfire keep things lively. From late June through mid-August, the show plays nightly except on Monday. Performances begin at 8 P.M., just as the sun starts to set. An admission fee is charged. You can reach the amphitheater by following the signs from U.S. 421, U.S. 321, U.S. 221, or N.C. 105 Extension. For information, call 828-264-2120 or visit www.horninthewest.com.

An Appalachian Summer Festival is a series of music, dance, art, and theater performances that spans the month of July. Past participants have included the Paul Taylor Dance Company, Willie Nelson, the Preservation Hall Jazz Band, Emmylou Harris, the Duke Ellington Orchestra, and the North Carolina Symphony. Workshops in writing, dance, and art are also offered. An admission fee is charged for most events, many of which are held on the campus of Appalachian State University. For information, call 800-841-2787 or visit www.appsummer.org.

Valle Country Fair has been held the third Saturday in October for over 20 years. Since the fair takes place during the height of the fall foliage season, thousands of tourists flock to Valle Crucis. Part craft show, part old-time cooking fair, this event attracts top craftsmen and the best canners of preserves in the area. Visitors enjoy old-time music and dancing. One of the highlights is the cooking of apple butter from scratch. For information, write P.O. Box 543 in Valle Crucis (28691). You can also call 828-963-4609 or visit www.vallecountryfair.org.

Places to Stay

It's important to note that lower rates are in effect on weekdays during summer and fall. In the off-season before skiing begins and after it ends, rates are even cheaper.

Resorts, Hotels, and Motels

Fairfield Inn & Suites. Deluxe/Expensive. 2060 Blowing Rock Road in Boone, 28607 (866-871-7425 or 828-268-0677; www.marriott.com/HKYFI). Fairfield offers lots of options for rooms and rates. In addition to standard rooms, larger rooms with refrigerators are available, as are suites with separate living and sleeping areas, refrigerators, microwaves, and whirlpools. Continental breakfast is included in the room rate. A heated indoor pool and an exercise room with a whirlpool are on the premises.

Holiday Inn Express. Deluxe/Expensive. 1943 Blowing Rock Road in Boone, 28607 (888-733-6867 or 828-264-2451; www.expressboone.com). Again, all sorts of room options and rates are available. You'll pay more for a suite or a room with a balcony or a whirlpool. Free continental breakfast is provided.

Best Western Blue Ridge Plaza. Expensive. 840 East King Street in Boone, 28607 (888-573-0408 or 828-266-1100; www.bestwesternboone.com). Each of the rooms here has a microwave and a refrigerator. Several have fireplaces and two-person Jacuzzis. An indoor heated pool is on the premises. A deluxe continental breakfast is included in the room rate.

The Broyhill Inn and Appalachian Conference Center. Expensive. On the Appalachian State campus at 775 Bodenheimer Drive in Boone, 28607 (800-951-6048 or 828-262-2204; www.broyhillinn.com). This inn has 83 guest rooms and suites. It is run by Appalachian State and serves primarily as a conference center. The full-service dining room is quite good; a lounge is also available for guests. During summer, visitors enjoy great views from the outdoor patios; during winter, they stay warm by the large native-stone fireplace. The inn occasionally offers special deals through its website.

Country Inn and Suites. Expensive. 818 East King Street in Boone, 28607 (800-456-4000 or 828-264-4234; www.countryinns.com/boonenc). Opened in summer 2006, this chain hotel has a variety of room types. A free continental breakfast is included. Each room has a microwave and a refrigerator. An indoor pool and a whirlpool are available.

La Quinta Inn & Suites. Expensive. 165 N.C. 105 Extension in Boone, 28607 (800-753-3757 or 828-262-1234; www.lq.com, then type in "Boone" for location). This chain offering opened late in 2008. All its rooms have high-speed wireless Internet, a microwave, and a refrigerator. Some have a whirlpool tub and a fireplace. A full breakfast is served.

Mast Farm Inn
PHOTOGRAPH BY CAROLYN SAKOWSKI

Inns and Bed-and-Breakfasts

Lovill House Inn. Deluxe. 404 Old Bristol Road in Boone, 28607 (800-849-9466 or 828-264-4204; www.lovillhouseinn.com). This inn is located just off West King Street on the western side of downtown Boone. Housed in an 1875 farmhouse with a wraparound porch, it offers a private bath, cable television, a ceiling fan, bathrobes, a hair dryer, a clock radio, and a telephone in each room. Some rooms have gas-log fireplaces. Early-morning coffee and tea are served before the complimentary breakfast. A cottage behind the farmhouse is available for rent. Lovill House has received a Four Diamond rating from AAA.

Mast Farm Inn. Deluxe. 2543 Broadstone Road/S.R. 1112 (P.O. Box 704) on the way to Valle Crucis, 28691 (888-963-5857 or 828-963-5857; www.mastfarminn. com). Mast Farm Inn is a huge, rambling, three-story farmhouse with a wraparound porch. Built in 1885, it began operating as an inn in the early 1900s. The eight guest rooms, most of which have private baths, are furnished with country antiques and old quilts; some have their original wood paneling. Seven guest cottages are also available for rent, including the farm's old loom house. A wonderful restaurant is on the premises.

The Baird House. Deluxe/Expensive. 1451 Watauga River Road in Valle Crucis, 28691 (800-297-1342 or 828-297-4055; www.bairdhouse.com). This Colonial-style farmhouse, located near the Mast General Store, was built in 1790. It rests on 16 acres of rolling pasture overlooking the Watauga River. A full country breakfast is served.

Taylor House Inn. Deluxe/Expensive. 4584 N.C. 194 South in Banner Elk, 28604 (800-963-5581 or 828-963-5581; www.taylorhouseinn.com). The Taylor House, built in 1910, has been described as "country elegant." Its seven rooms all have private baths and free WiFi. Two rooms are located in a nearby cottage and one in the inn-keeper's house. A two-course gourmet breakfast is served each morning.

Places to Eat

Boone is the High Country town where the chains are well represented.

Simplicity at Mast Farm Inn. Expensive. 2543 Broadstone Road/S.R. 1112 (P.O. Box 704) on the way to Valle Crucis, 28691 (888-963-5857 or 828-963-5857; www.mastfarminn.com). This restaurant is housed in the historic Mast Farm Inn. The chefs, who offer their own cooking classes through the inn, are advocates of the slow-food movement. As a result, they offer locally grown organic food, much of it raised on the Mast Farm. A fixed menu of four or more courses is offered at a fixed price; the menu changes daily. Breakfast is served daily and dinner Thursday through Saturday. Simplicity has two seatings from November to April and three seatings the rest of the year. Reservations are required because of the limited space.

The Dan'l Boone Inn Restaurant. Moderate. 130 Hardin Street in Boone, 28607 (828-264-8657; www.danlbooneinn.com). Opened in 1959, this family-style restaurant at the junction of U.S. 321 and U.S. 421 is an institution. In summer, the crowds line up across the porch and down the walk. The fixed-price meals begin with a salad in summer and soup in winter; they include three meats, five vegetables, homemade biscuits, a beverage, and desserts. Breakfast, lunch, and dinner are served daily.

Vidalia Restaurant and Wine Bar. Moderate. Across from the Watauga County Courthouse at 831 West King Street in Boone, 28607 (828-263-9176; www.vidaliaof-boonenc.com). Like most area restaurants, Vidalia uses locally grown organic foods whenever possible. The lunches focus on soups, salads, and sandwiches. Dinner features interesting treatments of traditional home cooking like porkchops and meat loaf. Lunch and dinner are served Tuesday through Saturday; brunch is offered on Sunday. Reservations are recommended.

Coyote Kitchen. Inexpensive. Next to Wal-Mart at 200 Southgate Drive in Boone, 28607 (828-265-4041; thecoyotekitchen.com). This restaurant bills its food as "Southwest and Caribbean Soul Food." An example of the creative cuisine is the "Havana Burrito," which includes red beans, Jerk chicken, jack cheese, roasted sweet potato, green chilies, grilled mushrooms, and roasted corn. Lunch and dinner are served daily.

Melanie's Food Fantasy. Inexpensive. 664 West King Street at the corner of Depot Street in Boone, 28607 (828-263-0300; www.melaniesfoodfantasy.com). Melanie's serves an eclectic assortment of egg dishes and pancakes for breakfast. A local favorite is the stuffed French toast, which looks like an extravagant dessert. Several vegetarian sandwiches are offered at lunch, as are burgers made from hormone-free beef. Melanie's takes care to prepare meat items separately from vegetarian entrées. Breakfast and lunch are served Tuesday through Sunday.

Peppers. Inexpensive. In the Shops at Shadowline at 240 Shadowline Road in Boone, 28607 (828-262-1250; www.peppers-restaurant.com). Opened in 1975, Pepper's has been a Boone staple ever since. The menu includes sandwiches, seafood, pasta dishes, and homemade desserts. Lunch and dinner are served daily.

Blowing Rock
COURTESY OF BOONE CONVENTION AND VISITORS BUREAU

Blowing Rock

At Blowing Rock's elevation of 4,000 feet, summer temperatures rarely climb over 80 degrees. The town began to attract summer residents in the 1880s. In the early days, most visitors spent the entire season. Some built beautiful Victorian summer homes, many of which still stand.

Blowing Rock has always catered to an upscale crowd. Because of this, it's been relatively easy for the town to maintain its quaint character through zoning regulations. Most of what passes for urban sprawl has been consigned to the bypass, while the downtown buildings have benefited from constant refurbishing.

The village is an easy drive from Boone. Because Blowing Rock literally hangs on the side of the mountain, you'll enjoy incredible views of the Johns River Gorge from various points in town.

JUST THE FACTS

Blowing Rock is located seven miles south of Boone where U.S. 321 and U.S. 221 join and become Blowing Rock Road.

For visitor information, contact the Blowing Rock Chamber of Commerce by writing P.O. Box 2445 (28605); you can also call 877-750-4636 or 828-295-4636 or visit www.blowingrock.com. The town's visitor center is located at

7738 Valley Boulevard/U.S. 321 Bypass (28605). It has an excellent selection of menus from area restaurants, in addition to the usual travel brochures.

The *Blowing Rocket* (www.blowingrocket.com) is the weekly newspaper. Events are also covered in the *Mountain Times*, a free weekly; for information, visit www.mountaintimes.com.

Things to Do

Special Shopping

Parkway Craft Center, located in the manor house at Moses H. Cone Memorial Park at Milepost 294 on the Blue Ridge Parkway, has served as a showcase for the Southern Highland Craft Guild for over 50 years. In this historic home built by Moses and Bertha Cone are weavings, baskets, pottery, woodcarvings, and glass and metal work. Craft demonstrations are usually going on. If you're up for a nice walk, ask how to get to the Cones' grave sites. The center is open daily from late March through November. Call 828-295-7938 or visit www.craftguild.org.

The *Shoppes on the Parkway*, located on U.S. 321, are a group of brand-name outlet stores. Some offer real bargains, so the parking lot is usually full. The shops are open daily year-round. For information, write the office at 270 Shoppes on Parkway Road, Suite 33 (28605). Or you can visit www.tangeroutlet.com or call 828-295-4444.

Recreation

The *Blowing Rock* is an immense cliff that hangs 3,000 feet over the Johns River Gorge. The rock walls form a flume that sweeps the northwest wind upward with such force that it blows light objects back up the mountain. You won't find much at this attraction other than the spectacular view. On clear days, you can spot Mount Mitchell, Grandfather Mountain, Table Rock, and Hawksbill. The Blowing Rock is located off U.S. 321 near the Green Park Inn. For information, write P.O. Box 145 (28605). Or you can call 828-295-7111 or visit www.theblowingrock.com.

Parkway Craft Center at Moses H. Cone Memorial Park
COURTESY OF BOONE CONVENTION AND VISITORS BUREAU

Hiking brochures are available at the Blowing Rock Chamber of Commerce. The hikes to Glen Burney Falls, the Cone Park carriage trails, and the hikes around the campground at Julian Price Park are all highly recommended.

For those who like to get their thrills on skis, *Appalachian Ski Mountain* is located near Blowing Rock. For information, write P.O. Box 106 (28605). Or you can call 800-322-2373 or 828-295-7827 or visit www.appskimtn.com. More ski slopes are listed in the chapter on Banner Elk, Beech Mountain, and Linville.

Seasonal Events

For almost 40 years, Blowing Rock Memorial Park has hosted a juried art-and-crafts festival one Saturday each month from May to October. *Art in the Park* has blossomed into a big attraction boasting over 100 exhibits. For information, call the Blowing Rock Chamber of Commerce at 800-295-7851 or 828-295-7851 or visit www.BlowingRock.com.

Held in late July, the *Blowing Rock Charity Horse Show* has been one of the top equestrian events in the Southeast since 1923. Centered at the Blowing Rock Equestrian

Preserve at 1500 Laurel Lane off U.S. 221 west of town, this two-week-long English saddle event features hunter jumpers and American Saddlebreds in competition. The preserve offers stables, a grandstand, an arena, campsites, and access to 25 miles of horse trails in Moses H. Cone Memorial Park. Unfortunately, the stables no longer rent horses for trail rides. For information, write P.O. Box 650 (28605). Or you can call 828-295-4700 or visit www.blowingrockequestrian.com.

Places to Stay

Resorts, Hotels, and Motels

Blowing Rock has several small motels that have been locally owned and operated for years. They are all lovingly maintained, and you will rarely go wrong with any of them. Most are located along Sunset Drive and North Main Street.

Bob Timberlake Inn at Chetola Resort. Deluxe. Off U.S. 321 on North Main Street (P.O. Box 17), 28605 (800-243-8652 or 828-295-5500; www.Chetola.com). Started in 1846, the manor house here is the centerpiece of a fabulous former summer estate. That house is now the Bob Timberlake Inn at Chetola. The inn features Timberlake's furniture-and-accessories line, his artwork, and personal mementos. Each room has a fireplace, a flat-screen TV, a DVD player, and a whirlpool tub. Breakfast is provided daily. The resort encompasses 87 acres of beautifully landscaped grounds surrounding a lake. The lodge, a modern addition, offers guest rooms. Guests can also rent one-, two-, and three-bedroom condominiums that have fireplaces, fully equipped kitchens, and outdoor decks. A first-class sports center, an indoor swimming pool, a whirlpool, a sauna, and massage therapy are offered. Guests can play tennis or racquetball, hike, fish, ride horses, or go mountain biking. Chetola offers meeting space and has a first-class restaurant.

Note: The next three inns have the same owner and call themselves *The Village Inns of Blowing Rock*. Call 800-821-4908 to make reservations; you can learn more about them at www.thevillageinnsofblowingrock.com. All three were renovated in 2005. Each room offers a refrigerator, a microwave, a coffee maker, and a hair dryer. Many of the suites and cottages have full kitchens, fireplaces, and Jacuzzis. Each accommodation offers complimentary continental breakfast and an afternoon wine-and-cheese reception.

Hillwinds Inn. Deluxe. On the corner of Ransom Street at 315 Sunset Drive, 28605 (828-295-7660). Hillwinds is a short walk from Main Street. In addition to regular rooms, it has two suites and two cottages. All feature 30-inch flat-screen TVs.

Ridgeway Inn. Deluxe. Near the intersection of U.S. 321 and U.S. 221 at 131 Yonahlossee Road, 28605 (828-295-7321). Ridgeway was the first inn in Blowing Rock. Today, it's known for the beautiful rose gardens that surround it. The guest rooms all have high-speed Internet access and sitting areas. The inn also offers two suites and two cottages that feature 30-inch flat-screen TVs, private decks or sunrooms, fireplaces, and Jacuzzis. This is a pet-free inn.

Village Inn. Deluxe. On the corner of Sunset Drive and U.S. 321 Bypass at 7876 Valley Boulevard, 28605 (828-295-3380). You may remember this location as Brookside Inn, but you won't recognize it now. The renovated inn features hardwood floors and rustic, elegant mountain decor. All rooms have private decks; some have hot tubs. The inn also offers two suites and three cottages. Some pet-friendly rooms are available. In front of the inn is a quarter-acre pond with an island and a gazebo.

Meadowbrook Inn. Deluxe/Expensive. 711 North Main Street (P.O. Box 2005), 28605 (800-467-6626 or 828-295-4300; www.meadowbrook-inn.com). This 61-room inn is a few blocks from Blowing Rock Memorial Park, the town's center. Each room has a terrace, a gas fireplace, and a whirlpool tub for two. Some suites have a wet bar, a refrigerator, and a microwave. The top-of-the-line pool suites are unique. What appears to be a closet leads down a spiral staircase to a private swimming pool. These are not Jacuzzis, but rather eight-foot-wide, 16-foot-long, four-foot-deep in-room pools. A fully equipped fitness center, a full-sized swimming pool, bicycles, and a Jacuzzi are available to all guests. A full-service restaurant, a bar, and meeting rooms are on the premises.

Azalea Garden Inn. Expensive. 793 North Main Street (P.O. Box 165), 28605 (828-295-3272; www.azalea-garden-inn.com). The first thing that will strike you about this inn is its landscaping. The owners have gone all out in covering the one-acre setting with flowering perennials. The rooms have either two full-sized beds or one king-sized bed, air conditioning, and cable television. An authentic log cabin is also available for rent; it has a log-burning fireplace, a kitchen, and two queen-sized beds. Guests enjoy complimentary morning coffee on the veranda, which offers a view of the abundant flowers.

Hemlock Inn. Expensive. 134 Morris Street (P.O. Box 422), 28605 (828-295-7987; www.hemlockinn.net). This cedar-sided motel has been owned and operated by the same family since 1994. All rooms have private baths, cable TV, microwaves, and refrigerators. Suites with fully equipped kitchens are available.

Inns and Bed-and-Breakfasts

Gideon Ridge Inn. Deluxe. 202 Gideon Ridge Road, 28605 (828-295-3644; www. GideonRidge.com). Housed in an elegant former summer home, this 10-room inn offers a spectacular view of the Johns River Gorge—the same view you'll pay to see at the nearby Blowing Rock attraction. *Country Inns Magazine* has called this "one of the ten best inns in America." Stone terraces are everywhere; most offer incredible views of the mountains or the perennial gardens. The library has a lovely stone fireplace. Breakfast is served in a room with a wonderful view of the surrounding mountains. Some rooms have Jacuzzis and fireplaces; all have first-class amenities. A three- or five-course fixed-price dinner is served each night at 7:30.

The Inn at Ragged Gardens. Deluxe. 203 Sunset Drive, 28605 (828-295-9703; www.ragged-gardens.com). This fully restored summer home built in the early 1900s sits in the center of an acre of colorful gardens just a block from Blowing Rock Memorial Park. The chestnut siding is a distinctive aspect of local architecture; unfortunately, it is no longer used, since the chestnut blight destroyed the source. Local granite was used in the entry columns, the flooring, and the staircase. Inside are chestnut-paneled walls and beams and a large rock fireplace. The rooms have goose-down comforters and pillows, fireplaces, private baths, ceiling fans, wireless Internet, and cable TV. Most offer balconies, sitting rooms, and one- or two-person whirlpools. Breakfast is served in a dining room that overlooks the rock-walled garden. The Best Cellar restaurant (see the "Places to Eat" section) is on the premises.

Maple Lodge Bed-and-Breakfast. Expensive. 152 Sunset Drive (P.O. Box 1236), 28605 (866-795-3331 or 828-295-3331; www.maplelodge.net). Maple Lodge is located a short walk from Blowing Rock Memorial Park. Its 11 rooms are furnished with a blend of antiques and family heirlooms. Each has a private bath and a goose-down comforter on a four-poster or lace-canopy bed. The library has a stone fireplace. A full breakfast is served in the dining room, which overlooks a wildflower garden.

Places to Eat

The Best Cellar. Expensive. In the Inn at Ragged Gardens at 203 Sunset Drive, 28605 (828-295-3466; www.thebestcellar.com). The Best Cellar has been one of the top restaurants in the area for over 30 years. All dishes, including breads and desserts, are prepared daily on-site. Lunch and dinner are served daily. Reservations are recommended.

Crippen's Country Inn and Restaurant. Expensive. 239 Sunset Drive (P.O. Box 528), 28605 (877-295-3487 or 828-295-3487; www.crippens.com). Crippen's has consistently received glowing reviews from food critics across the country, including those at *Southern Living* and the *New York Times*. The menu changes daily. Crippen's uses locally grown organic vegetables and prime meats including imported Kobe beef. The award-winning chef is known for his sauces, marinades, and vinaigrettes. All desserts are made on the premises. Dinner is served nightly from June through October and on Thursday, Friday, and Saturday the rest of the year; an expanded schedule is offered between Christmas and New Year's.

The Manor House Restaurant at Chetola. Expensive. Off U.S. 321 on North Main Street (P.O. Box 17), 28605 (800-243-8652 or 828-295-5505; www.chetola.com). This restaurant occupies a restored 1846 manor house. It serves mountain specialties in the dining rooms and on the patio overlooking the lake. Breakfast, lunch, and dinner are offered daily; Sunday brunch is an option during summer. Reservations are recommended for dinner.

Bistro Roca & Antlers Bar. Expensive/Moderate. 143 Wonderland Trail, 28605 (828-295-4008; www.BistroRoca.com). If you were a student at Appalachian State sometime from the 1960s to the 1980s, you'll probably remember Antlers Bar. But it doesn't look quite the same today. Renovated in 2005, it now has a wood-fired oven and an open kitchen. The proprietors also own the popular Gideon Ridge Inn, and the same attention to detail and quality is evident here. They take pride in using free-range meats, organic vegetables, homemade, naturally fermented pizza dough, and real—not prepackaged—stock for soups. The menu includes steaks, fresh fish, and hand-tossed, wood-fired pizzas. Be sure to check out the photos adorning the walls. These are professionally made photos of patrons' dogs, and sometimes of patrons and their dogs. Lunch and dinner are served Wednesday through Monday; brunch is offered on Sunday.

Storie Street Grille. Moderate. On the corner of Storie Street at 1167 Main Street, 28605 (828-295-7075; www.storiestreetgrille.com). For a great meal at a reasonable price, Storie Street Grille can't be beat. The bountiful salads and sandwiches are popular at lunch. Dinner features seafood, pasta dishes, and Mediterranean-inspired specialties. Lunch and dinner are served Monday through Saturday.

The Village Café. Moderate. Behind Kilwin's on Main Street at 146 Green Lake Court, 28605 (828-295-3769; www.thevillagecafe.com). You'll need to follow the stone walkway beside Kilwin's to reach this place. The café's gourmet breakfasts include such favorites as eggs Benedict and Belgian waffles. For lunch, you can get soups, salads, sandwiches, and homemade bread. You can dine on the stone patio or inside the turn-of-the-20th-century home. Breakfast and lunch are served Tuesday through Sunday.

Knight's on Main. Inexpensive. 870 Main Street, 28605 (828-295-3869; www.knightsonmainrestaurant.com). For decades, Knight's has been the place where the locals dine. At lunch, you can order burgers and sandwiches or get a "meat-and-two" plate with country ham, meat loaf, or fried flounder and home-cooked sides such as collard greens, baked apples, and pinto beans. On weekends during summer, lines frequently form for breakfast. Breakfast and lunch are served daily and dinner Monday through Saturday.

Woodlands BBQ. Inexpensive. On U.S. 321 Bypass at 8304 Valley Boulevard, 28605 (828-295-3651; www.woodlandsbbq.com). This establishment has been a Blowing Rock staple for years. It smokes its own ribs, chicken, beef, and pork (sliced or chopped) and offers a variety of sandwich and plate options. It also serves burritos, tacos, and nachos. A full-service lounge is on the premises. Lunch and dinner are served daily.

View of the North Carolina mountains from Grandfather Mountain
COURTESY OF BOONE CONVENTION AND VISITORS BUREAU

Banner Elk, Beech Mountain, and Linville

Avery County boasts several distinctly different communities.

The area around Newland, the county seat, is where many longtime year-round residents live. You won't find much evidence of a tourism boom here.

Linville, established in the late 1880s, was planned as an exclusive resort. It remains that today. Its lovely old homes have a distinctive architectural flavor, largely because of the chestnut siding on many of them. This community is still very private, as are the Grandfather Golf and Country Club and Linville Ridge Club. When these exclusive clubs came to the area, so did wealthy summer residents.

At 5,506 feet, Beech Mountain claims to be the highest town in eastern North America. Because it's a year-round tourist mecca, this is where you'll find the bulk of the county's high-end accommodations.

At the foot of Beech Mountain is Banner Elk. Because it is home to Lees-McRae College, the village has a bit of a college-town flavor. Here, you'll find quaint bed-and-breakfasts and excellent restaurants. Since the arrival of skiing as a winter draw, Banner Elk also claims many of the county's year-round citizens.

Today, retirees are discovering that the climate of the North Carolina mountains is not as severe as previously thought. Thanks to improved roads and crews that keep them open to serve the area's ski resorts, more and more people are coming here to live year-round.

Avery County has some of the strangest liquor laws in the country. Some clubs have been quite creative in getting exemptive legislation passed that allows them to serve alcoholic beverages. Visitors find it illogical when they walk into one convenience store and learn that beer and wine are not sold there, then visit another store owned by the same chain a mile down the highway and see those items stocked.

When you're traveling through Avery, note the strange building atop Sugar Mountain, one of the county's most prominent peaks. Although this structure spoils the view from all over the county, the good news is that it caused everyone throughout western North Carolina to wake up and pass a "ridge law" to prevent multistory buildings from being constructed on the ridge tops.

In Avery County, you'll find excellent accommodations and restaurants and attractions such as Grandfather Mountain, Linville Falls, and Linville Caverns. The county also claims more ski slopes than any other in the Southeast.

JUST THE FACTS

Banner Elk is less than 20 miles southwest of Boone at the intersection of N.C. 194 and N.C. 184.

To reach Beech Mountain, go to Banner Elk, turn onto Beech Mountain Parkway, and follow the signs to the ski resort.

Linville is located at the intersection of U.S. 221, N.C. 105, and N.C. 181 three miles west of Milepost 305.9 on the Blue Ridge Parkway.

For visitor information, contact the Avery County Chamber of Commerce, located in the Shoppes at Tynecastle at the corner of N.C. 105 and N.C. 184. The address is 4501 Tynecastle Highway, Suite 2, in Banner Elk (28604); call 800-972-2183 or 828-898-5605 or visit www.averycounty.com. The Beech Mountain Chamber of Commerce is headquartered in Beech Mountain Town Hall near the top of the mountain at 403-A Beech Mountain Parkway (28604); call 800-468-5506 or 828-387-9283 or visit www.beechmtn.com.

The weekly newspapers are the *Avery Journal* and the *Avery Post*. The Avery edition of the *Mountain Times* is included in the *Avery Journal*.

In the winter months, skiing is the big attraction.
COURTESY OF BOONE CONVENTION AND VISITORS BUREAU

Things to Do

Special Shopping

Fred's General Mercantile Company is located at 501 Beech Mountain Parkway in Beech Mountain (28604). Here, you'll find hardware, bird feeders, books, kites, sleds, gardening supplies, Christmas trees in season, fresh apples in fall, toys, crafts, clothing, snowshoes, and on and on. The store acts as a community center. In summer, customers can even enjoy live entertainment. Call 828-387-4838 or visit www.fredsgeneral.com.

Old Hampton Store and Grist Mill is located off N.C. 181 at 77 Ruffin Street in Linville (28646). This old country store offers corn and wheat products ground right on the premises in a gristmill. The big draw is hickory-smoked pork, beef, and chicken barbecue, served on homemade sourdough bread. The store is open daily from 10 A.M. to 5 P.M. Call 828-733-5213.

Recreation

The biggest attraction in Avery County, and perhaps the whole High Country, is

Grandfather Mountain, located on U.S. 221 two miles northwest of Linville, just off Milepost 305.9 of the Blue Ridge Parkway. In 2009, the state purchased almost 2,500 acres of undeveloped acreage from the Morton family, who had run the mountain as a tourist attraction since 1952. The family will continue to operate the nature center, wildlife habitats, and swinging bridge, but the state will maintain the back-country hiking trails.

Be forewarned that admission is charged by the person, not the carload, and is fairly expensive. After paying at the front entrance, you'll drive to the top of the mountain. Along the way, you can stop at the nature museum, which offers a short film about the mountain and exhibits about the area's flora, minerals, wildlife, and history; a gift shop and a snack bar are also on the premises. Next to the nature museum is the animal habitat, one of the top attractions on the mountain. Here, you can see black bears (and probably some cubs in the summer), rare cougars, golden eagles, bald eagles, otters, deer, and other wildlife. It is best to arrive soon after the park opens; the prime time to see the elusive cougars is right after they've been fed. Another highlight is the famous Mile-High Swinging Bridge, which stretches between two of Grandfather's peaks. You can glimpse this bridge from all over the area, but it's a whole new experience to walk across it and look into the gorge below.

Within the privately run part of the park and the current state park land are over 30 miles of hiking trails, some so steep that they employ ladders. Fees are no longer charged for the off-mountain trailheads. The trailhead for the Profile Trail is off N.C. 105 near its intersection with N.C. 184. The trailhead for the Boone Fork Trail is on the Blue Ridge Parkway; see the chapter on the parkway for the exact location. Visitors to the privately run part of Grandfather Mountain can explore the trail network within that section as part of the admission fee.

The entire mountain, which stands at 5,964 feet, has been named an international biosphere reserve because of the rare and endangered species found within its boundaries. Grandfather Mountain is open from 8 A.M. to 7 P.M. during summer, from 8 A.M. to 6 P.M. in spring and fall, and from 8 A.M. to 5 P.M. in winter. For information, call 800-468-7325 or 828-733-4337 or visit www.grandfather.com.

Linville Caverns is located four miles south of the Blue Ridge Parkway at 19929 U.S. 221 North near Marion (28752); take the Linville Falls Village exit at Milepost 317 and turn left on U.S. 221. The cave was discovered in 1822 when some fishermen decided to follow trout that seemed to be swimming into and out of the mountain. Once inside the mountain, the fishermen found various rooms filled with stalactites and stalagmites that had been forming for centuries. New rock continues to "grow" in the limestone cave today. The temperature is a constant 52 degrees year-round, so take a sweater. Linville Caverns is open daily from 9 A.M. to 6 P.M. June through Labor Day, from 9 A.M. to 4:30 P.M. during November and March, and from 9 A.M. to 5 P.M. during April, May, September, and October. It operates on weekends only during December, January, and February. An admission fee is charged. For information, call 800-419-0540 or 828-756-4171 or visit www.linvillecaverns.com.

Linville Falls cascades 90 feet into Linville Gorge, a national wilderness preserve. Located at Milepost 317.4 on the Blue Ridge Parkway, the falls are accessible by a series of trails that can accommodate all types of hikers and walkers. The 2.1-mile round-trip Linville Falls Trail allows visitors to see the upper and lower falls. The hike to the upper falls is the easy one. Viewing the lower falls is more strenuous, but these falls are the kind you usually see on postcards.

The Grandfather Ranger District of *Pisgah National Forest* contains a wealth of opportunities for outdoor lovers.

Linville Gorge Wilderness Area is a favorite hiking, camping, fishing, and hunting area for locals and tourists. Because its trails are not well marked, be sure to bring topographical maps, a compass, or a GPS device. For information about trails in

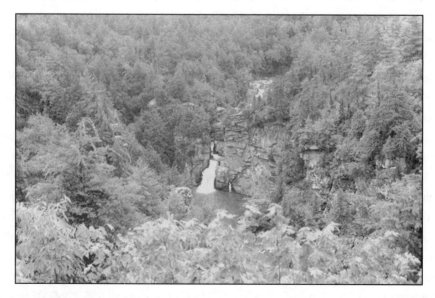

Linville Falls
PHOTOGRAPH BY CAROLYN SAKOWSKI

Linville Gorge Wilderness Area in Pisgah National Forest
PHOTOGRAPH BY CAROLYN SAKOWSKI

the gorge, consult the published hiking books on the area or call the Grandfather Ranger District office at 828-652-2144; the office is in Nebo, located at Exit 90 off Interstate 40.

If you want some relatively accessible but stunning views, consider a trip to **Table Rock** or **Wiseman's View**. To get to either, you'll have to drive on gravel forest-service roads. You won't need a four-wheel-drive vehicle, but you may not want to use your brand-new car. To reach Table Rock, take N.C. 181 to Gingercake Acres, where you'll see signs directing you to Table Rock Picnic Area. You'll drive through a residential area to F.R. 210, where the pavement ends. It's about four miles on F.R. 210 to Table Rock; the route is well marked. To reach Wiseman's View, take N.C. 183 North from Milepost 316.3 on the Blue Ridge Parkway. It is 0.7 mile from the community of Linville Falls to a road that runs four miles to the parking area.

Additional opportunities for fishing, hiking, camping, and hunting are available in the **Lost Cove, Wilson Creek**, and **Harper Creek** areas of Pisgah National Forest. In 1999, Wilson Creek was designated a wild and scenic area. You can reach the visitor center by taking Roseboro Road from Milepost 312.2 on the Blue Ridge Parkway to the Edgemont community. During summer, the center is open from 10 A.M. to 6 P.M. Monday through Saturday and from 1 P.M. to 6 P.M. on Sunday. From Labor Day to November 30, it is open from 10 A.M. to 4 P.M. Monday through Saturday and from 1 P.M. to 4 P.M. on Sunday. For information, write 7805 Brown Mountain Beach Road in Collettsville (28611). Or you can call 828-759-0005 or visit www.explorecaldwell.com.

In winter, the big attraction is skiing. Many of the area's slopes offer snowboarding, snow tubing, skating, and skiing; some even have night skiing. Equipment is available for rent at the slopes and at a number of area stores. Located in Avery County are *Ski Beech* (800-438-2093 or 828-387-2011; www.skibeech.com), at P.O. Box 1118 in Beech Mountain (28604), and *Ski Sugar Mountain* (800-784-2768 or 828-898-4521; www.skisugar.com), at 109 Sugar Mountain Drive in Banner Elk (28604). *Hawksnest*, located at 2058 Skyland Drive in Seven Devils (28604), offers snow tubing on over 20 lanes up to 1,000 feet long. For information, call 800-822-4295 or 828-963-6561 or visit www.hawksnesttubing.com.

Among Avery County's golf courses open to the public are *Mountain Glen* (828-733-5804), on N.C. 194 in Newland (28657), and *Sugar Mountain* (828-898-6464), at 109 Sugar Mountain Drive in Banner Elk (28604).

Sugar Mountain offers over 20 miles of single- and double-track mountain-biking trails during summer and fall. You can also mountain-bike a network of trails on *Beech Mountain*. A map is available at the Beech Mountain Chamber of Commerce.

You can book fly-fishing tours through *Foscoe Fishing Company & Outfitters*, located at 8857 N.C. 105 South in Foscoe (28607); call 828-963-6556 or visit www. foscoefishing.com. Another option is *Appalachian Angler*, located off N.C. 105 near Hound Ears Club at 174 Old Shulls Mill Road in Boone (28607); call 828-963-5050 or visit www.appalachianangler.com.

Several companies offer whitewater rafting trips on the Watauga and Nolichucky rivers. Try *Raft and Earth Adventures*, located at 1655 N.C. 105 in Boone (28607); call 866-411-RAFT or 828-963-5491 or visit www.raftcavehike.com. Another option is *Wahoo's Adventures*, located on U.S. 321 (P.O. Box 3094) in Boone (28607); call 800-444-RAFT or 828-262-5774 or visit www.wahoosadventures.com.

Seasonal Events

Two annual events take place on Grandfather Mountain.

Grandfather Mountain Highland Games and Gathering of Scottish Clans is held the second full weekend in July. This event has been in existence since 1956. Although

Crowd favorite Albannach performs during the Highland Games.
COURTESY OF BOONE CONVENTION AND VISITORS BUREAU

plenty of proud Scots in full regalia attend, you don't have to be of Scottish descent to enjoy the games. Traditional track and field events are held, but the real draws are the tossing of the caber (which resembles a telephone pole) and the throwing of sheep sheaves. The track is rimmed by brightly colored tents that house representatives from each clan. You can see Highland dancing, bagpipe competitions, and Border collie demonstrations. The festivities begin with the Torchlight Ceremony on Thursday, when all the clans march in. The events on Friday focus on music; a ceilidh (a concert of traditional Scottish music) is held Friday evening, as is the Celtic Rock Concert, featuring more contemporary Celtic music. Saturday sees further competitions, a Scottish dance, and another ceilidh and Celtic rock concert. The Parade of Tartans closes out the weekend on Sunday. Parking is restricted to certain areas off the mountain, so you'll have to use the shuttle buses to reach the games. An admission fee is charged. Unlike years past, alcoholic beverages and pets are no longer allowed. For information, call 828-733-1333 or visit www.gmhg.org.

The other event in MacRae Meadow on Grandfather is *Singing on the Mountain*. This all-day gospel sing has been held since 1924 on the fourth Sunday in June. It started as a modest gathering of families and friends from local churches. Today, thousands show up to hear the best in gospel music from all races and to hear such well-known ministers as the Reverend Billy Graham. At the 50th Singing on the Mountain, a record crowd of 100,000 showed up to hear Johnny Cash and to see

Bob Hope. Admission is free. Bring lawn chairs or blankets. Call 828-733-2013 or visit www.grandfather.com for information.

The ***Woolly Worm Festival*** is held in Banner Elk during a weekend in October. The woolly worm is actually a furry caterpillar with black and brown bands. Mountain folklore says you can predict what kind of winter lies ahead by examining the bands on these caterpillars right before the first frost. The festival includes food, live music, and crafts, but the real draw is the woolly worm races. You can bring your own or purchase a woolly worm; you then name it and enter it in one of the heats. Several worms are placed side by side at the bottoms of long strings. The winner is the worm that reaches the top of its string first. The event is fun to watch; kids love it. The winners of the heats compete until a grand champion emerges. The champion worm is then used to predict the forthcoming winter. For information on the festival, write 2 Shoppes at Tynecastle in Banner Elk (28604). Or you can call 800-972-2183 or 828-898-5605 or visit www.woollyworm.com.

Places to Stay

Resorts, Hotels, and Motels

The rates for most accommodations are less expensive on weekdays, even in summer. During summer and fall, the rates on Beech Mountain may be lower than those for similar accommodations in Boone and Blowing Rock.

4 Seasons at Beech. Expensive/Moderate. 608 Beech Mountain Parkway in Beech Mountain, 28604 (828-387-4211; www.4Seasons.Beech.net). Located at the top of Beech Mountain, 4 Seasons offers one- and two-room units, each with a telephone, a television, and a kitchen with a microwave, a refrigerator, and a dishwasher. Special packages are available during ski season.

The Inns at Beech Mountain. Expensive/Moderate. 700 Beech Mountain Parkway in Beech Mountain, 28604 (866-284-2770 or 828-387-2252; www.beechalpen.com). These two inns located next to each other are run by the same company. ***Beech Alpen Inn*** has 25 rooms with exposed beams and views of the mountains and ski slopes. Some rooms have queen-sized beds and French doors that lead onto balconies. Others have king-sized beds or two double beds, easy chairs, and window seats.

Some have stone fireplaces. All have private baths and cable television. The main floor of the Swiss-style *Top of the Beech* has a greatroom with a cathedral ceiling, a ski chandelier, a game table, sofas, and a large stone fireplace. All the guest rooms include two double beds, a table with seating, a private bath, and cable television. A restaurant is on the premises. For information, write the inns at 606 Beech Mountain Parkway in Beech Mountain (28604) or visit www.beechmountaininns.com.

Pinnacle Inn. Expensive/Moderate. 301 Pinnacle Inn Road in Beech Mountain, 28604 (800-405-7888 or 828-387-2231; www.pinnacleinnresort.com). Guests can rent a one- or two-bedroom villa or a ski suite at this resort. The villas have well-equipped kitchens, fireplaces, telephones, and color televisions. The inn offers an indoor heated pool, a sauna, a steam room, hot tubs, an exercise room, and opportunities for tennis, shuffleboard, and golf.

Inns and Bed-and-Breakfasts

The Blueberry Villa at Banner Elk Winery. Deluxe. Off N.C. 194 at 60 Deer Run Road near Banner Elk, 28604 (828-260-1790 or 828-898-9099; www.blueberryvilla. com). Situated on a 20-acre blueberry farm that boasts its own winery, this inn offers eight suites, each with a private bath and a Jacuzzi. Some of the beautifully appointed guest rooms have flat-screen TVs and gas fireplaces. The villa includes a game room, a gourmet kitchen, and expansive porches overlooking a trout pond and the vineyard.

Eseeola Lodge. Deluxe. 175 Linville Avenue in Linville, 28646 (800-742-6717 or 828-733-4311; www.eseeola.com). Eseeola Lodge is located near the intersection of U.S. 221, N.C. 105, and N.C. 181. It has received a Four Star rating from Mobil and has been recognized by *Golf Magazine* as a Silver Medalist Resort. Because of the chestnut siding and Tudor look, the lodge and its surrounding buildings are reminiscent of an English inn. Eseeola has been welcoming vacationers since 1892. In recent years, the rooms have been renovated and spacious suites have been added. Guests can arrange to play tennis or golf. A regulation croquet court is located across the street. The inn is open from mid-May to the end of October.

Archer's Mountain Inn. Expensive. 2489 Beech Mountain Parkway in Banner Elk, 28604 (828-898-9004; www.archersinn.com). This inn has 15 rooms with native-stone fireplaces, full private baths, and color televisions. Guests can rent a Jacuzzi suite, a room with a mountain-view balcony, an efficiency suite, rooms with vaulted ceilings, and traditional bed-and-breakfast-style rooms. The inn offers a full bar and the *Jackalope's View* restaurant, which serves fresh seafood, certified Angus beef, and exotic wild game. The restaurant is closed on Monday.

The Azalea Inn. Expensive. Behind the Village Shops at 149 Azalea Circle (P.O. Box 1538) in Banner Elk, 28604 (888-898-2743 or 828-898-8195; www.azalea-inn. com). Built in 1937, this inn has seven guest rooms, each with its own tiled bath and cable television. The carriage-house cottage has an upstairs and can accommodate four people; it includes a bedroom, a bath with a whirlpool, a living room with a sofa bed and a fireplace, and a full kitchen. The inn sits behind a white picket fence on a beautifully landscaped lot that features a birdhouse collection and brightly colored flowers in summer. Guests enjoy the fireplace in the living room and the wood stove on the sun porch.

The Banner Elk Inn. Expensive/Moderate. 407 Main Street East in Banner Elk, 28604 (888-487-8263 or 828-898-6223; www.bannerelkinn.com). This cozy historic inn has several rooms filled with antiques. All rooms include European down comforters; some have private baths. The inn has a greatroom, where guests can watch cable television or relax by the stone fireplace. The addition features its own kitchen, separate entrance, and private garden. Three cottages and three rental houses are also available. A full breakfast is served each morning.

The Perry House Bed-and-Breakfast. Expensive/Moderate. 153 Klonteska Drive (P.O. Box 2512) in Banner Elk, 28604 (www.perryhouse.com; 877-806-4280 or 828-898-3535). This 1903 farmhouse is conveniently located near the junction of N.C. 184 and N.C. 194 at the main stoplight in Banner Elk, across from Lees-McRae College and a block from the Village Shops. Each room has a private bathroom, cable television, a VCR, wireless Internet, and queen-sized beds. A full breakfast is included in the room rate.

Places to Eat

Artisanal Restaurant. Expensive. 1290 Dobbins Road in Banner Elk, 28604 (828-898-5395; www.artisanalnc.com). This restaurant boasts one of the hottest chefs in the High Country. It was previously located in the Shoppes at Tynecastle but has moved to a spectacular new location off Dobbins Road; call for directions, as it is off the beaten path. The cuisine here is contemporary American; you'll immediately recognize that the chef has worked at top restaurants. Dinner is served Tuesday through Sunday. Reservations are required; spots fill quickly on in-season weekends.

Eseeola Lodge. Expensive. 175 Linville Avenue in Linville, 28646 (828-733-4311; www.eseeola.com). A coat and tie are required for men at dinner at this grand old resort. The restaurant has won the prestigious Mobile Four Star Award. It features French and New American cuisine. Breakfast and dinner are served daily. Reservations are required.

Stonewalls. Expensive. On N.C. 184 (P.O. Box 569) in Banner Elk, 28604 (828-898-5550; www.stonewallsrestaurant.com). For over 25 years, Stonewalls has been known as a place to get good steaks and prime rib. The menu also includes seafood dishes, but this is primarily a meat place. Dinner is served daily.

Sorrento's World Famous Bistro. Moderate. In the Village Shops at 140 Azalea Lane in Banner Elk, 28604 (828-898-5214; www.sorrentosbistrohome.com). This restaurant bills itself as "a touch of Italy in the mountains." Sorrento's changes its menu monthly. Its nightly specials are usually excellent. It offers an extensive wine list. Lunch is served Wednesday through Sunday and dinner Wednesday through Monday.

Bella's Neighborhood Italian Restaurant. Inexpensive. 358 Tynecastle Highway in Banner Elk, 28604 (828-898-9022). Located in the Food Lion strip shopping center on N.C. 184, Bella's is deceptively good. It serves Italian dishes—pizza, lasagna, calzones—as well as such favorites as "Joe's Mussels" in a spicy red sauce. Lunch and dinner are served Thursday through Tuesday.

Fred's Backside Deli. Inexpensive. 501 Beech Mountain Parkway in Beech Mountain, 28604 (828-387-4838 or 828-387-9331; www.fredsgeneral.com). Located in Fred's General Mercantile Company, this deli serves sandwiches, salads, soups, pizzas, and homemade desserts. It also offers meats and cheeses for purchase. Breakfast, lunch, and dinner are served daily.

The Italian Restaurant. Inexpensive. 2855 Linville Falls Highway in Pineola, 28662 (828-733-1401). Located on U.S. 221 near N.C. 181 in a building that used to house a Tastee Freez, this restaurant might not inspire expectations of good food. But diners find themselves pleasantly surprised by the sandwiches, pasta dishes, pizzas, calzones, beer, and wine. Lunch and dinner are served Tuesday through Sunday.

River Dog Coffeehouse and Café. Inexpensive. In the Linville Village Shopping Center on N.C. 181 (P.O. Box 871) in Linville, 28646 (828-733-9333). This coffeehouse offers free wireless Internet, espresso, lattes, smoothies, and frappes. It serves breakfast and Reuben, Cuban, muffaletta, chicken salad, pimento cheese, and other sandwiches for lunch. It also offers gelatos and baked goodies. Breakfast and lunch are served Monday through Saturday.

Otway Burns statue in Burnsville's town square
PHOTOGRAPH BY CAROLYN SAKOWSKI

Spruce Pine and Burnsville

Until recently, few major highways reached Mitchell and Yancey counties, so development here was less than around Boone and Blowing Rock. Ironically, it seems this area should attract a great number of tourists, since it has some of the highest peaks in North Carolina. With the extension of Interstate 26 from Asheville into Tennessee and the projected expansion of U.S. 19E to four lanes, development is now starting here. Tourists and new residents are seeping into Burnsville more than

Spruce Pine, but both communities are still relatively undiscovered. Fortunately, this means you can still find unspoiled vistas.

Prominent in the area are the Black Mountains, where Mount Mitchell sits among a dozen peaks over 6,000 feet high.

Spruce Pine, the largest town in Mitchell County, has a long mining heritage that has evolved into a tourist industry. It is the site of the annual North Carolina Mineral, Gem, and Jewelry Festival. It is also home to many craftsmen, some of whom came to study at the Penland School of Crafts and stayed.

A short drive west is Yancey County, where Burnsville is the largest town. Its town square showcases a statue of the man for whom the town is named, Captain Otway Burns, a hero of the War of 1812. Burnsville, located about 35 miles from Asheville, markets itself as a place to escape traffic jams, urban blight, polluted air, and tainted water.

JUST THE FACTS

Spruce Pine is located at the intersection of U.S. 19E and N.C. 226 six miles from Milepost 331 on the Blue Ridge Parkway.

Burnsville is located at the intersection of U.S. 19 and N.C. 197. From Milepost 344 on the parkway, follow N.C. 80 to U.S. 19. From Asheville, take Interstate 26 North to U.S. 19E and go east.

For visitor information about the Spruce Pine area, contact the Mitchell County Visitors Center, located in the Museum of North Carolina Minerals at Milepost 331 of the Blue Ridge Parkway. The address is 79 Parkway Maintenance Road (P.O. Box 858) in Spruce Pine (28777); call 800-227-3912 or 828-765-9483 or visit www.mitchell-county.com. For information about the Burnsville area, contact the Yancey County/Burnsville Chamber of Commerce, located at 106 West Main Street in Burnsville (28714); call 800-948-1632 or 828-682-7413 or visit www.yanceychamber.com.

The weekly newspaper in Mitchell County is the *Mitchell News Journal*. In Yancey County, the weekly paper is the *Yancey Common Times Journal*.

Things to Do

Museums and Science Centers

The *Museum of North Carolina Minerals*, at Milepost 331 on the parkway, is part of the Blue Ridge Parkway Visitor Center. This is also the location of the Mitchell

County Chamber of Commerce's visitor center. Here, you can see exhibits on the wide range of minerals found in North Carolina. The gift shop carries books about gems and mining. The museum is open from 9 A.M. to 5 P.M. daily year-round. Admission is free. Call 828-765-2761 or visit www.nps.gov/blri.

Cultural Offerings

The *Penland School of Crafts*, located at 3135 Conley Ridge Road (P.O. Box 37) in Penland (28765), is open from early March to mid-December. The hours for its gallery and visitor center are 10 A.M. to 5 P.M. Tuesday through Saturday and noon to 5 P.M. on Sunday. To reach the school, take Penland Road off U.S. 19E between Spruce Pine and Burnsville. It is 2.9 miles to a left turn onto S.R. 1164, then 1.8 miles down the winding road to the school. See the sidebar about the school for further information, or call 828-765-6211 or visit www.penland.org.

Shopping

Home of the Perfect Christmas Tree is located at 262 Oak Avenue (P.O. Box 858) in Spruce Pine (28777). In 2003, author Gloria Houston gave a foundation in Spruce Pine the rights to her award-winning children's book, *The Year of the Perfect Christmas Tree*. The foundation used the funds to create 30 small businesses that produce handmade products. This store serves as a retail facility for the products. For information, call 828-765-0571 or visit www.homeoftheperfectchristmastree.org.

The *Toe River Arts Council* has galleries at 269 Oak Avenue in Spruce Pine (28777) and 102 West Main Street in Burnsville (28714). Both galleries feature works by local and nationally recognized contemporary and traditional craftsmen and artists. For more information, call the Spruce Pine location at 828-765-0520 or the Burnsville location at 828-682-7215 or visit www.toeriverarts.org.

Recreation

Emerald Village is located at McKinney Mine Road and Crabtree Creek Road in Little Switzerland, at the site of the Big McKinney and Bon Ami mines. From the Blue Ridge Parkway, take Exit 334 at Little Switzerland, go under the parkway bridge, and drive three miles. This attraction includes an underground museum in a former mine, where you can see equipment and learn about methods used for

The Penland School of Crafts

The Penland School of Crafts
COURTESY OF BOONE CONVENTION AND VISITORS BUREAU

The Penland School of Crafts has been described as one of the leading shapers of the American crafts movement and a producer of some of the best artisans in the country.

In 1914, Rufus Morgan founded the Appalachian School. Morgan wanted to include handicrafts in his program of instruction. In visiting area homes, he discovered high-quality woven articles that had been discarded when store-bought cloth became available. He convinced his sister, Miss Lucy Morgan, to come to Penland from Chicago and learn weaving from a local woman, Aunt Susan Phillips, so that Miss Lucy could teach the skill at his school.

Miss Lucy went on to instruct girls at the school and women in the community. She founded the Penland School with the goals of perpetuating the art of weaving and providing a source of income for local people. Miss Lucy also began collecting her students' wares and selling them to the outside world. In 1928, a pottery department was added to the school. In 1929, the sale of student-made goods totaled $18,000.

Today, the Penland School campus has over 40 buildings. It is open to students during spring, summer, and fall. Terms last one, two, or eight weeks, and the courses vary from year to year.

The curriculum usually includes work in wood, glass, fiber, clay, metal, paper-making, photography, and textiles. All are studied in rustic but professionally equipped studios.

Visitors can browse the Penland Gallery to get an idea of how important the Morgans' contribution was in preserving and encouraging traditional mountain crafts. Tours of the campus are offered on Tuesday at 10:30 A.M. and Thursday at 1:30 P.M.; no tours are given in January or February. Reservations are required.

mining gems a century ago. You can also mine your own gems—for a price. The mine offers enriched gravel and claims visitors will "find a gem every time." This is good if you have children, since they're sure to get excited about finding a "jewel." You can also see artisans at work cutting and mounting gems. Emerald Village is open from 9 A.M. to 5 P.M. on weekdays and from 9 A.M. to 6 P.M. on weekends from April through October; call for hours the remainder of the year. Fees are charged for mine tours and mining buckets. For more information, call 828-765-6463 or visit http://www.emeraldvillage.com.

The *Orchard at Altapass* is located near Spruce Pine on Orchard Road at Milepost 328.3 on the Blue Ridge Parkway. This working orchard produces heritage apples. The best time to visit is early fall, when the apples are ripe. The orchard offers hayrides, storytelling, mountain music, handmade crafts, jam, apple butter, cider, mountain honey, and dried fruits. Every Saturday and Sunday, free live music is showcased from 1 P.M. to 4:30 P.M. From May through September, the orchard is open from 10 A.M. to 6 P.M. Monday, Wednesday, Thursday, Friday, and Saturday and from noon to 6 P.M. on Sunday. During October, it is open every day. For information, write the orchard at P.O. Box 245 in Little Switzerland (28749). Or you can call 888-765-9531 or 828-765-9531 or visit www.altapassorchard.com.

Mount Mitchell State Park, accessible at Milepost 355 on the Blue Ridge Parkway, boasts the highest peak east of the Mississippi River. The park has picnic areas, nature trails, a 2009-vintage lookout tower offering spectacular mountain views, camping areas, a concession stand, and a ranger station. The park and the ranger station are open year-round except for Christmas; the concession stand is open May through October. For information, call 828-675-4611 or visit www. ncparks.gov/Visit/parks/momi/main.php.

Rivers Edge Outfitters, located at 280 Oak Avenue in Spruce Pine (28777), offers guide services including float trips for smallmouth bass, fly-fishing trips into the wilderness via horseback, fishing trips in private trophy waters, full-day wading trips on the Watauga and South Holston rivers, float trips on the French Broad and Nolichucky rivers, and canoe and kayak trips on the Toe River. For information, call 828-765-3474 or visit www.riversedgeoutfittersnc.com.

A popular summer activity in this area is tubing. *Loafers Glory Rafting & Tubing*, located at 2637 N.C. 226 North in Bakersville (28705), offers tubing trips on the

Elisha Mitchell

Not until Dr. Elisha Mitchell arrived in 1827 did anyone have much of an idea how tall the Black Mountains really were.

In 1825, Mitchell took charge of the North Carolina Geological Survey, the first statewide survey anywhere in the nation. In the course of fulfilling his duties, he made his first visits to the western part of the state. In an 1829 geological report, Mitchell stated his belief that the Black Mountains contained the highest land between the Gulf of Mexico and the White Mountains of New Hampshire.

When he returned to the Blacks in 1835, the first peak he climbed to take measurements was Celo Knob, elevation 5,946 feet. There, he noted "peaks considerably more elevated farther South." Mitchell took measurements of barometric pressure and temperature and compared them to measurements taken at his base in Morganton. He then used a formula to determine that the peak that later became known as Mount Mitchell stood 6,476 feet above sea level. He proclaimed it "the Highest Peak of the Black." It turned out that Mount Mitchell is actually 208 feet higher than Mitchell thought. He made the wrong measurements at his base. If those had been correct, he would have been off by only six feet.

General Thomas L. Clingman, a member of Congress and a man of sci-entific tastes, was taking measurements in the area at that same time. Clingman published a statement claiming that he had found a peak higher than the one measured by Mitchell.

Mitchell became obsessed with proving he was right and Clingman was wrong. He returned to the Blacks in 1857 to settle the matter, setting out alone. When he failed to meet his son as scheduled, a search party was organized. Ten days later, the frustrated group enlisted the aid of Big Tom Wilson, a legendary hunter and tracker who lived in the Cane River area, at the foot of the Blacks. The writer Charles Dudley Warner described Big Tom as "six feet and two inches tall, very spare and muscular, with sandy hair, long gray beard, and honest blue eyes. He has a reputation for great strength and endurance; a man of native simplicity and mild manners." The searchers agreed to let Wilson take the lead. Following seemingly invisible clues—broken limbs and faint impressions in the earth—Big Tom brought the group to a 50-foot waterfall. There, in a pool at the foot, was the perfectly preserved body of Dr. Mitchell. It was surmised that he must have become lost in the fog and fallen over the edge while following the stream. His body was buried in Asheville and later moved to the top of the peak that now bears his name.

Toe and French Broad rivers. For information, call 866-933-5628 or 828-208-9202 or visit www.ncrafting.com.

Carolina Hemlocks Recreation Area, located on N.C. 80 south of the community of Celo, has 36 campsites, each with a table, a fire ring with a cooking grill, and a lantern post. Activities here include trail hiking and fishing for brown and rainbow trout in the hatchery-supported Toe River. You'll also witness people bobbing along the river on inner tubes. The slow-moving current and gentle cascades lend just enough excitement to make the activity exhilarating but not too dangerous. You'll see signs for tube rentals at the stores near the recreation area.

Seasonal Events

The *North Carolina Mineral, Gem, and Jewelry Festival* is held the first week of August in Spruce Pine. It includes exhibits and demonstrations about gems, of course. For information, visit www.mitchell-county.com/festival or www.ncgemfest. com or call 800-227-3912 or 828-765-9483.

Places to Stay

Resorts, Hotels, and Motels

The Clear Creek Guest Ranch. Deluxe. Off N.C. 80 at 100 Clear Creek Drive south of Burnsville, 28714 (800-651-4510 or 828-675-4510; www.clearcreekranch. com). This is a little different from your typical accommodation because it's a dude ranch. The rates include three full meals a day, lodging, horseback riding, and ranch activities. Guests stay in one-, two-, or three-bedroom cabins that have porches with rocking chairs. All meals are served family-style in the main lodge. Lots of activities are available for children. The ranch is open from April to Thanksgiving.

Switzerland Inn. Expensive. 86 High Ridge Road (P.O. Box 399) in Little Switzerland, 28749 (800-654-4026 or 828-765-2153; www.switzerlandinn.com). Located on N.C. 226N where it meets the Blue Ridge Parkway at Milepost 334, this popular retreat has chalet-style architecture, paintings of storks on the chimney, and a magnificent panoramic view. An entire wall in the fieldstone-floored lobby is a window framing the Black Mountain Valley below. All the rooms have hand-painted murals that bring to mind the Swiss Alps. Most have balconies; all have cable television, telephones, and baths. Cottages are also available, as are large suites with air conditioning and separate sleeping and living areas. Room rates include a full breakfast and use of the swimming pool and tennis and shuffleboard courts. The inn is open from late April to the first week in November.

Pinebridge Inn and Executive Center. Moderate. 207 Pinebridge Avenue in Spruce Pine, 28777 (800-356-5059 or 828-765-5543; www.pinebridgeinn.com). This hotel is located in a converted schoolhouse, which allows for large rooms. All are equipped with cable TV, microwaves, and refrigerators.

Inns and Bed-and-Breakfasts

Richmond Inn. Expensive. 51 Pine Avenue in Spruce Pine, 28777 (877-765-6993 or 828-765-6993; www.richmondinn.com). This half-century-old inn boasts a Three Diamond rating from AAA. It is shaded by towering white pines and landscaped with native trees and shrubbery. You'll almost forget that the town of Spruce Pine is only three blocks away. The inn's terrace overlooks the valley of the North Toe River. A night's stay comes with a full breakfast.

Terrell House Bed-and-Breakfast. Moderate. 109 Robertson Street in Burnsville, 28714 (888-682-4505 or 828-682-4505; www.terrellhousebandb.com). This Colonial-style home was built in the early 1900s as a girls' dormitory for the Stanley McCormick School. It is situated in a quiet neighborhood within easy walking distance of the town square. It offers six guest rooms, each with a private bath. A full breakfast is served on fine china in the formal dining room.

Vance Toe River Lodge. Moderate. On N.C. 19E (P.O. Box 159) in Plumtree, 28664 (828-765-9696; www.vancetoeriverlodge.com). This place was built in 1919 as Vance General Merchandise. The owners moved here in 1996 and transformed the historic building into a lodge, restaurant, and campground. Located in the undeveloped part of Avery County along the Toe River only seven miles from the Appalachian Trail, this is a great getaway. The rooms have wireless Internet and satellite TV. Guests enjoy the swimming pool, the pool tables, and various activities. The campground includes a climbing tower, a ropes course, a zip line, and an 18-hole disk golf course. In 2007, the owners even opened their own winery. The Vance Toe

River Lodge Restaurant serves lunch Wednesday through Saturday, dinner on Friday and Saturday, and brunch on Sunday. Reservations are recommended because groups staying at the campground or lodge sometimes book the entire restaurant.

The Celo Inn. Inexpensive. 45 Seven Mile Ridge Road near Burnsville, 28714 (828-675-5132; www.celoinn.com). This inn is located off N.C. 80 some 7.8 miles from the Blue Ridge Parkway. It has five rooms in the upstairs of the main building, plus a separate cottage that sleeps five. The bathrooms are private but might be located across the hall from your room. Breakfast is offered for a small extra fee.

Places to Eat

Grassy Creek Golf and Country Club. Moderate. Off N.C. 226 at 2380 Swiss Pine Lake Drive north of Spruce Pine, 28777 (828-765-6589; www.grassycreek.com). This restaurant is located in the clubhouse of a semiprivate golf course. It serves lunch and dinner.

Garden Deli. Inexpensive. 107 Town Square in Burnsville, 28714 (828-682-3946; www.garden-deli.com). This family-owned and -operated restaurant, in business since 1987, offers sandwiches and salads. Lunch is served Monday through Saturday.

Switzerland Café & General Store. Inexpensive. Near Milepost 334 on N.C. 226 in Little Switzerland, 28749 (828-765-5289; www.switzerlandcafe.com). You'll find soups, salads, sandwiches, desserts, cheeses, imported beer, and wine here. The café is open for lunch and dinner daily from Easter weekend to November 1. It is open on weekends through December.

Upper Street Café. Inexpensive. 198 Oak Avenue in Spruce Pine, 28777 (828-765-0622). The luncheon menu here consists of burgers, sandwiches, and salads. Dinner entrées are limited. Desserts are provided by Sweet Buns Bakery. Lunch is served Monday through Saturday and dinner Friday and Saturday.

Quilt block in Yancey County
PHOTOGRAPH BY CAROLYN SAKOWSKI

Quilt Trails of Western North Carolina

While driving through the mountain counties, you'll most likely notice colorful quilt blocks painted on the sides of barns, houses, and even some franchise restaurants. Early in 2007, the Toe River Arts Council was inspired by projects in neighboring states that combined the artwork of quilt squares with trails that wound through the local scenery. That year, the council, with support from Handmade in America and the Blue Ridge Heritage Area, launched the creation of a series of paintings of individual quilt square designs. The project started in Yancey and Mitchell counties, where you'll still see the greatest representation. But you'll also see quilt blocks springing up in Avery, Watauga, and Ashe counties. Since the program's inception, visitors have taken to using the trails as an excuse to drive around the countryside.

The occupants or owners of the buildings where the quilt squares are placed select the prints. Each selection is linked to a story. A pattern might be part of a beloved family quilt, or it might be an artistic favorite. By summer 2009, squares had been placed on over 130 different buildings.

Be sure to stop by the Burnsville Chamber of Commerce, which houses a gift shop devoted to the quilt trails. There, you can view or purchase maps of the nine different tours that have been set up. For information about the project or about how to sign up for a block, or for updated information on the status of new blocks, write the Quilt Trails Project at P.O. Box 986 in Burnsville (28714). Or you can call 828-682-7331 or visit www.quilttrailswnc.org.

Asheville

By Sue Clark

T here is a peace that settles on my soul whenever I get away to the mountains. Driving west on Interstate 40 from my home in the Piedmont, it's easy to be fooled into thinking the blue images in the distance are a line of thunderstorms marching eastward. But as the engine of my car works harder as I climb, the mountains come into clearer view, and that familiar peace welcomes me. I have heard many people remark that traveling to the Blue Ridge Mountains is like coming home, even if it's the first time they've visited. These ancient peaks and valleys beckon with a warmth and understanding that comes from their age. In Asheville, as they like to say, "altitude affects attitude."

After the tortuous climb past Old Fort, the mountains are suddenly all around you. The road curves more sharply, but the reward is a new view with every turn. Drivers beware! It's easy to be distracted by the vistas you'll encounter for the next half-hour on your drive toward Asheville.

The city of Asheville, named for Governor Samuel Ashe, was incorporated in 1797. The influence of the Scots-Irish immigrants who settled this area is apparent. For example, many old bluegrass tunes sound quite similar to Irish jigs.

Asheville was an isolated town of only 2,600 before the coming of the railroad in the 1880s. Some of the first flatlanders to find their way here were the wealthy, who came to escape the oppressive heat of summer. They built large summer homes and elaborate resort hotels. Soon, Asheville's population was over 10,000.

In the 1920s, Asheville experienced another growth spurt. The popular Art Deco style of the day can still be seen in many downtown buildings. When city hall was erected, many citizens were disturbed by its opulent domed roof covered with green and pink tiles. The same architect was scheduled to build the county courthouse, but the pendulum swung in the opposite direction, and his contract was canceled. The courthouse looks like the straight-laced sibling of the neighboring city hall.

Asheville continues to attract visitors, as well as those who come to settle on this plateau between the Blue Ridge and Great Smoky mountains. And if the temperate weather and beautiful vistas aren't enough, the city offers a unique regional culture, a longstanding crafts tradition, a wide variety of shops and restaurants, outdoor recreation to suit even the most adventurous tastes, and first-class accommodations. Oh yes, and don't forget the French château and the five-star hotel and spa.

A trip to Asheville can be filled with shopping, dining, high culture, hiking, rafting, mountain climbing—the options are endless. Personally, watching sunsets is usually the activity that occupies my time.

JUST THE FACTS

Asheville is located at the crossing of Interstate 40 and Interstate 26.

It is served by Asheville Regional Airport; for information, call 828-684-2226 or visit www.flyavl.com.

The Greyhound bus terminal is located at 2 Tunnel Road (28801); call 828-253-8451 for information.

The Asheville Visitor Center is at 36 Montford Avenue (28801); take Exit 4C off Interstate 240. It is well staffed and open daily. For information, call 888-247-9811 or 828-258-6101 or visit www.exploreasheville.com.

The daily newspaper, the *Asheville Citizen-Times*, is a great source of information, as is *Mountain XPress*, a free weekly. You can also pick up *Bold Life*, a free monthly publication of arts and culture in the highlands.

Things to Do

Historic Places, Gardens, and Tours

You have a variety of options for tours, including a walking architecture and history tour of the Montford neighborhood, an auto rickshaw tour of Riverside Cemetery, an urban-trail tour, and a historic trolley tour. For something a bit different, try a Segway tour, the LaZoom Comedy Tour, or my husband's favorite, an Asheville

Brews Cruise. All are great ways to begin the Asheville experience, since they will give you the lay of the land and help you decide which places to explore further. For information about tours, contact the Asheville Visitor Center.

Biltmore Estate is located on U.S. 25 just north of Exit 50 off Interstate 40 at 1 Approach Road (28803). Words do little to describe this 16th-century-style château modeled after those in France's Loire Valley. The working estate is surrounded by rolling forestland, formal gardens, a winery, and a river. All of this is surprising, considering its proximity to Asheville's downtown.

Opened as a private home in 1895, Biltmore Estate boasted all the latest innovations, including central heating, indoor plumbing, electric lights, a bowling alley, a gymnasium, and an indoor pool—awe-inspiring features for its time. It has charmed its many visitors with its beauty, luxury, and amenities ever since.

George Vanderbilt, grandson of industrialist Cornelius Vanderbilt, purchased 125,000 acres near Asheville because he loved the mountain views and climate. He promptly hired architect Richard Morris Hunt and landscape architect Frederick Law Olmsted, two of America's leading designers, to plan his estate.

Biltmore Estate
COURTESY OF BILTMORE ESTATE

The 250-room mansion took hundreds of workers more than five years to build. The construction site had its own brick kilns and woodworking shops. Limestone was transported on a railroad spur laid just for Biltmore. Artisans and craftsmen were brought from Europe. Many of the men employed in the building of the home fell in love with Asheville and stayed after construction was finished. They settled easily into the area's strong crafts tradition.

While work was progressing on the mansion, the land was also getting attention. Vanderbilt wanted an estate that would include a productive farm and forest. His emphasis on land management is evidenced by the fact that most of the property was eventually sold to the federal government and became part of the Blue Ridge Parkway or Pisgah National Forest. Family descendants still own the mansion and 8,000 surrounding acres. Frederick Law Olmsted, most famous for his design of New York's Central Park, planned the gardens and the park surrounding the home, including the three-mile driveway.

After passing the Lodge Gate, you will make the beautiful drive to the visitor center, where you can purchase admission tickets. You may also view a short film about Biltmore, see a relief map of the area, check the menus of the estate's restaurants, and visit the restroom.

Your first view of the château will be across a long lawn with a reflecting pool in the center. The complex exterior features massive carved archways, columns, and gargoyles. This is but the beginning of the wonders to behold here.

You will enter Biltmore House just as George Vanderbilt's guests did over a century ago—through the main door and into the grand foyer, where you can purchase personal headsets that will allow you to tour the house at your own speed. It's well worth the fee, especially since the recent opening of new rooms on the second floor. Elevators are available for those who can't negotiate the staircases. The grand foyer is the hub of the mansion. Musical groups are often invited to perform in the winter garden on the right side of the foyer.

Each room in the mansion is distinctive. The medieval-style banquet room has a 70-foot arched ceiling, a table that seats 64, Flemish tapestries, numerous elk and moose heads, and a carved mantel that spans three massive fireplaces. The two-story Baroque library has elaborately carved paneling and an 18th-century painted ceiling imported from Venice.

Plan on spending at least half a day at Biltmore. The tour of the mansion lasts two-plus hours and covers everything from the third-floor guest suites to basement service areas such as the kitchens, pantries, and laundry. You'll also see the servants' quarters, the bowling alley, the gymnasium, and the indoor pool, complete with private changing rooms.

After touring the mansion, you can stroll the formal gardens. You may also want to visit the Biltmore Estate Winery, where a brief tour and a wine tasting are offered. The vintners are understandably proud of their award-winning wines. If you get hungry, your options include sandwiches, drinks, and ice cream at the Stable Café, located next to the mansion; baked goods and snacks at the bakery and the candy shop; and upscale dining at Deerpark Restaurant or the Winery Bistro, both located near the winery.

The house is open daily from 9 A.M. to 4:30 P.M. No one is admitted after 4 P.M.; the front door closes at 4:30 P.M. The winery is open daily from noon to 7 P.M. The admission fee may seem expensive until you realize you're paying for at least half a day's entertainment in a place unlike any other in America. For more information, call 800-411-3812 or 828-225-1333 or visit www.biltmore.com.

The *North Carolina Arboretum*, near Milepost 393 on the Blue Ridge Parkway at 100 Frederick Law Olmsted Way (28803), is nestled in one of the most beautiful natural settings in America. Within its 434 acres, the arboretum offers 65 acres of cultivated gardens, 10 miles of forested hiking and biking trails, a state-of-the-art greenhouse production facility, and the finest bonsai collection in the southeastern United States. A parking fee is charged except on Tuesday. The arboretum is open daily except Christmas, weather permitting. Its hours are 8 A.M. to 9 P.M. from April through October and 8 A.M. to 7 P.M. from November through March. Hours for the Visitor Education Center and the Bonsai Exhibition Garden are Monday through Saturday from 9 A.M. to 5 P.M. and Sunday from noon to 5 P.M. The greenhouse hours are Monday through Friday from 9 A.M. to 2 P.M. For more information, including a calendar of special events and educational programs, call 828-665-2492 or visit www.ncarboretum.org.

The ***Thomas Wolfe Memorial*** is located at 52 North Market Street (28801). The house suffered a fire at the hands of an arsonist on July 24, 1998. Over 85 percent of the personal belongings and artifacts of the Wolfe family escaped the flames but had to undergo extensive restoration from smoke and water damage. The home has now been completely restored.

Wolfe grew up in this 28-room house yet had no room of his own, since his mother used the majority of the building for a boardinghouse. In 1929, when Wolfe published *Look Homeward, Angel*, the residents of Asheville easily recognized the "Dixieland" boardinghouse in the town of "Altamont." They were not amused by Wolfe's less-than-flattering picture of his hometown. The local public library banned the book for more than seven years. Asheville eventually came to appreciate the talent of its native son. In 1948, some 10 years after Wolfe's death, the Asheville Chamber of Commerce helped purchase the house as a memorial to one of the 20th century's great novelists. In 1976, the memorial was designated a state historic site.

The visitor center is open Tuesday through Saturday from 9 A.M. to 5 P.M. and Sunday from 1 P.M. to 5 P.M. Check with the site for information on special events, especially those around October 3, Wolfe's birthday. Call 828-253-8304 or visit www. wolfememorial.com.

Botanical Gardens at Asheville, at 151 W. T. Weaver Boulevard (28804), is a beautiful setting for the preservation and display of trees, plants, and flowers native to the southern Appalachians. In 1960, several local garden clubs came together to help plant the grounds of this 10-acre preserve on the campus of the University of North Carolina at Asheville. Now operating as a nonprofit organization, the gardens provide a study area and information center for those interested in horticulture and those who simply appreciate a place of quiet beauty. Unpaved trails wind through the various areas, including the azalea garden and the garden for the blind. A wheelchair ramp is available. The gardens are open daily during daylight hours. Admission is free. For information, call 828-252-5190 or visit www.ashevillebotanicalgardens.org.

Museums and Science Centers

Pack Place, at 2 South Pack Square (28801), opened in 1992 at the cost of $14 million. It provides western North Carolina with a premier arts-and-sciences center, housing museums, offices for local arts organizations, and galleries and studios for artists. The *Asheville Art Museum* has a collection of contemporary and traditional paintings and sculptures by Southern artists. The *Colburn Earth Science Museum* displays 1,500 gems, semiprecious stones, fossils, and minerals, many from the area. Pack Place also houses an interactive museum called *Health Adventure*, which is popular with families. At 39 South Market Street within walking distance of Pack Place is Asheville's African-American cultural facility, the *YMI Cultural Center*. Pack Place is open Tuesday through Saturday from 10 A.M. to 5 P.M. and Sunday from 1 P.M. to 5 P.M. from June through October; it is closed on Sunday during winter. Hours vary for the partner museums, so check before you go. Call 828-257-4500 or visit www.packplace.org.

Pack Square Park, at 1 West Pack Square (28801), is the new jewel of downtown.

The 6.5-acre park is opening in stages through 2010. When completed, it will give Asheville a beautiful new gathering spot. The park will include a large lawn, an amphitheater, local artwork, benches, lush landscaping, and interactive fountains that promise giggling, splashing, and maybe even a soaking. Pack Square Park will provide a wonderful venue for new events, as well as Shindig on the Green, Bele Chere, the Greek Festival, the Fourth of July celebration, and other events throughout the year. Be sure to check out the 300 colorful tiles handmade by local middle-school students. Whether you're attending an event, shopping, or touring the town, the park is a perfect place to take a break in the shade and watch the world go by.

The ***Smith-McDowell House Museum*** is located on the campus of Asheville-Buncombe Technical Community College at 283 Victoria Road (28801). This brick mansion is the city's oldest home. Built in 1840, it has four stories and a double-tiered full-length porch with locally crafted columns. It was the home of mayors, a Confederate major, and friends of the Vanderbilts. The museum features restored period rooms, changing history exhibits, grounds designed by Frederick Law Olmsted, Jr., and the Buncombe County Civil War Memorial. It is open Wednesday through Saturday from 10 A.M. to 4 P.M. and Sunday from noon to 4 P.M. A small admission fee is charged. School programs and group tours can be arranged. For information, call 828-253-9231 or visit www.wnchistory.org.

Downtown Asheville
COURTESY OF ASHEVILLE CONVENTION AND VISITORS BUREAU

The *Western North Carolina Nature Center*, at 75 Gashes Creek Road (28805) on the grounds of the former Asheville Zoo, is designed to show the interaction between plants and animals in the southern Appalachians. The exhibits will interest both children and adults. One features the underground den of a live chipmunk beneath a tree's roots. The center presents animals in natural-habitat exhibits. Domestic animals are showcased at its Educational Farm, where, for example, children can see a cow being milked. A small gift shop offers nature books and souvenirs. The center is open daily from 10 A.M. to 5 P.M. A small admission fee is charged. For information, call 828-298-5600 or visit www.wncnaturecenter.org.

Cultural Offerings

Asheville has a thriving arts community with a long history. A visit would not be complete without taking in some of the galleries and studios. The Asheville Visitor Center has guides to the *River Arts District, Biltmore Village*, and the *Biltmore Antiques District,* as well as information on *Grovewood Gallery*. The *Gallery and Art Walks Guide* to downtown is also available.

The *Asheville Symphony*, headquartered at 87 Haywood Street (28801), is a fine regional orchestra founded in 1960. It offers a series of classical concerts usually featuring an internationally known guest artist. Call 828-254-7046 or visit www.ashevillesymphony.org for information and a schedule of performances.

Asheville Community Theatre, at 35 East Walnut Street (28801), presents 10 productions annually. These include comedies, dramas, and musicals. It also offers a reader's theater, a children's theater, and classes. For information, call 828-254-1320 or visit www.ashevilletheatre.org.

Special Shopping

Downtown Asheville is experiencing a very successful revitalization. The streets are dotted with a wonderful mix of coffeehouses, antique shops, boutiques, and restaurants. Call 828-768-5600 or visit www.downtownasheville.com for more information and the latest news and events.

Wall Street, part of which has been blocked off to create a pedestrian mall, has

Downtown Asheville at sunset
COURTESY OF ASHEVILLE CONVENTION AND VISITORS BUREAU

a great concentration of interesting shops and restaurants.

Just a short distance away at 55 Haywood Street (28801) is **Malaprop's**, one of those great independent bookstores that are becoming increasingly rare these days. Besides a fine selection of regional books, Malaprop's has a small, trendy café where you can sip a cappuccino while getting started on your latest literary purchase. Call 828-254-6734 or visit www.malaprops.com.

Grove Arcade, at 1 Page Avenue (28801), has been painstakingly restored to its original glory. Boasting more than 35 businesses at the time of this writing, with new ones coming in all the time, the arcade offers fresh foods, regional cuisine, locally made crafts, galleries, and a wide variety of restaurants. Built as a public market but inhabited by the federal government from World War II until the 1990s, the unusual Neo-Gothic building features griffins at the entrance, original phone booths, terrazzo tile, soaring ceilings, gargoyles, and friezes. A self-guided architectural and historical tour is available for download from the arcade's website. For the newest vendors and monthly events, call 828-252-7799 or check out www.grovearcade.com.

Biltmore Village, across U.S. 25 from the entrance to Biltmore Estate, is a quaint neighborhood of houses built for the artisans and craftsmen who helped construct the mansion. The two-story houses have been turned into restaurants and shops selling gifts, stationery, jewelry, clothing, knitting supplies, and household accessories. The little village is a nice setting for strolling and window shopping. More information is available at www.biltmorevillage.com.

The Screen Door, at 115 Fairview Road (28803), is a treasure hunter's haven. It is actually a collection of booths for area artisans, antique dealers, and craftsmen. The fun here is in the hunt. Treasures to be found include garden accessories, heirloom seeds, recycled metal sculptures, antique china and silver, estate jewelry, funky furniture, face jugs, books, toys. . . . Get the picture? Every trip is rewarded with something you didn't see the last time you stopped in. The Screen Door also holds seminars and workshops from time to time. It is open from 10 A.M. to 6 P.M. Monday through Saturday and from 1 P.M. to 6 P.M. on Sunday. Call 828-277-3667 or visit www.screendoorasheville.com for more information.

The *Folk Art Center* is located east of Asheville at Milepost 382 on the Blue Ridge Parkway. It features the work of the Southern Highland Craft Guild, an organization of artisans who make pottery, baskets, quilts, candles, brooms, weavings, furniture, jewelry, dolls, musical instruments, and woodcarvings, among other things. This low-roofed building opened in 1980 in a beautiful setting surrounded by flowering trees and azaleas. It serves as an educational center, a research library, a craft shop, and exhibition space. The guild hosts special events such as folk dancing, demonstrations of traditional crafts, and lecture series. The *Allanstand Craft Shop*, located on the premises, offers the largest and most diverse collection of high-quality handmade crafts anywhere in the North Carolina mountains. This is definitely a great place for gift shopping, even if the gift is for you! The center is open from 9 A.M. to 6 P.M. daily; it closes an hour earlier during January, February, and March. Admission is free. For information, visit www.southernhighlandguild.org or call 828-298-7928.

Western North Carolina Farmers Market, at 570 Brevard Road (28806) off N.C. 191 and Interstate 40, is a joy for the eye as well as the palate. This modern facility is operated year-round by the North Carolina Department of Agriculture. The feast for the senses begins with fresh local fruits and vegetables and continues with dried flowers, jams and jellies, and homemade crafts. The market is open daily from 8 A.M. to 6 P.M. April through October and from 8 A.M. to 5 P.M. November through March. Admission is free. For information, call 828-253-1691.

Recreation

If you like the great outdoors, Asheville's the place for you. Surrounded by three park areas containing more than a million acres, it offers plenty of opportunities for camping, hiking, fishing, horseback riding, and whitewater rafting.

If you plan to visit *Great Smoky Mountains National Park*, call 865-436-1200 or check out www.nps.gov/grsm. If you'd like to stay in one of the six campgrounds of the *Blue Ridge Parkway*, call 877-444-6777. If you want to camp in *Pisgah National Forest*, call 828-257-4200.

For hikers, opportunities don't get any better than the legendary *Appalachian Trail*, which cuts through Pisgah National Forest and Great Smoky Mountains National Park. Check with the park offices listed above or visit www.appalachiantrail. org.

Is fishing your passion? Head for *Lake Julian*, south of Asheville on N.C. 280 off U.S. 25; *Lake Powhatan*, on N.C. 191 just off the Blue Ridge Parkway south of Asheville; or *Lake Lure*, on U.S. 74 southeast of Asheville. You'll need a state fishing license. For information about hunting and fishing regulations, call 828-258-6101; for a list of area businesses that sell licenses, visit www.wildlife.org.

Whitewater rafting is popular from June through August on the French Broad River north of Asheville. Check out *French Broad Rafting Expeditions* (800-570-RAFT; www.frenchbroadrafting.com) or *Huck Finn Rafting Adventures* (877-520-4658; www.huckfinnrafting.com) for guided whitewater rafting excursions and calm-water float trips in the Asheville area. If you're a serious rafter and want to try other rivers, see the chapter on Franklin for companies that raft the Nantahala Gorge.

Skiing doesn't usually come to mind when visitors ponder the outdoor activities of North Carolina. However, the highest mountains in the eastern United States are here. *Wolf Laurel Ski Resort* (800-817-4111 or 828-689-4111; www.skiwolfridgenc.

com) is closest to Asheville. *Cataloochee Ski Resort* (800-768-0285 or 828-926-0285; www.cataloochee.com) is a short drive away in Maggie Valley. For information on other ski resorts, see the Boone chapter and the chapter on Banner Elk, Beech Mountain, and Linville.

Golf in the mountains presents its own special challenges and pleasures. Check out *Asheville Municipal Golf Course* (828-298-1867), *Black Mountain Golf Course* (828-669-2710), *Reems Creek Golf Club* (828-645-4393), and *The Grove Park Inn Resort & Spa* (800-438-5800).

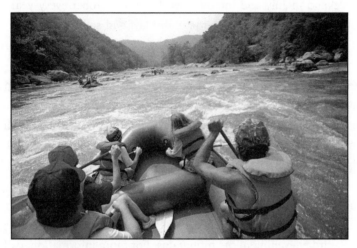

Whitewater rafting
COURTESY OF ASHEVILLE CONVENTION AND VISITORS BUREAU

Mountain golf
PHOTOGRAPH BY BEN CLARK

Seasonal Events

The *Mountain Dance and Folk Festival*, held at Pack Place the first weekend in August, is the oldest event of its kind in the nation. It showcases the best mountain crafts, musicians, and dancers—both cloggers and folk dancers. Started in 1927 by Bascom Lamar Lunsford, it is often called "the Granddaddy of Mountain Festivals." For information, call 800-257-1300 or 828-258-6101 or visit www.folkheritage.org.

The *Craft Fair of the Southern Highlands* is held in the Asheville Civic Center the third weekend in July and the third weekend in October every year. Over 100 craftspeople from the South demonstrate, display, and sell their works. Mountain music and dancing are part of the celebration. Call 828-298-7928 for information.

Bele Chere Downtown Community Celebration, held the last weekend in July, features bands (many of them nationally known), international food vendors, crafts, and contests. It is known as the largest free outdoor festival in the Southeast. The downtown area is closed to vehicles for the weekend. For information, call 828-259-5800 or visit www.belecherefestival.com.

Shindig on the Green is a series of free bluegrass concerts held on Saturday nights throughout the summer. They take place at Pack Square Park and are a great way to spend a Saturday evening in the mountains. For more information, call 800-257-1300 or 828-258-6107.

The *Mountain Sports Festival* is a three-day outdoor celebration in May featuring professional and amateur-level competitions in paddling, cycling, running, and climbing. Demonstrations and beginner-level events in various sports serve to educate and entertain. The festival is centered at Carrier Park on Amboy Road, where you'll find food, award presentations, demonstrations, retail vendors, and live entertainment. Admission is free to spectators; participation in competitions requires a registration fee. For more information, visit www.mountainsportsfestival.com or call 828-251-4029.

LEAF (Lake Eden Arts Festival), held at Camp Rockmont in neighboring Black Mountain, is a weekend festival in spring and fall that strives to connect cultures and create community through music and art. The three-day event includes a wide variety of handicrafts, folk art, culinary arts, healing arts, poetry, and outdoor activities

Dogwood trees along the French Broad River
COURTESY OF ASHEVILLE CONVENTION AND VISITORS BUREAU

like swimming, canoeing, kayaking, and hiking. Add to this workshops, folk dancing, and performances by world-renowned hip-hop, jazz, funk, folk, swing, blues, and zydeco acts and you have the makings of a great time for everyone. "LEAFers," as they are affectionately called, are involved in community outreach that pairs artists with youth in workshops, residencies, and interactive performances. Tickets are sold only in advance. For information, visit www.thelakeedenartsfestival.org or call 828-686-8742.

Places to Stay

Asheville has a great selection of accommodations. It offers 6,000-plus rooms in historic mountain retreats, country inns, bed-and-breakfasts, upscale downtown hotels, economy motels, national chain hotels, and everything in between. Reservations are highly recommended. You'll find Asheville a great home base for your mountain adventures, but don't even think about dropping in during fall leaf season or one of Asheville's popular festivals, when rooms have been reserved months in advance. Consider visiting in winter, when rates at many places are drastically reduced from summer and fall.

Resorts, Hotels, and Motels

The Grand Bohemian Hotel. Deluxe. 11 Boston Way, 28803 (877-274-1242; www. bohemianhotelasheville.com). Stepping into The Grand Bohemian is like entering an Old World hunting lodge, complete with stone archways, rich leather seating, antler chandeliers, and an inviting fireplace in the center of the lobby. Be prepared to be treated like aristocracy. Located in historic Biltmore Village, it is only a stroll away from art galleries, museums, shops, and restaurants. The Grand Bohemian offers 104 luxurious guest rooms and suites, state-of-the-art fitness equipment, 5,000-plus square feet of event space, and its own art gallery and gift shop. The Red Stag Grill serves breakfast, lunch, and dinner in a cozy street-side setting. From the beautifully appointed bar, you can admire the hotel's fine collections of steins and local artwork. Another thing worth admiring is the extensive wine list, which features vintages from around the globe. Each room has a flat-screen television, a surround-sound stereo, and an innovative RoomLinx interactive media and entertainment system. You can take a long soak in your room's massive bathtub or make an appointment for some pampering at the hotel's Poseidon Spa. This is the place to feed your desire to be treated like a royal.

The Grove Park Inn Resort & Spa. Deluxe. 290 Macon Avenue, 28804 (800-438-5800 or 828-252-2711; www.groveparkinn.com). The United States has only a handful of truly grand resort hotels. This is one of them. The attention to detail here comes from a long tradition. Back in the early 1900s, staff members used to polish every coin, so that no guest would be handed a tarnished piece of currency. While that is no longer the rule, it is an example of the kind of service that is still a part of the Grove Park.

The inn was the dream of E. W. Grove, the owner of a pharmaceutical firm famous for Grove's Tasteless Chill Tonic. Grove visited Asheville and found the climate beneficial to his health. His dream was to build the finest resort hotel in the world. After the inn opened in 1913, it became a favorite destination for the rich, the famous, and the powerful. One of the long hallways features photos of some of the inn's illustrious guests: Presidents Wilson, Taft, Coolidge, Hoover, Eisenhower, and Obama; business tycoons Henry Ford and Harvey Firestone; inventor Thomas Edison; and entertainers Enrico Caruso and Mikhail Baryshnikov. Many of the rooms have brass plaques on the doors that tell the year some famous person stayed there. One of the most requested rooms was used by F. Scott Fitzgerald.

The resort's golf course was redesigned by Donald Ross in 1924 and remodeled

The Grove Park Inn Resort & Spa
COURTESY OF THE GROVE PARK INN RESORT & SPA

in 2001. In 1973, the inn was listed on the National Register of Historic Places. That same decade, it added an indoor pool, a sports center, and a clubhouse. In the 1980s, wings were added to provide 512 deluxe rooms, two ballrooms, and a conference center. The new millennium has brought the most ambitious addition to date—a state-of-the-art spa complete with a lap pool, a mineral pool, several hot tubs, and an outdoor pool. The spa treatments are nothing short of luxurious. Located below the Sunset Terrace and between the two wings, the spa is mostly underground, so as not to spoil the view from the main inn.

The guest rooms are luxurious and the service outstanding. The inn offers outdoor activities, shopping and browsing, and award-winning dining. Many people who come for a once-in-a-lifetime experience wind up making a stay here a tradition.

Haywood Park Hotel. Deluxe/Expensive. 1 Battery Park Avenue, 28801 (800-228-2522 or 828-252-2522; www.haywoodpark.com). Haywood Park is an ultra-sophisticated suite hotel in the heart of downtown. The feel here is elegant and refined. The lobby, accented by polished brass railings, doesn't overpower guests with a lot of furniture. The huge rooms open into small common areas located on each floor. This is the type of hotel you'd expect to find in London or New York; the attention to detail and outstanding service are not bettered in any city. Haywood Park's location makes it the ideal spot from which to enjoy Asheville's boutiques and restaurants. It's also a popular choice for a front-row seat for the city's summer festivals.

Crowne Plaza Tennis and Golf Resort. Expensive/Moderate. 1 Resort Drive, 28806 (800-733-3211 or 828-254-3211; www.ashevillecp.com). While large chain properties are generally not listed in this guide, this one is worthy of an exception. Situated on 120 acres close to downtown, the resort and conference center has some unusual extras. The low-rise buildings allow an unobstructed view of the city and the surrounding mountains. Extensive meeting and banquet facilities are on the premises. But what makes this place unique are the options for play, such as the nine-hole championship golf course, the indoor soccer center, the 14 outdoor tennis courts, and the walking trails.

Inns and Bed-and-Breakfasts

Cumberland Falls Bed and Breakfast Inn. Deluxe. 254 Cumberland Avenue, 28801 (888-743-2557 or 828-253-4085; www.cumberlandfalls.com). Built in 1902, Cumberland Falls is in the heart of Asheville's historic Montford neighborhood. The inn has five luxury guest rooms, each with its own beautifully decorated ambiance. Some include a Jacuzzi, a fireplace, or skylights. But don't stay in your room all the time and miss out on the spectacular garden, complete with a footbridge, a koi-filled pond, a waterfall, comfortable seating, and gently playing music. This place of beauty and solace is the perfect setting for unwinding from the day's explorations. The innkeepers are very knowledgeable about the area and will be glad to offer suggestions for your vacation. Rates include a gourmet breakfast sure to fuel you for your adventures.

Inn on Biltmore Estate. Deluxe. 1 Antler Hill Road, 28801 (800-411-3812 or 828-225-1600; www.biltmore.com). Offering the only accommodations on Biltmore Estate, this inn continues a century-old legacy of hospitality begun by George Vanderbilt for his guests. Luxury and comfort reign here. Each of the 213 finely appointed rooms and suites has a breathtaking mountain view. Comfy chairs, fireplaces, terraces, a veranda, an outdoor pool, and exceptional service all come together to make this a true retreat experience. The dining room offers classic, yet innovative, cuisine centered around estate-raised beef, lamb, and veal, complemented by Biltmore Estate wines. The atmosphere is one of casual elegance, graciousness, and refined taste, all framed by the surrounding mountains.

1891 Cedar Crest Inn. Deluxe/Expensive. 674 Biltmore Avenue, 28803 (800-252-0310 or 828-252-1389; www.cedarcrestinn.com). Cedar Crest is one of the largest and most opulent residences surviving from Asheville's 1890s boom period. Perched on a hill three blocks north of the Biltmore Estate, this Queen Anne–style dwelling sits on four landscaped acres featuring English perennial gardens and a croquet lawn. Architectural details include a captain's walk, turrets, expansive verandas, carved oak paneling, and leaded glass. The guest rooms are appointed with satin-and-lace Victorian trappings and feature period antiques, canopied ceilings, claw-foot tubs, and fireplaces. Guests are treated to a sumptuous breakfast, afternoon refreshments, tea, coffee, desserts, and a true spirit of hospitality.

Chestnut Street Inn. Expensive/Moderate. 176 East Chestnut Street, 28801 (800-894-2955 or 828-285-0705; www.chestnutstreetinn.com). This large Colonial Revival home is located in the Chestnut Hill National Historic District. Its large porches are a beautiful accent to the mellow red-brick exterior. The high ceilings, ornate mantels, and antique furnishings and decorations transport guests back to a time when life had a relaxed quality. Amenities include private baths, down comforters, bathrobes, and fresh flowers. A full gourmet breakfast is served each morning. Guests enjoy late-afternoon tea on the veranda. If you're lucky, Mr. Bently, the inn's canine butler, may lead you through the English-style flower garden.

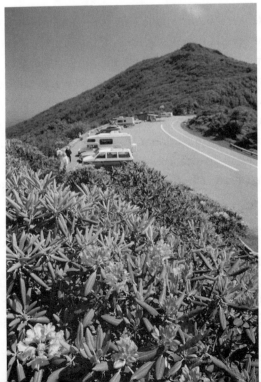

Scenic overlook on the Blue Ridge Parkway near Asheville
COURTESY OF ASHEVILLE CONVENTION AND VISITORS BUREAU

The Lion & the Rose. Expensive/Moderate. 276 Montford Avenue, 28801 (800-546-6988 or 828-255-7673; www.lion-rose.com). Comfort and elegance abound in this wonderful bed-and-breakfast, where no detail is overlooked. A Georgian mansion built around 1895, it has five elegant guest rooms, including a bridal suite with a balcony. Located in the historic Montford neighborhood, the inn has beautiful gardens for strolling and a veranda for relaxing. A full gourmet breakfast is served each morning. Afternoon tea is a great time to come together with other guests and share the day's adventures. The Lion & the Rose is a place to visit for a little pampering.

1847 Blake House Inn. Moderate. 150 Royal Pines Drive in Arden, 28704 (888-353-5227 or 828-681-5227; www.blakehouse.com). Blake House was built in 1847 in the Italianate-Gothic style. It originally served as the summer home of a wealthy lowland rice planter. It also saw service as a field hospital during the Civil War. The restored mansion boasts 22-inch-thick granite walls, heart-pine floors, original English plaster moldings, seven fireplaces, covered porches, and a patio. Each room has fine linens, cable television, a telephone, and a private bath. This is also a rare bed-and-breakfast that welcomes children.

Places to Eat

Curra's Dom. Expensive/Moderate. 72 Weaverville Highway, 28803 (828-253-2111; www.currasdom.com). Put this one in the GPS. A little off the beaten path but well worth it, the restaurant features authentic dishes from the interior of Mexico using local ingredients like homemade chorizo, duck, pasilla peppers, goat cheese, *pipian verde*, jicama, pork, beef, seafood, avocado, and a bunch of other things you've never heard of. Go with a sense of adventure, knowing that everything is prepared fresh. Don't miss the gazpacho, prepared with heirloom tomatoes, fresh pineapple, and cucumber. Curra's Dom even has an "Avocado Margarita"! Lunch and dinner are served Tuesday through Saturday; brunch is offered on Sunday. Reservations are strongly suggested.

Zambra. Expensive/Moderate. 85A Walnut Street, 28801 (828-232-1060; www.zambratapas.com). *Zambra* is Arabic for "flute." It is also an apt description of the "music" of this restaurant. The food here is exquisite—exotic, roughly beautiful, and delicious. The menu features the tastes of Spain, Morocco, and Portugal. The fun, innovative, and extensive tapas selections change frequently according to availability and the whim of the chef. And don't forget the wines, which hail from all over the world; guests have over 75 different Spanish and Portuguese vintages to choose from, as well as a wonderful list of ports and sherries. The eye-catching, comfortable Moroccan decor and the live entertainment make for a great evening. Dinner is served nightly; live entertainment is offered on Friday and Saturday.

Café on the Square. Moderate. 1 Biltmore Avenue, 28801 (828-251-5565). Overlooking historic Pack Square in the heart of downtown, this open, airy café is casual, yet elegant. It offers the freshest in produce, seafood, and meats. Lunch includes salads and a variety of sandwiches. Menu changes are frequent, so a trip here always offers something new. Shrimp étouffée and pork tenderloin with chipotle are among the dinner entrées. The café has an extensive wine list. Catering is available. Lunch is served Monday through Saturday and dinner daily.

Charlotte Street Grill and Pub. Moderate. 157 Charlotte Street, 28801 (828-253-5348 or 828-252-2948; www.charlottestreetgrill.com). Built in the early 1920s, this was northern Asheville's first drugstore. "The Pub" opened in 1976; the offerings in this festive, intimate setting lean toward appetizers and sandwiches. The building was later enlarged to include fine dining upstairs at the Charlotte Street Grill, which offers an extensive menu featuring meats, seafood, and pasta and tofu dishes. Whether you prefer "The Grill" or "The Pub," you will enjoy a unique and tasty dining experience here. Lunch and dinner are served Monday through Saturday.

Early Girl Eatery. Moderate. 8 Wall Street, 28801 (828-259-9292; www.earlygirleatery.com). The locals will tell you that no trip to Asheville is complete without a stop at Early Girl. The emphasis here is on healthy, made-from-scratch cuisine with a regional theme. Dishes range from house-made sausage, shrimp and grits, and "Vegan Tofu Scramble" in the morning to pan-fried chicken and "Black-Eyed Pea Cakes" at night. The folks at Early Girl believe in supporting local agriculture and work closely with nearby farms and dairies to bring guests the freshest ingredients possible. The atmosphere is comfortable, the food amazing, and the whole experience not soon forgotten. Breakfast, lunch, and dinner are served daily; a sumptuous Sunday brunch is also offered.

Flying Frog Café. Moderate. 1 Battery Park, 28801 (828-254-9411; www.flyingfrogcafe.com). Okay, how about this for different? This restaurant features French, Cajun, German, and Indian foods—and it works! The eclectic menu offers diverse specialties such as bouillabaisse, jambalaya, schnitzel, and crab cakes. All of the curries and delicious blends of seasonings and spices are prepared in-house. The extensive wine list reflects the café's international flair. Al fresco dining is available in the sidewalk café and more formal dining at the café downstairs; the full menu is available at the bar upstairs. Lunch and dinner are served daily in the sidewalk café and the bar. Dinner is served downstairs from Wednesday to Sunday.

Mayfel's. Moderate. 22 College Street, 28801 (828-252-8840; www.mayfels.net). Who says you can't get good Cajun food in the mountains? This is the best you'll find outside the bayou. All meals are made to order. The menu, which changes seasonally, takes advantage of as much of the local bounty as possible. Try the "Smoked Trout Spread" for a starter; it was featured in *Bon Appétit.* As for the entrées, you can't go wrong with the jambalaya, the seafood étouffée, the shrimp and grits, or "Loretta's Meat Loaf." And yes, muffalettas and po' boys are on the sandwich board. Vegetarians will find a wide variety of choices, too. Lunch is served Thursday through Monday and dinner Thursday through Sunday.

Tupelo Honey Café. Moderate. 12 College Street, 28801 (828-255-4863; www.tupelohoneycafe.com). This popular downtown eatery has it all. As part of Asheville's emphasis on local food, the executive chef established his own 12-acre farm to provide natural pesticide-free ingredients for the restaurant. An upscale but casual environment invites you to sample the authentic Low Country– and New Orleans–style delights. The unique appetizers, fun sandwiches, and tasty entrées are all prepared in an open kitchen. Breakfast, served anytime, is every bit as enticing as dinner. Leave room for dessert; the "Buttermilk Cheesecake" is like silk. Breakfast and lunch are served Tuesday through Sunday and dinner Tuesday through Saturday. Reservations are not accepted.

Jack of the Wood. Moderate/Inexpensive. 95 Patton Avenue, 28801 (828-252-5445; www.jackofthewood.com). This is the place to go for authentic pub fare and handcrafted ales. An Asheville favorite for more than 10 years, Jack of the Wood offers everything from shepherd's pie, fish and chips, and first-rate pub burgers to its highly acclaimed Green Man Ale. Throw in live Celtic, bluegrass, and traditional Appalachian music Wednesday through Saturday nights and you've got the makings for a great night out. The pub opens daily for dinner at 4 P.M.; a late-night menu is available after 10 P.M. Wednesday through Saturday.

Laughing Seed Café. Moderate/Inexpensive. 40 Wall Street, 28801 (828-252-3445; www.laughingseed.com). This popular downtown restaurant features a vegetarian menu that even meat lovers will find innovative and delicious. Pasta dishes, sandwiches, and daily specials are offered. You'll find Mexican, Indian, Asian, Mediterranean, and New American accents in the cuisine. Outdoor dining is available when weather permits. The atmosphere is open and casual. This is a great place to take a break from exploring Asheville's shops and boutiques. Lunch and dinner are served Wednesday through Monday.

Nearby

Black Mountain is a small community about 15 miles east of Asheville in the Swannanoa River Valley. The town has a history of attracting nonconformists and freethinkers. Oddly enough, it is also the center of the largest concentration of religious retreats in the United States; there are 20 in a 35-mile radius. Once a spiritual center for the Cherokee Indians, the area was the site of the experimental Black Mountain College from 1933 to 1956. Today, the town draws visitors who come to see the beautiful Montreat Conference Center and to enjoy shopping for crafts and antiques. To learn more, visit www.blackmountain.org.

When you're ready for a bite to eat, Black Mountain offers a great variety of lunch and dinner spots. For lunch, try *Veranda Café & Gifts*, at 119 Cherry Street

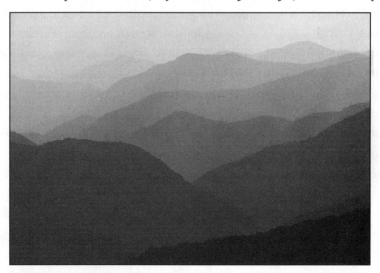

The Blue Ridge Mountains surrounding Asheville
COURTESY OF ASHEVILLE CONVENTION AND VISITORS BUREAU

(28711), which offers a relaxing atmosphere and a delicious assortment of sandwiches, salads, soups, daily specials, and tempting desserts; call 828-669-8864 or visit www.verandacafeandgifts.com. Al fresco dining and pizza, anyone? Head for *My Father's Pizza*, at 110 Cherry Street (28711), where you'll find gourmet pizzas, pasta dishes, subs, stromboli, and salads, all made from scratch; call 828-669-4944 or visit www.myfatherspizza.com. *Berliner Kindl German Restaurant,* at 121 Broadway (28711), has everything from schnitzels to brats, along with a deli, so you can take some authentic delicacies home with you; call 828-669-5255. A seasonal fine-dining menu is offered at *The Cellar Door*, at 117 Cherry Street (28711); call 828-669-9090.

After a day of shopping, you'll find no better way to unwind and ponder your purchases than a stay at the *Red Rocker Inn*, at 136 North Dougherty Street (28711). This favorite lodging and dining destination offers 17 comfortable, elegant guest rooms, each with a private bath. Twelve of the rooms are open year-round. Guests enjoy a mountain view from the red rockers lining the wide front porch. The Red Rocker Inn combines genuine hospitality, delicious Southern cuisine, and exceptional service. For information, call 888-669-5991 or 828-669-5991 or visit www. redrockerinn.com.

Weaverville, about 12 miles north of Asheville, is one of those quaint mountain towns just far enough from the bustle but close enough to everything the area has to offer. If you're staying in town, try the *Inn on Main Street*, located at 88 South Main (28787). A beautiful Victorian home built in 1900, it offers seven guest rooms, some with fireplaces and whirlpool tubs. All have private baths, air conditioning, and cable TV. Rates include a full breakfast made from scratch and complimentary evening refreshments. For information, call 877-873-6074 or visit www.innonmain.com.

At 911 Reems Creek Road in Weaverville (28787) is the *Zebulon B. Vance Homestead*, a state historic site featuring a reconstruction of the mountain home of one of North Carolina's preeminent statesmen. Vance is best known as North Carolina's governor during the Civil War. The two-story pine-log home has period furniture, some of it from the original house, built in 1790. Among the log outbuildings are a corncrib, a springhouse, a loom house, a slave house, a smokehouse, and a toolhouse. A guide is on hand to explain what life was like in the mountains for the Vances and other homesteaders. The visitor center offers displays that further illustrate the times. Guests are welcome to bring a picnic lunch to enjoy on the grounds. The homestead is open year-round Tuesday through Saturday from 9 A.M. to 5 P.M. Admission is free. For information, call 828-645-6706 or visit www.nchistoricsites. org/vance/vance.htm.

Craggy Gardens, located between Milepost 363 and Milepost 369 on the Blue Ridge Parkway, isn't really a garden at all. Instead, it's an ideal place for viewing wide slopes bursting with mountain laurel and rhododendron in June and the incredible display of fall colors in October. Trails wind among trees, shrubs, and flowers. The picnic area commands a striking view of the Blue Ridge. The visitor center has displays on local ecology. Rangers occasionally present interpretive programs. For information, call 828-298-0398.

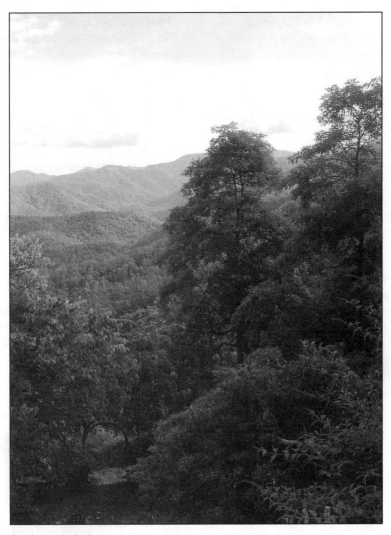

Scenic mountain view
PHOTOGRAPH BY BEN CLARK

St. Lawrence Basilica

The most beautiful building in Asheville may be the Spanish Baroque–style St. Lawrence Basilica, at 97 Haywood Street (28801). The most striking feature of the church is its central dome, which is built wholly of tiles and is entirely self-supporting. Measuring 58 feet by 82 feet, it is reputed to be the largest freestanding elliptical dome in North America.

St. Lawrence Basilica is filled with bas-relief and other sculptures, stained-glass windows, ornately carved doors, and glazed tiles from all over the world; some of the wooden statues come from Spain and the stained-glass windows from Germany, for example. The beautiful altar is topped with an 1,800-pound block of Tennessee marble.

St. Lawrence Catholic Church was designated a basilica by Pope John Paul II in April 1993. The basilica designation is given to certain churches because of their antiquity, dignity, historical importance, or significance as places of worship. At that time, only 33 basilicas were in the United States. As a basilica, St. Lawrence has the privilege of displaying the pontifical seal. The dominant feature of the seal is a pair of crossed keys, which symbolize the keys to the Kingdom. Basilicas also have special responsibilities, such as promoting the study of the documents of the pope and the Holy See, especially those concerning the sacred liturgy. Additionally, a basilica has the responsibility to promote the participation of the faithful in the Mass and the Liturgy of the Hours, especially matins (morning prayers) and vespers (evening prayers).

St. Lawrence Basilica is the only church built by the renowned Rafael Guastavino. The massive stone foundation and the brick superstructure give silent testimony to the architect's desire to construct an edifice that would endure for generations. There are no beams of wood or steel in the entire structure.

A visit to St. Lawrence Basilica offers a chance not only to view fine architecture, beautiful stained glass, and wonderful sculptures, but also to witness some of the sacred traditions of the Catholic Church that are not often on display in the modern world. For information, call 828-252-6042 or visit www.stlawrencebasilica.org.

The Southern Mountains

Hendersonville
Brevard
Highlands
Franklin

By Sue Clark

The southern mountains are an area of stark contrasts and rich beauty. Don't be deceived by what looks like a highway on your road map—it could just as easily be a winding, twisting way to get from one town to another. But arduous drives are rewarded by wonderful surprises here. Within easy walking distance of those "highways," you'll encounter waterfalls to slide down, waterfalls to walk behind, and even a waterfall you can drive under! In this four-county area south of Asheville, you'll find the home of one of America's greatest poets, a world-class music festival, boutiques, golf courses, and gem mines. A trip here provides many reasons for a return visit.

Hendersonville

Established in 1840, Hendersonville is ideally situated on a plateau between the Blue Ridge Mountains and the Great Smoky Mountains. Thanks to its mild climate and moderate altitude (2,200 feet), many people find this the perfect place to live and vacation. What's not to like? You can play golf 11 months of the year, you'll encounter little crime or pollution, and you'll find lots of friendly people. The area attracts many retirees.

Apples are the mainstay of Henderson County's economy. The North Carolina Apple Festival takes place in Hendersonville on Labor Day weekend. The county produces 70 percent of the state's leading fruit crop. Local farmers grow about 8 million bushels of Red and Golden Delicious, Rome Beauty, and Stayman apples, as well as many heirloom varieties, each year.

Downtown Hendersonville is great for walking. Small shops, boutiques, and restaurants line the main streets.

JUST THE FACTS

Hendersonville is 22 miles south of Asheville via U.S. 25 or Interstate 26. Both intersect U.S. 64 in Hendersonville.

The closest airport is Asheville Regional Airport; call 828-684-2226 for information.

The Henderson County Travel and Tourism office, at 201 South Main Street (28792), is a great place to start your planning; call 800-828-4244 or visit www.historichendersonville.org. You may reach the chamber of commerce at 877-836-1414 or 828-692-1413.

The daily newspaper is the *Hendersonville Times-News*. Current-events information, a shopping guide, and a dining guide are included in the free publication *This Week in WNC*.

Things to Do

Historic Places, Gardens, and Tours

Carl Sandburg Home National Historic Site is located south of Hendersonville at 81 Carl Sandburg Lane in Flat Rock (28731). The 264-acre farm called Connemara is where the Pulitzer Prize–winning poet and biographer spent the last 22 years of his life. In 1945, Sandburg bought the property and moved here with his wife, Paula, who was renowned for raising champion goats. In 1967, shortly after Sandburg's death at age 89, Connemara became a national historic site.

You'll get a sense of Connemara's peacefulness as you walk up the trail from the information center to the white three-story house. Built around 1838, the home is surrounded by trees and situated with a lovely view of the rolling countryside. Nearby are several outbuildings. About a quarter-mile away is the barn, where the goats were housed and tended. A few goats are still kept there.

In the reception area of the house, you can see a filmed interview of Sandburg conducted by Edward R. Murrow. The furnishings, family pictures, shelves of books, and huge stacks of papers and magazines in the living room and Sandburg's study have been left just as they were when he was in residence. On the dining-room table are his thermos and a handful of letters to be opened.

In summer, actors and actresses from the nearby Flat Rock Playhouse dramatize tales from Sandburg's *Rootabaga Stories*, a book of children's folk tales, in a small outdoor amphitheater located on the playhouse grounds. Performances of *World of Carl Sandburg* and *Sandburg's Lincoln* are also given. Shows are offered Tuesday through Saturday; admission is free.

The home is open daily except Christmas from 9 A.M. to 5 P.M. Admission to the grounds is free. Adults are charged a small fee for the house tour, but children under 16 are admitted free. The tour lasts about 30 minutes, after which you may enjoy walking the two marked trails on the property. For information, call 828-693-4178 or visit www.nps.gov/carl.

Oakdale Cemetery, on U.S. 64 West, is the site of "Wolfe's Angel." Thomas Wolfe's first novel, *Look Homeward, Angel*, contained numerous references to an angel statue carved from Italian marble. The statue in Oakdale Cemetery served as the inspiration. The author's father, W. O. Wolfe, sold it to the Johnson family to mark the family plot here. The angel holds a lily in her left hand while she extends her right hand upward. The statue is protected by a wrought-iron fence. A historical marker is located on the highway.

Museums and Science Centers

Be sure to check out the *Henderson County Heritage Museum*, located on Main Street in the lovingly restored courthouse at 1 Historic Courthouse Square (28792). It is open Wednesday through Saturday from 10 A.M. to 5 P.M. and Sunday from 1 P.M. to 5 P.M. For information, visit www.hendersoncountymuseum.org or call 828-694-1619.

The *Mineral & Lapidary Museum of Henderson County*, located at 400 North Main Street (28792), is open Monday through Friday from 1 P.M. to 5 P.M. and Saturday from 10 A.M. to 5 P.M. For information, call 828-698-1977 or visit www.mineralmuseum.org.

Cultural Offerings

Flat Rock Playhouse, located at 2661 Greenville Highway in Flat Rock (28731), is the state theater of North Carolina. It is a professional summer theater that presents eight or nine comedies, mysteries, and musicals from late May to mid-December. Periodically, Thomas Wolfe's *Look Homeward, Angel* is presented in honor of the local boy. For information, call 866-732-8008 or 828-693-0731 or visit www.flatrockplayhouse.org.

Special Shopping

Historic Downtown Hendersonville has experienced a revitalization in recent years. Within easy walking distance are antique shops, art galleries, and specialty stores. Visitors can go back in time at an old-fashioned soda shop located in a pharmacy that has occupied the same spot since the turn of the 20th century. Downtown shoppers will find everything from boutiques filled with local crafts to galleries featuring exhibits of modern art. Hendersonville's downtown is the perfect place to stroll, browse, shop, nibble, and enjoy a day in a lovely mountain community.

My favorite downtown spot is *Kilwin's Chocolate Shoppe*, located at 506 North Main Street (28792). My son and I consider ourselves fudge experts, so when a friend recommended a new place in Hendersonville as the home of the best fudge she'd ever tasted, we knew we had to check it out. Imagine my delight upon discovering that the "new" place was actually a beacon of my childhood. You see, the original Kilwin's is in Petoskey, Michigan, where my family had a summer home when I was a child. The owners in Hendersonville assured me it truly is the same Kilwin's; in fact, they had to travel to Petoskey to learn to make fudge the Kilwin's way. Don't limit yourself to just the fudge. The shop also sells ice cream, caramel corn, brittle, taffy, and candies, all of which live up to Kilwin's reputation for quality. For information, call 828-698-9794.

Henderson County Farmers Curb Market, at 221 North Church Street (28792), offers home-grown flowers, fresh fruits and vegetables, baked goods, handmade crafts, and an impressive array of pickles, relishes, jellies, and jams. It's also a great place to chat with the locals. The market is open Tuesday, Thursday, and Saturday from 8 A.M. to 2 P.M. from May to December; it is open Saturday only from January through March. For more information, call 828-692-8012 or visit www.curbmarket.com.

Recreation

Holmes Educational State Forest, located at 1299 Crab Creek Road southwest of Hendersonville (28739), is a managed forest that offers picnic areas, hiking trails, and sites for tent camping. Some of the trees have button-activated recordings describing aspects of the forest. The forest is open for visitors Tuesday through Sunday from mid-March to the Friday before Thanksgiving. For more information, call 828-692-0100 or visit www.ncesf.org/HESF/home.htm.

DuPont State Forest, located off U.S. 64 between Hendersonville and Brevard, encompasses over 10,000 acres of forestland. Hiking, biking, and horseback riding are allowed on designated trails. Demonstrations on soil and water protection, wildlife management, and forest management are offered throughout the year. Each spring and fall, the Friends of DuPont Forest offers their special Tour de Falls, during which guides take groups of 12 to 15 people into the forest for an up-close look at waterfalls and other points of interest. For information, call 828-877-6527 or visit www.dupontforest.com.

Seasonal Events

The ***North Carolina Apple Festival***, held Labor Day weekend, celebrates the apple harvest with street dancing and crafts for sale. The King Apple Parade rolls through downtown on Labor Day. For more information, call 828-697-4557 or visit www.ncapplefestival.org.

The *Garden Jubilee* is held the Saturday and Sunday of Memorial Day weekend. The emphasis is on plants and garden advice. Arts and crafts are available for sale. Call 800-828-4244 or 828-693-9708.

Art on Main, held the first weekend in October, features regional artists displaying and selling their fine arts and crafts. Call 828-693-8504.

Places to Stay

Inns and Bed-and-Breakfasts

Elizabeth Leigh Inn. Expensive. 908 Fifth Avenue West, 28739 (828-698-9707; www.elizabethleighinn.com). This 1893 mansion was one of the finest homes of old Hendersonville. Now fully restored and beautifully decorated, it is listed on the National Register of Historic Places. The Elizabeth Leigh Inn is the place to come for a quiet, luxurious, and highly pampered getaway. It offers a full gourmet breakfast, afternoon tea, private baths, homemade treats, and evening turn-down service. The inn can also host an exquisite garden wedding and reception or any other special event that requires that perfect touch of elegance.

Mélange Bed-and-Breakfast. Expensive. 1230 Fifth Avenue West, 28739 (800-303-5253 or 828-697-5253; www.melangebb.com). This beautiful old mansion, restored in 1996, offers Old World charm, tradition, and flair. High ceilings, marble fireplaces, ornate mirrors, Mediterranean porches, crystal chandeliers, and antique furnishings lend elegance and warmth. The large guest rooms and the two-room suite have either solid brass, old plantation oak, or French canopy beds; each room has a private bath. Room rates include a gourmet breakfast served in the rose garden, on the covered porches, or in the formal dining room.

Highland Lake Inn. Expensive/Moderate. 86 Lily Pad Lane in Flat Rock, 28731 (800-635-0979 or 828-693-6812; www.HLInn.com). This country retreat is a haven of hospitality, elegance, and unspoiled natural beauty. The choice of accommodations includes the elegant inn, the historic lodge, family-style cottages, and rustic cabins. Each room is distinctively decorated; some have whirlpool tubs, wet bars, canopy beds, and fireplaces. The rates include a sumptuous Southern breakfast, cable television, a newspaper, and full use of the extensive grounds, which include a lake, a swimming pool, tennis courts, a horseshoes pit, and a volleyball court; guests may use the canoes and paddleboats, ride bicycles, and fish. They'll even find a collection of barnyard animals; in the morning, they're welcome to watch the goats being milked. Highland Lake Inn is ideal for weddings, banquets, family reunions, and corporate retreats.

Woodfield Inn. Expensive/Moderate. 2905 Greenville Highway in Flat Rock, 28731 (800-533-6016 or 828-693-6016). Woodfield Inn has been receiving guests since 1852. It is a landmark establishment with a long tradition of Southern hospitality. A three-story frame hotel with a huge front lawn, it has an enormous entrance hall, a large sitting room, and three dining rooms downstairs. On the upper floors, which slant slightly, are Victorian bedrooms with high ceilings and French doors that open onto a veranda. Throughout the inn are antique furnishings, some of which have been here since the Civil War. Continental breakfast is included in the room rate.

Claddagh Inn. Moderate. 755 North Main Street, 28792 (866-770-2999 or 828-693-6737; www.claddaghinn.com). This three-story frame house with a wraparound veranda has been an inn for 90 years. It lends the same feeling you might get visiting your grandmother. Each of the 14 guest rooms and three suites is graciously appointed and has a private bath. A full country breakfast is served in the dining room.

The Waverly Inn. Moderate. 783 North Main Street, 28792 (800-537-8195 or 828-693-9193; www.waverlyinn.com). Located within easy walking distance of downtown, this lovingly renovated three-story house is listed on the National Register. The beautiful veranda filled with rocking chairs invites guests to enjoy the relaxing atmosphere. The 14 guest rooms are beautifully appointed. All have private baths. Room rates include a sumptuous home-cooked breakfast. Guests also enjoy the freshly baked cookies and hors d'oeuvres in the evening.

Places to Eat

Flight. Expensive. 401 North Main Street, 28792 (www.flightwoodgrill.com; 828-694-1030). Housed in an old bank building, Flight features wonderful international cuisine and specialties grilled over locally grown apple wood. The elegant, upscale atmosphere is accentuated by local artwork. Menu selections include applewood-grilled steaks, fresh seafood, pork, lamb, pasta dishes, fresh salads, and wood-grilled pizzas. Dinner is served Monday through Saturday. Reservations are suggested.

Season's at Highland Lake Inn. Expensive. 86 Lily Pad Lane in Flat Rock, 28731 (877-394-4945 or 828-696-9094; www.HLInn.com/Seasons). This place offers fine dining in a casual country setting. The vibrant, exciting menu features innovative cuisine that showcases the chef's creativity. Season's prides itself on fresh ingredients, including vegetables and herbs from its own gardens. Breakfast, lunch, and dinner are served Monday through Saturday. A brunch buffet and a dinner buffet are offered on Sunday. Reservations are requested.

Woodfield Inn. Expensive/Moderate. 2905 Greenville Highway in Flat Rock, 28731 (828-693-6016 or 828-693-6016). This inn has been a dining tradition since 1852, when it was a stop on the stagecoach line. Warm muffins are brought for you to enjoy while reading the menu, which includes fried chicken, baked ham, prime rib, and trout almandine. After one of the delicious homemade desserts, you'll want to linger on the veranda. The restaurant is open for dinner Wednesday through Sunday and for brunch on Sunday.

Blue Sky Café. Moderate. 3987 Hendersonville Road in Fletcher, 28732 (828-684-1247; www.iloveblueskycafe.com). This is the place to go for a relaxed, fun, family-friendly atmosphere where there's something on the menu for everyone, whether you crave a delicious vegetarian wrap or a big, juicy hand-pattied burger. And yes, the great kids' menu goes beyond mac 'n' cheese and chicken nuggets. Blue Sky has creative lunch and dinner specials and a really friendly staff. Guests can enjoy a cold beer or a glass of wine on the patio. The café is open for lunch and dinner Monday through Saturday.

Champa. Moderate. 437 North Main Street, 28792 (www.champanc.com; 828-

696-9800). Walking along Main Street, you'll find it hard to miss the wonderful aroma coming from this restaurant. Resistance is futile, so just give in. Champa serves a wide variety of sushi and Thai options in an upscale but casual setting. You'll have a hard time deciding among all the curry, rice, noodle, teriyaki, tempura, sushi, soup, salad, and appetizer choices. Or you can just do what my family did—everyone order something different and pass it around. Leave room for dessert; the "Tempura Cheesecake" is really special. Lunch and dinner are served daily.

Hannah Flanagan's Pub. Inexpensive. 300 North Main Street, 28792 (828-696-1665; www.theoriginalhannahflanagans.com). As in any good pub, the bar is the focus of this local hangout. Recently expanded to offer more table seating, Hannah Flanagan's is a great place to stop and take stock of your shopping expedition. Patrons enjoy the hearty soups, sandwiches, and other traditional pub fare, as well as the fine selection of imported beer. The fish and chips is simply the best you'll ever taste. This is one of those great pubs that makes you feel comfortable the minute you walk in the door. Lunch and dinner are served daily.

Margaritagrille. Inexpensive. 430 North Main Street, 28792 (828-692-3100). To me, comfort food means a friendly sports bar serving great pub food. If you agree, then wander into this Hendersonville hot spot since 1981. It boasts that its burgers are the best, and you'll probably agree. The appetizers are also great, as are the sandwiches and wraps. Margaritagrille does a mean BBQ pork and good seafood. Try the "Teriyaki Mahi Mahi" on a stick. Lunch and dinner are served daily. Live music is featured on weekends.

Nearby

To reach the famous *Chimney Rock* attraction from Hendersonville, take U.S. 64 East to Bat Cave, then turn right on U.S. 74. Or just type 431 Main Street in the village of Chimney Rock (28720) into your GPS and you'll get there. Located 15 miles east of Hendersonville, this attraction includes a massive rock formation known for its tall, narrow shape. Chimney Rock rises 315 feet above the entrance to Hickory Nut Gorge and provides a 75-mile panoramic view of Lake Lure and the Blue Ridge Mountains. Visitors cross the Rocky Broad River just past the entrance to the attraction; from there, they begin a three-mile drive to the base of the rock formation, after which they're transported to the top via an elevator that runs up a 26-story shaft hewn in the granite. For the more adventurous, a trail of plank steps also leads to the summit. Once on top, visitors can enjoy the view from the fenced-in overlook or from inside the Sky Lounge, which has a gift shop and a snack bar. The attraction also offers picnic areas with grills, a playground, an interpretive nature center, and hiking trails. Chimney Rock is part of the new, larger Chimney Rock State Park, though the original attraction is the only section accessible to the public at present. It is open daily, weather permitting, except for Thanksgiving, Christmas, and New Year's. An admission fee is charged. The ticket office is open from 8:30 A.M. to 5:30 P.M. during daylight saving time; otherwise, it's open until 4:30 P.M. The attraction closes 90 minutes after the ticket office. For more information, call 800-277-9611 or 828-625-9611 or visit www.chimneyrockpark.com.

If you'd like to stay in the area, you can't go wrong with the *1927 Lake Lure Inn and Spa*, located at 2771 Memorial Highway in Lake Lure (28746). This elegant inn, recently restored to its full splendor, offers a swimming pool, a full-service spa, and

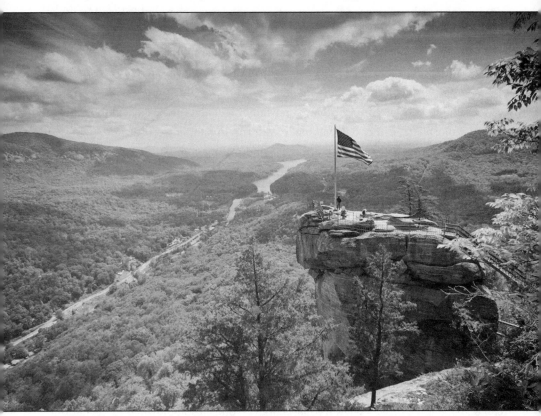

Chimney Rock and Lake Lure
COURTESY OF CHIMNEY ROCK PARK

an expansive veranda overlooking the lake. Call 888-434-4970 or 828-625-2525 or visit www.lakelure.com.

Saluda, on U.S. 176 approximately 12 miles southeast of Hendersonville, is a small community where a number of craftspeople live and labor. You can see some of their work and an array of regional country antiques in the town's old train depot, which has been converted into shops. Saluda is also the site of the famous Saluda Grade, the steepest main-line railroad grade in America. For information, visit www.saluda.com.

A noteworthy local hostelry is the _Orchard Inn_, located at 100 Orchard Inn Lane (28773). It occupies an old vacation retreat built for the Brotherhood of Railway Clerks. The nine guest rooms and five cottage suites are comfortably furnished with period pieces and antiques. Breakfast is served on the glassed-in dining porch overlooking the Warrior Mountains. For information, call 800-851-3800 or 828-749-5471 or visit www.orchardinn.com. Another option is the newly renovated _Saluda Mountain Lodge_, at 1793 Holberts Cove Road (28773), which offers 25 well-appointed rooms. Call 866-602-6973 or 828-749-4951 or visit www.saludamountainlodge.com.

As for dining, you have two excellent choices—the _Purple Onion_ (828-749-1179; www.purpleonionsaluda.com) and the _Saluda Grade Café_ (828-749-5854; www.saludagradecafe.com). Both are on Main Street and offer excellent food and a casual atmosphere. Either one will make your trip to Saluda worthwhile.

To reach _Pearson's Falls_, look for the sign directing you to turn off U.S. 176 approximately three miles from Saluda. You'll then need to travel one mile on S.R. 1102 and hike an easy quarter-mile trail to the 90-foot falls. The area is maintained by the Tryon Garden Club. A small admission fee is charged. The address for the falls is 2720 Pearson Falls Road in Saluda (28773). For information, call 828-749-3031 or visit www.pearsonsfalls.org.

Tryon, on U.S. 176 east of Saluda, is named for William Tryon, the British governor of the North Carolina colony. The town's pretty, steep Main Street offers a collection of great little shops and eateries. All in all, this small mountain town is a true gem. For information, visit www.tryon-nc.com.

Visitors come to Tryon for its gift and craft shops and to see works by local artists and craftspeople at the _Tryon Fine Arts Center_, at 34 Melrose Avenue (28782); call 828-859-8322 or visit www.tryonarts.org. Tryon is also renowned for its nationally and regionally sanctioned equestrian events, which take place at _FENCE_ (Foothills Equestrian Nature Center), located at 3381 Hunting Country Road (28782); for information, call 828-859-9021 or visit www.fence.org. If competition of a culinary nature is more your style, head to Tryon during the second week of June for the ***Blue Ridge BBQ Festival***. This event attracts over 25,000 people and features live music and a juried crafts exhibition. More than 70 teams participate in the two-day cooking event, which has been sanctioned by the governor as the official North Carolina State Barbecue Championship. For information, call 828-859-RIBS or visit www.blueridgebbqfestival.com.

If you plan to stay in town, try the ***Pine Crest Inn & Restaurant***, at 85 Pine Crest Lane (28782). Listed on the National Register, this inn has received 13 consecutive AAA Four Diamond awards. It offers affordable rooms, luxurious suites, private cottages, a modern conference center, and beautiful gardens. The restaurant is renowned for its relaxing atmosphere and its excellent cuisine featuring fresh seasonal ingredients. It has received *Wine Spectator* magazine's Award of Excellence for eight straight years; the extensive wine list is a perfect match for the expertly prepared cuisine. Call 800-633-3001 or 828-859-9135 or visit www.pinecrestinn.com.

Waterfalls
COURTESY OF TRANSYLVANIA COUNTY DEPARTMENT OF TOURISM

Brevard

On the edge of Pisgah National Forest sits the pretty little town of Brevard. Its permanent population of 7,000 swells to many times that number during the annual Brevard Music Festival. Brevard is in the heart of an area called "the Land of Waterfalls." It is the county seat of Transylvania County, whose name means "across the woods."

Brevard's downtown has shops, restaurants, a movie theater, antique malls, and a picturesque brick courthouse. Beyond downtown are attractive homes with big porches on shaded residential streets. Given the size of the town, Brevard's cultural offerings come as a surprise to many visitors. The mild climate and attractive landscape draw a large number of retirees, summer residents, and tourists.

Brevard is an ideal place to stay if you enjoy driving through the mountains and stopping at waterfalls. It is also the gateway to activities in Pisgah National Forest; many outfitters are ready to equip visitors for kayaking, tubing, hiking, and mountain biking. One of the best resources for exploring the national forest is National Geographic map #780. These waterproof, tear-resistant maps are available at most outfitters and at www.natgeomaps.com/trailsillustrated.

Transylvania County Courthouse in Brevard
PHOTOGRAPH BY JACK CHRISTFIELD

JUST THE FACTS

Brevard is three miles south of the intersection of U.S. 276 and N.C. 280, about 30 miles south of Asheville.

The Brevard Chamber of Commerce and Visitor Center is located at 175 East Main Street (28712); call 800-648-4523 or 828-883-3700 or visit www.brevardncchamber.org or www.visitwaterfalls.com.

The local newspaper is the *Transylvania Times*, published semiweekly.

Things to Do

Historic Places, Gardens, and Tours

The *Cradle of Forestry in America* is another legacy of George Vanderbilt. When Vanderbilt bought property in 1889 to create Biltmore Estate (see the chapter on Asheville), he hired Gifford Pinchot to manage the forestland. Pinchot was the first man in America to practice selective timber cutting. Pinchot's successor, Dr. Carl Schenck, started the first school of forestry in America, the Biltmore Forest School, which lasted from 1898 until 1913. In 1968, Congress established the 6,400-acre Pisgah National Forest.

The Forest Discovery Center at the Cradle of Forestry is located at 1001 Pisgah Highway/U.S. 276 in the community of Pisgah Forest (28768). This national historic site commemorates the birthplace of scientific forestry and forestry education in America. The visitor center has exhibits, an 18-minute film outlining the history of the forestry school, a gift shop, and a snack bar. Two interpretive trails are on the property. The Biltmore Forest School Campus Trail visits restored and reconstructed buildings that depict the life of the first forestry students at the turn of the 20th century. The Forest Festival Trail passes early forestry equipment, such as a 1915 logging locomotive and a steam-powered sawmill.

The Cradle of Forestry is open daily from 9 A.M. to 5 P.M. from April through November. A small admission fee is charged. Visit www.cradleofforestry.com or call 828-877-3130 for more information.

Cultural Offerings

Held for seven weeks each summer, the *Brevard Music Festival* presents a smorgasbord of more than 80 performances ranging from symphonies and pops to Broadway musicals and grand operas.

In 1936, Davidson College in Davidson, North Carolina, began a summer music camp. In 1943, the operation moved to an abandoned summer camp in Brevard. Three years later, the director and a few local students started the Brevard Music Festival, at that time a one-week series of performances by those attending the camp. The Brevard Music Camp subsequently built an 1,800-seat open-sided auditorium.

The camp offers private lessons, a concerto competition, an opera workshop, and performance experience with the Transylvania Symphony, the Brevard Music Center Orchestra, brass, wind, and woodwind ensembles, and a chamber choir. Students can earn college credit. During the festival, they have the opportunity to perform with guest artists.

Each summer, more than 400 of the nation's finest musicians gather to teach and perform. Guest artists have included Boston Pops conductor Keith Lockhart, vocalist Frederica von Stade, and the Louisiana Jazz Ensemble. Each season also promises four beautifully staged operas or musical theater productions, such as Lerner and Loewe's *Brigadoon*, Strauss's *Die Fledermaus*, and Verdi's *Aida*.

It's a good idea to purchase tickets in advance; the festival has many devoted followers who buy season tickets and attend every performance. If you intend to stay in the area during the festival, make room reservations well in advance. Some performances are free; a fee is charged for others. For more information, write the Brevard

Music Center at P.O. Box 312 in Brevard (28712); you can also call 888-384-8682 or 828-862-2105 or visit www.brevardmusic.org.

Special Shopping

The Heart of Brevard, as the locals like to refer to it, is brimming with boutiques, galleries, specialty shops, restaurants, and coffeehouses. Visitors can also find numerous outfitters' shops in the area, as well as guide services for mountain climbing, mountain biking, canoeing, and other outdoor pastimes. For information, visit www.brevardnc.org.

The *White Squirrel Shoppe*, at 2 West Main Street (28712), is housed in the historic McMinn Building. It features antiques, gifts, collectibles, custom pieces from Brevard and Transylvania County, home accessories, heritage lace, furniture, and more. The relaxing atmosphere includes a 12-foot waterfall! For information, call 888-729-7329 or 828-877-3530 or visit www.whitesquirrelshoppe.com.

Recreation

Pisgah National Forest is a land of mile-high peaks, cascading waterfalls, and heavily forested slopes. It is an ideal place for recreation. The forest gets its name from Mount Pisgah, a prominent peak in the area. In the 1700s, a Scots-Irish minister

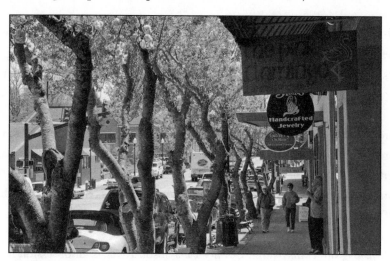

The Heart of Brevard
PHOTOGRAPH BY JACK CHRISTFIELD

saw the peak and named it for the biblical mountain from which Moses saw the Promised Land after 40 years of wandering in the wilderness.

The national forest is managed to provide the best combination of uses to benefit the general public while protecting the long-term quality of the forest. For more information on facilities, hiking, and biking, stop at the information center, located in the ranger station about a mile into the forest on U.S. 276 from U.S. 64. Or you can call the Pisgah National Forest supervisor at 828-257-4200 or visit www. pisgahforest.com/public-lands/pisgahnationalforest. This section of the forest lying southwest of Asheville between Brevard and Waynesville is the Pisgah Ranger District. The Grandfather Ranger District, northeast of Asheville, is covered in the chapter on Banner Elk, Beech Mountain, and Linville.

Waterfall viewing is a favorite activity in the area. The most popular drive goes north from Brevard on U.S. 276 through Pisgah National Forest to *Looking Glass Falls*. You can see the waterfall from the road, but parking your car and walking for a closer view is a much better way to experience this breathtaking natural wonder. U.S. 276 continues to *Sliding Rock*. Be sure to pack your bathing suit, because the best way to experience this water wonder is on your behind. A lifeguard is on duty in the summer, and a bathhouse is provided. You won't find a better means to cool off on a hot summer day. Another popular option is to drive west from Brevard on U.S. 64. You'll pass *Dry Falls*, where you can take an easy walk behind an 80-foot wall of water.

Hiking opportunities abound in the area. If you take U.S. 276 to the Blue Ridge Parkway, a right turn will lead you to Mount Pisgah, and a left will lead you past the Devil's Courthouse. Both areas offer hikes with breathtaking views. Information on hiking trails can be obtained at the outfitters' shops.

Brevard and Pisgah National Forest are quickly becoming one of North Carolina's premier destinations for *mountain biking*. *Bike* magazine recently called Brevard the perfect starting point for some of North Carolina's best single-track trails. With a million acres of terrain and 200 miles of trails just a few pedal strokes from the west side of town, it's easy to see why so many are coming to explore.

Fly-fishing on Transylvania County's Davidson River is an obsession to many. *Trout Unlimited* magazine ranks the Davidson one of America's top 10 trout streams. The Davidson and other area streams are stocked with brook, brown, and rainbow

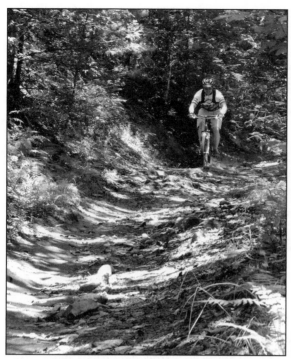

Mountain biking
PHOTOGRAPH BY TODD BRANHAM

trout from the Pisgah Fish Hatchery. If you plan to fish, you'll need a license, available at many of the outfitters' shops.

Places to Stay

Inns and Bed-and-Breakfasts

Greystone Inn. Deluxe/Expensive. Greystone Lane in Lake Toxaway, 28747 (800-824-5766 or 828-966-4700; www.greystoneinn.com). The magnificent mountains, beautiful Lake Toxaway—the largest private lake in North Carolina—a charming historic mansion, and fine cuisine are just a few of the superlatives at the Greystone Inn, located 17 miles west of Brevard. Built in the early 1900s, this mansion was converted into a luxury resort in 1984. Each of the 30 rooms is a perfect blend of comfort and elegance. The 16 rooms in the mansion range from cozy spaces with private baths, fireplaces, and great views of the lake to the spectacular Presidential Suite, which is large enough to accommodate a family (or two!). The Hillmont rooms, in a separate building, have private balconies overlooking the lake, marble baths, and extra space with fireplaces, wet bars, and hidden televisions, VCRs, and

The *Miss Lucy* cruising Lake Toxaway at the Greystone Inn
PHOTOGRAPH BY TIM SCHERMERHORN

stereos. From May 1 through October 31, this mountain aerie offers tennis, croquet, fishing, sailing, swimming, kayaking, and canoeing, as well as horseback riding and golf at nearby Lake Toxaway Country Club. The marina has boats, canoes, water skis, and fishing equipment. Hikers will be enticed by the winding paths along the Horsepasture River, which skirts a series of waterfalls including Rainbow Falls, a cascade nearly 200 feet tall. And don't forget the spa! What better way to experience mountain air and lake breezes than an afternoon of pampering chosen from the wide array of spa treatments? Room rates include breakfast, dinner, afternoon tea, evening hors d'oeuvres, and a nightly champagne cruise aboard a lovingly restored wooden boat, the *Miss Lucy*. The food here is every bit as enticing as the resort. The beautiful setting, the wide array of activities, and a staff that takes service to a new level combine to make this one terrific getaway.

Earthshine Mountain Lodge. Expensive/Moderate. 1600 Golden Road in Lake Toxaway, 28747 (828-862-4207; www.earthshinemtnlodge.com). Situated on an 83-acre farm, this lodge is built entirely of logs and decorated with log furnishings throughout. The 13 guest rooms have private baths and sleeping lofts. The real attraction, however, is the array of activities. The high-ropes and zip-line canopy tours resemble those at Outward Bound. Guests also have opportunities for hiking and rock climbing. A barnyard on the premises is filled with animals for the children. And entertainment is always provided after dinner. Room rates include all three meals.

The Sassy Goose. Expensive/Moderate. 1844 Reasonover Road in Cedar Mountain, 28718 (828-966-9493; www.sassygoose.com). Head south on U.S. 276 to the town of Cedar Mountain and you'll discover a wonderful under-the-radar retreat. "The Goose," as it is affectionately called, sits on 57 wooded acres including its own private Lady Falls, a six-acre lake complete with pontoon boat and canoes, a catch-and-release fishing hole, a "par-two" golf course, and opportunities for swimming, shuffleboard, and ping-pong. The main lodge has three rooms, each with a private bath. The cottage has two bedrooms, two baths, a living room with a fireplace, and a full kitchen. The two cabins each have a kitchen, a living room, a bedroom, and a bath. Breakfast is served in the main lodge. This is a great place for romantic getaways, family reunions, and old-fashioned mountain hospitality.

The Inn on Main Street. Moderate. 243 West Main Street in Brevard, 28712 (888-884-4770 or 828-884-4770; www.theinnonmainstreet.com). This New Orleans–style house two blocks from the middle of Brevard is where guests at the music festival often stay. Each of the six rooms has a private bath and cable TV. Guests can enjoy a gourmet breakfast in the inn's charming sunroom.

The Pines Country Inn. Moderate. 719 Hart Road in Pisgah Forest, 28768 (828-877-3131). This inn is located a short distance from Brevard in a peaceful farming area overlooking the Little River Valley. Guests can see horses grazing and wake to the songs of birds. The house, built in 1883, has been an inn since 1905. The atmosphere is homey and comfortable. The Pines offers 18 guest rooms, some in separate cottages. Room rates include breakfast.

The Red House Inn. Inexpensive. 412 West Probart Street in Brevard, 28712 (828-884-9349). The Red House Inn sits on a corner shielded from traffic by high hedges. Porches extend across the front of the two-story house, built in 1851 as a trading post. The oak woodwork is polished to a high gloss, and the comforters are fluffed on the antique beds. Room rates include a full breakfast served in the dining room.

Places to Eat

Hobnob. Expensive/Moderate. 226 West Main Street in Brevard, 28712 (828-966-4662; www.hobnobrestaurant.com). Big-city dining in an old family home awaits you at Hobnob. Al fresco dining is available for those beautiful mountain summer evenings. The menu is loaded with interesting appetizers, homemade soups, fresh salads, and New American cuisine inspired by local ingredients. Hobnob serves lunch and dinner Monday through Saturday and brunch on Sunday. Reservations are suggested.

The Falls Landing Bar & Restaurant. Moderate. 18 East Main Street in Brevard, 28712 (828-877-2835; www.thefallslanding.com). This restaurant specializes in fresh seafood such as grilled salmon, broiled trout, swordfish, mahi-mahi, Maine lobster, clams, oysters, jumbo shrimp, and steamed mussels. The menu also includes pasta dishes, top-grade steaks, chicken, and homemade soups and desserts. The Falls Landing is open for lunch and dinner Monday through Saturday.

Marco Trattoria. Moderate. 204 West Main Street in Brevard, 28712 (828-883-4841; www.marcotrattoria.com). Marco Trattoria serves Italian-inspired dishes and innovative wood-fired pizzas. You'll be comfortably seated on the patio or inside the family-friendly dining room, which features displays from local artists and businesses. The Sunday brunch menu includes such dishes as "Brioche French Toast" with blueberry syrup, eggs Benedict, a "Muffaletta Panini," subs, and pizzas. Marco Trattoria is open for lunch and dinner daily from Memorial Day through October. Call or check the website for off-season hours.

Dugan's Pub. Moderate/Inexpensive. 29 West French Broad Street, Suite 101, in Brevard, 28712 (828-862-6527; www.duganspub.com). Irish food, Irish beer, Irish smiles—what's not to like? The large bar and cozy booths make this a great place to hang out with friends. All of the food is prepared fresh. Dugan's specializes in authentic dishes such as shepherd's pie, "Bangers & Mash," and fish and chips. Lunch and dinner are served daily.

Bracken Mountain Bakery. Inexpensive. 42 South Broad Street in Brevard, 28712 (828-883-4034; www.brackenmountainbakery.com). This bakery specializes in European crusty breads and American sandwich breads. The breads and pastries are baked from scratch daily on the premises. While this is primarily a takeout operation, tables are available for those who wish to dine in. Flatbreads and filled pocket breads are available for a delicious lunch treat. Lunch is served Monday through Saturday from May to October and Tuesday through Saturday the rest of the year.

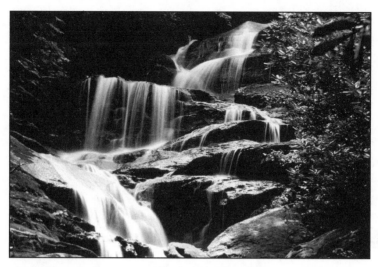

Waterfalls are abundant in the North Carolina mountains.
COURTESY OF ASHEVILLE CONVENTION AND VISITORS BUREAU

Highlands

The unique town of Highlands has a rich history, a wonderful climate, and an enviable way of life. Highlands stands tall in the mountains. Its altitude is 4,118 feet, making it one of the highest incorporated towns east of the Mississippi River. The surrounding mountains soar to over 5,000 feet. During July, the average temperature is a cool 67 degrees, making this a haven for those escaping the heat of the flatlands. Surrounded by Nantahala National Forest, the plateau on which Highlands rests is botanically and geologically unique.

Founded as a summer resort in 1875 by Samuel T. Kelsey and Clinton C. Hutchinson, Highlands has from its beginnings been a retreat from the fast pace of city life. While the year-round population is about 4,000, the summer population is over 20,000. Highlands has become a place of renewal for professionals and executives, who purchase land here and build beautiful summer homes. The cultural amenities during summer include live theater, chamber-music concerts, cabarets, and special dinners. Educational seminars and informative lectures are also offered. And shopping? The shopping in Highlands encompasses boutiques, specialty shops, antiques, jewelry, and handmade crafts and furniture.

JUST THE FACTS

Highlands is located at the intersection of N.C. 106/28 and U.S. 64, which makes a 90-degree turn at Main Street. The roads to Highlands from Brevard and Cashiers—and from anywhere else, for that matter—are twisting and demanding of drivers' attention. Leave the sightseeing to passengers.

The Highlands Visitor Center is located at 269 Oak Street (28741). Call 828-526-2112 or visit www.highlandschamber.org for information.

The area's semiweekly newspaper is called the *Highlander*.

Things to Do

Museums and Science Centers

Museum of American Cut and Engraved Glass, at 472 Chestnut Street (28741), is the collection of George and Bonnie Siek, who have graciously shared their passion with the Highlands community. The museum focuses on the display of "American Brilliant Period" cut and engraved glass. This period is generally acknowledged to have started with the 1876 Centennial Exhibition in Philadelphia and ended in 1916 with the American preparation to enter World War I. At any given time, the museum has over 400 pieces of glass on display. It is open Tuesday, Thursday, and Saturday from 1 P.M. to 4 P.M. from May to October. For information, call 828-526-3415.

Highlands Nature Center, a half-mile east of downtown at 950 Horse Cove Road (28741), is a small but informative center offering exhibits that interpret the area's flora and fauna. It has a small botanical garden with trails and a display of mineral samples and Cherokee artifacts. The center is open Monday through Saturday from 10 A.M. to 5 P.M. from May 23 to Labor Day; variable hours continue through October. Admission is free. For more information, call 828-526-2623 or visit www.wcu.edu/hbs/naturecenter.htm.

Cultural Offerings

The Bascom is located at 323 Franklin Road (28741). This brand-new center for the visual arts is the crown jewel in Highlands' rich history of arts and crafts. The six-acre campus presents changing exhibits and lectures. Artist-taught workshops and studio instruction take place in well-equipped, light-filled classrooms. The gallery shop showcases artwork, craft objects, jewelry, stemware, The Bascom's own vintage red and white wines, and more. Across the atrium, visitors can enjoy late-morning snacks, lunch, and late-afternoon fare, all provided by the Oak Street Café. From knitting to pottery to ceramics to jewelry making, The Bascom is the place for viewing, learning about, buying, and creating your own mountain arts and crafts. The exhibitions and the gallery shop are open Tuesday through Saturday from 10 A.M. to 5 P.M. For information, call 828-526-4949 or visit www.thebascom.org.

Highlands Playhouse, located at 362 Oak Street (28741), presents a summer season of professional theater featuring contemporary dramas and comedies. Call the ticket office at 828-526-2695 or visit www.highlandsplayhouse.org for the current schedule.

The *Highlands Chamber Music Festival*, which takes place from mid-July to the first weekend in August, features several concerts by renowned artists. They are held in different venues, including local churches. For information, call 828-526-9060 or visit www.h-cmusicfestival.com.

Recreation

Highlands is surrounded by *Nantahala National Forest*. If you're interested in hiking in the forest, call 828-524-6441 or write the United States Forest Service at 90 Sloan Road in Franklin (28734). Area outfitters are also a good source for hiking and biking information, equipment, and maps.

Since the main attraction in this area is the scenery, one of the favorite local pastimes is driving tours. Two routes through the national forest are particularly scenic.

From Highlands to Franklin, U.S. 64 follows the Cullasaja River Gorge. The river cascades over falls and ripples over rapids, all within sight of the road. The drive toward Franklin is downhill. The road starts out winding, then widens and curves more gently. Along the route, you may want to stop and photograph *Bridal Veil Falls*, where you can drive behind the 75-foot veil of water. The most spectacular waterfall on this route is *Lower Cullasaja Falls*, a dramatic series of cascades dropping more than 250 feet in a quarter-mile. Parking is hard to come by here because the narrow road hangs on a cliff. Drive past the waterfall and hike back to see it. You'll find it worth the effort.

From Highlands to Cashiers, U.S. 64 curves sharply but is well paved and marked. The trees and rhododendron are thick and close to the road except where a great vista opens to the south, revealing a bird's-eye view of nearby **Whiteside Mountain**, which rises 2,100 feet from the valley floor. Its summit has an elevation of 4,930 feet. Both the northern and southern faces feature stunning, sheer cliffs ranging from 400 to 750 feet in height. This route continues to the town of Cashiers, where you'll find pottery shops, gift shops, and resorts.

Places to Stay

Resorts, Hotels, and Motels

High Hampton Inn and Country Club. Deluxe/Expensive. 1525 N.C. 107 South in Cashiers, 28717 (800-334-2551 or 828-743-2411; www.highhamptoninn.com). This warm, family-oriented resort has a rustic style it has preserved since it was built in 1922. The exterior is covered with chestnut-bark shingles. Inside, the inn has log banisters in the stairwells and wood paneling on the walls and ceilings. The enormous lobby has four stone fireplaces around a central chimney and baskets of magazines and jigsaw puzzles for guests to relax over. The inn's 120 rooms have private baths but no telephones or televisions, so you can truly get away from it all. The inn also offers 40 vacation homes for rent. Meals are served buffet-style in the large dining room; it sounds casual, but men are expected to wear coats and ties for dinner and ladies to dress appropriately. The inn has an 18-hole golf course, outdoor tennis courts, and a lake with a sand beach. Canoes, sailboats, and fishing boats are available for rent. The latest addition is the state-of-the-art Hampton Health Club, which includes a gym and a full-service spa. The inn offers activities for children and teens and a long list of special seminars, golf and fishing schools, and art workshops. Adventurous souls should be sure to check out the new Beanstalk Climbing Tower. The room rates include three meals. The inn is open from April to Thanksgiving.

Old Edwards Inn and Spa. Expensive. 445 Main Street in Highlands, 28741 (866-526-8008 or 828-526-8008; www.oldedwardsinn.com). Old-World European charm and understated mountain elegance go hand in hand at this full-service mountain resort. Spanning several rolling acres in the heart of Highlands, the Old Edwards Inn and Spa boasts spacious guest rooms, suites, and cottages offering period antiques, fine Italian linens, and complimentary champagne upon arrival. The heated outdoor mineral pool and luxurious 25,000-square-foot spa—which uses herbs and botanicals directly from the spa's garden—guarantee a relaxing experience. The newly opened Old Edwards Club offers golf on one of the highest ridges on the East Coast. The resort features multiple on-site dining options, including the romantic Wine Garden with its patio-side waterfall. But if you wake up hungry at midnight, you'll appreciate the two 24-hour butler pantries full of treats and beverages for the taking. Guests can request a room with a private patio or terrace; some offer impressive rooftop views of nearby Highlands. For weddings and special events, the Farm at Old Edwards offers enchanted surroundings encompassing beautifully restored rustic buildings, an event pavilion, and spectacular gardens on lush, rolling hills just five minutes from Highlands.

Wyndham Sapphire Valley. Expensive/Moderate. 70 Sapphire Valley Road in Sapphire Valley, 28774 (828-743-3441; www.sapphirevalleyresort.com). This top-rated resort offers a range of activities year-round. Set on green, forested slopes, it looks like an attractive housing development of rows of townhouses behind stands of trees. The lodgings range from luxurious hotel rooms to efficiencies to one-, two-, and three-bedroom condos with separate living areas. All are comfortably furnished and attractively decorated; some have splendid views of the surrounding mountains. The kitchens are fully stocked, but if you prefer not to cook, the restaurant on the premises is open for lunch and dinner. Recreational facilities in the bracing air (the resort is 3,400 feet up) include an 18-hole championship golf course, one indoor and two outdoor pools, tennis courts, a lake beach, and a health club. You can also go horseback riding and rent bicycles, canoes, paddleboats, and fishing boats. Activities such as children's game days and weekly family bingo are offered in the community room. During winter, you may choose to try the resort's four ski slopes, which have a 425-foot vertical drop. Ski-equipment rentals are available.

Inns and Bed-and-Breakfasts

Fire Mountain. Deluxe. 700 Happy Hill Road (P.O. Box 2772) in Highlands, 28741 (800-775-4446 or 828-526-4446; www.firemt.com). This is one of the most spectacular mountaintop hideaways in America. Located at the highest point on Fire Mountain at an elevation of over 4,000 feet is a secluded retreat comprised of a sophisticated contemporary inn, private and intimate "Treehouses," and luxury mountaintop cabins, all with exquisite long-range mountain views. This retreat boasts springs, streams, ponds, waterfalls, and hiking trails. Rates include a full breakfast using ingredients from Fire Mountain's own gardens and local farmers.

Highlands House Bed and Breakfast. Deluxe. 101 Potter Lane in Highlands, 28741 (800-330-7316 or 828-787-1186; www.highlandshousebandb.com). Conveniently located just 1.5 miles from Main Street on N.C. 106, this newly renovated bed-and-breakfast offers comfort inside and out. The cozy guest areas have fireplaces that ensure a warm ambiance on cool mountain days. The several outdoor patios overlook a waterfall, a koi pond, and lovely gardens. Each room has a private bath and lush amenities. Rates include a full breakfast and an evening social hour.

4½ Street Inn. Expensive. 55 4½ Street in Highlands, 28741 (888-799-4464 or 828-526-4464; www.4andahalfstinn.com). This beautiful inn occupies a restored 100-year-old home on 1.3 acres five blocks from town. The inn has a hot tub, a wraparound porch, gardens, and a sun deck. Its 10 guest rooms include private baths; some have fireplaces. Guests are warmly welcomed with afternoon refreshments and home-baked cookies. In the evening, the hosts serve wine and hors d'oeuvres. Room rates include a gourmet breakfast, a morning paper, and fluffy robes. Bicycles are available for a trek into town. The bird feeders in the backyard provide great entertainment during breakfast.

Highlands Inn. Expensive. 420 Main Street in Highlands, 28741 (800-694-6955 or 828-526-9380; www.highlandsinn-nc.com). The Highlands Inn has been a cornerstone of this town since 1880. Listed on the National Register of Historic Places, it attracts a loyal crowd with its rocking chairs on the veranda and its flags extending from the second-floor railing. Each room has a private bath and is beautifully decorated with period furniture. An extended continental breakfast is included in the room rate.

Skyline Lodge and Restaurant. Expensive/Moderate. 4300 Flat Mountain Road in Highlands, 28741 (800-575-9546 or 828-526-2121; www.skylinelodge.com). Located atop 4,300-foot Flat Mountain, this lodge offers 43 guest rooms and suites and several two- and three-bedroom cabins on 50 private acres. The cabins have unique touches such as rough beam ceilings, birch-log stair rails, and decks built around the trunks of trees. The effect is one of stunning elegance amid rustic charm. The wide variety of recreational facilities includes a sauna, a steam room, a swimming pool, a gym, a game room, a conference center, and tennis courts. There's even a "Wedding Deck," designed for the perfect mountaintop nuptials. Hiking trails on the grounds lead to a 45-foot waterfall. A full-service restaurant, Jack's at Skyline, is open Tuesday through Sunday during high season and on weekends in the off-season. The full-service bar, the Loose Moose, is as fun as the name implies. Rooms are available from May through the first week of November. The cabins remain open year-round.

Places to Eat

Log Cabin Steak House. Expensive. 130 Log Cabin Lane in Highlands, 28741 (828-526-3380). This cabin was built in 1924 as a summer home for a family from Anderson, South Carolina. Most of the furniture was made by Tiger Mountain Woodworks of Highlands. The menu features entrées from the grill like New Zealand lamb chops and fried frog legs, seafood specialties such as North Carolina trout and barbecued shrimp, and a variety of pasta dishes. The freshly made desserts include coconut cake, "Snicker Doodle Pie," warm pear cake, and the famous "Brickle Basket," filled with a variety of surprises. Dinner is served daily in season. Check for off-season hours.

Ristorante Paoletti. Expensive. 440 Main Street in Highlands, 28741 (828-526-4906; www.paolettinc.com). This is fine dining Italian-style. Ristorante Paoletti offers homemade pasta, seafood, and prime cuts of meat in an intimate setting in downtown Highlands. Among the highlights are veal chops, chicken with prosciutto and mozzarella, and Colorado lamb. Nightly specials include the likes of venison rib chops, "Osso Buco with Risotto Milanese," and Carolina quail. The ravioli is made fresh every day. The menu includes a minimum of four fresh seafood dishes prepared in a variety of ways. The wine list, one of the largest in the country, includes over 850 selections from around the globe. Dinner is served daily. Reservations are suggested.

Wolfgang's on Main. Expensive. 474 Main Street in Highlands, 28741 (828-526-3807; www.wolfgangs.net). Presided over by an executive chef who has received numerous awards, Wolfgang's on Main is a dining adventure not to be missed. Guests can take advantage of the cool mountain air by dining in the garden pavilion or on the covered deck. Or they can enjoy their meal beside a fireplace in one of the cozy dining rooms of a home that dates to the 1890s. But the menu and the wine list are the highlights of this establishment. The chef offers signature specialties such as grilled venison loin prepared with apple-wood bacon and served with a sun-dried-cherry demi-glace. Diners can choose a main course from New Orleans specialties like crawfish étouffée or Bavarian specialties like wiener schnitzel or "Rostbraten." A winner of *Wine Spectator*'s Award of Excellence for the past several years, Wolfgang's has the perfect wines to go with such a varied and exciting menu. It also offers special events like wine dinners and holiday dinners. Check the website for a calendar of events. Wolfgang's is open year-round; the serving hours vary according to the season, so be sure to call in advance. Reservations are recommended.

Lakeside Restaurant. Expensive/Moderate. 531 Smallwood Avenue in Highlands, 28741 (828-526-9419; www.lakesiderestaurant.info). This place, which bills itself as "a casual restaurant with serious cuisine," comes highly recommended by locals. Fresh seafood, beef, veal, lamb, chicken, and pasta dishes are on the menu. The portions are generous and delicious. Daily specials are offered, as is a good wine list. Between June and October, Lakeside serves lunch daily and dinner Monday through Saturday. During April, May, and November, it is closed Sunday and Monday. Reservations are strongly recommended for dinner.

The Pizza Place of Highlands. Inexpensive. 365 Main Street in Highlands, 28741 (828-526-5660). Sometimes, you're just in the mood for a good pizza. If so, this is the place for you. Serving a wide variety of specialty and make-your-own pizzas, as well as appetizers, salads, and huge sandwiches, The Pizza Place is sure to please everyone in your crowd. Be sure to try the "MammaMia Cranberry Pizza." Hours vary with the season, so call to check before you head out.

Sports Page Sandwich Shoppe. Inexpensive. 314 Main Street in Highlands, 28741 (828-526-3555). This is the perfect place to grab lunch while shopping downtown. Sandwiches, salads, soups, and spuds are served in a relaxed, cozy room by an extremely friendly staff. You won't find frills here, just really good food. Sports Page even has a menu section labeled "Kids and Not-So-Hungry Adults" that caters to those planning a big dinner. Lunch is served Monday through Saturday.

Franklin

The town of Franklin is the center of a thriving gem-mining industry. No wonder the place is called "the Jewel of the Southeast."

In the latter part of the 19th century, the Cowee Valley, just north of Franklin, was found to contain a high occurrence of corundum—rubies and sapphires, for those of us who don't know our quartz from our carbonatite. Several commercial mining companies began digging exploratory mines. Rubies were found in all the gravel beds, but not in quantities sufficient to support extensive mining operations.

Commercial mining ended here around the turn of the 20th century. All the better for us, since the Cowee Valley has continued to yield hundreds of rubies, sapphires, and other gemstones. Visitors have the chance to unearth these treasures. The predominant business in Franklin is accommodating rock hounds. Several gem shops will sell you raw stones or cut and mount those you find at one of the many gem mines catering to tourists.

The other jewel in Franklin's crown is location. Just outside town are the beautiful Nantahala National Forest and Nantahala Gorge, which offer many recreational opportunities.

When you come to Franklin, notice the large, grass-covered mound at the bottom of the hill on U.S. 64 Business. This is all that remains of an 18th-century Cherokee village called Nikwasi. Many archaeologists have asked permission to excavate it, but in the end, Franklin officials have always decided to leave things as they are.

JUST THE FACTS

Franklin is located at the junction of U.S. 64, U.S. 23/441, and N.C. 28.

The Macon County Airport has one lighted runway; call 828-524-5529 for information.

The Franklin Area Chamber of Commerce is located at 425 Porter Street (28734). Call 866-372-5546 or 828-524-3161 or visit www.franklin-chamber.com.

The two local papers are the *Franklin Press*, published twice weekly, and the *Macon County News*, published weekly.

Things to Do

Museums and Science Centers

The *Franklin Gem and Mineral Museum*, at 25 Phillips Street (28734), is housed in the old city jail, built in the 1850s and used until 1972. The displays include a wide range of mineral specimens, fossils, and Indian artifacts. One room contains samples from all over North Carolina, while another has specimens from every other state in the union. One of the most interesting displays contains rocks under fluorescent light that continue to glow after the light is switched off. The museum was established and is maintained by volunteers of the Gem and Mineral Society of Franklin. From May through October, it is open Monday through Friday from noon to 4 P.M. and Saturday from 11 A.M. to 3 P.M. and 6 P.M. to 9 P.M. From November to April, it is open Saturday only from 11 A.M. to 3 P.M. Admission is free. Call 828-369-7831 or visit www.fgmm.org for information.

The *Scottish Tartans Museum and Heritage Center*, at 86 East Main Street (28734), celebrates the Scottish heritage of the North Carolina mountains. Displays document the evolution of the kilt and the influence of the Scots on Appalachian culture. If you are of Scottish descent, you can find your family tartan in the Tartan Room. The gift shop sells items from Scotland and handmade Appalachian crafts. The museum is open Monday through Saturday from 10 A.M. to 5 P.M. A small admission fee is charged for adults; children six and under are free. Call 828-524-7472 or visit www.scottishtartans.org for information.

Ruby City Gems and Minerals, at 130 East Main Street (28734), isn't strictly a museum. It's also a lapidary shop that sells raw and cut gemstones, lapidary equipment and supplies, and mineral samples such as geodes and amethyst crystals. The museum, located on the lower level, displays hundreds of mineral samples in well-lighted glass cases. The main attraction is a sapphire specimen that weighs 382 pounds. The shop and museum are open Monday through Friday from 9 A.M. to 5 P.M. and Saturday from 9 A.M. to 3 P.M. Admission is free, though donations are accepted. Call 800-821-RUBY or 828-524-3967 or visit www.rubycity.com for information.

Recreation

Franklin's main attraction is *gem mining*.

According to Indian legend, rubies appeared in the Cowee Valley because the beautiful daughter of a tribal chief fell in love with the son of her father's archenemy. When the chief found out, he was so enraged that he ordered the lovers put to death on the spot. The couple's love was so strong that their blood ran together into the earth and hardened into precious stones.

When you go mining for rubies and crystals, you'll pay for three or four buckets of rock and soil from the mine. Then, sitting at the edge of a flume line (a trough with gently flowing water), you'll rinse the soil from the rocks a scoop at a time and pick out the raw stones. Keep in mind that raw, uncut stones bear little resemblance to what you see in the jeweler's window. The mine operators will help you learn what to look for. Some mines enrich—or "salt"—the dirt with gravel known to contain some stones. If you've got children with you, choose one of these mines, where you'll have a better chance of keeping the kids' interest. You aren't likely to discover large gem-quality rubies, but you will have a lot of fun finding small, pretty stones to take away as souvenirs of your trip.

The chamber of commerce can provide a complete list of local gem mines. One that comes highly recommended is *Mason Mountain Mine*, at 5315 Bryson City Road (28734); call 828-524-4570. Another is *Rose Creek Mine and Campground*, at 115 Terrace Ridge Drive (28734); call 828-349-3774 or visit www.rosecreekmine.com.

Seasonal Events

The *Macon County Gemboree* is held twice each year, in late July and mid-October. Rock hounds gather from all over to display and sell gem and mineral specimens. Call 800-336-7829 or 828-524-3161 for information.

Places to Stay

Inns and Bed-and-Breakfasts

Buttonwood Inn Bed and Breakfast. Moderate. 50 Admiral Drive, 28734 (888-368-8985 or 828-369-8985; www.buttonwoodbb.com). This four-bedroom inn is furnished with antiques, country pieces, quilts, collectibles, and crafts. It offers a common room for guest conversation or reading and a back deck with rocking chairs. Rates include a full breakfast—but that does little to describe wonderful offerings such as "Dutch Babies with Rum Bananas," scones with homemade lemon butter, stuffed French toast, "Apple Sausage Ring," fresh herb-and-cheese soufflés, breads, coffee cakes, muffins, and more. Only a mile from downtown Franklin, this inn is ideally located near restaurants, shopping, golf courses, gem mines, waterfalls, hiking trails, and whitewater rafting opportunities.

Oak Hill Country Inn. Moderate. 1689 Old Murphy Road, 28734 (800-587-6374 or 828-349-9194; www.oakhillcountryinn.com). Take a step back and enjoy the leisurely pace of a forgotten time. This two-story frame Queen Anne–style house was built in 1888 for the Reverend John A. Deal, a missionary who established all of the Episcopal churches in western North Carolina. Each guest room features some of the gems found in the region—topazes, garnets, amethysts, and sapphires. Amenities include private baths, plush robes and towels, TVs with VCRs and DVD players, a library of movies, and more. Breakfast is included in the price of the room.

Places to Eat

The Frog & Owl Kitchen. Moderate. 46 East Main Street, 28734 (828-349-4112). Located in the heart of Franklin's downtown shopping district, The Frog & Owl Kitchen is the perfect place to take stock of your day's explorations. The menu includes raspberry citrus salad, lentil bean salad, a pesto chicken sandwich, a lamb burger, and mountain trout. A wine shop is on the premises, as is a deli, where gourmet pastas and salads are available for takeout. The desserts and breads are baked fresh every day. Lunch is served Monday through Saturday.

The Gazebo Creekside Café. Inexpensive. 44 Heritage Hollow, 28734 (828-524-8783; www.gazebocreeksidecafe.com). This lovely restored gazebo, located along a babbling creek, is a relaxing retreat in the middle of Franklin. The menu includes a wide variety of soups, salads, and sandwiches. For a cool drink, try a smoothie or a shake. The desserts include turtle cheesecake and Key lime pie, but don't miss the chunky apple pie—à la mode, of course. Lunch is served daily.

Nearby

Wayah Bald is a massive stone outcrop at an elevation of more than a mile in Nantahala National Forest. Its "baldness" is in dramatic contrast to the lush forest that surrounds it. You can see the bald from downtown Franklin, but the trip to experience it up close takes about an hour. Take U.S. 64 West to S.R. 1310, then turn right on S.R. 69, which will lead you deep into the forest, where you'll see wildflowers and streams cascading down hillsides. You can park close to the summit, then walk about a quarter-mile on a paved trail for a spectacular view from the top.

Dillsboro is about 20 miles north of Franklin on U.S. 441. The drive leads through a picturesque mountain valley to a lovely little town on a hillside.

Dillsboro has several shops that sell antiques, crafts, toys, and gifts. *Dogwood Crafters*, at 90 Webster Street (28725), is a crafts cooperative carrying the work of many artisans; call 828-586-2248. The nine outlets comprising *Riverwood Shops*, located across the railroad tracks on River Road, offer hammered pewter, leatherwork, weavings, and more; call 828-586-6996.

If you're staying overnight, consider the *Squire Watkins Inn*, located at 657 Haywood Road (28725), just off U.S. 441; call 828-586-5244. For a terrific meal, try the *Jarrett House*, located at 100 Haywood Road (28725). This regional landmark opened as a hotel in 1882. Famous for its family-style meals, it specializes in fried chicken, country ham, and mountain trout. Each meal comes with bowls of vegetables, slaw, stewed apples, and hot biscuits. Be sure to try the vinegar pie. For information, call 828-586-0265.

Rafting in the *Nantahala Gorge*, about 20 miles north of Franklin, will appeal to those who like thrills and outdoor excitement—and those who like getting soaked by cold mountain water. Several companies offer guided raft trips down the Nantahala River, which features class II and class III rapids. Don't let that intimidate you. Safety equipment is issued, and the guides tell you everything you need to do, so it's fun for even those with no rafting experience. The trips last about four hours and don't require special clothing except for something dry to change into afterward. Children must weigh at least 60 pounds to participate. Raft trips are offered from April through October. For a complete list of the companies that operate on U.S. 19 between Bryson City and Andrews, call 866-372-5546 or 828-524-3161.

The ***John C. Campbell Folk School***, located about 60 miles west of Franklin at 1 Folk School Road in Brasstown (28902), was founded in 1925 to preserve and teach traditional Appalachian crafts. During the Depression, it provided economic opportunities for farm families by selling their high-quality woodcarvings.

Week-long courses are offered year-round today. They include pottery, weaving, basketry, woodcarving, bookbinding, Appalachian dancing, and newer crafts such as jewelry making and kaleidoscope making. The school has recently started offering cooking classes, too. Students come back year after year and often sign up for several courses at a time. The craft shop sells a variety of pottery, weavings, decorative ironwork, split-oak baskets, and beautiful work by some of the original Brasstown carvers. The shop is open Monday through Saturday from 8 A.M. to 5 P.M. and Sunday from 1 P.M. to 5 P.M. Call 800-365-5724 or 828-837-2775 or visit www. folkschool.com for more information.

The Great Smoky Mountains

Great Smoky Mountains National Park

Bryson City

Cherokee

Maggie Valley

Waynesville

By Sue Clark

T raveling west from Asheville, you'll find the Blue Ridge Mountains in your rearview mirror and the Great Smoky Mountains ahead of you. The latter mountain range gets its name from the persistent haze that veils the rounded summits. These ancient mountains exude serenity while cloaking a rugged wilderness that, in many areas, remains untouched by modern hands.

Legend says the haze comes from a time when the Cherokees smoked the peace pipe with their enemies. The meeting continued for seven days, during which the parties continued to quarrel. The Great Spirit, becoming annoyed, turned the men into grayish white flowers called Indian pipes and made smoke cover the mountains to remind all men that they should live together in peace.

The scientific explanation is less interesting. It states that the haze is caused by an excess of oxygen and humidity created by the thick forestation. The oxygen and humidity mix with a microscopic mist of rosin-scented organic compounds called terpenes.

The Smokies are a naturalist's paradise. They are home to more than 1,000 varieties of flowering plants and hundreds of species of mosses and trees. The Smokies contain the largest stand of old-growth hardwoods in North America. The diversity of plants and animals is unmatched anywhere in the country.

Fortunately, much of this magnificence has been incorporated into a well-loved national park to ensure that its wild beauty will be preserved. However, tourism has indeed intruded. Even so, these mountains are considered by many—this author included—to be the most beautiful part of North Carolina.

Great Smoky Mountains National Park
PHOTOGRAPH BY BEN CLARK

Great Smoky Mountains National Park

The Grand Canyon receives over 4 million visitors annually and Yosemite and Yellowstone over 3 million each. But it is Great Smoky Mountains National Park that has more visitors than any other national park—over 9 million each year. The park encompasses more than a half-million acres along 70 miles of the North Carolina–Tennessee border. It contains some of the oldest mountains on earth. Within the park are 16 peaks more than 6,000 feet high—and only one road cuts among them. Between the park entrances at Cherokee, North Carolina, and Gatlinburg, Tennessee, Newfound Gap Road twists and turns, revealing one spectacular view after another. During fall color season, this road is so congested that the crossing can take twice as long as it does other times.

Great Smoky Mountains National Park was authorized by an act of Congress in 1926, but that was the easy part. Raising money to buy the property was difficult, and negotiations were complex. Within the proposed boundaries of the park, 85 percent of the property was owned by 18 timber companies and the rest in tiny parcels by nearly 6,000 homesteaders. Years of appropriations and private contributions netted only $5 million—half the necessary funds. John D. Rockefeller, Jr., matched that amount, and the park finally opened to the public in 1934.

Natural beauty is not the only thing you'll find here. More than 97 historic structures are maintained by the park. These include the log cabins, barns, mills, and stables of some of the families that settled in the mountains in the 19th century.

Ways to explore the park are endless. Those with only a little time can drive Newfound Gap Road, but they'll miss much of the park. A smaller road leads up to Clingmans Dome, the highest peak in the park, at 6,643 feet; those who make the half-mile climb on foot to the observation tower will be rewarded with a stunning view of the Smokies. Those who enjoy hiking or horseback riding will appreciate the more than 800 miles of trails. Back-country camping is also a great way to explore these majestic mountains. Regardless of your preference for exploration, Great Smoky Mountains National Park will leave an impression on you that will last a lifetime.

The park's busiest months are June, July, August, and October. At these times, the campgrounds are full and the roads accessing the park are crowded. It can get cool here even in summer, so remember to bring a jacket or sweater. Also note that the park gets 50 to 80 inches of rain annually, so rain gear should be part of your preparations. And one other word of warning: Bears roam this part of the country, and none of them is named Yogi. If you see one, enjoy watching it from a distance, but *never* attempt to feed it or entice it for a closer view.

JUST THE FACTS

Great Smoky Mountains National Park is 50 miles west of Asheville on U.S. 19. The North Carolina entrance is at the town of Cherokee. The Tennessee entrance is at Gatlinburg. Three visitor centers offer maps, guidebooks, museum displays, weather and road information, schedules of park activities (including ranger-guided walks and talks), and calendars of special events. The centers are open every day except Christmas. For information, write Great Smoky Mountains National Park at 107 Park Headquarters Road, Gatlinburg, Tenn. 37738. Or you can call 865-436-1200 or visit www.nps.gov/grsm.

Be sure to pick up a copy of *Smokies Guide* at one of the visitor centers. The official newspaper of the park, it is packed with information to make your visit the best possible.

Things to Do

Museums and Science Centers

The *Mountain Farm Museum* is located at the North Carolina entrance to the park. It consists of buildings typical of those found in the area around 1900. Corn is ground here every day; the meal is available for purchase at the water-powered Mingus Mill, located a half-mile north of the farmstead. For more information, call 828-497-1904 or visit www.nps.gov/grsm/planyourvisit/mfm.htm.

Cades Cove, on the Tennessee side of the park, is the site of a re-created pioneer mill community. Visitors can enjoy several cabins, three churches, and a mill. They can also drive the 11-mile loop around the settlement and the adjacent pastures, or stroll among the buildings and observe life as it was for the early settlers. Park rangers lead 30-minute guided walking tours daily during summer. A small bookstore offers material about the area and its history. After dark, old-fashioned hayrides delight the kids. The year-round campground has 159 sites.

Recreation

As with most outdoor recreation, information is the key to a great time. The park's visitor centers and the rangers who staff them are the best sources for up-to-date information on recreational opportunities.

Hiking is almost a religion at Great Smoky Mountains National Park. An endless variety of trails serves hikers of every taste and ability. The grandfather of them all, of course, is the *Appalachian Trail*, which zigzags for 70 miles through the park on the crests of the mountains between Davenport Gap, near the eastern boundary, and Fontana Dam, in the southwest.

If you're a serious hiker, you'll need serious maps, available at the visitor centers. *The Smokies Hiking Map and Guide* includes an up-to-date hiking map and information on back-country campsites. Another reliable source is *Hiking Trails of the Smokies*, which describes every hike in the park.

Camping is also popular in the park.

A permit—available from the visitor centers—is required for back-country camping. Back-country camping is free but is allowed only at designated campsites along the trails. If you wish to camp in the shelters along the Appalachian Trail, reservations are required. For more information, call the back-country office at 865-436-1231.

The park also offers 10 developed campgrounds with water but no showers, electricity, or trailer hookups. A fee is charged for the use of these campgrounds. For information or reservations, call 877-444-6777 or visit www.recreation.gov. Most of the campgrounds close in November and reopen in mid-March. Two stay open year-round.

Those who enjoy *picnicking* will appreciate the park's 10 picnic areas. Each has tables and fire grates. Please be aware of current fire conditions, and be conscientious about outdoor cooking. The same goes for trash, as no one wants four-footed guests crashing their party.

Horseback riding is offered through several licensed concession stables. Call 865-436-1200 for information.

Fishing for brown and rainbow trout is popular in park streams all year long. You must have either a North Carolina or a Tennessee fishing license, both of which are honored throughout the park regardless of which side of the border you're on. Check with the visitor centers for regulations regarding size and catch limits.

Naturalist programs are offered by rangers from May to October at the developed campgrounds and the visitor centers. Some are talks, some involve short walks, and some are geared for children. Topics include wildflowers, hardwood trees, animal habitats, and pioneer life. For a special treat, consider one of the walks offered at sunset or twilight. Call 865-436-1200 for more information.

Please be aware of park rules and considerate of the visitors who will come after you. Park regulations prohibit littering, defacing natural features, picking wildflowers, digging up plants, feeding wildlife, and letting pets run loose.

Places to Stay

Inns and Bed-and-Breakfasts

LeConte Lodge. Inexpensive. On top of Mount LeConte at 250 Apple Valley Road near Sevierville, Tenn. 37862 (865-429-5704; www.leconte-lodge.com). The only overnight facility inside the park, this lodge is accessible by a half-day hike. The premises are definitely rustic and the meals plain. Reservations are required. The lodge is open from late March through mid-November.

Bryson City

The county seat of Swain County, Bryson City shares a heritage with the Cherokee Indians, who once called this area home and still believe it to be the birthplace of the Cherokee people. The area has much to offer, including hiking, fishing, horseback riding, mountain biking, whitewater sports, camping, golf, a scenic railroad, and spectacular mountain vistas around every bend. *Outside* magazine named Bryson City one of the nation's top 100 places for outdoor enthusiasts. Don't worry if you're not the adventurous type, though. Bryson City recalls a less complicated time when the locals used to "roll up the streets" at night, after which the air was filled with nothing more than the sounds of crickets and tree frogs.

JUST THE FACTS

Bryson City is located about an hour west of Asheville on U.S. 19 at the doorstep of Great Smoky Mountains National Park.

The Chamber of Commerce is located at 210 Main Street (28713). For information, call 828-488-3681 or visit www.greatsmokies.com.

Things to Do

Recreation

Many people come to town for an excursion aboard the ***Great Smoky Mountains Railroad***, headquartered at 226 Everett Street (28713). One of the trips that departs from nearby Dillsboro travels along the Tuckasegee River. This three-hour ride visits the setting of the escape scene at the beginning of *The Fugitive*, starring Harrison Ford. The railway was hired by the film company to stage a derailment with an actual full-sized train. The crew had only one shot at it, and it went perfectly. The remains of the wreck are featured on the excursion, which also includes the 836-foot-long Cowee Tunnel. Other excursions depart from Bryson City and Andrews. One of the Bryson City trips crosses Fontana Lake on a trestle 791 feet long and 179 feet high. The Great Smoky Mountains Railroad also offers raft-and-rail trips, special excursions such as a "Santa Train" in December, a whole week devoted to Thomas the Tank Engine rides featuring a full-sized Thomas kids absolutely love, and mystery and dinner excursions. Call 800-872-4681 or 828-586-8811 or visit www.gsmr.com for more information.

Nantahala Outdoor Center, at 13077 U.S. 19 West (28713), is the place to go for all kinds of rafting, hiking, and biking adventures. NOH can plan excursions just about anywhere in the southern mountains of North Carolina and Tennessee. The guides are friendly, knowledgeable, and dedicated to tailoring something just right for you and your family. Whether you're a novice or an expert, NOH can plan an unforgettable mountain adventure that will keep you smiling for a long time. For information, call 888-905-7238 or 828-488-2176 or visit www.noc.com.

Places to Stay

Inns and Bed-and-Breakfasts

Hemlock Inn. Deluxe/Expensive. 911 Galbraith Creek Road, 28713 (828-488-2885; www.hemlockinn.com). This is a lovely one-level inn on a Great Smoky Mountains hilltop. If you sit in a rocker on the porch, all you'll hear is the songs of the birds. The inn offers 22 rooms and three cottages furnished country-style.

A favorite spot is the fireplace in the big family room, which boasts a breathtaking view of the mountains. This is a true getaway with no TVs or telephones in the rooms. Breakfast and dinner, included in the room rate, are served family-style at large tables with giant lazy Susans in the center. You can't help getting friendly with the other guests as the food is passed and shared. The emphasis here is on an old-fashioned, relaxing vacation that encourages you to stop, unwind, and gaze upon the beauty around you.

Charleston Inn. Expensive. 208 Arlington Avenue, 28713 (888-285-1555 or 828-488-4644; www.charlestoninn.com). Located in the heart of the Great Smoky Mountains, the Charleston Inn is perfect for a romantic getaway, an exciting outdoor adventure, or a relaxing vacation. The inn offers modern rooms with king or queen beds, private baths, Jacuzzis, private decks, porches, air conditioning, cable TV, and wireless Internet. A full breakfast is served in the dining room each morning. Open year-round, this inn is a great jumping-off point for a mountain adventure.

Fryemont Inn. Moderate. 245 Fryemont Street, 28713 (800-845-4879 or 828-488-2159; www.fryemontinn.com). Built in 1923 and listed on the National Register of Historic Places, the Fryemont Inn includes a beautiful poplar-bark-covered historic lodge with two enormous stone fireplaces, eight luxury fireplace suites, and a two-bedroom cabin. The dining room has been featured in national and regional publications. Except in winter, all rates include breakfast and dinner. The swimming pool, open in summer, is nestled in a grove of poplar and dogwood trees. The lodge and dining room are open from mid-April through Thanksgiving. The cabin and fireplace suites are open all year.

Places to Eat

Fryemont Inn Dining Room. Expensive. 245 Fryemont Street, 28713 (800-845-4879 or 828-488-2159; www.fryemontinn.com). The Fryemont Inn Dining Room has been featured in numerous magazines and publications, including *Bon Appétit* and *Travel and Leisure*. Built in 1923, it has a raftered ceiling, gleaming maple floors, and an enormous stone fireplace. Breakfast and dinner are served to inn guests; reservations from folks not staying in the inn are welcome. At breakfast, diners can choose from apple, blueberry, or pecan pancakes, French toast, omelets, biscuits and gravy, and all the favorite egg dishes. Dinner is a four-course meal that begins with the soup of the day and ends with a selection of wonderful cakes, pies, and cobblers. Entrées include prime rib, "Pecan-Crusted Trout in Lemon Cream," and country ham with red-eye gravy. Each is served with three side dishes of the day, always homemade. Breakfast and dinner are served daily. Reservations are recommended.

Relia's Garden. Moderate. In Nantahala Outdoor Center at 13077 U.S. 19 West, 28713 (800-232-7238 or 828-488-2175; www.noc.com). Located overlooking a garden of flowers and fresh herbs and featuring inspiring views and the rushing sounds of the Nantahala River, Relia's offers an unforgettable mountain dining experience. Entrées include country fried steak, pan-seared trout, buttermilk fried chicken, and "Smoked Beef Brisket in Blueberry Barbecue Sauce." The menu includes an innovative array of appetizers, salads, and desserts. Relia's serves dinner daily during summer and Friday through Monday in spring and fall; it is closed in winter.

Everett Street Diner. Inexpensive. 126 Everett Street, 28713 (828-488-0123). Breakfast at this well-known local favorite features omelets, eggs to order, waffles, French toast, pancakes, and breakfast burritos. The lunch menu includes sandwiches, soups, and salads, all made fresh on the premises. The desserts are said to be "like Momma used to make," so save room. Breakfast and lunch are served Monday through Friday.

Nearby

Fontana Dam is 35 miles west of Bryson City on N.C. 28. A project of the Tennessee Valley Authority during the early 1940s, the dam was built to fuel the effort for World War II. At 480 feet, it is the tallest dam in the eastern United States. Damming the Little Tennessee River created Fontana Lake, which takes up a sizable chunk of Swain County.

A few miles away at 50 Fontana Road/N.C. 28 North at the community of Fontana Dam (28733) is *Fontana Village*, a resort that grew from the housing units occupied by the workers who built the dam. Upon the dam's completion in 1945, the housing development was sold to private owners, who turned it into a family resort village. The village includes an inn with 94 rooms (some of which have fireplaces) and 250 rustic cottages equipped with kitchens. A restaurant, a buffet house, and a café all serve meals to those who choose not to cook. Recreational activities include miniature golf, swimming, boating, fishing, hiking, horseback riding, archery, and badminton. A playground, craft classes, and other organized activities are available for children. The mountains that surround Fontana Lake make a magnificent setting for an extended family vacation. The village is open year-round. For more information, call 800-849-2258 or 828-498-2211 or visit www.fontanavillage.com.

West of Fontana Lake is *Joyce Kilmer Memorial Forest*, which contains one of the last stands of virgin forest on the East Coast. The forest is left completely to nature's control; no plants or trees, living or dead, may be cut or removed. The result is a magnificent forest containing more than 100 species of trees, many specimens of which are over 300 years old. A two-mile recreation trail loops through the forest and the adjoining 14,000-acre Slickrock Wilderness Area. Fittingly, the forest is named for the author of the well-known poem "Trees." Joyce Kilmer was still a young man when he was killed in France during World War I. To reach the forest named in his honor, take U.S. 129 North from Robbinsville and follow the signs. For information, call the Cheoah Ranger Station at 828-479-6431.

Cherokee

The town of Cherokee is the largest community in the Qualla Boundary, the almost 56,000 acres of reservation land held in trust for the Eastern Band of the Cherokee Nation. The Cherokees are one of the "Five Civilized Tribes" of Muskogean-speaking people. They were the first Indians to have a written language, created by Sequoyah in 1821. At one time, they were an extremely powerful nation, controlling a territory of 135,000 square miles that stretched from the Ohio River southward into parts of what are now Georgia and Alabama. The forced removal of the Cherokees to the Oklahoma Territory has come to be called "the Trail of Tears." Several hundred Cherokees remained in the mountains during the removal. In 1866, they were finally granted the legal right to live in their homeland. About 8,200 members of the Eastern Band reside in communities throughout the Qualla Boundary today.

The town of Cherokee is undergoing some profound changes. Survival for the Native Americans used to depend on stereotypical tourist attractions that bore little resemblance to authentic Cherokee heritage. Ironically, the arrival of a large casino has pumped sorely needed revenue into the tribe. That revenue has been put to use improving the attractions that showcase the rich history and heritage of the Cherokee people.

JUST THE FACTS

Cherokee is located 48 miles west of Asheville at the intersection of U.S. 19 and U.S. 441. Just three miles north of Cherokee is the southern entrance to Great Smoky Mountains National Park.

The Cherokee Travel and Promotion Visitor Center is located at 498 Tsali Boulevard (28719). For information, call 800-438-1601 or 828-497-9195 or visit www.cherokee-nc.com.

The *Cherokee One Feather* is a weekly newspaper available throughout town.

Things to Do

Historic Places, Gardens, and Tours

Oconaluftee Indian Village, on Drama Road a half-mile north of U.S. 441, is a recreation of a Cherokee village as it was 250 years ago. Here, you can watch Cherokees making tools and decorations, carving weapons and cooking utensils, grinding corn, cooking, finger-weaving, making baskets and beadwork, and burning out dugout canoes. Cherokee guides escort visitors on a two-hour journey into the past. Visitors are welcome to linger, take pictures, and ask questions. One of the highlights of the tour is the seven-sided council house. Surrounding the village is a beautiful botanical garden with paths leading past mossy rocks, trickling water, and flower and vegetable gardens. The village is open daily from 9 A.M. to 5 P.M. from May and October. Admission is charged except for children under five. For more information, call 866-554-4557 or 828-497-2111 or visit www.cherokee-nc.com/oconaluftee.

Museums and Science Centers

The *Museum of the Cherokee Indian*, at 589 Tsali Boulevard/U.S. 441 North (28719) at the intersection with Drama Road, was totally renovated in 1998. Its state-of-the-art exhibits trace the history of the Cherokees, honor outstanding individuals, and show examples of traditional arts and crafts. Artifacts and relics are

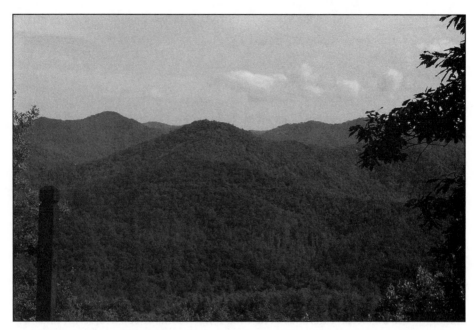

Snowbird Mountains in Joyce Kilmer Memorial Forest
PHOTOGRAPH BY BEN CLARK

presented in real-life settings of the time period. A seven-minute, three-screen, multi-sensory film presents the Cherokee creation story. In the exhibit halls, you can view maps of the Trail of Tears and read newspaper accounts of the removal. At the display on Sequoyah's syllabary, you can listen to audio samplings of the language. The gift shop carries books and souvenirs. From September through May, the museum is open daily from 9 A.M. to 5 P.M. From June through August, it is open from 9 A.M. to 7 P.M. Monday through Saturday and from 9 A.M. to 5 P.M. on Sunday. Admission is charged except for children under five. Call 828-497-3481 or visit www.cherokee-nc. com/museum for more information.

Special Shopping

Qualla Arts and Crafts Mutual, Inc., at 645 Tsali Boulevard (28719), was organized by Native American craftsmen in 1946. It has grown into the most successful Indian-owned and -operated craft cooperative in the United States. Among the items for sale are handmade Cherokee baskets, beadwork, pottery, woodcarvings, masks, and dolls. One room displays crafts made by Indians of other tribes. From June through August, the cooperative is open from 8 A.M. to 7 P.M. Monday through Saturday and from 9 A.M. to 5 P.M. on Sunday. From September to May, it is open from 8 A.M. to 5 P.M. daily. Call 828-497-3103 or visit www.cherokee-nc.com/qualla for more information.

Recreation

Harrah's Cherokee Casino, located at 777 Casino Drive/U.S. 441 (28719), has brought a great deal of revenue to the Eastern Band. The size of three football fields, the casino features 2,300 video gaming machines, three restaurants, a gift shop, and even a day-care facility. Neon lightning bolts flash across the ceiling whenever someone wins a jackpot over $1,000; the sound of thunder means the jackpot's even bigger. The 1,500-seat Cherokee Pavilion hosts live entertainment. The casino is where the action is 24 hours a day, seven days a week. Call 800-HARRAHS or 828-497-7777 or visit www.harrahscherokee.com for more information.

Oconaluftee Islands Park, on Tsali Boulevard/U.S. 441 North, is an oasis in the middle of the bustle of Cherokee. The mile-long Oconaluftee River Trail links the park to nearby Great Smoky Mountains National Park. Along the trail are handicapped-accessible walkways and fishing piers, benches and picnic tables, natural landscaping, and a picnic shelter. Most of the trail is smoothly paved. At Oconaluftee Islands Park, the outside world disappears and pure play takes its place. Wading, splashing, tubing, salamander hunting, picnicking, and lots of other opportunities for R and R are completely free here.

Fishing is popular around Cherokee. The streams and ponds on the reservation are stocked and overseen by Cherokee Fish and Game Management. While you don't need a state fishing license, you must purchase a tribal fishing permit, available at convenience stores, campground offices, and other locations throughout town. Call 828-497-5201 for more information.

Seasonal Events

Unto These Hills is performed at the 2,800-seat Mountainside Theatre on U.S. 441. This play by Kermit Hunter is the most popular outdoor drama in the state. It uses words and music to tell the story of the Trail of Tears. Performances are staged Monday through Saturday from mid-June to late August. The preshow starts at 7 P.M. and the drama at 7:30 P.M. Admission is charged. For more information, call 866-554-4557 or visit www.cherokee-nc.com.

Places to Stay

The town of Cherokee has a number of motels, rental cabins, and lodges, many of them along the Oconaluftee River. The arrival of the casino has brought many of the major chain hotels.

Inns and Bed-and-Breakfasts

Snowbird Mountain Lodge. Deluxe. 4633 Santeetlah Road in Robbinsville, 28771 (800-941-9290 or 828-479-3433; www.snowbirdlodge.com). This rustic mountain inn, built of chestnut logs and native stone, offers an excellent view of the Snowbird range from its terrace. But that doesn't begin to describe the experience. Upon arrival, guests are greeted in a massive but cozy front room where refreshments are available. The rooms and suites are luxuriously appointed and meant to help guests unwind. No phones or TVs are in the rooms. Guests can enjoy tennis, basketball, hiking trails, a screened reading deck, fountains, porches, and even a sunrise deck complete with a Japanese-temple-style prayer bell. And the food? Room rates include a four-course dinner that changes nightly and emphasizes local ingredients and exciting flavors. Breakfast, every bit as sumptuous, provides all the fuel needed for the day's adventures. And that's not all. When you are seated for dinner, you'll be given a lunch menu for the next day. In the morning, your lunch will be packed and ready for you to take on your excursions. The staff is knowledgeable about the area and more than willing to help with everything from hiking to kayaking to fishing and more. The Snowbird also offers classes ranging from watercolor painting to pottery. This is truly an all-inclusive resort.

Places to Eat

The Chestnut Tree. Moderate/Inexpensive. In the Holiday Inn Cherokee at 37 Tsaligi Road/U.S. 19 South in Cherokee, 28719 (828-497-9181). This is about the fanciest restaurant in Cherokee. It features mountain trout, steaks, chicken, and a good selection of sandwiches. It is open for breakfast and dinner Monday through Saturday and for all three meals on Sunday.

Grandma's Pancake and Steak. Inexpensive. On U.S. 19 at U.S. 441 in Cherokee,

28719 (828-497-9801). Grandma's is a casual family restaurant where you can get a great old-fashioned country breakfast any time of day and steak, shrimp, barbecue, flounder, and chicken for lunch and dinner. It features local favorites like "Indian Tacos," "Chili and Frybread," and mountain trout. Grandma's offers home-style vegetables and slow-cooked pinto beans seasoned with country ham and served with cornbread muffins. From June through October, it serves all three meals every day. The rest of the year, it serves breakfast and lunch Monday through Thursday and all three meals on Friday, Saturday, and Sunday.

The Trail of Tears

The facts are staggering: Some 14,000 Cherokees were forced to leave their ancestral home with whatever they could carry; they were led to the Oklahoma Territory in 20-plus separate detachments, many traveling in the dead of winter; no exceptions were made for the elderly, the sick, the pregnant, or the very young; approximately 20 percent died on the way.

In one of the most shameful episodes in this nation's history, the United States government decided to break numerous treaties with the Cherokees of the Blue Ridge and Great Smoky mountains. In 1828, President Andrew Jackson put through Congress the Indian Removal Act, which commanded that all Indians be led west of the Mississippi River. Cherokee land was confiscated when gold was discovered in the Appalachians. The 1835 Treaty of New Echota provided the Cherokees $5 million and land in what is now Oklahoma in exchange for their 7 million acres in the East. But by May 1838, only 2,000 of the 16,000 Cherokees had moved voluntarily. General Winfield Scott and a force of 7,000 men were sent to evict the remaining Indians. The tragedy that transpired eventually came to be called the Trail of Tears.

First, stockades were built to hold the Indians. Then small squads armed with rifles and bayonets were sent out to round up every Cherokee they could find. No time was allotted for packing—men were seized in the fields and women and children from their homes. The soldiers prodded and drove the Indians to the stockades. Behind the soldiers came bands of looters, who pillaged and burned the Cherokees' former homes.

From the time the detachments left the stockades, the 1,200-mile trek took as long as six months. The average distance covered was 10 miles a day. The Cherokees stopped only to bury those who died along the way—of disease, starvation, and exhaustion.

The numbers are indeed stark, but they do little to explain man's cruelty to man. When greed intercedes, there seems no end to the damage one people can inflict upon another.

Maggie Valley

Maggie Valley, a resort community at the base of the Balsam Mountains, was named for the daughter of the town's first postmaster. It is four miles from the Blue Ridge Parkway and 16 miles from Cherokee and the entrance to Great Smoky Mountains National Park. Maggie Valley has a permanent population of about 200, but that number swells in summer, when tourists stay in the many motels along U.S. 19/ Main Street and visit the Stompin' Ground. Cataloochee Ski Area is the big attraction during winter.

JUST THE FACTS

Maggie Valley is on U.S. 19 about 30 miles west of Asheville.

The Maggie Valley Chamber of Commerce is located at 2511 Soco Road (28751); call 828-926-1686 or visit www.maggievalley.com for information.

The newspaper that covers this area is Waynesville's *Enterprise Mountaineer*, which also puts out a tabloid of regional activities and advertising called *Adventure in the Smokies*.

Things to Do

Recreation

The wooden stage of the ***Stompin' Ground*** comes alive with professional clogging teams dancing to Appalachian music provided by fiddlers, guitar strummers, and banjo pickers. This is a great place to experience the folk dancing unique to the Appalachians. The audience is encouraged to participate, so don't be afraid to try clogging, line dancing, or even waltzing. The Stompin' Ground is located at 3116 Soco Road/U.S. 19 (28751). Its hours vary according to the performance schedule. An admission fee is charged. Call 828-926-1288 for more information.

As of this writing, ***Ghost Town in the Sky***, located at 10 Fie Top Road (28751), is once again offering tourists a day of Wild West fun. Ghost Town opened in 1961 as a theme park to mimic old towns of the American West. For over 40 years, it has offered rides fit for the youngest buckaroos to the bravest outlaws. It also features staged gunfights, live music, games, food, crafts, and more. A chair lift transports guests to the top of Buck Mountain, where their day of unabashed, good old-fashioned fun begins. For more information, call 800-GHOST-TOWN or visit www. ghosttowninthesky.com.

Cataloochee Ski Area, located at 1080 Ski Lodge Road (28751), was the first ski resort in North Carolina when it was built in 1961. It was so successful that it spawned a new industry. Now, ski areas dot the mountains from here to the Virginia border. Cataloochee's lodge and restaurant have a friendly atmosphere where families are welcome. The ski area has 14 slopes and a vertical drop of 740 feet. Ski instruction and equipment rental are available. Call 800-768-0285 or 828-926-0285 or visit www.cataloochee.com for more information.

Seasonal Events

Folkmoot USA is a 10-day cultural event in July that features traditional dance groups from all over the world. It is hosted in several western North Carolina cities. Folkmoot's Maggie Valley performances are held at the Stompin' Ground. For information and a calendar of performances, call 877-FOLKUSA or 828-452-2997 or visit www.folkmoot.com.

Places to Stay

Resorts, Hotels, and Motels

Cataloochee Ranch. Deluxe. 119 Ranch Drive in Maggie Valley, 28751 (800-868-1401 or 828-926-1401; www.cataloocheeranch.com). Located atop a mountain overlooking Maggie Valley, this is a special place with spectacular views. The lodge is rustic but well appointed. The staff is attentive to every detail. The seven cabins and two lodges contain 22 units with pine paneling and quilts on the beds. Horseback riding is the main activity here, but hiking trails and trout fishing are also offered. Rocking on the front porch and sitting before the fireplace in the lodge are also popular ways to spend time at Cataloochee Ranch. Generous country-style breakfasts and dinners, served April through November, are included in the room rate. The ranch is open year-round.

Maggie Valley Resort and Country Club. Deluxe/Expensive. 1919 Country Club Drive in Maggie Valley, 28751 (www.maggievalleyclub.com; 800-438-3861 or 828-926-1616). This resort is located a half-mile west of the intersection of U.S. 19 and U.S. 276 in a lush setting with a mountain backdrop. It offers 40 comfortable rooms, 11 private villas, 21 luxurious condominiums, a championship golf course, and an outdoor pool. Golf packages are available. The breakfast buffet and dinner, served in the resort's restaurant, are included in the room rate. Lunch is offered in the Pin High Lounge.

Inns and Bed-and-Breakfasts

The Swag Country Inn. Deluxe. 2300 Swag Road in Waynesville, 28785 (800-789-7672 or 828-926-0430; www.theswag.com). The Swag has earned a reputation as one of the most exclusive inns in the mountains. The drive to the top of its private peak is breathtaking. The rustic inn is made of hand-hewn logs taken from original Appalachian structures. The inn has a private entrance to Great Smoky Mountains National Park, an indoor racquetball court, a spring-fed swimming pond, and 250 acres of secluded land to explore. Special programs are offered throughout summer. The Swag is open from May through mid-November.

Jonathan Creek Inn and Villas. Expensive/Moderate. 4324 Soco Road in Maggie Valley, 28751 (800-577-7812 or 828-926-1232; www.jonathancreekinn.com). At first glance, this looks like many of the motels in Maggie Valley, but check deeper. The 44 spacious, comfortable rooms have back doors that open onto Jonathan Creek. They also have refrigerators, microwaves, and coffee makers. Some have whirlpools, hot tubs, fireplaces, and wet bars. The seven villas are an option for those desiring even more privacy. The beautifully landscaped grounds include several garden areas, hammocks, a picnic area, and a gazebo. The inn has an indoor heated pool.

Smokey Shadows Lodge. Moderate/Inexpensive. Fie Top Road (P.O. Box 444) in Maggie Valley, 28751 (866-926-0001 or 828-926-0001; www.smokeyshadows.com). The 12 guest rooms at this primitive-style lodge have chestnut paneling and beam ceilings. A separate cabin sleeps six. The long porch that extends across the back of the building offers a magnificent view. The country gourmet meals, not included in the room rate, don't leave anyone hungry. Smokey Shadows is open year-round.

Places to Eat

Maggie Valley Resort and Country Club. Expensive/Moderate. 1919 Country Club Road in Maggie Valley, 28751 (828-926-1616; www.maggievalleyclub.com). This is as fine a dining experience as you'll find in Maggie Valley. From freshly prepared eggs to homemade Belgian waffles, the breakfast buffet is the perfect way to start your day. You may wish to relax and enjoy a refreshing drink or light fare on the resort's scenic Clubhouse Terrace or in the quaint Pin High Lounge. A delicious lunch buffet is offered Monday through Friday. In the evening, you can feast on mountain trout, prime rib, chicken, and seafood in Season's Restaurant. The resort's restaurants are open daily to the public.

J. Arthur's Restaurant. Moderate. 2843 Soco Road in Maggie Valley, 28751 (828-926-1817; www.jarthurs.com). The big, rambling, ranchlike building that houses J. Arthur's welcomes families, who flock here after a full day of touring. Prime rib and steak are the specialties, but you'll find some surprises like "Gorgonzola Cheese Salad," too. Kids can satisfy their appetites with a range of burgers and sandwiches. The restaurant serves dinner daily in summer and from Wednesday through Saturday in winter.

Snappy's. Moderate. 2769 Soco Road in Maggie Valley, 28751 (828-926-6126). Snappy's is an unpretentious, comfortable restaurant that prides itself on serving the best pizza and Italian food in the area. It makes its own dough and sauce and blends its own cheeses to produce the kind of fare you would expect in more upscale locales. The portions are huge and the staff efficient and friendly. The menu also features appetizers, soups, salads, burgers, sandwiches, and just about every type of Italian entrée you can imagine. After dinner here, you're likely to leave with a doggie bag and a smile of satisfaction. Snappy's serves lunch and dinner from Monday through Saturday year-round. From May through October, it also serves Sunday dinner.

Butts on the Creek. Inexpensive. 1584 Soco Road in Maggie Valley, 28751 (828-926-7885). If you're a sucker for a catchy name, this one will certainly catch you. The "butts" here are pork butts slowly smoked to barbecued perfection. The "creek" refers to Jonathan Creek, which runs alongside the property. You can't get much closer to nirvana than sinking your teeth into great food while gazing at a babbling mountain stream. This place has that and more. Butts is open from April through November. It serves lunch and dinner Tuesday through Sunday.

Waynesville

Waynesville is an ideal mountain town. It doesn't have a manufactured tourist destination or a large business district. What it offers is a chance to get away from it all and still be close enough to visit area attractions. The downtown boasts a wonderful selection of retail shops, galleries, and restaurants. The streets are lined with shade trees and comfortable benches.

Waynesville plays host to a variety of street festivals in summer and fall. The entertainment at these outdoor celebrations includes parades, dance exhibitions, and craft displays. Thanks to plenty of charm and just the right amount of activity, Waynesville may become one of your favorite mountain getaways.

JUST THE FACTS

Waynesville is located at the intersection of U.S. 74 and U.S. 276 west of Asheville.

The Haywood County Chamber of Commerce, at 591 North Main Street (28786), is the place to go for information about the town. Call 877-456-3073 or 828-456-3021 or visit www.haywood-nc.com. You can also get information from the Downtown Association by calling 828-456-3517.

Waynesville's newspaper, the *Enterprise Mountaineer*, is published three times a week. The paper puts out *Adventure in the Smokies*, a tabloid of regional activities and advertising.

Things to Do

Museums and Science Centers

The ***Museum of North Carolina Handicrafts***, at 49 Shelton Street (28786), houses a fascinating collection of pottery, porcelain, baskets, woodcarvings, and turned bowls. Other treasures include hand-carved dulcimers, quilts, and a collection of Cherokee crafts and artifacts. The museum's gift shop sells a variety of crafts. An admission fee is charged. From May through October, the museum is open Tuesday through Saturday from 10 A.M. to 4 P.M.; call for winter hours. The number is 828-452-1551.

Special Shopping

Waynesville is one of those great mountain towns that entice you to stroll, browse, and shop. Main Street and the adjacent side streets offer hand-crafted furniture, galleries, boutiques, antiques, garden accessories, kitchen tools, clothing, books, and more.

The *Mast General Store and Candy Barrel*, at 55 North Main Street (28786), is familiar to anyone who visits North Carolina's mountains. The original store is in Valle Crucis, but many locations may be found from Boone to Hendersonville. Stop in to browse a wide variety of goods ranging from sweaters to cast-iron skillets. Of course, the kids won't let you leave without a visit to the Candy Barrel. The old-fashioned candies draw as many customers looking for nostalgia as people in search of a sweet morsel. Everyone enjoys browsing the bins for treats they haven't seen since childhood. The Mast General Store is open seven days a week; call 828-452-0075.

Seasonal Events

Local festivities include the *Smoky Mountain Folk Festival*, the *High Country Quilt Show*, the *Apple Harvest Festival*, and the *Church Street Arts and Crafts Show*. Check with the visitor center or the Downtown Association for information on these events.

Folkmoot USA, held during July, is a 10-day festival featuring international dance performances by guest groups from all over the world. Many of the performances are in Waynesville. This festival, over 15 years old, is recognized as one of the finest gatherings of international dancers in the country. Call 877-FOLKUSA or 828-452-2997 or visit www.folkmoot.com for more information.

Places to Stay

Inns and Bed-and-Breakfasts

The Windover Inn Bed and Breakfast. Deluxe/Expensive. 117 Old Hickory Street in Waynesville, 28786 (866-452-4411; www.windoverinn.com). Built in 1910, this late-Victorian home has original woodwork and hardwood floors that provide comfort from the moment you enter. Each room is lovingly decorated. Amenities include luxurious pillow top mattresses, fine linens, soothing whirlpool tubs, and romantic candlelit fireplaces. The inn offers warm, relaxing common areas for reading, conversation, and puzzles and games. Guests are invited to unwind along the garden footpath, on the wraparound porch, in the gazebo swing, or at the firepit. Coffee and tea are available on all three floors for guests to enjoy anytime. The room rate includes a delicious home-cooked breakfast with fruit, baked goodies, and entrées such as French toast, waffles, and quiche.

Balsam Mountain Inn. Expensive. Off U.S. 23/74 at 68 Seven Springs Drive in Balsam, 28707 (828-456-9498; www.balsaminn.com). This restored historic place is located a half-mile from the Blue Ridge Parkway. Opened in 1908 to serve the highest railway depot east of the Rockies, the inn offers beautiful mountain views from its two-tiered porch. It has 50 comfortable rooms with private baths, a library containing 2,000-plus volumes, a card-and-puzzle room, and a spacious lobby with two fireplaces. You won't find telephones in the rooms or a single television in the entire inn. The room rate includes a full country breakfast. The inn's restaurant serves breakfast and dinner Monday through Friday and all three meals on Saturday and Sunday.

Waynesville Country Club Inn. Expensive. 176 Country Club Road in Waynesville, 28786 (800-627-6250 or 828-452-2258; www.wccinn.com). This is one of Waynesville's most elegant lodgings. The three-story 1920s fieldstone inn is set against densely wooded mountains. Its 115 luxurious guest rooms offer views of the mountains or the 27-hole golf course. Tennis courts and a heated outdoor pool are on the premises. The wood-paneled dining room is open for all three meals. In-season rates include breakfast and dinner.

Mountain Creek Bed-and-Breakfast. Moderate. 146 Chestnut Walk Drive in

Waynesville, 28786 (800-557-9766 or 828-456-5509; www.mountaincreekbb.com). Finally, a bed-and-breakfast that's not filled with Victorian lace and antiques! The proprietors call the decor at Mountain Creek "retro 50s," and it's a refreshing and comfortable change of pace. A former corporate retreat lodge, the main house is situated above a rock-lined pond that makes for a beautiful view from the wrap-around porch and the window-lined den. The renovated pool house includes a Ja-cuzzi suite. The innkeepers are outdoor enthusiasts who will help organize hikes and bike trips. The room rate includes a gourmet breakfast prepared by a truly talented cook. Guests can arrange for an equally delicious special dinner.

Places to Eat

Balsam Mountain Inn. Expensive. Off U.S. 23/74 at 68 Seven Springs Drive in Balsam, 28707 (828-456-9498; www.balsaminn.com). The chef at Balsam prepares American cuisine to the highest standards, utilizing the bounty of local farms as well as fresh seafood from the Atlantic. The menu is constantly evolving accord-ing to the season and the availability of ingredients. Appetizers include "Smoked Trout Blini Stack," baked Brie, and fried green tomatoes. Entrées like "Coconut-Crusted Salmon," "Grilled Venison Loin with Blueberry and Port Wine Compote," and "Porkchops with Calvados" are equally mouth-watering. And just when you think you've been pampered enough, the waiter shows up with a dazzling array of desserts. Balsam Mountain Inn's cuisine has garnered many awards, most recently a perfect score from *Southern Living* for its shrimp and grits. The inn serves breakfast and dinner Monday through Friday and all three meals Saturday and Sunday. Res-ervations are recommended.

Lomo Grill and **Lomo's Bakery and Café**. Expensive/Moderate. 44 Church Street in Waynesville, 28786 (828-452-5222; www.lomogrill.com). Lomo Grill features au-thentic Italian and Mediterranean cuisine. Here, the finest meats are grilled in a wood-burning oven. The dining room's romantic ambiance complements the award-winning food and one of the finest wine cellars in the area. Lomo's Bakery and Café is patterned in the French style. Its delicious right-out-of-the-oven goodies include breads, pastries, and gourmet cookies. You can also enjoy specialty sandwiches, vegetarian entrées, homemade soups, unique quiches, and beautifully prepared salads. Dinner is served Tuesday through Saturday.

Ceviche's on Main. Moderate. 128 North Main Street in Waynesville, 28786 (828-246-0800). This is the perfect spot to stop while strolling downtown. Ceviche's menu is an eclectic mix of Mediterranean, Mexican, Tuscan, and American foods. Here, you'll find hummus, smoked trout dip, ceviche (of course), crab cakes, taco salads, Asian salads, grilled veggie sandwiches, black bean burgers, meat loaf, a "Cuban Bowl," penne pasta, tamales, and a wrap called "Red Hot & Blue." A full-service bar is offered. Ceviche's serves lunch and dinner daily.

Maggie's Galley. Moderate. 49 Hal Miller Road in Waynesville, 28786 (828-456-8945). When it comes to food—especially seafood—this place has it all. The appetizers include such treats as alligator, crawdads, onion straws, and nachos. The selection of main courses is just as eclectic: Hawaiian shrimp, North Carolina rainbow trout, the "Gator Dinner," and frog legs, as well as rib-eye steaks served with snow crab, lobster tail, or shrimp. Be sure to save room for dessert, when you'll get to choose from the likes of black walnut pie and "Coca-Cola Cake." Maggie's Galley serves dinner daily and lunch Tuesday through Sunday.

Pasquale's Pizzeria & Tapas Bar. Moderate. 1863 South Main Street in Waynesville, 28786 (828-454-5002). Great Italian food, a cozy bar that serves tapas, and a deck for al fresco dining combine for a memorable experience at Pasquale's. The restaurant serves Old World appetizers such as "Artichokes with Prosciutto," classic pizzas and calzones, and pasta, chicken, beef, and seafood entrées, all with an Italian flair. Dinner comes with a fresh salad tossed at your table and breadsticks perfect for getting every bit of sauce from your plate. Pasquale's is open for lunch and dinner Monday through Saturday.

Bogart's. Moderate/Inexpensive. 303 South Main Street in Waynesville, 28786 (828-452-1313; www.bogartswaynesville.com). This casual restaurant and tavern really hits its groove at night, when it gets pretty lively. The rustic interior is highlighted by stained-glass windows. Diners may choose from a good selection of burgers and sandwiches, as well as rainbow trout, stir-fried chicken, and sirloin tips. Lunch and dinner are served daily.

Whitman's Bakery and Sandwich Shoppe. Inexpensive. 18 North Main Street in Waynesville, 28786 (828-456-8271). This bakery has been serving downtown shoppers delectable goodies since 1945. The name Whitman (my maiden name) drew me in, but the aroma held me. The items I sampled were fresh, delicious, and deserving of such a fine name. Let me personally recommend the butter cookies with the pastel centers. Sandwiches are prepared to order by the friendly, inviting staff. Lunch is offered Tuesday through Saturday.

Appendix

The following pages contain key facts and phone numbers that should help answer travel queries and make it easier to plan a North Carolina vacation.

STATE AGENCIES

North Carolina Department of Commerce, Division of Tourism,
  Film and Sports Development
301 North Wilmington Street
Raleigh, N.C. 27626-2825
800-VISITNC or 919-733-8372; www.visitnc.com

This should be your first contact for information about North Carolina. The tourism office provides state maps and several useful publications. It publishes a full-color booklet of over 150 pages listing accommodations, campgrounds, events around the state, and state parks and historic sites. The booklet also contains a map. If you stop by the Raleigh office, you can pick up free brochures for many attractions statewide.

Division of Coastal Management
400 Commerce Avenue
Morehead City, N.C. 28557
888-472-6278 or 252-808-2808; www.nccoastalmanagement.net

North Carolina Aquariums
3125 Poplarwood Court, Suite 160
Raleigh, N.C. 27604-6434
800-832-3474; www.ncaquariums.com

North Carolina Department of Transportation
1 South Wilmington Street
Raleigh, N.C. 27601
877-368-4968 or 919-733-2520; www.ncdot.org

North Carolina Division of Forest Resources
512 North Salisbury Street
1616 Mail Service Center
Raleigh, N.C. 27699
919-857-4801; www.dfr.state.nc.us

North Carolina Division of Parks and Recreation
512 North Salisbury Street
1615 Mail Service Center
Raleigh, N.C. 27699
919-733-4181; www.ncparks.gov

North Carolina Division of State Historic Sites
430 North Salisbury Street, Suite 2050
4620 Mail Service Center (27699-4620)
Raleigh, N.C. 27699
919-733-7862; www.nchistoricsites.org

North Carolina Wildlife Resources Commission Headquarters
NCSU Centennial Campus
1751 Varsity Drive
Raleigh, N.C. 27606
919-707-0398 or 919-707-0391; www.ncwildlife.org

GENERAL SOURCES

Blue Ridge Parkway Superintendent
199 Hemphill Knob Road
Asheville, N.C. 28803
828-271-4779; www.nps.gov/blri

Cape Hatteras National Seashore Superintendent
1401 National Park Drive
Manteo, N.C. 27954
252-473-2111; www.nps.gov/caha

Cape Lookout National Seashore Superintendent
131 Charles Street
Harkers Island, N.C. 28531
252-728-2250; www.nps.gov/calo

Carolinas Association of RV Parks and Campgrounds
605 Poole Drive
Garner, N.C. 27529
800-906-0907 or 919-235-0239; www.campingcarolinas.com

Cherokee Welcome Center
498 Tsali Boulevard
P.O. Box 460
Cherokee, N.C. 28719
800-438-1601 or 828-497-9195; www.cherokee-nc.com

Great Smoky Mountains National Park Superintendent
107 Park Headquarters Road
Gatlinburg, Tenn. 37738
865-436-1200; www.nps.gov/grsm

National Forests in North Carolina Superintendent
160 Zillicoa Street, Suite A
P.O. Box 2750
Asheville, N.C. 28801
828-257-4200; www.cs.unca.edu/nfsnc

North Carolina High Country Host
1700 Blowing Rock Road
Boone, N.C. 28607
800-438-7500 or 828-264-1299; www.mountainsofnc.com

North Carolina Ski Areas Association
c/o Sugar Mountain Resort
P.O. Box 369
Banner Elk, N.C. 28604
800-SUGAR-MT or 828-898-4521; www.goskinc.com

Smoky Mountain Host of North Carolina
4437 Georgia Road
Franklin, N.C. 28734
800-432-HOST or 828-369-9606; www.visitsmokies.org

STATE HISTORIC SITES

Alamance Battleground
5803 N.C. 62 South
Burlington, N.C. 27215
336-227-4785; www.nchistoricsites.org/alamance/alamanc.htm

Aycock Birthplace
264 Governor Aycock Road
P.O. Box 207
Fremont, N.C. 27830
919-242-5581; www.nchistoricsites.org/aycock/aycock.htm

Battleship *North Carolina*
1 Battleship Road
P.O. Box 480 (28402)
Wilmington, N.C. 28401
910-251-5797; www.battleshipnc.com

Bennett Place
4409 Bennett Memorial Road
Durham, N.C. 27705
919-383-4345; www.nchistoricsites.org/bennett/bennett.htm

Bentonville Battleground
5466 Harper House Road
Four Oaks, N.C. 27524
910-594-0789; www.nchistoricsites.org/bentonvi/bentonvi.htm

Brunswick Town/Fort Anderson
8884 St. Philips Road SE
Winnabow, N.C. 28479
910-371-6613; www.nchistoricsites.org/brunswic/brunswic.htm

Charlotte Hawkins Brown Museum
6136 Burlington Road
P.O. Box B (27342)
Sedalia, N.C. 27349
336-449-4846; www.nchistoricsites.org/chb/chb.htm

CSS *Neuse* and Governor Caswell Memorial
2612 West Vernon Avenue
P.O. Box 3043 (28501)
Kinston, N.C. 28502
252-522-2091; www.nchistoricsites.org/neuse/neuse.htm

Duke Homestead
2828 Duke Homestead Road
Durham, N.C. 27705
919-477-5498; www.nchistoricsites.org/duke/duke.htm

Fort Dobbs
438 Fort Dobbs Road
Statesville, N.C. 28677
704-873-5866; www.fortdobbs.org

Fort Fisher
1610 Fort Fisher Boulevard South
P.O. Box 169
Kure Beach, N.C. 28449
910-458-5538; www.nchistoricsites.org/fisher/fisher.htm

Historic Bath
207 Carteret Street
P.O. Box 148
Bath, N.C. 27808
252-923-3971; www.nchistoricsites.org/bath/bath.htm

Historic Edenton
P.O. Box 474
Edenton, N.C. 27932
252-482-2637; www.nchistoricsites.org/iredell/iredell.htm

Historic Halifax
25 St. David Street
P.O. Box 406
Halifax, N.C. 27839
252-583-7191; www.nchistoricsites.org/halifax/halifax.htm

Historic Stagville
5825 Old Oxford Highway
Durham, N.C. 27712
919-620-0120; www.stagville.org

Horne Creek Farm
308 Horne Creek Farm Road
Pinnacle, N.C. 27043
336-325-2298; www.nchistoricsites.org/horne/horne.htm

House in the Horseshoe
288 Alston House Road
Sanford, N.C. 27330
910-947-2051; www.nchistoricsites.org/horsesho/horsesho.htm

North Carolina Transportation Museum
411 South Salisbury Avenue
P.O. Box 165
Spencer, N.C. 28159
877-628-6386 or 704-636-2889; www.nchistoricsites.org/spencer/spencer.htm

President James K. Polk State Historic Site
12031 Lancaster Highway
P.O. Box 475
Pineville, N.C. 28134
704-889-7145; www.nchistoricsites.org/polk/polk.htm

Reed Gold Mine
9621 Reed Mine Road
Midland, N.C. 28107
704-721-4653; www.nchistoricsites.org/reed/reed.htm

Roanoke Island Festival Park/*Elizabeth II*
1 Festival Park
Manteo, N.C. 27954
252-475-1500; www.roanokeisland.com

Somerset Place
2572 Lake Shore Road
Creswell, N.C. 27928
252-797-4560; www.nchistoricsites.org/somerset/somerset.htm

State Capitol
1 East Edenton Street
4624 Mail Service Center (27699-4624)
Raleigh, N.C. 27601-2807
919-733-4994; www.nchistoricsites.org/capitol/defaults.htm

Thomas Wolfe Memorial
52 North Market Street
Asheville, N.C. 28801
828-253-8304; www.nchistoricsites.org/wolfe/wolfe.htm

Town Creek Indian Mound
509 Town Creek Mound Road
Mount Gilead, N.C. 27306
910-439-6802; www.nchistoricsites.org/town/town.htm

Tryon Palace Historic Sites and Gardens
610 Pollock Street
New Bern, N.C. 28562
800-767-1560 or 252-514-4900; www.tryonpalace.org

Vance Birthplace
911 Reems Creek Road
Weaverville, N.C. 28787
828-645-6706; www.nchistoricsites.org/vance/vance.htm

OUTDOOR RECREATION

For most of the following, more complete information is provided in the text of this book; the index will tell you exactly where. This is intended as a quick-reference telephone list.

National Recreational Areas

Blue Ridge Parkway
828-271-4779

Cape Hatteras National Seashore
252-473-2111

Cape Lookout National Seashore
252-728-2250

Croatan National Forest
252-638-5628

Great Smoky Mountains National Park
865-436-1200

Nantahala National Forest
828-257-4200

Pisgah National Forest
828-257-4200

Uwharrie National Forest
910-576-6391

State Parks and Recreational Areas

Carolina Beach
910-458-8206

Chimney Rock
828-625-1823

Cliffs of the Neuse
919-778-6234

Crowders Mountain
704-853-5375

Dismal Swamp
252-771-6593

Elk Knob
828-297-7261

Eno River
919-383-1686

Falls Lake
919-676-1027

Fort Fisher
910-458-5798

Fort Macon
252-726-3775

Goose Creek
252-923-2191

Gorges
828-966-9099

Grandfather Mountain
828-297-7261

Hammocks Beach
910-326-4881

Hanging Rock
336-593-8480

Haw River
336-342-6163

Jockey's Ridge
252-441-7132

Jones Lake
910-588-4550

Jordan Lake
919-362-0586

Kerr Lake
252-438-7791

Lake James
828-652-5047

Lake Norman
704-528-6350

Lake Waccamaw
910-646-4748

Lumber River
910-628-4564

Mayo River
336-427-2530

Medoc Mountain
252-586-6588

Merchants Millpond
252-357-1191

Morrow Mountain
704-982-4402

Singletary Lake
910-669-2928

Mount Mitchell
828-675-4611

South Mountains
828-433-4772

New River
336-982-2587

Stone Mountain
336-957-8185

Pettigrew
252-797-4475

Weymouth Woods
910-692-2167

Pilot Mountain
336-325-2355

William B. Umstead
919-571-4170

Raven Rock
910-893-4888

FISHING AND HUNTING

You can get fishing or hunting licenses from any license agent, of which there are many. Look for them at hardware and sporting-goods stores. Some licenses expire June 30, while others expire one year from the date of purchase. For further information, contact the North Carolina Wildlife Resources Commission at 888-248-6834.

Resident inland fishing license—$15
Resident inland comprehensive fishing license (including trout)—$20
      Ten-day license—$5
      Trout license—$10
Nonresident inland fishing license—$30
      Ten-day license—$10
      Trout license—$10

Coastal recreational fishing requires a license (CRFL).
Resident coastal recreational fishing license—$15
      Ten-day license—$5

Nonresident coastal recreational fishing license—$30
  Ten-day license—$10

Resident sportsman license—$40

Resident hunting license—$15
  Big-game permit—$10
  Trapping license—$25
Nonresident hunting license—$60
  Big-game permit—$60
  Six-day hunting license—$40
  Six-day big-game permit—$40

BICYCLING

To help cyclists find safe and interesting places to ride, the Bicycle Program of the North Carolina Department of Transportation has identified primary and secondary roads that are relatively safe because of low traffic volume and good roadway conditions. Various routes encompassing over 3,000 miles have been mapped. Others will be available in the future.

Sample routes:

Mountains-to-Sea—700 miles from Murphy to Manteo
Piedmont Spur—200-mile east-west route
Carolina Connection—200-mile north-south route
Ports of Call—300 miles in the coastal area
Cape Fear Run—160 miles from Raleigh to the Cape Fear area
Ocracoke Option—175 miles from the Wilson area to the Cedar Island ferry
Southern Highlands—120 miles from the Blue Ridge Parkway to Lincolnton

Maps and tour routes are available for selected areas. To order one or more of these free guides, contact:

Bicycle Program
North Carolina Department of Transportation
1552 Mail Service Center
Raleigh, N.C. 27699-1552
919-733-2804

AID FOR HANDICAPPED TRAVELERS

Access North Carolina is an excellent travel guide for disabled persons. It provides accessibility information for virtually every tourist attraction in the state. It evaluates parking lots, entrances, indoor and outdoor sites, water fountains, and restrooms and also mentions special tours and access for blind and deaf persons. It is available at no charge from the North Carolina Division of Tourism, Film and Sports Development.

Index

A. J. Fletcher Institute, 227
Ackland Art Museum, 261–62
Adkins-Ruark House, 204
Admiral's Quarters Motel, 200
Advice 5¢, 24
Aerie, The, 131–32
African American Atelier, 349
Afro-American Cultural Center, 392
Air Bellows Gap, 418
Airborne and Special Operations Museum, 285, 289–90, 298
Airlie Gardens, 172–74
Alamance Battleground State Historic Site, 369
Allanstand Craft Shop, 497
Alleghany County Access Area, 438
Allen and Son Pit-Cooked Bar-B-Q, 271
Alligator Back rest area, 419
Alligator River National Wildlife Refuge, 39–40
Aloft Charlotte Uptown at the EpiCentre, 402
American Dance Festival, 250
American Tobacco Trail, 250
Amistad *Saga: Reflections, The*, 232
Amos Mosquito's Restaurant and Bar, 157
Amy's Coffee and Confections, 133
Ân, 277
Anchorage Inn, 70
Anchorage Marina, 68–69
Andrea's Troy-Bumpas Inn, 355
Angels & Antiques, 293
Angus Barn, 234
Annual Hang Gliding Spectacular and Air Games, 19
Annual Nags Head Surf Fishing Club Invitational Tournament, 19
Annual Outer Banks Stunt-Kite Competition, 20
Annual Peanut Festival, 103
Antiquing in Pittsboro, 279
Appalachian Angler, 471
Appalachian Ski Mountain, 459
Appalachian Summer Festival, 452
Appalachian Trail, 498, 553
Apple Harvest Festival, 570
Archer's Mountain Inn, 474–75
Arrowhead Inn, 252
Art Alliance, 349
Art in the Park, 459
Art on Main, 519
Artisanal Restaurant, 475–76
ArtsCenter, 263, 265
Artspace, 226
Artsplosure Spring Art Festival, 232
Ashe County Cheese Company, 440
Asheville Art Museum, 493
Asheville Community Theatre, 495
Asheville Municipal Golf Course, 499
Asheville Symphony, 495
Ashten's Restaurant & Pub, 311
Athena Greek Taverna, 335
Atlantic Coast Line Railroad Station, 288

Atlantis Lodge, 156
Attmore-Oliver House, 127
Augustus T. Zevely Inn, 333
Aurora Fossil Museum, 113–14
Avalon Fishing Pier, 15
Avon Golf and Fishing Pier, 56
Avon Motel, 58
Awful Arthur's Oyster Bar, 28–29
Ayr Mount, 277
Azalea Inn, 475

Back Porch, 72–73
Bad Bean Taqueria, 27
Badin Lake, 410
Baird House, 455
Bald Head Island, 160–61, 209
Bald Is Beautiful Convention and Contest, 140–41
Bald View Bed-and-Breakfast, 24
Ballantyne Resort Hotel, 401
Ballyhoo's Island Sports Grill, 158
Balsam Mountain Inn, 571, 573
Bank of America Corporate Center, 404
Bank of the Arts, 128
Banner Elk Inn, 475
Barbecue Festival, 373
Barker-Moore House, 100
Barn of Fayetteville, 297
Barnacles, 201
Barrier Island Kayaks, 158–59
Bascom, The, 536–37
Battle of Guilford Courthouse reenactment, 352–53
Battleship *North Carolina*, 177
Beaufort Antiques Show and Sale, 147
Beaufort Grocery, 149
Beaufort Historic Site, 145
Beaufort Inn, 148
Beaufort Old Homes and Gardens Tour, 147
Beaufort Wine and Food Weekend, 147
Bechtler Museum of Modern Art, 393
Beech Alpen Inn, 473–74
Beech Mountain, 471
Beggars and Choosers, 279
Bele Chere Downtown Community Celebration, 500
Belhaven Memorial Museum, 114–15
Bellamy Mansion, 170, 176
Bella's Neighborhood Italian Restaurant, 476
Ben F. Long Fresco Trail, 446
Bennett College, 341
Bennett Place State Historic Site, 242
Bennett Vineyards, 114
Bentonville Battleground, 298
Berliner Kindl German Restaurant, 510
Best Cellar, 463
Best Western Blue Ridge Plaza, 453
Best Western Coastline Inn, 182–83
Best Western Eldreth Inn, 443
Best Western High Point Hotel, 363
Bethesda Church and Cemetery, 311–12

Betty's Waterfront Restaurant, 207–8
Bicentennial Greenway, 363
Biennial Pilgrimage Tour of Homes and Country-
 side in Edenton and Chowan County, 103
Big Ed's City Market, 235
Big Rock Blue Marlin Tournament, 140
Biltmore Antiques District, 495
Biltmore Estate, 489–91
Biltmore Greensboro Hotel, 355
Biltmore Village, 495, 497
Birkdale Village, 395
Birthplace of Pepsi-Cola, 129
Bistro by the Sea, 142–43
Bistro Restaurant, 187
Bistro Roca & Antlers Bar, 463–64
Bistro Sofia, 356
Black Mountain, 509–10
Black Mountain Golf Course, 499
Black Pelican Oceanfront Café, 27
Blackbeard's Lodge, 70
Bleu Restaurant & Bar, 334
Blockade Runner Resort Hotel, 192
Blooming Garden Inn, 253
Blowing Rock Charity Horse Show, 459–60
Blowing Rock Equestrian Preserve, 459–60
Blowing Rock, the, 458–59
Blue, 405
Blue Heaven Bed-and-Breakfast, 183–84
Blue Moon Bistro, 149–50
Blue Point, 25–26
Blue Ridge BBQ Festival, 525
Blue Ridge Parkway Destination Center, 424
Blue Sky Café, 521
Blue Water Grille, 364
Blue Water Point Motel and Marina, 207
Blueberry Villa at Banner Elk Winery, 474
Blues 'n Brews Festival, 295
Bluff Mountain Trail, 419
Bluffs Coffee Shop, 419
Bluffs Lodge, 419, 433–34
Bob Timberlake Gallery, 373
Bob Timberlake Inn at Chetola Resort, 460
Bodie Island Lighthouse, 47–48
Bogart's, 573
Bonner House, 112
Bonnet's Creek, 204
Books to Be Red, 67
Boone Bike and Touring, 451
Boone Golf Club, 451
Botanical Gardens of Asheville, 493
Boundary House Restaurant, 210
Bowman Gray Stadium, 412
Bracken Mountain Bakery, 534
Brady C. Jefcoat Museum of Americana, 93
Breakwater Restaurant, 60–61
Breezeway Motel, 165
Breezeway Restaurant, 166
Brevard Music Festival, 528–29
Bridal Veil Falls, 537
BridgePointe Hotel and Marina, 131
Brightleaf Square, 248, 253, 254, 255

Brinegar Cabin, 419
British Cemetery, 65–66
Broad Creek Fishing Center & Marina, 40
Brookstown Inn, 332
Brown Mountain Lights, 422–23
Brown's Family Restaurant, 436
Broyhill Inn and Appalachian Conference Center,
 453
Brunswick Inn, 207
Brunswick Town, 209–10
Bryan Park, 352
Bryant House, 312
Buccaneer Inn Magnuson Hotel, 141
Buffalo Tavern Bed-and-Breakfast, 443
Bull Durham Blues Festival, 247, 250–51
Bullock's BBQ, 255
Burgwin Wright Museum House and Gardens,
 175
Burning Coal Theatre Company, 227
Buttonwood Inn Bed and Breakfast, 545–46
Butts on the Creek, 568–69
Buxton Woods Reserve, 57–58

Cabo Fish Taco Baja Seagrill, 407
Cades Cove, 553
Café on the Square, 507
Caffe Phoenix, 184
Calabash, 210
Calico Jacks Inn & Marina, 151
Cameo Art House Theatre, 291–92
Cameron House Inn, 43
Cameron Park Inn, 233–34
Camino Bakery, 337
Campbell House Galleries, 304, 305
Canadian Hole, 56
Candlelight Christmas Tour, 103
Candlelight Confection Perfection, 103
Cantina 1511, 406
Cape Fear Blues Festival, 182
Cape Fear Botanical Garden, 287–88
Cape Fear Kayaks, 193
Cape Fear Museum, 170, 178
Cape Fear Regional Theatre, 292, 297
Cape Fear River Boats, 172
Cape Fear Serpentarium, 178
Cape Fear Studios, 293
Cape Hatteras Bed-and-Breakfast, 60
Cape Hatteras Fishing Pier, 56
Cape Hatteras Lighthouse, 53–54
Cape Hatteras Motel, 58–59
Cape Lookout Lighthouse, 152
Cape Lookout National Seashore, 119, 151–52
Cape Lookout Studies Program, 146–47
Cape Lookout Village Historic District, 152
Cape Point, 152
Capital Area Greenway, 229
Capital City Bicycle Motocross Race Track, 231
Caprice Bistro, 184
Captain Ratty's, 133
Captain's Landing, 69
Captain's Quarters, 148–49

Captain's Quarters Inn, 104
Caribbe Inn, 157
Carl Sandburg Home National Historic Site, 516
Carmen's Cuban Café, 275–76
Carolina Aviation Museum, 389
Carolina Ballet, 227
Carolina Barnstormers, 250
Carolina Basketball Museum, 266
Carolina Beach State Park, 198
Carolina Beach Surf-Fishing Tournament, 199
Carolina Carriage Classic, 308
Carolina Coastal Adventures, 193
Carolina Cobras, 230
Carolina Creations, 129
Carolina Crossroads, 269
Carolina Hemlocks Recreation Area, 483
Carolina Horse Park at Five Points, 308
Carolina House Bed-and-Breakfast, 116
Carolina Hurricanes, 215, 230
Carolina Inn, 268
Carolina Mudcats, 281
Carolina Oceanfront, 21
Carolina Outdoors, 56
Carolina Raptor Center, 389
Carolina Renaissance Festival, 399
Carolina Sailing Unlimited, 136
Carolina Temple Apartments, 192
Carolina, The (Pinehurst), 309
Carolina, The (Whispering Pines), 307
Carolina Theatre (Durham), 247, 251, 253
Carolina Theatre (Greensboro), 350
Carolina Theatre and Grille (Elizabeth City), 91–92
Carol's Garden Inn, 253
Carowinds, 397
Carpe Diem, 406
Carr Mill Mall, 265
Carrboro Farmers' Market, 265
Carrboro Music Festival, 268
Carriage Tours of Pinehurst Village, 307
Cartwright House, 136
Cary, 276–77
Casablanca Café, 407
Cascade, 405
Cascades Nature Trail, 420
Castle Bed and Breakfast and Courtyard Villas, 71
Caswell Beach, 202
Cataloochee Ranch, 566
Cataloochee Ski Area, 499, 566
Cat's Cradle, 216, 267
Cedar Creek Gallery, 281
Cedar Island National Wildlife Refuge, 153
Cedar Rock Trail, 419
Cedars Inn, 148
Cellar Door, 510
Celo Inn, 485
Center City Walking Tour, 383
Center for Documentary Studies at Duke University, 248, 251
Center for Visual Artists, 349

Center, The (Elizabeth City), 86
Ceviche's on Main, 573
Champa, 521–22
Chandler's Wharf, 169, 180
Channel Marker, 157
Chapel Hill Museum, 263
Charleston Inn, 557
Charlotte Hawkins Brown Memorial State Historic Site, 370
Charlotte Marriott City Center, 401
Charlotte Marriott SouthPark, 402
Charlotte Motor Speedway, 412-13
Charlotte Museum of History, 383
Charlotte Nature Museum, 388
Charlotte Street Grill and Pub, 507
Chatham County Arts Council, 280
Chef Warren's, 311
Chelsea, The, 133
Chelsea Theatre, 264
Cherokee Adventures, 451
Chero's Market Café and Catering, 105
Cherry Point, 122
Chestnut Street Inn, 505
Chestnut Tree, 563
Chestoa View, 423
Chicamacomico Life Saving Station, 52–53
Children's Museum of Wilmington, 179–80
Children's Theater of Charlotte, 390
Childress Vineyards, 412
Chimney Rock, 522–23
Chimney Rock State Park, 523
Chowan Arts Council Gallery and Gallery Shop, 102
Chowan County Courthouse, 101
Chowan County Jail, 101
Chowan Golf and Country Club, 102–3
Christ Episcopal Church (Elizabeth City), 84
Christmas Candlelight Tour, 277
Christmas in July, 442
Church Street Arts and Crafts Show, 570
Circa 1922, 185
Circle 10 Art Gallery, 136
City Lake Park, 362
City Wine Seller Bakery and Deli, 92
Claddagh Inn, 520
Clamdigger Ramada Inn, 156
Clear Creek Guest Ranch, 483
Clearance Row, 366
Coastal Carolina Christmas Walk, 147
Coastal Ecology Sails, 147
Coker Arboretum, 260
Colburn Earth Science Museum, 493
Colington Island, 11
Comfort Inn Cross Creek, 296
Comfort Inn—Hatteras Island, 58
Comfort Suites Riverfront Park, 131
Community Thanksgiving Feast, 147
Concord Mills, 394
Cool Spring Baptist Church, 420
Cool Spring Tavern, 287
Copper, 406

Coquina Beach, 48
Core Sound Waterfowl Museum, 153
Corolla Wild Horse Museum, 12
Cottage Restaurant, 201
Cotton Exchange, 169, 180
Country Inn & Suites (Boone), 453
Courtyard by Marriott at Crabtree Valley, 233
Cove Bed and Breakfast, 71
Cow Café, 133
Coyote Kitchen, 456
Crabby-Oddwaters Restaurant, 208
Crab's Claw Restaurant and Oyster Bar, 157
Crabtree Falls, 423
Crabtree Meadows, 423
Cradle of Forestry in America, 527–28
Craft Fair of the Southern Highlands, 500
Craggy Gardens, 423, 511
Creekside Café, 73–74
Crippen's Country Inn & Restaurant, 463
Croatan National Forest, 119, 130
Crook's Corner Café and Bar, 270
Cross Creek Cemetery #1, 288
Crowders Mountain State Park, 410
Crown Center, 294, 296
Crown Coliseum, 294
Crowne Plaza Tennis and Golf Resort, 504
CSS *Neuse* State Historic Site, 137
Culpepper Inn, 90
Cumberland Falls Bed and Breakfast, 504
Cumberland Knob, 418
Cupola House, 100
Cupola House Wassail Bowl, 103
Curra's Dom, 506
Currituck Banks National Estuarine Research Reserve, 16
Currituck Beach Lighthouse, 5–6, 8
Currituck Club, 19
Currituck National Wildlife Refuge, 15–16
Cycling in Chapel Hill/Carrboro, 266–67
Cypress Creek Grill, 91
Cypress Moon Inn, 24

Dale Earnhardt Jr.'s Whisky River, 413
Daniel Boone Trace, 421
Dan'l Boone Inn Restaurant, 455–56
Dare Day Festival, 42
David R. Walters Antiques, 293
Davidson, 410-11
Davidson College, 410-11
Davie Poplar, 259, 260
Day at the Farm, 136
Days Inn (Elizabeth City), 89
Days Inn & Suites Mariner (Kill Devil Hills), 21
Deck House, 201
Deep Dish Theater Company, 264
Deep Gap, 420
Deepwater Pottery, 67
Deepwater Theater, 69
Delta Arts Center, 329
Deluxe Café, 184
Devil's Courthouse, 425

Diggs Gallery, 328
Dillsboro, 547
Discovery Diving, 146
Discovery Place, 387
Dismal Swamp Canal Welcome Center, 94
Dixie Classic Fair, 330
Docks at the Capitol, 293–94
Dockside Seafood House, 210
Dog Corner Park, 86
Dogwood Crafters, 547
Dogwood Festival, 294–95
Dogwood Trail, 295
Dolce Ristorante, 406
Dolphin Den, 61
Doughton-Hall Bed-and-Breakfast, 435
Doughton Park, 419, 432–33
Downeast Rover, 39
Downtown Arts District (Winston-Salem), 330
Downtown Thai, 334
Duck Town Park, 17
Duck Woods Country Club, 19
Dugan's Pub (Brevard), 534
Dugan's Pub (Pinehurst), 311
Duke Chapel, 239–40
Duke Forest, 250
Duke Homestead and Tobacco Museum, 242
Duke Mansion, 403
Duke of Dare Motor Lodge, 42–43
Duke University, 239–40, 242, 253
Duke University Lemur Center, 245
Dunhill Hotel, 401
Duplin Winery, 186–87
DuPont State Forest, 518
Durant Nature Park, 229
Durham Athletic Park, 249–50
Durham Bulls Athletic Park, 249, 253

E. B. Jeffress Park, 420
Early Girl Eatery, 507
Earthshine Mountain Lodge, 532
East Coast Classic King Mackerel Tournament, 199
East Franklin Street (Chapel Hill), 264–65
Eastern Music Festival, 349
Econo Lodge (Morehead City), 141
Edenton Coffee House, 106
Edenton Harbor, 102
Edenton National Fish Hatchery, 102
1847 Blake House Inn, 506
1891 Cedar Crest Inn, 505
82nd Airborne Division War Memorial Museum, 290
Elaine's on Franklin, 270
Elijah's Restaurant, 184
Elizabeth City Bed-and-Breakfast, 90–91
Elizabeth City commercial district, 84
Elizabeth City Historic Ghost Walk, 89
Elizabeth City State University Planetarium, 85
Elizabeth Leigh Inn, 519
Elizabeth II, 36
Elizabethan Gardens, 34–35

Elizabethan Inn, 42
Elizabeth's Café and Winery, 26
Emerald Grill, 158
Emerald Village, 479, 481
Emerywood Fine Foods, 365
EMF Fringe Series, 349
EpiCentre, 395
Episcopal Cemetery (Elizabeth City), 84
Eseeola Lodge, 474, 476
Evans Metropolitan AME Zion Church, 288
Everett Street Diner, 558
Executive Mansion, 221–22

F. W. Woolworth store (Greensboro), 358
Fairfield Inn & Suites (Boone), 453
Fairfield Inn & Suites (Elizabeth City), 89
Fairgrounds Flea Market, 228
Fairview Restaurant, 252
Falls Lake, 229
Falls Lake State Recreation Area, 281–82
Falls Landing Bar & Restaurant, 534
Farmers' Market (New Bern), 129
Fascinate-U Children's Museum, 290–91
Fayetteville Area Transportation Museum, 291
Fayetteville FireAntz, 294
Fayetteville Guard, 294
Fayetteville Museum of Art, 291
Fayetteville SwampDogs, 294
Fayetteville Symphony Orchestra, 292
Fearrington House Restaurant and Country Hotel, 279
Fearrington Village, 279
Federal, The, 255
FestiFall, 268
Festival for the Eno, 244, 251
1587, 45
Finley Golf Course, 267
Fire Mountain, 539–40
Firemen's Museum, 128
First Colony Inn, 24–25
First Horizon Park, 352
First Night Raleigh, 232
Flaming Amy's Burrito Barn, 185
Flat Rock Overlook, 422
Flat Rock Playhouse, 517
Flight, 521
Flying Burrito, 271
Flying Frog Café, 507–8
Flying Melon, 74
Folk Art Center, 424, 497
Folkmoot USA, 566, 570
Fontana Dam, 558
Fontana Village, 558–59
Foothills Brewing Company, 336
Foothills Equestrian Nature Center (FENCE), 524–25
Forest Theatre, 260–61, 268
Fort Anderson, 210
Fort Fisher State Historic Site, 195–97
Fort Fisher State Recreation Area, 199
Fort Macon State Park, 119, 153, 154–55

Fort Raleigh National Historic Site, 32–34
42nd Street Oyster Bar, 235
Foscoe Fishing Company & Outfitters, 471
Foster's Market, 255
Founders Hall, 392
4½ Street Inn, 540
4 Seasons at Beech, 473
Four Seasons Town Centre, 350
Four Square, 253–54
Fox Hunter's Paradise, 418
Fox Watersports, 56
Franklin Gem and Mineral Museum, 544
Franklin Square Art Gallery, 205
Fraser's, 444
Fred's Backside Deli, 476
Fred's General Mercantile Company, 467
Freeborne's Eatery and Lodge, 434
Freedom Park, 396
Frescoes, 445–46
Friendly Center, 350
Frisbee golf in Raleigh, 231
Frisco Native American Museum and Natural History Center, 55
Frog & Owl Kitchen, 546
Front Street Grill at Stillwater, 150
Front Street Inn, 183
Fryemont Inn, 557
Fryemont Inn Dining Room, 557–58
Full Frame Documentary Film Festival, 251–52
Full Moon Café, 45
Fun Junktion, 86–87
Furnitureland South, 359, 360–61

Gallery C, 227
Garden, The, 405
Garden Deli, 485
Garden Jubilee, 519
Gaston, Lake, 92
Gazebo Creekside Café, 546
General Store Café, 280
Genki, 185
George W. Dixon House, 126
Ghost Town in the Sky, 565–66
Gideon Ridge Inn, 462
Giggling Mackerel, 207
Gilbert Theater, 292
Glenn Eure's Ghost Fleet Gallery, 14
Golden Sands, 200
Goose Creek State Park, 116–17
Governors Club, 268–69
Grand Bohemian, 502
Grandfather Mountain, 421, 468
Grandfather Mountain Highland Games & Gathering of Scottish Clans, 471–72
Grandma's Pancake and Steak, 563–64
Grandover Resort and Conference Center, 353
Grandview Overlook, 420
Granville Queen Inn, 104
Grassy Creek Golf & Country Club, 485
Grave site of Aunt Bee, 280
Graveyard Fields, 425

Graveyard of the Atlantic Museum, 55
Graystone Inn (Wilmington), 183
Great Dismal Swamp, 93–94
Great Smoky Mountains Railroad, 556
Great Wolf Lodge, 402
Greek Isles, 406
Green Hill Center of North Carolina Art, 349
Green Valley Grill, 356–57
Greenfield Park & Gardens, 181
Greensboro Children's Museum, 347
Greensboro College, 341
Greensboro Cultural Center at Festival Park, 347–48
Greensboro Grasshoppers, 352
Greensboro Historical Museum, 358
Greensboro Marriott Downtown, 354
Greenwood Bed-and-Breakfast, 355–56
Greystone Inn (Lake Toxaway), 531–32
Grice-Fearing House Bed and Breakfast, 90
Grouper's Waterfront Seafood Grille, 91
Grove Arcade, 496–97
Grove Park Inn Resort & Spa, 499, 502–3
Guilford College, 341
Guilford Courthouse National Military Park, 343–45, 351
Guilford Native American Art Gallery, 349
Gullah Gullah Cuisine, 364

Hammocks Beach State Park, 119, 159
Hampton Inn (Elizabeth City), 89
Hampton Inn & Suites Outer Banks/Corolla, 21
Hampton Inn Morehead City, 141
Hanging Rock State Park, 374
Hanna House, 132
Hannah Flanagan's Pub, 522
Harkers Island Visitor Center, 151
Harmony Hill, 434–35
Harmony House Inn, 132
Harper Creek, 470
Harrah's Cherokee Casino, 562
Harvey B. Gantt Center for African-American Arts and Culture, 392–93
Harvey Mansion Historic Inn & Restaurant, 132–33
Harvey W. Smith Watercraft Center, 146
Hatteras Harbor Deli, 61
Hatteras Harbor Marina, 56
Hatteras Harbor Marina & Efficiencies, 59
Hatteras Island Fishing Pier, 56
Hatteras Island Sail Shop, 56
Hatteras Landing, 58
Hatteras Landing Marina, 56
Hawksnest, 471
Hawthorne Inn & Conference Center, 332
Hayti Heritage Center, 247, 251
Haywood Park Hotel, 503–4
Health Adventure, 493
Hemlock Inn (Blowing Rock), 462
Hemlock Inn (Tryon), 556–57
Henderson County Farmers Curb Market, 518
Henderson County Heritage Museum, 517

Henry F. Shaffner House, 333
Herbert Hoover Birthday Celebration, 42
Herons, 276
Herrings Outdoor Sports, 165
Hezekiah Alexander Homesite, 383
High Country Quilt Show, 570
High Hampton Inn and Country Club, 538
High Mountain Expeditions, 451
High Point Furniture Markets, 363, 365–66
High Point Museum and Historical Park, 360
Highland Lake Inn, 519–20
Highlander Café & Pub, 297
Highlands Chamber Music Festival, 537
Highlands House Bed and Breakfast, 540
Highlands Inn, 540
Highlands Nature Center, 536
Highlands Playhouse, 537
Hiking in the High Country, 451
Hilltop House Restaurant, 297
Hillwinds Inn, 461
Hilton at University Place, 401
Hilton Charlotte City Center, 402
Hilton New Bern Riverfront Hotel, 131
Hilton Wilmington Riverside, 182
Historic Bath State Historic Site, 112
Historic Bethabara Park, 322
Historic City Market (Raleigh), 228, 234, 235
Historic Edenton State Historic Site, 99
Historic Halifax, 92
Historic Hertford, 93
Historic Hillsborough, 216, 277–78
Historic Hope Plantation, 108–9
Historic Jackson, 92
Historic Latta Plantation, 384
Historic Murfreesboro, 93
Historic National Cemetery & Confederate Prison Site, 372
Historic Oakwood District, 222, 231, 233, 234
Historic Plymouth, 109
Historic Rosedale Plantation, 384
Historic Stagville, 243
Historic Washington, 115–16
Historic Williamston, 109
Historic Windsor, 108
History Place, 139–40
Hobnob, 533–34
Holden Beach, 203
Holiday Inn Bordeaux, 296
Holiday Inn Express (Boone), 453
Holiday Inn Express (Elizabeth City), 89
Holly Day Fair, 296
Holly Inn, 309
Holmes Educational State Forest, 518
Holy Trinity Episcopal Church, 440
Home Furnishings Center, 365
Home of the Perfect Christmas Tree, 479
Hong Kong Chinese Restaurant, 255
Horn in the West, 452
Horne Creek Living Historical Farm, 370
Horse-Drawn Carriage and Trolley Tours (Wilmington), 172

Hoskins House, 345
Hot Summer Nights, 227
Hotel Prince Charles, 296–97
House in the Horseshoe, 312–13
Howard House, 132
Howard's Pub and Raw Bar, 74
Hugh Mangum Museum of Photography, 244
Humpback Mountain, 423
Hurricane Mo's Restaurant and Raw Bar, 45
Huske Hardware House, 297

Ichiban, 336
Il Palio Ristorante, 269
ImaginOn: The Joe and Joan Martin Center, 390
Independence Day Fireworks Celebration, 369
Indigo Marsh, 166
Inlet Inn, 149
Inn at Bingham School, 269
Inn at Celebrity Dairy, 281
Inn at Corolla Light, 25
Inn at Oriental, 136
Inn at Ragged Gardens, 462
Inn at Teardrops, 278
Inn on Biltmore Estate, 504
Inn on Main Street (Brevard), 533
Inn on Main Street (Weaverville), 510
Inn on Pamlico Sound, 59–60
Innkeepers House, 152
Inns at Beech Mountain, 473–74
International Civil Rights Center & Museum, 358
International Folk Festival, 296
Iredell House, 101
Iredell House Groaning Board, 103
Island Ferry Adventures, 146
Island House of Wanchese, 44
Island Inn Restaurant, 74–75
Island Produce, 39
Island Style Adventure Company, 193
Italian Restaurant, 477

J. Arthur's Restaurant, 568
J. C. Raulston Arboretum, 223–24
J. H. Adams Inn, 364
J. P. Riddle Stadium, 294
Jack of the Wood, 508
Jack Spencer Goodwin Research Library, 140
Jackalope's View, 475
James Joyce, 255
James K. Polk Memorial, 385
Jarrett House, 547
Jefferson, 439
Jennette's Fishing Pier, 15
Jeremy's Lodge at Jefferson Landing, 442
Jesse Brown Cabin, 420
JFK Special Warfare Museum, 285, 290
Jockey's Ridge State Park, 17–18
Joel Lane House, 218, 222
John C. Campbell Folk School, 548
John S. MacCormack Model Shop, 146
John Wright Stanly House, 125–26

Johnny Mercer's Pier, 190–91
Johnson Lake, 229
Jolly Roger Pier, 164
Jonathan Creek Inn and Villas, 567
Jonathan Green, Jr., House, 158
Jones' Seafood House, 208
Jordan Lake, 229
Josephus Hall House, 372
Joyce Kilmer Memorial Forest, 559
Julian, Lake, 498
Julian Price Park, 421, 451, 459
Jumpinoff Rock, 420

Kannapolis, 412
Karen Beasley Sea Turtle Rescue and Rehabilitation Center, 164
Kathryn's Bistro and Martini Bar, 157–58
Kayak Carolina, 199
Kenan Auditorium, 180
Keziah Memorial Park, 204
Kilwin's Chocolate Shoppe, 517–18
King-Bazemore House, 108
Kings Creek Access Area, 438
Kitty Hawk Kites, 18
Kitty Hawk Sports, 14–15, 40
Knight's on Main, 464
Knollwood House, 310
Krankie's Coffee, 337
Krispy Kreme doughnuts, 323
K38 Baja Grill, 185

La Fiesta del Pueblo, 232
La Quinta Inn & Suites (Boone), 454
Lake Crabtree County Park, 275
Lake Eden Arts Festival (LEAF), 500–501
Lake Norman State Park, 411
Lake Wheeler Metropolitan Park, 229
Lakeside Restaurant, 542
Lakeview Park Fishing Pier and Campground, 294
Langdon House Bed-and-Breakfast, 148
Last Unicorn, 265
Latimer House Museum, 175–76
Latta Plantation Park and Nature Preserve, 395
Laughing Seed Café, 509
Laura A. Barnes, 48
Le Catalan, 185
LeConte Lodge, 555
Lees-McRae College, 465
Levine Museum of the New South, 386
Lexington, 373
Liberty Oak, 357
Liberty Point, 287
Lifesaving Station Restaurant, 26
Lighthouse Gallery and Gifts, 14
Lighthouse View Motel and Cottages, 59
Linn Cove Viaduct, 421–22
Linville Caverns, 468–69
Linville Falls, 423, 469
Linville Gorge Wilderness Area, 469–70
Lion & the Rose, 506

Little Glade Mill Pond, 418
Little Muddy Lake, 294
Little Richard's Barbecue, 337
Loafers Glory Rafting & Tubing, 481, 483
Loch Norman Highland Games, 399
Log Cabin Steak House, 541
Lois Jane's Riverview Inn, 207
Lomo Grill, 572
Lomo's Bakery and Café, 572
Looking Glass Falls, 530
Looking Glass Rock, 425
Lookout Cruises, 146
Loop, The, 191
Lost Colony, The, 40–42
Lost Cove, 470
Lost Cove Cliffs Overlook, 422–23
Louise Wells Cameron Museum of Art, 170, 178–79
Lovill House Inn, 454
Lower Cullasaja Falls, 537
Lump, The, 420
Lupie's Café, 408
Lure, Lake, 498

Macon County Gemboree, 545
Maggie Valley Resort and Country Club, 567, 568
Maggie's Galley, 573
Magic Cycles, 451
Magnolia Grill, 254
Magnolia Inn, 310
Main Street (Carrboro), 265
Malaprop's, 496
Mama Dip's Kitchen, 271
Manbites Dog Theater, 247
Manor House Bed-and-Breakfast, 369
Manor House Restaurant at Chetola, 463
Manor, The (Pinehurst), 309
Manteo Waterfront Marina, 40
Maple Lodge Bed-and-Breakfast, 462–63
Maple View Farm Country Store, 278
Marbles Kids Museum, 225–26
Marco Trattoria, 534
Margaritagrille, 522
Mariner's Wharf, 86
Marisol, 356
Market House, 285, 286–87, 291, 297
Martin Vineyards, 13
Mash House Restaurant & Brewery, 297
Mason Mountain Mine, 545
Masonboro Island, 193
Mast Farm Inn, 454–55
Mast General Store (Valle Crucis), 448
Mast General Store and Candy Barrel (Waynesville), 570
Mast Store Annex (Valle Crucis), 448
Mast Store Candy Barrel (Blowing Rock), 449
Mattamuskeet, Lake, 117
Matthew's 102 North, 444
Mattie King Davis Art Gallery, 145

Mayfel's, 508
McColl Center for Visual Art, 392
McDowell Nature Center and Preserve, 396
McIntyre's, 279
McLendon Cabin, 312
McLendon Hills Equestrian Center, 307
Meadowbrook Inn, 461–62
Meadows Inn, 132
Meet the Author Teas, 264
Melange Bed-and-Breakfast, 519
Melanie's Food Fantasy, 456
Mendenhall Plantation, 348, 360
Merchants Millpond State Park, 94–95
Meridian 42, 26–27
Merlefest, 374
Mert's Heart and Soul, 407
Metropolis, 26
Michael's Seafood Restaurant and Catering, 201
Microtel Inn & Suites (Elizabeth City), 89
Mid Pines Inn, 309
Mineral & Lapidary Museum of Henderson County, 517
Minnesott Beach, 137
Mint Museum of Art, 388
Mint Museum of Craft + Design, 388
Mint Museum Uptown, 388
Miss Annie's, 334
Mitchell Hardware, 129
Mollie's Restaurant, 166
Moncure, 278, 280
Montero's Restaurant, 91
Moonrise Bay Vineyard, 13
Mordecai Historic Park, 222–23, 234
Morehead Inn, 403
Morehead Manor Bed-and-Breakfast, 252–53
Morehead Planetarium, 262–63
Morgan's Tavern and Grill, 133
Morris Marina Kabin Kamps and Ferry Service, 151
Morrow Mountain State Park, 410
Moses H. Cone Memorial Park, 421, 451, 459, 460
Moss House, 116
Moth Boat Park, 86
Moth Boat Regatta, 87, 89
Mott Lake, 294
Mount Airy, 373
Mount Jefferson State Natural Area, 441
Mount Jefferson State Park, 420
Mount Mitchell State Park, 423, 481
Mount Vernon Mineral Springs, 278, 280–81
Mountain Creek Bed-and-Breakfast, 571–72
Mountain Dance and Folk Festival, 500
Mountain Farm Museum, 553
Mountain Glen, 471
Mountain Sports Festival, 500
Mountain View Lodge & Cabins, 435
Mrs. Willis' Restaurant, 142
Ms. Elsie's Caribbean Bed & Breakfast, 403
Muddy Lake, 294

Mumfest, 130
Museum of American Cut and Engraved Glass, 536
Museum of Anthropology of Wake Forest University, 326
Museum of Coastal Carolina, 203, 204–5
Museum of Early Southern Decorative Arts, 328
Museum of North Carolina Handicrafts, 569–70
Museum of North Carolina Minerals, 423, 478–79
Museum of the Albemarle, 84–85
Museum of the Cape Fear Historical Complex, 291
Museum of the Cherokee Indian, 560–61
Museum Store (Morehead City), 139–40
Music and Movies on Market Street, 267
Music Explorium, 249
My Father's Pizza, 510
Mystery Hill, 450–51

Nags Head Fishing Pier, 15
Nags Head Golf Links, 19
Nags Head Woods Ecological Preserve, 17
Nana's Restaurant, 254
Nantahala Gorge, 547
Nantahala National Forest, 537
Nantahala Outdoor Center, 556
NASCAR Hall of Fame, 413
NASCAR Trail, 411-13
Nasher Museum of Art at Duke University, 239, 244–45
National Hollerin' Contest, 298
National Opera Company, 227
Natural Science Center, 347
Natural Selections, 67
Net House, 150
Neuse River canoe launches, 229
Neuse River Recreation Area, 137
New Bern Academy Museum, 126
New Bern Civic Theatre, 128
New Bern Ghostwalk, 130–31
New Bern Tours, 123
New Hanover County Arboretum, 174
New River, 437–38
New River Canoe and Campground, 433
New River Country Club, 433
New River General Store, 441
New River Outfitters, 442
New River State Park, 433, 438, 442
New River Trail State Park, 433
Newbold-White House, 93
Newland, 465
Nikki's Fresh Gourmet, 185
1927 Lake Lure Inn & Spa, 523–24
Ninth Street (Durham), 248
Nixon Family Restaurant, 105
Noble's Grill, 334
NoDa, 394
NOFO on Liz, 407
NOMA, 336

North Carolina A & T State University, 342, 349, 358
North Carolina Apple Festival, 518–19
North Carolina Aquarium at Fort Fisher, 197–98
North Carolina Aquarium at Pine Knoll Shores, 155
North Carolina Aquarium at Roanoke Island, 37–38
North Carolina Arboretum, 491–92
North Carolina Azalea Festival, 182
North Carolina Black Repertory Company, 329
North Carolina Blumenthal Performing Arts Center, 390
North Carolina Botanical Garden, 261
North Carolina Collection Gallery, 263
North Carolina Colonial Heritage Center, 345
North Carolina Country Stampede, 109
North Carolina Crafts Gallery, 265–66
North Carolina Estuarium, 116
North Carolina Fourth of July Festival, 206
North Carolina History Education Center, 127
North Carolina Maritime Museum at Beaufort, 119, 145–46
North Carolina Maritime Museum at Southport, 202, 204
North Carolina Maritime Museum on Roanoke Island, 38
North Carolina Mineral, Gem, and Jewelry Festival, 478, 483
North Carolina Museum of Art, 215, 224, 251
North Carolina Museum of History, 224–25
North Carolina Museum of Life and Science, 244
North Carolina Museum of Natural Sciences, 225
North Carolina Mutual Life Insurance Company, 237, 243, 246
North Carolina Oyster Festival, 210
North Carolina Potato Festival, 89
North Carolina Renaissance Faire, 282
North Carolina Seafood Festival, 140
North Carolina Shakespeare Festival, 360
North Carolina State Capitol, 218, 220–21
North Carolina State Fair, 228, 231
North Carolina State Farmers Market, 228–29
North Carolina State Wolfpack, 230
North Carolina State women's basketball team, 231
North Carolina Symphony, 227
North Carolina Theatre (Raleigh), 227, 371
North Carolina Transportation Museum, 373
North Carolina Wine Festival, 369
North Carolina Zoological Park, 367
North Wilkesboro Speedway, 412
Northampton County Museum, 92
Northlake, 394
Northwest Trading Post, 420, 441
Not Quite Antiques, 293
Nothin Fancy Café & Market, 105–6
Novello Festival of Reading, 398

O. Henry Hotel, 353–54
Oak Hill Country Inn, 546
Oak Hollow Lake Park and Marina, 362
Oak Island, 202
Oak Island Nature Center, 206
Oakdale Cemetery (Asheville), 516–17
Oakdale Cemetery (Wilmington), 178
Oakwood Candlelight Tour, 231
Oakwood Inn, 233
Occaneechi Indian Village, 277
Ocean Isle Beach, 203
Oceanana, 156
Oceanana Fishing Pier, 156
Oceanic Restaurant, 192
Oconaluftee Indian Village, 560
Oconaluftee Islands Park, 562
Ocracoke Harbor Inn, 70–71
Ocracoke Lighthouse, 64–65
Ocracoke Preservation Society Museum, 67
Ocracoke Variety Store, 67
Ocracoke Visitor Center, 66–67
Ocrafolk Music and Storytelling Festival, 69
Oden's Dock, 56
Old Beaufort Shop, 145
Old Boone Mercantile, 449
Old Buggy Bed-and-Breakfast Inn, 310
Old Burying Ground, 145
Old East, 256, 259–60
Old Edwards Inn and Spa, 538–39
Old Greensborough & Downtown Historic District, 350
Old Hampton Store & Grist Mill, 467
Old North Durham Inn, 253
Old Salem Museum and Gardens, 321
Old Salem Toy Museum, 328
Old Sarge's Surplus, 293
Old Seaport Inn, 149
Old Well, 259
Old Wilmington City Market, 180
Olde Beau Golf Club, 433
Olde Southport Village, 205
Ole Log Cabin, 265
Olivia Raney Local History Library, 226
Ollie's Bakery, 337
Olympus Dive Center, 140
Opera House Theatre Company, 180
Operation Celebrate Freedom, 295
Orange Blossom Bakery & Café, 61
Orchard at Altapass, 481
Orchard Inn, 524
Oregon Inlet Campground, 49
Oregon Inlet Fishing Center and Full-Service Marina, 48
Oriental, 119, 136
Oriental Marina Motel, 136
Oriental School of Sailing, 136
Orton Plantation Gardens, 186
Otway House Bed-and-Breakfast, 148
Outer Banks Brewing Station, 28
Outer Banks Center for Wildlife Education, 11
Outer Banks Fishing Pier, 48

Outer Banks Pirate Festival, 19
Outer Barks, 13
Overmountain Victory National Historic Trail, 423

Pack Place, 493
Pack Square Park, 493–94
Palmer-Marsh House, 112–13
Parkway Craft Center, 458
Pasquale's Pizzeria & Tapas Bar, 573
Patterson's Mill Country Store, 248
Pea Island National Wildlife Refuge, 56–57
Pearson's Falls, 524
Pecan Tree Inn, 148
Pelican Lodge, 71
Penguin, The, 408
Penland School of Crafts, 478, 479, 480
Periauger, 93
Perry House Bed-and-Breakfast, 475
Pettigrew State Park, 106–7
Pewter Rose Bistro, 407
Pharmacy, The, 207
Piedmont Crafts Fair, 331
Piedmont Environmental Center, 363
Piedmont Farm Tour, 279
Pilot House Restaurant, 184
Pilot Mountain State Park, 373-74
Pine Crest Inn & Restaurant, 525
Pine Island Audubon Sanctuary, 16–17
Pine Needles Lodge and Golf Club, 306, 308–9
Pinebridge Inn & Executive Center, 484
Pinehurst Country Club, 301, 306
Pinehurst Harness Track, 302
Pinehurst Resort Hotel, 309
Pines Country Inn, 533
Pink Palace Bed-and-Breakfast, 165
Pinnacle Inn, 474
Piper's in the Park, 276
Pirate's Cove Marina, 40
Pisgah, Mount, 424–25
Pisgah National Forest, 451, 469–70, 498, 529–30
Pittsboro, 278, 279–80
Pizza Place of Highlands, 542
Pizzeria, The, 436
PlayMakers Repertory Company, 264
PlayMakers Theatre, 260, 268
Pleasure Island Seafood, Blues, and Jazz Festival, 199–200
Pocosin Lakes National Wildlife Refuge, 107–8
Pond House Inn, 89–90
Poplar Grove Historic Plantation, 186
Pop's Italian Trattoria, 254
Port Discover, 85–86
Port O' Call Restaurant and Gaslight Saloon, 27
Port O' Plymouth Civil War Museum, 109
Portsmouth Village, 151
Powhatan, Lake, 498
Price's Chicken Coop, 408
Progress Energy Center for the Performing Arts, 227

Provence, 270
Proximity Hotel, 354
Public Art Walking Tour, 383, 405
Pullen Park and Aquatic Center, 229–30
Purple Onion, 524

Quakers, 340, 341, 342, 348
Quality Inn (Elizabeth City), 89
Quality Inn (Morehead City), 141
Qualla Arts and Crafts Mutual, Inc., 561–62
Quilt Trails Project, 486

Rachel Carson Estuarine Research Reserve, 150
Radisson Governor's Inn, 275
Raft & Earth Adventures, 471
Raleigh City Museum, 226
Raps Grill and Bar, 143
Raven Rocks, 421
Ray's Splash Planet Waterpark, 397
RBC Center, 230, 234, 276
Red House Inn, 533
Red Rocker Inn, 510
Reed Gold Mine, 409
Reems Creek Golf Club, 499
Register Park, 206
Reid's Grocery, 390
Relia's Garden, 558
Replacements, Ltd., 350–51
Residence Inn by Marriott (Southern Pines), 309–10
Reynolda Gardens of Wake Forest University, 324
Reynolda House Museum of American Art, 324
Reynolda Village, 324
Richard Caswell Memorial, 137
Richland Balsam, 425
Richmond Inn, 484
Ride the Wind Surf & Kayak, 68
Ridgeway Inn, 461
Ristorante Paoletti, 541
River Arts District, 495
River Camp USA (Alleghany County), 433
River Camp USA (Ashe County), 442
River Dog Coffeehouse & Café, 477
River Forest Manor, 115
River House Country Inn, 443
River House Inn and Restaurant, 443
Riverfest, 182
Riverfront Park, 169
Rivergirl Fishing Company, 451
RiverRun International Film Festival, 331
Rivers Edge Outfitters, 481
Riverside Canoe, 442
Riverside Sports Center, 294
Riverview Café, 166
Riverwalk, 169
Riverwood Shops, 547
Roanoke Adventure Museum, 35–36
Roanoke Arts and Crafts Guild Holiday Fair, 109
Roanoke Island Festival Park, 35–37

Roanoke Island Inn, 43
Roanoke Marshes Lighthouse, 38
Roanoke River Lighthouse, 101
Roanoke River National Wildlife Refuge, 109
Roanoke Sound Pier, 15
Roast Grill, 235
Robert Hay House, 126
Roberts Market, 190
Roberts-Vaughan Village Center, 93
Rocks, The, 280
Rollingview Marina, 282
Rose Creek Mine and Campground, 545
Rosemary House Bed-and-Breakfast, 279–80
Rowan Museum, 372
Royal James Café, 150
Ruby City Gems and Minerals, 544
Rum Runners Dueling Piano Bar and Grill, 228
Rundown Café & Tsunami Surf Bar, 28

S & T Soda Shop, 279
Salem Tavern, 334
Salisbury, 371-72
Salty Dawg Marina, 40
Saluda, 524
Saluda Grade Café, 524
Saluda Mountain Lodge, 524
Sam and Omie's, 29
Sand Dunes Motel, 200
Sandbar & Grille, 60
Sanderling, 20–21
Sandhills Woman's Exchange, 305–6
Sandwich Pail Seaside Grill, 193
Sanford, 312–13
Sanford Pottery Festival, 312
Sanitary Fish Market, 142
Sans Souci Ferry, 108
Sarah P. Duke Gardens, 242, 244
Sassy Goose, 533
Savannah Inn, 200
Scarborough Faire, 13
Scarborough House Inn, 44
Schiele Museum of Natural History, 410
SciWorks, 327
Scottish Tartans Museum and Heritage Center, 544
Screen Door, 497
Scuba South Diving Company, 206
Sea Gull Motel, 59
Sea Scape Golf Links, 19
Sea View Pier, 164
Sea Vista Motel, 165
Seagrove, 368
Seahawk Motor Lodge and Villas, 156–57
Sean's Market & Restaurant, 105
Seaside Art Gallery, 14
Season's at Highland Lake Inn, 521
Second Empire Restaurant and Tavern, 234–35
Sertoma Arts Center, 227–28
Shallowbag Bay Marina, 40
Shatley Springs Inn, 444
Shaw House properties, 303–4

Sheets Gap, 419–20
Shelley Lake, 227, 229
Sheraton Atlantic Beach, 156
Sheraton Greensboro Hotel at Four Seasons, 355
Sheraton Imperial Hotel and Conference Center, 275
Sheraton Raleigh Hotel, 233
Shindig on the Green, 500
Shoppes at Farmers Hardware and Supply Company, 448
Shoppes on the Parkway, 458
Shops at Friendly Center, 350
Siena Hotel, 269
Silent Sam, 259
Siler City, 278, 280–81
Silver Coast Winery, 205
Silver Gull Oceanfront Resort Motel, 192
Simplicity at Mast Farm Inn, 455
Singing on the Mountain, 472–73
Sit-in demonstrations, 358
6th & Vine Wine Bar & Café, 336
Ski Beech, 471
Ski Sugar Mountain, 471
Skyline Lodge and Restaurant, 540–41
Slice Pizzeria, 28
Sliding Rock, 530
Smith Lake Recreation Area, 294
Smith Lake Riding Stables, 294
Smith-McDowell House Museum, 494
Smokey Shadows Lodge, 567
Smoky Mountain Folk Festival, 570
Snappy's, 568
Sneads Ferry, 166
Sneads Ferry Shrimp Festival, 166
Snowbird Mountain Lodge, 563
Solaris Tapas Restaurant and Bar, 357
Somerset Place State Historic Site, 106
Sorrento's World Famous Bistro, 476
South Brunswick Islands King Mackerel Classic, 206
Southbeach Grill, 192–93
Southeastern Center for Contemporary Art (SECCA), 326
Southern Highland Craft Guild, 458
Southern Lights, 357
Southern Roots, 365
Southern Season, 266
Southern Village Farmers' Market, 265
SouthPark, 394
Southport Riverwalk, 202
Southport Trail, 203
Spangler Children's Library, 390
Spencer Repair Shops, 371
Spirit Square Center for Arts and Education, 392
Sports Page Sandwich Shoppe, 542
Spotted Dog Restaurant & Bar, 270
Spouter Inn, 149
Spring Historic Home and Garden Tour (Hillsborough), 277
Spring Historic Homes and Gardens Tour (New Bern), 130

Springbrook Farms, Inc., 123
Squire Watkins Inn, 547
Squire's Pub, 311
St. John's Episcopal Church, 288–89
St. Joseph's Episcopal Church, 289
St. Lawrence Basilica, 512
St. Mary's Episcopal Church, 440, 445–46
St. Paul's Episcopal Church, 99–100
St. Thomas Episcopal Church, 113
Stamey's Barbecue, 357
State Street Station, 350
Station's Inn, 434
Stevens Center for the Performing Arts, 329
Stompin' Ground, 565
Stone Mountain Overlook, 418
Stone Mountain State Park, 411, 418, 432
Stonewalls, 476
Stoneybrook Festival and Steeplechase, 308
Storie Street Grille, 464
Storytelling Festival, 232
Streets at Southpoint, 248
Stripers Bar and Grille, 45
Sugar Creek Soundfront Seafood Restaurant, 28
Sugar Mountain, 471
Sugar Shack, 208
Summit Street Bed & Breakfast Inns, 333
Sunset Beach, 203
Surf City Pier, 164
Sutton's Drugstore, 271–72
Swag Country Inn, 567
Swan Quarter National Wildlife Refuge, 117
Swansboro, 158–59
Sweet Potatoes, 335
Switzerland Café & General Store, 485
Switzerland Inn, 483–84

Table Rock, 470
Talking Trees Walking Trail, 206
Tanawah Trail, 422, 451
Tanger Outlet Mall, 14
Tanglewood Park, 368
Tannenbaum Historic Park, 345
Taylor House Inn, 455
Teach's Hole, 67–68
Teach's Lair Marina, 56
Terrell House Bed-and-Breakfast, 484
Thai Moon, 75
Thai Peppers, 208
Thalian Hall Center for the Performing Arts, 170, 174–75, 180
Theodore Roosevelt State Natural Area, 154, 155–56
Thicket Lump Marina, 40
Thomas Wolfe Memorial, 492–93
Thunder Hill, 421
Thurston House Inn, 71–72
Toast Paninoteca, 256
Todd General Store, 449
Toe River Arts Council, 479
Top of the Beech, 474
Top of the Hill Restaurant & Brewery, 270–71

Topsail Island Museum: Missiles and More, 162–64
Tour de Moore Century Ride, 308
Town Creek Indian Mound, 301, 313
Townsend, Lake, 352
Trail of Tears, 564
Tranquil House Inn, 44
Trateotu, 142
Trestle House Inn at Willow Tree Farm, 104
Triad Stage, 350
Triangle SportsPlex, 277
Tryon, 524–25
Tryon Fine Arts Center, 524
Tryon Palace, 118, 122, 123–27
Tuba Exchange, 249
Tupelo Honey Café, 508
Tupelo's, 278
Tweetsie Railroad, 449–50
Twin Lakes Golf Course, 267

Umstead Hotel and Spa, 276–77
UNCC Botanical Gardens and Sculpture Garden, 385
Undercurrent Restaurant, 356
Underground Railroad, 348, 360
Unicorn Shoppe, 265
United Arts Council, 349
United States Army Corps of Engineers Field Research Facility, 12
United States Weather Bureau Station, 53
University of North Carolina at Chapel Hill, 216, 256–57, 258–63, 272–73, 284, 285, 286
University of North Carolina at Greensboro, 342–43, 349
University of North Carolina School of the Arts, 338
University of North Carolina Tar Heels, 266
Unto These Hills, 562
Upper Street Café, 485
U.S. National Whitewater Center, 397
U.S. Open King Mackerel Tournament, 206
U.S. 221 Access Area, 438
Uwharrie National Forest, 410

Valle Country Fair, 452
Valle Crucis, 447
Van der Veer House, 113
Vance Toe River Lodge, 484–85
Veranda Café & Gifts, 509–10
Verandas, The, 183
Vidalia Restaurant & Wine Bar, 456
Vietri Outlet Store, 277–78
Village Café, (Blowing Rock), 464
Village Inn (Blowing Rock), 461
Village Inns of Blowing Rock, 460–61
Village Tavern (Winston-Salem), 336
Villas, The (Pinehurst), 309
Vin Rouge, 254
Virginia Creeper Trail, 433
Visual Art Exchange, 228

W. Kerr Scott Reservoir, 411-12
Wagoner Road Access Area, 438
Wahoo's Adventures, 451, 471
Wall Street (Asheville), 495–96
Washington Duke Inn and Golf Club, 252
Watauga Kayak, 451
Waterfront Park (Elizabeth City), 202
Waterfront Park (Manteo), 86
Waterman's Grille, 105
Waterrock Knob Overlook, 425
Waverly Inn, 520
Waxhaw, 409
Wayah Bald, 547
Waynesville Country Club Inn, 571
Weatherspoon Art Gallery, 349
Weathervane, The, 266
Weaver Street Market and Café, 265, 272
Weavers Web Gallery, 129
Weaverville, 510
Weeksville Vineyard, 86
Wells Fargo Cultural Campus, 393
West End Café, 337
West Franklin Street (Chapel Hill), 265
West Jefferson, 439
West Point on the Eno City Park, 244, 251
Western North Carolina Farmers Market, 497–98
Westin Charlotte, 402
Weymouth Center for the Arts and Humanities, 304–5
Weymouth Woods–Sandhills Nature Preserve, 304
Whalehead Club, 8–10
Wheeler House, 93
White Doe Inn Bed-and-Breakfast, 43
White Pines Nature Preserve, 280
White Squirrel Shoppe, 529
Whiteside Mountain, 538
Whitewater rafting, 451
Whitman's Bakery and Sandwich Shoppe, 573–74
Wild horses of Shackleford Banks, 152
Wild ponies of Ocracoke, 66
Wild Woody's Store, 434
William B. Umstead State Park, 229
William Pugh Ferrand Store, 158
William's, 142
Willow Creek Golf Course, 451
Wilmington Adventure Walking Tours, 172
Wilmington Railroad Museum, 179
Wilmington Trolley Company, 172
Wilson Creek, 470
Windansea, 142
Windover Inn Bed and Breakfast, 571
Winds Resort and Beach Club, 206
Wing Haven Gardens and Bird Sanctuary, 386
Wingate Inn, 332
Wings Over Water, 20
Winston-Salem Dash, 330
Wiseman's View, 470
Wolf Laurel Ski Resort, 498–99

Wolfgang's on Main, 541–42
Woodfield Inn, 520, 521
Woodlands BBQ, 464
Woolly Worm Festival, 473
Worth House, 183
Wright Brothers National Memorial, 10–11
Wrightsville Beach King Mackerel Tournament, 191
Wrightsville Beach Museum of History, 189–90
Wrightsville Beach Park, 191
Wyndham Championship, 353
Wyndham Sapphire Valley, 539

Xia Asian Fusion, 335

Yacht Basin Provision Company, 208
Yadkin Valley wineries, 375-76
Yana's Ye Olde Drugstore and Restaurant, 158
YMI Cultural Center, 493

Zaloo's Canoes, 442
Zambra, 506–7
Zebulon B. Vance Homestead, 510
Zebulon Latimer House, 170